THE IRWIN/McGRAW-HILL SERIES IN MARKETING

CONSUMER AND BUSINESS CREDIT MANAGEMENT

Moore & Pessemier
Product Planning and Management: Designing and Delivering Value, *1/E*

Oliver
Satisfaction: A Behavioral Perspective on the Consumer, *1/E*

Patton
Sales Force: A Sales Management Simulation Game, *1/E*

Pelton, Strutton & Lumpkin
Marketing Channels: A Relationship Management Approach, *1/E*

Perreault & McCarthy
Basic Marketing: A Global Managerial Approach, *12/E*

Perreault & McCarthy
Essentials of Marketing: A Global Managerial Approach, *7/E*

Peter & Donnelly
A Preface to Marketing Management, *7/E*

Peter & Donnelly
Marketing Management: Knowledge and Skills, *5/E*

Peter & Olson
Consumer Behavior and Marketing Strategy, *4/E*

Peter & Olson
Understanding Consumer Behavior, *1/E*

Quelch
Cases in Product Management, *1/E*

Quelch, Dolan & Kosnik
Marketing Management: Text & Cases, *1/E*

Quelch & Farris
Cases in Advertising and Promotion Management, *4/E*

Quelch, Kashani & Vandermerwe
European Cases in Marketing Management, *1/E*

Rangan
Business Marketing Strategy: Cases, Concepts & Applications, *1/E*

Rangan, Shapiro & Moriarty
Business Marketing Strategy: Concepts & Applications, *1/E*

Rossiter & Percy
Advertising and Promotion Management, *2/E*

Stanton, Spiro & Buskirk
Management of a Sales Force, *10/E*

Sudman & Blair
Marketing Research: A Problem-Solving Approach, *1/E*

Thompson & Stappenbeck
The Marketing Strategy Game, *1/E*

Ulrich & Eppinger
Product Design and Development, *1/E*

Walker, Boyd & Larreche
Marketing Strategy: Planning and Implementation, *2/E*

Weitz, Castleberry & Tanner
Selling: Building Partnerships, *3/E*

Zeithaml & Bitner
Services Marketing, *1/E*

ELEVENTH EDITION

CONSUMER AND BUSINESS CREDIT MANAGEMENT

Robert Cole, Ph.D

Professor Emeritus of Marketing
University of Nebraska—Lincoln

Lon Mishler, M.A.

Northeast Wisconsin Technical College
President, CFP
Financial Planning and Information Services, Inc.

Boston, Massachusettts • Burr Ridge, Illinois • Dubuque, Iowa
Madison, Wisconsin • New York, New York • San Francisco, California • St. Louis, Missouri

Irwin/McGraw-Hill

*A Division of The **McGraw·Hill** Companies*

CONSUMER AND BUSINESS CREDIT MANAGEMENT

3 4 5 6 7 8 9 0 DOC/DOC 0 9 8 7 6 5 4 3

ISBN 0-256-18704-5

Editorial director: *Michael W. Junior*
Executive editor: *Craig S. Beytien*
Sponsoring editor: *Karen Westover*
Editorial coordinator: *Andrea L. Hlavacek*
Marketing manager: *Colleen J. Suljic*
Project manager: *Jim Labeots*
Production supervisor: *Scott M. Hamilton*
Designer: *Larry Cope*
Compositor: *Carlisle Communications, Ltd.*
Typeface: *10/12 Times Roman*
Printer: *R. R. Donnelley & Sons Company*

Library of Congress Cataloging-in-Publication Data

Cole, Robert Hartzell.
   Consumer and business credit management / Robert Cole, Lon
Mishler.—11th ed.
     p. cm.
    Includes index.
    ISBN 0-256-18704-5
    1. Credit—Management. 2. Consumer credit. I. Mishler, Lon.
II. Title.
HG3751.C64   1998
   658.8'8—dc21   97–10347

http://www.mhhe.com

To Carol, Amy, and Brian for their support, patience, and understanding.

PREFACE

Imagine the very first credit transaction in history. It certainly took place hundreds of years ago, before the existence of banks, credit bureaus, or credit departments. Perhaps a farmer asked his neighbor for some seeds to grow a crop promising to give the lender some of his produce. Perhaps a family breadwinner simply needed food for his or her family and promised to repay with a bonus to compensate the lender for this generosity.

The prospective lender would have been surprised and apprehensive. An element of trust would be needed, of course, and some guarantee of repayment would be nice. How could one evaluate the risk of making this loan? What compensation should be sought for delivering property for another person's use? How could one collect if repayment was not promptly provided?

If a farmer or businessperson obtains the means to produce employment opportunities and products, certainly the community would benefit. Loans and other credit programs have provided these opportunities throughout history. Financial institutions developed to put funds from savers into the hands of borrowers who used this value to create economic value. Credit has contributed to the economic growth of countries throughout the world as it makes goods and services available to consumers, businesspersons, and governments.

Although the basic tasks of evaluating risk, extending credit, and collecting payments have not changed, the mechanisms for marketing and conducting credit programs have changed dramatically over the years. Computers using sophisticated credit scoring programs often determine who will receive credit cards. Electronic payments systems speed up the disbursement and collection of account balances. Credit bureaus maintain vast databases of information about borrowers available on-line through computer networks. Lenders continue to find more ways to offer more credit options to businesses and consumers. Nearly everyone has the opportunity to use their creditworthiness to obtain goods and services, and most take advantage of the available programs to buy automobiles, houses, inventory, and services. As a result, modern businesspersons must understand the opportunities and challenges of extending credit.

This text, first published nearly 40 years ago, has chronicled these changes in credit management systems and practices. It continues to strive to help both providers and users of credit achieve responsible applications of this powerful invention of commerce. We try to merge theory with practice as we describe credit management for students, businesspersons, borrowers, and counselors. The Eleventh Edition incorporates many new and exciting features:

- New topics such as forms of business organization, negotiable instruments, and writing credit policies.
- Internet addresses for many credit organizations and agencies to allow students the opportunity to take virtual field trips to visit and learn about these credit participants firsthand.
- Additional case problems and an extension of the Bill and Betty Stevens comprehensive case problem.
- An updated glossary and improved listing of terms at the end of each chapter.
- More case problems and questions to help students practice what they have learned.
- Improved organization achieved by combining some chapters and expanding others.
- Enhanced teacher's manual.

Keeping up with the changes in this industry has been made possible by the recommendations and suggestions of the following reviewers whose ideas are incorporated in this revision: Stan Carson of Eastern Maine Technical College; John Gauthier of Gateway Technical College; Thomas C. Fryer of Northwestern Business College; and Frances L. Haldar of North Central Technical College. We are indebted to them for their help.

A sincere thank you also goes to the many executives who were willing to share their time and expertise in revising this Eleventh Edition. Special recognition is due:

- Robin Schauseil, Teresa Donohue, and Connie Cheak of the National Association of Credit Management.
- Janis Lamar of Experian Information Services.
- Kate Lohuis of Experian Business Information Services.
- John Ford and Kristen Petrella of Equifax Inc.
- Dwight Noyes of Northeast Wisconsin Technical College.

Finally, we appreciate the enthusiasm and administrative assistance provided by Linda Fletcher, Brian Mishler, and Jane Vondracek from Financial Planning and Information Services, Inc. Their insight, skills, and patience has been very helpful.

As always, suggestions from the readers of this book will be appreciated. We continue to strive for excellence in the production of a textbook addressing the training needs of both business and consumer credit.

Lon L. Mishler
Robert H. Cole

TABLE OF CONTENTS

CONSUMER AND BUSINESS CREDIT MANAGEMENT

PART I

INTRODUCTION TO CREDIT

1 | CREDIT IN THE ECONOMY

Learning Objectives

After studying this chapter, you should be able to:

- Define the term *credit* and explain the important aspects of a credit transaction.
- Explain how different types of credit can be classified.
- Explain the role of credit and its importance in our economy.
- Discuss the business cycle and the efforts by the federal government to stabilize the economy.
- Describe what credit does for consumers and business.
- Explain the dangers arising from credit use.
- Illustrate the need for more education regarding the extension and use of credit.

We live in a world of credit. Every day, in every way, we become more and more involved in various aspects of this credit world. As consumers, businesspeople, and voters, we are experiencing continued growth in using credit. All of us need to understand what credit is, how it is used, and the laws that regulate its use.

Historically, credit has contributed to the development of the American economy and to the high standard of living enjoyed by most Americans. Credit fosters the growth of business by providing the means to start, maintain, and transfer business enterprises. Businesses use credit extensively for sales among manufacturers, distributors, and retail outlets. Credit terms provide time to sell the inventory before payment is due. Business also benefits from the existence of credit programs for customers that help promote sales and open new markets. These sales have enhanced employment and helped the American economy move forward.

American consumers have been able to raise their standard of living in productive ways by obtaining homes, automobiles, and other durable goods when purchasing with cash was not an available option. Credit helps individuals handle emergencies and gives them a convenient way to manage their finances. Many college students use student loan programs to pay for their education.

Governments at all levels have greatly expanded their use of credit to finance government programs and facilities. New schools, expanding health and welfare programs, and new highways are examples of government spending. Local, state, and federal governments generally use debt securities to borrow funds if tax revenues are insufficient.

Attitudes toward the use of credit continue to change dramatically. Not long ago, many consumers would forgo purchases if they did not have cash. Today, most individuals and businesses embrace credit programs and will purchase goods and services quickly if credit is available. Even the growth of government deficits is tolerated with this new acceptance of credit and the readiness to borrow against future income.

The use of credit has become an important part of the American economy. It is the oil that lubricates our economic machinery. Its widespread use is not without dangers, however. Individuals have been tempted to use credit programs too often and have discovered that the misuse of credit can lead to bankruptcy, marital problems, stress, and other problems. Businesses have also found that allowing purchases without receiving cash can result in financial difficulties. We need to capitalize on the beneficial qualities of credit but avoid the pitfalls that can occur through uninformed and misguided expansion of credit.

DEFINITION OF CREDIT

The Credit Transaction

Before we can adequately define credit, we need to analyze the process and elements found in the credit transaction. Exhibit 1–1 outlines the participants, activities, and components of the credit process.

The Process
The process begins with a seller making goods, services, or funds (money) available to a buyer. The seller might be a retail firm, a distributor providing inventory to other businesses, or a financial institution offering loans.

The buyer examines the items offered and decides to complete an exchange or transaction. The purchaser then provides a **medium of exchange** (i.e., something of value acceptable to the seller) in exchange for the good or service delivered. The buyer also might offer cash to the seller. Cash enjoys universal acceptance and, therefore, the exchange is easily completed. The buyer may instead offer credit, however, by promising to pay for the items in the future. This credit, or promise to pay, has limited acceptance since the seller must decide if the promise of the buyer is indeed valuable and worth accepting in exchange.

If the credit is accepted, an agreement between buyer and seller will outline future payments over a period of time. Once the credit transaction is agreed to, the seller becomes a **creditor,** the party that is owed value or payment in a credit transaction. The buyer becomes a **debtor,** the party that owes value.

Exhibit 1-1   **The Credit Transaction**

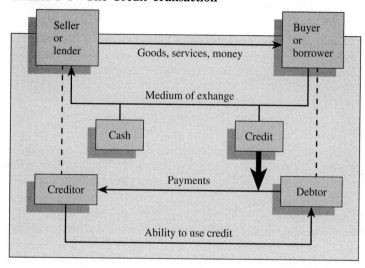

After payments are made to the creditor, the debtor's ability to use credit is restored or enhanced. The debtor demonstrates the legitimate value of a promise to pay in the future. **Creditworthiness** is the ability of a business or consumer to obtain goods, services, or money by using its promise to deliver payments in the future. This creditworthiness varies depending on the income of the applicant, indebtedness, and demonstrated willingness to pay past credit arrangements.

Components of the Credit Process

Many factors must be considered by creditors before accepting an applicant's promise to pay using credit instead of cash. They are unique to the credit transaction and define the tasks, responsibilities, and concerns of credit management personnel.

Risk

A cash sale results in immediate, guaranteed payment. In a credit transaction, however, the buyer or debtor may not pay in the end. If so, the seller will lose the value of the goods, services, and funds originally transferred to the debtor. Also lost will be any time and costs expended attempting to collect payment. An essential aspect of the credit process is trying to assess the amount of risk a particular customer represents.

Time

In a credit transaction, the seller will have to wait to receive payments. If the seller had received cash immediately, the cash could have been invested elsewhere by the seller for profit. The seller will lose investment earnings, and may be required to borrow funds to pay its own bills.

Security or Collateral

The seller or lender may require security or collateral as a part of the credit arrangement. **Collateral** is an item of value that the borrower owns (or is buying) as a pledge to reduce the risk of loss. The debtor assigns ownership rights to the credit grantor and agrees to surrender the item of value in the event of nonpayment. A credit manager or loan officer must become involved in assessing the value of any collateral offered.

Operating Expense

The seller will incur additional costs after accepting the debtor's promise to pay. Wages must be paid to credit personnel, extra processing costs will be incurred, and various printed forms will be required. Computers and other sophisticated equipment are required to successfully operate a credit department. Legal fees and other collection expenses are also inevitable.

Legal Considerations

The credit transaction is affected by laws that have been passed by state and federal legislatures to protect both the debtors and creditors. These laws must be understood to avoid the penalties and extra costs that are involved in litigation. Training is required to ensure that workers will conduct credit transactions properly. As these laws continue to change, someone must also accept the responsibility to monitor these changes in order to adjust the credit policies and procedures as needed.

Inflation

Inflation is a general rise in the prices of goods and services. If the repayment period extends for a period of time, and inflation is occurring, the purchasing power of the dollars returned will not be as great as the value of the dollars originally provided to the debtor. As prices go up, the real value of each dollar deteriorates since more will be needed to buy available goods and services. If you lend someone $1, a 5 percent inflation rate may result in your receiving only 95 cents in return after a one-year time period.

Finance Charge

The creditor may or may not require a finance charge as part of the credit transaction. A **finance charge** is an additional amount that must be paid over and above the value received by the debtor or borrower. The finance charge will help cover the costs mentioned above: losses due to nonpayment, operating expenses, lost investment earnings, inflation, and legal expenses. If finance charges are not specifically identified, they must nevertheless be incorporated in the prices of a firm's goods and services.

The Definition of Credit

Credit is a medium of exchange with limited acceptance. Because of the potential losses and components mentioned above, the credit manager or loan officer will not allow everyone to use credit programs. Credit is a medium of exchange to the extent that it facilitates the transfer of value from buyer to seller, but it is not available to everyone.

Credit personnel conduct investigations and assess the risk a particular client portrays before accepting a promise to pay. Credit is a privilege that must be earned and protected by those who wish to use this form of exchange.

CLASSIFICATION OF CREDIT

Credit transactions occur in many different forms. The classification of credit types is based on the purpose for the credit and the method of payment.

The two main classifications of credit are private and public credit. **Private credit** is credit used by individuals and businesses in order to carry on exchanges in the private sector of our economy. **Public credit** is credit extended, or used, directly by a level of government, such as state, local, or federal. Governments borrow money primarily through the sale of bonds and other securities if tax revenues are not sufficient to cover current spending needs. This book is primarily concerned with private credit.

Private credit
  Consumer credit
    Retail credit
      Revolving credit
      Retail installment credit
      Service credit
    Cash credit
      Installment loans
      Single-payment loans
      General-purpose credit cards
    Real estate credit
  Business credit
    Merchandise credit
    Financial capital for operations
Public credit

Exhibit 1–2 illustrates the chain of events that brings a product through the various stages of production and distribution until it is purchased by the ultimate user or consumer. At each step in the process, a business will purchase a good, enhance its value in some way, and sell it to the next business in the marketing chain. **Business credit** describes the credit relationships involved in purchasing goods for resale, or obtaining funds to operate, using credit as the medium of exchange. A distributor, for example, might purchase large quantities of products from a variety of related manufacturers and distribute related lines of products to retail stores. The distributor, and the other businesses, will likely be both a creditor and a debtor as goods move through the marketing chain.

EXHIBIT 1–2   **The Marketing Chain**

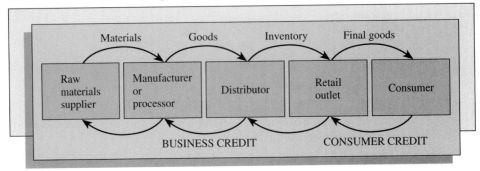

Consumer credit is illustrated at the very end of the marketing chain. **Consumer credit** is the use of credit as a medium of exchange for the purchase of finished goods and services by the ultimate user. A consumer, for example, will purchase a new automobile by signing an agreement to provide payments in the months or years ahead.

Consumer Credit

Consumer credit has been used for decades. Consumers with the desire or need to purchase items have often been willing to commit future income. Some families use credit only when needed, as for utilities and expensive durable goods that they must purchase; for example, automobiles and houses. Others use credit more easily to purchase a wide variety of luxuries, services, and other items they desire.

Retail Credit

Retail credit is a category of credit used by consumers to purchase final goods and services directly from sellers using revolving credit, installment contracts, or service credit. The underlying characteristic that ties these credit types together is that the credit of the buyer is accepted by the seller of the merchandise who agrees to wait for future payment. A large appliance store, for example, will sell a new refrigerator to a customer using a credit program that involves the seller collecting payments each month in the future during a specified time period.

Revolving Credit.   **Revolving credit,** also called *open-end credit* or *option-terms credit,* involves a credit agreement that allows consumers to purchase a variety of items using credit up to a predetermined maximum amount. A credit card is generally issued by the seller to identify the customer and can be used only for purchases from the issuer. Each month a statement is sent to the customer that lists previous purchases and amounts due. The customer can typically pay the entire outstanding balance within 25 to 30 days without additional finance charges. If the customer wishes, a minimum payment based on a standard formula can be paid instead, but a finance charge will be collected on the unpaid balance carried forward to the next monthly statement.

Retail Installment Credit.   **Retail installment credit** involves the purchase of a large ticket item by making a series of fixed, regular payments over a long period of time. There is generally a single contract for each item purchased with the payments, finance charges, and provisions for nonpayment specifically outlined in the agreement. Installment credit is also called *closed-end credit,* since the contract is generally marked "paid in full" and returned to the purchaser after the last payment is made as agreed.

Service Credit.   **Service credit** results from service providers agreeing to wait for payment from their customers. Doctors, dentists, plumbers, and others who furnish services will often send a bill or invoice at a later date requesting payment. There is often no formal contract and payment of the full amount of the invoice is expected by the service provider. Service providers in many cases will also accept general-purpose credit cards (described below) or set up retail installment plans for large debts.

Cash Credit

The second category of consumer credit is cash credit. **Cash credit** is an arrangement whereby a borrower obtains funds from a lender in exchange for an agreement to repay the funds later, generally with interest or finance charges. The funds that are borrowed may be used for a variety of purposes such as vacations, weddings, emergencies, and major purchases. Retail credit, the first category of consumer credit described above, involves the seller extending credit to facilitate the purchase of the good or service. In this category of consumer credit, the lender provides cash that will be used by the borrower.

Installment Loans.   **Installment loans** are loan arrangements where a series of fixed, regular payments are made by a borrower to repay funds over a period of time in the future. An installment loan customer might borrow money, for example, to buy an automobile from his or her neighbor. Student loans are also installment loans with the payments often commencing after graduation. After receiving the loan, the borrower will make regular payments to the lender to repay the principal along with any finance charge. The borrower will be required to provide evidence of income and financial security when applying for the loan so that the lender will feel confident that future payments will be forthcoming.

Single-Payment Loans.   **Single-payment loans** are generally short-term loans where funds are advanced for a year or less with an agreement that the funds will be repaid in one payment at the end of the period. Sometimes referred to as a *note* loan, the borrower will receive funds for the fixed time period, perhaps 90 days. He or she will return the funds in a single payment after the prescribed time period.

General-Purpose Credit Cards.   **General-purpose credit cards** are revolving credit arrangements where a borrower will pay for purchases using a credit card instead of cash. These credit cards, such as MasterCard, Visa, and Discover are accepted by a large number of vendors. The borrower receives an itemized statement each month that shows specific charges, purchases, and cash advances. The cardholder can typically pay the full amount each month without additional finance charges, or pay a minimum payment, in which case finance charges are later added to the account. These cards are examples of cash credit since they are used for a variety of purposes and are not necessarily issued by a specific vendor to facilitate a sale of a product or service.

Real Estate Credit

Real estate credit, the third consumer credit category, is credit that involves funds being extended to a borrower with a loan that uses real property as security or collateral for the loan. The funds may be used to purchase or improve a home or for any other purpose. A borrower may obtain a **mortgage loan,** a debt secured by real estate, to buy a family home. Also popular are other mortgage loans where the funds are used for any purpose: buying cars, college educations, or home improvements. These loans are popular because current tax laws often allow the interest on many such loans to be deducted from taxable income.

Business Credit

Business credit is the oldest form of credit. Suppliers, producers, vendors, and manufacturers need raw materials and inventory to carry on their enterprises. Because a time delay often exists between production and the delivery of funds upon sale, credit is often required. Farmers, for example, have used credit since the beginning of recorded history to purchase seeds with the debt being paid at harvest.

Merchandise Credit

Merchandise credit is used to obtain goods, raw materials, and inventory for resale. A business generally obtains the goods and agrees to pay according to various terms of sale provided by the seller that allow payment at a later date. In the meantime, the business may have the opportunity to sell the goods, thus generating the funds needed to pay for the original inventory purchase. A college bookstore, for example, may obtain notebooks from a distributor of school supplies that allows 30-day payment terms.

Financial Capital for Operations

Financial capital is the money needed to start, maintain, and operate a business. Funds are needed for a wide variety of purposes: salaries, marketing, overhead, and many other expenses that must be paid. Cash is needed to pay these expenses as they arise. The business expects, of course, that future profits from the sale of its products and services will provide the funds needed for repayment.

PUBLIC CREDIT

Public credit is borrowing by a level of government to finance the goods, services, and welfare programs it offers to its citizens. All levels of federal, state, and local governments borrow money when income from tax revenues is insufficient to pay for the programs they offer. Typically, the monies are raised through the sale of government bonds that promise to repay the funds to the investor(s) with interest over future time periods. Examples include school districts that issue bonds to build new schools, state governments that sell bonds to raise money for welfare programs, and the federal government selling securities to provide funds for national defense programs. The use of public credit has expanded greatly in recent years and the level of public debt continues to grow to record levels.

THE ROLE OF CREDIT IN THE ECONOMY

Credit has become an inescapable part of our everyday life. Its use can be both good or bad depending on the reason for its need and the ability of the borrower to repay in a timely manner. Business credit, for example, has often been considered **self-liquidating credit** since its purpose—obtaining goods and services for resale—automatically provides the means to repay when the goods are later resold. For example, a sporting goods store obtains an inventory of new bicycles with terms of sale that require payment within 60 days. During the first month, all the bicycles are sold, and the store owner has the funds needed to pay the account balance in full before it is considered past due.

What Credit Does for Consumers

Raise Standard of Living
Consumers generally benefit from using credit because they are able to use future income to pay for needed goods and services. They thus can raise their current standard of living based on their ability to earn or obtain funds in the future. A young, newly married couple, for example, can purchase needed furniture when they rent their first apartment. Students can obtain loans to attend college and use future income to repay the lender.

Handle Emergencies
Consumers are also able to deal with important emergencies and crises using credit. Unexpected automobile repairs, medical problems, and casualty losses must often be paid for immediately. Credit programs provide consumers the means to pay for these emergencies.

Convenient
Credit is also very convenient. Consumers can travel around the world using credit cards to pay for gas, hotels, airline tickets, and souvenirs. The need to carry large sums of cash is reduced. Travelers may never be caught short of cash if they carry a general-purpose credit card. An increasing number of vendors accept credit willingly and some, such as automobile rental agencies, actually prefer credit cards.

What Credit Does for Businesses

Expand Markets
Businesses rely on credit to expand their markets and find customers. If they provide credit purchase options for their customers, more people will be able to buy. Many

customers lack the funds to pay cash or prefer to use credit to purchase so they can pay later. A business soon realizes that many competitors offer credit plans. A business will need to accept credit use if it wants to survive.

Obtain Inventory and Supplies

Businesses also depend on the credit programs offered by their suppliers to obtain inventory and other items needed to operate their businesses. Businesses can expand product offerings and stock more goods if they are able to buy using credit.

Acquire Financial Capital

Finally, many businesses require capital to begin, maintain, and expand their operations. Many firms experience uneven cash flows where expenditures are required before funds arise from the sale of products and services. New locations, new employees, and marketing expenditures would often not be possible without the availability of business loans.

What Credit Does for the Economy

Credit has sometimes been referred to as the oil for our economic machinery. Credit enhances the flow of money and the factors of production within the economic system. The past economic growth of our nation with its expanding base of jobs, goods, and services has been due, in part, to our willingness to trust others for eventual payment. Credit has also provided a means to stabilize our level of economic activity by working to vary the interest rates charged for using credit.

Economic Stabilization Efforts

Exhibit 1–3 illustrates the business cycle. The **business cycle** refers to the up-and-down variations in the levels of total spending and productive activity that occur within our economic system. Although it is impossible to accurately predict the magnitude or duration of these swings in economic activity, the business cycle has occurred throughout history. During recessions, economic activity is at a low point and many problems occur, especially high unemployment and business failures. When the economy is in a recession, economists would like to see increased spending and activity. During peaks, the high levels of economic activity can lead to inflation, and economists generally want less spending.

The government attempts to smooth out these variations by using a combination of tools to change levels of spending and economic activity. These tools are classified as fiscal policy or monetary policy. The government monitors the economy by watching a series of economic indicators, and then tries to vary spending levels as needed. Basic economic theory provides that during recessions total spending should be increased, and during peak activity periods, spending should be moderated. The role of credit is especially important in monetary policy since the goal is to affect spending by controlling interest rates.

Fiscal Policy.   **Fiscal policy** is controlled by Congress as it implements laws to change taxes and the levels of government spending. Since government spending constitutes a large component of total spending, it can directly expand or reduce spending in the

EXHIBIT 1–3   The Business Cycle

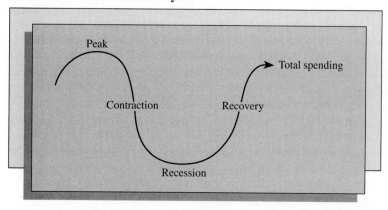

economy. During recessions, the president and Congress will often reduce taxes and expand government spending. This increased spending will stimulate economic activity and will generally lift the economy out of the recession. Fiscal policy is very powerful. If Congress votes to lower income taxes, for example, individual paychecks will increase very quickly as less is withheld for taxes. Many people will immediately spend this new income and the economy will rebound.

During inflationary periods, taxes should be raised and government spending should be reduced. It is politically unpopular to raise taxes and cut spending, however, so much of the burden for controlling inflation has been left for monetary policy.

Monetary Policy.   **Monetary policy** is controlled by the Federal Reserve System and involves several different policy tools designed to expand, or contract, the money supply to control interest rates. During recessions, when more spending is needed, the money supply will be expanded to lower interest rates and encourage spending. During inflationary periods, interest rates will be raised to discourage the high levels of spending that contribute to high prices. Interest rates and the money supply are controlled through the use of three primary tools: (1) changes in the Federal Reserve discount rate, (2) open-market operations, and (3) changes in reserve requirements.

The **discount rate** is the interest charged by the Federal Reserve System for loans made to commercial banks that belong to the system. Changes in the discount rate are widely published, and they generally indicate the direction the Fed wants interest rates to move. The announced changes usually result in corresponding changes in the interest rates charged by lenders throughout the economy. When these lenders increase their interest rates, auto, home, and other payments become higher immediately and less spending takes place.

Open-market operations include the buying and selling of government securities by the Federal Reserve System. If the Fed wishes to expand the money supply to lower interest rates, it will purchase government securities from the public, thus injecting more funds into circulation. More money in the economy will result in lower interest rates. Mortgage, auto, and other payments go down and more spending occurs. Selling government securities will reduce the money supply since funds are withdrawn from circulation as investors pay for the securities being sold. The reduced money supply causes interest rates to climb and discourages spending by business and consumers.

Reserve requirements are funds that depository institutions (i.e., banks, credit unions, savings and loan associations, and so on) must keep on hand or on deposit with the Federal Reserve System. By changing the reserve requirements, the Fed can either enhance or restrict the ability of the banking system to make loans and create additional spending. A financial institution needs to keep only a fraction of each deposit on reserve and can lend the excess amounts. These loans become deposits at other banks which can, in turn, make additional loans since they must keep only a portion in required reserves. This process of making loans, with the corresponding expansion of deposits within the banking system, is the primary method for expanding our money supply. Lowering reserve requirements during a recession is a powerful way to expand the money supply and lower interest rates.

DANGERS IN USING CREDIT

Certainly credit can be improperly used and cause many problems for businesses, consumers, and the community. All parties must be careful to ensure that credit is being used for productive purposes as well as being extended with appropriate care.

Dangers of Credit Use for Consumers

Consumers can use credit unwisely and experience disastrous outcomes. By overusing credit, some consumers find that they eventually cannot repay the borrowed funds or make their regular payments for merchandise. Credit is very tempting to the unwary consumer and the misuse of credit can result in bankruptcy, lost property, ruined marriages, and poor credit ratings. Some consumers find that they have committed too much of their future income and, in the process, lose their ability to save funds for important financial goals. As the availability of credit purchase options expands, it becomes even more important for families to learn budgeting and sound financial management practices.

Dangers of Credit Use for Business

Businesses must also be careful when using and extending credit. If too many customers use credit to purchase goods and services, and do not pay as agreed, many dollars of profit will be required to make up the losses. One of the most important reasons for a high failure rate among small businesses is the inability to implement good credit-management policies. Businesses must exercise extreme care in making sure that only qualified customers are given the opportunity to use credit programs. Effective collection departments must be organized to bring about positive cash flows from credit operations. Also, the costs of extending and collecting credit accounts must be controlled to make sure that important profits are not eroded.

Need for Education

It is clear that both providers and users of credit need to be careful. Credit is increasing in importance and seems to be replacing cash as a medium of exchange. Nearly everyone, such as consumers, businesspersons, and voters, will benefit from additional education regarding credit as an important part of our economic system.

The education for consumers should involve training in budgeting, understanding the terms of the various credit contracts, and the willingness to pay contracts as agreed. They should also understand their rights as outlined by the many consumer protection laws that have been passed in the area of credit management.

Businesses need to understand how to establish workable credit policies, how to investigate credit applicants, and how to collect the funds that are due following a credit transaction.

Important Terms

business credit   7

business cycle   12

cash credit   9

collateral   6

consumer credit   8

credit   6

creditor   4

creditworthiness   5

debtor   4

discount rate   13

finance charge   6

financial capital   10

fiscal policy   12

general-purpose credit card   9

inflation   6

installment loans   9

medium of exchange   4

merchandise credit   10

monetary policy   13

mortgage loan   10

open-market operations   13

private credit   7

public credit   7

real estate credit   10

reserve requirements   14

retail credit   8

retail installment credit   9

revolving credit   8

self-liquidation credit   11

service credit   9

single-payment loans   9

Discussion Questions

1. Describe how both cash and credit can function as a medium of exchange in a sales transaction.

2. Explain seven important components found in a credit transaction.

3. Describe the two main classifications of credit—private and public.

4. Discuss the stages a typical product passes through on its way to the ultimate consumer, and indicate how consumer and business credit is different.

5. List and describe three types of retail credit.

6. List and describe three types of cash credit.

7. Define real estate credit.

8. Discuss the differences between the two types of business credit.
9. Explain why business credit is often considered a "self-liquidating" credit.
10. Describe three advantages for consumers who use credit.
11. List and explain four advantages and uses of credit for businesses.
12. Describe fiscal policy and how it is used to change total spending within the economy.
13. List and explain the three policy tools used by the Federal Reserve System to control the money supply and interest rates.
14. Explain possible dangers of using credit for:
    a. Consumers
    b. Businesses
15. Why might credit be called the "oil that lubricates our economic machinery?"
16. Describe how the seven components of a credit transaction are incorporated in the following:
    a. An automobile loan from a bank
    b. A student loan
    c. The sale of business inventory to another business

CASE PROBLEM

Note: This case is used throughout the text and provides information used in later case problems.

Bill and Betty Stevens
123 Main Street
Anytown, USA

Family Information

The Stevens have been married for 21 years and have two children; Robert, age 17, and Sally, age 14. They expect both children to attend college, probably at a local state-supported university. They have already established a small savings account for each child, but expect to apply for financial aid when the time arrives for their children to attend college. Betty and Bill hope their children can earn grants or scholarships, but the Stevens are prepared to borrow money using student loans as needed.

Business Owned

Bill is the owner and manager of Office Supply, Inc., a local office supply store located near their home. Bill, 42, opened the office products store about three years ago. He purchased a franchise from a national chain store operation with personal savings and a business installment loan from a local bank, First National Bank. When Bill purchases inventory from the national warehouse, he has 30 days to pay for it, and if he pays within 10 days from the date of the invoice, he can subtract a 2 percent cash discount from the invoice total. These terms of sales are typical of other suppliers he often uses for the office supplies he stocks in his store. Bill employs two full-time and four part-time employees.

Customers of Office Supply, Inc., are generally small- and medium-sized businesses that buy paper products, office equipment, computers, and supplies.

The store accepts cash, checks, and credit cards from its customers. The store accepts MasterCard, Visa, the Discover Card, and a proprietary credit card, the Office Supply Card. Regular customers are invited to apply for the Office Supply Card that can be used at any Office Supply, Inc., branch in the United States. A sales finance company, Ace Finance, recently offered to assist the store in providing installment purchase options for customers wishing to buy computer systems.

Betty's Employment

Betty is an office manager for Mainstreet Dental Clinic where she supervises the work of three administrative assistants who work with patient accounts, file insurance claim forms, and maintain the accounting records for the clinic.

New customers who have dental insurance are asked to complete a short application form on their first visit to collect information about their insurance company and other financial data. The charges for dental services are then billed directly to the insurance company and the customer is given 30 days for the payment to arrive. If for some reason payment is not forthcoming, the customer is expected to pay the outstanding balance. Clients without insurance are encouraged to pay for their bill in full before leaving the office, but some credit will be allowed if they have good credit histories.

The Stevens's Home

The Stevens purchased their current home eight years ago with the help of a home mortgage loan from their bank. Last year they borrowed additional funds using a home equity loan (a second mortgage) to pay for home improvements and medical bills.

Other Credit Programs

The family has three credit cards, Visa, the Discover Card, and an oil company card. The Stevens purchased a new car last year from a local dealer and took advantage of a low-cost loan program offered by the manufacturer.

Credit in Action

List as many examples of credit use as possible. Using the Classification of Credit Types from Chapter 1, identify each type of credit illustrated.

a. Is the credit example business or consumer credit?

b. Who is the creditor and who is the debtor?

2

ROLE OF THE CREDIT MANAGER

Learning Objectives

After studying this chapter, you should be able to:

- Describe the reasons a business would offer credit purchase options.
- Describe three examples of outside providers of credit programs.
- Explain the factors that affect the decision to establish an internal credit department.
- Describe the goals of the credit manager.
- Explain the steps in the credit management process.
- Discuss the activities of professional associations for credit managers.
- Discuss important qualifications for a career in credit management.

The first chapter defined credit and discussed its role in our economy. Now, we consider the role of the credit manager: (1) the reasons a firm would require a credit manager, (2) the goals a credit manager works to attain, and (3) the duties and responsibilities performed by credit management personnel with emphasis on the stages involved in processing applications for credit. Finally, we will look at credit management as a career and discuss some of the qualifications and skills a good credit manager should possess.

THE BUSINESS DECISION TO OFFER CREDIT PROGRAMS

The business decision to offer credit programs, or options for purchase other than with cash, actually involves two basic questions. The first question is: Should we offer a credit purchase option or require cash sales only? Second, assuming a credit program is desired, Should we operate our own credit program or use an outside provider of credit management services?

Most businesses allow customers to purchase goods and services using credit. Although one occasionally finds a sign posted by a business, "No Credit Allowed," the offer of a credit program is almost universal. Manufacturers, distributors, and retailers have found that sales will generally increase if they offer credit programs. Businesses also find that their customers desire credit options because of the convenience involved and the need for additional time to pay. Many customers will buy only from those sources that offer alternatives to cash purchases. If competitors offer credit programs, a business may not be able to escape offering credit options and will have to match the competition. If a dentist requires cash before providing dental care, or if an office supplies wholesaler requires cash in advance from every customer, the actual level of sales may be too low to sustain the business. Customers will automatically migrate to those businesses that provide time payment plans. Finally, some businesses depend on finance charges as an important source of revenue and will offer credit programs to improve profits.

Reasons a Business Offers Credit Programs

- Generate additional sales.
- Satisfy customer desires.
- Improve customer service.
- Meet competition.
- Improve profits.

Most businesses need to offer credit programs to generate sufficient sales. Perhaps the more important decision for a business is whether to develop in-house credit programs or to use an outside provider of credit purchase options.

USING OUTSIDE PROVIDERS OF CREDIT PROGRAMS

Many businesses decide to transfer the credit management functions to others. Examples include accepting general-purpose credit cards, selling installment contracts to indirect lenders, or subcontracting the credit management functions.

General-Purpose Credit Cards

Some firms will accept general-purpose credit cards, such as VISA or MasterCard, instead of cash. A financial institution, or other financial service provider, makes the decision to issue the credit card after conducting an investigation of creditworthiness. It generally assigns a credit line to each customer to limit total purchases at stores or businesses that accept the card. The business that accepts the credit card may be required to conduct credit authorization checks to make sure the proper person is using the card and that the card has not been lost or stolen. The business will generally receive less than the full amount of the purchase to cover transaction costs. Also, the business may be required to purchase equipment used in processing charges.

Indirect Lenders

Other businesses will offer installment purchase options for large ticket items. They will help a customer fill out an application for credit, but will send the application to an indirect lender. An **indirect lender** is a financial institution (e.g., bank or consumer finance company) that purchases installment credit contracts as they are created by the seller of the goods. A customer might pick out a new refrigerator in an appliance store, for example, and complete an application along with an installment purchase contract. Later, the customer receives a payment book from the consumer finance company that "purchased" the credit agreement. The appliance store receives funds immediately and the finance company collects the payments and finance charges outlined in the contract. The indirect lender (finance company in this example) will typically be involved in the decision to accept the customer. Once the contract is sold, the indirect lender will be responsible for servicing and collecting the account.

Factoring

As we will learn in later chapters, some business credit departments decide to transfer the entire credit and collections functions to other providers by using the services of a factor. A **factor** is a financial institution, or other agency, that purchases the accounts receivable of a business from clients and assumes all credit risks involved. A perfume distributor, for example, might send all orders to a factor that decides if the order should be filled based on the creditworthiness of the purchaser. If the order is approved, the perfume distributor is immediately given access to the funds and the factor becomes responsible for collecting the amounts owed. The business that uses a factor may not need a full-time credit manager.

These programs, provided by others outside the firm, will be more fully explained in the chapters that follow. The business that uses other agencies to provide credit programs may not need an internal credit department. However, these outside programs will carry fees and other costs. The business may suffer from customer complaints, lost goodwill, and lost time for workers to process the necessary applications, contracts, and sales vouchers. The business will also find that while these costs must be paid, it will receive no interest or earnings from the credit operation. In spite of these costs, some businesses will decide to use an outside provider rather than operate their own credit department.

THE DECISION TO DEVELOP AN INTERNAL CREDIT DEPARTMENT

The decision to operate an internal credit department is often difficult because a new department requires increased costs of operation and qualified personnel. These employees need specific knowledge and experience in credit management. Other important considerations include the amount of capital available, type of goods sold, legal restrictions, and the availability of outside providers of credit programs. The most important factor affecting the decision to offer credit programs is the effect a self-managed credit program has on sales and profits.

Costs of Operations

There are many costs involved in operating an internal credit department. Salaries must be paid to credit workers. Funds must be spent to provide equipment, supplies, and printed materials to support the credit activity. There are also costs associated with promoting credit programs, conducting credit investigations, and collecting accounts. Occasionally, amounts may have to be "written off" as uncollectible. Finance charges may offset some of these costs. In business credit, however, this income may not exist or will be insufficient to cover the costs. The businessperson must consider these costs carefully in deciding whether to offer credit purchase options through an internal credit operation.

Amount of Capital Available

A business that offers customers additional time to pay for goods and services is investing financial capital as it waits for them to repay the funds. The accounting records for the firm will now include an **accounts receivable,** an accounting entry that records the funds due on accounts from customers arising from sales or services provided. In many business credit arenas, and occasionally in consumer credit, no interest is charged during the time the funds are owed. Yet the firm may be required to pay its own bills before the funds have been collected from its customers. The business must have the capital available to pay its own bills and wait for customers to pay.

Availability of Qualified Credit Personnel

One of the leading causes of small business failures is the problems associated with accounts receivable. Many business owners lack skills and experience in credit management. Policies need to be developed that help employees determine which customers qualify for new accounts. Other procedures are needed to manage credit activities. Experienced credit workers are needed to make decisions, work with customer accounts, and employ effective collection techniques. A myriad of laws and restrictions require compliance, or the firm may experience numerous legal problems. If the owner is unable to provide this knowledge and experience, additional employees may be required.

Legal Restrictions

Many state and federal laws influence credit activities. Most laws, as we will learn in later chapters, deal with disclosure of credit terms, unfair discrimination in credit decision making, contract terms, and unfair collection practices. Some state laws, for example, set maximum repayment periods and interest rates on installment credit contracts. The business owner must be willing to follow changes in these laws and comply with the legal provisions in the many laws that exist.

Type of Goods and Services Offered

One of the basic principles of credit management is that the value of the goods financed should never fall below the amount owed. In other words, a customer may not pay for an item if the benefits of owning it have disappeared or been significantly reduced. For instance, allowing customers to charge groceries carries an additional risk since, once consumed, the desire to pay later may vanish. Borrowers are more likely to make regular payments on a home mortgage or automobile loan because the good purchased continues to provide an economic benefit. Before offering a credit purchase option, the business must make sure that the product or service offered is valuable, and that the value is sustained over the repayment period.

Availability of Outside Credit Providers

As we have seen above, a business may be required to offer credit programs as a result of competition and the desires of its customers. Occasionally, no outside provider of credit programs is available for a business, and the business may have to offer credit programs itself.

Factors Affecting Decision to Develop an Internal Credit Department

- Effect on sales and profits.
- Costs of operations.
- Amount of capital available.
- Availability of qualified credit personnel.
- Legal restrictions.
- Type of goods and services offered.
- Availability of outside providers.

CREDIT MANAGEMENT FUNCTIONS

Once the decision to establish a credit department has been made, attention must be directed toward the responsibilities, duties, and goals of the credit manager. A **credit manager** is an individual within a business organization responsible for evaluating customer applications for credit and who holds the power to commit business resources in a credit transaction. Although the term *credit manager* is used in many business credit situations, this definition also applies to many others whose titles might be loan officer, business manager, comptroller, among others. A loan officer in a financial institution, for example, evaluates applications for loans and decides if loan proceeds will be advanced. A retail credit manager will decide, based on the information provided, if a customer will be allowed to purchase items using credit. The common link is the challenge to evaluate risk and decide if a credit relationship is possible between the creditor and the applicant.

The credit manager must balance many different, and sometimes competing, concerns. A marginal customer who wants to open a credit account offers an opportunity or a threat. If the customer pays bills in a timely manner and handles the credit account well, the credit program offers an opportunity to increase sales. On the other hand, the customer may not handle the credit account well, and the decision to offer credit purchase options will result in additional costs for the business.

GOALS OF THE CREDIT MANAGER

The credit manager is empowered to commit business resources after an evaluation of the customer's willingness and ability to pay. Throughout the investigation and decision-making process, the credit manager must concentrate on many different goals.

Increase Sales Revenue

The credit manager is in an important position within the organization's strategy to increase sales. Every business enterprise sells a good or service. If more credit applications are approved, more sales will result. An organization will not survive long without a constant flow of customers willing and able to buy the firm's product. The credit manager will try to approve as many applications as possible.

Monitor and Control the Volume of Receivables

In most financial institutions, the loan or other credit arrangement is the product being offered. Here, the credit manager will work to expand the volume of receivables by making more loans, issuing more credit cards, or establishing more accounts with quality customers. In most business credit environments, however, no interest is paid by customers who pay invoices within the time frame allowed. In this case, an important challenge for the credit manager is keeping the outstanding receivables as low as possible. The volume of receivables will grow automatically as a business grows, but the growth must be monitored and controlled. Serious cash flow problems will develop if too many customers delay or withhold payments.

Bad debt expense is a category in a firm's financial records for recording uncollectible debts. This situation occurs when the prospect of collecting the amount due has vanished, or the costs involved in further collection efforts are greater than the funds owed. Bad debt expense is very difficult to absorb since the loss usually includes the value of the merchandise sold in addition to any finance charges outstanding. The credit manager must continually monitor the effectiveness of collections activities to uncover trends and improve results.

Control Operating Costs and Expenses

The credit process requires human effort, capital expenditures for equipment, and payments for outside services that contribute to credit operations. Salaries, supplies, computers, investigation expenses, and collection costs must be paid. The credit manager must decide if the benefits from a particular expenditure outweigh the costs.

Reduce Collection Expenses and Bad Debt

After the loan is made, or the credit purchase approved, the credit manager must wait for payments on the account. Effective collection efforts involve carefully monitoring accounts and responding early when payments are not made. Research clearly indicates that the longer an account is allowed to languish without a follow-up, the less likely full payment will be made. Collection expenses include the time used in collections efforts, legal fees, mail expenses, and possible payment for outside assistance such as collection agencies.

Develop Credit and Collections Policies

Most modern business credit departments have well-defined credit and collections policies. A **credit policy** is a written guideline for employees that defines the basic qualifications and requirements for deciding which customers will be offered credit purchase options. A **collections policy** defines the collection process, collection devices used, and the time line for implementing specific collection activities.

Train and Supervise Other Employees

Any manager must be involved in the basic management functions of planning, organizing, directing, and controlling. Within the credit department, the credit manager must develop the strategies, policies, and procedures necessary to accomplish basic department goals. Employees must be placed in positions that will use their individual strengths and, if needed, additional training must be available. Performance appraisals and other control measures must be implemented to ensure that employees are working up to their potential.

Cooperate with Other Departments

The credit manager must also train others in the firm about the credit functions and the decision-making process. In business credit situations, for example, the credit manager may have limited personal contact with the customers. The sales representatives for the firm call on customers and attempt to gather orders. These representatives must understand the credit process so they can assist the credit manager in gathering information. They must also explain the credit programs available and the basic requirements for opening a credit account. The credit and sales departments must work closely together since credit programs are needed to complete sales. Also, the credit manager must cooperate with those who monitor the firm's cash flow. The credit manager helps improve this flow of cash by assisting with the collections of accounts receivable.

Maintain Good Customer Relations

The credit granting and collections activity provides many opportunities to earn or ruin customer satisfaction. Good human relations skills must be practiced by everyone who comes in contact with customers. Many times, the conversations and requests for payments require negotiation skills. The employees must be friendly, but they must also deal with customers in a firm, businesslike fashion. Developing understandable policies and consistent procedures to deal with questions helps employees work with customers.

Goals of the Credit Manager

- Increase sales revenues.
- Monitor and control receivables.
- Control operating costs and expenses.
- Reduce collections expenses.
- Develop credit and collections policies.
- Train and supervise employees.
- Cooperate with other departments.
- Maintain good customer relations.

THE CREDIT MANAGEMENT PROCESS

Exhibit 2–1 shows the different steps involved in the credit- granting process. The **credit management process** is a series of steps that involves promoting credit purchase options, analyzing the risk of credit applicants, and collecting the payments after the debt is created. The process is universal and applies to both consumer and business credit operations. At each stage, the credit manager must develop operating policies that will help ensure that each credit account is handled in a consistent, cost-effective manner.

Promotion describes any effort undertaken to encourage product sales or to increase the number of customers using credit purchase options. The promotion of credit programs is undertaken to increase sales as more people will purchase products if credit programs are available. Once the credit programs are in place, promotion may be needed to attract appropriate customers. The credit manager must oversee these activities to ensure that quality customers are attracted using acceptable promotion activities. Direct mail, special sales and terms, direct solicitation by company sales staff, and media advertising are used

EXHIBIT 2–1   **Steps in Granting Credit**

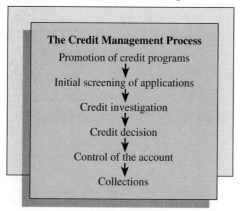

The Credit Management Process

Promotion of credit programs

Initial screening of applications

Credit investigation

Credit decision

Control of the account

Collections

to encourage customers to open credit accounts. Existing customers with good credit histories must also be encouraged to use their credit accounts more often. Higher credit volume generally results in lower costs per credit customer and, if finance charges are levied, more customers (and sales) will increase the income from credit operations.

The promotion activity also requires that the application process is relatively easy. The application form must be short, but it must collect enough information to allow an adequate investigation. A steady flow of applications will allow the credit manager to improve credit sales.

Initial Screening of Applications

Initial screening describes the efforts by credit personnel to make quick, cost-effective checks to see if an applicant meets the basic criteria for opening a credit account. The promotion activities will generate applications for new credit accounts. Most credit departments will first use various internal screening activities to determine if a more in-depth, more costly credit investigation is suggested.

Many consumer credit grantors now use credit scoring systems to screen new applications for credit. A **credit scoring system** is a statistically based form, or computer program, that assigns points to different facts reported in the credit application, financial statements, or the credit bureau report. The guide typically assigns values to specific credit qualities; that is, income, years at the same address, and time on the job. In business credit, the points may be based on financial ratios, which are calculated using the assets, liabilities, and earnings of the business credit applicant. If the credit score is high enough, a more complete investigation will continue. Some retail credit card issuers use computerized credit scoring systems to make the decision to offer the credit card and to assign a credit line to the account.

In business credit, the prescreening often includes studying and analyzing the financial statements of the firm requesting a credit purchase. **Financial statement**

analysis involves the calculation of various financial ratios, and other computations, using numbers drawn from financial statements. The results are used to evaluate the liquidity, profitability, and financial health of the firm applying for credit.

Credit Investigation

A **credit investigation** involves a series of steps undertaken to verify information on the credit application and determine how the customer has handled past financial obligations. The credit investigation involves many activities to gather the information needed to make a sound decision. Usually the credit manager will verify the income and financial health of the applicant. The challenge for the credit manager is to gather enough information without spending too much time and money on unnecessary investigation efforts. Also, the credit manager may develop specific policies to guide the investigation effort. One example of a policy would be to require verification of at least two years' employment history for each applicant.

The credit manager will generally contact commercialized reporting agencies during this stage of the credit management process. **Commercialized reporting agencies** collect, retain, and sell information about the credit histories of consumers and businesses. Large nationwide databases are maintained that include demographic information, employment histories, credit payment records, public record information, and other data related to a consumer's credit history. Dun and Bradstreet, along with other business reporting agencies, gathers credit-related information about business customers. The fees for reports vary depending on the type of report requested, the agency that provides the reports, and the methods used in delivering the information to the user.

The credit investigation stage will also involve **direct inquiry,** that is, the process of contacting employers, credit grantors, and other individuals who can verify facts and provide information about an applicant's willingness and ability to pay. Direct inquiry requires the permission of the applicant and is generally obtained with the application. The credit manager must realize that wages paid for the time credit personnel spend conducting direct inquiry contribute to the cost of the credit investigation.

Credit Decision

The **credit decision** is a judgment made by the credit manager to accept or reject an application for a credit purchase. Credit is a medium of exchange with limited acceptance due to the time and risk involved in collecting payments. After the investigation is completed, the credit manager must decide if the promise to pay later is valid.

The decision may also require setting a credit line. A **credit line** is a pre-authorized spending limit assigned to a customer that automatically allows additional purchases up to a certain amount. The credit manager may not look at the credit applicant's file again unless a new purchase will cause the debt to exceed the credit line. The credit line acts like a red flag to show that credit purchases may be getting too high. The credit manager may, however, extend the line as needed if the customer has been handling the account well. In the meantime, credit assistants can approve all orders that keep the account below the established credit line.

The credit manager must constantly balance the need for more credit customers with the need to control costs and losses. The ability to make a good decision is based on a combination of art and science. The science often involves the ability to analyze the financial health of the applicant. The art evolves with experience and includes the ability to ask the right questions to predict payment results.

Control of the Account

Control functions are used to monitor an account to ensure that total indebtedness is appropriate for an individual customer. The debt may drift too high, or good customers may not be using enough credit. Control activities involve "watching" the accounts to verify that payments are being made as planned and that the relationship between the customer and the credit grantor continues to be productive. Part of this activity requires the credit manager to update customer information occasionally to make decisions to expand or restrict credit lines. Methods need to be developed that will assist credit personnel in identifying accounts that are falling behind in their payments. Authorization procedures are required to prevent credit extensions beyond the approved credit lines. Other techniques may be useful in soliciting more business from customers who are handling their accounts in a responsible fashion.

Collections

Collection activities include any effort to get credit customers to pay their bills, or payments, in a timely manner. This is one of the most important aspects of effective credit management. A disciplined, responsive collections program will improve cash flow, maintain good customer relations, and increase sales. This activity requires contacting past-due customers, making reasonable arrangements for payment, and following up if the arrangements are broken. Collection devices include invoices, letters, telephone calls, and legal efforts depending on the severity of the collection problem. Research shows that the longer a bill goes without payment, the more difficult it becomes to collect an account.

A CAREER IN CREDIT MANAGEMENT

The Demand for Credit Managers

As the use of credit has expanded throughout our economy, the importance of trained, qualified credit managers has also grown. Many credit managers enjoy the challenges of credit risk analysis and decision making. Their positions are often essential to the success of their firms, since credit programs are an important ingredient for increased sales and quality customer service. Every day presents a variety of tasks and rewards. Credit managers also enjoy helping consumers and business customers improve their own economic status through the responsible use of credit. The need for credit management professionals is being recognized more and more as business owners become aware of the specific skills and qualities needed in this field.

Most credit managers initially receive training and education in other areas such as accounting, finance, or general business administration. Once employed, however, they may develop an interest in credit operations and the specialized skills that bring about promotions into credit management positions. Although a few educational institutions in the United States offer specialized degree programs in credit management, a considerable amount of training occurs in individual business firms and credit managers must often develop their own training programs. Much of the training burden is also carried by professional associations that offer seminars, correspondence courses, and other continuing education offerings.

PROFESSIONAL ASSOCIATIONS FOR CREDIT MANAGERS

Nearly every occupational group organizes its members by creating a professional association. Professional associations provide many services to their members, including educational offerings, lobbying activities, publications, information exchange, and public relations efforts. Some of the professional associations related to credit management appear in Exhibit 2–2.

Educational Offerings

Most professionals encounter ongoing changes in legislation, technology, and approaches to doing their jobs. Professional associations usually sponsor a continuous flow of seminars, workshops, and other training events to keep members up-to-date. A credit management organization, for example, might offer seminars to explain recent changes in bankruptcy laws, or explain new techniques for analyzing financial statements. Workshops might be conducted to train credit workers in microcomputer applications for the credit departments. Many other educational offerings are possible to help both experienced and inexperienced credit managers improve their skills and knowledge.

EXHIBIT 2–2   Professional Associations for Credit Managers

- National Association of Credit Management
- American Bankers Association
- American Collectors Association
- Credit Union National Association
- Society of Certified Credit Executives
- International Credit Association
- American Financial Services Association
- Consumer Bankers Association

Lobbying Activities

Members of a professional association generally have a similar set of goals, interests, and desires regarding legislative changes. Bankers, for example, might universally agree that bankruptcy laws are already too liberal and should not be amended to provide more protection for bankruptcy petitioners. Most professional associations will engage in lobbying activities to influence the future of proposed legislation. A professional lobbyist may be employed to discuss important bills with legislators, testify before legislative committees, and work to put forth the wishes and desires of the association he or she represents.

Publications

Most professional associations publish newsletters, magazines, or books to help members stay informed. The current events that are reported will generally address issues and techniques that are important to the members. Advertising may be included that will help the members learn about new products or new service providers. Articles are also included to explain new methods of accomplishing tasks and to offer suggestions for improving credit management results.

Information Exchange

Some professional associations arrange formal methods for the exchange of information between members. For example, the National Association for Credit Management (NACM), primarily an organization of business credit managers, has maintained a credit interchange bureau for many years that allows credit managers to exchange information about the payment records of mutual customers. Even without a formal exchange mechanism, the regular meetings of a professional association allow networking to occur with the opportunity to talk with others involved in similar activities.

Public Relations

Sometimes the professional association will launch efforts to improve the image of the profession. Such activities may indirectly improve the ability of a credit manager to do the job if the public gets a better understanding of what they do and why it is important to the community. Public relations activities may also be instrumental in attracting qualified workers to the field and improving the quality of workers.

IMPORTANT QUALIFICATIONS FOR CREDIT MANAGERS

Credit managers need a variety of skills and a specialized information base to do their jobs well. At this point, we will summarize some of the more important qualities, techniques, and understandings that make individuals good credit managers.

Careful Attention to Detail

Since the essence of credit management activities is risk analysis and decision making, credit managers need to be very detail conscious. They cannot afford to overlook important facts that may seriously affect the outcome of a particular credit decision. Applications, and other forms, must be completed carefully. Contracts must be signed, legal rights recorded, and financial records must be accurate. These duties require careful attention to the details of each task.

Ability to Make Decisions

Credit managers obviously make many decisions. A good credit manager will be able to make decisions based on the information available. Many times more information will be desired, but will be unavailable or too costly to obtain. One of the biggest challenges in credit management is the task of making decisions quickly with the information at hand. Of course, a good decision will not be made if too much information is missing, but time and money cannot be wasted gathering additional, unnecessary details. Unfortunately, few decisions seem obvious and easy to make for many beginning credit managers.

Persistence

A good credit manager must be persistent. Sometimes important investigation steps need to be completed before a decision can be made. Collections activities also require patience and persistence in locating customers, uncovering the true reasons for nonpayment, and making acceptable arrangements for payment. Disciplined, consistent follow-up is the key to success in collections efforts and sales.

Good Human Relations Skills

Many credit management activities require good human relations skills. A loan officer, for example, must use empathy and understand how nervous applicants may be when they apply for a loan. A collector must obviously mix patience with firmness when dealing with customers who have fallen behind in their repayment schedules. Good communications skills are also required in nearly every credit management activity.

Important Qualities for Credit Managers

- Careful attention to details.
- Ability to make decisions.
- Persistence.
- Good human relations skills.

ORGANIZATION OF THIS TEXTBOOK

This textbook is divided into two main sections, one for consumer credit and another for business credit. Within each section, the chapters will first describe the credit types discussed earlier in the classification outline from Chapter 1. In the "Consumer Credit" section, for example, the chapters will first describe the differences and main features of retail credit, cash loan credit, and real estate credit. In the "Business Credit" section, the early chapters will address the two main types: merchandise credit and obtaining financial capital for operations.

After the credit types are described, the text will look at the steps involved in risk analysis and decision making in both consumer and business credit. The credit management process described earlier will provide the general framework for the chapters that follow. A separate section will discuss the collections process, common collection tools, devices, and techniques that are used in both consumer and business credit.

Important Terms

bad debt expense   24
collection activities   29
collections policy   25
commercialized reporting agencies   28
control functions   29
credit decision   28
credit investigation   28
credit line   28
credit manager   23

credit management process   26
credit policy   25
credit scoring system   27
direct inquiry   28
factor   21
financial statement analysis   27
indirect lender   21
initial screening   27
promotion   26

Discussion Questions

1. Explain four reasons a business might decide to offer credit purchase options to its customers.

2. List and describe examples of outside providers of credit programs that allow customers to use credit purchase options without the seller having to operate its own credit department.

3. Describe some disadvantages of using outside providers of credit programs.

4. List and describe six factors that affect the business decision to develop and manage an internal credit department.

5. Explain seven important goals for a credit manager.

6. Identify and describe the six steps in the credit management process.

7. What activities does a professional association typically engage in to help the members of the organization?

8. Name seven professional associations that currently assist credit managers in different fields.

9. Describe four important qualifications for a career in credit management.

Suggested Readings—Part I

Callahan, Terry. "The Changing Role of the Credit Professional?" *Business Credit,* September 1996, p. 14.

Cleaver, Joanne and Frances Martin. "Pass or Fail for Credit Education." *Credit Card Management,* September 1996, p. 110.

Davies, Glyn. "Credit: 6,000 Years Old and Still Evolving Vigorously." *Business Credit,* June 1996, p. 16.

DeLapa, Gina. "Financial Literacy is Everyone's Job." *Credit World,* July/August 1996, p. 32.

Glade, Carole. "Credit Education—A Challenge in Creativity." *Credit World,* November/December 1995, p. 9.

Kaufman, Richard. "Credit Management: The Value-Added Function." *Business Credit,* November/December 1996, p. 40.

Ladwig, Kit. "The Scramble for Credit Managers." *Collections and Credit Risk,* July 1996, p. 23.

Naff, Kevin C. "Customer Service and the Credit Department." *Business Credit,* May 1995, p. 25.

Schauseil, Robin. "The NACM National Education Department: Serving Your Needs." *Business Credit,* May 1996, p. 51.

Schuchardt, Jane; Cynthia Needles Fletcher; and Linda Kirk Fox. "Improving Consumer Credit Literacy—A Public-Private Responsibility." *Credit World,* November/December 1996, p. 21.

Susswein, Ruth. "College Students and Credit Cards: A Privilege Earned?" *Credit World,* May/June 1995, p. 21.

"The Federal Reserve System." *Business Credit,* July/August 1995, p. 21.

Thorpe, Paula. "The Credit Manager: Adapting to Change." *Business Credit,* September 1996, p. 12.

Whelan, Kevin J. "Credit and Collections: A Paradigm Shift?" *Credit World,* July/August 1996, p. 20.

Wolner, Dan A. "Death of the Bean Counter." *Business Credit,* May 1995, p. 17. (Role of Credit Manager)

Internet Sites

http://www.pueblo.gsa.gov/money.htn
> This site includes a catalog of free and inexpensive government publications related to personal finance, credit laws, and money.

http://www.dfi.state.in.us
> Indiana Department of Financial Institutions, Consumer Credit Division, provides information on many topics related to credit use and consumer protection laws.

Professional Associations:

http://www.aba.com
> American Bankers Association

http://www.collector.com
> American Collectors Association

http://www.scsn.net/users/cpi
> Credit Professionals International

http://www.cuna.org
> Credit Union National Association

http://www.ica-credit.org
> International Credit Association

http://www.ibaa.org
> Independent Bankers Association of America

http://www.nacm.org
> National Association of Credit Management

Federal Reserve Banks:

gopher://town.hall.org
   Federal Reserve Board Data
http://www.bog.frb.fed.us
   Board of Governors
http://www.frbchi.org
   Federal Reserve Bank of Chicago
http://www.stls.frb.org
   Federal Reserve Bank of St. Louis
http://woodrow.mpls.frb.fed.us
   Federal Reserve Bank-Minneapolis

Data:

http://www.census.gov
   Census Bureau
http://stats.bls.gov
   Bureau of Labor Statistics
http://www.fedworld.gov
   List of Government Agencies

CASE PROBLEM

Refer to the Bill and Betty Stevens's case problem in Chapter 1. Make a list of different credit management positions indicated in the problem and list some of the tasks they are required to complete. (One example is shown.)

Credit Management Position	Tasks
Loan Officer at bank:auto loan	

UNDERSTANDING CONSUMER CREDIT

3 RETAIL AND SERVICE CREDIT

Learning Objectives

After studying this chapter, you should be able to:

- Distinguish between "retail credit" and "cash credit."
- Explain the benefits of providing retail and service credit and potential problems.
- Explain the characteristics, benefits, and pitfalls of 30-day retail charge account programs.
- Explain the characteristics, benefits, and pitfalls of retail installment credit.
- Discuss the principles of retail installment credit.
- Explain the important features and operating characteristics of retail revolving credit.
- Discuss the variations in computing finance charges in revolving credit plans.
- Show how to compute the approximate annual percentage rate (APR), and rebates for prepayment in installment transactions.
- Explain the growing importance of service and professional credit.

RETAIL CREDIT—GENERAL PURPOSE AND CONCERNS

As described in Chapter 1, **retail credit** is a category of credit used by consumers to purchase final goods and services directly from sellers. This type of credit differs from cash credit because the purpose of the retail credit transaction is to facilitate the sale of a product or service. **Cash credit** provides the user with cash or more generalized purchasing power to use for a variety of purposes. Retail credit is often offered by the store or service provider to furnish an alternative means of payment if the purchaser does not wish to use cash. Of course, some buyers may not have the cash and wish to commit future income to the purchase. Thus, they wish to "buy now, pay later."

Benefits of Providing Retail and Service Credit

Regardless of the specific credit program offered, the retailer or service provider benefits from offering credit purchase options. Most important is the opportunity to increase sales since a new category of buyers is now available—those without available cash. Customers using retail credit tend to spend more and generally purchase better-quality products than cash purchasers. Better-quality products often result in fewer returns and increased customer satisfaction. Retail credit options help a business match the offerings of its competitors and will attract customers who prefer to use credit for convenience. Some retailers also believe that offering credit programs provides an opportunity to strengthen customer loyalty.

Benefits of Providing Retail and Service Credit

- Increase sales volume.
- Better quality products sold.
- Match competition.
- Attract convenience-oriented customers.
- Strengthen customer ties.

Potential Problems Arising from Retail Credit Programs

There are many problems and challenges that occur for retailers offering credit programs. Operating costs will increase along with the need to promote credit plans, investigate applications for credit, manage accounts, and collect past-due amounts. Extra equipment, space, and personnel will be required to conduct the credit operations. Collection problems will occur since some customers will fail to pay and may require legal action to provide payment. The retailer may have to borrow additional funds to pay for merchandise if the time frame for customer payments does not match the terms of sale for the inventory. Disagreements about credit activities can adversely affect customer relations and the image of the retailer in the community.

An especially important challenge for retail credit grantors has been fraudulent use of credit cards. Most fraud involves the use of credit accounts by unauthorized users. It is extremely important that clerks and other customer service representatives be trained in fraud prevention measures. Identification should be verified by checking signatures and by following other procedures required by credit grantors.

RETAIL 30-DAY CHARGE ACCOUNTS

Although retail 30-day charge accounts are becoming less prevalent today, this program was once very popular. A **retail 30-day charge account** provides a customer with the opportunity to charge a series of purchases to an account operated by a retailer who will send one bill or statement at the end of a predetermined time period (usually once a month). The accounts were maintained primarily as a convenience for the customer who benefited from the ability to "charge" purchases throughout the month with a single bill sent at a later date. Sometimes people refer to this credit plan as maintaining a "tab" at the retail establishment that offers this opportunity. These accounts were often offered by grocery and clothing stores and also gasoline service stations, where many purchases were made at different times throughout the month. Although these accounts can still be found in most communities, the retail revolving accounts and the universal-purchase credit cards have largely replaced 30-day charge accounts.

Important Features of 30-Day Charge Accounts

Retail charge accounts normally run 30 days. However, in practice, bills may be outstanding for a longer period, depending on general economic conditions, the season, the type of store involved, and the type of customers.

- Purchases are charged to the account and a single bill is sent each month. The account is generally used to purchase less-expensive nondurable goods with title passing to the buyer at the time of purchase. The retailer often has no rights to repossession.
- Payment in full is expected by the merchant on receipt of the statement.
- No interest or finance charges are generally levied except in those cases when payments fall significantly behind.
- No formal contract typically exists, and the privilege of continuing to use the account requires that payments be made in a timely fashion.

Benefits and Pitfalls of 30-Day Charge Accounts

Retail charge accounts involve several types of costs not found in cash sales. Bad-debt losses occur despite the merchants' best efforts to weigh the risks involved. If proprietors devote time to this function, they limit the time they can devote to buying, selling, and other administrative duties. Another factor is the additional cost of merchandise returns, which charge account customers look on as a special privilege. Retailers who accept credit thus walk a tightrope; a new account may either increase profits through increased sales or expand the store's uncollectible accounts. In many stores, however, and in smaller stores in particular, pressure of personal friendship, lack of knowledge of economic conditions, difficulty obtaining credit information, pressure of other duties, and lack of adequate recordkeeping, all combine to make retail credit acceptance a somewhat careless operation.

Delayed payments have troubled retail merchants for years, and they continue to present a problem—whether to charge a fee on accounts that are not paid by the end of the normal 30-day period. Most stores undoubtedly prefer to do so, but they are restrained by competition. Also, simply because a store threatens to add a carrying charge if accounts are not paid within a specified time—often 60 days after receipt of the statement—there is no guarantee that such a policy will be indiscriminately enforced. Many stores screen their overdue accounts and are very careful not to offend their "good but slow" customers by imposing charges and writing collection letters. If a store decides to place a finance charge on late accounts, it must decide on the amount and be careful to comply with state and federal regulations.

For some smaller firms, charge accounts are still a factor in credit policies and practices. But retail charge account credit has declined rapidly in importance in the expanding consumer-credit picture. Today, retail charge account credit accounts for an estimated 2 to 3 percent of total consumer credit outstanding.

RETAIL INSTALLMENT CREDIT

Retail installment credit has been the subject of more praise and criticism than any other type of consumer credit. Retail installment credit is a credit plan or program that allows purchasers to pay for goods in the future by making a series of fixed, regular payments. A new automobile, for example, is often purchased by signing a credit agreement that will require monthly payments for a three- to five-year period of time in the future. Since most American families use installment credit, often to purchase the more expensive items in the family budget, it is important to them, to the business and financial institutions concerned, and to society in general that installment credit is used wisely and correctly.

Important Features of Retail Installment Credit

The important features of a retail installment credit are discussed as follows:

- Regular payments, often on a monthly basis, are required.
- Payment amounts are generally fixed and include principal, interest, and other charges for additional loan services (i.e., credit insurance).
- A separate contract or conditional sales agreement is signed for each item purchased using installment credit. A **conditional sales agreement** is a contract that outlines the terms and payments required to purchase an item on credit and also provides that actual ownership of the item does not pass to the buyer until all payments have been made.
- Retail installment credit is often referred to as closed-end credit since the credit program ends with the final payment.

Increased Use of Installment Credit

Exhibit 3–1, which breaks down consumer installment credit by type, indicates its increasing frequency of use. To what factors can we attribute this rapid growth in installment credit? First, an expanding variety of consumer products is adaptable to installment selling. Second, consumer attitudes changed with respect to this type of credit. And third, retailers changed their attitudes over the years with respect to this powerful selling tool.

Exhibit 3–1   Consumer Installment Credit Outstanding 1980 to 1995 (in billions)

Type of Credit	1980	1985	1990	1995
Installment credit outstanding	$298.2	$517.7	$734.9	$1024.8
Automobile	112	210.2	283.1	353.3
Revolving	55.1	121.8	223.5	395.2
Other	131.1	185.7	228.3	276.2

Source: Board of Governors of the Federal Reserve System, *Federal Reserve Bulletin,* monthly; and *Annual Statistical Digest.*

Changing Attitude of Consumers

In the early days of installment credit, the sales techniques used by some vendors damaged customer goodwill. Exaggerated claims, misunderstandings between vendor and customer, and threats of force to collect overdue accounts contributed to the stigma associated with this type of selling. Not until this stigma was removed did installment buying become commonplace. Fortunately, the early abuses were short-lived, and the industry recognized that customer goodwill was essential to its success.

Changing Attitude of Retailers

Many retailers built up the same prejudice against installment selling as consumers had against installment buying. Retailers shunned this type of selling because of the industry's prevailing low standards and because they failed to recognize it as a productive merchandising tool. However, as consumers' attitudes changed, so did retailers! The adoption of high standards by the sales finance industry soon convinced retailers of the sales possibilities of installment selling.

PRINCIPLES OF RETAIL INSTALLMENT CREDIT

The installment credit principles discussed below successfully serve both vendors and customers. These guidelines help to ensure a successful credit relationship between the parties involved.

Type of Goods

The best items to sell on an installment basis are durable and large ticket items. **Durable goods** are manufactured products with a relatively long life and long-term utility. In general, goods of high-unit value are consumed over a relatively long period; therefore, consumers have many months or years of enjoyment from them. Consumers tend to feel more responsibility to pay a debt when they are still using and enjoying the merchandise. Goods that are consumed immediately place a creditor in a more difficult position from the collection standpoint.

Down Payment

A **down payment** is a cash payment made by the buyer to cover a portion of the full purchase price. The remaining amount required for purchase is financed or provided by the retail installment agreement. The down payment should be sufficient to create a sense of ownership. This sense of ownership creates pride of possession in the customer's mind and provides a safety margin for the vendor. If customers have no sense of ownership, they may face their debts with discouragement and spite. The safety margin may be important if the item is eventually repossessed, or otherwise sold to pay off the outstanding balance of the purchase contract. Most new products immediately lose value as they become used products.

The amount of down payment varies with the type of goods financed. For years, the customary down payment on new cars ranged from one-fifth to one-third of the original purchase price. Customers with excellent credit standing or with large equity in their cars being traded in were generally allowed to make lower down payments. Also, down payment amounts, manufacturers' rebates, and special interest rates have become important marketing tools. Rebates, for example, may be accepted and used as the down payment in an effort to sell more automobiles in the competitive market that currently exists.

The Installment Terms and Schedule of Payments

Installment terms as found in the installment credit agreement outline the amount, frequency, and timing of the regular payments. Both the retailer and the purchaser need to be aware of several important considerations, as discussed below.

- The amount of each payment should be affordable and related to income and other outstanding obligations.
- The value of the item being financed should never fall below the unpaid balance of the agreement. Neither the seller nor the purchaser will be able to sell the item to pay the outstanding balance of the contract if the value falls below the amount owed. The time period of the credit agreement is obviously related to the life of the item being purchased.
- The payments should be convenient. This may involve matching the payment due date to the customer's payday or other payment obligations.
- The repayment period should not be too long. As discussed above, a long repayment period may result in the item being purchased losing too much value. Finance charges are also higher, collection problems may be increased, and the buyer may lose interest in the item purchased if payments extend too far into the future. Some state laws also limit the amount of time an installment loan or installment purchase agreement can run, depending on the value financed.

Finance Charges

A finance charge is the extra cost or expense charged to the buyer who uses credit to purchase goods or services or to borrow funds. The finance charges included in the installment purchase agreement should be adequate to defray the operational costs of the credit department. These charges should also cover inflationary costs, since the value of

Box 3–1 Credit Management Tips

Calculating the Approximate APR

Bill Stevens purchases a television set for $415. He signs a retail installment credit contract that requires a $25 down payment and 10 monthly payments of $42.50.

Amount financed (P) = $415 – $25 = $390

Finance charge (F) = ($42.50 × 10) – $390 = $35

Number of payments in this contract (N) = 10

Number of payments in one full year (M) = 12

Approximate APR = $\dfrac{2MF}{P(N+1)}$ $\dfrac{2 \times 12 \times \$35}{\$390 \times 11}$ = 19.58%

Note: This calculation is not accurate enough to satisfy the requirements of the Truth-in-Lending Act.

---

dollars paid over an extended period of time may fall if inflation occurs. The finance charge should also provide a reasonable return on the investment the seller makes when giving the customer additional time to pay for goods and services. Numerous laws exist, however, that limit the allowable finance charges that can be collected in most credit transactions.

To avoid misunderstandings, vendors should spell out all finance charges to their installment customers. Note that a finance charge may be called a *service charge,* a *carrying charge,* or an *interest charge.* The Consumer Credit Protection Act (Truth in Lending) became effective July 1, 1969. The main purpose of this law was to assure meaningful disclosure of credit terms (primarily the finance charge and the true annual percentage rate) so that consumers would be able to compare credit terms more readily and use credit more wisely.

Consumers seldom understand interest charges and the actual cost of credit. The cost of credit is significant for both consumers and vendors, but for different reasons. Consumers should know the cost of credit so they can decide if the installment purchase is a wise move. Vendors must decide if the finance charge will cover their costs and earn a profit. Box 3–1, "Credit Management Tips," shows one method used to approximate the annual percentage rate (APR) on an installment credit arrangement.

Repossession

Under an installment arrangement, sellers have an added protection. If the customer does not comply with the terms of the agreement, the article may be repossessed. **Repossession** is the ability of the seller to regain possession of the item financed by the credit agreement if a prescribed number of payments are not paid. However, this is the last action most sellers want to take. Repossession can be complicated by a number of strict legal requirements and is often difficult to accomplish without loss.

Rebates for Prepayment

A customer should always be allowed to prepay in full the unpaid balance of any installment obligation at any time without penalty. Each payment includes both interest and principal, with the interest expense related to the time period the contract is supposed to run. Since the original installment contract assumed that the full time frame would be used, the actual amount due (the payoff amount) will be different than the total of the remaining payments if the contract is being paid early. A **rebate for prepayment** is the return of a portion of the total precomputed interest included in an installment credit agreement if it is paid early. Although no money changes hands, the resulting payoff figure is less than the total payments remaining.

The **Rule of 78s** is a method used to calculate the amount of the rebate of precomputed finance charges when an installment credit agreement is paid early. The task involves calculating the appropriate portion of each preceding payment that should be allocated to interest expense. The remaining payment amount is therefore used to reduce the outstanding principal. This allocation process is necessary to calculate the remaining principal balance when a credit customer wishes to pay the installment contract early. "Credit Management Tips" (Box 3–2) uses an example to show how the actual calculation would be made.

Box 3–2 Credit Management Tips

Calculating Finance Charge Rebates: Rule of 78s

Bill Stevens paid his installment loan in full after only two payments. Eight out of 10 total payments ($42.50 each) remain. The total finance charge on the contract is $35. He is entitled to a refund of a portion of the precomputed finance charge using the Rule of 78s. The equation used to find the finance charge refund and the amount due to pay off the contract in full is as follows:

$$\frac{\text{Sum of number of payments remaining}}{\text{Sum of total number of payments}} \times \text{Finance charge} = \text{Refund}$$

$$\text{Total of payments remaining} - \text{Refund} = \text{Balance due}$$

$$\frac{1+2+3+4+5+6+7+8}{1+2+3+4+5+6+7+8+9+10} \times \$35 = \frac{36}{55} \times \$35 = \$22.91$$

$$(8 \times \$42.50) - \$22.91 = \$317.09 = \text{Balance due}$$

Note: A quick way to sum any string of digits is:

$$\frac{n(n+1)}{2} \quad \text{where } n \text{ is number of digits.}$$

EXHIBIT 3-2   Loan Amortization Table

					Lender Name — Any Bank				
Pmnt #	Start of Period	Annual Interest Rate	Scheduled Balance	Actual Balance	Scheduled Payment	Interest Portion	Principal Portion	Additional Principal
1	01/98	10.00%	6,000.00	6,000.00	(527.50)	(50.00)	(477.50)	
2	02/98	10.00	5,522.50	5,522.50	(527.50)	(46.02)	(481.47)	
3	03/98	10.00	5,041.03	5,041.03	(527.50)	(42.01)	(485.49)	
4	04/98	10.00	4,555.54	4,555.54	(527.50)	(37.96)	(489.53)	
5	05/98	10.00	4,066.01	4,066.01	(527.50)	(33.88)	(493.61)	
6	06/98	10.00	3,572.40	3,572.40	(527.50)	(29.77)	(497.73)	
7	07/98	10.00	3,074.67	3,074.67	(527.50)	(25.62)	(501.87)	
8	08/98	10.00	2,572.80	2,572.80	(527.50)	(21.44)	(506.06)	
9	09/98	10.00	2,066.75	2,066.75	(527.50)	(17.22)	(510.27)	
10	10/98	10.00	1,556.47	1,556.47	(527.50)	(12.97)	(514.52)	
11	11/98	10.00	1,041.95	1,041.95	(527.50)	(8.68)	(518.81)	
12	12/98	10.00	523.14	523.14	(527.50)	(4.36)	(523.14)	
			-	-	-	-	-	

Many installment contracts today use a **simple interest method** of determining the interest portion of each payment made. The simple interest method refers to the practice of charging interest based on the most recent principal owed and the number of days since the last payment. No method for calculating a rebate is required because the interest is not precomputed.

Sometimes the lender provides an amortization table for the borrower. An **amortization table** is a listing of payments for an installment loan that shows the interest paid, the principal due, and the remaining balance for each payment in the contract. These tables generally assume that payments occur each month without further adjustments for the exact number of days between payments. Many financial institutions use the power of their computer systems to charge interest on this more accurate basis. An typical amortization table is shown in Exhibit 3-2.

Acceleration Clause

Some installment contracts incorporate an acceleration clause. An **acceleration clause** is a credit installment contract clause, which provides that in the event a specified number of payments is past due, all remaining payments are due and payable at once, or on the demand of the contract holder. The purpose of this clause is to provide the seller with an alternative to accepting the precomputed interest amount if the buyer takes longer than agreed to make his or her payments. Upon "acceleration," the contract is typically converted to a simple interest contract, and interest is charged on the outstanding balance for the number of days between payments.

Credit Investigation

The credit investigation is uniquely important in installment credit transactions. Installment credit accounts usually represent a high average sale and extend over a relatively long time. In the sale of cars, for example, the sum to be financed is quite large. These factors present a risk peculiar to this type of credit. The principal created by these conditions is that the credit investigation should be thorough enough to diminish the inherent risk. Even though the right of repossession may offer the creditor considerable protection, profit in installment sales really depends on completion of the payments. Repossessions can be costly and even disastrous if they occur too frequently. Creditors should rely on the quality of the risk as revealed by the credit investigation rather than on other contingent factors.

Principles of Retail Installment Credit

- Type of goods.
- Down payment.
- Installment terms.
- Finance charges.
- Repossession.
- Rebates for prepayment.
- Acceleration clause.
- Credit investigation.

BENEFITS AND PITFALLS OF INSTALLMENT CREDIT

Installment credit has been a profitable and effective tool for retailers who wish to increase sales. It has also created much enjoyment and satisfaction for consumers. The real danger in installment credit, as in so many other things, is not in its use but in its abuse. Consumers can easily overextend themselves with this type of credit, and a few have installment debts out of proportion to their ability to pay. Such a situation is damaging to the credit industry and demonstrates the need for consumer education in the use of credit.

Retailers must be aware that the customer's credit qualities are more crucial elements to the risk than the lien retained. Retailers must accept credit wisely. Some customers are imprudent or impetuous, and others are dishonest. By adhering to sound principles of credit management, retailers can do much to avoid individuals who do not have the ability or character to pay.

Retail Revolving Credit

One of the most popular credit plans is the retail revolving credit plan. A **revolving credit plan** allows the credit buyer to (1) pay the full amount due each month resulting from previous charges, or (2) pay a minimum payment and spread the remaining amount due over a future time period. Revolving credit, sometimes called the *option-terms plan,* is a hybrid of installment credit and the 30-day charge account. The account is treated like a 30-day account with no interest if the full amount is paid monthly. If the customer chooses to spread payments out into the future, the account becomes similar to a retail installment credit arrangement.

In May 1956, J. L. Hudson's Department Store in Detroit introduced its "30-Day Account with Optional Terms." Under this plan, customers could pay in full in 30 days without a finance charge, or they could pay as little as one-fourth of the balance each month with a minimum monthly payment of $10 if the balance was $50 or less. If the customers chose to extend their payments past 30 days, the store added a finance charge.

Important Features of Retail Revolving Credit

The most important features of a typical, present-day option-terms revolving credit plan are listed below. Exhibit 3–3 shows an example of a retail revolving credit agreement.

- Customers apply for a revolving credit account and are assigned a credit line or limit that defines the maximum amount they are allowed to have outstanding at any given point in time.
- There is no down payment required and customers are issued a credit card for identification and authorization of purchases.
- If they stay under their credit limit, customers are encouraged to charge purchases on a regular basis using a credit card in lieu of cash.
- Monthly statements are mailed that outline a minimum payment due and the full outstanding balance. If customers pay the full balance each month, no interest is charged. Any amounts carried forward to the next month, however, are subject to a finance charge.
- Finance charges are typically governed by state law. Referred to as "open-end" credit, other federal laws also govern some of the relationships and activities that occur between issuer and user.
- Under the option-terms revolving credit plan commonly found today, customers usually have the option of paying their bills within 25 to 30 days (from billing date) without any finance charge. The plan provides a schedule of payments for amounts carried beyond the prescribed time. For each range of unpaid balances (e.g., $10.01–$200), a specific monthly payment such as $10 or $11 is due. In the example shown in Exhibit 3–4, when the account balance is over $500, the monthly payment is 1/28th of the account balance, which includes the finance charge. Payment due is predicated on the balance owed, providing for reduced monthly payments as the balance outstanding declines. Repayment schedules vary among retail organizations.

EXHIBIT 3–3   A Retail Revolving Credit Agreement

SEARSCHARGE CREDIT ACCOUNT APPLICATION ID 63

STORE NO.

Please indicate below name in which account is to be carried. Applicant, if married, may apply for a separate account.

INFORMATION ABOUT YOURSELF

(COURTESY TITLES ARE OPTIONAL)	FIRST NAME	MIDDLE INITIAL	LAST NAME

☐ MR. ☐ MRS. ☐ MISS ☐ MS.

ADDRESS (TO WHICH YOU WANT YOUR BILLING MAILED)	APT.	CITY	STATE	ZIP CODE

RESIDENCE ADDRESS	APT.	CITY	STATE	ZIP CODE

HOME TELEPHONE	BUSINESS TELEPHONE	SOCIAL SECURITY NUMBER	AGE	NO. OF DEPENDENTS (EXCLUDE YOURSELF)
( )	( )			

ARE YOU A U.S. CITIZEN? ☐ YES ☐ NO (IF NO, EXPLAIN IMMIGRATION STATUS) | ARE YOU A PERMANENT RESIDENT? ☐ YES ☐ NO | HOW LONG AT PRESENT ADDRESS ☐ YEARS ☐ MOS. | DO YOU: ☐ OWN ☐ BOARD ☐ RENT ☐ L/W PARENTS ☐ OTHER | MONTHLY RENT OR MORTGAGE $

PREVIOUS ADDRESS (IF LESS THAN 2 YEARS AT PRESENT ADDRESS) | APT. | CITY | STATE | ZIP CODE | HOW LONG? ☐ YEARS ☐ MOS.

EMPLOYER (RETIRED/STUDENT, INDICATE: HOW LONG/YEAR IN SCHOOL) | ADDRESS | CITY | STATE | ZIP CODE | HOW LONG? ☐ YEARS ☐ MOS.

OCCUPATION (FORMER OCCUPATION IF RETIRED) | NET INCOME (TAKE HOME PAY) ☐ PER MONTH ☐ PER WEEK | PREVIOUS EMPLOYER (IF LESS THAN 1 YEAR WITH PRESENT.) | HOW LONG? ☐ YEARS ☐ MOS.

OTHER INCOME* $ ☐ PER MONTH ☐ PER WEEK | SOURCE OTHER INCOME | *Note: Alimony, child support or separate maintenance income need not be disclosed if you do not wish to have it considered as a basis for paying this obligation.

FINANCIAL INFORMATION

MAJOR CREDIT CARDS (VISA, MASTERCARD, ETC.) | ACCOUNT NUMBER | MO. PAYMENT $ | AUTO LOAN? NAME OF LENDER ☐ YES ☐ NO | MO PAYMENT $

OTHER CREDIT CARDS (DEPT. STORES, ETC.) | ACCOUNT NUMBER | MO. PAYMENT $ | PREVIOUS SEARS ACCOUNT? ☐ YES ☐ NO | ACCOUNT NUMBER

DO YOU HAVE A: CHECKING ACCOUNT? ☐ YES ☐ NO | NAME OF BANK/FINANCIAL INSTITUTION | ACCOUNT NO (OPTIONAL) | IS THIS AN INTEREST PAYING OR NOW ACCOUNT? ☐ YES ☐ NO

DO YOU HAVE A: ☐ SAVINGS ACCOUNT ☐ CD ☐ MONEY MARKET ☐ OTHER | NAME OF BANK/FINANCIAL INSTITUTION | ACCOUNT NO (OPTIONAL)

RELATIVE OR PERSONAL REFERENCE NOT LIVING WITH YOU | ADDRESS | CITY | STATE | RELATIONSHIP

Complete this section if you want cards issued to additional buyers on your account.

1. FIRST NAME | LAST | RELATIONSHIP | 2. FIRST NAME | LAST | RELATIONSHIP

SPOUSE INFORMATION

Complete this section if: (1) your spouse is an authorized buyer, **(2)** you reside in a community property state (AZ, CA, ID, LA, NV, NM, TX, WA, WI), or **(3)** you are relying on the income or assets of a spouse as a source for payment.

SPOUSE, FIRST NAME | MIDDLE INITIAL | LAST NAME | AGE

EMPLOYER | ADDRESS | CITY | STATE | ZIP CODE

HOW LONG? ☐ YEARS ☐ MOS. | OCCUPATION | SOCIAL SECURITY NUMBER | NET INCOME (TAKE HOME PAY) $ ☐ PER MONTH ☐ PER WEEK

> I agree to pay Sears in accordance with the credit terms disclosed to me and to comply with all terms of the SearsCharge Agreement. A copy of the SearsCharge Agreement will be given to me to keep when my application is approved. Sears will retain a security interest where permitted by law under the Uniform Commercial Code on all merchandise charged to the account. Sears is authorized to investigate my credit, employment, and income references and to report to proper persons and credit bureaus my performance of the account. Finance charges not in excess of those permitted by law will be charged on the outstanding balance from month to month.
>
> X _____
> APPLICANT'S SIGNATURE   DATE

IMPORTANT SEARSCHARGE CREDIT TERMS

The information below includes the costs associated with a SearsCharge Account. It is accurate as of October 1989, but may change after that date. To find out what may have changed write to: Sears Telemarketing Center, 2269 Village Mall Dr., Mansfield, OH 44906. A copy of the entire SearsCharge agreement for you to keep, with all terms applicable to your state of residence, will be sent to you with the credit card(s). You need not accept the card and are not required to pay any fee or charge disclosed unless the card is used.

Annual Percentage Rate	The annual percentage rate is 21% unless you reside in a state shown below:	
	Alabama 21%	Massachusetts 18%
	to $750, 18% on excess	Michigan 20%
	Alaska 18%	Minnesota 18%
	to $1000, 10.5% on excess	Missouri 20.04%
	Arkansas 12%	Nebraska 21%
	(See Variable Rate Information)	to $500, 18% on excess
	California 19.2%	No. Carolina 18%
	Connecticut 18%	No. Dakota 18%
	Florida 18%	Pennsylvania 18%
	Hawaii 18%	Puerto Rico 20.4%
	Iowa 19.8%	Rhode Island 18%
	Kansas 21%	Texas 18%
	to $1000, 14.4% on excess	Washington 18%
	Louisiana 18%	W. Virginia 18%
	Maine 18%	Wisconsin 18%

Variable Rate Information	(Arkansas Residents Only) Your Annual Percentage Rate may vary. The rate is determined by adding 5% per annum to the Federal Reserve Discount Rate on 90 day commercial paper in Arkansas.
Grace Period To Repay Balance	You have 30 days from your billing date to repay your balance before being charged a finance charge.

Balance Calculation Method For Purchases	The Average Daily Balance method (including new transactions) is used in all states except Maine, Massachusetts, Minnesota, Mississippi, Montana, New Mexico and North Dakota where the Average Daily Balance method (excluding new transactions) is used.
Minimum Finance Charge	A minimum monthly finance charge of 50¢ applies in all states except Arkansas, Connecticut, Hawaii, Maryland, Nebraska, Nevada, No. Carolina, No. Dakota, Rhode Island, Virginia, Dist. of Columbia, and Puerto Rico.
Late Payment Fees	Late payment fees vary from state to state. They range from zero to the lesser of $5 or 5% with a minimum of $1 on payments more than 10 days late.
Annual Fees	None
Over-The-Credit-Limit Fees	None
Transaction Fees	None

Exhibit 3–4   An Option-Terms Revolving Credit Plan

Schedule of minimum monthly payments. The required minimum monthly payment is based on the highest New Balance on the account.

When the Highest New Balance Reaches:	The Minimum Monthly Payment Will Be:	
$.01 to $10.00	Balance	You may always pay more than the required minimum monthly payment. The minimum payment will change only if charges to the account increase the balance to a new high. The minimum payment will not decrease until the new balance is paid in full.
10.01 to 200.00	$10.00	
200.01 to 240.00	$11.00	
240.01 to 280.00	$12.00	
280.01 to 320.00	$13.00	
320.01 to 360.00	$14.00	
360.01 to 400.00	$15.00	
400.01 to 440.00	$16.00	
440.01 to 470.00	$17.00	
470.01 to 500.00	$18.00	

Over $500.00: 1/28th of highest account balance rounded to next higher whole dollar amount.

Variations in Computing Finance Charges

Different stores use various methods to compute finance charges on revolving credit accounts: previous or opening balance, average daily balance, and adjusted balance methods.

In the oldest of the three methods, the **previous balance method,** the finance charge is based on the previous month's balance without deducting payments or credits made during the month if the account is not paid in full.

In the **average daily balance method,** the finance charge varies according to the point in the billing cycle when the customer makes a payment. A fairly recent development, this method is a by-product of the computerization of retail accounts receivable. The average daily balance is the sum of the actual amounts owed each day of the monthly billing period, including charges made during the current monthly billing period but excluding unpaid finance or insurance charges, if any, divided by the number of days in the billing period. All payments and other credits are subtracted from the previous day's balance.

The **adjusted balance method** bases the finance charge on the previous month's ending balance less any payments or credits. Few stores use this method although it may be best for the customer.

"Credit Management Tips" (Box 3–3) compares the three revolving credit card billing methods. As the example shows, the finance charge may vary considerably for the same pattern of purchases and payments on a revolving credit card account. Even when the annual percentage rate is the same, the amount of the finance charge depends on how the creditor treats the payments.

Since customers can avoid finance charges on revolving credit card accounts by paying within a certain time, it is important that they receive the bill promptly and get credit for paying promptly. Customers should also check the payment date on the

Box 3–3 Credit Management Tips

Calculating Finance Charges Using the Three Methods

Bill Stevens uses a retail revolving account that has an 18 percent APR (1.5 percent monthly). His outstanding balance at the beginning of the month was $400. On the 15th, Bill pays $300. There are no other payments or charges. The following calculations show the finance charge using the three methods.

	Adjusted Balance	*Previous Balance*	*Average Daily Balance*
Monthly rate	1.5%	1.5%	1.5%
Previous balance	$400	$400	$400
Payments	$300	$300	$300 (15th)
Finance charge	$1.50	$6.00	$3.75
	(1.5% × $100)	(1.5% × $400)	(1.5% × $250)

Note:

$$\text{Avg daily balance} = \frac{\text{Sum of daily balances}}{\text{Number of days in billing cycle}}$$

$$= \frac{(\$400 \times 15) + (\$100 \times 15)}{30}$$

statement; in most instances, creditors must credit payments on the day received. Customers should also follow the creditor's instructions as to where, how, and when to make payments in order to avoid delays that may result in finance charges.

Other Important Characteristics

It is illegal for a revolving charge creditor (this also applies to credit cards as discussed in Chapter 4) to send a customer a credit card unless the customer asks or applies for one. However, a card issuer may send a customer, without request, a new card to replace an expired one. The customer also may be sent an application for a card in the mail or be asked to apply by phone.

The customer's risk for unauthorized charges on lost or stolen cards is limited to $50 on each card, even if someone charges hundreds of dollars before the card is reported missing. The customer does not have to pay for any unauthorized charges made after the customer notifies the issuer of the loss or theft of the card.

Customers may withhold payment on any damaged or shoddy goods or unsatisfactory services purchased with a credit card, as long as they make an effort to solve the problem with the merchant.

Benefits and Pitfalls of Revolving Credit

A revolving credit plan does not automatically assure higher profits. However, many of the advantages for the store are disadvantages for the customers.

To the Customer

Customers who use a revolving credit plan can usually charge more than under a 30-day plan because they have more time to pay. They are free to buy at any time up to a limit set by the store without having their credit rechecked with each purchase, as is the case with the usual installment buying. In addition, customers have the option to pay the entire amount due with no finance charge or pay the amount owed in a series of payments with a finance charge added.

Despite the advantages, customers encounter certain pitfalls. Because it is so easy to buy, some people find themselves continually in debt to the store. In fact, some customers look on revolving credit payments in the same way as income tax and other types of payroll deductions.

Another factor is the finance charge. The most commonly used finance charge, 1.5 percent per month on the unpaid balance, results in a true annual rate of approximately 18 percent. This is considered by many to be an expensive rate to pay on credit purchases.

Some customers do not understand the finance charges they are paying or certain provisions in the contract they sign. For example, a store usually claims title to merchandise purchased under its revolving credit agreement until paid in full. Each payment is applied to merchandise and services as follows: first, to unpaid finance charges; then, if items are purchased on different dates, the first purchased is the first paid; if items are purchased on the same date, the lowest priced is first paid. Different contracts have different provisions as to title.

To the Store

A store's primary purpose in introducing revolving credit is to increase sales and, in turn, profits. In addition, the store gains added income from finance charges.

By offering a revolving credit plan, a store can meet its competition, attract new customers, and encourage current customers to make more purchases. Many stores adopt a revolving credit plan to decrease bad-debt losses; customers not only purchase more but also can pay off the amount they owe much more easily through small but regular monthly payments.

Revolving credit plans require more capital investment because customers pay over an extended period of time. Some stores incur more bad-debt losses due to "skips." The type of clientele, which may change with the introduction of revolving credit, may call for more careful and costly credit investigation. But "calling for" a different type of investigation and actually "making it" are two different things. Revolving credit also involves additional bookkeeping, billing, and other related tasks, thus adding to the store's operating expenses.

Current Status of Retail Revolving Credit

In the 1970s and early 1980s, retail chains and oil companies pushed their own retail revolving credit plans. As time passed, however, more retailers have begun to accept general purpose credit cards such as VISA, MasterCard, and others.

Exhibit 3–5 reflects the number of credit cardholders, the number of cards outstanding, and the dollar amount of credit card debt for 1980, 1990, and projections for 2000.

Major Oil Company Plans

Major oil companies were initially very strict in their acceptance of individuals as credit risks. And customers were allowed to charge only items normally asked for in a service station (i.e., gas, oil, tires, repairs). A company consolidated a customer's purchases over a period of time (generally 30 days) on one bill to be paid as a regular 30-day open account with no finance charge, even for late payment. This situation changed, however, when the major oil companies adopted the revolving credit type of plan. Interest rates are determined by the law in the consumer's home state, not the state where the card-issuing company is located, or the state in which the purchase is made.

Service stations also honor bank credit cards, although some major oil company stations manage their own credit plans in addition to the bank card plan. Such an arrangement, they believe, encourages customer loyalty. In fact, several major oil companies recently decided to accept only their own company cards, to the exclusion of all other credit plans.

The top six oil company card issuers are Shell, Chevron, Mobil, Amoco, Exxon, and Texaco. Only a small percentage of these cards carry an annual fee, typically $20 per year. In addition to providing revolving credit on oil station purchases, Amoco and Shell provide credit at certain restaurants and hotels.

Exhibit 3–5   Credit Cards—Holders, Numbers, and Debt 1980, 1990, and Projections, 2000

Type of Credit Card	Cardholders (millions)			Number of cards (millions)			Credit card debt (billions)		
	1980	1990	2000 (Proj.)	1980	1990	2000 (Proj.)	1980	1990	2000 (Proj.)
Total	$ 86	$113	$141	$526	$1026	$1344	$80.2	$236.4	$660.9
Bank	63	79	106	111	217	469	25.0	154.1	486.0
Oil company	69	85	82	110	123	105	2.2	3.3	4.1
Phone	NA	97	132	NA	141	203	NA	1.7	3.0
Retail store	83	96	121	277	469	476	47.3	51.0	98.9
Travel and entertainment	11	23	26	10	28	32	2.7	13.8	35.3
Other	13	11	10	19	48	60	3.0	12.5	33.7

NA—Not Available Cardholders may hold more than one type of card.

Includes airline, automobile rental, Discover (except for cardholders), hotel, motel, and other miscellaneous credit cards.

SOURCE: HSN Consultants, Inc., Santa Monica, CA, *The Milson Report* (Santa Monica, CA), bimonthly. Copyright used by permission.

OTHER VARIATIONS AND TYPES OF RETAIL CHARGE ACCOUNT CREDIT

There are many variations of retail credit accounts. The various types of credit purchase options are limited only by the ability of retailers to invent new programs. Credit programs are often added as marketing and sales incentives to help convince purchasers that the offer is an unusually good deal.

90 Days Same as Cash

This variation generally involves having the customer sign a regular installment sales contract with the additional understanding that if the buyer pays in full within 90 days from the date of sale, no finance charges will be levied. Not only does this help promote the sale, but the retailer may also have some customers who intend to pay in full later change their minds. They may, instead, decide to pay the regular installments once the contract is set up.

Divided Payments

These programs typically divide the "cash price" of the merchandise into monthly, quarterly, or other payment configurations. For example, an item selling for $120 might require three payments: $40 in 30 days, another $40 at 60 days, and a final $40 payment at 90 days. The advertisements often point out that there is no finance charge since the cash price is simply divided into payments. The "zero percent finance plans" are sometimes challenged, however, since some critics maintain that the finance charges are buried in the original cost of the merchandise.

SERVICE CREDIT

Although service credit is an important segment of the total consumer credit picture, it has been practically ignored in consumer credit literature. Service credit is the amount owed by individuals to professional practitioners and service establishments. In the past decade, the amount of noninstallment service credit has increased an estimated three to four times.

Professional Credit

Professionals of all types accept credit from their customers. Doctors, dentists, accountants, attorneys, and others provide advice or process papers for a fee. Often the clients are given time to make payments.

Credit is a customary method of doing business with physicians, dentists, and other health care providers. Private practitioners and clinics generally accept credit from their patients, and most of them expect to collect most of the amount due. However, some patients' fees are entered as receivables on the books, even though the practitioner knows that the recipients may be unable to pay at any time in the future.

Thirty-day accounts are the most common type of credit in the medical and dental professions. The services are delivered, sometimes on an emergency basis, and bills are sent later. Full payment is obviously preferred, but some professionals may allow patients to arrange installment payments for protracted treatments or services. If the bill is large, the patients may not be able to pay within 30 days.

The vast growth of hospital, medical, and surgical insurance plans has permitted millions of people to take care of their health needs on a "cash basis" by shifting the financial burden—or a large part of it—to insurance companies. A major activity for many clinics and practitioners is dealing with insurance companies to procure payments on behalf of their patients. Medicare and Medicaid are government-sponsored health insurance plans that help pay bills for the elderly and those without sufficient assets or income.

Credit arrangements also are found in the legal profession; services are rendered for a client, who is billed at some later date. In those cases where the client benefits from the outcome of a legal action, e.g., receiving payment for injury, the attorney fee may be a percentage of the court award and is relatively easy to collect. Of course, in some cases, the legal action is not successful, yet payment is still required by the attorney.

Credit in Service and Repair Establishments

Basically, credit in a service establishment is like credit in a retail establishment. In many instances, it is difficult to separate the two because thousands of retailers offer repair and other services that may be purchased on credit. Auto dealers, for example, offer repair services in addition to selling new and used automobiles.

Note that the word *service* does not mean the various devices a store uses to attract and hold customers (e.g., free delivery, credit arrangements, parking lots, and so on). A service establishment fills some need or performs some operation or task on a customer's goods. The term *service* may also apply to individuals who do not have a so-called place of business, but who are handy with tools and have an ability to fix things. Plumbers, carpenters, landscape technicians, and furnace repairpersons are examples. These service people may operate from their car or truck, have regular customers for whom they perform certain services, and generally provide bills after the services are delivered. Another example of service credit is providing utility services to users, such as electricity.

Problems and Challenges in Service Credit

There are several problems that occur in service credit. Many times, there is no tangible good attached to the credit transaction. After the service is delivered, the individual's material situation is generally unchanged. Fixing an automobile, for example, does not provide the recipient the same satisfaction that comes from buying a new item of clothing or a new appliance. Also, without a good involved, there may be nothing to repossess or claim in the event of nonpayment and the service cannot be retracted. Furthermore, many healthcare services are delivered on an emergency basis, and payment becomes a secondary consideration to alleviating pain or saving a life.

Service providers may be poorly equipped to deal with credit operations. Many are sole proprietors of small businesses that cannot afford to hire professional credit managers. They generally have little or no training in credit investigations, decision making, or collections. As a result, many service establishments have begun to accept general-purpose credit cards or other methods to transfer the credit activities to others.

The number of service establishments has increased rapidly over the years, and a large segment conducts business on credit. The cost of services continues to take a larger share of the American consumer's budget and will continue to do so in the years to come.

Important Terms

acceleration clause   47
adjusted balance method   51
amortization table   47
average daily balance method   51
cash credit   39
conditional sales agreement   42
down payment   44
durable goods   43
installment terms   44

previous balance method   51
rebate for prepayment   46
repossession   45
retail credit   39
retail 30-day charge account   40
revolving credit plan   49
rule of 78s   46
simple interest method   47

Discussion Questions

1. How does retail credit differ from cash credit?

2. List and describe five important benefits for the retail firm providing retail and service credit.

3. List and describe five potential costs or problems arising from retail credit programs.

4. Describe the important features of retail 30-day charge accounts.

5. Describe the important features of retail installment credit.

6. How have the changing attitudes of consumers and retailers contributed to the increase in retail installment purchases?

7. Discuss the eight principles of retail installment credit. What should the customer and retailer be aware of regarding each principle?

8. Describe the important features of retail revolving credit or option-terms credit.

9. Contrast the three methods for computing finance charges on retail revolving credit plans.

10. What are the advantages of the option-terms plan to the store and to the customer? The disadvantages?

11. Describe two variations of retail credit plans: the divided payment plan and the 90-days same as cash plan. How are they different from 30-day, installment, and revolving credit plans?

12. An appliance store sold Mr. Lynn a stereo for $495. A down payment of $50 was required, and the payment period was set to cover 24 months. The store added a finance charge of $83 with a total of payments equal

to $528 (24 at $22). What is the approximate annual percentage rate of interest paid by Mr. Lynn? Would this rate be legal in your state?

13. How do you account for the changing importance of 30-day retail charge account credit?

14. What is service credit? Why should it be recognized and fully understood?

15. Discuss the problems and challenges of service credit.

CASE PROBLEM

Office Supply, Inc. Contemplates Installment Sales

Bill Stevens is considering offering a retail installment purchase option for customers at his office supply store. Although a local consumer finance company has offered to handle the credit operations, Bill is wondering if he should offer his own program. Here are some important questions:

1. What products at an office products store would be appropriate for an installment purchase program? Why?
2. What activities would Bill need to be involved in if he started his own credit program?
3. What advantages would likely occur for the store? What possible problems?

4

FINANCING RETAIL AND SERVICE CREDIT TRANSACTIONS

Learning Objectives

After studying this chapter, you should be able to:

- Describe alternatives for financing retail and service credit transactions when retailers do not offer internal credit purchase options.
- Describe universal credit card programs and the various issuers that provide them to the public.
- Discuss travel and entertainment charge cards.
- Describe the services and uses related to debit cards and electronic funds transfer systems.
- Explain the methods available to a commercial bank for acquiring installment business.
- Spell out the variety of financing plans for installment transactions available to the retail dealer.
- Trace the development of sales finance companies and illustrate how such companies operate.

This chapter looks at alternatives to financing retail and service transactions in those cases where a retailer does not wish to develop, maintain, and operate an internal credit program for its customers. Chapter 3 looked at the various forms of credit offered by sellers to its customers who seek an alternative to cash purchase. To introduce and expand a credit plan, a store needs additional capital. This capital may be furnished by the store's own reinvested earnings or by loans from commercial banks or other types of financial institutions. Either of these methods may enable retail merchants to carry their own accounts until they receive payments from customers. Loans may be based solely on the store's unsecured credit position, but the store usually has to put up certain assets as collateral.

In recent years, however, most retail and service concerns have sold part or all of their installment credit activities and have used credit card plans, such as Visa, MasterCard, Discover, and Optima, and charge card plans, such as American Express, Diners Club, and

Carte Blanche. The distinction between credit card plans and charge card plans appeared in the Fair Credit and Charge Card Disclosure Act of 1988. Under this act, a *charge card* is defined as "a card, plate, or other single credit device that may be used from time to time to obtain credit which is not subject to a finance charge." A credit card is subject to a finance charge. This distinction will be explained in detail in Chapter 6.

This chapter considers credit plans available for consumers when the retailer does not offer its own program. Many firms in the financial services industry have developed unique products and methods for helping finance consumer purchases, both large and small. These financing methods can be divided into two main categories: credit card programs and indirect financing, which involves the purchase of installment contracts negotiated between buyer and seller.

CREDIT CARD PROGRAMS

The growth in the variety and use of credit cards by American consumers has been phenomenal. There is an increasing number of different "credit cards" that assist consumers in their purchases. Those who use credit cards enjoy the convenience of not having to carry large sums of money. They also appreciate receiving an itemized billing statement on a regular basis, which may be useful in recordkeeping. In some cases, the customer also has the option to spread payments into the future, which is helpful for larger, more expensive purchases. The term *credit card* is used to describe a wide array of different plans, however, and an initial discussion of the more important types is worthwhile.

Classification of Credit Cards

I. Proprietary store cards

II. General-purpose cards
   A. Bank cards
   B. Nonbank cards
   C. Corporate brand-name cards

III. Travel and entertainment cards

IV. Debit cards

Proprietary Store Cards

A **store card** is a retailer owned and operated credit card program designed to facilitate sales in its own retail outlets. These limited-purpose retail credit cards were discussed in Chapter 3. Store cards, generally issued by national chains, can only be used in the specific subsidiaries of the issuer, i.e., the Sears Card will only be accepted at Sears stores. Examples include Sears, J.C. Penney, Montgomery Ward and many other national chain department stores that offer their own credit cards. Oil cards are also offered by major oil companies like Amoco and Shell. These cards are typically part of standard option-terms, open-end-type accounts that allow the customer to pay for purchases in full each month, or extend payments into the future with additional finance charges.

General-Purpose Cards

General-Purpose Cards are credit cards used to purchase a wide variety of goods and services from merchants that have agreed to accept these cards in lieu of cash. These cards, originally issued by banks, are now issued by a growing number of firms that hope to strengthen customer ties, increase sales, and generate income.

The general-purpose cards are issued to individual consumers who apply for them by completing a short application form. An annual fee may be required by the issuer, but competitive pressures continue to diminish these fees, especially for those that charge a minimum amount each year. The credit card permits the holder to charge purchases at firms (this can include retail outlets, service dispensers, medical facilities, educational institutions, and tax-collecting agencies) that are participating members. The cardholder is usually assigned a **credit line,** the maximum amount the issuer is willing to extend at any given time. The issuer bills the cardholder for all purchases made during a month. Cardholders can pay the full amount due within a specified grace period, usually 25 to 30 days after the billing date, without any finance charge. If they prefer, cardholders can make a minimum payment and the account is placed on a revolving basis, which carries a finance charge that varies from state to state. Note that the state in which the card-issuing bank is located determines the interest rate charged, regardless of where the consumer resides or where the purchase is made.

The card plays a dual role. It gives the merchant evidence that a consumer has been granted a line of credit, and it is a convenient, accurate means of imprinting sales drafts. The merchant submits these sales slips to the card issuer. Merchants receive an immediate payment, less a discount, in their own accounts. The discount is usually determined by the dollar volume of credit purchases the merchant generates, the average draft size, and type of merchant. The range of this discount is usually between 1 and 5 percent, although the amount may be even less for large-volume merchants, i.e., airlines.

Bank Cards

Bank credit card plans evolved largely because of greatly increased demand for consumer credit after World War II. The early 1950s saw a sporadic development of bank card plans, with a rapid increase from 1951 to 1952 followed by a rapid decline by 1955. Profits did not live up to bankers' expectations, and high administrative start-up and processing costs coupled with low volume caused many of them to abandon their plans.

MasterCard.   In July 1967, the California Bankcard Association created Master Charge. Also in 1967, 11 banks in the state of New York instigated another joint effort in bank credit cards. This plan, called "Interbank Card," was an arrangement for coordinating banks throughout the country in the credit card field. By January 1968, Master Charge ownership had passed to the Interbank Card Association. In early 1981, the name was changed to MasterCard International and Master Charge cards were replaced.

Visa.   The Bank of America introduced its program in 1958 and began licensing its card in 1966 through Bank of America Service Corporation. This led to the formation of National BankAmericard, Inc. (NBI), in July 1970. NBI was formed as an independent, nonstock membership corporation to administer, promote, and develop the BankAmericard system throughout the United States. The name BankAmericard was changed to Visa on January 1, 1977.

MasterCard and Visa, and the banks they are associated with, have dominated the general-purpose credit card market for many years. Beginning in the mid-1980s, however, other retailers, manufacturers, and service providers started issuing general-purpose cards in competition with the banking sector. A bank credit card application is shown in Exhibit 4–1.

EXHIBIT 4–1   A Bank Credit Card Application

Application For MasterCard/Visa

I would prefer MasterCard ☐   or Visa ☐   or Both ☐

Yes, I'm interested in your Auto Pay service ☐

☐ NEW ACCOUNT ☐ REISSUE REQUEST ☐ REQUEST LIMIT INCREASE

ACCOUNT NUMBER

IMPORTANT

Read these Directions before completing this Application and Check Appropriate Box.

☐ If you are applying for an individual account in your own name and are relying on your own income or assets and not the income or assets of another person as the basis for repayment of the credit requested, complete only Sections A and C.

☐ If you are applying for a joint account or an account that you and another person will use, complete all Sections, providing information in B about the joint applicant or user.

☐ If you are applying for an individual account, but are relying on income from alimony, child support, or separate maintenance or on the income or assets of another person as the basis for repayment of the credit requested, complete all Sections to the extent possible, providing information in B about the person on whose alimony, support, or maintenance payments or income or assets you are relying.

SECTION A—APPLICANT

FIRST NAME	MIDDLE NAME	LAST NAME	SOCIAL SECURITY NUMBER	BIRTHDATE MO/DAY/YR

STREET ADDRESS · APT. NO. · CITY · STATE · ZIP · HOW LONG? · HOME PHONE NO. (   )

☐ OWN ☐ BUYING · ☐ RENT ☐ LIVE W/RELATIVES · PREVIOUS STREET ADDRESS · CITY · STATE · ZIP · HOW LONG? · NO. DEPENDENTS: AGES:

EMPLOYED BY · HOW LONG? · ADDRESS · MONTHLY SALARY $

BUSINESS PHONE (   ) · POSITION · PREVIOUS EMPLOYER · ADDRESS · CITY · STATE · HOW LONG?

NAME OF NEAREST RELATIVE NOT LIVING WITH YOU · STREET ADDRESS · CITY · STATE · PHONE NO. (   ) · RELATION

BANK WITH · BRANCH · ☐ CHECKING ACCOUNT NO. · ☐ SAVINGS ACCOUNT NO. · ☐ LOAN · ☐ CREDIT CARD

Alimony, child support, or separate maintenance income need not be revealed if you do not wish to have it considered as a basis for repaying this obligation.

OTHER INCOME $ · SOURCE(S) OF OTHER INCOME · ALIMONY, CHILD SUPPORT, SEPARATE MAINTENANCE, RECEIVED UNDER: ☐ COURT ORDER ☐ WRITTEN AGREEMENT ☐ ORAL UNDERSTANDING

SECTION B—JOINT APPLICANT

FIRST NAME	MIDDLE NAME	LAST NAME	SOCIAL SECURITY NUMBER	BIRTHDATE MO/DAY/YR	HOME PHONE NO. ( )

STREET ADDRESS · APT. NO. · CITY · STATE · ZIP · HOW LONG? · NO. DEPENDENTS: AGES:

☐ OWN ☐ BUYING · ☐ RENT ☐ LIVE W/RELATIVES · PREVIOUS STREET ADDRESS · CITY · STATE · ZIP · HOW LONG? · RELATION TO APPLICANT IF ANY

EMPLOYED BY · HOW LONG? · ADDRESS · MONTHLY SALARY $

BUSINESS PHONE (   ) · POSITION · PREVIOUS EMPLOYER · ADDRESS · HOW LONG?

NAME OF NEAREST RELATIVE NOT LIVING WITH YOU · STREET ADDRESS · CITY · STATE · PHONE NO. (   ) · RELATION

BANK WITH · BRANCH · ☐ CHECKING ACCOUNT NO. · ☐ SAVINGS ACCOUNT NO. · ☐ LOAN · ☐ CREDIT CARD

Alimony, child support, or separate maintenance income need not be revealed if you do not wish to have it considered as a basis for repaying this obligation.

OTHER INCOME $ · SOURCE(S) OF OTHER INCOME · ALIMONY, CHILD SUPPORT, SEPARATE MAINTENANCE, RECEIVED UNDER: ☐ COURT ORDER ☐ WRITTEN AGREEMENT ☐ ORAL UNDERSTANDING

EXHIBIT 4–1   *(concluded)*

PLEASE LIST BELOW ALL DEBTS, INCLUDING ANY ALIMONY OR CHILD SUPPORT. YOU MAY ALSO LIST ANY ACCOUNTS (PAID OUT OR OPEN) WHICH YOU WISH THE BANK TO CONSIDER AS A CREDIT REFERENCE. USE SEPARATE SHEET IF NECESSARY

NAME OF COMPANY OR BANK		ACCOUNT NUMBER	PRESENT BALANCE	MONTHLY PAYMENT	ACCOUNT IN NAME OF
RENT OR MORTGAGE PAYABLE TO					☐ APPLICANT ☐ JOINT APPLICANT ☐ OTHER
AUTOMOBILE FINANCED BY	YEAR				☐ APPLICANT ☐ JOINT APPLICANT ☐ OTHER
	MAKE				
	YEAR				☐ APPLICANT ☐ JOINT APPLICANT ☐ OTHER
	MAKE				
					☐ APPLICANT ☐ JOINT APPLICANT ☐ OTHER
					☐ APPLICANT ☐ JOINT APPLICANT ☐ OTHER
					☐ APPLICANT ☐ JOINT APPLICANT ☐ OTHER

SECTION C—OBLIGATIONS AND REFERENCES

Are you a co-maker, endorser, or guarantor on any loan or contract?   Yes ☐   No ☐   If "yes"

For whom? _____   To whom? _____

Are there any unsatisfied judgements against you?   Yes ☐   No ☐   If "yes" to whom owed? _____

Have you been declared bankrupt in the last 10 years?   Yes ☐   No ☐   If "Yes" where? _____   Year _____

FOR ARMED FORCES PERSONNEL ONLY–HOME OF RECORD Service Member is   ☐ Applicant   ☐ Joint Applicant

Address of Home of Record	City, State, Zip	Expiration of Category	Rank

CREDIT LIMIT REQUESTED: _____

The applicant and joint applicant, if any, hereby request a MasterCard/Visa, affirm that everything stated in this application is true and correct, understanding that the Bank will retain this application whether or not it is approved, authorize the Bank to check the above credit and employment history and to answer questions about the credit experience with the account, and agree to be obligated by the terms and conditions of the MasterCard/Visa Agreement and Disclosure required by Federal Law as amended from time to time delivered to them. Should a MasterCard/Visa be issued and without limiting the generality of said agreement they specifically agree, jointly and severally to pay for credit extended through the use of the card and all costs incurred in collecting that indebtedness, including a reasonable attorney's fee.

_____   _____   _____   _____
Applicant's Signature   Date   Other Signature (where Applicable)   Date

FIRST FLORIDA BANK

Member FDIC   Please fold and tape securely; postage is paid. Or, bring into your local First Florida Bank branch.

Nonbank Cards

In 1986, Sears introduced its Discover Card, a general-purpose credit card designed to compete with both Visa and MasterCard. The Discover Card coexists with Sears Card, the proprietary store card issued by Sears. The Discover Card offered some interesting incentives to encourage the public to sign up, including no annual fee and a cash-back bonus based on purchases. Exhibit 4–2 lists some of the financial services available with the Discover Card.

During the 1980s, Sears launched an effort to become a one-stop financial services firm that would provide consumers with a complete package of financial products and services. Existing subsidiaries, and some new acquisitions, provided the means to offer this package: Dean Witter for brokerage services, Allstate for insurance products, Coldwell Banker for real estate franchises, the Discover Card, and the traditional Sears retail stores. Observers noted that a consumer could buy a house, furnish it, purchase insurance, open a brokerage account, get a credit card, and fill their dresser drawers through a single corporate network. In 1995, however, Sears began restructuring this network by spinning off subsidiaries and selling shares to the public.

In 1987, American Express introduced its Optima Card, a revolving, general-purpose credit card. Previously, American Express had only issued a travel and entertainment card

In 1985, the AFL-CIO sponsored a labor-related affinity credit card that provided members with favorable interest rates while promoting organized labor's image. Today this card is one of the most successful in the affinity card market.

Other successful groupings include public service employees, clothing and textile workers, steel workers, mail handlers, letter carriers, electrical workers, hotel and restaurant employees, golfers and tennis players, and church organizations.

Prestige cards.   In recent years, both MasterCard and Visa have experienced record growth in their gold card or prestige card programs. A **prestige card** is a premium credit card that offers a wide array of bank products (such as higher credit card limits, personal check-cashing services, travel-accident insurance, emergency cash, free traveler's checks, and car rental discounts) into a single prestige product.

Previously, each bank credit card plan designed its own prestige card with its own attractive features, thus preventing the promotion of the cards through national marketing campaigns. Once their cards were launched, Visa and MasterCard encouraged growth by subsidizing issuers' direct mail, print advertising material, and TV and radio spots.

Prestige cards are profitable for banks because many customers pay fees that average 50 percent higher than those on so-called standard cards; customers charge more per purchase than regular cardholders; and customers maintain considerably higher-than-standard account balances and thus pay more in deferred payment charges.

Secured-card programs.   Traditionally, bank credit card accounts have been structured as unsecured lines of credit available through the use of plastic cards. A fairly recent development, however, is the offering of secured-card programs. A **secured credit card** is a credit card secured by some form of collateral that becomes available to the issuer in the event of default by the cardholder. The security is typically a deposit account or a certificate of deposit with the issuing bank. The credit line on the card generally equals the amount of the deposit provided by the applicant. Interest rates are typically higher than with unsecured cards, application fees may be required, and annual fees must be paid. The cards appeal to higher-risk clients in need of credit repair who would not otherwise qualify for unsecured credit cards.

Unfortunately, various schemes and scams have developed as aggressive telemarketers and others sell these programs to anxious customers. Unsupported guarantees of credit cards, exorbitant processing fees, and the use of expensive "900" numbers have damaged the image of secured credit cards. Some reputable issuers exist, however, who find this sector very profitable. Secured credit card issuers must document their security interest in the deposit accounts and they must be careful to comply with federal and state legislation.

Benefits of General-Purpose Credit Cards

The popularity and use of general-purpose credit cards continues to grow. Both customers and merchants benefit from the generalized purchasing power that is incorporated in these payment mechanisms.

To Customers.   As more and more firms participate in these plans, customers can use their cards at an ever-widening assortment of merchants. An increasing number of service establishments accept general-purpose credit cards. Some educational institutions accept them for tuition payments, and governmental agencies for tax payments. With the cash-advance feature, customers can obtain cash loans quickly and conveniently. More businesses are installing unattended 24-hour terminals (cash dispensers and automated tellers) for cash-advance loans.

To Participating Merchants.   The advantages of increased sales and profits, improved cash position, and freedom from credit department detail continue to benefit participating merchants. As credit becomes a way of life in this country, many merchants who had a cash-only policy are finding credit a necessity for survival. General-purpose credit card plans provide the means for such merchants to switch to a cash or credit policy.

To Credit Card Issuers.   Credit card plans continue to help banks and other firms develop new business from participating merchants, "cross-sell" other services to cardholders, and create a progressive image. Card issuers contend that credit cards allow them to offer a new service to existing customers, provide a means of penetrating new consumer and merchant markets, and increase the opportunities for additional income. The newer nonbank and corporate brand name issuers are especially interested in improving their image and increasing sales.

Travel and Entertainment Cards

As their name implies, "T&E" cards are used primarily for purchases related to travel and entertainment, especially by businesspersons. The Fair Credit and Charge Card Disclosure Act of 1988 defined a *charge card* as "a card, plate, or other single credit device that may be used from time to time to obtain credit which is not subject to a finance charge." A **travel and entertainment card** is a charge card that allows the cardholder to charge goods and services at member establishments, and then receive one itemized monthly statement of the charges which is paid in full each month. The monthly statement gives the customer an itemized record of expenditures and travels and proof of legitimate business expenses for tax purposes. Firms that agree to honor the cards pay a stipulated percentage discount in order to be reimbursed for the customer's charges. The cardholder also is required to pay an annual fee to the issuing organization.

American Express and Citicorp Diners Club are the leaders in the travel and entertainment charge card field. A major market for these cards is found in the business community, as large corporations provide them to sales representatives and others for business expenses. The corporation pays the monthly bills and benefits from the documentation provided by the T&E card issuer. Charge card issuers are currently competing vigorously for this corporate market and are developing sophisticated reporting services that show expenditures itemized by region, by employee, and by department to help businesses control costs. Card issuers are also interested in capturing individual consumer users, of course, with a marketing message that often emphasizes the prestige of carrying one of these cards. Diners Club (see Exhibit 4–4 for a Diners Club application form) is the granddaddy, dating back to 1950; American Express entered the field in 1958.

EXHIBIT 4–4   Application for the Diners Club Card

Apply Today for the Diners Club Card

Place your silver
sticker here.

Don't pass up this opportunity to apply for Diners Club
Card membership. Apply for the Card that gives you Club
Rewards℠, $350,000 Automatic Air Travel Accident Insurance,
and thousands of dollars in future purchasing privileges.

Diners Club Membership Form
Fill in this Form completely and mail in enclosed envelope.

Please print your full name as you wish it to appear on the Card. (25 spaces maximum)

Please print your business title or company name if you wish it to appear on the Card.

ADDITIONAL CARD: Please issue an additional Diners Club Card, $30 each annually, with separate monthly itemized listing for the above family or household member. **Married Applicants may each apply for separate accounts.**
Please indicate whether or not you wish Additional Cardmember to also have access to the Club Cash℠ Account. ☐ YES ☐ NO

Social Security Number   Birth Date   Number of dependents (include yourself)

Highest Level of Education Completed:
☐ Graduate School   ☐ College   ☐ High School

Home Address   Street

City   State   Zip

( )   Years at current address:_____   own ☐ rent ☐ other ☐
Home Telephone (include area code)

Previous Home Address (if less than 1 year at present address)

City   State   Zip

Indicate your banking relationships:
☐ Checking ☐ Money Market ☐ Savings ☐ NOW ☐ Other
Bank Name
☐ Checking ☐ Money Market ☐ Savings ☐ NOW ☐ Other
Bank Name

Check which charge cards you have:
American Express ☐   Visa ☐   MasterCard ☐   Oil Company Cards ☐
Sears ☐   Ward's ☐   J.C. Penney ☐   Other Store Cards ☐

Employer Name   Your Position

Employer Address   Street

City   State   Zip

( )   Self-employed: Yes ☐ No ☐
Business Telephone (include area code)

Annual Wages or Salary (must be provided): _____

If your annual salary is less than $25,000—indicate source and amount of other income, and individual (Banker, Broker, Employer, etc.) we may contact for confirmation. Please understand that your total annual income from all sources must be at least $25,000 to be considered for Cardmembership.

Disclosure of income from alimony, child support or separate maintenance required only if you wish it to be considered for purposes of this application.

Other income $_____   Source_____

Name of individual for additional income verification.   ( )   Phone

Address   City   State   Zip

Please provide all requested information so your Membership Form may be promptly processed. Send no money now. Upon our approval, we will bill you for the non-refundable $55 annual MEMBERSHIP FEE (subject to change).

I have read both sides of this application and agree to its terms.

X
Signature of Primary Applicant   Date

X
Signature of Additional Applicant, if any   Date

SEE REVERSE SIDE FOR IMPORTANT INFORMATION

The major charge card companies vary in the number of outlets serviced; the annual fee charged customers; the plan followed for extended payments, if any; the cash-advance feature allowed; and the minimum income of applicants.

American Express issued its green card in 1958, its gold card in 1966, and its platinum card in 1984. Each card carries a different annual fee and a different array of financial services. Exhibit 4–5 compares the three American Express cards.

EXHIBIT 4–5   **How American Express Charge Cards Compare**

Green Card	Gold Card (Includes all Green Card Features)	Platinum Card (Includes all Green and Gold Card Features)
Introduced 1958	Introduced 1966	Introduced 1984
Annual Fee: $55	Annual Fee: $75	Annual Fee: $300
No preset spending limit	$2,000 line of credit	Travel emergency assistance
Signed receipt with bills	Nonresident membership in 90 private U.S. clubs	Personalized travel service
24-hour customer service	Envoy personalized travel service	Minimum $10,000 line of credit
AmEx Travel Service Office Network		Nonresident membership in 26 exclusive clubs worldwide
Emergency card replacement		Preferred Welcome
Buyer's Assurance Protection Plan		Worldwide Personal Assistance to locate goods and services
Purchase Protection Plan		
Global Assist Hotline		
Car rental loss and damage insurance		
$100,000 travel accident insurance		
Baggage insurance plan		
Express cash		
$1,000 emergency fund		
Assured reservations		

Debit Cards

Debit cards are not credit cards or charge cards. A **debit card** is a plastic card used to access funds stored elsewhere for payment for goods and services. Debit cards, sometimes referred to as **check cards,** may be used to access a checking account, for example. The cards often look like a regular credit card and are readily accepted by merchants. The funds to pay for the purchase are immediately deducted from the debit cardholder's bank account, however, when the purchase ticket arrives at the bank.

These cards may also operate as a part of an electronic funds transfer (EFT) system that incorporates automated teller machines (ATMs) and/or point of sale (POS) terminals. **Electronic funds transfer systems** utilize telephone lines and electronic messages to transfer funds. A debit card holder uses an ATM to access his or her bank accounts, withdrawing and depositing funds, moving funds around, and perhaps making loan payments. A point of sale terminal will typically be found in a retail store, such as a grocery store. The customer uses a debit card to pay for groceries immediately by moving funds electronically from his or her bank account to the store's bank account. The card is "read" electronically to determine the account number and the user is asked to input a Personal Identification Number (PIN) before the transfer is executed. The PIN is a security measure that requires the debit card user to input this memorized number before funds are actually transferred. The payment process is very convenient and the store benefits since the funds are transferred instantaneously (no more bad checks). Since many credit card users pay their balances in full each month anyway, the debit cards may become more common in the future.

A variation of the debit card system is a smart card. A **smart card** is a debit card that stores value that can be accessed for purchases electronically. Where these systems are currently used, college students and employees of large corporations will "load" their cards up at a centralized location and then use these cards to purchase cafeteria food, books, and vending machine products. The value is stored electronically on a magnetic strip or in a computer chip embedded in the card. Again, the interest in these cards revolves around the convenience offered, especially for reoccurring purchases of inexpensive items.

Credit Card Fraud

Credit card and charge card fraud is a growing problem. Any business that issues or accepts credit cards is a potential target for credit card fraud. Types of fraud include the following:

Application Fraud

The perpetrator uses a fictitious or stolen identity to obtain a credit card. Purchases are charged and, for a time, bills are paid to build a credit line. Eventually, the cardholder disappears. The best defense is to carefully investigate every new application to verify identity and other facts.

Lost or Stolen Cards

Hotel workers and others may steal credit cards, which are later used or sold to other dishonest individuals. The cards are used as quickly as possible to charge items to the original cardholder's account. Since lost cards are often reported soon after they are lost, a more desirable method for thieves is to steal "never received" cards from the mail. Card issuers often require that new cards be activated by calling a special number from a home telephone to guarantee the cards arrived at the intended destination.

Counterfeit Cards

Sometimes credit cards are manufactured using sophisticated equipment to stamp out plastic cards and program magnetic strips. Card issuers are adding graphical features that are difficult to copy and, in some cases, using a photograph of the cardholder. Eventually, a method will be available to carry the fingerprints of the cardholder to prevent duplication.

Loading Up

This unusual term is used to describe the process of charging large amounts of goods and services prior to filing bankruptcy. The individual cardholder knows that unsecured debts will generally be wiped out by the bankruptcy action. Fortunately, recent changes to the bankruptcy laws have recognized this fraudulent behavior and include provisions to prevent this activity.

Telemarketing Fraud

Unsuspecting cardholders may be asked to provide their account numbers over the telephone, perhaps because they have supposedly won a free vacation. The actual intent is to charge large sums to the credit card account for items or services that are never provided. Obviously, the best protection for the individual is to never give your credit card account number to anyone that calls unless you initiate the conversation with a reputable firm.

The best protection for everyone involved is to check identification carefully and to be aware of fraudulent activities. Modern authorization processes require sales clerks to scan the magnetic strips on most credit cards and, using a computerized modem, obtain permission to accept the credit card on every sale. The card should be retained by the clerk until the authorization is approved.

FINANCING RETAIL INSTALLMENT TRANSACTIONS

Large ticket items, e.g., automobiles, major appliances, and expensive furniture, are generally not appropriate purchases for credit cards or charge cards. The customers often prefer an installment purchase option that will provide fixed regular payments extending months, and sometimes years, into the future.

Since many shoppers pick out an item first, and decide how to pay for it later, it was a natural development for retailers to become more involved in the creation of a signed installment contract. Retailers take the customer's credit information, execute the security agreement, and complete other tests necessary to establish the installment account. Retailers also inform the customer of the terms of the contract and answer the customer's questions. If the retailer does not wish to carry this "paper" themselves, they will seek a financial institution, or other agency, to purchase the contract.

Retailers who carry their own paper need more capital to compensate for a decline in their working capital. They also need more capital if they increase sales volume by offering installment credit services. Retailers who want a faster turnover of their own capital and desire to shift much of the credit risk burden may sell their paper to a sales finance company, commercial bank, or other type of consumer finance institution. Those who do so transfer the credit function to specialists in installment credit and free their own organization to concentrate on merchandising.

Today retailers carry only a small portion of the debt they are influential in creating. Commercial banks and finance companies hold most installment paper.

Financing by Commercial Banks

Today's high standard of living would not be possible without bank credit, particularly bank installment credit.

Many bankers think that the Federal Housing Administration (FHA) was the major factor in influencing banks to enter the field of installment credit. Under the blanket insurance arrangement provided by the FHA in the early 1930s, commercial banks were able to handle direct property improvement loans and acquire paper from contractors and dealers who supplied materials and labor. Banks' satisfactory experience in this area provided the impetus to explore other fields of installment credit.

Basically, a commercial bank has different methods available for acquiring install-ment business—the direct approach and the indirect approach. Banks may also use a combination of both methods.

Direct Method

Direct loans generally involve only two parties: the bank and the borrower. In this approach, the bank solicits the customer directly and makes loan commitments to creditworthy borrowers. The bank in turn can control its credit policies, as well as the ratio and volume of business it accepts.

Direct lending has many advantages over indirect installment lending:

1. The bank can apply its credit policies consistently.
2. The bank has greater flexibility in its operations.
3. Only two parties are involved.
4. The bank can better determine and evaluate the borrower's financial and personal characteristics.
5. The bank can influence the size of the loan.
6. Direct lending broadens a bank's base of operation within its trading area.

The principal disadvantage of direct lending is smaller volume generated at a slower pace. In addition, the bank's trading area may be too small to generate a large volume of walk-in direct installment loans, and the bank may have more difficulty with repossessions because it lacks a relationship with a dealer.

Indirect or Dealer Method

This method involves three parties: the dealer, the borrower, and the bank. The dealer takes the credit application and prepares the necessary contracts and other forms. The dealer presents the paper to the bank for discount and, if approved, receives from the bank the amount financed by the borrower. In most cases the bank sends the borrower a payment coupon book. Banks need to recognize the following fundamental differences between direct and indirect (or dealer) methods when considering a dealer arrangement:

1. The bank doesn't see the installment purchasers and thus doesn't have an opportunity to appraise them.
2. The attitude of many installment purchasers toward their obligations is different from the attitude of direct borrowers. When borrowers receive money from a bank in a direct loan transaction, they realize they must repay the obligation in money. When installment purchasers buy goods through a dealer, however, they sometimes think they can cancel their obligation by returning the goods, or they feel justified in refusing to make their installment payments if the goods are unsatisfactory.
3. Fraud, forgery, and misrepresentation are possible in any credit transaction where the bank doesn't see the obligor personally.

All experienced installment credit department managers in commercial banks know that the risks involved in indirect financing are substantially greater than they are in direct installment credit. Dealers have to be carefully policed in indirect financing, and often, the bank doesn't know as much as it would like about prospective borrowers. Yet indirect business can produce a high volume fairly quickly. As a result, indirect business offers the bank an opportunity to generate substantial loan volume with little effort.

In formulating policy on indirect installment sales, an installment loan department first considers the quality of the retail paper. In most cases, this paper is only as good as the dealer that initiates it. As a result, the dealer's moral and financial qualifications are extremely important and must be reviewed carefully. Most banks spend considerable time reviewing the dealers' "track records," including details about their financial and business history. When deciding whether to finance a dealer's paper, the bank generally investigates the following areas of the dealer's background:

1. Current and past financial operating statements.
2. Deposit relations with the bank.
3. Trade references.
4. Distributor or manufacturer relations.
5. Credit reporting agencies.
6. Experiences with other financial institutions.
7. Standing with local office of the Better Business Bureau.

Once a bank accepts a dealer relationship, it must consider a wide range of other policies, including the following:

1. The ability to give speedy and prompt decisions on loans the dealer submits to the bank.
2. The development of experienced bank personnel who thoroughly understand the dealer's selling and credit problems.
3. Effective and economically feasible collection practices.
4. The adoption of competitive rates and terms.
5. Provisions for an adequate inventory-financing program for the dealer.
6. The maintenance of adequate bank records to be able to review the condition of each dealer's accounts.
7. The ability to extend additional bank services to the dealer.

A variety of financing plans are available. Those selected depend on the competitive conditions prevailing and on the bank's credit policy. Some commercial banks offer their dealers a choice of several plans; others make only one program available and handle all paper purchased under that plan. The purchase of installment paper by commercial banks comes under three major classifications: the full recourse plan, the nonrecourse plan, and the repurchase plan. In each of these three plans, consumer default "triggers" the plan's provisions.

Full Recourse.   Under the full recourse plan, dealers sell or sign over to the bank the installment sale paper that they originate. They do so with an unconditional guarantee:

they accept full responsibility for the paper should the purchaser become delinquent. In the event of default, the dealer must repurchase the obligation from the bank for the balance due. The dealer is also responsible for reconditioning and reselling the product. Dealers like full recourse arrangements because of the lower bank discount rate—particularly if the consumer is a good credit risk.

Nonrecourse.   Under the nonrecourse plan, dealers have no responsibility if the customer defaults. They only have to warrant the genuineness of the paper, terms of sale, title, and so forth. The commercial bank buys the paper solely on the credit quality of the installment purchaser. In the event of repossession, the commercial bank assumes the full responsibility of retaking, reconditioning, and reselling the product.

Repurchase.   Under this plan, if the consumer defaults, the dealer has to buy back the property for the unpaid balance after it has been repossessed by the bank. The property must be delivered to the dealer's place of business within a specified number of days after maturity of the oldest unpaid installment. Generally, the bank has 90 days to locate the property and return it to the dealer.

Bank installment credit department managers and others involved in these decisions should judge dealer paper based on its individual merits. Banks should maintain a flexible credit policy at all times and make allowance for the financial strength of the dealer, the plan in effect, the quality of the paper purchased, the reserves available, and the borrower's equity. Some retailers request the privilege of a nonnotification plan. Under this plan, the dealer's customers have no knowledge that their sales contracts have been discounted at a commercial bank. Banks usually restrict nonnotification plans to highly reputable dealers with strong financial responsibility. The dealer's full recourse endorsement is generally required.

Dealer Reserve

A **dealer reserve** is an account maintained at a bank as part of an agreement between a retailer who wishes to sell installment contracts and the financing organization that will be purchasing contracts. In consideration of the dealer's part in originating the business and also to offset whatever liability the dealer assumes, banks frequently establish a reserve from a portion of the finance charge. Under a dealer participation arrangement, the finance charge to the customer must be higher than the bank rate to the dealer. The difference between the two is frequently set aside in a reserve account, giving the bank some protection on the dealer's contingent liability. The reserve will be drawn on to help cover losses the bank suffers upon repossession of the merchandise and prepayment of installment contract. Funds generally accumulate in the reserve account until the account balance achieves a certain percentage of the total outstanding paper that the dealer maintains with the bank. From time to time the bank will pay the dealer any excess.

Dealer reserve accounts are a policy decision, and they frequently differ from one type of dealer to another and often with the same dealer class. Although some states regulate dealer reserves, banks retain some flexibility. They often base their percentage of outstandings for a certain dealer on their judgment of the dealer's creditworthiness.

Inventory Financing

Also known as flooring, floor planning, and wholesale floor plan, **inventory financing** is a form of credit extended by a lender to a retail dealer to enable the dealer to carry an adequate supply of goods for display and sale.

Most commercial banks don't consider inventory financing as a separate activity but rather an integral part of the installment sale financing relationship with the dealer. The low yield the bank obtains from this type of financing is a trade-off to the higher yield derived from the dealer's installment paper. Floor planning thus is an accommodation granted to retail dealers for two basic reasons: (1) in consideration for their agreement to discount with the bank the majority of their retail installment contracts and (2) to gain other cross-selling business activities.

Inventory financing first developed for car dealers, and they utilize it to a great extent. Car dealers have to pay cash for cars delivered to the dealership. The manufacturer draws a sight draft on the dealer, and this draft is payable on receipt of the cars. If dealers used their own capital to pay for the cars, many would have all of their working capital tied up in inventory, thus seriously limiting the quantity of cars they could purchase. Commercial banks thus floor plan the shipments from manufacturers by paying the manufacturer for the dealer. In exchange for this financing, the dealer delivers a security interest in the cars it acquires to the bank. As a result, the commercial bank has title to the cars but the dealer retains possession. Dealers store the cars or use them for display or demonstration. When the dealer sells a car, the dealer must immediately or within a stipulated period satisfy the bank's lien. Of course, the commercial bank involved would also like to handle the buyer's car loan.

In extending flooring credit, the soundness of the dealer is vitally important. Although there are exceptions, experienced dealers with proven managerial ability offer the best risk.

Financing by Sales Finance Companies

A **sales finance company** is a specialized type of institution that (1) engages primarily in buying consumer installment contracts from retail dealers, (2) provides wholesale financing for these dealers, and (3) charges rates competitive with those of commercial banks and other lenders for equivalent services. The sales finance company is not to be confused with cash lending institutions such as small loan companies, consumer finance companies, and personal loan companies, which lend money directly to consumers and operate under special state legislation. Some consumer finance companies, however, operate sales finance company subsidiaries and use existing branch locations and personnel for these operations. Others operate subsidiaries for their manufacturing firms to accomplish the same outcomes: (1) assisting dealers in obtaining inventory and (2) assisting customers with their installment purchases. The major automobile manufacturers, for example, have each launched these financing subsidiaries, e.g., General Motors Acceptance Corporation, Ford Motor Credit Corporation, and others.

Sales finance companies originated in the early 1900s. The *Saturday Evening Post,* in its March 31, 1900, issue, carried its first "horseless carriage" advertisement, but not until

1909 did the production of motor vehicles (both passenger cars and trucks) exceed 100,000. The first sales finance companies supplied working capital to manufacturers and wholesalers by buying open accounts and purchasing drafts and notes receivable. It was not until the increased acceptance of the automobile that sales finance companies, as we know them today, were organized.

When buying a car or some other high-priced durable good with installment credit, customers usually have to fill out application forms that request fairly detailed information on employment, income, and other pertinent factors. These application forms vary, however, from retail dealer to retail dealer. After the buyer signs the application, it is usually witnessed and signed by a salesperson or the dealer. The usual installment sale contract is then prepared.

If the retail dealer decides not to carry the paper to maturity, the contract may be offered to a sales finance company based on a prearranged agreement between the dealer and the sales finance company. The sales finance company usually performs the credit investigation (although the dealer may do it at certain times) to make sure all the documents are in order and, if everything is acceptable, to make the purchase. The customer's account is then opened, and the customer usually is notified that the sales finance company purchased the contract. The customer makes payments directly to the sales finance company.

As with commercial banks, the purchase of installment paper by sales finance companies comes under three major classifications: the full recourse plan, the nonrecourse plan, and the repurchase plan. In case of customer default, the provisions of these plans come into effect in the same manner as described under commercial bank financing.

In the recourse plan, the dealer reserve protects the dealer to some extent against losses. This fund, set aside by the sales finance company out of the finance charges, is refunded to the dealer under specified conditions. The dealer reserve covers expenses of repossession and other encumbrances against the vehicle. The dealer reserve account, which is set up in the accounting records of the sales finance company, ordinarily totals about 1.5 percent on the amounts advanced on new cars and approximately 2 to 3 percent on used cars. Thus, the retail dealer can be reimbursed on repossession from two sources: the car resale and the accumulated dealer reserve.

When buying installment contracts, sales finance companies' methods, contract forms, and procedures are similar to commercial banks. The interest rates of both are highly competitive in most communities.

In addition to buying installment paper from retailers, particularly car dealers, sales finance companies provide wholesale financing to durable-goods dealers. Such financing arrangements are similar to those provided by commercial banks.

Sales finance companies have changed and expanded over the years and have diversified in at least four ways:

1. In addition to cars, they now deal in installment paper on manufactured homes, boats, aircraft, and farm machinery.
2. They are moving into other types of financing, such as small loans and commercial lending.

3. They are moving into new fields that may or may not be related to the finance industry. An example of this would be the acquisition of a bank by a sales finance company.

4. Some independent sales finance companies are establishing insurance subsidiaries.

COMPETITION FOR INSTALLMENT CONTRACT FINANCING

The competition among buyers of installment contracts has escalated in recent years. This competition has placed considerable pressure on banks and other financial institutions that purchase installment contracts to buy more contracts, to lower the interest rate differentials to give more to the dealers, and to improve services.

A dealer will typically work primarily with one financial institution and will send all contracts to that organization first. Others, however, will offer to look at any contracts rejected by the primary contract purchaser to see if they might be able to approve the transaction. They, in fact, may approve some tentative deals to demonstrate their flexibility and service in an effort to win the primary spot. This activity may place undue pressure on all the financing organizations to approve shaky deals, which contributes to poor loans being made and to eventual losses.

Other competitive pressures work to increase the amounts contributed to the dealer reserves by having the bank reduce its own interest rates and the amount it collects from the contract. A small interest rate differential may cause a dealer to switch installment financing sponsors.

There is also pressure on the contract purchasers to improve service and the speed with which they make decisions. New computer networks link the dealers and the financing organization electronically. The dealer types in the customer application on-line and the information appears on a computer screen in the bank. A credit bureau file is electronically obtained at the same time, a credit score may be calculated by the computer, and a decision is often made in a matter of minutes (sometimes without loan officers even involved—the computer decides). If a positive decision is made, the installment contract and other documentation is printed, with the blanks automatically completed, back in the dealer's office.

Important Terms

affinity cards   66
check cards   70
credit line   62
credit card bank   66
dealer reserve   75
debit card   70
electronic funds transfer system   70
general purpose cards   62

inventory financing   76
prestige card   67
sales finance company   76
secured credit card   67
smart card   71
store card   61
travel & entertainment card   68

Discussion Questions

1. List and describe four reasons consumers use credit cards.

2. What is a proprietary store credit card and how does it differ from a general-purpose credit card?

3. Describe the typical rules for charges, payments and finance charges with general-purpose credit card plans. For a T&E card?

4. What are the advantages of using credit cards for consumers, for issuers, and for retailers?

5. What are the primary differences among bank cards, nonbank cards, and corporate brand-name general-purpose credit cards?

6. Explain the characteristics of specialized credit cards: affinity cards, prestige cards, and secured credit cards.

7. What are ATMs, POS terminals, debit cards and smart cards?

8. Explain the various ways retailers can finance their installment accounts.

9. What factors should retailers consider in choosing a method of financing installment accounts?

10. Contrast the two methods available to a commercial bank for acquiring installment business: direct and indirect financing. Explain each method.

11. Distinguish clearly between the full recourse, the nonrecourse, and the repurchase plans of buying paper. Which plan is best for the consumer? For the retailer? For the commercial bank or the sales finance company?

12. What is the primary purpose of a dealer reserve?

13. What is inventory financing? Why is it especially important in the automobile industry?

14. What is the primary reason for the existence of sales finance companies?

15. What is the holder in due course doctrine? Explain how this doctrine affects you as a consumer.

16. How does the growing competition among installment contract purchasers affect this business?

17. Discuss the growing importance of credit card fraud.

18. Explain the difference between a credit card plan and a charge card plan. Give an example of each.

5

TYPES OF CONSUMER CREDIT— CASH LOAN CREDIT

Learning Objectives

After studying this chapter, you should be able to:

- Explain why consumers need cash loans.
- Describe the characteristics of cash loan plans in commercial banks.
- Illustrate the changing character of commercial banks and their customers.
- Trace the origin, development, and growth of credit unions.
- Explain the operations of consumer finance companies.
- Compare the relative costs of consumer lending institutions.

Cash loans are created when consumers approach a financial institution or another lender seeking funds for a variety of uses. Consumers eventually repay the money they receive along with additional amounts charged as finance charges. They sign a contract that outlines the payments, interest rate, and other terms related to the repayment of the funds borrowed. The consumer is committing future income or assets to the repayment and has decided that the immediate use of the funds justifies paying extra amounts in the future. This chapter describes cash loan credit, which is credit in the form of money. Two other types of consumer credit are retail credit, which facilitates the purchase of goods, and service credit, which allows consumers time to pay for services.

A system of financial institutions has evolved to supply most people with various types of cash loans. Commercial banks, consumer finance companies, credit unions, industrial banks, savings and loan institutions, and a number of other institutions (including philanthropic organizations and illegal lenders) supply cash loans to consumers.

USE OF CASH LOANS BY CONSUMERS

Consumers borrow money for a variety of reasons. They may want to consolidate existing debts into one larger loan, pay for emergency services, or purchase merchandise and services with cash. Loans made to cover this broad range of purposes, for example, may be used for medical and dental expenses, home repair and modernization, tax bills, and educational expenses, as well as for furniture, appliances, and cars.

Individual consumers, with their varied needs and desires, differ greatly in their ability to satisfy their wants. Some borrowers need small sums of money; others require larger sums. Some are able to repay their loan in a matter of 60 to 90 days; others need longer terms. Some prudently compare interest and service charges; others regard immediate cash as more important than cost. A number of borrowers need the security of a co-maker, while others are able to borrow on their signature alone. In addition, consumer borrowers differ in their ability to handle funds wisely. These differences among cash loan purposes, and the differences that arise from the variety of loan applicants, explain the variety in cash loan providers and the types of loans available. Some lenders specialize in a particular type of loan, others concentrate on making loans to a particular type of applicant, e.g., higher-risk borrowers.

Why do consumers borrow money to purchase goods and services when they can use other types of retail credit? Sometimes the cost of obtaining a direct loan from a financial institution is the least-expensive option. Financing a new automobile through a dealer involved in indirect lending may, for example, result in a higher interest charge designed to compensate the dealer for generating the business. Many consumers calculate the cost of other types of retail credit, for example, credit cards, compare this cost with that of a direct personal loan, and use the cheapest money available.

Also, retail financing programs are not always available. Merchandisers may demand cash only and expect the purchasers to raise the funds from some other source. A good example is the individual who wishes to buy a used car from another individual. A cash loan will be required if the buyer does not have sufficient savings. Smaller firms without credit programs, companies selling their inventory as they go out of business, and income taxes that must be paid are other examples where credit plans are not available.

Some consumers prefer to transact all credit-related business with a single bank or credit institution. This may be due to customer loyalty, habit, or because they simply prefer to deal with an organization that knows them. Some loan applicants arrive at a point where they wish to consolidate a lot of retail accounts and other loans into a single debt consolidation loan. The debt consolidation loan often reduces the monthly outflow of cash and may be used to clear up current delinquency.

Why Use Cash Loan Credit versus Retail Credit?

- Debt consolidation.
- Lower interest expense.
- Retail credit programs not available.
- Preference and habit.

CONSUMER CASH-LENDING INSTITUTIONS

Commercial banks, credit unions, consumer finance companies, and industrial banks are the principal sources of cash loans made to consumers. Each of these institutions was originated either to serve a particular consumer segment or to meet specific consumer needs not being met by existing credit facilities. The types of loans offered by lending institutions are so varied and numerous that most American consumers have a ready source of cash credit. The variety of cash-lending institutions exemplifies the ability of our economy to develop services and products to meet diverse consumer needs.

Cash-lending institutions can be thought of as "sellers of money." This concept clearly establishes them as merchandisers of credit. The supply and cost of money for cash-lending institutions have a parallel in the supply and cost of goods for retail firms. In other words, the inventory of a financial institution is money that is purchased using depository accounts or borrowed at a cost lower than the interest charged. Cash-lending institutions build a customer group that seeks cash loans and will return when the need again exists, just as retailers of other commodities strive for goodwill, promotion, and repeat sales to satisfied customers. The interest rates and service charges of the cash-lending institutions represent the cost of money to the borrower, as prices of goods represent costs to the buyer of goods and services. Furthermore, the profit motive attracts capital, business firms, and personnel to the lending industry just as it lends impetus to most economic activity. Consequently, sellers of money are confronted with many of the same problems facing other types of merchandising establishments. They must develop and market products, concentrate on customer service, and manage their businesses efficiently. The degree of their success frequently hinges on the same methods that are used by successful merchandisers of other goods and services.

Commercial Banks

Commercial banks were slow to adopt the practice of lending cash to consumers. Before 1930, commercial banks were active in the real estate loan field but made only a few customer loans to individuals, and these were single-payment loans made to individuals with high incomes.

In the late 1920s, banks began consumer cash lending. By this time they were fairly sure that consumer credit was a mature economic force. More importantly, they could see the profitable experience of the pioneering sales finance and consumer loan institutions. Consumer finance companies, discussed later in this chapter, had successfully made consumer cash loans since 1879. The National City Bank of New York opened the first consumer loan department in 1928. Prior to this time, the only "good" loan was a business loan, which automatically carried the likelihood of repayment since its purpose was tied to making a profit. Gradually the early stigma of consumer credit diminished, and cash lending to consumers became as accepted and commonplace as loans to businesses.

Cash credit, as offered by commercial banks, has changed considerably in recent years, and many credit plans have been developed. These present-day plans, while varied and ingenious, can best be classified into three forms of cash loan plans: (1) installment loans, (2) open-end revolving loans, and (3) single-payment loans.

Installment Loans

As described earlier, an **installment loan** is a loan arrangement where a series of fixed, regular payments are made by a borrower to repay funds over a period of time in the future. At the end of the repayment period, the loan is considered paid in full, and the contract is generally returned to the buyer. This type of credit is referred to as *closed-end credit* since the transaction comes to a definite end.

Conventional Installment Loans.   Commercial banks often lend money for the purchase of durable consumer goods such as automobiles, mobile homes, and recreational equipment. If the funds are being used to purchase a tangible durable good, the bank will generally use the item as collateral and will want to take a security interest in the item. The bank will also require that the borrower maintain insurance coverage to prevent loss. Sometimes, there is not a tangible good involved and the commercial bank must decide if an applicant's signature (promise to repay) is sufficient. Loans for vacations, wedding expenses, medical bills, and education are a few examples where collateral does not exist.

Home Equity Loans.   A **home equity loan** is an installment loan secured by the equity, or net worth, in real estate after subtracting the outstanding first mortgage balance from the market value. It is generally a second mortgage loan where a single real estate property is used as security for both loans. Typically, the commercial bank will lend only 75 percent to 80 percent of the appraised value of a home minus the outstanding first mortgage balance. For example:

Appraisal of home	$100,000
Percentage	× 75%
Percentage of value	$ 75,000
Less mortgage debt	−$ 40,000
Maximum loan	$ 35,000

A payment schedule is created and the customer pays regular installments for the specified period. The popularity of this type of loan has increased significantly since the Tax Reform Act of 1986 which removed the tax deductions for nonmortgage interest. Consumers began using mortgage instruments to fund expenditures that typically have been financed by consumer loans. In addition, borrowing against home equity carried a favorable interest rate compared with rates on many types of consumer credit, particularly credit cards and charge cards. Borrowers are now using home equity loans to buy cars, consolidate bills, and otherwise obtain loans that continue to enjoy interest deductibility within the limits prescribed by tax laws.

Student Loans.   **Student loans** are made to help pay tuition and the other costs related to education. Over the years various federal student loan programs have been developed to encourage higher education. The federal support of these lending programs arose from a desire to invest in future human capital and the willingness to help educational institutions by increasing the number of "paying" customers. Some student loan programs involved government subsidies which paid the interest on the loans until after the student graduated. The banks that made these loans collected the interest directly from the government and also received payments for servicing the loans once the repayment period had begun. A federal agency, the Student Loan Marketing Association (called Sallie Mae), was also begun to purchase these loans with funds raised from the sale of government bonds.

Open-End Revolving Loans

These loans incorporate preapproved lines of credit that allow the bank customer to draw on a maximum amount of credit and to borrow as needed by writing a check or by using a credit card. A formula generally determines the amount of the monthly payment and the interest rate is often a variable rate tied to some index, such as the prime rate. As long as the customer makes the regular payments as agreed, the credit relationship continues and no specific end exists. The three basic types of open-ended revolving loans are discussed below.

Cash Advances on Bank Credit Card Plans.   A common addition to bank credit cards is the cash advance feature. A **cash advance** is a loan obtained with a bank credit card that provides the borrower with cash up to the existing credit limit and at terms specified at the time the card is issued. In some instances, banks have used this feature to consolidate processing of all their small personal loans through their bank credit card operations. If a customer approaches the bank for a $300 loan for example, the bank personnel will often recommend that the customer apply for a bank credit card and use the cash advance feature for a loan of this size. The total dollar amount that can be loaned by this method to an individual consumer depends on the bank's policy and the customer's creditworthiness. Finance charges usually are imposed from the date of the cash advance—that is, the consumer is not given the "free" period generally given in retail and service transactions. In addition, some banks have installed 24-hour teller services, enabling customers to use machines to obtain cash advances by using their bank credit card with a magnetic strip on the back.

Overdraft Plans.   An **overdraft plan** provides a borrower with a preapproved loan reserve, generally incorporated into a checking account, that is used at the convenience of the borrower when funds are needed. Overdraft plans, which are basically a form of installment credit, developed independently of bank credit cards. These plans have appeared in a variety of forms and names.

Some plans give customers a choice of two methods of drawing on the reserve: (1) customers simply write a check for any amount up to the agreed maximum, regardless of their checking account balance; or (2) customers give prior notification to the bank to transfer funds from the loan reserve to their checking account, when they anticipate using the reserve. If the checking account's balance falls to zero, the bank may also transfer funds automatically to prevent nonsufficient funds (bounced) checks. In some plans, the bank provides a loan that is exactly the amount of the overdraft. In others, the bank credits the account with loans in increments of $50 or $100. The individual then repays the loan on a revolving basis, sometimes liquidating it by making ordinary deposits to a checking account or by making more formal, separate loan repayments to the bank.

In evaluating these plans, it is important to look at the potential benefits accruing to the customers as well as to the bank. Customers need to apply for credit only once. If their application is approved and if this credit is handled in the designated manner, they may continue to revolve within the line as long as they want. In addition, these plans are easy and convenient for customers to use; customers are not limited to "certain" merchants, as with bank credit card plans. Such a credit arrangement is often viewed as a prestige type of borrowing in that only customers who measure up to certain credit criteria can secure it. This service appeals to many customers as a way to meet recurring need for short-term financing of small purchases and vacation needs and as a contingency reserve.

There are some disadvantages, however. Customers not only face the temptation to spend more money than they have in their checking accounts and to stay in debt for longer periods, but they also must pay an interest charge for this privilege.

Home Equity Lines of Credit.   The home equity line of credit is similar to the closed-end home equity loan discussed above. A **home equity line of credit** is an open-end credit plan with a loan reserve based on the equity owned by the borrower in real estate. The primary difference is that a home equity line uses the net worth available in real estate to determine the size of a credit line that can be drawn upon as needed by the borrower. This is a form of open-end credit, however, since no predetermined payment schedule or time frame exists. A formula determines the amount of monthly payments, the interest rate is often variable rather than locked in, and the program will continue indefinitely until terminated by either the bank or the borrower. The attractiveness of this type of credit line is, again, the deductibility of the interest for tax purposes since this is a form of mortgage debt. Some financial advisors caution consumers to be careful with using these open-end home equity lines of credit. It is very tempting to use these lines; however, the homeowner may end up "spending" the only significant asset he or she have managed to acquire.

Single-Payment Loans

Single-payment loans are generally short-term loans where funds are advanced for a year or less with an agreement that they will be repaid in one payment at the end of the period. Single-payment loans are frequently made for 30, 60, or 90 days and for longer periods such as six months, nine months, or even one year. These loans may be made on either an unsecured or a secured basis, depending on the overall quality of credit risk relative to the amount of the loan. The collateral for these loans, if requested, is usually government bonds and other securities, cash value of life insurance policies, savings accounts, cars, and other personal property that can readily be converted to cash in the event of default.

Typical Bank Consumer Loans

I. Installment loans
  a. Conventional loan
  b. Home equity loan
  c. Student loan
II. Open-end revolving loans
  a. Cash advance bank credit card
  b. Overdraft plan
  c. Home equity line of credit
III. Single-payment loan

Interest Rates

There are a variety of methods used to quote and collect interest charges. Whether or not the quoted percentage actually is the true rate depends on the method and time of collecting the interest. In the past, single-payment loans were sometimes negotiated as discount loans. A **discount loan** is a loan arrangement where the interest for the entire loan period is deducted at the time the loan proceeds are distributed. If the interest is discounted at the time the loan is made, the borrower has use of the principal less the interest; hence, the actual rate will be somewhat higher than it would be if interest and principal had been paid on the loan's maturity date. The financial institution may require that the interest be divided and paid monthly, quarterly, or at the end of the loan period.

Two common methods of charging interest on installment loans are the simple interest method and the add-on method. The simple interest method is challenging the add-on (or discount) method for figuring interest on installment loans. The **simple interest method** charges interest on a daily basis using a daily interest rate, usually 1/365th of the annual finance charge, which is deducted first from each payment. The dollar amount of interest varies depending on the number of days between payments. If a customer pays $100 as a scheduled payment, the interest charge deducted will depend on the outstanding loan balance, the number of days since the last payment, and the daily interest rate. If a customer makes payments early, or pays the loan in full, this method of charging interest is most beneficial. If a borrower falls behind, or delays payments, the interest will be a larger amount.

Under the **add-on method** of figuring interest, the amount of the finance charge is computed before the loan is made and is added to the loan amount. For example, 10 percent interest on a $1,000 loan is $100. The monthly payment would be $1,100 divided by 12 or $91.67 per month. The customer repays the loan proceeds, plus the interest, in a series of installment payments. The annual percentage rate (APR) for the add-on method is nearly twice the indicated rate because the customer only has average use of about half the loan proceeds.

The Changing Character of Commercial Banks and Their Customers

From the customer's viewpoint, today's commercial bank is a very different institution than it was two or three decades ago. Historically, commercial banks were established to serve the financial needs of businesses. Dealings with business usually involve fairly large sums of money, and the risk element can be rather accurately appraised. Banks' services to the needs of commerce are still their main function; change and adjustment to current needs of business contributed to their growth and overall importance to our economy. Traditionally, banks have been conservative financial institutions and were so regarded by most consumers. The conservative nature of their management, the early stigma associated with consumer installment financing, the legal requirements, and, in general, their preoccupation with commercial needs all tended to slow the banks' entrance into the financing of consumer needs.

Most present-day banks set out to overcome such negative attitudes and now pursue all kinds of consumer credit. In adopting the policy that consumer financing was sound and in aggressively seeking consumer credit customers, they have gradually become one of the dominant sources for consumer loans.

In expanding their present-day customer group, banks had to compete against other aggressive consumer loan institutions. They accomplished much of this expansion through sales promotion. Banks adjusted their hours to customers' convenience; provided friendly, convenient, comfortable, and attractive loan quarters; and used the most effective advertising media and techniques. Using the "full-service" banking concept, some banks adopted the so-called personal banker plan in which each customer is assigned a bank officer who is responsible for the bulk of the customer's relationships with the bank. The specific objective of such a plan is to eliminate inconvenience, runaround, and loss of customer identity. In addition, banks provide customers with an array of banking services, including checking accounts, overdraft privileges on their checking account, traveler's checks, safe-deposit boxes, trust services, installment loans, and notary services. Savings programs include savings accounts, savings certificates with different maturities, and IRA deposit accounts. The community bank continues to offer a broad array of services that many competitors cannot duplicate.

Bankers face increasing competition for deposits, however. Money market and other mutual funds have attracted billions of dollars that were once on deposit with financial institutions. A **mutual fund** is an investment company that pools the funds of a group of investors and buys securities of a particular type. The income and capital gains from these investments are distributed to the investors in proportion to the size of their investment. A **money market mutual fund** invests funds in short-term, unsecured money market investments such as corporate bonds, treasury securities, and commercial paper (notes). Deposits in money market mutual funds are not insured by the FDIC, the interest rate fluctuates daily, and some checking privileges are generally available. Money market funds attracted large sums from bank accounts in the early 1980s when they were able to pay more interest than banks, who were restricted by law from paying higher interest. Insurance companies, brokerage firms, and others have also joined the field in recent years as they attempt to sell investment products, thus attracting bank deposits. Banks have begun selling mutual funds and insurance annuities in an effort to at least share in the commissions that result from the sale of these products.

FDIC Protection

One of the strongest promotional features of commercial banks is the Federal Deposit Insurance Corporation (FDIC) deposit protection. Deposit guarantee legislation, beginning with the 1933 establishment of the FDIC, was enacted to prevent bank system failures like those of the Great Depression of the 1930s. This remained virtually unchanged until enactment of the Depository Institutions Deregulation and Monetary Control Act in 1980. This act covers a variety of credit activities, one of the most important being increased coverage for all federal deposit insurance from $40,000 to $100,000.

Bank Holding Companies

Closely connected to the future of commercial banking operations is the bank holding company movement, which is of increasing interest to both economic and political sectors. A **bank holding company** is a company that holds a controlling interest in one or more commercial banks. Historically, formation of a bank holding company was used to overcome many restrictions on banking activities and expand services to the public. A bank holding company can provide many services to its subsidiary banks. Examples are auditing, investment counseling, data processing support, volume purchasing of supplies, sophisticated equipment, and shared technical expertise. As electronic funds transfer systems become more prevalent, thus eliminating the need for consumers to keep their funds in local banks, the size of financial service conglomerates and bank holding companies will undoubtedly continue to expand.

Automated Teller Machines (ATMs)

In the early 1970s automated teller machines began to grow in popularity. **Automated teller machines** are electronic terminals that enable consumers to perform various banking transactions such as deposits, cash withdrawals, account balance inquiries, and account transfers using remote terminals without the aid of a human teller. Certain states have mandatory sharing laws that require institutions that own ATMs to share their off-premises machines for a "reasonable fee" with any other financial institution in the state. The use of these machines has not lived up to expectations, however, as many customers—even active ATM users—still prefer the human teller.

How Banks Have Expanded Consumer Credit Activity

- Tailoring services to customer needs.
- Offering broad array of services.
- Selling mutual funds & insurance annuities.
- Increased FDIC protection.
- Bank holding companies.
- Using automated teller machines and electronic funds transfer systems.

Internet Banking

A growing phenomenon today is the increased use of the Internet for a variety of purposes. The **Internet,** sometimes called the "information super-highway," is a vast, worldwide network of computers that is accessed through telephone lines. Anyone with a computer and a modem, can "log on" and find access to unlimited amounts of information and opportunities to communicate with others.

An emerging use of the Internet is commercial transactions and home banking activities. Although security is still an important concern, observers are predicting that many banking transactions, including loans, will be handled electronically. Banks and other financial institutions will probably expand their service offerings and will provide more advisory-type services once financial transactions become more automated.

Credit Unions

A **credit union** is an association of people who decide to save their money together and make loans to each other at relatively low interest rates. In other words, it is a cooperative financial institution. A credit union is organized by people who share a common bond—for example, employees working for the same employer, members of a fraternal order or labor union, or residents of the same community. Some credit unions serve multiple groups, but each group has its own common bond.

The credit union industry has changed dramatically. Many credit unions have obtained community charters, adopted practically every service and loan type offered by commercial banks, and built outstanding full-service facilities. The community charters generally specify geographical bonds among members, so anyone living or working in a certain area may join the credit union. This approach has broadened the potential membership group and resulted in credit unions being strong competition for other lenders.

Origin of Credit Unions

Credit unions began in Germany in 1849. A mayor of a small town reasoned that the citizens could save money together and make loans to each other at low interest rates. The idea spread rapidly, and by 1888 more than 425 credit unions had been formed. In 1900, Alphonse Desjardins founded the first credit union in North America in Levis, Quebec.

Credit unions came to the United States in 1909, due largely to the efforts of Edward A. Filene, a well-known Boston merchant. In 1921, Filene hired Roy F. Bergengren to direct the Credit Union National Extension Bureau and oversee the rapidly growing credit union movement. In 1934, the Credit Union National Association was formed to serve the needs of the thousands of established credit unions.

Structure and Organization of the U.S. Credit Union Movement

More than 90 percent of U.S. credit unions are affiliated through an extensive system of state and national credit union service organizations. Members of affiliated credit unions govern this service organization structure through their democratically elected representatives. Credit unions in a community or specific geographic area may join or form a chapter. Chapters sponsor educational programs and undertake joint promotion and public relations projects.

Leagues are voluntary associations of credit unions within a given state or geographic area. Leagues are governed by their member credit unions and offer management advice and bookkeeping assistance, legal counsel, legislative and regulatory support, training programs, public relations, insurance counseling, and other essential services.

The Credit Union National Association, Inc. (CUNA) is the national credit union confederation of U.S. leagues. It provides legislative, public relations, research, educational, and development support for the national credit union movement. By joining a league, credit unions become affiliated with CUNA and have access to the services provided by its affiliates, including data processing and investment, lending, and liquidity management programs, as well as marketing assistance and printing and supply materials.

The CUNA Mutual Insurance Society, the credit union insurance company, serves credit unions and their members with an insurance program wholly oriented to the purposes and objectives of the credit union movement. As a mutual company, it returns all income, after operating expenses and reserves, to policyholders in the form of dividends.

The CUMIS Insurance Society, Inc., a stock insurance company, is the property, casualty, and fidelity insurance arm of the credit union movement. Ownership of the company is vested in credit union members, credit unions, chapters, credit union leagues, and CUNA Mutual. In addition to providing the nonlife insurance needs of credit unions and their organizations, CUMIS offers them homeowner and tenant insurance plans and life, health, and car insurance.

Characteristics of Credit Unions

Credit unions may be chartered under either state laws or the Federal Credit Union Act of 1934 and its subsequent amendments. The organizing group should consist of at least 300 persons. The common bond of membership may be employment, church affiliation, residence, labor union membership, and the like.

Credit unions adhere to the basic principles commonly associated with other cooperative ventures. The savings and loan facilities are their main function, and they operate only for the benefit and use of their members. Credit unions acquire capital from membership savings, which are invested in credit union shares. Besides shares, credit union capital consists of reserves and undivided earnings. Shares usually accumulate in $5 units, and amounts deposited that are less than this are applied to the purchase of a share. The credit union's capital is available for loans to shareholding members. Each member, irrespective of the amount of holdings in the credit union, is entitled to one vote in the election of its board of directors and its committee members who manage the organization. Additional dividends may be declared on members' shares after expenses are paid and legal reserves set aside.

State laws regulating the operation of credit unions vary substantially, but the more common requirements and general provisions of the federal law indicate their characteristics. Both federal and state laws emphasize protection of the members against imprudent management, while still providing them with a ready source of cash credit at relatively low interest rates. The credit union's accounting records are examined regularly by government authorities. Surety bond requirements give the members further protection. The treasurer and each officer who handles money must be bonded. The National Credit Union Administration supervises credit unions operating under federal charter, and in most states the state banking commission supervises those under state charter. The Federal Share Insurance Act, enacted in the fall of 1970, requires federal credit unions and permits state-chartered credit unions to provide share insurance on members' savings comparable to the FDIC program offered by banks and savings and loan associations. A number of share and deposit insurance plans also provide coverage to savers in state-chartered credit unions.

The most controversial aspect of credit unions rests in their long-time exemptions from the corporate income taxes that must be paid by commercial banks and other financial institutions. The tax-exempt status is related to the credit unions' history of not-for-profit operations for the benefit of its members. Commercial banks, and other tax-paying financial institutions, have been lobbying Congress to end this tax-exempt status since credit unions, especially those with geographic-based membership, no longer deserve this exemption. Credit unions in many communities have expanded their business to offer nearly identical services to those offered by commercial banks.

Character of Loans

A credit union member is one who owns one or more credit union shares, which earn dividends; a shareholder is eligible for the credit union's lending services. The credit committee, which is elected by the members, meets as often as necessary to approve or reject loan applications. Authority to approve loans within specified limits may also be delegated to staff loan officers. Installment loans are normally granted and repaid in equal installments according to a schedule established by the organization. Small amounts may be repaid in 6 months, in 12 months, or over longer periods, depending on the amount borrowed and requirements of the borrower. The borrower may repay the entire remaining balance of a loan at any time without penalty and thus save interest. Most credit unions offer loan protection insurance, primarily through CUNA Mutual Insurance Society. The credit union generally pays the premium for this insurance out of earnings, at no additional charge to the borrower. If the insured borrower dies or is disabled before the loan obligation is fully met, the insurance pays off the loan balance.

Individuals borrow money from credit unions for essentially the same reasons they borrow money from other sources: for cars, home repairs, debt consolidation, taxes, medical expenses, vacations, and education, and to take advantage of various financial opportunities.

Growth and Increasing Importance of Credit Unions

Since 1921 credit unions in the United States and Canada have grown rapidly. Except during the war years of 1943–1945, credit unions have increased in members and assets practically every year. At the same time, services have increased gradually.

Much of the growth and present-day success of credit unions is due to their relatively low rate of interest, which is made possible by the low cost of operation. Credit unions, at times, enjoy the privilege of free office space provided by the sponsor. They are exempt from some taxes because of their cooperative nature. Frequently, they receive the services of management (except for the treasurer) free because elected officers serve voluntarily without pay. The larger credit unions, which are growing in number, maintain scheduled and longer hours of operation and are staffed with paid employees. Members regard the saving feature of credit unions as advantageous, because dividends paid to shareholders have at times been higher than interest on similar savings in commercial banks and savings and loan associations. Exhibit 5–1 is a typical list of services and products available from a credit union. Share drafts, a unique type of financial instrument, have become popular among credit union members (see Exhibit 5–2). Some of its characteristics are as follows:

1. The share draft is payable by the credit union out of the member's share draft account.
2. The share draft is payable through a bank or some other clearing facility. This is the same type of payable-through system used for drafts on nonbank institutions such as insurance companies. Recently, some large credit unions have begun clearing their own share drafts.
3. The request for payment of the draft is transferred electronically from the payable-through bank to the credit union—the draft itself is not transferred.
4. Members are given statements that list share drafts in numerical order by share draft number.
5. The member has a carbon copy of each share draft for recordkeeping.
6. A microfilm copy of each original draft is available on request to the member who wrote the draft, but no copy is returned to the member by the credit union.
7. Dividends on share draft accounts are typically paid monthly on the low balance for the month, but some credit unions pay interest on the average daily balance. Seventy-five percent of credit unions offering share drafts levy no routine charges on these accounts.

Despite the apparent advantages enjoyed by credit unions, there are some limitations on most ventures of a cooperative nature. At times, it is difficult to recruit spokespersons and workers for organizations of this type because they are not paid for their time and effort. Another limitation on credit union growth is the number of people with a common bond needed before a credit union can be organized. Groups of this size are not easy to organize in many professional, trade, and clerical fields. In 1982, however, the National Credit Union Administration amended its chartering policies to allow existing federal credit unions to take in small employee and association groups as members. This has significantly extended credit union service to groups previously too small to have their own credit union.

An increasing number of credit unions offer a variety of consumer credit and savings plans. They also participate in the new electronic payments systems and give their customers the convenience of automated teller facilities and bill-paying plans at their credit union locations.

EXHIBIT 5–1   **A Typical List of Credit Union Services and Products**

MEMBER SERVICES

SAVINGS
Passbook Savings
Certificate of Deposits (CD's)
Individual Retirement Accounts
  (IRA's)
IRA Passbook Account
Money Market Account
Christmas Club Account
Funeral Trust Account
Children's Accounts

MISCELLANEOUS SERVICES
Payroll Deduction Program
MasterCard
Safe Deposit Boxes
  (Ashwaubenon only)
TYME
FST&T– telephone banking
Money Orders
Cashier's Checks
Travelers Cheques
Direct Deposit
  (Government Checks)
Notary Public
Night Deposit
Wire Service
U.S. Savings Bonds
Group Accident Insurance –
  $1000 free for members 18-69
Photo Copies
Check Safekeeping
Coin Counter
Telephone Transfers
Quest – Travel Savings
  Program
MasterPhone

CHECKING
Interest Checking
Regular Checking
Simple Checking
No Minimum Checking
Nifty Fifty Checking
Fee-Free Checking
Overdraft Protection
Pre-Authorized Payments
Kwik Cash Line of Credit

CLUB ACCOUNT
Nifty Fifty Club

LOANS
Auto & Truck Loans
Boat & RV Loans
Student Loans
Debt Consolidation
Personal Loans
Home Improvement
Home Equity Loans
Home Chequity Line of Credit
Home Loans –
  First and Second
Credit Life and Disability
  Insurance
Revolving Credit (Open-end)
Loan Applications by Phone
New & Used Car Value
  Information
Kwik Cash Line of Credit

SOURCE: First Security Credit Union.

Consumer Finance Companies

Consumer finance companies (often referred to as *small loan companies, personal finance companies,* and *licensed lenders*) are corporations that make loans to consumers under state-enacted regulations. The characteristics of their loans, their customers, their methods of operation, and the state statutes under which they do business are the principal distinguishing features of these institutions.

EXHIBIT 5-2 **Example of a Share Draft**

Principal Types of Loans

Consumer finance companies are almost exclusively installment loan providers of relatively small loans; the average amount of their loans is considerably less than commercial bank loans. Through sales finance subsidiary operations, they are also often involved in buying installment contracts from local retailers who want to provide their customers with installment purchase options. The relatively small loan balances (along with higher risk clientele) is one reason consumer finance companies have traditionally charged higher interest rates on their loans. A larger percentage charge is needed to cover operational costs and other expenses when the loan amount is small.

The Consumer Finance Customer

Borrowers from consumer finance companies generally come from different occupational groups than do borrowers from commercial banks. Most finance company loans are made to laborers, operatives, crafts workers, lead workers, and kindred workers. They borrow funds for the same reasons that other occupational groups borrow, such as consolidation of overdue bills; refinancing existing obligations; payment of medical, dental, and hospital bills; and other financial emergencies.

In general, consumer finance company customers represent higher risks. Historically, customers of the small loan business are wage earners and others of limited means. It is this group that the finance company has so successfully attracted and served. Generally, the customer's income and occupation are less stable than those of the commercial banks' customers. The security accepted for loans is often of lesser value or more difficult to accurately appraise, e.g., household goods. Many times customers are turned down by commercial banks, credit unions, and others before they find their way to a consumer finance company.

Services and Methods of Operation

The services of consumer finance companies frequently differ from those of commercial banks. Finance companies are usually located for the customer's convenience and are likely to have many small branches in a single city. They do not accept deposits, maintain safe deposit boxes, or provide many of the other services offered by financial institutions. Thus, their offices can be relatively small, sometimes staffed by only a few workers, and are often located in malls and other convenient locations. Their offices accept loan applications, investigate applicants, accept payments by mail and on the premises, and handle delinquencies and other necessary matters.

A consumer finance business conducted under the Uniform Small Loan laws may be an individual proprietorship, a partnership, or a corporation. The incorporated company was at first rare, but with the enactment of the Uniform Small Loan Law in most states, the corporate enterprise has become the dominant form of organization. Typically, large corporations operate on a national scale, with licensed offices in hundreds of cities of all sizes. Smaller companies usually operate regionally, while the smallest firms with one or a few offices operate locally.

State Statutes

Consumer finance companies' rapid growth and present-day position in the lending industry are a direct result of the small loan laws enacted by most states. Before the enactment of such laws, this business was characterized by deceptive interest charges and abusive collection practices. In 1907 and 1908, the Russell Sage Foundation, a philanthropic organization, financed studies that dealt with existing small loan conditions and the demand for loans of this type. These studies disclosed a large demand for small loans by wage earners and other consumers of small means, the need for legitimate lending agencies to supply the demand, and the necessity of subjecting the business to state supervision. In 1916 the foundation, in cooperation with a group of moneylenders, drafted a model small loan law known as the Uniform Small Loan Law. Improved drafts of the model law have been made from time to time by the foundation and by the National Consumer Finance Association.

The first Uniform Small Loan laws tended to reduce the number of lenders subjected to regulation, because some lenders found it unprofitable to operate at the interest rates permitted by law. Before long, however, lenders who formerly shunned this business were attracted to the small loan field, and large numbers of new companies were organized to transact small loans under regulation. The small loan industry encourages state regulation as the basis for attracting ethical personnel and sufficient capital to meet the demand for small loans. The industry's support of the model Uniform Small Loan Law testifies to its opposition to illegal lenders who prey on wage earners and charge usurious interest rates in states without effective legislation. Today the National Consumer Finance Association promotes effective state legislation.

Provisions of an Effective Small Loan Law

An effective small loan law must provide for an interest charge that is sufficient to attract capital to the business and at the same time protect borrowers from abusive practices. Most states have enacted laws that meet this requisite. Many states have modified the model Uniform Small Loan Law to suit local conditions or particular interests.

Interest charges for cash loans generally vary from 36 percent annually on the smallest to 18 percent on larger, well-secured loans. The Russell Sage Foundation originally recommended a maximum loan size of $300. The need for larger loans readily became apparent, and in some states today the loan ceiling is $25,000.

The lender must be licensed, and each office operated by a chain company must be licensed by the state in which the business is conducted. Each office is subject to annual and special examinations, must be bonded, and usually must submit to a test of ethical and financial fitness.

Under the provisions of the Truth in Lending Act (see Chapter 7), the lender has to disclose the amount financed, the finance charge, the annual percentage rate, the prepayment procedure and total of payments, delinquency or early payment charges, the rebate calculation procedure, and whether a security interest is taken in connection with the extension of credit. The lender may collect no fees other than recording fees. The licensee must accept payment from the customer in advance of the due date, and interest charged can be only for the time the borrower has had use of the money. Civil and criminal penalties are provided for violation of the provisions of the act.

While the above are the principal provisions of the Uniform Small Loan Law (in association with the Truth in Lending Act), there are many other important specific requirements. States that have enacted small loan legislation have varied from these provisions, but essentially with the same fundamental objectives. Some states prohibit any other business to be operated in conjunction with a small loan office; others permit insurance writing to minimize the degree of risk; and still others stipulate somewhat different methods of interest computation.

Changing Consumer Attitudes

General acceptance of the small loan business accompanied the widespread change of consumer attitudes and the acceptance of consumer credit of all types during the first half of the 20th century. Most consumers, at some time, experience a temporary need for a small loan when obligations exceed income and savings. This need would exist whether or not the Uniform Small Loan laws existed.

An individual who borrows $100 from a consumer finance company at a monthly rate of 3 percent and repays the loan in 12 equal monthly installments will pay a total interest cost of $20.60, or 36 percent true rate of interest. This amount appears high unless the cost of lending small amounts is clearly understood. The cost of capital for these businesses is higher than it is for commercial banks. The alternative to the Uniform Small Loan Law, which has attracted capital and ethical businesses to this field, is the loan shark and illegal lender. From the standpoint of social necessity, it is better for consumers to have convenient and fair access to small loans rather than be subjected to the lending and collection methods of illegal lenders. Also, the small loan company is the only available cash credit source for many families, whereas typical commercial bank customers can easily qualify for and borrow funds from several sources. Consequently, if a state wishes to make small consumer loans available to its wage earners and lower-income borrowers, it must sanction interest charges that will cover the high expenses this kind of business incurs. If it wants this business to be conducted ethically, it must provide for effective regulation and supervision.

The phenomenal growth in both the number of lenders and the number of consumer borrowers is some indication of the American consumer's widespread acceptance of the small loan business. Today consumer finance companies range from a single-office company to vast chains that operate hundreds of offices throughout the country. However, finance companies now face increased competition among themselves and with commercial banks and credit unions.

Industrial Banks and Loan Companies

Industrial banks are banking companies organized under the industrial loan laws that exist in some states primarily for the purpose of making consumer installment loans. They are governed by nonuniform state laws. In some states, they are similar to commercial banks. In others, their services are restricted by law, and they operate like small loan companies or the consumer loan departments of commercial banks.

In some states the firm may use the word *bank* in its advertising, contracts, and general literature. The laws of these states authorize such banks to accept deposits and make loans, and the banks may become members of the Federal Deposit Insurance Corporation. Other states do not authorize industrial banks as such, but do permit the operation of industrial loan companies. In these states, such firms are commonly known as industrial loan companies or industrial credit corporations, and the use of the term *bank* is prohibited. The remaining states have no specific legislation covering industrial banks. If industrial banks want to conduct business in one of these states, they must be awarded a charter under the laws applicable to commercial banks. Or, they may secure a license and comply with the state small loan law and operate as consumer finance companies.

Except in states that authorize industrial banks to accept deposits, "investment certificates" or "shares of stock" are used to circumvent usury laws. These institutions devised this method because state banking laws, as originally conceived, did not cover interest paid on loans that were repaid in installments. A borrower from an industrial bank must subscribe to an equal amount of noninterest-bearing investment certificates to be "purchased" through a schedule of deposits. When the amount of the deposits equals the value of the investment certificates, the certificates revert to the industrial bank and the loan is thereby paid off. Today industrial banks operate under one of the several methods suggested, depending on the legislative restrictions of the particular state. Some accept deposits from borrowers and nonborrowers and make loans for both consumer and commercial purposes. Others use the investment certificate device to avoid being accused of usurious interest rates. In some states, industrial loan companies neither accept deposits nor use investment certificates, but they lend money to consumers or businesses in a manner similar to other consumer lending institutions. Many industrial banks and industrial loan companies originated with Arthur J. Morris during the early 1900s. His company evolved into the largest group of industrial banks, known as the Morris Plan Banks or Companies.

Savings and Loan Associations

Savings and loan associations are depository thrift institutions originally organized to accept savings deposits and provide mortgage financing. Historically, savings and loan associations (S&Ls) did not make commercial loans or consumer loans but were primarily engaged in mortgage lending. To encourage home ownership and mortgage lending, Regulation Q, which at one time controlled interest rates on savings accounts, allowed S&Ls to pay slightly higher interest rates. When savings and loan associations operated primarily as mortgage lenders, they did not represent significant competition within the commercial bank arena.

The issue of savings and loan associations as competitors of commercial banks resurfaced in the 1980s when Congress granted all thrifts, including savings and loans, the power to make consumer and commercial loans and to issue transaction accounts. Congress passed the Depository Institutions Deregulation and Monetary Control Act (DIDMCA) in 1980 (see Chapter 7) to help the thrift industry retain its deposit base and to improve its profitability. This 1980 law allowed thrifts to make consumer loans up to 20 percent of their assets, issue credit cards, accept negotiable order of withdrawal (NOW) accounts from individuals and nonprofit organizations, and invest up to 20 percent of their assets in commercial real estate loans.

Further deregulation took place in 1982 with passage of the Garn-St Germain Depository Institutions Act. This law increased the proportion of assets that thrifts could hold in consumer and commercial real estate loans and allowed thrifts to invest 5 percent of their assets in commercial loans (7.5 percent for savings banks) until January 1, 1984, when this percentage increased to 10 percent.

This deregulation created tremendous problems for the savings and loan industry and was one of the causes of savings and loan failures in the 1980s and of the resultant federal government actions. Many former savings and loan associations have changed their names to "savings banks" to regain some of their lost credibility and to attract additional business. Some have been purchased by commercial banks. Although they can make a wide variety of loans, the most common loan involves mortgage lending. The savings and loan associations have been increasingly active in the second mortgage and home equity lending arena.

Other Types of Lenders

No estimate has been made of the volume of loans made by friends and relatives, philanthropic organizations, church societies, and fraternal orders, but the amount is believed to be sizable. Some people have the distinct advantage of borrowing from friends and relatives, thereby enjoying less formal contractual arrangements and, on most occasions, strict secrecy. The interest charge and enforcement of payment depend almost entirely on the relationship and mutual trust between the individuals.

Philanthropic or charitable organizations, church societies, educational institutions, foundations and fraternal orders make loans to individuals under special circumstances. These institutions function to provide temporary financial assistance to deserving people. Some loans may take the form of an outright gift, while others are made with the understanding that complete repayment will be made at some future date. Variations exist from institution to institution.

The pawnbroker is another source of cash loans to individuals. A **pawnbroker** is a lender licensed to loan money at a specified interest rate with personal property left with the pawnbroker as security. Interest rates may run as high as 360 percent (or more), but no inquiry is made into an individual's credit standing. Insurance companies are still another source; individuals can often borrow on their life insurance polices, paying an interest rate of approximately 4 to 8 percent. Some investment houses lend up to 50 percent of the market value on some blue-chip stocks.

In defiance of state laws, some illegal lenders charge interest rates as high as 700 percent. Typically, illegal lenders are more interested in earning exorbitant charges than in actually collecting the principal. They prefer victims who will obligate themselves deeply and be submissive to the lenders' collection methods. Collections are enforced by threat of wage assignments, loss of employment, and even physical violence. The debtor is frequently of limited means and "buys off" the threats, at least temporarily, by paying interest charges; but the debtor seldom has enough to meet the full principal and exorbitant interest charges.

Sources of Consumer Cash Loans

- Commercial banks.
- Credit unions.
- Finance companies.
- Industrial banks & loan companies.
- Savings & loan associations.
- Others (churches, pawnbrokers, etc.).

Relative Costs of Consumer Lending Institutions

To fully appreciate the interest rates charged by various consumer lending institutions, we must examine their costs of operation. Interest rates charged customers, or the "price of borrowed money," are usually relative to the costs of doing business and the degree of risk the lender assumes. The costs of conducting consumer loan activity may be quite high or relatively low, depending largely on the number and extent of the functions performed. Furthermore, relative costs of capital have an important influence on the interest rate. The factors that influence the costs of conducting a cash loan business are discussed in the following paragraphs. These brief discussions cover only legal lenders.

Types of Risk Accepted

The average loan made to wage and salary earners by consumer finance companies is small. When the amount of the loan is modest, the dollar cost per loan of acquiring and servicing customers is relatively high. Because consumer finance companies usually deal with borrowers of limited means, the greater risk they incur influences their ability to attract capital, bad-debt ratios, and costs of investigation. Commercial banks, in particular, and credit unions accept credit from more stable customer groups and therefore incur less risk. Some occupations have greater income stability than others. The occupational groups attracted by banks and credit unions are qualitatively more acceptable from the credit risk standpoint. This factor alone contributes heavily to the higher cost of credit from consumer finance companies.

Investigation Costs

The cost of investigation incurred by commercial banks and credit unions is generally less than the cost incurred by consumer finance companies. The types of risk accepted by the latter mean that those who are dishonest and those who can't or won't pay must be screened out by investigation. The borrower's identity, stability, and general reputation must be verified. Also, income, expenses, and outstanding obligations must be established. On the other hand, commercial banks and credit unions frequently appraise former applicants. Each of these institutions accepts deposits, and in many instances someone in the organization knows the loan applicant. Furthermore, each institution realizes that the apparent risk governs the extent and intensity of investigation. Consequently, consumer finance companies conduct rather extensive and costly investigations because of the higher risk element associated with their customers.

Cost of Capital

The cost of capital for commercial banks, credit unions, and some industrial banks is less than that for consumer finance companies. The three former institutions accept deposits, and their deposits are several times as large as their own capital. They have been able to attract capital more successfully because of the lower risk of their lending operations. Consumer finance companies, on the other hand, cannot accept deposits and must borrow from commercial banking facilities or other financial institutions or supply their own funds. They thus pay higher rates for their capital irrespective of the source. For these same reasons, consumer finance companies need somewhat higher net profit to attract investors.

Bad-Debt Losses

The greater degree of risk incurred by consumer finance companies is reflected in higher bad-debt losses. Another factor that contributes to a high bad-debt loss ratio is the low average loan size. Even though a consumer finance company has a well-managed collection system, the cost of collecting nominal sums that are about to become bad-debt losses is usually prohibitive. Furthermore, numerous legal actions against wage earners and others of small means might threaten the social acceptance and goodwill the small loan industry has built. The threat of legal action by a commercial bank or credit union to collect larger average sums usually results in a settlement because the customers they deal with prefer to avoid embarrassment. Interest rates to be charged must take into account the relative amount and frequency of bad-debt losses.

Collection Costs

The collection costs on an installment account are much higher than those of a single-payment loan. Commercial banks have a large volume of single-payment loans, while consumer finance companies primarily make installment loans. In addition, other installment lenders are not subject to the same expenses as consumer finance companies. In an effort to protect borrowers from abuse, the Uniform Small Loan laws of the various states impose costly procedures on this type of business. Consumer finance companies must account for each installment loan in detail, make many individual calculations, and give the borrower detailed informative receipts. The consumer finance company also has accounts that require special handling. Again, the modest amount of its loans makes for higher collection costs. Delinquencies must be remedied by constant reminders, personal letters, and even personal contact with the debtor.

Sources of Income

Commercial banks have many sources of income. They receive income from operation of their lending and trust departments, from their bank credit card operations, from the purchase and sale of federal government and municipal securities, from safe-deposit boxes, from the sale of traveler's checks, and from the operations of the companies that are part of bank holding arrangements. On the other hand, consumer finance companies' income is derived almost exclusively from interest on consumer loans.

Services Provided

Consumer finance companies, by the nature of their business, establish offices for their customers' convenience. These offices are not generally housed within another institution, as are consumer credit departments of commercial banks and credit unions. The services rendered frequently involve more time and relatively more personnel. Most consumer finance companies have gone to considerable expense to establish debt amortization programs for their customers. Each borrower who needs this service presents different problems.

Many, if not most, commercial banks have expanded their customer services. They now advise and counsel their customers on money matters and arrange for debt amortization on a level competitive with that of other types of cash-lending institutions. Commercial banks' introduction of the many new installment loan plans illustrates that they see the necessity of being more customer conscious.

Factors Influencing Interest Charges

- Types of risk accepted.
- Investigation costs.
- Cost of capital.
- Bad-debt losses.
- Collection costs.
- Sources of income.
- Services provided.

Convergence and Consolidation of Financial Institutions

An important trend among financial institutions is an increasing number of mergers and acquisitions. Many of the emerging bank services are technology based and, as a result, are expensive to offer. Automated funds transfers and many other services offer important economies of scale, that is, the opportunity to lower costs by becoming a larger-scale firm. Small banks, for example, find it increasingly more difficult to offer the array and depth of services that larger, nationally franchised financial institutions are offering.

Financial institutions are also becoming more alike. As credit unions obtained community charters and expanded service offerings, they look and operate more and more like commercial banks. Many savings and loan associations whose image was tarnished by the many S&L failures in the 1980s, have changed their names, and sometimes, their charters to banks. Commercial banks are selling mutual funds, insurance products, and other nontraditional opportunities for customers to invest savings. As the regulations are relaxed further, banks may begin underwriting new stock issues, operating their own mutual funds, and selling more services. National brokerage firms are offering mortgage loans through 800-number telephone systems and department stores are issuing general-purpose credit cards. Commercial banks are also operating small loans under the state small loan acts to capture the higher risk, higher interest rate market. As long as active competition is found in the financial services industry, consumers will continue to benefit from a wider variety of providers and services.

Important Terms

add-on method   86

automated teller machine (ATM)   88

bank holding company   88

cash advance   84

consumer finance companies   93

credit union   89

discount loan   86

home equity line of credit   85

home equity loan   83

industrial banks   97

installment loan   83

internet   89

money market fund   87

mutual fund   87

overdraft plan   84

pawnbroker   98

savings & loan associations   97

simple interest method   86

single-payment loan   85

student loan   83

Discussion Questions

1. How does cash loan credit differ from retail credit? From service credit?

2. List and describe 10 reasons consumers might seek a cash loan.

3. Why do some consumers borrow money to purchase goods and services when they could use other types of retail credit to make these purchases?

4. What is meant by the phrase: "A commercial bank is a merchandiser of money"?

5. List and describe three types of installment cash loans made by commercial banks.

6. Describe three loans offered by commercial banks that can be referred to as "open-end revolving loans."

7. Explain the characteristics of a single-payment loan.

8. Check the laws in your state to discover the interest rates allowed on cash loans to consumers.

9. What is the difference between the simple interest method and the add-on method of collecting interest on an installment cash loan?

10. What are the potential benefits of overdraft plans to the individual customer? To the bank?

11. Explain the cash-advance feature on bank credit card plans.

12. Explain the history and development of U.S. credit unions.

13. How do you account for the growth and increasing importance of credit unions?

14. Explain why a share draft is a unique type of financial instrument.

15. What provisions should a small loan law have in order to be effective?

16. How do you account for consumers' changing attitude toward consumer finance companies?

17. How is a home equity loan different from a home equity line of credit? What are the advantages and disadvantages of each?

18. What is meant by a bank holding company?

CASE PROBLEM

Bill and Betty Stevens—Financial Statements

Businesses routinely submit financial statements along with credit applications when applying for loans or credit terms. Most consumers do not maintain or provide financial statements to lenders, although many loan officers attempt to construct these statements from the information they obtain from the loan applications. Use the information below to complete the financial statement forms provided.

Name: Bill and Betty Stevens
Date: December 31, 19XX

Cash and liquid assets:	
Bank checking account	$ 3,000
Credit union savings account	5,000
Investments:	
Bank certificate of deposit	6,000
Bill's Individual Retirement Account	12,000
Betty's 401K retirement savings account	4,000
Individual stocks	2,000
Business interests—Office Supply, Inc.	10,000
Personal use assets:	
Household Goods	30,000
Automobiles	$20,000
Residence	95,000
Short-term liabilities:	
General-purpose credit card—Visa	2,300
Department store credit card	500
Installment loan for appliances	1,000
Medical bills	200
Long-term liabilities:	
Automobile loan	12,000
Home mortgage loan	75,000
Home improvement loan (2nd mortgage)	6,000
Annual income:	
Bill—Office Supply, Inc. salary	35,000
Betty—Mainstreet Dental Clinic wage	28,000
Interest and dividends	300
Expenses:	
Food and groceries	5,200
Utilities	2,600
Home maintenance	1,000
Transportation expenses	3,000
Insurance—Life, health, auto	2,000
Insurance—Homeowner's	400
Gifts and contributions	3,000
Recreation	$ 4,000
Clothing	2,000
Income taxes	12,600
Property taxes	2,300
Social security taxes	4,800
House payments—12 @ $750	9,000
Automobile payments—12 @ $525	6,300
Home equity loan payments—12 @ $125	$ 1,500
Payments—Credit cards, etc.	400
Savings and investments	3,200

PERSONAL BALANCE SHEET

Name _____

Date _____

ASSETS

Cash and Liquid:
Cash and checking _____
Savings accounts _____
Other   _____

Total Liquid Assets _____

Investment Assets:
Bank certificates _____
Individual stocks _____
IRA accounts   _____
401K savings   _____
Business interests _____
Other   _____

Total Investment Assets _____

Personal Use Assets:
Residence   _____
Automobiles   _____
Household goods _____

Total Use Assets _____

Total Assets   _____

LIABILITIES AND NET WORTH

Short-Term Liabilities:
Credit card accounts _____
Installment credit   _____
Other   _____

Total Short-Term Liabilities _____

Long-Term Liabilities:
Automobile loan balance _____
Home mortgage   _____
Home equity loan   _____

Total Long-Term Liabilities _____

Total Liabilities _____

NET WORTH
Total assets
Less total liabilities

_____

Total Liability + Net Worth _____

Income Statement

Name _____

For Period Ending _____

Income: _____
    Wages
    Wages   _____
    Interest & dividends   _____
    Other income   _____

Expenses:
    Food and groceries   _____
    Transportation   _____
    Clothing   _____
    Recreation   _____
    Gifts and contributions   _____
    Insurance—Life, etc.   _____
    Insurance—Homeowner's   _____
    Utilities   _____
    Home maintenance   _____
    Income taxes   _____
    Social security taxes   _____
    Property taxes   _____
    House payments   _____
    Automobile loan payments   _____
    Home equity loan payments   _____
    Credit card payments   _____
    Savings and investments   _____
Net Income   _____

6

REAL ESTATE CREDIT

Chapter Learning Objectives

After studying this chapter, you should be able to:

- Explain how a home may be financed.
- Clarify the differences between fixed rate mortgages and adjustable rate mortgages (ARMs).
- Discuss special programs designed to encourage home ownership, FHA loans, VA loans, and private mortgage insurance.
- Discuss the secondary mortgage market and the activities of second-layer lenders.
- Compare savings and loan associations, commercial banks, and various other sources as places for the consumer to go for home financing.
- Describe the point system in mortgage lending and important clauses that are often found in a mortgage agreement.
- Explain two mortgage lending standards: the housing expense ratio and the debt payment ratio.
- Describe home equity loans and home equity lines of credit

The high rate of home ownership in the United States represents a response to many social, historical, demographic, and economic forces. Home ownership is one of the outstanding characteristics of our society: approximately 65 percent of the nation's homes are owner-occupied. Owning a home is one of the most important financial goals for most families.

The American consumer usually goes through three steps when buying a home:

1. Locating a desirable home and negotiating for the purchase. This step includes the preparation of and agreement to the contract in which the price and terms of sale are included.

2. Arranging for a loan, usually from a savings and loan association, a commercial bank, a mortgage company, an insurance company, relatives, or friends. An application is completed, the home is appraised, the buyer's credit is checked, and the loan is approved or denied.

3. Closing the sale, usually with the help of the real estate agent involved and the lawyers representing the seller and the buyer. The "happy day" of taking possession is now at hand.

The purchase of a home is probably the largest monetary transaction in the life of the American consumer. This chapter is primarily concerned with Step 2 in this important process.

RESIDENTIAL FINANCING

The prospective home buyer will approach a lender and ask for a mortgage loan. If the loan application is approved, the borrower will sign a mortgage note agreeing to repay the full amount to the lender over a period of time with interest. A **mortgage** is a debt secured by real estate. A **first mortgage,** which arises with the initial purchase of real property, provides the lender with the first claim on the value of the real estate in the event the borrower defaults on the loan and cannot pay. A **foreclosure** is a legal procedure in which the lender exercises its security interest in the property and forces the sale of the property to try to pay off the mortgage if the borrower does not pay.

Special Programs to Assist Borrowers

Conventional fixed-rate mortgages often require a down payment of 20 percent of the purchase price. This down payment is required to provide a safety margin for the lender in the event of a foreclosure. A 20 percent down payment is difficult for many families to acquire, so the federal government has encouraged various agencies to offer **default insurance,** which provides a mortgage payoff on behalf of the borrower if he or she does not pay. This insurance reduces the risk for the lender, who will then be more inclined to accept a lower down payment, perhaps only 5 or 10 percent of the purchase price.

Federal Housing Administration Programs

The National Housing Act of 1934 created the Federal Housing Administration (FHA), which was established primarily to increase home construction, reduce unemployment, and operate various loan insurance programs.

The FHA makes no loans, nor does it plan or build houses. As in the veterans (GI) loan program, the applicant for the loan must make arrangements with a lending institution. This financial organization then may ask if the borrower wants FHA insurance on the loan or may insist that the borrower apply for it. The federal government, through the Federal Housing Administration, investigates the applicant and, having decided that the risk is favorable, insures the lending institution against loss of principal in case the borrower fails to meet the terms and conditions of the mortgage. The borrower, who may pay an insurance premium of one half of 1 percent on declining balances for the lender's protection, receives three benefits: a careful appraisal by an FHA inspector, a lower down payment (often 3 percent to 5 percent), and a lower interest rate on the mortgage than the lender might have offered without the protection.

GI Loans (VA-Guaranteed)

The original Servicemen's Readjustment Act, passed by Congress in 1944, extended a wide variety of benefits to eligible veterans. The loan guarantee program of the Veterans Administration (VA) has been especially important to veterans. Under the law, as amended, the Veterans Administration is authorized to guarantee or insure home, farm, and business loans made to veterans by lending institutions. The VA can make direct loans in certain areas for the purpose of purchasing or constructing a home or farm residence, or for repair, alteration, or improvement of the dwelling. The terms and requirements of VA farm and business loans have not induced private lenders to make such loans in volume during recent years.

Despite a great deal of confusion and misunderstanding, the federal government generally doesn't make direct loans under the act. The government simply guarantees loans made by ordinary mortgage lenders after veterans make their own arrangements for the loans through normal financial circles. The Veterans Administration then appraises the property in question and, if satisfied with the risk involved, guarantees the lender against loss of principal if the buyer defaults at no cost to the veteran.

Private Mortgage Insurance

Private mortgage insurance (PMI) guarantees the repayment of conventional home mortgage loans in exchange for a one-time premium paid by the mortgage holder. This private business loan program is equivalent to the FHA and the VA loan programs.

The PMI company insures a percentage of the consumer's loan to reduce the lender's risk; this percentage is paid to the lender if the consumer does not pay and the lender forecloses the loan. Lenders decide if they need and want the borrower to have private mortgage insurance. If so, it becomes a requirement of the loan.

Special Programs for Borrowers Who Lack 20 Percent Down Payment

	Fee Charged?
• FHA insurance	Yes
• GI loans	No
• Private mortgage insurance	Yes

The Secondary Mortgage Market and Second-Layer Lenders

The federal government, in an effort to encourage home purchase and mortgage lending, has helped establish a **secondary mortgage market** where mortgage contracts are purchased by various federal agencies and later sold to investors. These federal agencies, using funds obtained from bond issues, will buy mortgages after they are negotiated and finalized by lenders and borrowers. The lending institution will sell the mortgage in order to receive the face amount immediately. This allows the institution to make another loan, collect loan origination fees from a new client, and sell the new loan once again in the secondary market.

These federal credit agencies, which include the Federal Home Loan Mortgage Corporation, the Federal National Mortgage Association, and the Government National Mortgage Association, are referred to as **second-layer lenders.** They conduct secondary market activities in the buying and selling of loans and provide credit to primary lenders in the form of borrowed money. They do not have direct contact with the individual consumer.

Federal Home Loan Mortgage Corporation

In 1970, the Federal Home Loan Mortgage Corporation, sometimes known as "Freddie Mac," was established. This corporation is designed to promote the flow of capital into the housing market by establishing an active secondary market in mortgages. It may by law deal only with government-supervised lenders such as savings and loan associations, savings banks, and commercial banks. Its programs cover conventional whole mortgage loans, participations in conventional loans, and FHA and VA loans.

Federal National Mortgage Association

Known in financial circles as "Fannie Mae," this association was chartered as a government corporation in 1938, rechartered as a federal agency in 1954, and became a government-sponsored, stockholder-owned corporation in 1968. Fannie Mae, which has been described as "a private corporation with a public purpose," basically provides a secondary market for residential loans. It fulfills this function by buying, servicing, and selling loans that, since 1970, have included FHA-insured, VA-guaranteed, and conventional loans. However, purchases outrun sales by such a wide margin that some observers view this association as a lender with a permanent loan portfolio rather than a powerful secondary market corporation.

Government National Mortgage Association

This association, which is often referred to as "Ginnie Mae," operates within the Department of Housing and Urban Development. In addition to performing the special assistance, management, and liquidation functions that once belonged to Fannie Mae, Ginnie Mae has an important additional function—that of issuing guarantees of securities backed by government-insured or guaranteed mortgages. Such mortgage-backed securities are fully guaranteed by the U.S. government as to timely payment of both principal and interest.

SOURCES OF MORTGAGES AND REAL ESTATE CREDIT

The housing market is one of the largest users of borrowed funds in the American economy. In fact, the need for residential mortgage credit has grown more rapidly over the past quarter-century than has any other single type of capital or credit requirement.

Savings associations have been, and continue to be, the major source of residential credit. However, the so-called second-layer lenders (organizations such as the Federal National Mortgage Association and the Federal Home Loan Mortgage Corporation) have become a significant source of credit in recent years as these organizations buy mortgages in the secondary market.

Loans outstanding on one- to four-family homes, which represented the largest segment of mortgage loans as of the close of 1995, totaled $3,640 billion. Exhibit 6–1 shows mortgage debt outstanding, by type of property and holder, for selected years from 1970 through 1995.

The family seeking assistance in buying or constructing a home generally has several possible loan sources available. A qualified home buyer or builder can obtain a mortgage from savings and loan associations, commercial banks, savings banks, mortgage bankers and brokers, life insurance companies, credit unions, federal agencies, individual investors, and builders. In deciding on the most advantageous source, applicants should consider a number of factors, such as the size of the loan needed, maturity of the loan, interest rate, method of paying off the loan, and other characteristics.

Savings and loan associations lead by a wide margin in the total amount of credit provided to owners and buyers of homes. Their loans exceed the combined holdings of commercial banks, savings banks, and life insurance companies.

Savings and Loan Associations

The most important purpose of these institutions is to make mortgage loans on residential property. These organizations, which also are known as "savings associations," "building and loan associations," "cooperative banks" (in New England), and "homestead associations" (in Louisiana), are the primary source of financial assistance to a large segment of American homeowners. As home-financing institutions, they give primary attention to single-family residences and are equipped to make loans in this area.

EXHIBIT 6–1   Mortgage Debt Outstanding, by Type of Property: 1970 to 1995
(In billions of dollars. As of December 31. Includes Puerto Rico and Guam)

Type of Property and Holder	1970	1980	1990	1995
Mortgage debt, total	$474	$1,463	$3,804	$4,724
Residential nonfarm	358	1,110	2,966	3,929
One- to four-family homes	297	969	2,676	3,640
Savings institutions	167	487	600	488
Mortgage pools or trusts	3	125	1,046	1,754
Commercial banks	42	160	456	665
Individuals and others	36	117	408	498
Federal and related agencies	22	61	153	226
Life insurance companies	27	18	13	8
Five or more units	60	141	290	289
Commercial	86	255	759	710
Farm	30	97	79	84

SOURCE: Board of Governors of the Federal Reserve System, *Federal Reserve Bulletin,* monthly.

Some of the traditional characteristics of a savings and loan association are:

1. It is generally a locally owned and privately managed home financing institution.
2. It receives individuals' savings and uses these funds to make long-term amortized loans to home purchasers.
3. It makes loans for the construction, purchase, repair, or refinancing of houses.
4. It is state or federally chartered.

For most of its history, the savings and loan institution was a remarkable success. Started in 1930, it grew from a small, mutually owned organization into the prime supplier of mortgage money for the American home buyer. Beginning in 1980, Congress granted all thrifts, including savings and loan associations, the power to make consumer and commercial loans and to issue checking accounts along with other consumer credit products. For a variety of reasons, many savings and loan associations experienced difficulty adjusting to the new environment and hundreds of savings and loan associations failed. The Financial Institutions Reform, Recovery, and Enforcement Act (FIRREA) of 1989 was passed to deal with the crisis. The act, among other things, established the Resolution Trust Corporation (RTC) to liquidate failed S&Ls it acquired as a result of federal deposit guarantees. The failed institutions were liquidated or merged with the total price tag for the cleanup running into the billions. Many savings and loan associations have been purchased by commercial banks and others have changed their names to include the word *bank* instead of *savings and loan.*

Commercial Banks

In the past, commercial banks have not been greatly interested in real estate loans and have placed only a relatively small percentage of their assets in mortgages. As their name implies, such financial institutions secured their earnings primarily from business and consumer loans and left the major task of home financing to others. However, due to changes in banking laws and policies, commercial banks are increasingly active in home financing.

Changes in banking laws now allow commercial banks to make home mortgage loans on a more liberal basis than ever before. In acquiring mortgages on real estate, these institutions follow two main practices. First, some of the banks maintain active and well-organized departments whose primary function is to compete actively for real estate loans. In areas lacking specialized real estate financial institutions, these banks become the source for residential and farm mortgage loans. Second, the banks acquire mortgages by simply purchasing them from mortgage bankers or dealers.

In addition, dealer service companies, which were originally used to obtain car loans for permanent lenders such as commercial banks, wanted to broaden their activity beyond their local area. In recent years, however, such companies have concentrated on acquiring mobile home loans in volume for both commercial banks and savings and loan associations. Service companies obtain these loans from retail dealers, usually on a nonrecourse basis. Almost all bank/service company agreements contain a credit insurance policy that protects the lender if the consumer defaults. The service company usually receives 1.5 percent per year of the scheduled terms of the original amount financed. In addition, most service companies perform other functions, including collection efforts after the loan becomes more than 30 days past due, repossession if necessary, sale of repossessed collateral, and collection of monthly payments.

Savings Banks

These depository financial institutions are federally chartered, primarily accept consumer deposits, and make home mortgage loans. Historically, these institutions were of the mutual (depositor-owned) form and were chartered in only 16 states, the majority being in New England.

Mortgage Bankers and Brokers

Mortgage bankers are companies or individuals who originate mortgage loans, sell them to other investors, service the monthly payments, and may act as agents to dispense funds for taxes and insurance.

Mortgage brokers basically present the consumer home buyer with their attempts to find the best loan from a variety of sources. They may also become involved with repairing credit bureau reports, consolidating debts with personal loans, and, in general, helping people qualify for mortgage loans. Some are very active in trying to service those borrowers who would be turned down for a mortgage by commercial banks and other traditional sources for mortgage credit. Their income comes from the lender making the loan plus an extra fee, usually 1 percent of the mortgage.

Life Insurance Companies

Life insurance companies are another source of financial assistance. These companies lend on real estate as one form of investment and adjust their portfolios from time to time to reflect changing economic conditions. Formerly, farm loans were looked on with favor by life insurance companies. In recent years, however, these institutions have reduced their activity in residential mortgages. Individuals seeking a loan from an insurance company can deal directly with a local branch office or with a local real estate broker who acts as loan correspondent for one or more insurance companies.

Credit Unions

These cooperative financial institutions are organized by people who share a common bond—for example, employees of a company, a labor union, or a religious group. (See Chapter 5 for a detailed description of the activities of a credit union.) Some credit unions offer home loans in addition to other financial services.

Federally Supported Agencies

As previously discussed, under certain conditions and fund limitations the Veterans Administration makes direct loans to creditworthy veterans in housing credit shortage areas designated by the VA's administrator. Such areas are generally rural areas and small cities and towns not near the metropolitan or commuting areas of large cities—areas where GI loans from private institutions are not available.

The federally supported agencies referred to here do not include the so-called second-layer lenders who enter the scene after the mortgage is arranged between the lending institution and the individual home buyer.

Other Sources

Individual investors constitute a fairly large but somewhat declining source of money for home mortgage loans. Experienced observers claim that these lenders prefer shorter term obligations and usually restrict their loans to less than two-thirds of the value of the residential property. Likewise, building contractors sometimes accept second mortgages in part payment of the construction price of a home if the purchaser is unable to raise the total amount of down payment above the first mortgage money offered.

Finally, real estate investment trusts (REITs), which began when the Real Estate Investment Trust Act became effective January 1, 1961, are available. A **real estate investment trust** operates like a closed-end mutual fund that sells shares to investors, and then purchases a portfolio of mortgages or real estate properties. REITs, like savings and loan associations, are committed to real estate lending and can and do serve the national real estate market, although some specialization has occurred in their activities.

Source of Real Estate Credit

- Savings & loan associations
- Commercial banks
- Savings banks
- Mortgage bankers/brokers
- Life insurance companies
- Credit unions
- Veterans Administration
- Other
  - Builders
  - Real Estate Investment Trusts

Provisions of Home Mortgages

Types of Mortgage Loans

Fixed-Rate Mortgages

A **fixed-rate mortgage** is a loan secured by real estate that carries a predetermined, fixed rate of interest for the term of the repayment period. The borrower, for example, may obtain a $100,000 loan with a 30-year repayment period and a locked-in interest rate of 7.0 percent. The monthly payment of $665.30 will not vary and will be divided each month to pay the interest on the loan and to reduce the principal owed. In the early months of a mortgage loan, nearly all of the payment goes toward the payment of interest. The advantages of fixed-rate mortgages are that they are easy to understand and they help the borrower plan for the future since the payment is predetermined and will not change. The disadvantages are that these mortgages may carry higher interest rates than other types of mortgages, and if interest rates in general decline after the borrower obtains a fixed-rate mortgage, the locked-in rate may be a problem. During the early 1990s, interest rates had fallen to their lowest levels in 20 years, and many borrowers were requesting fixed-rate loans for their purchases or for refinancing existing mortgages.

Adjustable Rate Mortgages

An **adjustable rate mortgage** (ARM) is a real estate loan that provides for periodic adjustments in the interest rate during the repayment period. Adjustable rate mortgages are often more difficult to understand since the mortgage contracts include a variety of provisions related to the size and timing of the interest rate fluctuations. For example, the loan officer might tell a prospective borrower:

> "The initial rate for your adjustable rate mortgage will be 7 percent. The base rate is 8 percent with annual adjustments based on the 6-month treasury bill index, currently 6 percent. The interest rate margin is 2 percent and the loan carries an annual monthly payment cap of 1 percent and a lifetime interest rate cap of 5 percent."

The key features referred to by the loan officer outline typical features of an adjustable rate mortgage.

1. **Initial interest rate.** This is the beginning interest rate for the loan which may be used as a marketing device to attract borrowers. It is generally very low and will be in effect only until the first adjustment in the mortgage rate takes place. Borrowers are often interested in these lower interest rates because the lower initial mortgage payments help them qualify for larger loans and more expensive homes.
2. **Base interest rate.** Sometimes called the *contract rate,* this is the interest rate that the various caps are figured on and is generally the sum of the index and the margin rate at the time the loan is applied for.
3. **Index.** This is an arbitrary index that is outside the control of the lender and is used to determine the changes in the interest rates when each adjustment occurs with an adjustable rate mortgage. An index is often a government securities rate or a published cost-of-funds index for the classification of the lending institution involved, e.g., savings and loan associations.
4. **Margin rate.** The interest rate at each adjustment point will equal the index plus the margin rate. For example, the new interest rate at each adjustment point in the above example will be the treasury bill rate plus 2 percent.
5. **Adjustment period.** This describes how often the interest rate on the mortgage will be adjusted. It might be adjusted every 6 months, once a year, or some combination of periods such as locked in for the first three years, and adjusted annually thereafter.
6. **Monthly payment cap.** This is a limit on the annual increase in monthly payments. For example, the mortgage contract may provide that payments cannot increase more than 1 percent in any given year. The monthly payment

cap may prevent the payment from increasing enough to cover the interest charges due each month if the base rate increases substantially. In some cases, this can result in **negative amortization,** which means the total amount owed on a mortgage contract actually increases each month since the payment doesn't cover the interest charges due.

7. **Lifetime interest rate cap.** This clause in an adjustable rate mortgage will limit the total increases during the lifetime of the mortgage and will define a maximum interest rate. A lifetime cap of 5 percent and a base rate of 8 percent, for example, means that the interest rate can never be greater than 13 percent. Sometimes, an interest rate cap will exist for each adjustment period, e.g., no adjustment will exceed 1 percent. If an interest rate cap exists for each adjustment, there is usually no monthly payment cap mentioned above.

Adjustable rate mortgages are especially attractive to borrowers who expect to sell their homes and move in a relatively short period of time. They benefit from the lower initial rates and are less concerned about the possible long-term increases above the rates available on a fixed basis. Of course, there is always a possibility that rates will decline, and a borrower who believes this will choose an adjustable rate mortgage to take advantage of lower rates in the future.

Amortization

Amortization may be defined as the systematic and continuous payment of the principal balance on an obligation through installments until the debt has been paid in full. All government mortgage financing institutions, such as the FHA, insist on the amortized form of mortgage lending. This direct-reduction mortgage provides for a fixed monthly payment that not only covers interest—and perhaps taxes and insurance—but also reduces the principal of the mortgage debt. Exhibit 6–2 shows an amortization schedule.

Using the material in Exhibit 6–3, it is easy—and amazing—to figure how much a buyer actually pays for the home over the years. In Examples A and B, comparative figures are shown for an 11.5 percent mortgage over 15 years and over 30 years. The difference between Example A and Example B (same home, same down payment, same interest rate, but longer payoff period) is $188,380 [–] $115,210 = $73,170.

Example A: $60,000 home with $10,000 down payment for 15 years at 11½%

Monthly payment	$ 11.69	per $1,000
	× 50	
	$ 584.50	for $50,000 mortgage
For 15 years or	× 180	
180 months	$105,210	total dollar payments
Down payment	+$ 10,000	
	$115,210	total cost of home*

*Does not include taxes and insurance.

EXHIBIT 6–2   Loan Amortization Table

Loan amount: $5,000
Term of loan: 12 months
Interest rate: 9.00 %

Payment Number	Payment Amount	Interest Amount	Principal Amount	Remaining Balance
0				$5,000
1	$437.26	$37.50	$399.76	$4,600
2	437.26	34.50	402.76	4,197
3	437.26	31.48	405.78	3,792
4	437.26	28.44	408.82	3,383
5	437.26	25.37	411.89	2,971
6	437.26	22.28	414.97	2,556
7	437.26	19.17	418.09	2,138
8	437.26	16.03	421.22	1,717
9	437.26	12.88	424.38	1,292
10	437.26	9.69	427.56	865
11	437.26	6.49	430.77	434
12	437.26	3.26	434.00	0

EXHIBIT 6–3   Payment Schedule

	Monthly Payment to Amortize $1,000 Loan, Including Interest at Rate of—					
	8½%	9½%	10½%	11½%	12½%	15%
In 15 years	$9.85	$10.45	$11.06	$11.69	$12.33	$14.00
In 20 years	8.86	9.33	9.99	10.67	11.37	13.17
In 25 years	8.06	8.74	9.45	10.17	10.91	12.81
In 30 years	7.69	8.41	9.15	9.91	10.68	12.65

Example B: $60,000 home with $10,000 down payment for 30 years at 11½%

Monthly payment	$ 9.91	per $1,000
	× 50	
	$ 495.50	for $50,000 mortgage
For 30 years or	× 360	
360 months	$178,380	total dollar payments
Down payment	+$ 10,000	
	$188,380	total cost of home*

*Does not include taxes and insurance.

The "Point" System in Mortgage Lending

Over the years mortgage lenders have frequently charged "points." This practice, while generally misunderstood and often ignored, is vitally important to understanding mortgage lending operations. A **point** equals 1 percent of the face value of the mortgage and is an additional charge required to obtain a mortgage loan. Points may be collected as a one-time prepaid interest charge so the contract rate will be lower than it would otherwise be. Also, loan processing, or loan origination fees, charged by the financial institution will be expressed and collected at points. If a homeowner is charged four points on a $20,000 loan, the lender deducts $800 and the home buyer receives only $19,200. However, the home buyer has to repay the entire 20,000. This, of course, means that the true annual rate of interest is more than the stated rate.

Points may also be charged to the seller. These points, however, do not affect the interest rate; they simply reduce the amount the seller receives. Points may be charged as prepaid interest in some loans, often in order to get a more attractive rate for the term of the loan. Some lenders also express their loan origination (or processing) fees as points. In this case, some points are included in the amount financed, whereas other points represent out-of-pocket costs that the buyer pays when the loan is closed.

Home buyers should seek expert advice as to the terms of their mortgage and the points charged before making any final decision.

Balloon Clause

A **balloon payment clause** in a mortgage will require that a fixed-rate, long-term loan be paid off at the end of a specified time period. For example, the loan may initially be amortized over a 15- or 30-year period of time, but this clause requires that the loan is due in as early as three years. The loan may or may not have a provision to refinance at the time of the balloon. Otherwise, it is the buyer's responsibility to locate new refinancing.

Assumption Clause

An **assumption clause** means that a prospective buyer of a home may be able to keep the mortgage currently in force for the seller. In other words, the buyer takes over the payments and continues the mortgage as it exists. If the home purchase price is considerably higher than the existing unpaid balance, however, the buyer may be required to come up with a substantial cash payment. Sometimes the seller will agree to accept a second mortgage and receive payments personally over time. The assumption clause normally provides that the new buyer must be acceptable to the lender. The lender, of course, will do a complete credit investigation before it allows the mortgage to be assumed by another party.

Prepayment Clause

A **prepayment clause** requires the mortgage holder to pay specified fees or penalties if the mortgage is paid off early.

Box 6–1   Credit Management Tips

Adjustable Rate Mortgages

Adjustable rate mortgages offer some significant advantages for borrowers. Lenders generally charge lower initial interest rates for ARMs than for fixed-rate mortgages. Borrowers may, as a result, qualify for a larger loan since payments will initially be lower. Also, if rates stay low, the total interest paid over the life of the mortgage will be lower.

However, there is also the risk that interest rates will move higher. This will result in higher monthly payments in the future. Here are some important questions for the borrower . . .

• Is my income likely to rise enough to cover higher mortgage payments if interest rates go up?

• Will I be taking on other sizable debts, such as a loan for a car or school tuition, in the near future?

• How long do I plan to own this home? (If you plan to sell soon, rising interest rates may not pose the problem they do if you plan to own the house for a long time.)

• Can my payments increase even if interest rates generally do not increase?

SOURCE: Adapted from "Consumer Handbook on Adjustable Rate Mortgages," prepared by the Federal Reserve Board, Office of Thrift Supervision, undated.

MORTGAGE LENDING STANDARDS

As in any lending situation, the lender is obligated to determine that the borrower show the willingness and financial ability to repay the mortgage. As the number of mortgages being sold in the secondary market has increased in recent years, fairly specific lending standards, or income ratios, have developed.

Monthly Housing Expense-to-Income Ratio

This ratio requires that expenses related to housing be totaled. These expenses typically include:

1. Principal and interest payments on the mortgage.
2. Hazard or homeowner's insurance premiums.
3. Real estate taxes.
4. Payments on secondary financing.

5. Mortgage insurance premiums.
6. Other costs specifically related to housing, e.g., condominium maintenance fees or dues.

The sum of these monthly housing costs is then divided by gross monthly income to determine the ratio or percent of income spent for housing. Secondary market guidelines generally state that this ratio should not exceed 25–28 percent of stable monthly income. A family with monthly income of $3,000, therefore, should not be spending more than $840 (28 percent of $3,000) on housing expenses. This calculation is often used to estimate how much a family can afford to pay for a new home.

Monthly Debt Payment-to-Income Ratio

This ratio begins with a calculation of the total monthly debt repayment obligations of the mortgage loan applicant. This total generally includes:

1. Monthly housing expense (see above).
2. Payments on all installment debts.
3. Alimony, child support, or maintenance payments.
4. Revolving charge account payments.
5. Payments for second homes.

This sum is again divided by monthly income to determine the debt-payment ratio. This ratio, or percentage, should generally not exceed 33–36 percent of stable monthly income. The family mentioned above with a $3,000 income cannot have more than $1,080 in total debt payments (36 percent of $3,000) in order to meet this lending guideline.

In some cases the borrower may be allowed to exceed one or both ratios, but the exceptions would require special documentation. Generally, the debt-payment ratio is the most important, but exceptions are possible in certain circumstances.

CLOSING COSTS

It is important that prospective home buyers and mortgage borrowers understand the types and magnitude of closing costs and come to the closing meeting with sufficient cash. Also called **settlement costs,** these are costs associated with the transfer of ownership to the real estate property and the settling of accounts with the buyer, seller, real estate agent, financial institution, and others who deliver services required by the transfer of title. The Real Estate Settlement Procedures Act of 1974 requires a lender to give advance notice to the borrower of the closing costs, or a reasonable estimate. Some of the more important costs are:

1. Sales/brokers commission. This is the total dollar amount of sales commission usually paid by the seller. Fees are usually a percentage of the selling price of the home.

2. Loan origination fee. This is a fee paid by the borrower, often stated as points, designed to compensate the lender for processing the application.

3. Loan discount points. This is a one-time charge used to adjust the interest rate on the mortgage note to equal the current market rate of interest. It represents prepaid interest and will compensate the lender for accepting a contract rate below the normal rate.

4. Appraisal fee. This is a fee paid to a professional appraiser who verifies the value of the property being purchased. The appraiser inspects the house and the neighborhood, and checks the selling prices of comparable houses. The appraisal is most beneficial to the lender who is interested in the true value of the property in the event they must foreclose.

5. Credit report fee. The lender will order an updated credit bureau report to check the borrower's credit history and other credit-related facts. This information is used in conjunction with the loan application to help the lender arrive at a decision.

6. Mortgage insurance premium. The lender may require the borrower to pay the first premium, or a lump-sum premium for the life of the loan, at the time of closing.

7. Hazard insurance premium. Because the lender needs to be sure the hazard insurance is in place to protect the property against loss, they may require that the first premium be paid in advance at closing.

8. Real estate taxes. The lender may require that monthly payments be made to a reserve or escrow account to cover local property taxes.

9. Title search. These expenses cover the costs of the examinations of records of previous ownership to determine whether the seller can convey a clear title to the property.

10. Title insurance. This is a lump-sum premium for a title policy that will protect the lender, and sometimes the borrower, against loss due to defects in connection with the title.

11. Survey. This is the cost of a surveyor that may be required to determine the exact location of the home and the property lines.

12. Inspection costs. Other inspections may be required to look for problems with pests, well, septic systems, and environmental hazards.

HOME EQUITY LOANS

The Tax Reform Act of 1986 dramatically increased the interest among borrowers in using their homes as security for loans. This act phased out the deductibility of the interest for tax purposes with other forms of consumer debt. Within specific guidelines, the interest on loans secured by real estate continues to be deductible for federal income tax purposes. Since passage of this act, many consumers have been paying off automobile loans, credit card balances, and other consumer debt with funds obtained from home equity loans and home equity lines of credit.

A home equity loan is a second mortgage where the lender agrees to stand in line behind the first mortgage holder in the event of liquidation. An appraisal of the property to be used as collateral is often required along with other closing costs. A home equity line of credit is an open-end, revolving-type debt that allows the homeowner to draw upon a preapproved amount of indebtedness as needed. The maximum credit line is often based on a percentage of the value of the property, e.g., 75–80 percent of its market value, minus the outstanding first mortgage amount.

There are limits on the amount of interest that is deductible and most borrowers are encouraged to see a tax advisor to determine the allowable deductions.

DISCRIMINATION IN MORTGAGE LENDING

As pointed out in Chapter 7, the Equal Credit Opportunity Act prohibits credit discrimination on the basis of race, color, religion, national origin, sex, marital status, and age (provided that a person has the capacity to enter into a binding contract); because all or part of a person's income derives from any public assistance program; or because a person in good faith has exercised any right under the Consumer Credit Protection Act. The provisions of this act apply in any decision-making activity in regard to home mortgage lending.

Likewise, some mortgage lenders have been the target of criticism because of certain **"redlining"** practices—that is, setting aside certain areas in a community as undesirable credit risk zones.

Important Terms

Discussion Questions

1. Why might home mortgage loan credit be considered as a type of consumer credit? Why might it be considered business or investment credit?

2. Why would you want to buy a home? When would you rent?

3. What is the difference between a first mortgage and a second mortgage?

4. Distinguish between an FHA-insured, a VA-guaranteed, and a conventional fixed-rate mortgage loan.

5. What is meant by the term *second-layer lenders* and the secondary mortgage market?

6. What are some of the traditional characteristics of savings and loan associations?

7. What sources are available to the American family to finance the purchase of a home?

8. Check with a savings and loan association, a life insurance company, a commercial bank, and a savings bank (if there is one in your area) as to their requirements for home financing.

9. What is the basic difference between a fixed-rate mortgage and an adjustable rate mortgage?

10. What are the important features and provisions in an adjustable rate mortgage that a borrower must know?

11. What are the advantages and disadvantages of the adjustable rate mortgage to the home buyer? To the lending institution?

12. What is meant by the "point" system in home mortgage lending?

13. What is private mortgage insurance (PMI)?

14. Explain the housing-expense ratio and the debt-payment ratio as they are used to determine who might qualify for a mortgage loan. Provide numerical examples.

15. Discuss the attraction and operations of home equity loans and home equity lines of credit.

15. What is meant by amortization?

16. Distinguish between a fixed-rate mortgage and an adjustable rate mortgage.

17. What are the disadvantages of a balloon mortgage? The advantages?

18. Explain the most important basic features of ARMs.

19. Would you want to take out a home equity loan? Why or why not?

CASE PROBLEM

This weekend Bill and Betty Stevens attended an open house and fell in love with a home currently for sale. They discussed the property with the real estate agent and are convinced they can sell their home quickly and buy the new home if they can arrange the financing. Here are some details:

Selling Price of existing home	$ 80,000
Less: Real estate commission	−4,800
First mortgage balance	−45,000
Second mortgage balance	−9,000
Equals the amount for down payment	$ 21,200
Cost of the new home	$120,000
Less: 20% down payment	−24,000
($21,200 + savings withdrawal)	
Equals the amount of new mortgage	$ 96,000
Other information:	
Annual real estate taxes = $3,700.00	
Hazard Insurance = 500.00	

Using this and the other information about the Stevens family and their financial situation, answer the following questions:

1. What is the new monthly mortgage payment if the Stevenses could arrange a 10.5 percent, 25-year mortgage at a local financial institution? (See Exhibit 6–3)

2. What is the housing expense-to-income ratio for the Stevenses if they move into this new home? What will their monthly debt payment-to-income ratio be?

3. Would you recommend that the mortgage loan be approved? Discuss your conclusion with a mortgage loan officer.

7

REGULATION OF CONSUMER CREDIT

Learning Objectives

After studying this chapter, you should be able to:

- Trace the historical development of consumer credit regulation.
- Point out the provisions of laws:
    Truth in Lending Act
    Credit Card Issuance Act
    Fair Credit Reporting Act
    Fair Credit Billing Act
    Equal Credit Opportunity Act
    Fair Debt Collection Practices Act
    Electronic Fund Transfer Act
    Depository Institutions Deregulation and Monetary Control Act
    Garn-St Germain Depository Institutions Act
    Competitive Equality Banking Act
    Fair Credit and Charge Card Disclosure Act
    Home Equity Loan Consumer Protection Act
    Financial Institutions Reform, Recovery, and Enforcement Act
    Home Mortgage Disclosure Act
    Community Reinvestment Act
- Trace the passage of state regulations of consumer credit.

Credit is an easy way for people to purchase items they want now but can't afford to pay for immediately. Almost all credit carries a cost, in the form of either interest or carrying charges. Consumers must weigh the enjoyment they will derive from the things they wish to purchase today against the necessity of having to pay for those items—at a cost—in the future. Because not all consumers use good judgment in their use of credit, and because credit grantors may take advantage of borrowers, federal and state laws have been passed to protect credit users from unfair practices. Other social and economic goals are also promoted through credit legislation. This chapter traces the history of federal and state credit regulation in the United States.

FEDERAL REGULATION OF CONSUMER CREDIT

The Goals of Credit Regulation

Promote Stability Within the U.S. Economy

Some laws have been passed to provide a stable money supply and to prevent the disruption that would occur if widespread bank failures were to occur. The protection for depository accounts provided by the Federal Depository Insurance Corporation (FDIC), for example, was designed, in part, to prevent bank runs in which many depositors demand the return of their funds at the same time. Other laws are designed to protect the safety and integrity of the financial institutions that collect and hold the savings of citizens by protecting depositors from improper or fraudulent acts by the institutions. Laws regulate, for example, the types of permissible bank loans and the amounts that can be lent to any one borrower. The Credit Control Act attempted to address problems associated with inflation by controlling the amount and types of credit extended to borrowers. The reserve requirements and other tools used by the Federal Reserve System (discussed in Chapter 1) are also examples of government economic stabilization efforts tied to credit transactions.

Consumer Protection

Some laws are designed to protect consumers from their failures to understand credit transactions and from unfair practices that might be used by credit grantors. Laws exist to prohibit unfair discrimination in credit granting, to provide contract terms that the average person can understand, and to restrain collectors from using overzealous, unfair collection methods. State laws often control interest rates and the terms of credit contracts so borrowers will be treated fairly. Many laws are directed toward disclosure so consumers can more accurately understand finance charges, credit bureau information, and the reasons they have been declined a credit account.

Promote Social Goals

Some laws in the credit management arena have been passed to accomplish various social goals deemed important by legislators and others. For example, some sectors of the economy have been identified as having special importance and laws ensure that credit will be made available. Examples include laws that impact lending for housing, small business, agriculture, and minority groups. The laws take the form of tax credits, guarantees against default, outright subsidies, and other provisions that make more loans available for the supported social or economic sector. Federal programs exist, for example, to assist students with loans for college educations. The government and legislators believe that society and the economy will benefit from more college graduates and has developed special lending programs to encourage this investment in education.

> ### *Goals of Credit Regulation*
>
> • Promote economic stability
> • Protect consumers
> • Promote social goals

Federal regulation of consumer credit began during World War II. Much new federal credit legislation was passed during the 1960s, 1970s, and 1980s. Each law attempted to reduce the problems and confusion surrounding consumer credit, whose complexity increased with its wider use. These laws are designed to set a standard treatment for individual consumers in their financial dealings.

The financial services sector of our economy is perhaps the most heavily regulated industry in this country. Many complain that the burden of regulations has created undue hardship and excessive costs for lenders. Others believe that many regulations have interfered with the ability of American financial institutions to compete in worldwide financial markets. The other point of view, of course, is that the desirable goals of economic stability, consumer protection and social improvement have been facilitated.

The Regulating Agencies—Federal and State

A network of regulators has developed, resulting in extensive supervision of financial institutions and other credit grantors. The network of regulators became larger with passage of more new credit laws. To date, there are five key groups of regulators.

Office of the Comptroller of the Currency (OCC)

This agency was established by the National Currency Act of 1863 and is the oldest regulator in the group. Although the agency was originally set up to provide a safe and uniform currency, these responsibilities have largely been passed to the Federal Reserve System. Today the OCC is primarily responsible for granting national bank charters, approving mergers and branches, and supervising national banks. Banks with national bank charters comprise only about 30 percent of the total number of banks, but because they tend to be larger than average, these banks account for the majority of total deposits. The OCC can remove officers, revoke charters, and levy fines.

Federal Reserve System

The "Fed" is an independent agency established in 1913 to promote a stable currency and to ensure the economic health of our monetary system. As discussed in Chapter 1, the Federal Reserve System tries to maintain stable price levels and encourage economic growth by using open market operations, changes in the discount rate, and changes in reserve requirements. The Federal Reserve System is also generally responsible for developing the regulations needed to implement the various credit laws passed by Congress.

Federal Deposit Insurance Corporation (FDIC)

The FDIC was established in 1933 as an independent agency of the federal government. It provides insurance that currently protects individual deposits up to $100,000 from loss due to the failure of a depository institution. This protection is generally available for deposits in banks, savings and loan associations, and credit unions through the FDIC or similar insurance corporations. The financial institutions pay an insurance premium generally based on the level of total deposits. The FDIC primarily supervises state-chartered banks that are not members of the Federal Reserve System. The FDIC, and the other insuring agencies, acquire their powers through the need to supervise the financial institutions controlling the deposits they must insure. The FDIC is also active in disposing of failed financial institutions by arranging a merger or liquidating the assets.

Other Federal Regulators

Other federal regulatory authorities have arisen to supervise credit-granting agencies other than commercial banks. The Office of Thrift Supervision, for example, charters and supervises savings and loans associations. The National Credit Union Administration likewise oversees federally chartered credit unions. The Department of Justice is concerned with business mergers, including financial service firms, that might violate antitrust legislation and result in restraints of trade. The Federal Trade Commission is generally interested in consumer protection measures and truth in advertising of all types of credit-granting institutions.

State Regulators

Many of the authorities and agencies discussed above are concerned with banks and financial institutions. Other credit grantors, such as consumer finance companies, state-chartered credit unions, and retail credit grantors, are supervised by state agencies. Other credit-related firms such as collection agencies are also supervised by state regulators, e.g., the state banking commissioner.

Major Credit Regulators

- Office of the Comptroller of the Currency (OCC)
- Federal Reserve System
- Federal Deposit Insurance Corporation (FDIC)
- Other Federal Regulators
  - Office of Thrift Supervision
  - National Credit Union Administration
  - Department of Justice
  - Federal Trade Commission

Early Consumer Credit Legislation

Passage of Regulation W during World War II was the first attempt at consumer credit regulation. The regulation (1) dealt with the amount of down payments and the length of the repayment periods in installment selling and (2) prohibited continued activity on 30-day charge accounts that were past due for a specified period. The actual results of Regulation W are questionable. During World War II, few consumer durable goods were available and consumer income was unusually high. Consequently, sales declined for goods targeted by Regulation W for reasons other than the regulation.

The effect of regulation during the postwar period and the Korean conflict was mild. Perhaps only lower-income groups and those with heavy obligations on their incomes had to delay purchases of durable goods. The incomes of the major portion of consumers were high enough and their savings sufficient to meet the regulatory standards. Further, a scarcity of goods prevailed for several years after World War II, and by the time the United States was involved in the Korean conflict, the ineffective results of the previous regulations were well understood. Regulation during the Korean conflict was mild and applied only to the down payment and length of the repayment periods on installment sales contracts. In this instance the goods under regulation were very limited; most goods were free of controls.

Credit Control Act

The Credit Control Act was one of the many credit-related federal laws that appeared during the 1960s and 1970s. Signed into law December 24, 1969, this legislation empowered the president "at any time at his discretion to authorize complete and total control of all forms and types of credit by the Federal Reserve Board—even over rates and licensing." To enforce the provisions of this act, the Federal Reserve Board was empowered, with permission from appropriate courts, to issue permanent or temporary injunctions or restraining orders against violators or suspected violators and to assess civil penalties or bring criminal charges against willful violators.

President Carter invoked the Credit Control Act in 1980 as part of a program to control inflation and imposed restraints on the growth of certain types of consumer credit extended by banks, retailers, finance companies, and others. The controls were only in effect for a few months and the act has not been used since.

Truth in Lending Act—Title I of the Consumer Credit Protection Act

In 1960, the federal government made a serious but unsuccessful attempt to regulate consumer credit activities in the form of a "consumer credit labeling bill" (S. 2755). This bill, among other things, would have required that a statement of the total finance charges in dollars and cents and of the "simple" annual rate accompany every consumer credit transaction. According to its sponsors, the bill would "assist in the promotion of economic stabilization by requiring the disclosure of finance charges in connection with extension of credit." Throughout the early 1960s other bills were introduced and hearings conducted. Finally, in January 1967, the Truth in Lending Act was passed and signed into law. It became effective July 1, 1969.

As originally passed, the Truth in Lending Act is Title I of the Consumer Credit Protection Act. Title II deals with extortionate credit transactions. Title III is concerned with wage garnishment. Title IV provides for the creation of a National Commission on Consumer Finance. **Extortionate credit transactions** are transactions with exorbitant or excessive charges. **Wage garnishment** is a legal proceeding whereby money or property due to a debtor (wages) but in possession of another (employer) is applied to the payment of a debt. For most consumer–business transactions, compliance with the law is under the general supervision of the Federal Trade Commission, which has been given part of the responsibility for enforcing Regulation Z. This regulation, which implements the Truth in Lending Act, was issued by the Board of Governors of the Federal Reserve System and is designed to tell business executives how to comply with the act.

The main purpose of the truth-in-lending portion of the act is to assure a meaningful *disclosure of credit terms* so that consumers will be able to readily compare the various credit terms available to them and to avoid the uninformed use of credit. The Truth in Lending Act is simply a disclosure law; it does not set maximum interest rates. It does specify, however, that the most important credit terms—the dollar amount of the finance charge and the annual percentage rate—be disclosed to the customer. Later amendments added other provisions such as a right of rescission in certain consumer credit transactions. A **right of rescission** provides buyers an opportunity to change their mind about a transaction and to cancel a contract.

Types of Credit Covered

The Truth in Lending Act applies to loans where the money, property, or service extended is for personal, family, or household purposes. A finance charge is imposed in covered transactions and a written agreement exists that requires four or more installments. Loans to businesses, commercial enterprises, and agriculture are not covered. Loans in excess of $25,000 are also exempt, except in those cases where the loan is secured by a dwelling or real property.

Disclosure Statement

The law provides that a disclosure statement must be given to the borrower before the transaction is completed. The disclosure statement will outline the charges that are included in the total finance charge and will show the annual percentage rate. The **total finance charge** is a total of interest, fees, and charges payable by the loan customer and required as a condition of the credit. Although there are some variations determined by the type of loan, these charges include interest, points, loan fees, credit report fees, document preparation fees, and others. The **annual percentage rate** is a standardized calculation that incorporates interest and other fees to show the total cost of the loan averaged over the entire loan term. With this information, the borrower is in a good position to compare the loan rates at different institutions or firms.

Right of Rescission

If any consumer credit transaction involves a security interest in real property that is used, or expected to be used, as the customer's principal residence, the customer has the right to cancel the transaction until midnight of the third business day following the date the transaction is consummated or the date the disclosure forms are delivered. If the borrower decides to exercise these cancellation rights, the lender must be notified in writing within the three-day time frame. Most lenders will not disburse funds until the rescission period has passed.

Other Provisions

Any advertisement relating to extensions of credit repayable in more than four installments without an identified finance charge must state that the cost of the credit is included in the price of the goods or services. A maximum limit on class-action liability is set at $500,000 or 1 percent of the creditor's net worth, whichever is less. A **class action suit** occurs when a plaintiff initiates a lawsuit on his or her own behalf and on behalf of any others who may have the same claim against the defendant. Fraudulent use of a credit card to obtain money, goods, or services having a value aggregating $1,000 is made a federal crime, enforceable by the Justice Department.

Penalties

If any creditor fails to disclose information required under truth in lending or gives inaccurate information, it may be sued for actual damages (any money loss suffered). In addition, the individual can sue for twice the finance charge in the case of a credit transaction. In any successful lawsuit, the individual is entitled to court costs and attorney fees.

The Truth in Lending Act makes it fairly easy for the consumer to understand the terms creditors are offering, but it is difficult at times to estimate the dollar difference from various terms. Assume a consumer is buying a $7,500 car, puts down $1,500, and needs to borrow $6,000. Compare the three credit arrangements shown in Exhibit 7–1. How do these choices compare? The answer depends on what the buyer actually needs:

1. The lowest cost loan is available from Creditor A.
2. If the buyer is looking for lower monthly payments, he or she could get them by paying off the loan over a longer period. However, the buyer would have to pay more in total costs. A loan from Creditor B will add about $488 to the finance charge.
3. If that four-year loan were available from Creditor C, the APR of 15 percent would add another $145 to the finance charges as compared with Creditor B.

The buyer should look at all the terms before making the credit choice.

Exhibit 7–1   Three Possible Credit Arrangements

	APR	Length of Loan	Monthly Payment	Total Finance Charge	Total of Payments
Creditor A	14%	3 years	$205.07	$1,382.52	$7,382.52
Creditor B	14	4 years	163.96	1,870.08	7,870.08
Creditor C	15	4 years	166.98	2,015.04	8,015.04

Credit Card Issuance Act—Title V of the Consumer Credit Protection Act

In October 1970, a federal law on credit card issuance became effective. Under this law, no credit card may be issued except in response to a request or application. This requirement, however, does not apply to renewals or substitutions for previously accepted cards. The law applies to all card users, including banks, oil companies, and entertainment firms.

In addition to stopping the mailing of unsolicited cards, the law limits the consumer's liability on lost or stolen credit cards. After the consumer has notified the credit card company of the loss or theft of any credit card, he or she does not have to pay any unauthorized charge. Regardless of how much is charged before the missing card is reported, the most the consumer will have to pay for any unauthorized charges is $50 on each card. A card company may not collect any loss from the consumer—even the first $50—unless it can prove the following four things:

1. The card was issued at the consumer's request, the card was issued as a renewal or substitute for an accepted card, or the consumer used it at least once before it was lost or stolen.
2. The consumer was provided something on the card, such as a signature line, to identify the consumer as the authorized party to use it.
3. The consumer was notified of the potential $50 liability.
4. The consumer was notified he or she may give oral or written notification that the card was lost or stolen. The consumer must be given a means of notification, such as a telephone number, an address, or both.

Fair Credit Reporting Act—Title VI of the Consumer Credit Protection Act

This amendment to the Consumer Credit Protection Act became law in April 1971. The provisions of this act affect all grantors of consumer credit and all local retail credit bureaus. One of the major requirements on credit grantors is the provision making it mandatory for the business to inform consumers whenever credit is refused on the basis of a credit report and, further, to inform them of the name and address of the bureau making the report. If credit is denied on the basis of information received from a source other than a credit bureau, the business must inform consumers of their right to request in writing the nature of the information on which the denial was based.

The act places new restrictions on credit bureaus as to the inclusion of obsolete information in any consumer report they release; spells out the conditions under which bureaus must disclose in-file information to consumers; prescribes the procedure to follow in case of dispute about the accuracy of information contained in a report; places certain restrictions on investigative consumer reports; and sets forth the bureaus' liability in connection with their operations.

More details of the act as amended and as interpreted by the Federal Trade Commission, which has the responsibility for enforcement of the act, will be covered in Chapter 10 on consumer credit reporting agencies.

Fair Credit Billing Act

The Fair Credit Billing Act became effective in October 1975, as a result of an amendment to the Truth in Lending Act. The act is designed to protect consumers against inaccurate and unfair credit billing practices by credit card issuers and other "open-end" creditors. Revolving, flexible, option, 30-day, 90-day, and other types of credit accounts are included under the definition of open-end accounts if a credit card is used or a finance charge imposed. The act provides procedures for prompt resolution of billing disputes.

The major provisions of the act are as follows:

1. If a customer thinks a bill is wrong or wants more information about it, he or she should notify the creditor in writing within 60 days of the bill's mailing date. The letter should include the customer's name and account number, a statement indicating the bill contains an error, an explanation of why it is believed there is an error, and the suspected amount of the error.

2. While waiting for an answer, the customer does not have to pay the disputed amount or any minimum payments or finance charges that apply to it. The customer, however, is still obligated to pay all parts of the bill that are not in dispute.

3. The creditor must acknowledge the customer's letter within 30 days, unless the bill is corrected before that. Within two billing periods—but in no case more than 90 days—either the account must be corrected or the customer must be told why the creditor believes the bill is correct.

4. If the creditor made a mistake, the customer does not have to pay any finance changes on the disputed amount. The account must be corrected either for the full amount in dispute or for a part of that amount along with an explanation of what is still owed. If no error is found, the creditor must promptly send the customer a statement of what is owed. In this case, the creditor may include any finance charges accumulated and any minimum payments missed while the bill was being questioned.

5. If the customer still is not satisfied, the creditor should be so notified within the time specified to pay the bill.

6. Once the customer has written about a possible error, the creditor may not give out information about the customer to other creditors or credit bureaus or threaten to damage the customer's credit rating. Until the letter is answered, the creditor also may not take any collection action on the disputed amount or restrict the account because of the dispute.

7. The customer may withhold payment of any balance due on defective merchandise or services purchased with a credit card, provided a good faith effort has been made to return the goods or resolve the problem with the merchant from whom the purchase was made. If the store that honored the credit card was not also the issuer of the card, two limitations apply to this right: the original amount of the purchase must have exceeded $50, and the sale must have taken place in the customer's state or within 100 miles of the customer's current address.

Creditors must provide customers with a complete statement of their fair credit billing rights when the customers first open an account and at least twice annually (or send a shorter version with each billing).

A creditor who fails to comply with rules applying to the correction of billing errors automatically forfeits the amount owed on the item in question and any finance charges on it, up to a combined total of $50—even if the bill was correct. The customer also may sue for actual damages plus twice the amount of any finance charges, but in any case not less than $100 or more than $1,000. Court costs and attorney fees are allowed in a successful lawsuit. Class action suits also are permitted.

Private enforcement of the act is supplemented by administrative enforcement by several federal agencies. Compliance by banks, for example, is enforced by the appropriate bank regulatory agency. The Federal Trade Commission has enforcement responsibility for all creditors not specifically assigned to other federal agencies (for example, department stores and other retailers, consumer finance companies, and all nonbank credit card issuers).

Equal Credit Opportunity Act (ECOA)—Title VII of the Consumer Credit Protection Act

The Equal Credit Opportunity Act (ECOA), effective in October 1975, became Title VII of the Consumer Credit Protection Act. Implementing regulations—Regulation B—have been issued by the Federal Reserve Board. The act and regulations apply to all who regularly extend or offer to extend consumer credit or who arrange consumer credit for any purpose or in any amount. The Women's Business Ownership Act extended the notice and recordkeeping provisions of the ECOA to apply to some commercial loan applications. The Equal Credit Opportunity Act is designed to provide an equal opportunity to apply for credit.

The act does not require a lender to make bad loans or poor credit decisions. The lender collects appropriate data, conducts a credit investigation and analysis, and determines if an applicant is eligible for a loan. The decision, however, must be based on creditworthiness without consideration of sex, marital status, race, religion, age, and other information outlined below.

The principal provisions of Regulation B are as follows:

1. Creditors may not discriminate against a loan applicant on the basis of race, color, religion, national origin, sex, marital status, or age (although a customer must be of a legal age to sign a contract).
2. Creditors may not discriminate on the grounds that an applicant's income is derived from public assistance programs or on the grounds that an applicant has exercised his or her rights under the Consumer Credit Protection Act.
3. Creditors may not make statements discouraging applicants from applying for a loan based on the considerations outlined above.
4. Creditors may not refuse, based on these considerations, to grant a separate account to a creditworthy applicant.

5. Creditors may not ask the marital status of an applicant applying for an unsecured separate account, except in a community property state or as required to comply with state law governing permissible finance charges or loan ceilings. A **community property state** refers to a state that has laws that provide equal ownership of all property by spouses obtained during a marriage regardless of how the property is titled.

6. The creditor may not request information about a spouse unless:
   a. The spouse will be allowed to use the account; or
   b. The spouse will be liable according to the contract for the account; or
   c. The applicant is relying on the spouse's income as a basis for repayment, or
   d. The applicant resides in a community property state; or the property on which the applicant is relying for repayment is located in a community property state; or
   e. The applicant is relying on alimony, child support, or separate maintenance payments as a basis for repayment.

7. Neither sex nor marital status may be used in credit scoring systems. Credit scoring systems must be statistically sound. Even in a sound credit system, creditors may not assign a negative factor or value to the age of an elderly applicant.

8. Creditors may not inquire into childbearing intentions or capability or birth control practices. They may not assume from an applicant's age that an applicant or an applicant's spouse may drop out of the labor force due to childbearing and thus have an interruption of income.

9. With certain exceptions, creditors may not require or use unfavorable information about a spouse or former spouse where an applicant applies for credit independently of that spouse and can demonstrate that the unfavorable credit history should not be applied.

10. A creditor may not discount part-time income but may examine the probable continuity of an applicant's job.

11. A creditor may inquire about and consider whether obligations to make alimony, child support, or maintenance payments affect an applicant's income.

12. A creditor may ask to what extent an applicant is relying on alimony or child support or maintenance payments to repay the debt. The applicant must first be informed that such disclosure is unnecessary if the applicant does not rely on such income to obtain the credit.

13. Creditors who deny credit must notify the applicant within 30 days of the decision. The applicant should also be informed of the reasons for the denial or of the right to request the reasons.

14. Creditors must inform holders of existing accounts of their rights to have credit history reported in both names.

15. Creditors must, with certain exceptions, give applicants the following written notice: "The Federal Equal Credit Opportunity Act prohibits creditors from

discriminating against credit applicants on the basis of sex or marital status. The federal agency which administers compliance with this law concerning (insert appropriate description—bank, store, etc.) is name and address of the appropriate agency."

16. With certain exceptions, creditors may not terminate credit on an existing account because of a change in an applicant's marital status without evidence that the applicant is unwilling or unable to pay.

If an applicant thinks he or she has adequate proof of discrimination by a creditor for any reason prohibited by the act, the individual may sue for actual damages plus punitive damages of up to $10,000 if the violation is proved to have been intentional. Court costs, attorney fees, and class action suits also are possible.

In total, the Equal Credit Opportunity Act requires that all credit applicants be considered on the basis of their actual qualifications for credit and not be turned away because of certain personal characteristics.

Regulation Q

Federal Reserve Regulation Q established interest rate ceilings on deposits at commercial banks that are members of the Federal Reserve System. Ceilings at insured nonmember banks were set by a regulation of the Federal Deposit Insurance Corporation (FDIC) and were the same as for member banks. The Banking Acts of 1933 and 1935 were the basis

---

Box 7–1   Credit Management Tips

A Few Suggestions for Loan Officers

- Take a Loan Application from Everyone. Get the applicant to state the purpose of the loan and complete an application to document the interview.
- Don't Make Promises of Prejudge Loan Decisions. If you are at a party and a friend asks you about getting a loan, simply invite them to the financial institution to complete a loan application.
- Stick to the Basic Questions Found on the Loan Application. For example, use the terms married, unmarried, or separated. Don't ask for details about a divorce or marital status.
- You Cannot Require a Spouse to Sign in Most States. If an applicant requests unsecured, individual credit and meets the lender's tests of credit worthiness, you cannot inquire about the spouse or their level of income.
- Always Provide a Notice of Adverse Action. This is required when credit is denied, credit is offered with terms different than originally requested, credit privileges are terminated, or credit line extension is refused. A standard form is published by the Federal Reserve Board.

of these regulations. Until 1966, there were no explicit nationwide regulations on interest and dividend rates at savings and loan associations and savings banks. In that year, legislation brought rates paid by federally insured mutual savings banks under the control of the FDIC, and rates paid at savings and loan associations that are members of the Federal Home Loan Bank Board were placed under the control of the board.

Under the provisions of the Depository Institutions Deregulation and Monetary Control Act of 1980, Regulation Q's interest rate controls ended March 31, 1986.

Fair Debt Collection Practices Act—Title VIII of the Consumer Credit Protection Act

The Fair Debt Collection Practices Act, which became effective March 20, 1978, covers the collection practices of third-party debt collectors—those who collect debts for others. This law applies only to collectors dealing with individuals, not to agencies seeking payment from businesses.

The major provisions of the law are as follows:

1. Collectors may not phone debtors at inconvenient times or places. This provision forbids calls between 9 PM and 8 AM.
2. If a debtor engages an attorney, the collector must deal only with the attorney.
3. The collector may not call a debtor at the debtor's place of work if it is known or suspected that the debtor's employer prohibits such communication.
4. If the collector is notified in writing that the debtor refuses to pay the debt, the collector must stop communicating with the debtor, except to describe the additional measures that are being taken.
5. The collector is obliged to give a debtor the following information in writing: the amount owed; the creditor's name; a statement that the debt amount is assumed to be correct, unless the debtor informs the collector otherwise within 30 days; a promise that if the debt is disputed, the debtor will be sent verification of the debt or a copy of the judgment entered against the debtor.

Electronic Fund Transfer Act

Electronic fund transfer (EFT) involves transferring funds between parties electronically rather than through the use of checks or cash. An employer, for example, will use an on-line computer system to instruct its bank on payday to deduct funds from its account to add funds to employee accounts. While EFT is designed to displace some cash payments, it is primarily an alternative to checks.

The Electronic Fund Transfer Act was passed in October 1978, as an amendment to the Financial Institutions Regulatory and Interest Rate Control Act. It provides for required disclosures, receipts, notices, and periodic statements as consumer safeguards, including penalty provisions. Limits are placed on the liability of consumers in the event of unauthorized transfers or lost or stolen EFT cards. It prohibits both financial institutions and others from requiring a consumer to establish an EFT account, particularly the making of an extension of credit conditional on repayment by EFT or employers forcing employees to use EFT in direct deposit of paychecks. It also gives the Federal Reserve Board rule-making authority to implement its requirements and prohibitions.

The Electronic Fund Transfer Act applies to all types of financial institutions that offer EFT services to consumers, including banks, savings and loan associations, credit unions, savings banks, finance companies, and firms that install EFT point-of-sale terminals or other similar devices.

If a financial institution fails to comply with any provisions of the EFT Act, the individual concerned may sue for actual damages (or, in the case of failure to correct an error or credit an account, three times actual damages) plus punitive damages of not less than $100 nor more than $1,000. If an institution fails to make an electronic fund transfer, or to stop payment of a preauthorized transfer when properly instructed to do so, the individual concerned may sue for all damages following from the failure. The individual also is entitled to court costs and attorney fees in a successful lawsuit; class action suits also are permitted.

Depository Institutions Deregulation and Monetary Control Act (DIDMCA)

On March 31, 1980, the president signed into law the Depository Institutions Deregulation and Monetary Control Act. This legislation marked the culmination of many years of effort to change some of the rules under which U.S. financial institutions operated for nearly half a century.

The provisions of this act cover a wide variety of credit activities, the most important of which are:

1. Increased the maximum coverage for all federal deposit insurance from $40,000 to $100,000.
2. Gave statutory authority for banks' automatic services for transfers from savings to checking accounts, saving and loan remote service units, and credit union share drafts.
3. Imposed federal override of state usury ceilings on residential mortgages, including mobile homes.
4. Gave authority for NOW accounts to be offered nationwide; required full reserve requirements on NOW accounts.
5. Increased the interest rate credit unions could charge for consumer loans from 12 to 15 percent.
6. Gave authority for state and national banks to charge interest on business and agricultural loans of more than $25,000 at up to 5 percentage points more than the Federal Reserve district bank's discount rate plus surcharge.
7. Gave authority to repeal Regulation Q on March 31, 1986.

The Garn-St Germain Depository Institutions Act

This complex and detailed act, effective October 15, 1982, dealt with different areas of financial reform. It became a rapid step toward a deregulated financial system. At the time of passage, many observers viewed the Garn-St Germain Act as primarily a rescue operation for the savings and loan institutions and the savings banks. The act also increased the options of other depository institutions, however, and gave regulators greater flexibility in handling crisis situations in which banks and thrifts ceased to be viable.

The provisions of the act were directed toward widening the sources of depository institution funds, contributing to the removal of interest rate ceilings, permanently expanding the uses of funds and other powers, and temporarily granting regulators emergency powers to deal with current depository institution crises.

Debt Collection Act

In October 1982, the president signed the Debt Collection Act of 1982, allowing government agencies to report delinquent debtor information to credit bureaus and to contract with third-party collection agencies in an effort to recoup approximately $33 billion in delinquencies.

Beginning November 1983, the Office of Management and Budget began requiring government agencies to comply with the Debt Collection Act of 1983 by reporting delinquent debts to credit reporting agencies. Government agencies also have to purchase credit reports on prospective borrowers.

Competitive Equality Banking Act

Federal regulatory agencies' rulings in 1987 granted commercial banks certain additional securities underwriting powers. **Underwriting securities** refers to the practice of an investment banker purchasing the newly issued securities of a corporation with the expectation that the securities will be sold later at a profit. The first of these rulings was by the Federal Reserve, which ruled in April 1987 that banks could underwrite commercial paper, municipal revenue bonds, and mortgage-backed securities. These activities were to be conducted through nonbank subsidiaries that are owned by a bank. In July 1987, the Federal Reserve Board also approved the underwriting of securities backed by consumer receivables. However, Congress imposed a moratorium beginning in March 1987 prohibiting all federal bank agencies from granting any new nonbanking powers for one year.

This moratorium, contained in the Competitive Equality Banking Act of 1987 (CEBA), prohibited regulatory approval of any new securities, real estate, or insurance activities. The congressional moratorium ended without any legislative action on this issue, so the ban on further regulatory approvals was lifted. However, clarification of this issue is pending.

Fair Credit and Charge Card Disclosure Act

The distinction between credit card plans and charge card plans appeared in the Fair Credit and Charge Card Disclosure Act of 1988. Under this act, which was signed into law November 4, 1988, a **charge card** is defined as "a card, plate, or other single credit device that is not subject to a finance charge." On the other hand, a **credit card** is subject to a finance charge.

This law requires that disclosures be made on applications and brochures, in mailed solicitations for credit cards and charge cards, in published advertisements for these cards, and in telephone solicitations. These regulations apply only to applications for consumer credit. Exhibit 7–2 shows a guide to the disclosure provisions of the law.

Telephone solicitations for new accounts can be handled differently. All of the disclosures shown in Exhibit 7–2 (except for the late fee, cash-advance fee, and the over-limit fee) are required for telephone solicitations. Disclosures can be mailed within 30 days after a request for the card but not later than the card itself. This federal law is tougher than most of the state application disclosure laws in effect.

Home Equity Loan Consumer Protection Act

As was pointed out in earlier chapters, a home equity line is a form of revolving credit in which a consumer's home serves as collateral for a loan. The Home Equity Loan Consumer Protection Act (HELCPA) was enacted in November 1988. This law and the implementing regulations adopted by the Federal Reserve Board require extensive new disclosures to the consumer at an early stage in the loan application process.

Financial Institutions Reform, Recovery, and Enforcement Act

The Financial Institutions Reform, Recovery, and Enforcement Act (FIRREA) dramatically altered the savings and loan industry. This act was passed in response to the many savings and loan association failures in the late 1980s. As discussed earlier, the deregulation of the financial services industry allowed many savings and loan associations to invest in new, speculative ventures. Many of the commercial real estate ventures, along with others, turned out to be poor investments. When the deals fell apart, the savings and loan associations involved became insolvent. Because the deposits of nearly all S&L depositors were insured by the Federal Savings and Loan Insurance Corporation, the federal government was compelled to step in and take control of the failed

---

EXHIBIT 7–2   A Guide to Disclosure Provisions

Credit Card Issuers Must Reveal . . .	*Charge Card Issuers Must Reveal . . .*
• APR and how determined.	• All items at left, except APR.
• Balance-calculation method.	• That all charges are payable on receipt of statement.
• Grace period.	
• Annual, transaction, and account-maintenance fees.	
• Minimum finance charge.	
• Cash-advance fee.*	
• Late fee.*	
• Fee for exceeding credit limit.*	

*Does not apply to telephone solicitations.

institutions. FIRREA is a comprehensive law that attempted to restructure this industry by strengthening U.S. depository institutions and the deposit insurance corporations. Some of the highlights of this legislation, passed on August 9, 1989, are as follows:

1. The Federal Home Loan Bank Board, which functioned in a manner similar to the Federal Reserve Board, was replaced by the Office of Thrift Supervision, which operates as part of the U.S. Treasury Department. The OTS charters federal S&Ls, establishes regulations, and supervises all savings and loan associations.

2. FIRREA established the Resolution Trust Corporation to manage the assets and liabilities of failed savings and loan associations. The RTC tries to liquidate assets, arrange mergers, and develop other solutions to the problems tied to the failures. The RTC is managed by the Federal Deposit Insurance Corporation. Funds are raised by the sale of long-term bonds and from appropriations from Congress.

3. The Federal Savings and Loan Insurance Corporation (FSLIC), which previously insured the deposits of nearly all savings and loan association depositors, was replaced with the Savings Association Insurance Fund (SAIF). The SAIF is controlled by the FDIC.

The Home Mortgage Disclosure Act of 1975

This act, which is implemented under Federal Reserve Regulation C, requires depository institutions to disclose information related to mortgage loans made in their communities. The act applies to banks, savings associations, credit unions, and other mortgage lending institutions that have assets of more than $10 million and are located in Standard Metropolitan Statistical Areas. They are required to maintain data related to their mortgages and to make this information available to regulators and the general public. Information gathered includes date and purpose of the application (home purchase, home improvement, or refinancing), action taken, property location, and information about the race, sex, and income of the applicant. The purpose is to guard against redlining, a practice of refusing to make loans in certain undesirable neighborhoods in a community and unwarranted discrimination.

The Community Reinvestment Act of 1977

This act, implemented by Federal Reserve Regulation BB, requires financial institutions to establish methods of determining and meeting credit needs in their communities, especially the needs of low- and moderate-income customers. The act is unique in that it speaks to the federal supervisory agencies and requires that, as part of their examinations, they assess the institution's record of meeting the credit needs of its entire community, including low- and moderate-income neighborhoods. The financial institutions are expected to (1) define the community it serves, (2) determine its credit needs, and (3) take steps to help meet those needs. Outreach programs should be in place that help the financial institution identify needs among local governments, businesses, and organizations. In order to remain in full compliance of this law, financial institutions generally must be able to document their efforts and they must focus on the needs of low- and moderate-income customers when they define the needs of their communities.

STATE REGULATION OF CONSUMER CREDIT

Uniform Consumer Credit Code (UCCC)

The Uniform Consumer Credit Code was drafted by the National Conference of Commissioners on Uniform State Laws. At its annual meeting in August 1974, the conference approved the code for enactment in all states. Currently 10 states (Colorado, Idaho, Indiana, Iowa, Kansas, Maine, Oklahoma, South Carolina, Utah, and Wyoming) and Guam have enacted the code. The main purposes of the code are:

1. To simplify, clarify, and modernize the law governing consumer credit and usury.
2. To provide rate ceilings to assure an adequate supply of credit to consumers.
3. To further consumer understanding of the terms of credit transactions and to foster competition among suppliers of consumer credit so that consumers may obtain credit at reasonable cost.
4. To protect consumers against unfair practices by some suppliers of consumer credit, having due regard for the interests of legitimate and scrupulous creditors.
5. To permit and encourage the development of fair and economically sound consumer credit practices.
6. To conform the regulation of disclosure in consumer credit transactions to the federal Truth in Lending Act.
7. To make uniform the law, including administrative rules, among the various jurisdictions.

In the areas of consumer sales, leases, and loans, the major protective provisions of the UCCC are found in six categories: rate ceilings, disclosure of finance charges, limitations on multiple agreements between the buyer and the seller, limitation on various practices (such as default payments and balloon payments), rules governing home solicitation sales, and limitations on the creditors' remedies.

Uniform Commercial Code

The Uniform Commercial Code is a uniform body of rules designed to deal with all situations ordinarily arising in the handling of a commercial transaction. It was designed by the National Conference of Commissioners on Uniform State Laws and the American Law Institute. Passed at the state level, this law affects all commercial transactions.

The Uniform Commercial Code, 1962 Official Text with variations, is the law in all states (except Louisiana), the District of Columbia, and the Virgin Islands. The code is

---

Box 7–2   Credit Management Tips

How to Determine the Credit Needs of Your Community

Appoint a Program Coordinator

To keep your board of directors informed, you will need a community program coordinator. You should choose an individual who has a strong interest in the community.

Locate Sources of Information

Information about community credit needs may come from a variety of sources.

Identify Contacts

Make a list of people and organizations in your community that might be helpful.

Make Contact with the Sources

Call upon the individuals and organizations you have identified to see what they are doing in the community. Find out their goals and their attitudes toward your financial institution.

Establish a Productive Dialogue

Do more than merely tell community residents about the services of your financial institution; involve them in developing and planning additions to those services.

People may need to know more about your financial institution. If they are unaware that it is willing to lend them funds, they won't come to your institution for a loan. If they believe its terms are unfair, they will go across town to another lender. Mistaken beliefs can be identified and changed through good communications with your community.

SOURCE: Pamphlet prepared and distributed by the Federal Reserve System, undated.

---

divided into 10 articles as follows: General Provisions; Sales; Commercial Paper; Bank Deposits and Collections; Letters of Credit; Bulk Transfers; Warehouse Receipts, Bills of Lading, and Other Documents of Title; Investment Securities; Secured Transactions, Sales of Accounts, Contract Rights, and Chattel Paper; and Effective Date and Repealer.

Important Terms

Discussion Questions

1. Categorize each law discussed in Chapter 7 according to the three goals and purposes of credit regulation: economic stability, consumer protection, and attainment of social goals.

2. What do you believe are the most important provisions of the Truth in Lending Act? Why did you choose the ones you did?

3. What is the main purpose of the Credit Card Issuance Act?

4. What are the main provisions of the Fair Credit Reporting Act?

5. Explain what you believe the Fair Credit Billing Act has attempted to accomplish.

6. What effect has the Equal Credit Opportunity Act had on you as a consumer?

7. What are the main purposes of the Home Mortgage Disclosure Act and the Community Reinvestment Act?

8. What did the Fair Debt Collection Practices Act and the Debt Collection Act attempt to accomplish?

9. Explain the main provisions of the Electronic Fund Transfer Act.

10. How did the DIDMCA and the Garn-St Germain Act affect the country's financial system?

11. What did the Competitive Equality Banking Act attempt to accomplish?

12. Explain the main provisions of the Fair Credit and Charge Card Disclosure Act.

13. Check with three financial institutions in your community and see what effect the Home Equity Loan Consumer Protection Act has had on their operations.

14. What effect has FIRREA had on the operations of savings and loan institutions in your community?

15. Discuss what is meant by the cash price–time price doctrine.

16. What is the status of the Uniform Consumer Credit Code in your state? Are there state laws with similar provisions in your state?

17. What is the Uniform Commercial Code?

Suggested Readings—Part II

Government Publications on Credit Laws and Credit Rights
Address: Consumer Information
P.O. Box 100
Pueblo, CO 81002
"Buying and Borrowing: Cash in On the Facts" (425R)
"Choosing A Credit Card" (587R)
"Fair Credit Reporting Act" (426R)
"Fair Debt Collection" (427R)
Address: Publication Services
Division of Support Services
Board of Governors
Federal Reserve System
Washington, DC 20551

"Consumer Handbook to Credit Protection Laws"
"What Truth in Lending Means to You"
"How to File a Consumer Credit Complaint"
"The Equal Credit Opportunity Act and Age"
"The Equal Credit Opportunity Act and Women"
"The Equal Credit Opportunity Act and Doctors, Lawyers, and Small Retailers"
"The Equal Credit Opportunity Act and Credit Rights in Housing"
"Fair Credit Billing"
"Truth in Leasing"
"If You Use a Credit Card"
"Alice in Debitland: Consumer Protections and the Electronic Fund Transfer Act"

Bibliography

Adler, Jane. "The FCRA's Sudden Makeover." *Credit Card Management,* December 1996, p. 74.

Allen, Catherine A. "Smart Cards: Impact on Financial Services Strategies for Payment and Virtual Banking." *Credit World,* March/April 1996, p. 24.

Brugger, John C. "Neither Snow . . . Nor Rain . . . Nor Credit Card Theft." *Credit World,* November/December 1995, p. 14.

Evanoff, Douglas D. and Lewis M. Segal. "CRA and Fair Lending Regulations: Resulting Trends in Mortgage Lending." *Economic Perspectives,* Federal Reserve Bank of Chicago, November/December 1996, p. 19.

Frank, John N. "How Rewarding Are Rewards Cards?" *Credit Card Management,* June 1996, p. 24.

Good, Barbara A. "The Credit Union Industry—An Overview." *Economic Commentary,* Federal Reserve Bank of Cleveland, May 15, 1996.

Kaplan, Jeffrey M. "Corporate Ethics/Compliance Programs: The New State of the Art." *Credit World,* March/April 1995, p. 9.

Linnen, Beth M. "Dressing Up the Store Card." *Credit Card Management,* March 1996, p. 40. (Credit card enhancements)

Lowe, Janet and David E. Whiteside. "No Longer on the Fringe." *Collections and Credit Risk,* July 1996, p. 53. (Pawnbrokers, etc.)

Middleton, Martha. "Fighting Fraudulent Applications." *Collections & Credit,* April 1996, p. 53.

Middleton, Martha. "Reforming the Reforms." *Collections and Credit Risk,* January 1996, p. 23.

Morris, Trisha. "Multicultural Home Buyers Create New Business Opportunities." *Credit World,* July/August 1996, p. 17.

Punch, Linda. "An Encore for an Old Fraud Problem?" *Credit Card Management,* July 1996, p. 38.

Rutledge, Gary. "Taming the Fraud Monster." *Credit World,* September/October 1996, p. 10.

Sherry, Linda. "Debit Cards Can Be Convenient—If You Know the Rules." *Credit World,* March/April 1996, p. 30.

Skouby, Larry D. "Fair Lending & Discrimination." *Credit World,* March/April 1995, p. 24.

"Smart Cards 101." *Credit Card Management,* April 1996, p. 22.

"The Big Score For Mortgage Scoring." *Collections and Credit Risk,* January 1996, p. 9.

Internet Sites

http://www.smartcrd.com
Answers to frequently asked questions about Smart Cards
http://www.fanniemae.com
Fannie Mae

http://www.hud.gov
Department of Housing and Urban Development (FHA home page and mortgage limits)
http://www.va.gov
Veterans home loan guarantees

MANAGEMENT AND ANALYSIS OF CONSUMER CREDIT

8

MANAGEMENT AND PROMOTION OF CONSUMER CREDIT

Learning Objectives

After studying this chapter, you should be able to:

- Explain the need for sound credit management practices in attaining credit department goals.
- Discuss the differences and similarities in managing credit functions in retail, cash, and service credit departments.
- Explain the use of credit policies, rules, and procedures.
- Discuss the advantages and disadvantages of different methods of organizing a credit department.
- Describe the importance of developing control measures in credit management activities.
- List and describe important professional associations for consumer credit managers.
- Discuss the need for additional credit customers and the sources for obtaining them.
- Describe the marketing mix which combines product, price, place, and promotion in credit management operations.

The next four chapters deal with the management and analysis of consumer credit. In Part I, the different types of credit were outlined along with the universal steps involved in promoting, investigating, and extending credit—both consumer and business credit. The credit management process, discussed in Chapter 2, involves promoting credit, screening applications, investigating and evaluating risk, controlling the accounts, and collections. The credit management process is summarized in Exhibit 8–1.

Exhibit 8–1

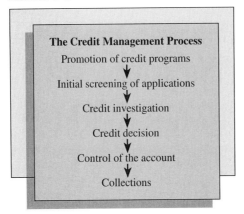

The Credit Management Process

Promotion of credit programs
↓
Initial screening of applications
↓
Credit investigation
↓
Credit decision
↓
Control of the account
↓
Collections

Chapter 8 begins a detailed consideration of this process in consumer credit. We will look more carefully at the goals and activities of the consumer credit manager. We will consider some of the unique aspects of managing consumer credit and discuss how the credit manager develops guidelines and procedures to help reach these goals.

This chapter will also look at the first step in the credit management process: promotion of credit programs. Retail credit programs present a unique situation since they are often a part of the overall retail promotion programs that attempt to encourage the sale of goods and services offered by a firm. By offering "easy credit terms," a firm can sell more appliances, automobiles, and other goods to customers who lack the cash to buy the items outright. Once the credit plans are in place, however, the credit program itself becomes a marketable product since a larger credit customer base will often bring about more efficient operations, more sales, and improved income. Cash lending institutions, of course, must also promote their credit programs heavily since lending money is their basic trade.

The Need for Sound Credit Management

The activity we call management basically involves attaining goals and accomplishing work through the efforts of others. Chapter 2 outlined the goals of both consumer and business credit managers. Credit managers, even those who work alone in small businesses, need to develop methods to accomplish the goals listed in Exhibit 8–2. If other workers are involved, the credit manager must certainly develop credit management guidelines that will ensure consistent, effective activities. Even a sole business owner, however, needs to concentrate on credit-related activities to be successful.

The need for sound credit management policies and procedures differs little among the three types of consumer credit: retail credit, cash credit, and service credit. Sometimes

Exhibit 8–2

Goals of the Credit Manager

- Increase sales revenue.
- Train and supervise other employees.
- Control operating costs and expenses.
- Monitor and control the volume of receivables.
- Reduce collection expenses and bad debt.
- Cooperate with other departments.
- Maintain good customer relations.

---

credit policies and other management activities are more visible in larger credit departments and within financial institutions because of the need for communication with many credit workers. In a very small business, credit policies may not be written down, but they must exist nevertheless in successful operations. One of the leading causes of failures among small businesses is the inability of the manager to deal with accounts receivable and the credit-related aspects of selling goods and services. Certainly, the management of credit is important in most lines of trade that accept more than cash payments.

Retail Credit Management

Credit management in retail credit is often a part of a large effort to sell goods and services. Ads may emphasize that "easy credit plans are available" to increase customer traffic and sales. In the credit area, the emphasis is often on speed in making decisions, authorizing purchases, and moving products with credit operations comprising only a part of the process. Indeed, if enough profit is being made on the items being sold, additional risk may be acceptable among those approved for credit use. An organized approach to gathering information, conducting investigations, and controlling receivables is still very important and good credit management activities are necessary.

Managing Cash Lending Activities

Cash lending also requires sound credit management practices. Financial institutions are often larger and typically have very visible, well-established policies and procedures. Smaller branches, such as those of a consumer finance company, may be staffed with only a few credit workers, but the credit policies are usually dictated by the larger corporation that controls the lending processes. The type of customer sought and the kinds of loans that are made often determine the credit management policies and practices that will be used. A lender that accepts higher than normal risks, for example, may conduct more extensive investigations or react more quickly to a past-due payment.

Service Credit Management

The essential difference in service credit management is that credit programs and credit customers are often considered undesirable. In retail credit management, the various credit programs were originally implemented to increase sales. Once the programs were in place, however, an ever-expanding customer base is desired to lower costs and perhaps enhance profit from additional revenue from finance charges. In service credit, however, the provider is obligated by tradition and practice to give the customer additional time to pay. A dentist or doctor who requires cash payments at the end of every customer visit will soon run out of patients. Especially in the medical arenas, the existence of third-party payers, e.g., insurance companies, has brought on the common practice of service credit. Competition continues to encourage service providers to emphasize their credit programs, however, as they discover that the credit program itself will increase business. Plumbers, auto repair shops, lawyers, accountants, and many others who provide services to customers need to carefully consider their credit management activities and provide effective guidelines.

CREDIT MANAGEMENT ACTIVITIES

Developing Policies, Rules, and Procedures

A credit manager should develop various policies or guidelines to help achieve the goals of the credit department. These policies are used by the credit manager and others to make decisions and determine which actions to take. Policies help ensure consistency and are designed to promote the most efficient, profitable activities. These policies are guidelines, however, and the specific characteristics of an individual case may dictate that alternative actions be taken. The policies allow the credit manager to delegate many routine activities and, unless an unusual case arises, credit workers can generally carry on the required functions. Some policies, rules, and procedures are dictated by credit laws and must be carefully adhered to in order to prevent problems in compliance.

Credit Policy

A **credit policy** is a written policy statement used by a credit department to define the types of credit offered and to state the basic characteristics of an acceptable risk. The credit policy will explain the types of credit plans or loans offered. It may define what the credit department views as an acceptable purpose for credit and outline the types of customers it seeks. The policy should define acceptable credit terms and describe satisfactory collateral if appropriate. In many respects, the credit policy will outline the mission and basic purpose for the credit department. See Chapter 17 for a more detailed description of writing a business credit policy.

Investigation Policy

An **investigation policy** is a written guideline to help credit investigators gather sufficient information to arrive at a sound decision. The investigation policy should define the credit qualities that are considered important and establish minimum investigation standards. The policy might require, for example, that residence histories be verified for a minimum of two years. The policy might also require that credit bureau reports be obtained on all customers and that salaries be verified by contact with employers. The actual details, of course, will vary depending on the type and volume of credit offered by the individual credit department.

Collection Policy

A **collection policy** is a guideline to help credit workers decide which collection devices to employ and how to proceed when attempting to collect amounts owed to the firm. We will learn in later chapters that effective collection utilizes various tools, techniques, and devices to convince customers to pay as agreed. The collection policy will typically cover the various collection stages and devices and indicate how long an account will stay in each stage. If a payment is 10 days past due, for example, a telephone call might be made. If the payment becomes 120 days past due, however, the policy might require that legal action be initiated to collect the debt. The collection policy will also outline acceptable methods to use and indicate how the department wants certain activities accomplished.

Rules

Rules are statements that outline prohibited activities and define acceptable behavior. In the credit department, many rules are established to ensure compliance with various state and federal laws. A rule, for example, might prohibit a collector from making a telephone call to a customer at unusual hours to ensure that customers are not harassed as determined by law. Rules might also require that applications be taken for every customer that inquires about a credit account to help the department comply with the Equal Credit Opportunity Act. Generally, there can be no variation nor departure from the actions outlined in rules.

Procedures

Procedures are step-by-step instructions that are designed to bring about a consistent course of action when performing a task. Procedures will be established for crediting an account with a payment, for example. Other procedures will involve adding a new customer to a database or establishing a new file. These instructions ensure that complex actions are completed with a minimum of errors and that specific guidelines are adhered to.

Major Credit Management Activities

- Developing policy.
  - Credit policy.
  - Investigation policy.
  - Collection policy.
- Outlining rules of behavior.
- Establishing procedures.

Organizing the Credit Department

Organizing the credit department requires that the credit manager decide who does what duties in the department. **Organizing** is a management function that involves grouping activities and assigning them to individual employees. Obviously, a very small credit department will not require extensive organization since only a few workers handle all the activities. In larger departments, however, organization is essential in order to capitalize on the talents of the employees and to ensure that the department goals are attained.

Functional Organization

Organizing a department on a functional basis means that different workers, or groups of workers, will be assigned a specific function for all customers. For example, a credit department might have a collections department to work with past-due customers. An investigations department would conduct all the credit investigations for credit applications. The advantage of a functional approach is to develop expertise in a particular activity among those assigned to this function, e.g., the workers become collections specialists. The functional organization also allows the firm to utilize a worker's best skills in a specific area or activity.

Customer Organization

A customer-based method of organizing a department will assign selected customers to different credit workers. For example, an alphabetical approach may be used, with all customers whose last names begin with letters A through F assigned to a particular employee. This employee may take the application, conduct the investigation, make the decision, and be responsible for collecting the payments from the same customer. This method of organization is especially useful in training and developing employees, since they are becoming cross-trained. They operate as generalists, rather than as specialists, and learn to do many more things. They are also more difficult to replace, however, and they may not be able to accomplish every activity in the most efficient manner.

Most firms use a combination of organization methods. Some departments may be organized on a geographic basis, for example, with different branches spread throughout a community. Within each branch, the basic organization might be on a product basis, i.e., consumer loans and business loans. The consumer lending department might be organized on a functional or customer basis described above. The credit manager must balance the advantages and disadvantages of each method to decide which is best for the overall task at hand.

Developing Control Measures

An important part of any activity is the development of methods for watching the progress toward a goal. **Controlling** is a management activity that involves developing standards for measuring progress, monitoring the activity, and finding ways to get the activity back on track if a deviation from the standard is detected. The efforts of individual employees must be appraised and training may be required to enhance skills. New methods or technology may improve performance in a particular area. Numerous statistics are often gathered about collection results, the number of applications taken and accepted, and the expenses involved in operating a credit department. Basically, the credit department needs to know if progress toward the goals outlined above is occurring. Some of these control measures will be discussed in later chapters.

PROFESSIONAL ASSOCIATIONS FOR CONSUMER CREDIT MANAGERS

The credit management task is very challenging and complex. As discussed in Chapter 2, various professional organizations and groups exist that help promote a particular profession or occupation. Numerous professional associations have been established to provide education, services, and other activities that will help credit managers improve the results of their efforts. These organizations represent a cooperative effort to enhance each profession and to help the members do a better job. Described below are some of the more important associations related to consumer credit.

International Credit Association (http://www.ica-credit.org)

In 1912, retail credit managers recognized the need for closer cooperation among themselves and with the organizations that furnished consumer credit data. As a result, the Retail Credit Men's National Association was formed. In 1927, the name of this trade association for retail credit granters was changed to the National Retail Credit Association. The focus of the association continued to expand until it grew to cover all facets of the credit industry. Today this association is known as the International Credit Association (ICA) and is located in St. Louis, Missouri. Through its local and district associations, it conducts a continuing program of education and service for the personnel of credit-related companies. Its membership is comprised of approximately 9,000 credit executives located throughout the world and representing a broad cross section of credit industries. The ICA has identified three primary concerns and strategic directions for the 1990s: consumer education, industry education and certification, and legislation.

Consumer Education
The Challenge 2000 program is administered by the Education Foundation, which was established by the International Credit Association in 1985 as a nonprofit educational organization. The Challenge 2000 program is a comprehensive effort to deliver quality credit education to high school students and targeted adult populations. A series of initiatives has been developed to train high school teachers, provide credit personnel as resources, and develop useful training materials.

Industry Education and Certification
The ICA offers members a variety of educational opportunities: local association meetings and seminars, district conferences, international conferences, and industry forums on critical issues. The ICA has also published educational materials that enhance the skills of credit workers in all areas of the credit industry.

The ICA provides a certification program administered by the Society of Certified Credit Executives (SCCE). This division of the ICA offers four different certifications for credit professionals at different stages in their careers. Level 3 requires that the applicant pass a comprehensive certification examination.

Legislation

The ICA monitors proposed legislation that is likely to impact the credit industry. The association will lobby Congress and will work to ensure that the voices of credit executives are heard and that the resulting laws will address the needs of the industry and consumers.

Credit Professionals International (http://www.scsn.net/users/cpi)

Credit Professionals International is primarily a club organization with more than 250 local associations. The focus of the association is on credit education and peer contacts. Its primary purpose is to develop a closer contact among those working in the credit industry. More than 9,000 members have joined, and they represent a variety of credit professions.

Retail Merchants Association

An organization of retail credit personnel is the National Retail Merchants Association's Credit Management Division. This association includes department, specialty, dry goods, and apparel stores among its members. Since 1934, when it was established, the Credit Management Division of the association has furnished a special research service to the credit managers of member stores. Through meetings, surveys, and publications, this division constantly works to keep its members up to date on new developments and changing techniques in the retail credit field.

American Bankers Association (http://www.aba.com)

The American Bankers Association (ABA), organized in 1875, is a national organization representing about 90 percent of the nation's banking assets. This association has carried out a diverse program designed to meet the many different needs for education as a basis for career development in the banking field. As part of the association's educational program, the Consumer Credit Division of the ABA has prepared a variety of manuals on the important aspects of installment credit policies and procedures. Many banks also find that they need further assistance. As a result, ABA offers a national Consumer Credit Conference where bankers exchange ideas and information regarding their consumer credit programs and procedures.

The American Bankers Association also has been active in establishing, developing, and promoting an off-duty banking educational program offered by the American Institute of Banking (AIB). The institute sponsored its first classes in 1902 and was the first formal educational program of its type directed toward the education of a large adult group.

Hundreds of additional educational programs for bankers are available each year, covering many areas and carrying a variety of titles. A number of these programs are called *banking schools,* and the American Bankers Association maintains an up-to-date listing of resident banking schools, classified by broad category. Some state banking associations sponsor banking schools primarily designed for local bankers, while other associations concentrate on conferences, clinics, and other shorter programs.

The Institute of Financial Education
(http://www.theinstitute.com)

This organization is a nonprofit educational association aligned with the savings and loan industry. The Institute of Financial Education (IFE) offers classes and information in a variety of formats. Coursework is offered through correspondence study, in-company classes, or chapter classes. The IFE has identified eight individual career path award programs with specific course requirements, including: teller, senior teller, financial counselor, financial services supervisor, branch manager, banking operations specialist, lending associate, and lending specialist.

Credit Union National Association, Inc.
(http://www.cuna.org)

The Credit Union National Association, Inc. (CUNA) is the national confederation of U.S. credit union leagues. It provides legislative, public relations, research, educational, and developmental support for the national credit union movement. By joining a league, credit unions become affiliated with CUNA. CUNA also offers a wide variety of educational opportunities, including schools and conferences, educational materials, and correspondence courses.

American Collectors Association, Inc.
(http://www.collector.com)

The American Collectors Association, Inc. (ACA) was organized in 1939 and is an international organization of professional collection services. It is the world's largest organization of debt collection services. Its international voluntary membership serves more than 11,000 communities throughout the United States, Canada, and over 100 other nations.

   Membership in ACA signals clients that their collection agency subscribes to high operating standards. ACA members serve credit grantors by contacting consumers with past-due accounts and counseling them on ways to repay their debts. ACA is organized into several departments, including public affairs, public relations, education, communications, membership, management resources, insurance, and sales. ACA offers its members a discount long-distance program, and it also has specialized divisions for healthcare collections and check collections. Another association, the International Association of Billing Services, Inc., is owned by ACA. Its members are companies that provide billing of current account services to their clients.

   ACA publishes *Collector* magazine, which updates members monthly on developments in the collection industry. The ACA education program consists of separate schools. Each school is designed to be presented as a one-day seminar so that students can improve their knowledge without a great time commitment. Some schools also are available as half-day seminars in conjunction with unit meetings. The schools are divided into three groups: collector track schools, sales track schools, and management track schools. The education department also offers a number of award-winning, self-paced training programs designed for use in the collection office.

Associated Credit Bureaus, Inc.
(http://www.acb-credit.com)

The Associated Credit Bureaus, Inc. (ACB) is the national association of retail credit bureaus. It offers its members such widespread benefits as interbureau reporting rosters, standardized reporting forms, trade publications, national public relations, educational services, credit bureau research, special information reporting services, and annual meetings and conventions.

Other Associations

In May 1971, consumer finance companies, sales finance companies, and industrial banks, through their respective trade associations, joined forces to become the American Financial Services Association. This organization has established a school for the personnel of its member firms; the school is held at Marquette University and is known as the Consumer Credit Institute. Another financial association is the Consumer Bankers Association. Like the American Financial Services Association, the Consumer Bankers Association has established its School of Consumer Banking to raise the standards of credit management among its members.

The Credit Research Center
(http://www.purdue.edu/UNS...Research_Center.html)

The Credit Research Center (CRC) was established at Purdue University in 1974. The center was launched with the stated purpose of compiling, analyzing, summarizing, and disseminating information affecting all aspects of the consumer credit industry. The four major directions for the center's activities are to:

1. Look into the future issues of "consumerism."
2. Identify strategic problems common to various segments of the industry.
3. Provide hard, impartial research data and analysis for responsible decision making by credit grantors, legislators, and the courts.
4. Broadly communicate research findings relevant to important credit problems.

MARKETING CREDIT PROGRAMS

Marketing is an essential activity for any business. **Marketing** is the process that facilitates the movement of goods and services from the producer to the ultimate consumer. As we will learn later, there are four basic components to marketing: product, price, place, and promotion. Credit programs are no different from any other

Exhibit 8–3   **Newspaper Ad Promoting Use of Credit**

Introducing at all
Jubilee Foods...

• MASTERCARD   • VISA   • DISCOVER   • TYME

NOW YOU CAN PAY FOR YOUR GROCERIES WITHOUT WRITING A CHECK OR USING CASH.

USE YOUR MASTERCARD ON
•THURSDAY, OCTOBER 7 •FRIDAY, OCTOBER 8
•SATURDAY, OCTOBER 9 AND
**GET AN UNLIMITED 5% OFF OF YOUR
TOTAL FOOD BILL AT THE REGISTER!**

AT JUBILEE FOODS "YOU'RE GONNA LOVE WHAT WE HAVE INSTORE!"
SO CHECK OUT OUR OTHER GREAT FEATURES.

Source: Green Bay *Press Gazette*, October 6, 1993.

product or service. Once credit plans are established, businesses want to increase the number of users and customers.

Should Credit Customers Be Sought?

A basic question for many businesses concerns the desirability of more credit customers. Do the advantages outweigh the disadvantages? Credit operations generally result in greater costs, potential public relations problems, and cash flow problems. Cash lenders, of course, must constantly work to attract new borrowers since credit extension is the basic purpose for their existence. Retail and service firms can decide, however, whether to "push" or not to push credit programs. Exhibit 8–3 shows a newspaper ad promoting the use of credit run by a grocery store. Credit customers are often good customers, however, and they provide numerous benefits to the firm that is able to attract them.

Increase Sales Revenue

Credit customers generally spend more than cash customers. If people are short of funds immediately before payday, they will undoubtedly shop where they have established credit. Offering credit programs will also open up an entire market comprised of individuals willing to spend future income if they do not have available cash. Of course, overall profit will only increase if credit customers are carefully selected and if costs are controlled.

Sell Better-Quality Merchandise
Credit customers are also likely to buy better-quality goods since they are not restricted by the amount of cash available. In general, credit customers are less price conscious and are willing to spend more money. The purchase of better-quality goods will enhance profits, reduce returns and allowances for poor-quality items, and will improve overall customer satisfaction.

Enhance Customer Loyalty
Customers tend to develop loyalties to individual stores and lenders. They like to return to the places of business that know them. The additional knowledge that they are creditworthy, and that they have gained the approval that comes with opening a credit account, will only increase this loyalty. Credit customers are more likely to return and will do much of their business at establishments that have adopted credit programs.

Stabilize Cash Flow
Credit programs will help smooth out the ups and downs of cash flow. If a customer buys merchandise from a seller that utilizes its own credit program, the payments will stretch out for many months following the actual purchase. Seasonal variations in sales volume, e.g., large sales during Christmas, will be leveled as customers make payments in the months that follow. Credit users will often use credit cards and other programs to stabilize their own spending if they experience periods of reduced income.

Reduce Operational Costs
Once credit programs are established, a larger number of credit customers will often lower operational costs. An efficient, computerized credit authorization system, for example, can handle thousands of customers, and the cost per transaction will be lowered as more transactions occur. Overhead costs, wages and salaries of credit workers, and collection costs often increase more slowly than the growth in customers. Therefore, adding more customers will lower total costs.

Why Seek Credit Customers?

- Increase sales revenue.
- Sell better-quality merchandise.
- Enhance customer loyalty.
- Stabilize cash flow.
- Reduce operational costs.

Sources of Additional Credit Sales

Once a business has determined that additional credit sales and customers are desired, methods must be developed to market credit programs and promote increased credit volume. These sales will come from new customers, inactive credit customers, and active users.

New Customers

If more customers apply for and receive credit privileges, credit sales will likely increase. Whether the business firm makes cash loans, sells goods with installment contracts, or issues credit cards, new customers will result in greater credit volume. The sources of new customers include cash customers who have not used credit, potential customers living in your community, and new residents. Since credit plans are widely used, the addition of new customers often means convincing them that your program is somehow better than those they already have available to them. For example, you may need to convince a customer who already has three other credit cards, that your program is better and more desirable. Some customers will be new users. Methods should be developed to identify new residents in the community, newly married couples, and others who will be looking for their first ventures into credit use. Recently, general-purpose credit card issuers have been offering credit cards to college students. Even though students have minimal income in many cases, the card issuers set low credit lines and are willing to take additional risks in exchange for the opportunity to establish lifelong customer ties.

Inactive Customers

Many firms have approved credit accounts and loans for customers in the past who have stopped using the available credit. Perhaps a credit card account was established but the customer has not charged anything for several months. In this case, the issuer has already expended funds and energy in the approval process, so increased use is very desirable. These customers may have been tempted by other firms' offers and have been drawn away from your credit programs. The challenge, of course, is to regain their confidence and loyalty.

Active Customers

The customers that are currently using your credit programs can often increase their use if they believe it is in their best interests. A loan customer can perhaps consolidate other bills by increasing the loan amount with your firm and paying off the other accounts. A general-purpose credit card or bank card can also be used more heavily by many customers. If they carry several different bank cards in their wallet, perhaps they can be convinced to reach for one rather than another. Control measures must be used, of course, to prevent a credit customer from extending account balances beyond a reasonable amount. Many active customers, however, can be safely trusted with more credit outstanding.

The Marketing Mix

The marketing mix of product, price, place, and promotion will help a firm analyze its approach to enhance credit sales or credit program use. The four P's represent a simplified structure for looking at the complex mix of ingredients involved in marketing products and services.

Product

The credit product is a more complicated concept than is often believed. The banker, for example, provides more than just a cash loan in most circumstances. The loan may be a home equity loan that results in additional tax deductions for the borrower. Perhaps the loan was made with less red tape, fewer expenses, or more speed. Even the addition of friendly service and the belief that the firm cares for the well-being of the customer will change the nature of the product offered. Each firm must carefully analyze what a particular group of customers is looking for. The same product might be marketed in different ways, by emphasizing different features, in an attempt to reach a particular segment of the market. Each product is a complex combination of features, services, and advantages. Once the firm understands what a particular group of customers needs, it can proceed with promoting its set of offerings.

Price

The price of many credit programs and products is fairly uniform. Given a specific risk profile, a customer can obtain a loan or credit account from many sources that all charge about the same amount. There are, of course, some variations. One credit card might carry a lower interest rate than others. A customer buying furniture from a high-volume retailer might be convinced that the credit is free even though the cost of the credit is included in the price of the merchandise. Home mortgage loans, however, vary little from one lender to another. In these cases, other parts of the marketing mix must be emphasized.

Place

This consideration involves the channels used to distribute the product and services. A firm might build several branch offices around the community to improve access for customers. A credit card issuer will make credit applications available at many locations where they will be easily seen and perhaps picked up. A telephone application will streamline the process and make the products offered more attractive. Part of the marketing process involves looking at ways to improve the distribution of the good or services offered.

Promotion

Promotion is the combination of factors that convinces a customer to buy or take advantage of your particular credit plan. This activity is especially important in those industries where product, place, and price are not much different. Methods must be established to draw customers to your place of business.

Advertising is generally required to tell customers about your goods and services. A vast array of advertising media is available and includes printed materials, direct mail, billboards, radio and television ads, and others. Advertising informs potential customers of new products and provides many useful educational functions. Its basic purpose is to get customers to do something or buy something. Exhibit 8–4 shows a direct mail advertisement for a general-purpose credit card.

Ехнівіт 8–4

Only the GE Rewards Card rewards you with guaranteed savings* and much, much more.

Everybody likes to save money. And that's just what you'll do with the GE Rewards MasterCard. We guarantee it! When you receive the GE Rewards MasterCard, you'll get $250 worth of coupons right away—and another $250 worth every three months. That's $1,000 worth of savings opportunities good at thousands of GE Rewards Partners' retail locations.

The rewards keep coming...with 2% back.

In addition to your $1,000 in savings coupons, you'll receive 2% back in GE Rewards Checks on purchases made with your card. Rewards Checks are good for purchases at GE Rewards Partners. So the more you spend with your GE Rewards Card, the more you'll earn!

No annual fee

Unlike other credit cards that charge from $20 to $40 in annual fees, the GE Rewards MasterCard has no annual fee.

The purchasing power of MasterCard

Accepted at over 10 million locations worldwide, your GE Rewards Card will save you money on shopping, dining, traveling and entertaining. And you'll enjoy the convenience of 24-hour ATM access and cash advances from over 200,000 financial institutions worldwide.

And guaranteed savings* from a name you trust!

You trust GE to deliver quality products and superior service. And now you can be sure the GE Rewards MasterCard will save you money through the exclusive GE Rewards programs!

To apply for your GE Rewards MasterCard, simply sign and return the enclosed application today—and start making shopping more rewarding with major savings, guaranteed.

Questions? Call 1-800-GE REWARD

We bring good things to life.

* If, after the first 12 months of cardmembership, you find that you haven't saved money by using the GE Rewards Checks and coupons, call us and we'll close your account and send you $10–no questions asked. Certain conditions and limitations apply to GE Rewards Checks and coupons. Please see the coupons and Program Guidelines (which you'll receive shortly after you receive your credit card) for complete details.

Source: Reprinted with permission from Monogram Bank, Cincinnati, OH.

Personal selling is very important in contemporary business settings. Although some businesses employ professional sales representatives, all employees must develop a sales-oriented approach to their jobs. They must be prepared to increase customer purchases by pointing out other products or increasing product use among qualified customers. A bank customer mentions to a teller that they are taking a trip and the teller proceeds to sell traveler's checks. A customer calls a loan officer to ask for a few extra days to make a payment since the customer's automobile has broken down. The loan officer immediately invites the customer to apply for another loan to purchase an automobile. Sometimes these efforts are referred to as "cross-selling," which involves looking for opportunities to sell other services offered by the firm. These sales opportunities are numerous, but must be recognized as opportunities by those involved.

Marketing Mix

- Product
- Price
- Place
- Promotion
  - Advertising
  - Personal selling
  - Incentives
  - Public relations

Incentives may be used to promote additional sales or credit use. A retailer might advertise additional price reductions if credit customers use their credit accounts or credit cards. Special "back-door sales" might be offered, when only credit customers are invited to shop during times when the store is normally closed. Some firms offer small items as gifts if the credit user charges at least one purchase during a given time period. Currently, a rash of rebate offers is available from different general-purpose credit cards tied to manufacturers of large ticket items. Rebates on automobiles, airline tickets, and appliances are offered which represent a small percentage of the total amounts charged on the general-purpose credit card.

Developing good public relations programs is another part of effective sales promotion. Many credit institutions encourage their employees to become involved in community organizations. Many also donate time and money to charitable causes and worthy community projects. The image of a particular firm or credit grantor is an important part of the overall marketing task.

Important Terms

collection policy   153
controlling   154
credit policy   152
cross-selling   164
investigation policy   152

marketing   158
organizing   154
procedures   153
rules   153

Discussion Questions

1. What is credit management and what goals does a credit manager attempt to attain?

2. How does the importance of credit management activities differ among retail, cash, and service credit operations?

3. List and describe the three primary types of credit policies that should be established by the credit manager.

4. What are rules and procedures? Give examples of each that might be found in a credit department.

5. Describe the different ways a credit department might be organized. What are the advantages and disadvantages of each?

6. What does developing control measures involve? Give examples.

7. List and describe several professional associations available to consumer credit managers. What are these associations trying to accomplish in most instances?

8. What advantages do credit customers provide a firm or business?

9. Discuss the various sources of increased credit sales in a typical firm.

10. What are the four P's found in the marketing mix?

11. Describe the concept of a credit product and discuss some of the features that may be important to prospective customers.

12. What is involved in determining "place" and the methods of distribution of a product or service?

13. What are four aspects of sales promotion and describe how different promotion techniques are used in the field of credit.

Case Problem—
Cross-Selling Bank Products and Services

Betty Stevens stops by the bank today to pick up some cash for a short trip the Stevens family will be taking this weekend. They are traveling to a college in a community a few hundred miles away that their son, Robert, is considering attending next fall. Mrs. Stevens comments that the college is expensive, but they will try to help their son with the expenses. She has stopped by to pick up a few hundred dollars to use during their travels.

You are the person Betty Stevens has approached at the bank. Make a list of other bank products or services that you could mention to Mrs. Stevens for the trip and for Robert's attendance at college next fall. Describe some of the features and benefits for each product or service you could mention.

Check with a local banker to see if he or she can add anything to your list.

The Consumer Credit Investigation

Learning Objectives

After studying this chapter, you should be able to:

- Identify the credit qualities that should be investigated.
- Outline the information the credit applicant supplies to the credit analyst.
- Summarize the advantages and disadvantages of direct inquiry.
- Discuss the information supplied from in-file facts.
- Explain the differences between facts and opinions.
- Point out the importance of economic conditions in decision making.
- Explain the differences between investigation and verification.

A **credit investigation** is a series of steps undertaken to verify information provided in an application for credit and to determine how the customer has handled past financial obligations as an aid in making a sound credit decision. It is not an activity to satisfy curiosity. It has a much more immediate and practical purpose. Credit analysts must ask themselves what they need to know in order to make a proper credit decision. The extent of the investigation should be governed by the degree of certainty necessary for a proper decision.

At all times credit executives also must weigh the value of additional information about a credit prospect against the cost of obtaining such information. They are faced on the one hand with needing sufficient information from which to make valid decisions. On the other hand they must pay the cost of acquiring that information. Credit managers must carefully decide when they have enough information from the viewpoint of completeness, accuracy, and cost. It is a continuing problem to determine when sufficient information has been obtained in each credit investigation.

FACTS OR OPINIONS

Credit investigators must keep in mind that references, informants, and credit reporting agencies do not create credit information. Credit information is created only by consumers through their conduct and activities. Such information becomes credit information when it can be used to predict a credit applicant's future behavior. Credit information is important when, if known, it would influence a credit decision.

Some information will be fact and some will be opinion. A **fact** is information that has been objectively verified as real information. For example, an applicant's prior history of being late with 50 percent of payments on a new TV set is fact. It could be verified by reviewing dates of payments received. An **opinion** is a belief or conclusion that is not substantiated by proof or positive knowledge. For instance, a statement that the applicant "does not make payments on a regular basis" is an opinion unless it is supported with true data. Opinions may rest on facts or prejudice or imagination. An opinion may be soundly based on objective facts and be the result of careful and logical analysis of the situation. It may be also be based on prejudice or limited information.

Credit managers who substitute the opinions of others for their own judgment have permitted these outsiders to become credit managers for their departments and have themselves become merely credit clerks. The use of opinions may also result in illegal discrimination prohibited by current legislation. Such opinions, soundly based or not, do affect the quality of the credit performance expected and so have a place in the analysis. But these opinions should be regarded as simply a category of facts. In the analysis they should be weighed in the same way as any other factual category.

When making a credit investigation, the credit executive should do so in a manner designed to collect facts rather than opinions. Questions should be phrased to induce informants to reply factually rather than with loosely stated opinions or judgments. Informants should be asked questions for which they are likely to know the answers. Asking informants questions about things they are not likely to know invites opinion rather than fact and also tempts informants not to reply at all.

WHAT TO INVESTIGATE

On the question of what to investigate the custom is to recite the C's of credit analysis. These so-called C's of credit have been cited by thousands of credit managers and have been discussed over and over again in textbooks, articles, and speeches. The more common approach is to discuss four C's of credit: character, capacity, capital, and conditions. Other C's are sometimes cited, however, such as collateral and common sense. These C's help the credit manager complete a quick mental check to determine if any category of information has been overlooked. More specific credit qualities also need to be investigated, however, before most credit decisions can be made.

Character

Character is an intangible sum of personal attributes related to integrity and the moral strength of a person. The elements entering into character are concerned with personal habits and attitudes such as drinking, gambling, and so forth. Character also may be revealed by business or professional conduct, such as payment of obligations, tendency to make unwarranted claims or to return goods without cause, attitude toward obligations, speculative tendencies, and respect for the rights of others. **Credit character** is best described as the *willingness* of a credit customer to pay his/her payments as agreed.

Character is an inward thing that probably cannot be measured or appraised exactly by even those most intimately associated with an individual. Certainly, it is difficult for a credit manager to determine and evaluate character. Nevertheless, the credit investigation can come closer to interpreting this quality correctly when it asks for specifics that can be verified. "How has this individual paid a bill with you?" is a better question than "What is the individual's credit reputation?" It becomes an even better question by asking the year the account was opened, the balance now owing, the highest recent credit, and the number of times the account has been past due. Attitude toward obligations is better revealed by a question asking whether the person makes unjustified claims or acts in accordance with the contract than by general questions about attitude toward obligations. Evidence that is largely factual can be gathered about the payment record of an applicant and is generally the best predictor of credit character.

Capacity

Capacity is the *ability* of a credit applicant to pay a specific dollar obligation when it is due. Measuring the capacity of an applicant generally involves investigating income and employment. The ability of an applicant to pay as agreed is also determined by the level of expenditures and other indebtedness. An applicant, for example, can have insufficient income to cover existing debts. This may be because income is too low or debt levels are too high. Income must also be sustainable and predictable. Capacity will be threatened if an individual becomes unemployed or if income is significantly reduced.

Capital

Capital is the financial strength of a credit applicant, primarily determined by the level of reserve assets. These assets may be tangible, such as savings account balances, or they may be intangible. An intangible asset might be the ability to find another job quickly because of specialized skills and knowledge. These assets, in either case, are available for the credit applicant to rely on if financial adversity strikes. If individuals become unemployed, for example, they will continue to make credit payments as agreed by drawing funds from their savings account. They might also quickly find another job.

Collateral

Collateral is the assignment of ownership rights in property in the event a credit customer does not pay. The collateral, often referred to as the security for a loan or credit obligation, may be the item being purchased using credit or property already owned. For example, a borrower who already owes an expensive automobile may ask for a bank loan secured by the automobile. If the borrower does not repay the loan, the bank will have ownership rights in the automobile. The bank will, of course, want to make sure that the automobile is indeed owned by the person and is not being used as collateral on any previous loans.

Conditions

Conditions is a credit analysis category that looks at how the applicant fits into the economic system and how economic events will affect the ability and willingness to pay. A construction worker, for example, should be asked to explain what he or she does during the winter months to maintain income. Employees destined for layoffs may have reduced income and reduced willingness to pay if they blame society for their misfortunes. Age, obsolete work skills, lack of education, and other conditions affect the ability of an applicant to maintain income.

Common Sense

Common sense is simply good judgment. This credit analysis tool is normally mentioned after an account has been determined to be an uncollectible bad debt. The credit analyst will then remark that common sense should have been used to avoid the credit relationship in the first place. Relatively simple observations and calculations may often demonstrate that a loan or credit account should not be created. Many times it is the responsibility of the credit grantor to determine that a credit extension is not appropriate. Some borrowers who lack control of their spending habits will continue borrowing up to the point where no more credit is allowed. Credit analysts may have to substitute their own common sense for the borrowers'.

C's of Credit Analysis

- Character
- Capacity
- Capital
- Collateral
- Conditions
- Common Sense

Relative Importance of the C's of Credit Analysis

In consumer credit, the credit analyst gives more weight to credit character and capacity than to factors that reflect an applicant's capital. Most credit managers would rather receive payments from a willing and able applicant than depend on repossession. **Repossession** is the legal process used to reclaim security or collateral in the event of nonpayment of a loan. Acquiring capital through repossession and other channels can be difficult, expensive, and may adversely affect the image of the credit grantor. Even though the legal means to collect an account exists, the best outcome arises from granting credit to applicants who possess the willingness and ability to pay.

Most credit analysts will identify character as the most important of the C's of credit analysis. If borrowers have the willingness to pay, they will overcome impaired capacity and will eventually pay the account in full. If borrowers lack credit character, however, they can often avoid or slow down payment even if sufficient capacity is present. Again, legal channels for collection often exist, but the willingness to pay as agreed is the most important quality in seeking credit clients.

CREDIT QUALITIES TO INVESTIGATE

The C's of credit analysis provide a general framework for the credit investigation. The credit manager must use a more specific list of credit qualities to investigate, however, if he or she needs to gather the facts required to make a good credit decision. Credit applications are used to collect detailed information that helps credit analysts evaluate the risk involved in lending funds or opening accounts for applicants. Exhibit 9–1 gives an example of the questions asked on an application form of a retail department store chain. These credit qualities are related to the C's of credit but represent more specific concerns. The following credit qualities are often considered to be important in the risk analysis process.

Most large firms process a tremendous volume of credit requests. They may use a credit scoring system as a preliminary screening device and turn down applicants who do not attain some minimum score. **Credit scoring systems** are statistically based systems that assign points to characteristics reported on the application and on the credit bureau report. Many of the credit qualities listed below are included in typical credit scoring systems. For example, more points would be added to an applicant's total for being employed at the same job for 10 years than for 1 year. Other characteristics are considered and the points are then totaled to determine the score for the credit applicant. If a certain score is not obtained, the applicant may be turned down without further investigation. Each firm using such a system will have its own schedule of assigning points and setting the number required for credit acceptance.

Many large volume credit grantors have computerized the credit scoring process. A data entry clerk inputs the application information into the computer system and the computer calculates a credit score. If a sufficient score is available, the computer may actually authorize a new account, assign a credit line, issue the credit card, and establish the recordkeeping files without further intervention by a credit analyst.

Credit scoring has limitations, however. Although preferred by many credit executives, it still is not a perfect predictor of creditworthiness. This topic will be discussed in more detail in connection with decision making in Chapter 11.

Payment Record

The most important point to consider here is not whether the consumer can pay but whether he or she *will* pay. Some individuals have the money available to meet credit payments, but they simply do not want to or will not let go of that dollar. Character thus plays a vital role.

Exhibit 9–1   **Application Form for a Department Store**

JBYRONS   **Application for Credit**   To find out about changes in the information in this application for credit you may call us at 1 (800) 821-1111.

FOR OFFICE USE ONLY

☐ **Individual Account** — Is based on your own creditworthiness. Complete sections A, B, C, E. You may designate one authorized user, for whose payments you will be responsible, by writing only his/her name and relationship in section D.

☐ **Joint Account** — Is based on the creditworthiness of both parties, and both will be responsible for payment. Complete sections A through E.

STORE   ASSOCIATE NO.   DATE

Section A – Tell us about yourself

LAST NAME   FIRST NAME   MIDDLE   SOCIAL SECURITY NO.   AGE

HOME ADDRESS   APT.   NO. OF DEPENDENTS (EXCLUDING SELF)

CITY   STATE   ZIP CODE   HOME PHONE ( )

☐ OWN   ☐ ROOM & BOARD   ☐ LIVE WITH PARENTS   ☐ RENT FURNISHED   ☐ RENT UNFURNISHED   ☐ MOBILE HOME   ☐ OTHER   TIME AT THIS ADDRESS YRS. MOS.   MONTHLY RENT OR MORTGAGE PAYMENT $

PREVIOUS HOME ADDRESS (IF LESS THAN 3 YEARS AT PRESENT ADDRESS)   TIME AT PREVIOUS ADDRESS YRS. MOS.

NAME AND ADDRESS OF NEAREST RELATIVE NOT LIVING WITH APPLICANT   RELATIVE HOME PHONE ( )

Section B – Tell us about your employment

BUSINESS OR EMPLOYER   TYPE OF BUSINESS ( )   BUSINESS PHONE ( )   EXT.

BUSINESS ADDRESS   CITY   STATE   ZIP CODE   EDUCATION ELEMENTARY   HIGH SCHOOL   COLLEGE   POST COLLEGE

POSITION OR TITLE   HOW LONG WITH THIS EMPLOYER YRS. MOS.   ANNUAL SALARY $

IF SELF EMPLOYED, PLEASE GIVE YOUR BUSINESS BANK REFERENCE AND ACCOUNT NUMBER

PREVIOUS BUSINESS/EMPLOYER (IF LESS THAN 3 YEARS AT THIS JOB)   HOW LONG YRS. MOS.   POSITION OR TITLE

OTHER INCOME: ALIMONY, CHILD SUPPORT, OR SEPARATE MAINTENANCE INCOME NEED NOT BE REVEALED IF YOU DO NOT WISH TO HAVE IT CONSIDERED AS A BASIS FOR REPAYING THIS OBLIGATION.   ANNUAL AMOUNT $ SOURCE

Section C – Tell us about your credit and banking relationships

BANK REFERENCES – NAMES OF BANKS AND BRANCH LOCATIONS   ACCOUNT NUMBERS

1.   CHECKING   SAVINGS NOW/MONEY MKT. (CHKG. & SAVINGS)

2.   CHECKING   SAVINGS NOW/MONEY MKT. (CHKG. & SAVINGS)

CREDIT REFERENCES – ACCOUNTS WITH DEPT. STORES, BANK CARDS, OIL COMPANIES   ACCOUNT NUMBERS   BALANCE

1. $

2. $

3. $

OUTSTANDING LOANS (NAME OF CREDITOR/CREDIT UNION/FINANCE COMPANY)

OTHER CREDIT REFERENCES   HAVE YOU EVER HAD ANOTHER JBYRONS ACCOUNT YES NO   ACCOUNT NUMBER (IF KNOWN)

Section D – Information regarding joint applicant or authorized user

LAST NAME   FIRST NAME   MIDDLE   SOCIAL SECURITY NO.   AGE

BUSINESS OR EMPLOYER   TYPE OF BUSINESS   BUSINESS PHONE ( )   EXT.

BUSINESS ADDRESS   CITY   STATE   ZIP CODE   EDUCATION ELEMENTARY   HIGH SCHOOL   COLLEGE   POST COLLEGE

POSITION OR TITLE   HOW LONG WITH THIS EMPLOYER YRS. MOS.   ANNUAL SALARY $

RELATIONSHIP TO APPLICANT   OTHER INCOME: ALIMONY, CHILD SUPPORT, OR SEPARATE MAINTENANCE INCOME NEED NOT BE REVEALED IF YOU DO NOT WISH TO HAVE IT CONSIDERED AS A BASIS FOR REPAYING THIS OBLIGATION.   ANNUAL AMOUNT $ SOURCE

Section E – Please sign below and on reverse side

I (We) understand that you may investigate my (our) credit record and may report information concerning the credit experience of the Account for individual and joint accountholders and authorized users to consumer reporting agencies and others.

If Applicant signs on behalf of Joint Applicant, Applicant represents that he or she is authorized to make this application and enter into this Agreement on behalf of Joint Applicant.

I (We) agree to terms of the **RETAIL INSTALMENT CREDIT AGREEMENT** on reverse side.

X   APPLICANT'S SIGNATURE   DATE

X   JOINT APPLICANT'S SIGNATURE   DATE

Source: Courtesy of JByrons

Payment record usually is considered the most important factor revealed in an investigation. It shows not only the manner of the consumer's payments and thus is important as a predictor of behavior, but it shows past payment habits as well. The credit investigation should seek facts about the types of account involved, the amount currently owed, the amount past due, the highest recent credit, and the manner of payment. The manner of payment should be stated specifically—pays in 30 to 60 days, pays in 90 days, and so forth. The adjectives prompt, good, and slow can have a variety of meanings; 60 to 90 days may be considered prompt by one firm and slow by another, depending on the type of account involved.

The date of the experience also should be established. This is especially important when an applicant has a varied record containing some derogatory data. It is important to know whether the profit and loss charge-off, the collection through judgment, or the repossession occurred in the past or is the most recent experience. Investigators draw a different conclusion if the bad record occurred some time ago and the applicant has a good current record than from the opposite sequence.

Income

Since most customer debts are to be paid from income, investigation of income is essential. A credit investigator should find out the amount of an applicant's income and its regularity, and should estimate the probability of its continuance. Income must be evaluated relative to the demands placed on it by individual or family needs and obligations. Such demands may include prior commitments, such as retail installment purchases, installment cash loans, home mortgage loans, contingent obligations that result from agreeing to be a comaker on another person's loan, and alimony payments.

There are differences of opinion as to how income should be defined. For instance, should investigators count overtime pay, unemployment compensation, bonuses, and profit-sharing plans?

Under the Equal Credit Opportunity Act of 1975, creditors cannot discount part-time income but can examine the probable continuity of an applicant's job. In addition, creditors can inquire about and consider whether obligations for alimony, child support, or maintenance payments affect an applicant's income. Likewise, creditors can ask to what extent an applicant is relying on alimony, child support, or maintenance payments to repay a debt. However, applicants must first be informed that such disclosure is unnecessary if they do not rely on such income to obtain the credit.

Indebtedness and Expenditures

An important part of the credit investigation involves trying to uncover the total outstanding debts, the amounts of payments, and other obligations that can drain income. Some credit investigators, for example, will ask credit applicants to provide a recent paycheck stub which shows information about employer deductions, credit union payments, and other obligations. A careful look at expenditure levels may be needed since applicants may not always realize they will have trouble making payments in a timely manner. The adequacy of income should be tested by comparing it with the individual's current contractual obligations and present expenditure pattern.

Employment

Employment is probably the principal source of income, so it should be investigated along with income. Employment information should include, at minimum, the name of the employer, the type of business, and the applicant's position. The credit analyst should be interested in a wide variety of information regarding employment. How long has the employee been employed? If less than three to five years, what is the prior employment history? Is he or she well thought of or likely to be terminated? Is the position full-time or part-time? How is the employee compensated? How much does the person earn and how stable is the income? How secure is the position and what is the outlook for the industry?

For self-employed applicants, information is often gathered from income tax records and, with permission, from accountants involved in the bookkeeping functions. Investigation of credit prospects who are self-employed should be especially extensive, since applicants themselves supply their own employment and income information.

Residence

Check of residence is, first of all, a routine verification of identity. In addition, residence information should show the length of time at the present location and any previous residences in the last three to five years. If necessary, these facts can be used as the basis for more intensive investigation in the local area. They also may reveal certain information about the other credit qualities of the applicant. In addition, the investigation should determine whether the applicant owns or rents the property. If the applicant owns the property, the investigator should determine the amount of the mortgage and the mortgage payment. The amount of the rent and the manner of payment should be determined if the property is rented.

Marital Status

This area has been the subject of a great deal of controversy in recent years. Marital status used to be considered a significant quality in most consumer credit transactions, so credit investigators sought this information. Now, under the Equal Credit Opportunity Act of 1975, a firm cannot refuse to grant a person credit on the basis of sex or marital status. However, the firm can inquire about a person's marital status to determine the rights and remedies available under applicable state law. Likewise, a firm can ask for joint signatures from a married couple on a credit application in order to comply with state legal requirements involving liens, garnishments, or wage-assignment situations. In addition, a husband and wife can ask for separate credit accounts voluntarily, in which case the accounts cannot be combined for billing purposes.

Under the provisions of the Housing and Community Development Act of 1974, lenders are required to consider the combined incomes of husband and wife in extending mortgage credit.

It should be noted that the three types of acceptable terms are unmarried, married, or separated. Previous terms such as divorced or widowed are no longer acceptable.

Age

With the young, the investigation should establish that the applicant is of legal age to sign a contract. With most investigations, age is not an important credit quality. However, extremes of youth or age can be crucially important. Under the 1976 amendments to the

Equal Credit Opportunity Act, creditors can ask about and consider an applicant's age in order to favor the applicant. However, they can't use age in a credit scoring system unless the system is demonstrably and statistically sound and the age of an elderly applicant is not assigned a negative factor or value. Some studies show that credit risk generally decreases with increasing age, especially above 50.

Reserve Assets

In only a few instances should a creditor rely on reserve assets for payment of a consumer credit obligation. In most cases reserve assets are additional surety that both debtor and creditor hope will not be needed. In some cases, especially with older customers who are living on a pension or on income from investments, the investigation of reserve assets may be essential in order to establish capacity to handle the credit obligation. However, when considering property ownership, analysts must avoid attributing a positive effect to something that, when carefully analyzed, should be given negative weight. Homeowners may have such heavy mortgage payments that, instead of the home being an addition to reserve assets, they are earmarking too much current income to assume any additional commitments. Analysts need sufficient detail about such situations to assure they don't overlook a recurring heavy payment.

Equity in Purchase

An additional credit quality, equity in the purchase, is a major concern, especially in consumer installment purchasing. Most large ticket purchases financed through installment credit involve a conditional sales contract. A **conditional sales agreement** is a contract that outlines the terms and payments required to purchase an item on credit and which also provides that actual ownership of the item does not pass to the buyer until all payments have been made. The item belongs to the seller until the last payment has been made. Strictly speaking, equity in purchase concerns the market value of the property. The presence of this market value, as it is available to the creditor through the terms of the contract, may raise an otherwise unacceptable credit risk well above the level of acceptability. When the equity is large and is maintained by the amount and frequency of payment, the major question may not be, "Will the individual pay?" but instead, "Can the property always be found and retaken?" If the equity is smaller and is not maintained by the amount and frequency of payments, personal credit qualities should be analyzed more carefully and should be correspondingly stronger to attain equal safety.

In addition, the proportion of the initial equity may affect the attitude of the buyer toward the obligation. When the initial equity or ownership is large, through a significant down payment, the buyer may be more likely to complete the contract as agreed. If the initial equity is small, the buyer may have less interest in paying the payments to the end. The relationship becomes more like a rental transaction than a purchase transaction.

Collateral

While collateral, an element of capital, is lacking in most retail and service credit transactions, it is often involved in cash loans made to consumers. Collateral—some tangible asset owned by the individual and offered as additional security to the lending institution—is another credit quality to consider. The value of the collateral varies, however. Commercial banks prefer savings, bonds, stocks, and insurance policies, followed by real estate, automobiles, mobile homes, boats, aircraft, and further down the list, various types of unsecured collateral.

Purpose for the Credit

The purpose for the loan or credit account is also a credit quality. Some purposes represent investments that may actually improve the financial status of the applicant. A home improvement loan, for example, will typically result in an increase in the value of the real estate. Other purposes, e.g., vacation loans, represent pure consumption expenditures without any return in value after the funds are spent. Worse yet, some requests for funds may result from poor money management practices. Loan consolidations to help a family lower monthly payments, which also extend the time of indebtedness, may result from previous overindebtedness. Likewise, asking for funds to pay regular expenses such as rent payments that are past due will lend insight into the financial management skills of the applicant.

INFLUENCE OF ECONOMIC CONDITIONS

While credit analysts today can obtain a fairly reliable picture of an individual through a series of specific questions, they always face the problem of interpreting this information in terms of the current economic environment.

Credit Qualities to Investigate

- Payment record
- Income
- Indebtedness and expenditures
- Employment
- Residence
- Marital status
- Age
- Reserve assets
- Equity in purchase
- Collateral
- Purpose for the credit

Knowledge of the economic environment must be part of the analyst's general knowledge. Some of this knowledge is secured by keeping abreast of local business and community affairs. Are strikes affecting certain industrial plants? Are layoffs predicted? Is the weather too dry or too wet, and is the farmer going to be hurt as a consequence? Are some area businesses expanding rapidly and thus drawing new residents to the community? In other words, credit analysts must know "How's business?" in their own industry, other industries, their own town, and surrounding towns.

Perhaps a knowledge of this short-term economic climate is easier to acquire than the ability to predict the long-term economic picture. The background, experience, and training of credit managers will be vital factors in how they look at the future. Their political beliefs, their international views, their financial position, and their experiences in attaining their present position also color their views.

Consistent with their short-run and long-run views of economic conditions, credit managers must interpret the information they obtain about a credit applicant to make the decision to accept or to reject the credit.

INVESTIGATION AND VERIFICATION

The investigation accomplishes two purposes. First, it is a way to develop information not at hand. It is also a way to verify the information supplied. Most credit verifications start when an individual asks for credit and supplies some personal credit information in an application. If an investigation is necessary, good credit managers use this process to verify the information supplied by the applicant. Although most credit applicants are honest, a few make fraudulent statements, lie about their true financial situation, or try to obtain funds illegally. The credit executive should confirm the most vital and important facts from several separate and independent sources. The credit executive has to judge how much verification is needed based on the overall quality of the credit applicant and the manner in which the information supplied coincides with that already known or easily secured.

HOW MUCH TO INVESTIGATE

A **credit investigation** is undertaken to aid in making a sound credit decision. Now the credit analyst must face the problem of how much investigation is needed because every bit of information secured through investigation costs money. Credit executives always walk a tightrope in deciding when they have enough information in terms of completeness, accuracy, and cost.

Insufficient information can cause errors in judgment. Inadequate information means that some pertinent fact was not known that, if known, would have caused a different decision. An even more probable cause of error is that the analyst either did not give sufficient weight to certain information or, even worse, interpreted the information incorrectly.

Extensive investigations cost money and take time; meanwhile, a decision is delayed, with consequent loss of customer goodwill and friction with salespeople. The accumulation of additional bits of information is costly, whether the information is purchased from sellers of credit information or developed by direct inquiry. Unless the information is useful, it is not worth what it costs in either time or money. A mass of factual data may actually interfere with the analysis and decision. The sheer extent of the evidence may result in its being incorrectly weighed or misinterpreted. More pertinent evidence may be buried under a mound of nonpertinent detail.

The proper time to seek information from the applicant and to decide on the extent of the investigation is when credit is first requested. Should the information supplied by the applicant be unusually complete and the case appear sound, the investigation may be limited to payment experience only or to payment experience and verification of employment and residence. Should the information obtained from the applicant be limited, as it sometimes is with retail charge accounts, the investigation should be much more extensive. It is possible for an account to be accepted without investigation—that is, without verification of the information supplied by the applicant. In some cases the "no investigation" policy is advisable. In fact, creditors often waste money verifying the obvious. It is far better to save investigation budgets for cases where there is a probability of trouble.

It is not desirable to gather all possible evidence before reaching a credit decision. The desirable amount is just the amount needed to reach a decision based on the judgment and experience of the credit executive.

WHERE TO INVESTIGATE

What, then, should the investigation do? It should seek specific information from sources that possess the information or can get it accurately, completely, quickly, and at minimum cost. (Note: Since information is the raw material of credit decisions, the credit managers must give as well as get credit information. The best basis for a full flow of clear credit information is an exchange of information.)

Information sources that are accurate, complete, speedy, and reasonably priced include credit applicants themselves, direct investigation, in-file ledgers, and consumer credit reporting agencies, banks, and other miscellaneous sources.

INFORMATION SUPPLIED BY APPLICANTS

Most consumer credit investigations start with information supplied by the applicant. Such information, which should be regarded as a part of the credit investigation, is treated as statements of fact that have not been verified. Certain facts may be accepted without verification; others may be verified through further investigation. The first credit decision is whether any facts need to be verified. If so, a second and third determination becomes necessary: which facts to verify through investigation and what sources to use.

The Credit Application

Most credit departments use a formal procedure for opening a credit account—usually involving an application for credit signed by the applicant. The signature is a vital factor in credit transactions (particularly installment and revolving credit) that result in a finance charge. Exhibit 9–2 shows a warning to the buyer before signing a credit agreement. The extent of the information sought varies considerably, depending on the firm's policies, the type of account requested, and the customs of the trade and region.

The Case for a Formal Application

A **formal application** process involves a comprehensive form that is used to gather information about the applicant's credit qualities followed by a personal interview with a credit analyst to go over the facts outlined. Those who argue for a formal application procedure have a number of reasons for their view.

Complete information can best be obtained by asking the applicant to fill out a comprehensive application. Certain facts are likely to be known only to the applicant. Unless asked for at the time the account is opened, such facts may not be developed through the investigation. In fact, they may not even be sought. It is more economical to obtain such leads from the applicant and simply verify them through further investigation if verification is considered desirable.

An applicant may have a more serious attitude toward credit obligations if the application is rather formal and complete. When the opening of the account seems a

---

EXHIBIT 9–2   Warning to Buyer before Signing Agreement

NOTICE TO THE BUYER: 1. DO NOT SIGN THIS CREDIT AGREEMENT BEFORE YOU READ IT OR IF IT CONTAINS ANY BLANK SPACE. 2. YOU ARE ENTITLED TO A COMPLETELY FILLED IN COPY OF THIS CREDIT AGREEMENT. 3. KEEP IT TO PROTECT YOUR LEGAL RIGHTS.

A copy of this Retail Installment Credit Agreement, along with information regarding your rights to dispute billing errors, will be delivered with your credit card if this application is approved.

Vice President
Chief Financial Officer

X _____
Buyer Signs   Date

X _____
Co-Buyer Signs   Date

rather minor or routine procedure, the applicant may not be properly impressed with the value of credit or with the necessity of conforming to the terms established. When an account is opened, the creditor has an unusual opportunity to educate the customer in proper credit behavior. First, if they are impressed with the fact that not everyone can receive credit, they are more likely to regard the account as a privilege and not as a right. Second, the best time to establish sound habits or behavior patterns is with the first transaction. Payment according to terms is a habit that should be established early. By making the opening of the account a formal process, applicants take the first step toward establishing good credit habits. Third, the customer is more likely to respect a credit department that operates in a careful and businesslike manner. A casual attitude toward the acceptance of credit is likely to impress the customer as being typical of all operations of the business. The best way to achieve this serious attitude is to combine a personal interview between the credit prospect and the credit manager with the completion of the credit application blank.

The Case for an Informal Application

An **informal application** process involves a relatively short credit form that is completed by the customer and delivered to the credit grantor for processing. Some firms strongly believe that informality in credit investigation is more desirable. They point out that credit is just as much a sales promotional tool as advertising. Advertising is easily viewed and read by customers; thus credit should be made easily obtainable. A brief application form for credit may be made readily accessible to the credit prospect at various convenient points. The prospect simply fills out the short form, mails it to the credit department, and usually has no direct contact with anyone in the credit department.

Such stores count on the idea that the vast majority of people pay their accounts. Thus, they reason, why bother to spend money on interviews? To these stores it appears better to conserve funds to secure payment from those who don't live up to the provisions of the credit arrangement. Of course, such a view presupposes that the credit department will know exactly when and how to go after reluctant payers and that these collection efforts (which cost money) will be successful.

What Information Should Be Requested?

The bare minimum is simply identifying information—the name and address of the credit prospect. For the sake of accurate posting to the account, it is desirable to secure the complete given name and at least the middle initial. Some retail stores handle thousands of accounts and may have a number of Carl Johnsons, Edward Smiths, or Mary A. Smiths. A minimum addition to the identifying information is place of employment and occupation, as well as the length of time at each (and previous address or employment if less than one year). A rule of thumb often used in retail credit departments is that residence and employment should be known for five previous years. Such information enables investigators to develop facts or verify information over a sufficient period of time to satisfy doubts as to current behavior. Investigation at earlier places of residence or employment may then be undertaken whenever there is reason to question the consistency of credit behavior. With the widespread movement of population, such caution seems indicated.

Sales finance companies and cash lenders commonly use more detailed application blanks than retailers. They often need the additional information because their credit transactions involve larger amounts and longer time periods. Additional questions may cover the regularity and reliability of an applicant's income and more information about assets. These lenders are likely to ask about real estate owned, bank balances and other savings, and insurance carried. They seek information as to past credit dealings by asking for other installment contracts and other cash loans currently open and recently paid. They usually ask for a list of business references (best asked by the heading "firms with which you have had recent credit transactions") and for a list of personal references. Some also ask the customer's bank and type of account carried. Exhibit 9–3 shows a detailed application form used by a commercial bank. Exhibit 9–4 shows a less detailed form used by a retail firm.

Some questions may be precautionary in the event the lender has to trace a **skip**—a debtor who deliberately disappears and leaves no forwarding address. When a lender has a lien on property purchased on an installment contract or used as collateral for a loan, both the debtor and the property may be sought. If the property under lien is a car, it may facilitate the debtor's disappearance. Since such a disappearance is deliberate, tracing the debtor involves some detective work. Certain classes of information supplied when the account is opened can be the leads needed to initiate a search. Such requests as "name and address of nearest relative" are used for this purpose.

Signature and Contract

It is good credit practice to have the applicant sign the application. Some credit departments add words above the signature to make the application a formal written contract. This clause may be an affidavit that the information is given for the purpose of obtaining credit and that the facts are complete and correct. The clause may also recite the credit terms and be drawn as a contract between creditor and debtor.

The Credit Interview

Obviously, the nature of the credit interview should be consistent with the character of the application and the philosophy of the credit department. Opinions differ as to the best procedures for conducting a credit interview, especially the procedures for completing an application. Some prefer to develop the answers to questions through the interview and to record the information on the application form themselves. Other credit departments ask the applicant to fill out the form first followed by a brief interview with a credit analyst who looks over the form and asks additional questions. The ability of the credit personnel available for interviewing and the firm's physical facilities are important in deciding these questions.

If applicants fill out the form, a firm needs fewer skilled credit personnel and can accommodate more customers in the same space. A skilled credit interviewer can secure much more information and can also stress the rights and wrongs of credit behavior. If a credit interviewer fills in the application, the form should provide space for recording any extra information (the interviewer should record this additional information after the customer leaves). If the customer fills in the application, the interviewer should look over the form to be sure it's complete and probe more deeply into questionable areas.

EXHIBIT 9–3 **Detailed Form Used by a Commercial Bank**

FIRST FLORIDA BANK

Select the accounts for which you are applying by checking the appropriate boxes. Flex-Line Home Equity Line of Credit and Mortgages require special applications. See your Personal Banker for details.

☐ Flex-Line Executive ☐ Redichek ☐ Gold MasterCard ☐ Visa Gold ☐ Regular MasterCard ☐ Classic Visa ☐ Installment Loan

Credit Amount Request $_____ Purpose _____

☐ NEW ACCOUNT ☐ REISSUE REQUEST ☐ REQUEST LIMIT INCREASE ACCOUNT NUMBER ☐☐☐☐☐☐☐☐☐☐☐☐☐☐

IMPORTANT;
Read these Directions before completing this Application and Check Appropriate Box

☐ If you are applying for an individual account in your own name and are relying on your own income or assets and not the income or assets of another person as the basis for repayment of the credit request, complete only Sections A, C, D.

☐ If you are applying for a joint account or an account that you and another person will use, complete all Sections, providing information in B about the joint applicant or user.

☐ If you are applying for an individual account, but are relying on income from alimony, child support, or separate maintenance or on the income or assets of another person as the basis for repayment of the credit requested, complete all Sections to the extent possible, providing information in B about the person on whose alimony, support, or maintenance payments or income or assets you are relying.

SECTION A — APPLICANT

FIRST NAME	MIDDLE NAME	LAST NAME	SOCIAL SECURITY NUMBER	BIRTHDATE MO/DAY/YR

| STREET ADDRESS | APT. NO. | CITY | STATE | ZIP | HOW LONG? | HOME PHONE NO. ( ) |

☐ OWN ☐ RENT ☐ BUYING ☐ LIVE W/RELATIVES | PREVIOUS STREET ADDRESS | CITY | STATE | ZIP | HOW LONG? | NO. DEPENDENTS: Ages:

| EMPLOYED BY | HOW LONG? | ADDRESS | MONTHLY SALARY $ (GROSS) |

| BUSINESS PHONE ( ) | POSITION | PREVIOUS EMPLOYER | ADDRESS | CITY | STATE | HOW LONG |

| NAME OF NEAREST RELATIVE NOT LIVING WITH YOU | STREET ADDRESS | CITY | STATE | PHONE NO. ( ) | RELATION |

| BANK WITH | BRANCH | ☐ CHECKING ACCOUNT NO. / ☐ SAVINGS ACCOUNT NO. | ☐ LOAN / ☐ CREDIT CARD |

ALIMONY, CHILD SUPPORT, OR SEPARATE MAINTENANCE INCOME NEED NOT BE REVEALED IF YOU DO NOT WISH TO HAVE IT CONSIDERED AS A BASIS FOR REPAYING THIS OBLIGATION.

OTHER INCOME Source(s) of other income: $ | ALIMONY, CHILD SUPPORT, SEPARATE MAINTENANCE, RECEIVED UNDER: ☐ COURT ORDER ☐ WRITTEN AGREEMENT ☐ ORAL UNDERSTANDING

SECTION B — JOINT APPLICANT

| FIRST NAME | MIDDLE NAME | LAST NAME | SOCIAL SECURITY NUMBER | BIRTHDATE MO/DAY/YR | HOME PHONE NO. ( ) |

| STREET ADDRESS | APT. NO. | CITY | STATE | ZIP | HOW LONG? | NO. DEPENDENTS: AGES: |

☐ OWN ☐ RENT ☐ BUYING ☐ LIVE W/RELATIVES | PREVIOUS STREET ADDRESS | CITY | STATE | HOW LONG? | RELATIONSHIP TO APPLICANT IF ANY

| EMPLOYED BY | HOW LONG? | ADDRESS | MONTHLY SALARY $ (GROSS) |

| BUSINESS PHONE ( ) | POSITION | PREVIOUS EMPLOYER | ADDRESS | HOW LONG |

| NAME OF NEAREST RELATIVE NOT LIVING WITH YOU | STREET ADDRESS | CITY | STATE | PHONE NO. ( ) | RELATION |

| BANK WITH | BRANCH | ☐ CHECKING ACCOUNT NO. / ☐ SAVINGS ACCOUNT NO. | ☐ LOAN / ☐ CREDIT CARD |

ALIMONY, CHILD SUPPORT, OR SEPARATE MAINTENANCE INCOME NEED NOT BE REVEALED IF YOU DO NOT WISH TO HAVE IT CONSIDERED AS A BASIS FOR REPAYING THIS OBLIGATION.

OTHER INCOME Source(s) of other income: $ | ALIMONY, CHILD SUPPORT, SEPARATE MAINTENANCE, RECEIVED UNDER: ☐ COURT ORDER ☐ WRITTEN AGREEMENT ☐ ORAL UNDERSTANDING

SECTION C — OBLIGATIONS AND REFERENCES

PLEASE LIST BELOW ALL DEBTS, INCLUDING ANY ALIMONY OR CHILD SUPPORT. YOU MAY ALSO LIST ANY ACCOUNTS (PAID OUT OR OPEN) WHICH YOU WISH THE BANK TO CONSIDER AS A CREDIT REFERENCE. USE SEPARATE SHEET IF NECESSARY.

NAME OF COMPANY OR BANK		ACCOUNT NUMBER	PRESENT BALANCE	MONTHLY PAYMENT	ACCOUNT IN NAME OF
RENT OR MORTGAGE PAYABLE TO					☐ APPLICANT ☐ JOINT APPLICANT ☐ OTHER
AUTOMOBILE FINANCED BY	YEAR: MAKE:				☐ APPLICANT ☐ JOINT APPLICANT ☐ OTHER
	YEAR: MAKE:				☐ APPLICANT ☐ JOINT APPLICANT ☐ OTHER
					☐ APPLICANT ☐ JOINT APPLICANT ☐ OTHER

Are you co-maker, endorser, or guarantor on any loan or contract? Yes ☐ No ☐ If "yes"

For whom? _____ To whom? _____

Are there any unsatisfied judgments against you? Yes ☐ No ☐ If "yes" to whom owed? _____

Have you been declared bankrupt in the last 10 years? Yes ☐ No ☐ If "yes" where? _____ Year _____

The applicant and joint applicant, if any, hereby request a Revolving Line of Credit, affirm that everything stated in this application is true and correct, understanding that the Bank will retain this application whether or not it is approved, authorize the Bank to check the above credit and employment history and to answer questions about the credit experience with the account, and agree to be obligated by the terms and conditions of the Agreement and Disclosure required by Federal Law as amended from time to time delivered to them. Should a Line of Credit be issued and without limiting the generality of said agreement they specifically agree, jointly and severally to pay for credit extended through the use of the card or any other credit device and all costs incurred in collecting that indebtedness, including a reasonable attorney's fee.

_____ (Seal) _____ _____ (Seal) _____
Applicant's Signature | Date | Other Signature (where Applicable) | Date

What appears more important is to develop the right attitude toward the credit interview rather than to prescribe a single procedure for completing the application. The credit interview should be a part of the credit department promotion of credit sales. It is an opportunity to convert a credit prospect into a credit customer. Accordingly, the credit interview should not be an inquisition; rather, it should be a business procedure for

EXHIBIT 9–3   (concluded)

FILL OUT SECTION D ONLY FOR UNSECURED CREDIT REQUESTS IN EXCESS OF $5,000

(When you are relying solely on your present income and credit record as the basis for approval, without including any form of collateral, i.e., property and/or assets, it is considered an Unsecured Credit Request.)

	ASSETS		LIABILITIES AND NET WORTH	
1.	CASH On hand, and unrestricted in banks		18. Notes Payable to Banks, Unsecured Direct borrowings only	$
2.	U. S. Government Securities (Guaranteed)		19. Notes Payable to Banks, Secured Direct borrowings only.	
3.	Government Agencies Securities		20. Notes Receivable, Discounted With banks, finance companies, etc.	
4.	Accounts and Loans Receivable (See Sched. No 1)		21. Notes Payable to Others, Unsecured	
5.	Notes Receivable, Not Discounted (See sched. No 1)		22. Notes Payable to Other, Secured	
6.	Notes Receivable, Discounted With banks, finance co., etc. (See Sched. No 1)		23. Loans Against Life Insurance (See Sched. No 2)	
7.	Life Insurance, Cash Surrender Value (Do not deduct loans) (See Sched. No 2)		24. Accounts Payable	
8.	Stock and Securities Other Than Guaranteed U. S. Gov't and Gov't Agencies (See Sched. No 3)		25. Interest Payable	
9.	Real Estate Registered in own name (See Sched. No 4)		26. Taxes and Assessments Payable (See Sched. No 4)	
10.	Automobiles Registered in own name		27. Mortgage Payable on Real Estate (See Sched. No 4)	
11.	Other Assets (Itemize)		28. Brokers Margin Accounts	
12.			29. Other Liabilities (Itemize)	
13.	Sub Total $		30.	
14.	Less Line No. 31 $		31. Total Liabilities	
15.	Net Worth (To be shown on line No. 33) $		32.	
16.			33. Net Worth	$
17.	TOTAL ASSETS	$	34. TOTAL LIABILITIES and NET WORTH (Line 31 plus line 33)	$

(Left margin: SECTION D – PERSONAL FINANCIAL STATEMENT)

No. 1 Accounts Loans and Notes Receivable   (A list of the largest amounts owing to me.)

Name and Address of Debtor	Amount Owing	Age of Debt	Description of Nature of Debt	Description of Security Held	Date Payment Expected

No. 2 Life Insurance

Name of Person Insured	Name of Beneficiary	Name of Insurance Co.	Type of Policy	Face Amount of Policy	Total Cash Surrender Value	Total Loans Against Policy	Amount of Yearly Premium	Is Policy Assigned

No. 3 Stocks and Securities Other Than Guaranteed U. S. Government Securities and Government Agencies

Face Value (Bonds) No. of Shares (Stocks)	Description of Security	Registered in Name of	Cost	Present Market Value	Income Received Last Year	To Whom Pledged?

No. 4 Real Estate *The legal and equitable title of all the real estate listed in this statement is solely in the name of the undersigned, except as follows:*

Description or Street No.	Dimensions or Acres	Improvements Consist of	Mortgages or Liens	Due Dates and Amounts of Payments	Assessed Value	Present Market Value	Unpaid Taxes Year	Amount

No. 5 I have credit accounts with   (List most frequently used accounts)

Name	Address	Name	Address

The undersigned certifies that each side hereof and the information inserted herein have been carefully read and is true and correct.

Date _____   Signed _____

SOURCE: Courtesy of First Florida Bank

EXHIBIT 9–4   Less Detailed Form Used by a Retail Firm

JCPenney instant credit Application

For Office Use Only

To apply for Instant Credit, fill out the application below. If you have applied for a JCPenney account within the past 60 days, please do not complete this application.

Store Number | Account Number | Type Of Account You Want: Individual / Joint

Credit Insurance Enrollment

☐ YES — I wish to protect my JCPenney Account with Credit Insurance for the cost as described above. I understand the insurance is not required.

☐ NO — I waive my right to enroll for Credit Insurance at this time.

APPLICANT (SIGN TO ENROLL) | Date Of Birth
SPOUSE'S NAME | Date Of Birth

In signing this enrollment form, I authorize J.C. Penney Company, Inc. to advance to J.C. Penney Life Insurance Company and J.C. Penney Casualty Insurance Company amounts equal to the premiums becoming due under the policy applied for and bill such amounts with my JCPenney Credit Account. I agree to pay such amounts when billed.

General Information (Please Print All Information)

Name Of Applicant To Whom Our Billing Statements Should Be Sent (First, Middle Initial, Last) | Applicant's Social Security Number

Name And Relationship(s) To Applicant(s) Of — ☐ Co-Applicant ☐ Authorized Buyer(s)

Present Address — Street/Apt. ☐ Own ☐ Rent ☐ With Parents ☐ Other | City, State | Zip

Former Address (If At Current Address Less Than One Year) — Street/Apt. | City, State | Zip

Home Phone ( ) | Business Phone ( ) | Date Of Birth | Co-Applicant's Date Of Birth

Bank Account ☐ Checking & Savings ☐ Checking ☐ Savings ☐ Loan

Picture I.D. (Driver's License, Student I.D., Etc.) | Number | Major Credit Card | Account Number

Sign here to complete your JCPenney Instant Credit Application.
Your signature(s) mean(s) that you have read, understood, and agree to the terms of the above Retail Installment Credit Agreement.

Applicant's Signature | Date | Co-Applicant's Signature | Date

SOURCE: Courtesy of JC Penney Company, Inc.

establishing that a credit relationship between the lender and the borrower is mutually beneficial. The interviewer should proceed with the quiet confidence that the prospect is a valued customer.

Analyzing the Application

The credit application is a source of credit information that has not been verified. One goal in analyzing the application involves the need for verification. Certain information can be verified by everyday references and sources. For example, an address can be confirmed in a telephone directory or a city directory. In some cases, a directory may also confirm an applicant's occupation. Other verifications involve contacting the employer, the landlord or mortgage holder, and listed creditors.

Brevity of residence or employment may indicate the need for more extensive investigation. Knowledge of employment policies in the community can help direct the extent of the investigation. Certain employers may have a policy of carefully screening employees, and employment with such a firm may permit some inference of reliability.

Sometimes an occupation may indicate the need for more complete investigation. Occupations that are seasonal or that experience considerable fluctuation in income or high turnover call for more complete investigation than do more stable occupations. Some credit scoring systems attempt to assign point values to different occupations.

Certain characteristics do seem to prevail among those in higher-rated occupations (largely professional and highly skilled workers). Stability of income and better utilization of income are two. These are important factors in accepting credit from these groups. Although there are exceptions among all occupations, the sense of responsibility an occupational group may have substantially affects its paying habits. This fact may be attributed to the kind and amount of education or training necessary to perform these better-rated jobs—sometimes years of formal education and personal discipline.

Some occupational groups are made up of transient workers. Such workers have always been regarded as doubtful credit risks because they may have less sense of credit responsibility. This is true of workers who move frequently from one town to another—e.g., unskilled factory workers, section hands, and common laborers. Until recently, it was a relatively simple matter for a worker to skip out on debts and assume another name in a new community. The network of credit bureaus throughout the nation, strong union affiliations, social security registration, and income tax laws have significantly hampered this practice.

Stability of income is as important as the amount of income in credit risk appraisal, so it plays an important role in credit study. Credit selling is most effective when directed toward those who have the financial ability to pay installment or revolving credit purchases or the recurring amounts due on open account purchases. Selling techniques should attract the largest number of people with a reasonably regular income to move the product from the retailers' shelves.

Indicating the Investigation to Make

The decision whether to make a further credit investigation and, if so, to what extent is based on an analysis of the application. Of course, a distinction must be made between an initial application for credit and a request from an established credit customer for a larger amount of credit. The application and interview are the primary sources for determining further action with the initial credit applicants. On the other hand, payment record data from in-file information plays a dominant role in deciding whether to expand a customer's credit.

What to investigate and what sources of credit information to use should be carefully considered by the credit analyst. Selection must be made between the various sources, and each source must be selected on the basis of type of information desired; speed, accuracy, and completeness of the response; and relative cost of obtaining the information.

Information Supplied by Direct Inquiry

Direct inquiry is the process of contacting employers, credit grantors, and other individuals who can verify facts and provide information about an applicant's willingness and ability to pay. The credit analyst, or a representative, gathers the information by telephone, by mail, or in personal conversations. For example, a credit investigator might call an employer to verify employment and gather information related to pay, years of service, and reliability. Direct inquiry is a common method of obtaining information to verify facts presented on an application or during an interview. Likewise, direct inquiry is also used to obtain additional facts needed to decide whether to accept the credit of an initial applicant or to enlarge the amount of credit accepted from an established customer.

Some information may be purchased from consumer credit reporting agencies. A **credit bureau** is a firm that collects, retains, and sells information related to the creditworthiness of community members. Often, lenders and credit grantors must join the credit bureau and pay fees for the information they are provided. Credit bureaus and other credit reporting agencies are considered in Chapter 10.

Although investigation may be done by direct inquiry or by purchase of reports from professional sources of credit information, direct inquiry is not free. Direct inquiry incurs costs in time and personnel, and purchase fees in some instances may be lower. But direct inquiry may be faster, and it gives the investigator the ability to ask specific questions, develop additional information as needed, and confine the response to pertinent information. For instance, on the basis of preliminary analysis of the application, a credit analyst may decide to verify only the applicant's employment and its duration. A telephone call or a letter to the employer may suffice, and the case is closed in a matter of minutes. If an inquiry doesn't confirm the information supplied by the application or raises some additional questions, the investigation can be extended.

Direct inquiry can result in duplication, and the information supplied may be incomplete and not uniform for all accounts. When a number of people possess the same information, a middleman is usually the most efficient way to exchange such information. For each creditor to know the experience of six other creditors, for example, each must send out six inquiries and reply to six inquiries. If they all submit information to a central clearing agency, each creditor only has to make one inquiry and submit one reply—a total of only seven inquiries and seven replies.

Inquiry by Mail

Direct inquiry by mail may be directed to the employer, firms that have had credit dealings with the applicant, the applicant's bank, attorneys who might have had contact with the applicant, and other references. In each case, the reference letter should be carefully framed to solicit information that the informant is expected to have that is pertinent to the credit decision. The questions should be phrased as specifically as possible and the form designed so it is easy for the respondent to reply. In all cases an offer to reciprocate should be made and a self-addressed, stamped envelope supplied for reply. While communication by letter is more common, some firms use double-return postcards with the name of the applicant coded on the reply card to avoid possible legal complications. It is usual to indicate that the information is needed because of a request for credit, and in some cases the nature of the transaction is indicated. Since such information should be and usually is on a give-and-get basis, some firms submit their own experience when asking for the experience of others. It also is usual to state if the inquiry is directed to a person whose name was supplied as a reference.

Questions should be phrased to permit specific and unequivocal answers. So far as possible, the questions should require factual response rather than opinion or judgment. The questions should not indicate or invite bias in either inquiry or reply. The whole tone should be tactful and considerate of the respondent.

Appropriate questions to be directed to the employer include:

Employed since? _____ or How long employed? _____
Position or occupation? _____
Confirmation of salary given by applicant: Yes ___ No___

And if a former employer, it is appropriate to ask:

Employed? From _____ to _____
Position or occupation? _____
Reason for separation? _____

Appropriate questions to trade creditors include:

Type of account? _____
When account was opened? _____
Original payment terms? _____
Present balance? $ _____
Highest recent credit? $ _____
Amount past due? $ _____
Payment experience: _____
     Pays when due _____
     Within 30 days _____
     In 30 to 60 days _____
     In 60 to 90 days _____
     Other _____
(If experience has been unsatisfactory, please state the nature of the difficulty, the manner of collection, and if there was a charge to profit and loss.) $ _____ Date? _____

Appropriate questions to banks include:

Is applicant a depositor? Yes? _____ No? _____ Checking?_____
Savings? _____
Approximate amount of the usual balance? $ _____
Have you had lending experience with applicant? Yes _____ No _____
Was the lending experience satisfactory? Yes _____ No _____
Would you recommend? _____

This last question, which violates the precept not to ask for opinion, is included because some bankers won't answer specific questions but will make a recommendation.

Developing Additional Informants

Specific questions can glean usable information even from biased sources, since few reputable business executives actually falsify credit information. They are more likely to bias their reply by not mentioning any unfavorable points or by being vague, even generous, in response to requests for opinion or judgment. It is sometimes surprising to the credit analyst—and would be even more surprising to the prospect—how frank some answers can be.

Despite these mitigating factors, such predictable bias impels skillful investigators to develop evidence from informants not supplied by the prospect. Ingenuity and knowledge of the market often help the investigator to add sources. For example, utilities usually have experience records. Public record information can also be used. Ownership of property can be checked against tax records. The presence of liens can be determined by examining public records. Police records are sometimes revealing. While every case doesn't warrant such a costly and time-consuming investigation, when circumstances indicate it, the investigation can be extended in unusual directions.

Inquiry by Telephone

Inquiry by telephone can be used in place of a mail inquiry and is generally preferred by credit grantors. The same questions outlined above are asked in a telephone call to the person or firm that possesses the information. The interviewer records replies on a form similar to that used in mail inquiries. Standard questions result in uniform responses, but trained telephone investigators should be skilled enough to probe further if indicated.

Telephone inquiry has an advantage over mail: replies are received immediately. The cost per completed inquiry compares favorably with the cost of a mail inquiry. The use of mail inquiry may be required, however, if telephone inquiry is not possible. Sometimes a firm will have a policy that states that employment verifications will be done by mail only. The employer recognizes that verifying employment is a useful activity for its employees, but does not want to deal with the disruption of business that occurs with numerous telephone requests.

Inquiry by Outside Representative

Some firms, particularly cash lenders and sales finance companies, use their own employees as credit investigators. The employees, or outside representatives, may be assigned the dual task of outside or personal collector and credit investigator. They usually are supplied with the names of employer, landlord, and business firms and are expected to call these people and ask questions similar to those asked in a mail investigation. Here, too, there is an advantage in using standardized questions and a standard form for recording answers.

Outside representatives should be aggressive in developing additional informants and in extending the depth of the inquiry. Although a mail investigation cannot readily be extended, good outside representatives analyze the information supplied as it accumulates. They thus extend their inquiries to the point where they decide that they have sufficient information to accept or to reject. By discreet inquiries, they may develop information that no other means of direct investigation can match. Inquiries can be made of neighbors and local tradespeople, even the mail carrier or a police officer.

Some cash loan companies, lending on the collateral of household effects, believe that personal examination of the home can supply useful credit information. Such information as the type and quality of the furnishings, quality of housekeeping, and pride or lack of pride in the home can indicate the credit quality of the applicant. In a similar situation, a loan officer may want to examine an automobile that is being offered as collateral. The mileage and general condition of the automobile may be important in determining the true market value.

Inquiry through Credit Group Meetings

The technique of group meetings is more common in business credit transactions, but in some communities creditors selling consumer goods use it to exchange ledger facts and other valuable information. While such meetings are often held under the auspices of the local retail credit bureau, the technique is a result of direct inquiry.

The purpose of such group meetings, which often are held in conjunction with a social luncheon or dinner, is to provide a quick and easy means of exchanging information about initial applicants for credit, slow-pay customers, and other accounts exhibiting unusual behavior. Usually, each participating store is limited in the number of names it can bring up in discussion.

INFORMATION SUPPLIED FROM IN-FILE LEDGER FACTS

In-file ledger facts, the payment record a firm already has on an applicant, are one of the most important sources of information in deciding whether to accept or reject a larger amount of credit from an established credit customer. Applicants applying for additional credit have already been interviewed, investigated, and had their applications analyzed and verified. The important facts should still be reviewed with existing customers, however, because significant changes may have occurred in the financial lives of these individuals.

In-file records indicate the firm's experience with the customer. Credit analysts know the customer's payment habits, any complaints registered, and any collection efforts needed. In many cases such information is sufficient. In others, the credit executive will seek more information, called *purchased information,* from professional sources. Such sources will be covered in the next chapter.

Important Terms

Discussion Questions

1. What is meant by the statement "Credit information is created only by the subject of the credit inquiry"?

2. What is the basic purpose of a credit investigation?

3. Distinguish between facts and opinions.

4. Explain the statement "The credit investigation brings together historical information which, through analysis, is used as a basis for a prediction of future behavior."

5. Explain the difference between credit character and moral character.

6. List and describe the qualities credit investigators normally evaluate.

7. What additional qualities would you recommend be applied to the list appearing in the text?

8. Check with several firms (retail, service, and financial) in your community as to the importance they place on each of the credit qualities suggested.

9. Distinguish between collateral and equity in purchase.

10. Why are economic conditions an important factor in determining credit risk?

11. Why is the question "How much to investigate?" difficult to answer?

12. Distinguish between direct inquiry and in-file ledger information.

13. Explain the statement "The extent to which consumer-supplied information is verified or expanded through additional investigation depends on the judgment of the credit analyst."

14. Should credit applications be signed? Why or why not?

15. How would you conduct a credit interview? Why did you include the steps that you did?

16. Why do sales finance companies and cash lenders use more detailed application forms?

17. List the C's of credit in the order of importance. Which is most important to a credit grantor? Least important?

10

CONSUMER CREDIT REPORTING AGENCIES

Learning Objectives

After studying this chapter, you should be able to:

- Describe the basic purpose of consumer credit reporting agencies.
- Explain the difference between consumer credit reporting agencies and investigative reporting agencies.
- Describe typical products and services offered by credit bureaus.
- Trace the history, development, organization, and operation of local credit bureaus.
- Discuss activities of Associated Credit Bureaus, Inc. (ACB).
- Describe the sources and types of information gathered by credit bureaus.
- Point out the legal restrictions on credit bureau operations under the Fair Credit Reporting Act.
- Explain the activities of Experian Information Services (formerly TRW), Trans Union, and Equifax, Inc.

Information about the credit history or paying habits of individuals and families may be secured from many sources. As described in Chapter 2, the credit manager will use direct inquiry methods to gain information. The manager may also purchase information about an individual's credit history from commercialized credit reporting agencies. Each source, direct inquiry or credit reporting agencies, has its own special merits as well as some disadvantages.

The direct method of investigation is "free" only in the sense that the creditor pays no fee to an outside organization. If one considers the time, wages, and other expenses involved in gathering and verifying information, direct inquiry may be more costly than a fee service, and the product supplied may be inferior. Yet, in any credit investigation, the quality of information is a prime consideration. Most credit investigations will also include information obtained from specialized credit reporting agencies.

CLEARINGHOUSES OF CREDIT INFORMATION

Consumer credit reporting agencies, also called *credit bureaus,* are firms that collect, retain, and sell information related to the credit histories of consumers. These firms function as clearinghouses of information. Creditors feed information into the credit bureaus, which make the information available to other creditors who have a business need-to-know. Creditor X, for example, provides payment information to the credit bureau. Later, Creditors Y, Z, and any other creditors request the credit bureau file and get the information supplied by the first creditor. A **credit bureau report** contains payment histories supplied by creditors, along with other information gathered from public records, collection agencies, and others. Credit information in the files of credit reporting agencies can be used more than once; in fact, multiple use of the same information is the principle on which this type of organization is founded. Credit information gathered by direct methods is available only to the firm doing the investigation.

TYPES OF CREDIT BUREAUS

There are two basic types of credit bureaus or reporting agencies. *Consumer credit reporting agencies* generally have their own computer database which typically contains files for millions of credit users throughout North America. The primary source of their data is accounts receivable information that is routinely supplied by credit grantors. They also obtain public record data from court records. There are three major firms in the United States today: Experian Information Services (formerly TRW), Trans Union, and Equifax, Inc. These three competing firms operate their own branch offices and provide information to other independently owned credit bureaus that have arranged for immediate access to the databases of these firms.

Another kind of reporting organization, termed an *investigative credit reporting* company, produces investigative consumer reports that contain information about a consumer's character, general reputation, personal characteristics, or mode of living obtained through personal interviews as well as traditional sources. These reports are developed primarily for employers and insurance firms to use in evaluating applicants for employment or insurance. Equifax, Inc., a leader in this field, offers detailed investigations by its staff of field representatives. An investigative report contains the standard credit bureau information, along with information gathered by field reporters.

Any credit bureau has immediate access to the records of all other credit bureaus, through a long-standing arrangement. A credit bureau worker can, for example, enter a name and social security number at a terminal anywhere in the nation and obtain a file from a national database. The credit file of a family that moves to another community is thus available to credit grantors in the new location through interbureau reporting arrangements.

Three Major Credit Bureau Computerized Databases in the U.S.

- Experian (formerly TRW)
- Trans Union
- Equifax, Inc.

CREDIT BUREAU PRODUCTS AND SERVICES

The traditional product provided by credit reporting agencies is a **written credit report** describing the payment history, public records, and other information about individuals who use credit programs. As technology has advanced, reports originally mailed in written form are now delivered to most inquirers electronically—computer to computer.

With the large databases of information, credit reporting agencies have developed other services desired by credit grantors. Examples include:

- Point scoring systems to predict account delinquencies and bankruptcies.
- Alert messages to pinpoint file discrepancies or unusual credit activities that call for further investigation. Some agencies, for example, will notify creditors if an unusually large number of inquiries or charges occur within a particular file.
- Fraud databases to protect against illegal activities.
- Search features to locate customers who have moved, changed their names, or "skipped." **Skips** are debtors who move in an effort to avoid repayment of debts.
- Reports that provide credit grantors, financial institutions, and marketing organizations with information on how, where, and by who   credit is being used in their markets.
- Direct marketing and mailing list services. Prescreening identifies creditworthy consumers, per the customer's criteria, before a mailing is made, and "cluster groups" of people of similar affluence and lifestyles can be targeted. Other services involve identifying those with new addresses and members of specific demographic groups.

In the future, credit bureaus may become a one-stop shopping place for all of a credit grantor's solicitation and promotion marketing needs—from targeting of customers, to preparing and distributing mailings, to processing of responses.

Other expanded capabilities within the credit bureau industry include automated credit application processing and score card monitoring products. These systems can compile, analyze, score, and evaluate all the application information necessary to make an informed credit decision and pass it on to the credit grantors with a recommendation for approval, rejection, or further review, based on the credit grantor's criteria. The application can be entered on-site by the client, or at a processing center. Loan decisions can be made in minutes.

HISTORY AND ORGANIZATION OF CREDIT BUREAUS

Credit bureaus are one of the most important sources of information about consumers' paying habits. Credit grantors need such information to extend credit privileges promptly and knowledgeably.

Beginning and Development of Local Credit Bureaus

Local credit bureaus are primarily a twentieth-century development. The first so-called credit bureau was organized as early as 1860 in Brooklyn, but credit bureaus grew and developed slowly before World War II. Until then, few retailers sold on credit, and those that did confined their credit business to well-known customers. Movement of people was limited because of the lack of rapid transportation and communication facilities. The reputations and bill-paying habits of community members was fairly well known. Some credit exchanges maintained lists of poor credit risks, but the mechanisms for gathering and sharing information were not well developed.

From this humble beginning, credit bureaus grew to the position of importance they now occupy. Credit bureaus have become the principal clearinghouses for information furnished by their subscribers, members, and other outside sources. They are one of the best examples of close cooperation among business firms serving the American public.

Origin and Growth of the Trade Association for Credit Bureaus

The organized exchange of consumer credit information between local areas started about the turn of the century. In 1906 William H. Burr, owner of a "credit company" in Rochester, New York, asked the managers of several other consumer credit reporting agencies to meet with him to discuss the possibility of forming a national association of credit bureaus. Before that time there were no rosters of credit bureaus, no system for interchanging reports between bureaus, and no standardized forms. This 1906 meeting resulted in the formation of the only national organization of credit bureaus, then called the *National Association of Retail Credit Agencies* but now known as **Associated Credit Bureaus, Inc.** (ACB). The need for closer cooperation between credit bureaus and credit grantors soon became evident, and in 1912 the Retail Credit Men's National Association (now known as the International Credit Association) was formed as a trade association of retail credit managers.

From its 1906 beginning, when six small credit reporting agencies incorporated and agreed to exchange credit information, ACB has grown rapidly. Today it is the only trade association in the consumer credit reporting industry, offering its members traditional trade association benefits such as lobbying, group purchasing, national public relations, and training aids for employees through seminars, forums, and institutes.

ACB also operates a comprehensive certification program so that credit reporters and consumer interviewers receive thorough training in the laws that govern their activity. The certification, which is usually renewed every two years, is often used to prove the operational procedures and the employees are carefully monitored. (See http://www.acb-credit.com)

Organization and Ownership of Local Credit Bureaus

In the past, most credit bureaus were community cooperative or nonprofit associations operated for the benefit of users. Others were owned by local chambers of commerce, which operated them for the benefit of their members. Today most credit bureaus are owned by individuals and corporations and operated for profit.

As with any private business, credit bureaus may change owners. Most bureaus are incorporated. The three major databases mentioned earlier acquire new branch offices occasionally when they purchase bureaus formerly affiliated by contract arrangements. The number of offices owned by Trans Union, Experian, and Equifax increases steadily.

Regardless of ownership, the principle of credit bureau operation is constant. All credit bureaus rely on the cooperation of credit grantors to contribute information about their credit customers and to purchase credit reports. All bureaus interview consumers, explain their function to all who are interested, attempt to reconcile differences between consumers and credit grantors, and correct errors as they are detected. The **Fair Credit Reporting Act** (FCRA), effective in 1971, regulates the credit reporting agencies, provides access to information by consumers, and includes mechanisms for correcting errors. The FCRA crystallized the methods and formats, so that today treatment of consumers is uniform.

At one time reporting firms needed a physical location. Today computers have made that unnecessary. All a credit grantor—or even another credit bureau—needs is access to a computer terminal.

Credit bureaus are conscious of the need for security measures to protect the integrity of their data. Each credit bureau develops a security program tailored to its own needs. Depending on the bureau's experience, the security systems range from complex automated systems to simple precautions to prevent unauthorized access to credit records.

Security programs need constant updating to provide better protection and to become as standardized throughout the industry as different operating environments permit.

Security touches almost all aspects of credit bureau operations. ACB requires certain basic security measures of its members and recommends others depending on the size and location of the credit bureau. Computerized bureaus, especially, adopt stringent methods to prevent unauthorized access to stored data.

The residents who live in a wide area around any city where a credit bureau is located will find that their credit files are readily available because the data from the national credit grantors are accessible from the three major firms through the affiliated bureaus.

OPERATION OF CREDIT BUREAUS

Credit bureaus must maintain control of the data they collect. To comply with the Fair Credit Reporting Act, credit bureaus must carefully verify the identity of all who request credit information, whether it be a credit grantor, an employer, or even the subject of the report itself.

Principal Sources of Credit Information

Since the primary activity of a credit bureau is to furnish credit reports on consumers applying for credit, it is important to explore the principal sources of data for such reports.

Credit information is gathered from a variety of sources located in one or more trading areas that are willing to exchange information. The credit bureaus arrange to secure the necessary data from as many creditors and other sources as possible. Many creditors automatically provide accounts receivable information in computer-ready format or download information from the credit grantor's computer to the credit bureau's computers at prearranged time intervals. Some creditors will provide machine readable computer disks or tapes that contain the most recent account information of its credit customers. The credit bureau computers "read" and input the information into bureau files in minutes. In addition, affiliate bureaus arrange for banks, finance companies, retailers, and so on to add their computerized information to the files and enrich the credit histories in the bureau. Bureaus also add new and current employment information to each person's file as that information becomes available, usually from a credit application. Other information is gathered from public records.

Types of Information Gathered

The credit bureau gathers data that relates to the payment history and creditworthiness of the individual whose data file is being constructed. The information will be used to help a credit decisionmaker evaluate an applicant's willingness and ability to pay his or her financial obligations.

Credit files may be drawn up on computer screens or printers located in the credit grantors' offices. Each of the three major database firms has customized the once-standard credit report format so it provides all of the information needed. Although the information in each database is theoretically identical, the display of the information and its treatment will be different, depending on the database source. A Trans Union format, for example, will look different from an Exquifax format. A format devised by the Associated Credit Bureaus, Inc. (ACB), called *Crediscope,* is designated Form 2000 (See Exhibit 10–1). A credit bureau report generally contains the following information.

Ledger Information
Ledger information is the recorded monetary transactions of a business and, in this context, shows how an individual credit customer has handled his or her credit accounts.

EXHIBIT 10–1   Sample Form 2000

NAME AND ADDRESS OF CREDIT BUREAU MAKING REPORT

☐ SINGLE REFERENCE   ☐ IN FILE REPORT   ☐ TRADE REPORT
☒ FULL REPORT   ☐ EMPLOY & TRADE REPORT   ☐ PREVIOUS RESIDENCE REPORT
☐ OTHER_____

Credit Bureau of Anytown
1311 Main St.
Anytown, Anystate 12345

FOR   First National Bank
Anytown, Anystate 12345

Date Received	10/11/91
Date Mailed	10/12/91
In File Since	1973
Inquired As:	2

CONFIDENTIAL
crediscope® REPORT

Member
Associated Credit Bureaus, Inc.

REPORT ON: LAST NAME	FIRST NAME	INITIAL	SOCIAL SECURITY NUMBER	SPOUSE'S NAME
Consumer	Robert	B	123-45-6789	Betty

ADDRESS: CITY	STATE:	ZIP CODE	SINCE:	SPOUSE'S SOCIAL SECURITY NO.
812 Elm St. Anytown	Anystate	12346	1975	987-65-4321

PRESENT EMPLOYER:	POSITION HELD:	SINCE:	DATE EMPLOY VERIFIED	EST. MONTHLY INCOME
Research Engineer Inc.	Sr. Vice Pres.	5/81	3/21/89	$ 3600

DATE OF BIRTH	NUMBER OF DEPENDENTS INCLUDING SELF:			
4/48	2	☒ OWNS OR BUYING HOME	☐ RENTS HOME	OTHER: (EXPLAIN) ☐

FORMER ADDRESS:	CITY:		STATE:	FROM:	TO:
123 Oak St.	Thattown	Anystate		1973	1975

FORMER EMPLOYER:	POSITION HELD:	FROM:	TO:	EST. MONTHLY INCOME
Sun Research	Engineer	1978	1981	$ _

SPOUSE'S EMPLOYER:	POSITION HELD:	SINCE:	DATE EMPLOY VERIFIED	EST. MONTHLY INCOME
Gift World	Owner	1984	3/21/89	$ 1800

WHOSE	KIND OF BUSINESS AND ID CODE	DATE REPORTED AND METHOD OF REPORTING	DATE OPENED	DATE OF LAST PAYMENT	HIGHEST CREDIT OR LAST CONTRACT	PRESENT STATUS BALANCE OWING	PRESENT STATUS AMOUNT	PAST DUE AMOUNT	NO. OF PAYMENTS	NO. MONTHS HISTORY REVIEWED	TIMES PAST DUE 30-59 DAYS ONLY	TIMES PAST DUE 60-89 DAYS ONLY	TIMES PAST DUE 90 DAYS AND OVER	TYPE & TERMS (MANNER OF PAYMENT)	REMARKS
3	D-608 Jones Department Store	9/91A	2/83	6/91	$172	$85	$34		2	12	1	1		R-$17	
1	B-319 Bank of Anytown	9/91M	8/85	8/91	2400	00	00			24				I-$100	
2	C-526 Styles of Today, Inc.	9/91A	1980	7/91	$1264	100	50		1	12	2	1		R-$50	
3	N-772 Ready-Credit	9/91A	2/81	7/91	$350	160	–		–	12	1		0		DRP
0	D-490 Everybody's Dept. Store	5/89M	1979	6/90	$700	00	0		–					R-$150	

Public Record
County Small Claims Court Case SC-1001, 5/31/91.
Plaintiff Ace Stereo Sales $825 Paid 8/91.

This information is furnished in response to an inquiry for the purpose of evaluating credit risks. It has been obtained from sources deemed reliable, the accuracy of which this organization does not guarantee. The inquirer has agreed to indemnify the reporting bureau for any damage arising from misuse of this information, and this report is furnished in reliance upon that indemnity. It must be held in strict confidence, and must not be revealed to the subject reported on, except as required by law.

FORM 2000-5/80

Information on Form 2000 shows, in outline form, the manner in which individuals meet their credit obligations. The present status of the consumer is of paramount importance, but the reader of a credit report is vitally interested in the historical status—how often the consumer was significantly late in paying bills. The period covered by each tradeline is expressed in months under the column heading "No. of months history reviewed."

The credit history section of Form 2000 tells the reader many other facts:

1. Who is responsible for paying the account. This information is necessary to comply with the Equal Credit Opportunity Act and is discussed at length later.
2. The kind of business reporting the information. Actual names of credit grantors are shown on automated bureau reports.
3. The date the credit bureau received the information. Bureaus with computer access to major creditors' automated accounts receivable files receive updated data every 30 days.
4. The method of reporting.
5. The date the account was opened.
6. The date of the last payment.
7. The highest amount of credit extended or the amount of credit represented by the last contract with the customer.
8. Whether the account is open charge, revolving, or installment. If known, the amount of monthly payments agreed to is shown.
9. Explanatory remarks to help the reader obtain a clearer picture of the consumer's paying habits. The explanatory remarks are three-letter abbreviations that amplify and explain the reference on that line.

Demographic Information

Demographic information is data related to the identity and location of the family. The credit bureau report, for example, will include the most recent and former address of the person, the social security number, date of birth, number of dependents, and whether the residence is rented or owned. Information about a spouse is also normally included, although the spouse will typically have a separate file under his or her own name. The social security number, if it can be obtained, is especially useful to the credit bureaus who often end up with duplicate files for the same person who uses slightly different names when applying for credit. The social security number is needed to verify that the individual is the same person when reported by two different creditors.

Employment Information

Employment information is data related to the name of an individual's employer, position held, income, and length of service. When a credit bureau receives a request for an updated report, the bureau routinely checks with the employer of record to verify and update employment information. If the report ordered is an "in-file" report, the bureau furnishes the name of the last known employer along with other employment information stored in the file. If it has been a long time since an individual has applied for credit, the employment information (especially income) will be of limited value since it is likely out of date.

Public Records

Public record information is the data maintained by governments, the court system, and other public agencies that make this information available to anyone who is interested. Credit bureaus check public records regularly to gather credit-related data. A bankruptcy petition, judgment for money due, or a tax lien may affect a consumer's paying ability, regardless of his or her previous record.

Credit Bureau Inquiries

The credit bureau also records and reports inquiries. **Credit bureau inquiries** are listings that show what creditors or parties have requested a particular file. These inquiries can provide information about other applications for credit that were recently submitted and perhaps declined. A large number of inquiries is sometimes considered unfavorable since it may indicate overuse of credit. Accounts or debts that are not indicated on an application for credit will sometimes show up in the credit bureau files.

Credit Bureau Information

- Ledger information
- Demographic data
- Employment information
- Public records
- Inquiries

Need for Facts—Not Opinions

Credit bureaus have long distinguished between facts and statements of opinion. In the distant past, credit reports included opinions of credit grantors and even comments about the subject's parents. Credit bureau files were once maintained in individual envelopes for different community members and contained news clippings and any other information the credit bureaus wanted to keep in these files. To ensure compliance with the Fair Credit Reporting Act, bureaus now refuse to place in their files anything other than verifiable data.

The Equal Credit Opportunity Act changed how credit reports are prepared. Before passage of the ECOA, almost all files, both credit grantor and credit bureau, were in the name of the husband. The ECOA requires creditors, when reporting credit history, to make clear what responsibility the subject has toward the accounts listed. Separate, individual files are maintained for both husband and wife. Form 2000 provides several options coded in the extreme left-hand column headed "Whose." The most widely used designations are:

1. Individual account for individual use.
2. Joint account with contractual liability.
3. Authorized user (usually a spouse).
4. Comaker of a promissory note.

Scope of Bureau Operation

The primary purpose of the credit bureau is to supply information. How this information is furnished to credit grantors is explained in the following sections.

Preparation and Maintenance of the Bureau File

The bureau files are the source of credit information from which data can be obtained quickly and easily and in turn, transmitted to inquirers. The basic stock-in-trade of a bureau is its information obtained from two major sources: local creditors and national or regional creditors' accounts receivable information.

Local firms that have credit experience with the subject of an inquiry are asked for current information covering their recent experience with that subject. Subjects usually name credit references when filling out a credit application. The contract credit grantors sign to become bureau subscribers specifies that they will provide their ledger experience promptly and accurately.

When the process works properly, the basic file accumulates automatically and reflects the credit experience of creditors with information about the subject's paying habits. Obsolete data, as defined in the Fair Credit Reporting Act, are deleted.

A bureau file reveals such data as details of each creditor's last transaction with the customer, the current status of the account, and a historical status that may cover varying lengths of time.

In addition to ledger experience, the credit bureau files contain information about each credit user, such as current and past addresses and current and former employment data. Public records of civil judgments for money, bankruptcy filings, and tax liens are added as they are obtained from court records.

Types of Credit Reports

Credit bureaus offer several kinds of credit reports either in printed form or orally. An **in-file credit report** is the most common report and involves the credit bureau providing all the information as it currently exists in the bureau files. There is no effort to verify, update, or manipulate the information further.

When an oral in-file report is requested by a member credit grantor, he or she identifies his or her company by a prearranged code to ensure confidentiality of the information. Then the credit grantor provides complete identification of the subject to include name, address, social security number, spouse's name, employment, and previous address. This information, read from a recent credit application, is used by the bureau to update the demographic and employment data. The credit bureau operator then reads the file to the credit grantor.

An increasing number of credit grantors are electronically linked to the credit bureau network. They will use an applicant's name or social security number to request a credit bureau file using a computer terminal in their own place of business. The in-file report will then be displayed and printed almost immediately on their equipment. In fact, in today's computerized environment, oral reports can be more expensive than computer terminal displays and printouts.

Credit bureaus are prepared to provide many specialized reports. For example:

Residential Mortgage Credit Report. This comprehensive report contains more information than a regular consumer credit report. A credit bureau employee will often make direct inquiries to verify almost everything in the file. The cost of this credit report is often charged to the borrower as a closing cost related to a home sale.

Business Reports. Usually prepared in response to a specific request, the business report contains all the information the bureau is able to collect on smaller commercial firms. The business report may be supplemented by credit reports on the owners, although great care is exercised to separate consumer credit histories from business credit transactions.

Personnel Reports. Usually prepared in response to requests from prospective employers, the reports may contain academic records, employment history, public records, and a consumer credit history. Where items of public record become part of a personnel report, up-to-date revision of this data is required by the Fair Credit Reporting Act to ensure that an employment or promotion opportunity is not jeopardized by incorrect or outdated public information.

Standardization of Terminology

Standardization of terminology within the credit industry was once a problem. Credit language was ambiguous, confusing, and sometimes misleading. A department store with a lenient credit policy might state that the consumer was "slow but satisfactory," yet a bank with a strict policy would describe the same paying habit as "very unsatisfactory."

With computerization, standardized language was vital between credit grantors and credit bureaus. For this reason, ACB and a cross section of the country's credit grantors devised "Crediscope," and by mutual cooperation, the present terminology emerged. Crediscope simplifies credit reporting and guarantees consumers that all creditors use the same criteria to judge paying habits. It provides one of the most thorough means available for including only objective information in a credit report.

Exhibit 10–1 shows a completed sample credit report Form 2000. An explanation of the credit history shown on sample Form 2000 is given in Exhibit 10–2. Exhibit 10–3 explains the terms that might appear on any Form 2000. Each of the three large database bureaus has its own format and each is significantly different than the Form 2000. This format is a good illustration, however, of the type of information found in a credit bureau report.

Charges for Credit Bureau Services

Whether operated as a merchant-owned service or a profit-oriented corporation, credit bureaus must charge for their services. Most bureaus charge a monthly fee or "dues" billed to all members according to the membership contract. Usually, the fee is a base charge only; the bureau depends on the sale of credit reports for its income. Each report the bureau furnishes to a subscriber is counted and listed on a monthly statement showing the quantity and price. Each bureau establishes its own prices.

EXHIBIT 10-2 **Explanation of Credit History on Sample Form 2000**

Trade line 1. This is a shared account that Mr. Consumer's wife is permitted to use. Department store (D608) last reported the account on computer tape September 1991 with a high credit of $172; the account owes $85, of which $34, amounting to two payments, is currently past due. The creditor reviewed the last 12 months' history of the account. Under historical status, note that in addition to the two payments currently past due, the account has also been past due on the other occasions. This is a revolving account with a $17 monthly payment. Bureaus assign internal code numbers to help them keep each firm separate. One department might be D608, while another might be D853.

Trade line 2. Individual account with a bank (B319) in the husband's name. Trade reported manually 9/91. The creditor reviewed 24 months' history with installments of $100 monthly. The account was never as much as 30 days past due and is now paid in full.

Trade line 3. Clothing firm (C526) revolving account, high $1,264, for which both spouses are contractually liable. The account currently owes $100, of which one $50 payment is past due. In addition, note that on two other occasions in the past 12 months, the account balance became 30 to 59 days past due and that once it became 60 to 89 days past due.

Trade line 4. A national credit card account on which the spouse is an authorized user. All or part of the present balance of $160 is disputed and was reported by the creditor as DRP (disputed—resolution pending). Under the Fair Credit Billing Act, the creditor suppresses any information as to the amount past due and the number payments past due. The "1" in the 30—59 days past-due column under historical status does not refer to the current condition of the account. Rather, it indicates that at one other time within the 12 months reviewed, the account was in this condition and that it was not disputed at that time.

Trade line 5. Legally, favorable information can be reported indefinitely, but users of credit reports prefer that it not be retained so long that it distorts the consumer's present paying trends. In this instance the data is over one year old, and the account is inactive.

CREDIT BUREAU OPERATIONS AND THE LAW

The Fair Credit Reporting Act (Title VI amendment of the Consumer Credit Protection Act) regulates the credit reporting industry. It became effective in 1971.

According to the authors of the bill, Congress explained the need for such a law in these words:

1. The banking system is dependent upon fair and accurate credit reporting. Inaccurate credit reports directly impair the efficiency of the banking system, and unfair credit reporting methods undermine the public confidence which is essential to the continued functioning of the banking system.

2. An elaborate mechanism has been developed for investigating and evaluating the creditworthiness, credit standing, credit capacity, character, and general reputation of consumers.

3. Consumer reporting agencies have assumed a vital role in assembling and evaluating consumer credit and other information on consumers.

4. There is a need to ensure that consumer reporting agencies exercise their grave responsibilities with fairness, impartiality, and a respect for the consumer's right to privacy.

EXHIBIT 10–3   Explanation of Abbreviations Used in Sample Form 2000

Terms of Sale

Open account (30 days or 90 days)	O
Revolving or option (open-end a/c)	R
Installment (fixed number of payments)	I

Kind of Business Classification

Code	Kind of Business	Code	Kind of Business
A	Automobile	O	Oil companies
B	Banks	P	Personal services other than medical
C	Clothing	Q	Mail-order houses
D	Department and variety	R	Real estate and public accommodations
F	Finance	S	Sporting goods
G	Groceries	T	Farm and garden supplies
H	Home furnishings	U	Utilities and fuel
I	Insurance	V	Government
J	Jewelry and cameras	W	Wholesale
K	Contractors	X	Advertising
L	Lumber, building materials, hardware	Y	Collection services
M	Medical and related health	Z	Miscellaneous
N	National credit card companies and air lines		

A. Column 1, whose account, provides a means of showing how a credit grantor maintains the account for ECOA purposes. Examples: 0—Undesignated, 1—Individual account for individual use, 2—Joint account contractual liability, 3—Authorized user spouse, 4—Joint, 5—Comaker, 6—On behalf of account, 7—Maker, 8—Individual account of spouse, 9—Subject no longer associated with account.

B. Column 3, method of reporting, indicates how a trade item was placed in file: A—Computer tape or TVS, M—Manual.

C. When inserting dates, use month and year only (example: 12–90).

D. Remarks codes (examples):

ACC—Account closed by consumer.
AJP—Adjustment pending.
BKL—Account included in bankruptcy.
CCA—Consumer counseling account.
    Consumer has retained the services of an organization
    that is directing payment of his accounts.
CLA—Placed for collection.
DIS—Dispute following resolution.
DRP—Dispute resolution pending.
JUD—Judgment obtained for balance shown.
MOV—Moved. Left no forwarding address.
PRL—Profit and loss write-off.

RLD—Repossession. Paid by dealer.
RLP—Repossession. Proceeds applied to debt.
RPO—Repossession.
RRE—Repossession, redeemed.
RVD—Returned voluntarily. Paid by dealer.
RVN—Returned voluntarily.
RVP—Returned voluntarily, proceeds applied to debt.
RVR—Returned voluntarily, redeemed.
STL—Plate stolen or lost.
WEP—Wage earner plan account (Chapter 13 of the
    Bankruptcy Act).

E. Account numbers, if shown, should appear on second line just below each trade item.

F. Disputes and comments associated with specific trade lines should be printed on second or third line in cases where account numbers are printed.

The Fair Credit Reporting Act established, among other things, the length of time that adverse information may remain in a consumer's credit file:

1. Bankruptcies which, from date of adjudication of the most recent bankruptcy, antedate the report by more than 10 years.
2. Suits and judgments which, from date of entry, antedate the report by more than seven years or until the governing statute of limitations has expired, whichever is the longer period.
3. Paid tax liens which, from date of payment, antedate the report by more than seven years.
4. Accounts placed for collection or charged to profit and loss which antedate the report by more than seven years.
5. Any other adverse item of information which antedates the report by more than seven years.

The Fair Credit Reporting Act distinguishes between "consumer report" and "investigative consumer report" because these are radically different in context. This chapter deals almost exclusively with the former. As explained earlier, investigative consumer reports contain information on a consumer's character and reputation, whereas consumer credit reports are composed of factual ledger experience only. Investigative consumer reports are used mostly by insurance companies to evaluate applicants for their insurance policies. The Fair Credit Reporting Act provides that underwriting is the specific permissible purpose for this kind of report, so it may not be used when claims are filed.

The Federal Trade Commission, which is responsible for enforcing the act, has announced interpretations that have affected credit bureaus' mode of operation. Two of the more interesting are:

1. Prohibition of books containing credit ratings of individual consumers (called *credit guides*), unless the ratings are coded to ensure that consumers can't be identified by name.
2. Permission to credit bureaus to offer promotional lists (described earlier in this chapter) so long as the user of such a list certifies that every person on the list will receive the solicitation and a firm offer of credit will be extended.

If a credit grantor declines credit privileges to an applicant based on information in a consumer credit report, the credit grantor must advise the applicant and provide the name and address of the credit bureau. This applies even if the credit report was only partly responsible for the decision. Notification is customarily provided in writing.

The business is not required to give any information to the consumer as to what the report contains. The applicant is generally better served by contacting the credit bureau directly for more detailed information. One reason is that the firm that compiles the report (the bureau) is in a much better position to explain it and to be helpful to the declined applicant.

Further, if the credit grantor denies credit based on data from sources other than a credit bureau, the consumer must be informed at the time of denial of the right to request in writing, within 60 days, the information that led to rejection. For example, a jewelry store might have asked the credit department of a hardware store how regularly the applicant pays. The intent of the law is that the consumer be given enough facts to be able to refute or challenge the accuracy of the information. The law does not require the credit grantor to tell the consumer the names of the sources checked.

Since the FCRA became law, credit grantors have been acutely conscious of the definition of a credit reporting agency. Legally, if a credit grantor relays third-party data as distinguished from its own ledger information, it becomes a credit reporting agency itself. For example, suppose a jewelry store calls a hardware store about a consumer's paying habits and the hardware store passes along secondhand information learned from a clothing store. The hardware store is then considered to be a consumer reporting agency and is liable for all the record keeping and interview procedures in the FCRA.

One of the most important provisions of the act is the right of consumers to know what is on file about them in credit bureaus. The law provides that every consumer reporting agency reveal the following on request and proper identification of the consumer:

1. The nature and substance of all information (except medical information) in its files on the consumer at the time of the request.

2. The sources of the information; except that the sources of information acquired solely for use in preparing an investigative consumer report and actually used for no other purpose need not be disclosed: Provided, that in the event an action is brought under this title, such sources shall be available to the plaintiff under appropriate discovery procedures in the court in which the action is brought.

3. The recipients of any consumer report on the consumer that it has furnished—
   a. for employment purposes within the two-year period preceding the request, and
   b. for any other purpose within the six-month period preceding the request.

The law states that consumers cannot be charged for an interview if, within the past 30 days, they have been denied credit because of a credit report from a credit bureau or have received a notice from a collection department affiliated with a credit bureau. The credit reporting industry has extended this 30-day time period to 60 days through current policy statements. Bureaus usually charge for interviews if the consumer just wants to find out what the file contains and has not been refused credit. Bureaus have generally agreed to charge no more than $8 for this service.

Individuals can sue any creditor or credit reporting agency for violating the law about who can have access to its credit records and about correcting errors in its files. The individual is entitled to actual damages plus punitive damages as allowed if the violation is proved to be intentional. In any successful lawsuit, court costs and attorney fees are awarded. An unauthorized person who secures a credit report—or a credit reporting agency employee who supplies a credit report to unauthorized persons—may be fined up to $5,000 or imprisoned for a year, or both.

During September 1996, the Fair Credit Reporting Act was amended as part of the Omnibus Appropriations Act of 1996. Among the major provisions are the following:

1. Entities that furnish information to a credit bureau may be liable if the furnisher knows the information is inaccurate.

2. Furnishers of data to credit bureaus are required to reinvestigate errors within a specified period of time.

3. Prescreening is specifically permitted. Also the creditor can post-screen respondents to see if they still qualify and they may deny the credit application.

4. State laws are preempted until January 1, 2004.

5. Consumers and credit reporting agencies may take legal action against individuals who obtain a consumer report without a permissible purpose.

6. Banks and their affiliates can share consumer information without having to comply with the law as long as the consumer is given the opportunity to prohibit this sharing.

EXPERIAN INFORMATION SERVICES

Experian (http://www.experian.com) (formerly TRW) is a supplier of consumer and business credit, direct marketing, and real estate information services. TRW, Inc. concluded the sale of its information businesses in September 1996. In November 1996, Great Universal Stores PLC purchased Experian and merged the company with the CCN Group of Nottingham, United Kingdom. This new global information provider employs more than 3,500 people in almost 100 locations throughout the United States.

Experian, one of the nation's largest consumer credit bureaus, provides computerized credit reporting services to qualified subscribers as permitted by law and company policy. The subscribers include credit grantors, employers, and insurers. Experian's consumer credit database contains factual credit history information on nearly 190 million consumers nationally.

In order to access the database, subscribers must transmit a subscriber code and password in addition to the required identifying information about the consumer. Identifying information includes the following: full name (including generation, such as junior or senior), current and previous addresses for the past five years, social security number, and year of birth. The information is transmitted from the subscriber's computer terminal to Experian's data center in Allen, Texas (outside Dallas), over a private data communications network. Within two to three seconds, the credit information is retrieved from Experian's database and transmitted back to the subscriber in the form of a credit report.

Experian's consumer credit report is provided in an easy-to-read format for consumers who request a copy of their credit bureau file (see Exhibit 10–4). The TRW Profile Summary shows selected information from the full report provided to subscribers which contains coded information and risk scores (see Exhibit 10–5). Information that identifies a consumer is used to locate and display a complete credit history about the consumer. Name, addresses, social security number, year of birth, and employer's name are all part of the identifying information. The main portion of the report contains factual credit history information about open and closed credit accounts as well as selected public record information, limited to bankruptcies, judgments, and tax liens. All of this information is reported to Experian at least monthly. Some lenders report data more frequently; public record data is often reported as it is filed with the court.

Box 10–1   Credit Management Tips

Requesting a Credit Bureau Report

The three major credit reporting agencies listed below will provide anyone with a copy of their current credit bureau file. If you have not been denied credit recently, there may be a small charge to receive your report. All three will respond if the following information is provided in writing.

Last Name, First Name, Middle Initial, Generation (Jr, III, etc.)
Spouse's First Name
Social Security Number   Date of Birth
Present Home Address with Zip Code
Previous Address for the Last Five Years with Zip Codes
Phone Numbers: Day and Evening

Print neatly, but sign the request with a signature. Some credit reporting agencies require a verification of your name and address by enclosing a photocopy of a current billing statement from a major creditor, a utility bill, or a driver's license.

The addresses, phone numbers, and current charges appear below. The charges in some states may be less, call for a current price.

Experian
PO Box 2104   Charge = $8
Allen, TX 75013   1-800-682-7654

Trans Union
PO Box 700   Charge = $8
N. Olmsted, Ohio 44070   1-800-851-2674

Equifax
PO Box 740241   Charge = $8
Atlanta, GA 30374   1-800-685-1111

Experian Information Services does not collect information about race, religious preference, personal lifestyle, medical history, or criminal records.

Open, current accounts remain on the report indefinitely while closed or paid accounts are removed within 10 years. As set by federal law, adverse credit information remains on file for a maximum of seven years, with the exception of bankruptcies, which remain for a maximum of 10 years. Inquiries to a consumer's file are retained up to two years.

In addition to its base product credit report, Experian Information Services offers a variety of services that assist subscribers with account management through account monitoring and statistical modeling. Experian has in-house statisticians who develop models that assess a consumer's future credit risk. One of the company's newest products

EXHIBIT 10–4

THIS IS YOUR TRW CONSUMER IDENTIFICATION NUMBER. PLEASE REFER TO THIS NUMBER WHEN YOU CALL OR WRITE TRW.

ID# 6030929418361222

JONATHON QUINCY CONSUMER
10655 NORTH BIRCH STREET
BURBANK, CA 91502

HOW TO READ THIS REPORT:

AN EXPLANATORY ENCLOSURE ACCOMPANIES THIS REPORT. IT DESCRIBES YOUR CREDIT RIGHTS AND OTHER HELPFUL INFORMATION. IF THE ENCLOSURE IS MISSING, OR YOU HAVE QUESTIONS ABOUT THIS REPORT, PLEASE CONTACT THE OFFICE LISTED ON THE LAST PAGE.

YOUR CREDIT HISTORY:

THIS INFORMATION COMES FROM PUBLIC RECORDS OR ORGANIZATIONS THAT HAVE GRANTED CREDIT TO YOU. AN ASTERISK BY AN ACCOUNT INDICATES THAT THIS ITEM MAY REQUIRE FURTHER REVIEW BY A PROSPECTIVE CREDITOR WHEN CHECKING YOUR CREDIT HISTORY. IF YOU BELIEVE ANY OF THE INFORMATION IS INCORRECT, PLEASE LET US KNOW. INSTRUCTIONS FOR REINVESTIGA-TION ARE INCLUDED ON THE LAST PAGE OF THIS REPORT.

AT YOUR REQUEST:

TRW INCLUDES THE FOLLOWING STATEMENT IN ALL REPORTS OF YOUR CREDIT HISTORY.

"MY IDENTIFICATION HAS BEEN USED WITHOUT MY PERMISSION ON APPLICATIONS FOR CREDIT. PLEASE CHECK WITH ME AT 213.999.0000 OR 714.555.0000 BEFORE APPROVING ANY CREDIT IN MY NAME."

ITEM	ACCOUNT NAME	DESCRIPTION	STATUS/PAYMENTS
1	* CO SPR CT SANTA ANA 123 MAIN STREET SANTA ANA, CA 92765 CASE# 7505853	THE ORIGINAL AMOUNT OF THIS COURT ITEM IS $1,200. THE PARTY THAT BROUGHT THIS ACTION AGAINST YOU OR THE COURT REFERENCE NUMBER IS ALLIED COMPANY.	THIS JUDGMENT WAS FILED IN 10/88 AND PAID IN FULL ON 10/19/89.
2	* BAY COMPANY 98 PIER BLVD SAN FRANCISCO, CA 94041 DEPARTMENT STORES ACCT# 4681123R101	THIS CHARGE ACCOUNT WAS OPENED 05/85 AND HAS REVOLVING REPAYMENT TERMS. YOU HAVE CONTRACTUAL RESPONSIBILITY FOR THIS ACCOUNT AND ARE PRIMARILY RESPONSIBLE FOR ITS PAYMENT. THE CREDIT LIMIT OF THIS ACCOUNT IS $1,600. THE HIGH BALANCE AMOUNT OF THIS ACCOUNT IS $1,285.	AS OF 01/95 THIS ACCOUNT IS CURRENT AND PAYMENTS ARE BEING PAID ON TIME BUT WAS PAST DUE 60 DAYS IN 04/93. YOUR BALANCE AS OF 01/21/95 IS $0. THE LAST PAYMENT REPORTED TO TRW WAS MADE ON 09/13/94. PAYMENT HISTORY: NNNCC1CCCCCC/CCCCCCCC21CC
3	* CENTRAL BANK 1456 E. RANGER DR DALLAS, TX 75221 BANKING ACCT# 4590345859403	THIS CREDIT CARD ACCOUNT WAS OPENED 07/88 AND HAS REVOLVING REPAYMENT TERMS. YOU ARE OBLIGATED TO REPAY THIS JOINT ACCOUNT. THE CREDIT LIMIT OF THIS ACCOUNT IS $6,000. THE HIGH BALANCE AMOUNT OF THIS ACCOUNT IS $1,624.	AS OF 12/94 THIS ACCOUNT IS PAID IN FULL BUT WAS 30 DAYS PAST DUE IN 07/94. THE LAST PAYMENT REPORTED TO TRW WAS MADE ON 12/22/94. PAYMENT HISTORY: CCCC1CCCCCCC/CCCCCCCCCCCC

EXHIBIT 10-4 *(continued)*

ID# 6030929418361222

JONATHON QUINCY CONSUMER
10655 NORTH BIRCH STREET
BURBANK, CA 91502

ITEM	ACCOUNT NAME	DESCRIPTION	STATUS/PAYMENTS
4	HILLSIDE BANK 651 MAIN ST SMALL OAK, AR 72657 BANKING ACCT# 291445C8119	THIS AUTO LOAN WAS OPENED 04/94 AND HAS 48 MONTH REPAYMENT TERMS. YOU ARE THE CO-MAKER ON THIS ACCOUNT AND HAVE GUARANTEED THE ACCOUNT SHOULD THE MAKER DEFAULT. THE ORIGINAL LOAN AMOUNT OF THIS ACCOUNT IS $16,300.	AS OF 01/95 THIS ACCOUNT IS CURRENT AND ALL PAYMENTS HAVE BEEN PAID ON TIME. YOUR BALANCE AS OF 01/15/95 IS $14,748. THE LAST PAYMENT REPORTED TO TRW WAS MADE ON 01/15/95. COLLATERAL: 1994 FORD TAURUS. PAYMENT HISTORY: CCCCCCCCCC
	ACCOUNT WAS IN DISPUTE - NOW RESOLVED - REPORTED BY SUBSCRIBER		
5	* MOUNTAIN BANK PO BOX 322 DENVER, CO 80217 BANKING ACCT# 3562A0197325346R5	THIS SECURED LOAN WAS OPENED 08/92 AND HAS 60 MONTH REPAYMENT TERMS. YOU ARE OBLIGATED TO REPAY THIS JOINT ACCOUNT. THE ORIGINAL LOAN AMOUNT OF THIS ACCOUNT IS $43,225.	AS OF 03/95 THIS ACCOUNT IS 30 DAYS PAST DUE AND WAS 30 DAYS PAST DUE 2 OTHER TIMES. YOUR BALANCE AS OF 03/26/95 IS $19,330 WITH $956 PAST DUE. YOUR SCHEDULED MONTHLY PAYMENT IS $956. THE LAST PAYMENT REPORTED TO TRW WAS MADE ON 01/03/95. PAYMENT HISTORY: CCCCCC1C1CCC/CCCCCCCCCCCCC

YOUR CREDIT HISTORY WAS REVIEWED BY:

THE FOLLOWING INQUIRIES ARE REPORTED TO THOSE WHO ASK TO REVIEW YOUR CREDIT HISTORY.

ITEM	ACCOUNT NAME	DATE	REMARKS
6	CAL AUTO 10 ALLEN STREET NEWARK, NJ 09987 AUTOMOTIVE	03/24/94	INQUIRY MADE FOR ACCOUNT CREDIT EXTENSION, REVIEW OR COLLECTION FOR UNSPECIFIED REPAYMENT TERMS. THE AMOUNT IS UNSPECIFIED.
7	HILLSIDE BANK 651 MAIN ST SMALL OAK, AR 72657 BANKING	04/18/94	INQUIRY MADE FOR AN AUTO LOAN FOR 48 MONTHS. THE AMOUNT IS $18,000.

THE FOLLOWING INQUIRIES ARE NOT REPORTED TO THOSE WHO ASK TO REVIEW YOUR CREDIT HISTORY. THEY ARE INCLUDED SO THAT YOU HAVE A COMPLETE LIST OF INQUIRIES.

ITEM	ACCOUNT NAME	DATE	REMARKS
8	BAY COMPANY 98 PIER BLVD SAN FRANCISCO, CA 94041 DEPARTMENT STORES	02/10/95	INQUIRY MADE FOR AN ACCOUNT REVIEW.

EXHIBIT 10–4   *(continued)*

JONATHON QUINCY CONSUMER
10655 NORTH BIRCH STREET
BURBANK, CA 91502

PLEASE HELP US HELP YOU:

AT TRW WE KNOW HOW IMPORTANT YOUR GOOD CREDIT IS TO YOU. IT'S EQUALLY IMPORTANT TO US THAT OUR INFORMATION BE ACCURATE AND UP TO DATE. LISTED BELOW IS THE INFORMATION YOU GAVE US WHEN YOU ASKED FOR THIS REPORT. IF THIS INFORMATION IS NOT CORRECT, OR YOU DID NOT SUPPLY US WITH YOUR FULL NAME, ADDRESS FOR THE PAST FIVE YEARS, SOCIAL SECURITY NUMBER AND YEAR OF BIRTH, THIS REPORT MAY NOT BE COMPLETE. IF THIS INFORMATION IS INCOMPLETE OR NOT ACCURATE, PLEASE LET US KNOW.

Your Name:	JONATHON QUINCY CONSUMER	Social Security #:	548603388
Address:	10655 NORTH BIRCH STREET BURBANK, CA 91502	Spouse:	CONSUMER, SUSAN
Other Addresses:	1314 SOPHIA LANE SANTA ANA, CA 92708	Year of Birth:	1951

IDENTIFICATION INFORMATION:

THE FOLLOWING ADDITIONAL INFORMATION HAS BEEN PROVIDED TO US BY ORGANIZATIONS THAT REPORT INFORMATION TO US.

Address:	1314 SOPHIA LANE SANTA ANA, CA 92708 Reported 11/84 by a TRW MEMBER	235 EAGLE POINT BLVD BUFFALO, NY 14202 Reported 04/84 by a TRW MEMBER
Employers:	AJAX HARDWARE 2035 BROADWAY LOS ANGELES, CA 90019 First Reported 4/89	BELL AUTOMOTIVE First Reported 11/80
Other:	Spouse Initial --- S AKA Name --- Smith Nickname --- Jack	

From 01/01/95 the number of inquiries with this Social Security # = 8
Social Security number you gave was issued: 1965-1966

CKPT: TELEPHONE ANSWERING SERVICE ON FACS+ FILE/COMMERCIAL BUSINESS ADDRESS/ABC ANSWER ALL, 10655 BIRCH ST, BURBANK, CA 91502 213 555 1212

*** END OF THE REPORT ***

Exhibit 10–4 *(concluded)*

JONATHON QUINCY CONSUMER   Year of Birth: 1951
10655 NORTH BIRCH STREET
BURBANK, CA 91502

SS# 548603388

If you believe an item on your TRW credit report to be inaccurate, we will recheck it with the source of the information and notify you of the results. This process will take about 30 days.

Full identification information including Social Security number is needed to begin the reinvestigation process.

TRW DOES NOT ALTER OR DELETE HISTORICALLY ACCURATE DATA.

> **At your request we will re-check the information you have
> disputed and send the results to organizations who have
> reviewed your credit history in the past 6 months (12 months
> for MD, NY and VT residents) or to employers who have
> inquired in the past 2 years.**

For credit inquiries, our hours are Monday-Friday. The best time to reach an agent is 9 a.m. to 4 p.m. Tuesday through Thursday at 1.800.422.4879 or write to us at TRW IS&S-NCAC, PO BOX 2106, ALLEN, TX 75002-9506.

CONSUMER CREDIT REPORT (CDI) TRW – FORM 1.05W   03/15/95 16:42:19   PAGE 4

TRW Information Services Division
505 City Parkway West
Orange, CA 92668
800.854.7201

Exhibit 10-5   The TRW Profile Summary

The TRW Profile Summary

The TRW Profile Summary contains 16 significant calculations from the Profile report.

1 The total number of public record items.

2 Total installment loan account balance owed by the consumer.

3 Total real estate loan account balance owed by the consumer.

4 Total revolving charge account balance owed by the consumer.

5 Total dollar amount of past due payments owed by the consumer.

6 The combined total of scheduled and estimated monthly payments owed by the consumer.

7 Total dollar amount of real estate payments owed by the consumer.

Note: An **asterisk** following a Profile Summary total indicates not all tradelines had an amount which could be included in the total.

8 Total percentage of revolving credit still available to the consumer.

9 Total number of inquiries.

10 Total of inquiries made within six months preceding the date of the Profile report.

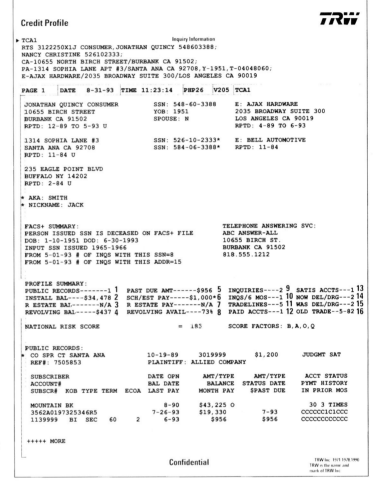

11 Total number of tradelines on the Profile report.

12 Total of accounts which have been paid satisfactorily or paid after having been previously delinquent.

13 Total of accounts which are current or paid satisfactorily.

14 Total of accounts which are now delinquent or derogatory.

15 Total of accounts which were delinquent or derogatory, and either have been paid in full or brought current.

16 The date the oldest tradeline on the report was opened.

TRW Information Services Division
505 City Parkway West, Suite 800
Orange, CA 92668
1.800.854.7201

©TRW Inc. 1994
TRW is the name and
mark of TRW Inc.
Printed in the USA

1224/1229
01/94

values loan portfolios and identifies the amount of cross-sell opportunities. This automated evaluation results in written reports.

Experian (formerly TRW) was the first credit reporting agency to use artificial intelligence in combination with an expert system to monitor access to its database. In 1989 TRW purchased one of its primary competitors, Dallas-based Chilton Corp., and strengthened its file in the Midwest and South. Chilton's consumer credit database was merged with TRW's that same year. Both Information Services and Business Credit Services are headquartered in Orange, California.

TRANS UNION

Trans Union (http://www.tuc.com) is one of the nation's leading consumer credit information companies. It maintains more than 220 million names from all 50 states, Puerto Rico, the Virgin Islands, and Canada in its computerized database at corporate headquarters in Chicago. The database is comprised of accounts receivable data from national, regional, and local credit grantors. Trans Union also has many subsidiaries and divisions abroad.

Trans Union Divisions and Subsidiaries include the following:

Ameri-fact, a subsidiary that specializes in nationwide pre-employment background verifications, e.g., criminal record checks, social security number verifications, credit reports, and verification of employment references.

Residential Services Division, which uses consumer credit information to meet the appraisal, equity loan evaluation, property search, and residential mortgage credit reporting needs of the financial and mortgage banking community.

Flood Zones, Inc. offers flood zone determinations.

The Insurance Division, Communications & Energy Group, and EcoGroup Inc., offer information, risk management services, fraud detection, collection tools, and marketing strategies to assist firms in the insurance, communications, energy, and utility industries.

List Services and Marketing Services provide prescreened lists to creditors and direct marketers.

Tfi is a joint venture of Trans Union Corporation and Fair, Isaac and Company, Inc., the world's leading predictive and decision control software company. Information and computer models are uses by companies worldwide to make better decisions.

Trans Union gathers and continuously updates accounts receivable information from credit grantors at all levels, even those that do not maintain large mainframe computer systems. It also collects full public record information in every county and state in North America.

Trans Union introduced the Credit Reporting On-Line Network Utility System (CRONUS) in 1970. It was the first on-line information storage and retrieval data processing system to complement the automated techniques used by credit grantors. CRONUS provides credit grantors across the country with fast and accurate one-source credit information on consumers. Each bureau within CRONUS electronically maintains and enriches consumers' credit reports continuously, both on-line and off-line.

Most inquiries are made on-line using computers although oral inquiries are also available. With oral inquiries, an operator keys in the subject's identifying information: name, current address, previous address, social security number, and name of spouse. Within seconds, the consumer's credit file is displayed on the screen. The operator then reads the information to the prospective credit grantor. Printed reports are also available with on-line systems and can be automatically printed in the credit grantor's place of business.

Because operators can access any of the credit bureau's databases, they can get information on consumers residing in any city served by Trans Union. By adding or reconciling file information, the operators can update a consumer's file on line.

EQUIFAX, INC.

Equifax, Inc. (http://www.equifax.com), founded by Guy and Cator Woolford in 1899, was formed to provide local Atlanta businesses with individuals' credit histories. Today Equifax is one of the world's leading providers of decision support information services and systems that facilitate consumer financial transactions. Headquartered in Atlanta, Georgia, the company today employs 14,000 people throughout North and South America, the United Kingdom, and continental Europe, serving more than 100,000 customers.

Equifax's consumer reporting activities are concentrated in two operational areas: credit services and insurance information services.

1. **Credit services.** Equifax operates one of the largest credit reporting networks in the country including company owned and affiliated credit bureaus located throughout the United States. Some of its more important divisions include: Credit Reporting Services offers consumer credit information, decision support, and credit management services.

Decision Systems provides modeling and analytical services along with marketing information and customer segmentation systems.

Equifax Card Services offers credit card marketing enhancements, and credit card and debit card processing for financial institutions.

Check Services provides check verification and an on-line guarantee of checks written at the point of sale.

2. **Insurance information services.** Equifax is the largest provider of risk management information to the insurance industry in the U.S. and Canada. The variety of automated and traditional information services supports both the underwriting and claims processes of all types of insurance. In the U.S., services include: personal life, health, auto and property underwriting reports; health measurements; medical history reports; claims investigations; motor vehicle reports; automated claims information; hospital bill audits; and commercial property inspections and surveys. Services offered in Canada include life and health underwriting reports, motor vehicle reports, commercial property inspections,

and automated claims information. Customers include most life and health, property and casualty, and commercial insurance companies and many agents throughout the U.S. and Canada.

SPECIALIZED CREDIT BUREAUS AND OTHER SOURCES

There are many specialized credit reporting agencies throughout the United States. Some of these serve particular professional groups, while others handle specialized types of reporting. The medical and dental professions can often use a medical credit bureau, which has a collection service as well as a credit reporting service.

Small loan companies and a few other financial institutions have established lenders' exchanges. These exchanges operate in some metropolitan markets for the express purpose of servicing particular types of lending and financing institutions. They keep master records of all loans or contracts financed by their members so they can rapidly check outstanding loans against a prospective loan customer. Subscribers can make telephone inquiries and receive immediate reports consisting of lists of outstanding loans against a potential debtor and the names of the lenders. Then lenders can be questioned about their experience with the subject. Subscribers or members of the exchange must disclose their borrowers by name, so that a complete record of the subject's similar dealings is available. Exchanges frequently service the small loan industry in a particular metropolitan area. In some cities, banks and sales finance companies also use similar facilities.

Important Terms

Associated Credit Bureaus, Inc.   194
business reports   201
consumer credit reporting agencies   192
credit bureau inquiries   199
credit bureau report   192
credit bureaus   192
demographic information   198
employment information   198
Fair Credit Reporting Act (FCRA)   195

in-file credit report   200
investigating credit reporting   192
ledger information   196
personnel reports   201
public record information   199
residential mortgage credit report   201
skips   193
written credit report   193

Discussion Questions

1. Explain why credit bureaus are needed by creditors.

2. What is the difference between an investigative report and a consumer credit report?

3. What are typical products and services offered by modern credit reporting agencies?

4. What effect has the Fair Credit Reporting Act had on credit bureaus? On credit grantors? On consumers?

5. Trace the beginning and development of the local credit bureau.

6. What are the principal activities of Associated Credit Bureaus, Inc.?

7. Discuss the principal types and sources of credit bureau information.

8. What data are reported on Form 2000?

9. Explain the operations of Experian Information Systems, Trans Union and Equifax and their services.

11 DECISION MAKING AND CONTROL

Learning Objectives

After studying this chapter, you should be able to:

- Explain the importance of decisions in credit operations.
- Describe reasons for poor credit decisions.
- Explain the development and use of a credit standard.
- Discuss the development and use of a credit grading device.
- Describe the use of a credit scoring system.
- Comment on discrimination in decision making.
- Explain the nature and types of control techniques in credit operations.
- Describe the use of credit lines and credit limits.
- Discuss automated approaches to credit control.

Decisions are the heart of all credit work. Customers offer credit for goods, services, and money, and credit managers must decide whether to accept or refuse the credit transaction. Judgment should be based on the information that is readily and economically available. This information should be pertinent to the problem and should be sufficiently penetrating to yield the greatest help possible in arriving at a correct decision. Once collected, however, the information must also be used properly if good credit decisions are going to be the result of the analysis.

The credit investigation brings together the raw materials that are processed through the credit analysis in order to get the final product—the credit decision. This end product is the objective of all the efforts directed toward gathering information and all the skill exercised in analyzing the information.

Once the credit decision has been made, and the credit account is opened, mechanisms must be developed to watch the account to ensure that payments are being made as agreed. Procedures must also be in place so that the account is properly used by those authorized to do so. This chapter also considers these and other control measures used to minimize losses for credit grantors.

DECISION MAKING IN CREDIT OPERATIONS

Importance of Decisions

The credit offered by a customer or borrower must be examined before a decision is made to accept or reject it. Making such decisions is the single most important credit activity. The success of the credit operation rests squarely on the appraisal and acceptance of the credit offered; the activities of the credit department in administering its work and collecting accounts may make the operation more successful or less successful, but they cannot replace decisions.

Reasons for Poor Credit Decisions

At the time the application for credit is approved everyone, both lender and borrower, expects that payments will be made in full and at the predetermined time intervals. Only in the case of outright fraud would a borrower plan not to repay the funds advanced. The lender, or credit grantor, believes that payments will be made or a loan or account application would not be approved.

However, events occur in the lives of customers and borrowers that may make payment impossible. Disability, financial misfortune, death, and economic loss of many varieties will leave some customers without the means to repay. Some customers will use the legal channels available in bankruptcy courts to avoid repayment of their debts. One could argue that these examples of failed credit accounts are unavoidable. The credit manager may have had sufficient facts and, at the time the loan was made, used good judgment in the extension of credit.

Some bad loans, unfortunately, will be the result of poor decisions. These errors generally involve insufficient information or the misuse of good data regarding the risk presented by a particular application for credit. Errors in decision making are probably unavoidable, but every effort should be made to carefully analyze the available information and uncover missing information.

Insufficient Information

Some errors in decision making will occur because important facts were not known at the time of the decision. Information will never be perfect, of course, and the decision must always be made with some facts missing. Perhaps a particular creditor cannot be contacted to verify the amount owed or an employer will not verify the employment of an applicant due to their firm's policy. Sometimes the pressure of time, and the speed required by the customer or a third party, will prevent the credit investigator from getting all the information needed. Sometimes the applications taken by a loan officer will not be as complete as they should be. Customers will often legitimately forget some credit accounts or loans, i.e., a credit union loan paid by payroll deduction. Perhaps the loan applicant has been a customer for many years and the loan officer does not want to impose on the client needlessly when, in fact, the situation has changed substantially. Obviously, a clearly written investigation policy will help establish a minimum standard regarding the type and amount of information to be collected.

Misleading or False Information

Nearly all customers are honest and will not knowingly withhold or misrepresent information. Some, however, will be dishonest and will try to obtain funds or an account using fraud. Some applicants for credit will understate their indebtedness, lie about their identities, or withhold information that they suspect will prevent the extension of credit. They may be desperate for money due to a hardship or they may suffer from simple greed. One of the reasons information on the application should be verified is to make sure of the facts. When loan applications are taken and documents signed, proper identification should be required to ensure that applicants are indeed who they say they are. Although this is a fairly rare occurrence, some provisions should be made to safeguard against false identity.

Improper Interpretation of the Facts

Sometimes the information is correct and sufficient, but the decision maker misinterprets the facts. Facts are thought to be unimportant at the time the decision is made, but after the account is delinquent, become clear indications that the credit should not have been approved. Perhaps a decision maker will suffer from the **halo effect**, the failure to consider all facts because one fact is so over-powering that it interferes with the ability to make a good decision. For example, a large income earned by a respected medical doctor may restrict the ability of a lender to consider other derogatory credit factors. Most loan officers and credit managers will agree, as they look over the original applications of charged-off bad debts, that they "should have known better." These errors in interpretation are difficult to avoid, but a structured approach to the decision using a credit grading form or credit scoring system (discussed below) will help overcome the problem.

Failure to Establish a Credit Standard

The most basic requirement in making decisions is to have a standard that can be used to determine if the risk evidenced by a credit applicant is too high. Exhibit 11–1 illustrates the variety of risk profiles that will be present and the need to draw a line to determine which applications will be accepted and which will be denied. Of course, some decisions are easy because the financial health, collateral, and payment record of the applicant is very strong. Other decisions are easy because the applicant is obviously not qualified. The greatest challenge is to work with applications in the "gray" zone where the applicants are closer to the limits imposed by the credit standard.

Some credit standards are very specific, i.e., the mortgage payment cannot exceed 25 percent of gross income. Others are left up to the judgment of business owner, manager,

EXHIBIT 11–1   **Establishing a Credit Standard**

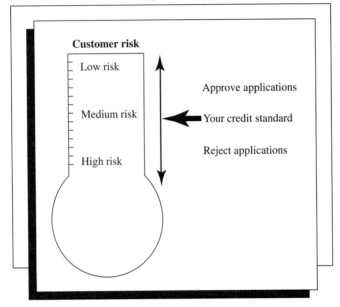

or other person who develops the basic credit standard. Many new small business ventures fail, however, because the owner gives credit to everyone and fails to develop standards for decision making. Credit and investigation policies need to be developed to ensure that the needed information is available regarding qualified prospects. Once the information is available, however, some standard needs to be developed to determine who will receive an approval.

Developing a Credit Standard

The development of a credit standard is a challenging, but important task. If the standard is too high, sales will be lost and some valuable customers will go elsewhere for products, loans, or services. If the standard is too low, collection expenses and bad debt may be unacceptable.

   The credit standard may also need some flexibility and may change over time with different situations. If economic conditions are poor, the firm may have to lower its standards to keep sales at a minimum level. Certain products may attract riskier clientele and the credit standard, as a result, will have to be raised for credit buyers. A strong collections department may allow a credit grantor to lower credit standards. Sometimes, the decision to market goods on a high volume, low markup basis will entail fairly easy credit standards. If high markups are available on expensive merchandise, high credit standards might be used. Although standards may differ with different economic conditions or products, the decision should be based on an identifiable standard.

Judgmental versus Numerical Decision Making

Judgmental decision making describes the decision-making process based primarily on experience, personal knowledge, and intuition. Some observers will visualize this approach as a "gut feeling" method whereby a credit manager looks over an application, perhaps makes a few quick calculations, and decides if credit should be extended.

The decision maker might calculate a debt ratio and complete a cash flow estimate as a part of the decision process. A **debt ratio** is the total monthly debt payments divided by the total monthly income of an applicant. This calculation shows the percent of monthly income that is currently committed to debt repayment. In cash loan situations, it is a good idea to calculate the debt ratio both before and after the potential loan is made. Each loan officer or credit grantor generally establishes the criteria, but a debt ratio exceeding 30 percent is often considered too high.

Many credit grantors also attempt to estimate the applicant's cash flow before and after the credit application is approved. A **cash flow estimate** is a calculation that subtracts estimated family expenditures for debt repayment, living expenses, and other typical costs from income to estimate the amount of discretionary income. Basically, the question is whether the applicant can afford the new payment or credit obligation. The judgmental method may be more highly structured with the use of a credit grading form, or a disciplined checkoff procedure, to help the user consider all aspects of the application for credit. Those who favor the judgmental method point out that the ability to develop information, especially in those situations where the credit analyst meets the applicant face-to-face, is very worthwhile. The major disadvantage is that it often requires substantial experience on the part of the credit manager who must analyze and mentally compare the application with others he or she has seen.

Numerical decision making is a number-based decision-making approach that assigns weighted values or credit scores to different qualities drawn from a credit application. As discussed in earlier chapters, a credit scoring system will typically be used to calculate a total credit score that is used to make the actual credit decision or as an aid for the decision maker. Different point values are assigned to length of employment, length of residence, type of occupation, or a variety of other factors. The resulting credit score may be used to approve an application, assign a credit limit, or indicate that further investigation is needed. The advantage of a numerical system is that it generally eliminates personal prejudices and inappropriate values on the part of the decision maker from the process. It is also easier to establish an identifiable standard for decision making since a required total score can be pinpointed.

Many credit managers believe that a combination of approaches is most beneficial. An applicant may not be able to earn a high enough score, yet in the judgment of the credit manager, be a worthwhile credit risk. This customer can perhaps be salvaged if the credit manager has the ability to override the negative decision produced by the credit scoring guide. If a numerical evaluation system is used exclusively, a potentially good customer will be lost because the score was not high enough. A good credit manager can often gather additional information and, using experience-based intuition, approve good accounts that would otherwise be rejected.

Likewise, an application for credit approved using the judgmental approach might be subjected to a numerical analysis and receive a poor credit score. This score might direct the credit manager to a more detailed look that would, in fact, lead to a different decision. Many credit managers report that although they were at first skeptical of credit scoring systems, they eventually learned to appreciate the ability of these systems to accurately predict the success or failure of the credit relationship.

Grading as an Analytical Device

The judgmental approach to credit decisions can often be made easier by using a credit grading form. A **credit grading form** is a preprinted form used to record the subjective evaluations of a credit manager regarding the various credit qualities found in a credit application. An example is shown in Exhibit 11–2.

Using a Credit Grading Form

The credit manager completes the credit investigation and analyzes the facts on the application. One by one, each listed credit quality is appraised as excellent, good, fair, or poor. Generally, three or four divisions are sufficient and more would confuse the process. The following guidelines can be used to assign grades:

Excellent: Superior, of the highest or finest quality.

Good: Above average, having desirable qualities, but not superior.

Fair: Average quality. Not particularly good or bad.

Poor: Generally undesirable. Below average or of questionable quality.

EXHIBIT 11–2   Credit Grading Form

Credit Quality	Grade			
	Excellent	Good	Fair	Poor
Income				
Employment				
Reserve assets				
Payment record				
Reputation				
Collateral				
Loan purpose				
Debt ratio				
Cash flow				
Summary grade				

The judgment of the credit manager is required to define "average," but the determination will generally be based on experience and the analysis of similar applications for credit. Beginning decision makers will often complete the grading forms and show them to a more experienced credit grantor as a part of their training program.

After each credit quality is evaluated, a separate grade is given to the overall application for credit. The summary grade will indicate if the applicant is good, fair, or poor based on the combination of the individual grades indicated above.

A credit grading form can be designed in many different ways. The number and types of credit qualities evaluated can vary in different credit departments. Its main purpose is to make sure that the credit decision maker looks at the individual qualities listed.

Advantages

Using a credit grading form in judgmental decisions has many advantages. The structured approach to the decision helps avoid the halo effect described earlier. The credit grading form is also very useful for beginning credit managers since they are required to use an orderly approach and record their thoughts as the decision is being made. Later on, the actual performance of the approved accounts can be correlated with the grading evaluations originally made. The form can also be used to evaluate the performance of experienced credit managers and will help collectors individualize collection responses. For example, an applicant with a lower credit grade might be contacted more quickly if a payment is missed. The collector may also decide to employ more assertive measures in these cases. The quality of business coming from a particular geographic region, or as a result of an individual advertising campaign, or from a sales finance dealer can be evaluated based on the credit grades generally observed.

Advantages of Using a Credit Grading Form

- Avoid halo effect.
- Aid beginning managers.
- Judge account performance.
- Judge credit manager performance.
- Individualize collection responses.
- Judge quality of business from various sources.

Disadvantages

The credit grading form requires substantial experience-based judgment. For example, John Doe receives an income of $375 a week. Is this good, fair, or poor? With these limited facts, it is difficult to grade his income; we know nothing of the certainty of its continuance or the demands on it. If we call Doe's employer and find out that Doe is a cutter in a local shoe factory, has been employed there for 7 years, and is 31 years old, we can judge that his income is likely to continue based on age and length of employment. We can make a better judgment if we know something about the shoe business and the market position of the local shoe factory. Knowledge is further improved when we know something about the employment policies of the local company. These comments illustrate how valuable general knowledge of local and national business conditions is to credit analysts.

Even with additional facts, different credit managers may reach different conclusions. The credit grading form helps direct the credit analyst to a more complete evaluation of the applicant, but the process still requires the use of informed, experience-based judgment. Of course, the true test of a credit manager's judgment is the eventual success of individual decisions and the profitability of the credit department.

Credit Scoring Systems

Credit scoring systems represent an attempt to bring a more scientific, numerical basis to the decision-making process. Henry Wells, a statistician who worked for Aldens, Inc. and Spiegel, Inc. in the late 1930s and early 1940s, was the first to use statistical methods to evaluate a credit applicant's repayment potential. He devised a point scoring system for new mail-order time payment applications.

Applying mathematical and statistical models to the credit-granting decision gained recognition when David Durand of the National Bureau of Economic Research in New York published his 1941 study entitled "Risk Elements in Consumer Installment Financing." He was the first to use discriminant analysis to measure credit risk. Subsequently, various attempts were made to investigate statistical credit systems, but the credit industry did not seriously consider credit scoring models until the mid-1960s.

The following statistical procedures are necessary to develop a point scoring system:

1. Application samples are taken to include those that would be approved with and without a credit report and those rejected with and without a credit report.
2. Factors on the application are correlated with the performance of these accounts over a period of time—6 months, 12 months, 18 months, and so on.
3. Weights are derived from statistical techniques and the position of the particular group of applicants characterized by these factors.
4. Statistical methodologies will attempt to measure the discriminating power of any single application factor, or any combination of factors, to the degree that the success or failure of the factor by itself indicates possession of the ability being measured. In credit point scoring, the ability being measured or predicted is payment ability.
5. Certain predictions are inferred from payment performance measured over time for each group of applicants characterized by certain factors.
6. Numerical weights are assigned to factors and the total of these weighted factors is plotted on a curve.[1]

---

[1] Stanley L. Mularz, "Statistical Origins and Concepts of Point Scoring," *The Credit World,* March–April 1987, p. 50.

Using a Credit Scoring Guide

The credit scoring guide will list the statistically valid credit qualities and characteristics to be drawn from the application for credit. Different point values are assigned to an individual application based on that person's history and current situation. For example, living at the same address for an extended period of time might be found to have a high correlation to good payment histories. A score guide will assign increasing point values to applicants as the years at the same address increase. The point values of all scored qualities are added together to arrive at a total score. If the credit score is above a certain amount, the application will be approved. An application with a score below a predetermined total will be rejected, and in between these numbers that bring either immediate rejection or approval, a more extensive investigation might be conducted. Some high-volume credit grantors use the credit score to also assign credit limits and credit lines for an open-end credit account.

Exhibit 11–3 shows an example of a credit scoring guide.

Advantages

Credit scoring guides are very useful for screening applications and quickly eliminating those that are not likely to be approved. By foregoing investigations, the credit department may reduce operational costs significantly. Some good customers may be lost if the applications are turned down prematurely, but the savings in investigation costs will often exceed the lost income from these few creditworthy customers that are turned down.

As mentioned earlier, a good statistically valid credit scoring guide should result in better credit decisions. The scoring guide eliminates the problems of inappropriate prejudices and personal values on the part of the decision maker. The scoring process can be delegated to nearly anyone, and in fact, is sometimes incorporated into a computerized analysis program. Also, the credit standard created by the required total point score can be easily adjusted to respond to different situations. If the number of approved applications needs to be increased, the required total score can be lowered. Different total scores can also be required given different credit programs, different products, or different customer types. Illegal discrimination is still not allowed, however, and the different credit score values must always be statistically related to the credit grantor's own experience.

Disadvantages

The use of a credit scoring guide can create some problems for a credit grantor. The scoring process can become too mechanical. Too many good customers can be lost if no one analyzes the applications. There is always the possibility that the credit scoring guide is not valid and poor customers are approved for credit while good customers are declined. Also, customer service may suffer as the credit department concentrates too much on numbers and forgets to look at the character and capacity of the customer.

Automated Credit Decision Making

Computers are being used in credit decision making more frequently and efficiently than ever before. Some of the reasons for this increase include greater availability of software, lower costs for equipment, and the need to capitalize on the speed and efficiency of computerization.

EXHIBIT 11–3   **Credit Scoring Guide**

Credit Information	Application Information Points Assigned			
Years at same address	Less 1 year	1–3 years	3–8 years	8 years +
	2	8	15	25
Years at same employer	Less 1 year	1–3 years	3–8 years	8 years +
	4	10	27	43
Age of principal automobile	Less 1 year	1–3 years	3–6 years	6 years +
	32	21	10	2
Housing status	Owner	Renter		
	20	10		
Age	18–27	28–40	41–61	62 +
	11	5	12	15
Monthly debt payment as percent of gross income	Less 20%	20–30%	30–40%	40% +
	35	25	10	0
Frequency of wage payment	Weekly	Biweekly	Monthly	
	15	20	25	
	Total points			
	Bankruptcy, Judgment, Charge-off			−50
	Final total			

NOTE:
Less than 80 points = Turndown
60–150 points = Investigate
Above 150 = Approve

In the most advanced systems, the credit decision can be made in a matter of minutes. For example, a customer applies for credit at an automobile dealership that uses indirect lending services provided by a financial institution. At the auto dealer's location, the application information is keyed into an on-line computer terminal. The information appears electronically on the screen of a loan officer at the financial institution. The lender electronically pulls in the information from the credit bureau, a credit score is automatically tallied, and a decision can be made very quickly. If the application is approved, an on-line message can be sent back to the dealer's office which results in the loan documents being printed for the customer's signature.

Once an organization computerizes its decision making, it can expect to realize several benefits:

1. Ability to use more complex mathematical scoring models.
2. Immediate updating of scoring criteria.
3. Access to on-line credit bureau information.
4. Faster turnaround time for customers to be notified whether their application has been accepted.
5. Better tracing of customer data to prevent duplicate applications, fraud, or inaccurate customer information. This information also will provide a data bank of information that can be tapped for possible sale of other products or services.
6. More time to spend on the percent of applications that fall into the questionable acceptance range.
7. Employees' lack of knowledge about the weight being given to specific scoring criteria. This eliminates employees' doctoring applications based on their personal feelings versus the actual situation.[2]

While the benefits of computerizing the credit decision process are many and profound, there are some disadvantages. These include training costs and lost productivity during the training period. Also, customers may feel alienated by having a computer decide their acceptance. Although not as likely today as in the past, management might resist trying credit scoring systems. Because developing a truly accurate system is costly, some firms take shortcuts and never gain full benefit.

As the volume of new credit applications continues to increase and more firms develop some automated system of credit control, an increasing number of firms will begin to experiment with and adopt some type of numerical scoring plan.

Discrimination in Decision Making

The 1975 Equal Credit Opportunity Act prohibits discrimination by creditors on the basis of sex or marital status. Extensive amendments in March 1976 expanded the act's prohibition of discrimination to include color, race, religion, national origin, age, receipt of income from public assistance programs, and the good faith exercise of rights under the Consumer Credit Protection Act. As a result of this amended federal act and various state laws, certain credit qualities have diminished in importance or disappeared as factors in credit decisions.

However, the Equal Credit Opportunity Act did specify that credit grantors can employ credit scoring techniques that are "demonstrably statistically sound" and "empirically derived" if they do not include factors prohibited by law. The board of governors of the Federal Reserve System is responsible for developing the criteria for a "statistically sound and empirically derived" credit scoring system.

---

[2]The author thanks Richard L. Cole, vice president of Cole Enterprises, Inc., Clearwater Beach, Florida, for his help in preparing this section.

On April 1, 1983, the Federal Reserve Board adopted an interpretation dealing with the treatment of income on credit scoring systems. This interpretation "prohibits creditors from discounting or excluding the income of an applicant (or the spouse of an applicant) from consideration because of a prohibited basis or because the income is derived from alimony, child support, separate maintenance, part-time employment, retirement benefits, or public assistance. A creditor may consider, however, the probability of any income continuing in evaluating an applicant's creditworthiness and may consider the extent to which alimony, child support, or separate maintenance is likely to be consistently made." The board also made another interpretation, this time regarding the selection and disclosure of reasons for adverse action. The board stated "the reasons for adverse action must relate to factors actually scored or considered by the creditor" in both credit scoring systems and judgmental systems. Thus, if a creditor takes adverse action because of bankruptcy, the specific factor must be disclosed.

CONTROLLING THE CREDIT RELATIONSHIP

Control is one of the major management functions carried on in all types of business environments. **Control** describes the act of verifying or checking progress of an activity followed by efforts to correct deviations. Control measures compare the current state of affairs with some benchmark to determine if progress is occurring and if the activity remains on track. In credit management, this activity involves providing information to the parties involved in the credit relationship. Credit control measures also help ensure the proper use of a credit account and serve to prevent overextensions.

Information Processing

Both parties in the credit relationship, debtor and creditor, need information to verify that the credit account is being paid as agreed. It is also important to provide the means to check on the current status of the account to determine if too much (or too little) credit is being extended.

Billing the Customer

Perhaps the most basic form of information processing in credit transactions is to bill the customer on a timely, regular basis. The bills may take the form of a regular monthly statement for a credit card account, or they may be comprised of payment stubs collected in a coupon booklet delivered to the customer after a cash loan is extended.

A proper billing statement for an open-end credit account will show the amount currently owed, the history of account activity since the last statement, and information about the remaining credit available for use. In the past, credit grantors sent copies of the actual charge slips signed by the customer during the month as proof of the amounts charged to the account. Today, nearly all credit card and retail creditors use a descriptive statement that simply lists the transactions. Of course, the credit customer can generally request, and receive, actual signed documentation if they suspect a billing error has occurred. Exhibit 11–4 shows an example of a descriptive billing statement.

EXHIBIT 11–4   **Example of Descriptive Billing**

BANK CARD SERVICE CENTER
PO BOX 80999
LINCOLN NE 68501-0999

1W   7 15 2

VISA	MINIMUM PAYMENT DUE	PAST DUE AMOUNT	PAYMENT DUE DATE	NEW BALANCE	ACCOUNT NUMBER	PLEASE WRITE IN AMOUNT OF PAYMENT ENCLOSED
	83.00	0.00	05/17/90	1667.81		$.

Payments received at the mailing address below before 2:00 p.m. will be credited to your account as of the date of receipt. Payments received at any other location may be subject to a delay in crediting of up to 5 days after the date of receipt. Use enclosed envelope and make payment to:

PLEASE DETACH AND ENCLOSE
TOP PORTION WITH PAYMENT.

BANK CARD SERVICE CENTER
PO BOX 80999
LINCOLN NE 68501-0999

4413 0000 3008

V000441300125009200083006016678150004413001250092

See Billing Rights Summary on reverse side regarding telephone calls. TELEPHONE NO.   402-471-1433

PAGE 2 OF 2

ACCOUNT NUMBER	CREDIT LIMIT	AVAILABLE CREDIT	DAYS IN BILLING CYCLE	BILLING CYCLE CLOSING DATE	PAYMENT DUE DATE	MINIMUM PAYMENT DUE
4413 001 250 092	3750	2070	32	04/22/90	05/17/90	83.00

DATE OF TRANS	POST	REFERENCE NUMBER	CHARGES, PAYMENTS AND CREDITS SINCE LAST STATEMENT	AMOUNT
0415	0422	A7H2600FZMEU00332	HOWARD JOHNSONS NO 157 COLUMBIA MO	8.70
0420	0422	B041300G008QFRGVN	MILLER & PAINE GATEWAY LINCOLN NE	26.25
		FINANCE CHARGE *PURCHASES $11.00 *CASH ADVANCE $0.00		11.00

PREVIOUS BALANCE	PAYMENTS	CREDITS	PURCHASES AND CASH ADVANCES	DEBIT ADJUSTMENTS	FINANCE CHARGE	NEW BALANCE
551.59	27.00	0.00	1132.22	0.00	11.00	1667.81

AN AMOUNT FOLLOWED BY A MINUS SIGN (–) IS A CREDIT OR A CREDIT BALANCE UNLESS OTHERWISE INDICATED.
TOLL FREE CUSTOMER SERVICE NUMBER.
(NEBRASKA) 1-800-742-0107 (OUTSIDE NEBRASKA) 1-800-228-9145
TO REPORT LOST OR STOLEN VISA OR MASTERCARDS CALL:
(LINCOLN RESIDENTS) 475-0577 (OMAHA RESIDENTS) 399-3600
(NEBRASKA RESIDENTS) 1-800-642-9370
(OUTSIDE NEBRASKA RESIDENTS) 1-800-228-1122
Send Notice of Billing Errors to: BANK CARD SERVICE CENTER P.O. BOX 81068 LINCOLN, NE 68501

	UNDER RATE CHANGE POINT		DOLLAR POINT AT WHICH RATES CHANGE	OVER RATE CHANGE POINT		1. Total Current Billing Cycle Purchases	2. Average Daily Balance of Previous Billing Cycle Purchases
	CASH ADVANCES	PURCHASES		CASH ADVANCES	PURCHASES	1132.22	192.63
ANNUAL PERCENTAGE RATES	18.00%	18.00%	N/A	N/A %	N/A %	3. Average Daily Balance of Old Purchases	4. Average Daily Balance of Cash Advances
MONTHLY PERIODIC RATES	1.500%	1.500%		%	%	541.46	0.00

VISA 1W

FINANCE CHARGE
FINANCE CHARGE

NOTICE See reverse side for important information.

Finding Past Due Accounts

From the credit department's perspective, some system must also be developed to collect information about past due accounts. As payments come into a credit department, they are posted to the account. Some means must also exist, however, to identify those accounts that are not receiving regular payments.

If a regular billing statement is sent and a payment is not received within the projected time frame, i.e, 30 days, a system must be in place to pinpoint the nonpayment. Computerized accounting systems have greatly enhanced the ability of businesses to quickly produce lists of customers who have not provided payments within a specified time period.

Once a past due or slow account is located, policies and procedures should be implemented to (1) make the customer aware of the problem and (2) provide for more careful attention to the particular account involved. Financial institutions, for example, maintain problem loan lists so that lenders and other personnel watch these accounts more carefully. In the case of retail or credit card accounts, the customer may be asked to refrain from using credit privileges until the past due status is cleared.

Some credit grantors, especially high-volume credit card issuers, have developed sophisticated computer models that attempt to predict bankruptcies based on payment records. These systems go beyond simply locating past due customers. They actually help the firm prepare for future problems.

Setting Credit Lines and Limits

Simply saying yes or no regarding the extension of a cash loan may be sufficient. Even in these cases, however, it is often good for the lender to ask, "What is the most I would lend to this particular borrower?" If the borrower does deserve more credit, some lenders will code the account to encourage employees to solicit more loans at every opportunity.

In the case of open-end credit, such as a retail charge account, the applicant needs to be told how much they will be allowed to charge and how much can be owed at any given point in time. A **credit limit** is the maximum dollar amount that can be charged to a credit account for the account to remain in good standing. If the credit limit is used as a red flag to prompt reconsideration of this maximum amount established for a particular customer, the limit is operating more like a credit line. A **credit line** is a temporary dollar limit for amounts charged to a credit account that may be extended at the request of the customer or after a client has demonstrated responsible use of the account. Many credit limits are, in fact, credit lines since the customer often is given additional credit to use if the line is crossed.

Advantages of Credit Lines and Limits

The use of credit lines allows maximum delegation. The credit manager can set a credit line for an individual customer and afterwards, entrust the daily decisions regarding additional charges to anyone in the firm. This relieves credit managers of the routine work of handling daily transactions, so they can concentrate on other difficult tasks. The credit line also instructs customers regarding their creditworthiness. In some cases, customers will spend more after they learn that more credit spending power is available. Credit limits also provide the opportunity to restrict credit use for questionable applicants. Many prospective credit customers will start with a modest credit line in those cases where the credit manager is not totally sure the account should be opened. As the customer performs well and meets payment schedules as agreed, the credit line can be extended. Modern computer-based accounting systems constantly analyze the pattern of posted payments and will automatically extend credit lines when payments are regular and sufficient. If the payments fall behind, the credit limit can also be lowered to reduce the lender's exposure as a credit customer begins to experience financial difficulties.

Disadvantages

Occasionally an applicant for a credit account will be offended if the assigned credit line is too low. Credit lines, in fact, may be too low if the credit manager is too strict in the decision-making process. This will restrict sales to creditworthy customers. Sales to existing customers will also be dampened if the credit manager fails to review credit lines on a regular basis. Good quality customers should be given sufficient room to buy goods and services using credit programs.

Methods for Setting Credit Lines

The best time to set a credit line is when the original application is approved. At the time an account is opened, it is subjected to the most complete review and examination it is likely to have for some time. The credit manager has completely analyzed the information available and has thought carefully about the account's payment possibilities. The effort to set a specific amount also requires the decision maker to make a more careful and penetrating analysis.

Although the advantages of using limits are well recognized, no one method is best for setting the limit. Methods are necessarily inexact and, in many instances, arbitrary. Variations occur between the types of credit plans involved—for example, between the option-terms revolving credit plan, the installment plan, and the open charge account plan. An installment plan, for example, with excellent security provided by the item being purchased, will allow a higher limit than an unsecured account. Variations also occur between retail transactions, service transactions, and cash loans from financial institutions.

Some credit departments attempt to limit the account to a certain period of time—a month's purchases, a week's purchases, and so on. Utilities, such as the water, light, and phone companies, are almost compelled by the nature of the business to follow such a procedure. Utilities often annualize payments by determining a fixed, year-round payment that smooths out the variations from high heating bills during the winter months. They may reduce the risk exposure somewhat by requiring a meter deposit or advance payment.

Some credit managers, in the course of the credit interview for opening a regular 30-day account, persuade customers to set their own limit. This is sometimes accomplished by asking, "What do you want as a limit on your purchases?" or "Do you have any amount you want to place as a limit on your purchases?" Others approach the matter a little more tactfully by asking, "About how much do you think you will buy in the course of the month?" After the customer gives an amount, the next question may be, "Shall we then consider this as the limit you place on your purchases?"

The computer-based credit scoring systems used by some high-volume credit card issuers use the credit score to approve an account and to assign the initial credit line. As mentioned earlier, the computer-determined line can later be adjusted based on the actual payment record of the customer.

Completely uniform standards are not necessary for the creditor firm to determine the quantity of credit acceptable from any one debtor. These matters are determined by individual firms and enforced through the operations of their credit departments. The policy on the quality of credit to be accepted should be adjusted to the firm's general sales policies, clientele, location, line of goods carried, and local and general business conditions. The policy on the quantity of credit to be accepted from any one debtor should be adjusted to the financial resources of the creditor, the credit standing of the debtor, and the type of credit plan involved.

Identification and Authorization

Once the account is established and a credit line has been set, policies and procedures must be developed to ensure that the account is being used properly. Identification involves making sure that current users are indeed allowed to use the account. There is always the possibility of fraud, especially in those cases where a customer charges items that they immediately take with them when they leave the store. Identification methods should be speedy and relatively simple since many customers are upset by lengthy procedures designed to verify they are who they say they are.

Authorization procedures help control the amount of credit used by making sure the current credit purchases do not push the total amount owed beyond the credit line. If a particular purchase does indeed extend the total beyond the line, a quick method should be developed to extend the credit line on the spot if the customer is worthy.

Identification and Authorization by Credit Card

Identification may be handled by issuing credit cards or some similar device. This method is commonly used by credit card and charge card plans and certain retail stores. When presented to the salesperson, the card serves to identify the customer. In the past, most credit card issuers furnished listings of lost or stolen credit cards to credit grantors. Credit grantors could then compare the number on an offered card with those reported lost or stolen. The issuer sponsoring the plan sometimes gave salespeople a financial reward for recovering a card that a customer is attempting to use fraudulently. Also, if the purchase was larger than a certain amount, the clerk was required to call an authorization center to make sure the credit purchase was approved.

Modern on-line, computerized authorization systems require the clerk to slide the credit card though a magnetic strip reader. This device reads the account number and automatically contacts the computerized database of account holders using telephone lines. This communication electronically verifies that the card has not been stolen and checks the credit line to see that the purchase is appropriate. The clerk reads an authorization number from a small message screen on the device and records the control number on the charge slip.

Identification by Signature

Another identification technique is having the customer sign the sales ticket. Should the customer claim that the purchase was not made, the signature on the sales ticket proves otherwise or is good evidence in case the creditor has to institute legal action.

Identification by Personal Recognition

In some smaller stores, the clerk or store manager recognizes customers personally, and there is no need for more elaborate identification systems.

Computerization and Credit Control

Computers are being used by more retail businesses and to a greater degree than ever. And this increase is expected to continue. Computer programs help credit managers achieve more effective control over operations and better decision making. In addition, a purely objective, carefully customized system enables credit managers to express their credit policies in concrete numerical terms.

Retailers can use computer programs to analyze sales from store level down to individual items, reduce labor costs, gather useful information for soliciting credit accounts and for collections follow-up, review inactive accounts, and improve record-keeping accuracy.

Thus the increasing use of on-line management systems affects every aspect of credit management, integrating initial decision making, identification, authorization of credit purchases, and control functions.

The decreasing cost of computers and the availability of prepackaged software eliminates the need for in-house programmers, so smaller retailers can now realize the benefits of computerizing their credit operations.

Electronic Funds Transfer

Consumers also benefit from computerized retail operations in the form of expanded customer services. One of these expanded customer services is electronic funds transfer (EFT) or point-of-sale (POS) technology. The retail industry has made considerable progress in developing and implementing point-of-sale transaction processing systems. Across the entire spectrum of retailing—food, drug, specialty store, and mass merchandising—these innovative retail information systems have provided many benefits to management, store personnel, and customers.

POS is the electronic transfer of funds—initiated from the point of sale at a retailer (hence the name)—from a consumer's account to a retailer's account to pay for purchases or services.

It works like this: A customer walks up to the counter with a basket of food. The cashier rings up the items as usual. The customer then puts his order bank card (a debit card, probably an ATM card) through a slot on a card-reading device and enters his or her personal identification number on a keypad. If there are sufficient funds, the account is debited for the amount of the purchase, and the store's account is credited for the same.

EXHIBIT 11–5   Electronic Funds Transfer Systems

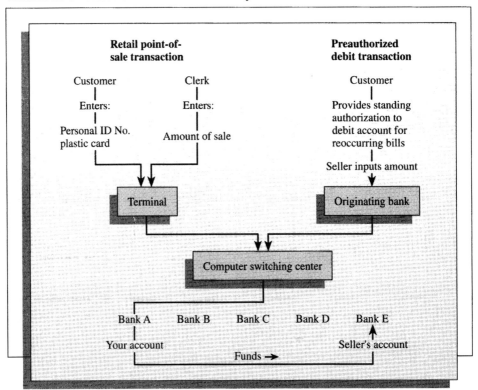

This on-line transaction is completed at the time of the sale or at least by the end of the day. POS transactions can also be made using an off-line system.[3]

Exhibit 11–5 illustrates a POS transaction. The POS technology yields the following advantages:

- Eliminates delay at checkouts caused by writing and cashing of customer checks.
- Provides customer with an additional payment option.
- Deducts payment automatically from customer's bank account in a debit card transaction.
- Requires minimum checker/cashier intervention.
- Provides easy-to-follow, lead-through instructions in POS terminal display.
- Creates potential increase in sales.
- Improves cash flow.

---

[3]Alec Smit, "POS: Where Have We Been? Where Are We Going?" *ABA Banking Journal,* September 1988, p. 104.

- Creates potential source of revenue from financial institutions.
- Eliminates check cashing charges.
- Reduces amount of cash and checks subject to theft at store level.

One drawback to electronic funds transfer is that it requires three primary participants: the bank, the retailer, and the consumer. If any one is missing, it will not operate. All of these participants must realize benefits over current methods of payment to make the change profitable. POS and EFT technology have been discussed in the literature for the past 20 years and yet the complete success many predicted has not been realized. But the limited use it enjoys today merits the discussion in this edition.

The main disadvantages to computerizing credit operations for retailers include training costs, the possibility of acquiring so much information that it becomes difficult to identify pertinent data, and the possibility that some consumers may view additional automation as another step away from the more personalized service they once enjoyed and expected.

Time and Expense Problems

In identification, authorization, and billing, emphasis generally is placed on speed and cost of operation and on maintaining customer goodwill. At times this necessarily means a relaxation in credit safeguards. Most stores believe this is justified, since the savings of time and money may more than compensate for the small number of customers who take advantage of a lax system. The systems described here are primarily large-store systems. In many smaller stores, the same results can be accomplished with less formal procedures because the store manager (or owner) is usually personally acquainted with most of the store's customers. In any event, whether the system is formal and routinized or whether it is informal and nonroutinized, the essential features of the task remain the same.

Important Terms

cash flow estimate   221
control   228
credit rating form   222
credit limit   230
credit line   230

debt ratio   221
halo effect   219
judgmental decision making   221
numerical decision making   221

Discussion Questions

1. Explain the statement, "Decisions are the heart of all credit work."
2. List and describe important reasons for poor credit decisions.
3. What is a credit standard and how is it used? Explain why different credit standards might be used for different products or in different situations.

4. Discuss the differences between judgmental and numerical decision making.

5. Explain how a credit grading form is used.

6. Describe the advantages and disadvantages of using a credit grading form.

7. Explain the development and use of a credit scoring guide. What are the advantages and disadvantages?

8. What activities are involved in the management function "control"? Explain credit control functions.

9. Explain the advantages and disadvantages of credit lines. How does a credit line differ from a credit limit?

10. List and describe common methods for setting credit lines.

11. Discuss three methods used to properly identify credit customers before they are allowed to use a credit account.

12. Explain how electronic funds transfer systems are employed in point of sale systems. What are the advantages for the customer and the retailer?

13. Discuss how computers are being used in credit decision making and control.

Suggested Readings—Part III

Management and Analysis of Consumer Credit

Altman, June. "The Word About Print." *Credit Card Management,* September 1996, p. 68. (Promotion of Credit)

Cellura, Alan. "Digital Imaging: A New Role for Data Processing Companies." *Credit World,* January/February 1996, p. 22.

Clancy, Rockwell. "Self-Service Banking: Directing the Consumer to Interactive Services." *Bank Management,* November/December 1995, p. 50.

Frank, John N. "Scoring Takes on a New Meaning." *Credit Card Management,* September 1996, p. 155.

Geary, Steven M. "Credit Repair, Practice vs. Promise." January/February 1995, p. 14.

Johns, Constance C. "Credit Bureaus and Limited Credit Services Partner to Provide Customers Truly Quick Credit." *Credit World,* November/December 1995, p. 21.

Kahn, Paul. "Pacing the Quality Race." *Credit World,* May/June 1995. p. 24.

Kryston, Mike. "Predicting Profitability: Finding and Keeping the Right Customers." *Credit World,* November/December 1995, p. 27.

Ladwig, Kit. "Weaving the Web." *Collections and Credit Risk,* July 1996, p. 45.

Novotny, Ann and Marvin H. Shaub. "How to Make a Dark Horse Shine." *Credit World,* September/October 1996, p. 9. (Marketing)

Rowland, Jan. "Credit Scoring: Big Opportunities for Small and Start-up Businesses." *Credit World,* September/October 1995, p. 21.

Snyder, Jesse. "Who's On First?" *Collections and Credit Risk,* September 1996, p. 63. (Credit Bureau Competition)

Solomon, Matt. "Marketing on the World Wide Web." *Credit Union Magazine,* February 1996, p. 27.

Tannenbaum, Fred M. "Big Potential in Small-Business Scoring Models." *Collections and Credit Risk,* January 1996, p. 59.

Totty, Patrick. "Credit Scoring Offers Multiple Benefits." *Credit Union Magazine,* March 1996, p. 62.

Whiteside, David E. "More Than Just a Credit Bureau." *Collections and Credit Risk, July 1996, p. 39.*

Whiteside, David E. "The Scoring Revolution." *Collections & Credit,* April 1996, p. 37.

Internet Sites

Credit Reporting Agencies:

http://www.equifax.com	Equifax Financial Information Services
http://www.tuc.com	Trans Union Corporation
http://www.experian.com	Experian (formerly TRW)
http://www.acb-credit.com	Associated Credit Bureaus, Inc.

Professional Associations:

http://www.aba.com	American Bankers Association
http://www.collector.com	American Collectors Association
http://www.scsn.net/users/cpi	Credit Professionals International
http://www.cuna.org	Credit Union National Association
http://www.ica-credit.org	International Credit Association
http://www.ibaa.org	Independent Bankers Association of America
http://www.nacm.org	National Association of Credit Management

Others:

http://www.wisbank.com	Good information on credit bureaus from Wisconsin Bankers Association

Case Problems

The following case problems provide an opportunity for readers to test and compare their decision-making skills.

1. Read each problem and complete a credit grading form for each case. Record additional facts that you are interested in knowing. (Note: Be careful about violations of credit laws regarding illegal discrimination.)
2. Decide if you would grant or refuse the loan or credit account.
3. Discuss your decision with others. What are the possible outcomes of approving or not approving the loan requests? If you have the opportunity, ask a local loan officer or credit manager if they would approve the loan application.

BILL AND BETTY STEVENS

Bill and Betty Stevens (see Chapter 2) have approached your bank and want a debt consolidation loan for $10,000. They bought a new house recently (see Chapter 6) and have had a few more expenses than they originally anticipated. The following is a list of the debts they would like to consolidate and pay off with a new loan from your bank.

XYZ Finance Company	Carpet loan	$2,000
Visa	Miscellaneous	$2,000
MasterCard	Miscellaneous	$1,500
Ace Appliance	Appliances	$3,000
City	Property taxes	$1,500

They are certain they can get back on their feet financially if they can pay these bills off, reduce their cash outflows by consolidating these bills, and lower their interest expense. They must also start a savings program for sending their children to college.

Amount Requested = $10,000;
Payment = $212.80;
36 mos/11 percent.

Review the facts discussed in earlier case problems regarding the Stevens family. You may want to construct a new financial statement before completing the credit grading form.

JENNIFER SMITH

Jennifer is 21 years of age and works at a local insurance company home office as a claims approver. She attended the local technical college after graduating from high school and completed a two-year associate degree program in secretarial science. She lives at home with her parents in a nearby small town and commutes 15 miles each day to her job. She pays no rent and her parents provide most of her basic support.

She wants to buy a new automobile. She has been driving one of her parent's cars and feels that she can afford the payments now that her full-time job is secure. Her only other credit experience is a loan to purchase her own furniture with an original loan balance of $4,615. The contract was actually initiated at a furniture dealer who eventually sold the contract to a consumer finance company, ABC Finance. A credit check reveals that she currently owes $2,466 and has paid the account as agreed (none over 30 days past due).

A check at her financial institution, the bank in her small town, shows a checking account with an average balance in the low three figures and a savings account with $2,200. The credit bureau file is clean. It shows only the outstanding loan at ABC Finance and a previous loan, now paid, at another finance company.

She is interested in moving her banking accounts to your bank located in the town where she works. She points out immediately that she does not want to ask her parents or anyone else to co-sign. At 21, she feels she can handle her own financial affairs.

Name: Jennifer Smith   Age 21
Unmarried
Dependents: None
Address: 123 Main Street   Small Town, WI
How Long? 21 years
Landlord: William Smith (Dad)   Rent? $0
Previous Address: None
Employer: National Casualty Insurance   Big Town, WI
       Position: Claims Approver   How Long? 1 year
       Income: $12,000 per year
Previous Employer: Ace Manufacturing   How Long? 3 months
Other Income: None
Loan Request: $7,824 ($9,624 less $1,800 down payment)
       New Payment = $256.15;   36mos/11 percent
Purpose/Collateral: New compact automobile
Debts: ABC Finance Company   Furniture
                       Original terms: 36 @ $166.84/month
                       Owes: $2,466

BETTY CLEENE

Betty tells you immediately that she was recently divorced and asks you if she should even bother applying for a loan. Her old car has died and she wants to purchase a 6-year-old Ford Escort from her neighbor for $6,500.

For three years she has been a self-employed house cleaner and operates under the name, Executive Housekeeping. She does not have any employees and claims that she has plenty of work to keep her busy. In fact, she often must turn down new jobs because her time slots are filled. She also explains that her tax records will verify her income for the last three years.

Betty still owes $2,300 on a 1979 Oldsmobile that was financed by your bank one year ago. Betty claims the engine has blown up and the body has rusted away. She jokes that she'll give it back to you if she can't finance another car.

A check at your bank reveals that she has a checking account with a $350 balance and a savings account with a balance of $660. Her account has been paid as agreed with no payments past due.

Her credit bureau report shows nothing new or unusual. The department store charge accounts are listed in the report and correspond to the information from the application. The finance company loan was taken two months ago (Betty explains she needed this for car repairs) and shows the same balance as the application. There are two collection accounts, $28 and $36, due at two different clinics in the city. All accounts are rated as agreed. Collateral listed indicates she has used co-signers in the past. Betty explains that the collection accounts resulted from disputes she had with an insurance company over the payment of medical claims and have since been satisfied. Betty also states that the co-signer she used previously has indicated that she would rather not co-sign another loan.

Name: Elizabeth Cleene   Age 42   Unmarried
Dependents: 2 children—Ages 4 and 7
Address: 555 Maple Street   Anytown, USA
How Long? 3 years
Landlord: Alan Wilson   Rent? $450
Previous Address: 444 Elm Street   Anytown, USA   2 years
Employer: Executive Housekeeping   Anytown, USA
        Position: Owner/Employee   How Long? 3 years
        Income: $24,000 per year
Previous Employer: Housewife   How Long? 15 years
Other Income: Child support from Tom Jones—$300 per month
Loan Request: $6,500; New Payment = $212.80;   36mos/11 percent
Purpose/Collateral: Ford Escort   6 years old
Debts: ABC Finance Company   Furniture $2,000 $249/month
        Sears   Charge Acct.   1,000   40/month
        Ace Department Store   Charge Acct.   500   20/month
        Your Bank   '79 Oldsmobile   2,000   148/month

JOHN AND JUDY ADAMS

John and Judy need $2,000 to buy new furniture. You can't help noticing that Judy is pregnant. John has an excellent work record and his family, including his father and his grandfather, have been bank customers for many years. They own a modest, but adequate three-bedroom home. John's employer hopes to eventually give him more responsibilities and an increase in his pay, but needs more growth in his business to accomplish this. Judy also receives high marks from her employer and expects a 5 percent increase in her salary next month.

They have been married for 10 years and, as far as you can determine, have never been late with a single payment. Their credit bureau report is absolutely clean and supports all the figures included in the loan application.

Name: John Adams   Age 31
Co-applicant: Judy Adams   Age 29
Dependents: 1, Age 3
Address: 123 Main Street   Small Town, WI
How Long? 3 years
Mortgage Holder: BC Savings and Loan
Payments: $350.00 Principal/Interest—Taxes: $2,000 per year
Previous Address: 233 Oak Street   Small Town, WI 2 years
Employer: Bigtime Office Supply
   John   Position: Equipment repair
          How long: 3 years
          Income: $18,000 per year (gross)
   Judy   Midwest Dentists
          Position: Receptionist
          How long: 2 years
          Income: $12,000 per year (gross)
Previous Employer: ABC Beverage   4 years   None
Other Income: None
Loan Request: $2,000; New Payment = $93.22;   24mos/11 percent
Purpose/Collateral: Furniture

Debts:				
First National Bank	86 Chevrolet	$4,000	$214/month
Sears	Revolving Acct.	900	36/month
JC Penney	Revolving Acct.	1,500	60/month
MasterCard	Bank Card	2,000	80/month
ABC Finance Co	Personal Loan	1,000	148/month

Credit Grading Form

Credit Quality	Grade			
	Excellent	*Good*	*Fair*	*Poor*
Income				
Employment				
Reserve assets				
Payment record				
Reputation				
Collateral				
Loan purpose				
Debt ratio				
Cash flow				
Summary grade				

IV | UNDERSTANDING BUSINESS CREDIT

12 | BUSINESS USE OF MERCHANDISE CREDIT

Learning Objectives

After studying this chapter, you should be able to:

- Describe merchandise credit.
- Discuss the development and contributions of merchandise credit.
- Describe typical terms of sale in merchandise credit.
- Discuss the factors influencing terms of sale.
- Establish a classification of terms of sale.
- Explain cash discounts and the equivalent rates of interest involved.
- Describe the nature and types of negotiable instruments.

The last nine chapters have covered consumer credit, and the next seven chapters are devoted to business credit. The classification of credit used in Chapter 1 shows that business credit is divided into two types: merchandise credit and financial capital for business operations. This chapter covers business use of merchandise credit.

Merchandise credit involves a firm's ability to obtain merchandise, inventory, and services in exchange for its promise of future payment. Merchandise credit is distinguished from credit for financial capital for business operations, because the value received includes merchandise generally obtained for resale. Financial capital is used to pay operating expenses when revenue is insufficient or delayed.

Merchandise credit is used by many different institutions, such as manufacturers, wholesalers, retailers, and cooperative enterprises. It is a form of business credit since the credit relationship exists between two businesses and because the credit is used to make a profit. Merchandise credit is the most important type of short-term credit used and accepted by businesses, by virtue of the number of transactions, the policies associated with accepting it, and the accounting procedures necessary to manage it accurately.

FUNCTION OF MERCHANDISE CREDIT

Merchandise credit facilitates the movement of goods through successive production and distribution stages. While this important function is frequently supplemented by other forms of credit, businesses rely on merchandise credit more than other sources.

Financing the Movement of Goods

Exhibit 12–1 illustrates the use of merchandise credit as goods move through the stages of production and distribution. When producers of raw materials sell to processors and manufacturers, the goods may be financed in several ways. If these original producers are financially capable, they may accept their customers' credit and provide additional time to pay. The seller provides specified **terms of sale,** a description of the conditions for payment in a merchandise credit transaction. If raw materials suppliers are financially weak, the burden of financing the goods falls on the purchasers, who may use their own capital or borrow from a bank or some other lending institution.

As the raw materials are processed or converted into semi-processed goods, they are sold to manufacturers of finished goods who may offer their credit in exchange. This is known as merchandise credit because the manufacturers are acquiring goods for further fabrication or for resale. As the goods are manufactured into finished products, they are sold to wholesalers or industrial supply houses. These businesses typically order large quantities of related products and distribute these goods to businesses who need smaller quantities for their inventory. This transfer is again accomplished by merchandise credit—wholesalers offer their credit to the manufacturer in exchange for the goods. Finally, retailers offer their credit to obtain an inventory of finished goods. Merchandise credit transactions take place each time goods change ownership until they are purchased by the final consumer.

Merchandise credit, then, is used by all kinds of business enterprises to finance the acquisition of goods or services. The transaction appears to be very informal: one business orders goods or services and another delivers. Evidence of the transaction is an account receivable or a note receivable claim in the seller's accounting records. The buyer's evidence of the transaction is an account payable or note payable obligation in its accounting records. Few businesses are free from frequent credits and debits to these asset

EXHIBIT 12–1   The Marketing Chain

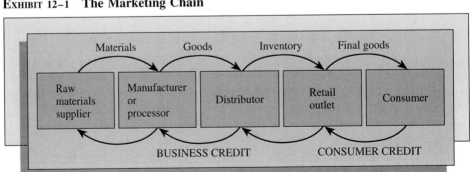

and liability accounts. Although there seems to be a lot of faith and trust involved, our laws do support these transactions and, if properly documented, provide the seller with specific rights when a business fails to pay for the goods. The vast majority of all goods and services flowing through the production and marketing processes are financed this way.

Essential to a Mass-Distribution Economy

Some method of facilitating payments in the various stages of production and distribution is essential to the effectiveness of a mass-distribution economy. Merchandise credit has become essential to the smooth operations of our economy, as described below.

Allows Businesses to Obtain Inventory.   If businesses depended exclusively on bank loans and their own capital, they could not acquire the same volume of inventory. New businesses, especially, would confront large start-up costs if the beginning inventory required cash payment. Instead, a business obtains merchandise with a promise to pay and, after the goods are sold, pays the invoice in full.

Facilitates Distribution of Manufactured Goods.   The widespread use of merchandise credit and much of its importance as a form of business finance stem from the nation's economic developments. In a simple, single community-based economy, retailers might drop by their suppliers and pay cash for each day's inventory for resale. As the nation grew, so did the distances between manufacturers and their customers. With the development of transportation and communication systems, population and businesses scattered over vast geographic areas. As mass production methods developed, manufacturers needed new ways to move more merchandise than would be possible through cash-only sales. Retailers also increased in number, and large-scale distribution became necessary to meet the wants of a growing population. Sales volumes increased at all levels and more efficient payment mechanisms were required to facilitate distribution.

Fosters Cooperation Among Businesses.   Creditors who deal with businesses today regard themselves more as business partners than as people in a position to ruthlessly enforce a claim. Credit between business enterprises is recognized as mutually profitable. In a sense, then, because both have risk capital invested, an attitude of partnership is fostered. As trust develops, the open account transaction, as evidence of a merchandise credit transaction, replaces the trade acceptance, promissory note, and draft. An **open account transaction** is a credit sale documented by accounting entries in the business records of both buyer and seller. This relationship between manufacturers and distributors, based on trust and supported by laws, has contributed to the rapid growth and development of the American economy.

TERMS OF SALE

In each merchandise credit transaction, the seller and buyer must understand the conditions for payment, generally known as **terms of sale, credit terms, or payment terms.** It is sound business practice to quote terms of sale on all invoices covering the

MISHLER ENTERPRISES, INC
123 Main Street
Anytown, State 12345

Invoice

Invoice Number
Invoice Date

Sold to:

Shipping Method: Purchase Order No:

Payment Terms: 2% 10 days, Net 30 days

QUANTITY	DESCRIPTION	DISCOUNT	UNIT PRICE	AMOUNT

Total Amount Due:

shipment and all instruments associated with the sales contract (see Exhibit 12–2 for an example of an invoice with terms of sale). If specific terms of sale are not quoted, the buyer can legally presume that any terms customary in that line of trade are applicable. The buyer's obligation to meet the terms of sale arises when the seller delivers the goods or services or meets other specified conditions of the sale. The terms of sale applicable in merchandise credit transactions are peculiar to this type of credit.

Establishing Terms of Sale

Credit terms offered to customers should be determined by executives responsible for policy decisions. Credit policies deserve just as careful consideration as other elements of the sales program. While credit policies and terms may vary in particular situations, certain general principles are common.

Two major variables are involved in all terms of sale. The first is the **credit period,** also called the *net credit period,* which is the length of time allowed before payment is considered past due.

The second major variable is the **cash discount.** This is a reduction in the total amount due allowed if payment is made before the end of the net credit period. The period of time the cash discount is allowed is known as the **cash discount period.** Not all firms allow cash discounts, but they are common in many trades. The cash discount should not be confused with the **trade discount,** which is a pricing device and bears no relationship to the time of payment.

In addition to the importance of quoting terms of sale, seller and buyers need a clear understanding as to the credit instrument employed. The most frequent evidence of a merchandise credit transaction is the seller's accounts receivable ledger. However, in some instances the seller may use a promissory note, trade acceptance, or time draft, all of which require the buyer's signature. Use of one of these instruments should be specified. To avoid disputes and eventual loss of customers, sellers must be sure that buyers understand the terms of sale, the credit instrument, delivery dates, and all other details of the credit transaction.

Another detail of the credit transaction is known as **anticipation,** a deduction some sellers allow for paying the amount due early. The deduction usually equals the interest at the current prime rate for the number of days the payment is early. Generally, the cash discount provides a higher return, but if the cash discount period has expired, anticipation provides some reward for paying before the date due. For example, an invoice for $2,000 is paid 10 days early after the cash discount period has expired. The amount due after an anticipation discount of 6% would be as follows:

Amount of invoice = ... $2,000.00

Anticipation discount = $2000 $\times$ .06 $\times \dfrac{10}{360} =$ 3.33

Amount due = ... $1,967.67

Factors Influencing Terms of Sale

Even though American industries use various terms of sale, many trades tend toward standardized selling terms, referred to as *customary or regular terms of sale.* Competition and other factors often influence the members of a trade to adopt similar selling policies over time.

Despite this trend, most companies have several terms of sale that serve as credit department guideposts. Once a company establishes its selling terms, they are likely to correspond to the selling terms of the rest of the trade. Established terms, however, often have to be adjusted for a particular customer or circumstance. The following factors are the most important influences on the adoption of particular selling terms and their occasional adjustment.

Effect on Sales and Profits

The decision regarding terms of sale depends primarily on the effect on sales and profit that the business firm expects these terms to have. If a firm's terms of sale are too costly because the firm must borrow funds to pay its own bills, stricter terms might be offered to its customers. On the other hand, more liberal terms might draw customers away from a firm's competitors resulting in higher sales and profits.

Rate of Stock Turnover

Sellers commonly finance buyers through at least a portion of their stock turnover periods, which are the time it takes to sell the merchandise. Accordingly, there is a relationship between the time it takes to convert merchandise into cash and the time allowed for payment of the indebtedness. Lines of trade with rapid turnover of merchandise generally have a short credit period, and those with relatively slow rates of stock turnover generally have a longer credit period. For example, most food products have a short credit period and clothing items have a relatively longer credit period.

Location of Customer and Transportation Facilities

Sellers dealing in distant markets are often at a disadvantage compared to local producers. Shipping goods over long distances takes time, and if the time for payment starts from the date of the invoice, distant customers do not have as much time to pay after they receive the shipment. To overcome this handicap, sellers may attempt to equalize the distance and transportation factors by allowing a longer credit period or by allowing terms starting with receipt of goods. In this way, the seller's terms of trade compensate for time lost in transportation and the expense of carrying a larger stock.

Regional Differences

When selling in certain sections of the country, sellers may have to adjust terms to local conditions. While not as important today as it was in the past, this influence is still real in many areas. Crop farming, for example, is more seasonal than dairy farming. Merchandise credit selling terms should be adjusted to this condition. Sellers may have to make a similar adjustment in industries where customers' income is very irregular.

Character of the Goods

Adoption and adjustment of terms may be based on the character of the goods. If a firm sells a wide variety of products, a single selling term may not apply equally well to all of them. Different products on the same invoice may or may not carry a cash discount. Likewise, the credit period may vary from one line of goods to another even though the goods are all sold by the same supplier. Variations in terms of sale may thus be the result of such factors as profit margin, perishability, the novelty of the product, and even seasonal characteristics. For example, goods that are very perishable and those that afford a narrow profit margin usually have a short credit period and little or no cash discount. Conversely, sellers usually grant a longer credit period and a larger cash discount when goods are seasonal, new, and yield a wide margin of profit.

Nature of Credit Risk

The terms of a particular trade may not be uniformly applied to all customers. Terms may vary according to the nature of the credit risk. Thus, buyers who are poor credit risks may be sold on a cash basis or on COD (cash on delivery) or CBD (cash before delivery) terms, whereas better credit risks get more liberal terms of sale. When most buyers in a particular trade are weak credit risks, the above terms may become standard practice, and sellers may continue to use them even after this reason ceases to exist.

Class of Customer

Variations in selling terms may also exist because of customer differences. Customers can be classified in numerous ways—for example, by size of order, by type of buyer (wholesaler or retailer), and even by type of wholesaler or type of retailer. Customers who make small purchases are frequently allowed shorter terms than the standard terms for the trade. On the other hand, large buyers who represent an important portion of the supplier's total volume may be given terms that are more lenient than is customary. A related factor is the customer's ability to perform important marketing functions for the supplier. Large buyers, for example, are frequently in a position to assume the storage function, provided the selling terms are adjusted to their requirements and other discounts are made available. Usually, as a matter of industry trade practices, wholesalers get different terms than retailers.

It should be emphasized, however, that different terms of sale for different customers must be justified on the basis of cost savings for the seller. The **Robinson-Patman Act** is a federal law that prohibits price discrimination that restricts competition or promotes monopolies. The courts have determined that *price* incorporates terms of sale and, thus, must be the same for similar buyers in the same category.

Competition

Competition often has the strongest influence on selling terms. Sellers frequently modify customary terms of sale to meet the actions of their competitors. Because of this, they grant extra datings or seasonal datings (datings designed to delay the buyer's payment date) to various customers. Certain customers, because of the competitive pressures they are able to exert, may also be granted terms of MOM (middle of month) or EOM (end of month). Too frequently, competition causes a departure from an originally sound policy. A firm may offer more attractive terms to attract customers from its competitors. Competitors, however, come to adopt the same terms, so the more lenient terms generally become standard trade practice. When this happens, terms of sale are no longer effective in stimulating sales, and the entire trade may find itself following unsound practices without any firm deriving special benefit.

Financial Resources of the Seller

The seller's ability to carry accounts receivable may force some modification of terms. A new business venture that is short of working capital has to sell on shorter terms than a well-established business with adequate resources to carry large accounts receivable. If many firms in a particular industry are financially weak, this policy may be adopted by the entire industry. For example, the shortage of working capital of the early car manufacturers led the industry to adopt cash terms. The same policy persisted long after car manufacturers had adequate working capital.

Economic Conditions

Business activity is influenced by economic conditions, and hence some business practices are modified according to the business cycle. Firms tend to adjust selling terms in periods of prosperity or recessions. Probably the ideal adjustment to cyclical changes is to tighten terms during prosperity and to liberalize them during recessions.

Unfortunately, credit managers often tighten credit terms during recessions as the general mood is pessimistic. As sales fall off during recessions, however, some customers simply take longer to pay and collections activities become more important. During periods of prosperity, credit managers are often swept along by the optimism incorporated in the economic peaks in the business cycle. Too much optimism, of course, can lead to problems when the business cycle turns down again and accounts receivables include many financial weak customers.

Attitude of Credit Managers

Credit managers can influence selling terms. Their degree of influence, however, depends on their position in a company relative to other policy-making positions and the relationship they have with other selling departments. If credit managers consider it their sole responsibility to eliminate bad-debt losses, and if they impose this attitude throughout a company, the seller may unduly shorten the credit terms. Likewise, a credit manager may be too lenient by offering too much credit and liberal terms of sale for too many customers.

Factors Influencing Terms of Sale

- Effect on sales and profits.
- Rate of stock turnover.
- Location of customer and transportation facilities.
- Regional differences.
- Character of the goods.
- Nature of the credit risk.
- Class of customer.
- Competition.
- Financial resources of the seller.
- Economic conditions.
- Attitude of the credit manager.

TERMS OF SALE CLASSIFIED

Terms of sale can be classified into the following groups:

Prepayment Terms

This class of terms includes **CBD (cash before delivery), COD (cash on delivery), CWO (cash with order), CIA (cash in advance),** and **SD-BL (sight draft with bill of lading attached).** Technically, prepayment terms are not common in merchandise credit transactions. When prepayment terms are used, the element of risk inherent in credit transactions is absent or slight.

Aside from a few instances where they are customary in certain lines of trade, the above terms indicate the seller's unwillingness to accept the credit risk. The buyer may have always been a poor credit risk, or the buyer's creditworthiness may have deteriorated to the point of being unacceptable. Not only is the seller unwilling to accept the buyer's credit, but the buyer also is often required to submit payment by certified check or cashier's draft; thus the seller does not even assume the risk of check clearance.

Unlike the other prepayment terms, COD terms and SD-BL terms are not entirely free of risk. The risk involved centers on the possibility that the buyer may reject the shipment after it arrives at its destination. In such instances the seller will have to pay the round-trip transportation costs, enter into a questionable credit arrangement with the original buyer, or, as a last resort, seek out another customer nearby. Sellers should insist on cash or a certified or cashier's check in payment of COD shipments.

SD-BL terms involves an order bill of lading, a document that verifies title to merchandise, attached to a sight draft. A sight draft must be paid when presented to the person named as payee. The seller sends these instruments to a bank in or near the buyer's city. When the merchandise arrives, the buyer may check the condition of the shipment and then pay the sight draft at the bank. In return for paying the sight draft, the buyer receives the bill of lading, which grants title and possession of the shipment. Once a shipment is made on SD-BL terms, the seller should be wary of buyers who plead lack of funds when the goods arrive. Coupled with this claim, such buyers usually encourage the seller to permit the bank to release the shipping papers, promising payment in 10 days. Since the alternatives are so unattractive, the seller may be strongly tempted to accept this arrangement. However, to do so means accepting credit from a customer whose credit was unsatisfactory a few days earlier.

Cash Terms

Cash terms do not indicate an immediate cash payment but the acceptance of credit for approximately 10 days from the date of invoice. Cash terms are a step removed from prepayment terms, as the credit period is very short. The time interval allows the buyer time to inspect and accept the shipment, and the seller's risk is lessened compared to more common, longer terms. With cash terms the buyer usually gets no discount privilege. Since the seller has no special recourse if the buyer fails to pay, the seller incurs the usual degree of credit risk. Bill-to-bill terms are a variation of cash terms that require the purchaser to pay for the current shipment when the next shipment arrives. An example would be a retailer receiving inventory deliveries each week and being required to pay for the last shipment each time new inventory arrives.

Net Terms

Net terms require full payment at the end of the stated credit period and allow no cash discount. For example, *net 30 days* means the invoice must be paid in full within 30 days from the date of the invoice.

Ordinary Terms

In many lines of trade, the terms of sale (referred to as ordinary terms) are the net credit period, the cash discount, and cash discount period. One of the frequently used ordinary terms is "²∕10, net 30" (2 percent discount if paid within 10 days, full amount due in 30 days). If a customer receives an invoice for $300 dated March 15, terms ²∕10, net 30, the customer has the choice of paying $294 on or before March 25 or $300 by April 14. By electing to pay the $300, the buyer pays $6 for the use of $294 for 20 days—a figure equivalent to 36 percent annual interest. Buyers should take advantage of all cash discounts.

Single-Payment or Lumped-Order Terms

In a number of industries, sellers permit customers to accumulate their obligations over a short period of time. These arrangements are used when individual buyers purchase and repurchase frequently. Rather than bill the customer for each order, the seller accumulates orders, usually for a month, and bills the customer as of one date.

Single-payment terms are really a special form of dating. The terms used may be based on EOM (end of month), MOM (middle of month), and proximo (a specified date in the following month). If EOM terms are used, all sales made during a given month are dated as of the first day of the following month. The cash discount period and net credit period commence with this date. Under terms of ⁸∕10 EOM, common in the apparel trades, all deliveries in the month of October are included in the statement rendered as of the last business day of October, and payment must be made by November 10 to take advantage of the 8 percent discount.

A common variation of EOM terms is to consider orders after the 25th of each month to be orders in the following month. For example, an order on May 26 is considered a June order and would not be invoiced until the end of June. This practice undoubtedly developed to encourage buyers to order in the last few days of each month. Otherwise, they would wait until the next month to get more time to pay.

MOM (middle of month) terms allow for a shorter total credit period. Under MOM terms, all purchases made between the 1st and the 15th of any month are consolidated and a statement rendered as of the 15th. Purchases made between the 16th and the end of the month are similarly consolidated as of the last day of the month (or the first of the next month). Hence, all purchases invoiced during the first half of a month with terms 2 percent/10 days, net 30 days are to be paid less discount as of the 25th (10 days beyond the 15th of the month). Likewise, purchases accumulated during the last half of the month are due the 10th of the following month to earn a cash discount.

Proximo terms specify a date in the month following shipment by which payment must be made. Terms of net 10th proximo, for example, mean that payment of October shipments must occur before November 10th (the next month). A cash discount period may also be included, e.g., 2 percent 10th proximo, net 30th. This provides a cash discount if payment is made before the 10th day of the following month, and full payment would be due 20 days later, on the 30th of the following month. In many instances, there is no distinction between proximo terms and EOM terms; one or the other just becomes customary in a particular trade.

Special Datings Terms

Special datings, which extend the credit period, are used to adjust terms to conditions peculiar to a trade or its customers. **"Season" dating** and **"extra" dating** are two common credit terms denoting special dating.

If the demand for a product is seasonal, sellers use season dating to induce buyers to purchase and accept delivery well ahead of their selling season. Sellers benefit because they can plan their production more in accord with their sales curve, and they can shift some of the storage burden to the buyer. Buyers have the goods on hand without an immediate investment of their own funds. This type of dating compensates the buyer for the storage burden and brings the payment date closer to the buyer's selling season. Summer wearing apparel, for example, may be purchased in October and delivered in January on terms of $2/10$, net 60, but the invoice may be dated May 1. These terms permit the discount on or before May 10 and establish the net due date as no later than July 1. This same arrangement can be accomplished by extending the regular selling terms an additional 30, 60, or 90 days during the preselling season months.

Extra dating is another method of giving customers long discount and credit periods. Extra dating terms treat the discount period and credit periods as identical, but rather than state the terms as 2 percent 70 days, net 70 days, they are customarily stated as 2 percent 10-60 extra. Under these terms, the purchaser is expected to pay the stated amount of the invoice, less 2 percent, 70 days after the date of invoice.

ROG (receipt of goods) and **AOG (arrival of goods)** terms and a few similar arrangements are used to compensate for disadvantages imposed on distant buyers. Such terms, in effect, adjust the beginning date of the discount period and often of the net credit period. Since terms may start with the date of the invoice, ROG and AOG terms adjust the entire discount period so that the first day of the discount period corresponds to the receipt or arrival of goods, whichever is applicable. Terms of this type are often competitively necessary for sellers dealing with distant customers.

Consignment Terms

Consignment terms are most often used for other than credit reasons. Agricultural products are customarily sold on consignment terms with commission agents. New products, and for that matter any merchandise for which a distributing organization refuses to accept the purchase risk, may be handled on consignment terms. And some goods of very high unit value move through marketing channels under these terms. Sellers also use consignment terms when the buyer's creditworthiness doesn't justify ordinary terms of sale and when the buyer lacks the resources for prepayment arrangements such as COD or SD-BL. Title to consigned goods remains with the seller, while the recipient acts as an agent for the seller. Because of the legal implications, credit managers must use consignment terms cautiously. Consigned goods must be physically segregated from other goods; proceeds from the sale of such goods must be separately accounted for; the shipper must carry insurance on the merchandise in the name of the consignor; and periodic sales and inventory reports and remittances by the consignee must be provided for. Credit managers should seek legal help to draw up consignment contracts and prepare the necessary directions to the consignee.

CASH DISCOUNTS AND EQUIVALENT RATES OF INTEREST

Cash discounts are very attractive to buyers. If the equivalent interest rate is higher than current interest rates, businesses should borrow money to take advantage of discounts rather than forgo this attractive return. In some businesses, particularly retail enterprises, the discounts taken can make the difference between a profit and a loss. Several offices of the National Association of Credit Management distribute complete tables to inform their members of the advantage of taking all cash discounts.

Terms of Sale Classified

- Prepayment terms.
- Cash terms.
- Net terms.
- Ordinary terms.
- Single-payment or lumped-order terms.
- Special datings.
- Consignment terms.

For example, an invoice with ordinary terms of 2 percent 10 days, net 30 days provides a 2 percent return for a 20-day investment period. The investment period is based on the assumption that the purchaser would wait until the last possible day (the 10 day) to take advantage of the cash discount and that the net credit period requires full payment 20 days later. Since there are 18 periods of 20 days each in a 360-day year (360/20 = 18), the annualized return is 36 percent (2 percent × 18 periods). See Exhibit 12–3 for rates of interest equivalent to selected cash discounts.

Furthermore, if the invoice above is for the amount of $2,000, the cash discount is worth $40. The cost of a loan at 12 percent would equal only $12.40 (interest = $1,860 × .12 × 20/360). Stated in monetary terms, it is also clear that the cash discount offers a profitable opportunity to save money.

EXHIBIT 12–3	Rates of Interest Equivalent to Selected Cash Discounts*

Terms	Annual Rate
½/10, net 30	9 %
1/10, net 30	18
2/10, net 60	14.4
2/30, net 60	24
2/10, net 30	36
3/10, net 30	54
3/30, net 60	36
4/10, net 60	26.8

*To compute such equivalents, find the number of days' differences between the cash discount period and the net credit period. This represents the number of days the seller gains in the use of funds when the buyer remits within the discount period. The potential number of times this is apt to occur is 360 days × the rate of discount = the equivalent rate of interest per year. For example, for terms 2/10, net 30, 360 ÷ 20 = 18 × 2% = 36%.

THE PROBLEM OF UNEARNED DISCOUNTS

Some retailers take unearned discounts—that is, they send the manufacturer a check for the amount due less the cash discount even though the cash discount period has expired. The seller then has to decide whether to accept the payment as a completed transaction, bill the buyer for the cash discount erroneously taken, or return the uncashed check and demand the net amount due. There is no one correct procedure; sellers have to consider customer goodwill, competitive conditions, and their own capital position.

TERMS OF SALE AND FEDERAL LEGISLATION

As mentioned earlier, sellers can use terms of sale to practice price discrimination. Price discrimination exists when sellers vary discounts to buyers in the same class. Credit terms came under the scrutiny of the federal government during the 1930s, when the **Robinson-Patman Act** became law. The Robinson-Patman Act prohibits price discrimination that results from discriminatory credit terms. Sellers are allowed to grant uniform discounts to all customers of the same class (i.e., all manufacturer customers, all wholesaler accounts, and all retailer customers). They cannot give larger cash discounts to one buyer than to another of the same class, accept terms insisted on by "terms chiselers," and allow late discounts when not applicable uniformly to all customers of the same class.

Cash Discounts or Trade Discounts?

The cash discount is a reward to prompt-paying customers for (1) saving the seller additional costs associated with a slower turnover of receivables and (2) avoiding the collection difficulties involved in handling slow-paying accounts. It is also a penalty assessed against slow-paying customers to compensate for the higher costs and inconveniences of handling their business. In the former case, the quoted price is considered the list price, and the cash discount allowed roughly equals the expenses saved by doing business with prompt-pay customers. In the latter case, the net price is the true realized price; the penalty collected from slow-paying customers approximately equals the expense of doing business with them.

Sellers would have difficulty collecting this penalty if it were so labeled, and efforts to enforce "fines" for delinquency would be strongly resisted and cause much ill will. Psychologically, it is better to collect the penalty as a benefit withdrawn. Loss of the discount then appears to buyers as the withdrawal of a gain that, through their own fault, they did not obtain. As a penalty assessed against slow-paying customers, the cash discount, to be equitable, must be no longer than necessary to recover the additional costs involved.

The costs to be recovered by the penalty are for: (1) use of the seller's capital during the extra time allowed for payment, (2) the assumed risk of potential bad-debt losses, and (3) increased billing and collection costs. Most trades allow a cash discount of 1, 2, or even 3 percent, an amount that seems to correspond to the cost savings incurred. Yet, under the guise of a cash discount, many sellers offer discounts as high as 6, 7, or 8 percent, and higher. And some accept these discounts even though payment is late. Such liberal discounts are trade discounts—not cash discounts—and so are special-dating terms if the discount is not disallowed because of late payment. Similarly, when the discount period and the net credit period are synonymous, some credit managers view the cash discount as a trade discount.

Negotiable Instruments

Closely related to the activity of paying invoices, raising capital, and accepting payments is the subject of negotiable instruments, or commercial paper. **Negotiable instruments** are promissory notes, checks and drafts used in business transactions to borrow funds, pay for purchases, or transfer value to another. Various rules and requirements concerning the validity, transfer, and character of different trade documents developed over the years and were eventually organized in Article 3 of the Uniform Commercial Code, a law adopted by virtually every state to standardize the ways businesses interact.

In order to qualify as a negotiable instrument, a document must comply with seven requirements. If one of the required elements is missing, the document may still be valid and enforceable between the parties involved, but the document is not negotiable. A negotiable instrument owned by and payable to a person may be *negotiated* by the owner, an activity that transfers value to another.

The seven requirements for negotiable instruments includes the following:

1. The instrument must be in writing and signed by the party executing it.
2. The instrument must contain either an order to pay or a promise to pay.
3. The order or the promise must be unconditional.
4. The instrument must provide for the payment of a certain sum of money.
5. The instrument must be payable either on demand or at a fixed or definite time.
6. The instrument must be payable to a payee or to bearer.
7. The payee and the drawee must be designated with reasonable certainty unless the instrument is payable to bearer.

Promissory Notes

A **promissory note** is a written *promise to pay* money at a specified time. Two parties are involved, the maker, the one who signs the note and promises to pay and, the payee, the one to whom the promise is made. The promissory note may, or may not, include provisions for the payment of interest.

Some specific types of notes are known by different names. A **bond** is a written contract that contains a promise to pay a sum certain in money at a fixed future time. Bonds are issued by corporations, municipalities, or governments, and may be secured by property or future revenue from a project funded by a bond issue.

A **collateral note** is a promissory note secured by personal property. The claim on the personal property is freed on payment of the note. If the note is not paid, the creditor may sell the property as prescribed by law. Any excess proceeds from the sale must be returned to the debtor and, if the proceeds are not sufficient, the debtor may be sued for the deficiency.

Real estate mortgage notes are promissory notes secured by real property, i.e., land and the buildings on the property. **Debentures** are notes issued by businesses that are basically unsecured and, as such, are backed only by the earning power and general ability of the business to pay the debt.

Drafts

A **draft,** sometimes called a *bill* or *exchange,* is *an order to pay* a sum certain on demand, or at a definite time, to another person. A **sight draft** is payable at sight or upon presentation by the payee or holder of the draft. A **time draft** orders the payment after a certain time period after presentation. A **trade acceptance** is a special type of draft that is prepared by the seller of goods on the purchaser. By signing the trade acceptance, the buyer agrees to the payment terms contained in the draft.

Checks are examples of drafts that are drawn on a bank and that are payable on demand. The check is an order by the drawer (a depositor), to the bank (drawee), to pay another person (payee). Some special types of checks are the following:

A **certified check** is an ordinary check that has been accepted by an official of the drawee bank. The check is generally stamped "certified" and the funds are set aside for the payment of the check, generally from the drawer's account. The bank is afterwards liable for the payment of the check.

A **cashier's check** is a draft issued by a bank drawn on its own funds and signed by an official or officer of the bank. This type of check is especially helpful when a personal check or cash payment is not desired by the recipient of the payment.

If a check is drawn with the intent to defraud another person, the drawer is liable for payment and may be subject to criminal prosecution under the bad check laws of the state. A **bad check** is a check for which payment is refused by the bank, usually due to insufficient funds. The challenge for the recipient of the check who wishes to bring forth criminal charges is the need to prove fraud. Sometimes, state law directs that if a person is notified of the nonpayment, and a fixed time period elapses, i.e., 10 days, a presumption of intent to defraud is made.

Important Terms

anticipation   249
AOG (arrival of goods)   255
bad check   260
bond   259
cash discount   249
cash discount period   249
cashier's check   260
CBD (cash before delivery)   253
certified check   259
CIA (cash in advance)   253
COD (cash on delivery)   253
collateral note   259
consignment terms   255
credit period   249
credit terms   247
CWO (cash with order)   253
debentures   259
draft   259
extra dating   255

merchandise credit   245
negotiable instruments   258
net credit period   249
open account transaction   247
payment terms   247
promissory note   259
real estate mortgage notes   259
Robinson-Patman Act   251, 257
ROG (receipt of goods)   255
SD-BL (sight draft with bill of lading attached)   253
season dating   255
sight draft   259
special datings   255
terms of sale   246
time draft   259
trade acceptance   259
trade discount   249

Discussion Questions

1. Explain the function of merchandise credit.
2. Why do receivables difficulties rank first as a fundamental cause of business failure?
3. Comment on the changing attitudes toward merchandise credit.
4. What are the major variables involved in terms of sale?
5. Explain the 11 factors influencing the terms of sale.

6. What is the six-way classification of terms of sale?

7. Why does the rate of anticipation tend to vary directly with the prevailing interest rate at commercial banks?

8. Why would a manufacturer use consignment terms?

9. How do you compute rates of interest equivalent to selected cash discounts?

10. Describe the seven requirements a document must satisfy to be a negotiable instrument.

11. What is the difference between a promissory note and a draft? Provide examples of each.

PROBLEMS AND APPLICATIONS

Complete the following table:

Terms of Sale	Date of Invoice	Last Date for Cash Discount	Amount Due Less Discount	Net Amount
2/10 net 30	Sept 15			
1/10 net 60	June 1			
1/15 net 45 EOM	April 1			
Net 30 days	May 15			

CASE PROBLEM

Bill Stevens's office products store orders supplies and inventory from several different vendors, each with different terms of sale. He needs to determine if he should borrow funds to take advantage of the cash discounts offered, or pass up the opportunity since he must borrow the funds. Complete the following chart assuming an invoice amount due of $5,000 and an interest expense of 12 percent annually with a 360-day year.

Terms of Sale	Amount Saved (Cash Discount)	No. of Days Loan Will Be Outstanding	Interest (Cost To Borrow)	Net Savings
2/10 net 30				
1/10 net 60				
1/15 net 45 EOM				
Net 30 days				

13 | FINANCIAL CAPITAL FOR BUSINESS OPERATIONS

Learning Objectives

After studying this chapter, you should be able to:

- Distinguish between financial and merchandise credit.
- Explain the differences between various types of business loans made by commercial banks.
- Point out what compensating balances do to the actual rate of interest paid for a loan.
- Distinguish between ordinary accounts receivable financing and factoring of accounts receivable.
- Explain how commercial paper acts as a source of funds.
- Discuss the need for long-term borrowing.
- Explain the activities of the Small Business Administration (SBA).
- Explain the individual's interest in starting or expanding his or her own business.

While merchandise credit is used to finance some of a firm's current assets, e.g., its merchandise inventory, most businesses require additional financial assistance to carry on operations. Businesses need **financial capital for operations,** the money needed to start, maintain, and operate a business. Borrowing may be short-, intermediate-, or long-term. Businesses use short-term borrowing to acquire current assets not covered by merchandise credit or by the owners' investment. They use intermediate- and long-term borrowing, on the other hand, to finance both current and fixed assets. Commercial banks and business finance companies (primarily factors and commercial finance companies) are the principle sources for short- and intermediate-term loans. Another source of funds for short-term needs is the issuance and sale of commercial paper. Long-term loans are available from such sources as insurance companies, investment houses, trust companies, and, to some extent, the Small Business Administration (SBA), wealthy individuals, and commercial banks.

This chapter is designed to discuss the business need for capital to operate and the various sources for this capital. The primary sources mentioned here are commercial banks, accounts receivable financing, the Small Business Administration, and commercial paper.

Although not as commonly used as the above-mentioned sources of financial assistance, recognition should be given to the fact that corporate stock issuance, the use of long-term corporate bonds, and nonbank lenders are other sources that are at times utilized to provide financial capital for business operations.

MERCHANDISE CREDIT MANAGEMENT VERSUS FINANCIAL CAPITAL FOR BUSINESS OPERATIONS

Merchandise credit management concerns a highly specialized type of business credit—facilitating the sale of merchandise and services in exchange for credit. With such specialization, individual managers tend to concentrate on terms of sale, collections, and cash discounts. They often see these activities as separate, and different, from the credit management needs related to the acquisition of funds to operate. In some firms, a treasurer or controller is given the responsibilities associated with monitoring cash flow and finding the best source for funds when cash flows are temporarily deficient. Other times, the credit manager also manages the cash position of the firm and operates as both a credit grantor (offering terms of sale) and as a credit user (finding funds to operate). Obviously, the two activities are closely tied together since the extension of too much credit, or the failure to collect funds aggressively, may have a detrimental effect on cash flow.

Whether credit executives are directly involved with their companies' financial needs frequently depends on their position in the organizational structure. Organizational structures vary according to the number and types of functions to be performed. A small- or medium-sized enterprise may employ a single executive to deal with both merchandise credit administration and the company's working capital requirements. This person may be designated as the treasurer, with a subtitle, credit manager. To work both sides of the fence—that is, customers' credit and the company's credit—the executive must be intellectually equipped to cope with the several types of business credit. Large businesses, on the other hand, often divide financial responsibilities among several executives. Merchandise credit management may be established in a separate department headed by a credit manager. The short-, intermediate-, and long-term capital requirements of the company may be administered by an executive designated as the treasurer or by the treasurer and a select group of company officers. Whatever policy the company follows, these executives need specialized knowledge to perform their tasks effectively. Because of the close relationship between credit and debt management, such executives need knowledge of all phases of business credit.

The need for operating funds *must be temporary.* Eventually a firm must collect sufficient revenue and profits to repay all loans and provide a positive return on the investment of the owners. A home builder, for example, may need to borrow funds to pay the carpenters since the building effort takes time and income is delayed until the home is sold. Ultimately, however, the home is sold and the funds are available to repay all loans and profit remains. A firm that does not generate sufficient cash flow to pay its expenses will eventually fail.

Many loans for business operations are thus short term. They exist to carry firms through these time periods when revenue is delayed. Of course, some loans and credit relationships are longer-term arrangements used to finance long-term assets and business expansion activities. Those who lend these funds must analyze the risk each borrower represents to ensure that their own firms prosper.

Irrespective of titles, organizational structure, and company size, executives responsible for merchandise credit management frequently advise credit customers on their financial problems. The increased tendency for credit managers to counsel their business customers is fostered by the present-day partnership concept of creditor and debtor. Many credit managers report that the customer-counseling aspect of their credit departments is one of the most valuable services they render. Their clear understanding of other sources of working capital and their ability to recommend these sources often give new life to a marginal or deteriorating customer. Similarly, cash loan managers must recognize the financial role played by merchandise credit in financing a portion of their customers' current assets.

The parts of this book devoted to business credit can be a valuable source of information for cash-lending executives. Selling merchandise and services on credit and handling business loans have a marked degree of similarity. They use similar credit information, a decision-making process, and collection policies. Differences between the two involve dependence on various sources of credit information, differences in credit standards, methods of controlling customers' accounts, and various governmental regulations.

NEED FOR LOANS

A business executive may turn to a lender for the following reasons:

- To increase volume by extending longer or more generous credit terms for desirable business.
- To manufacture and launch a new seasonal product at the right moment.
- To phase production in advance of peak seasonal demands, thus eliminating overtime and reducing costs.
- To pay bills promptly or in advance and gain cash discount or price, delivery, and service concessions.
- To increase production and cut costs by purchasing new, more efficient machinery and equipment.
- To expand production and sales by increasing the number of employees.

- To help finance the purchase of another company.
- To buy out a partner.
- To save on transportation costs by buying carload lots.
- To take advantage of favorable raw material prices.

COMMERCIAL BANK LOANS

As a source for short- and intermediate-term loans, no other institution is as dominant as the **commercial bank.** The tremendous financial resources of our commercial banking system make it the largest and most frequently used source for borrowed capital.

Credit Policy of Commercial Banks

A business firm can enjoy a long and continuous financial relationship with its commercial bank. Other than acting as a depository for business funds, the bank stands ready to serve its customers by providing an important segment of their financial needs. A commercial bank, however, usually has higher credit standards than those involved in merchandise credit transactions. Businesses that cannot meet the standards must acquire cash by borrowing from other, frequently less attractive, sources.

Banks have high credit requirements because they are entrusted with the public's money. A bank must guard this trust above all else to maintain its reputation and its customers' confidence. A Federal Reserve member bank cannot ask for extensions of its obligations without impairing its position in the system. And the liquidity of banks depends largely on the liquidity of their customers. The requirement that banks always be in a position to meet their obligations limits the extensions they can grant their customers. Banks do grant extensions, but the number cannot exceed a safe limit without impairing the bank's liquidity.

Another factor that contributes to banks' credit standards is that their stock-in-trade is money and not merchandise. Merchandise creditors have a wider margin of profit from the sale of merchandise than banks have from the lending of money. Because of this, merchandise creditors may be more willing to accept marginal risks and grant extensions not considered prudent by a bank. Furthermore, the amount of credit involved in a merchandise credit transaction may represent only a small portion of the debtor's total obligations; bank loans frequently represent a major portion of the firm's total debt. An extension granted by a merchandise creditor has very different implications from an extension granted by a bank.

Finally, banks are subject to supervision of state and federal banking authorities. They are restricted on the size of loan made to any one borrower; they are not permitted to lend on the security of their own stock; and they are limited in the amount they may lend to an officer of the bank. There are exceptions to the above restrictions; but, more important, bank loans are examined periodically. Bank examiners and their supervisors are responsible for enforcing the numerous administrative regulations that affect bank loan activities. To be regarded highly by the Federal Reserve System and its examining bodies, a bank must not have a record of lending money to a high proportion of weak credit risks. Thus legal regulations are another factor affecting the standards imposed on business borrowers.

Kinds of Loans

Single-Payment Loans

Traditionally, businesses obtained loans to finance their short-term needs, and loan maturities corresponded to the normal terms of sale (30, 60, or 90 days). A business would sign a short-term promissory note with repayment required after a short time period. During the 1930s, commercial banks changed their policies with respect to loan maturities and adjusted their lending terms to conform to the needs of borrowers. Short-term loans left many business firms with inadequate funds for continuous working capital and capital to refinance their bond issues. Since that time banks have also been making intermediate-term loans, with maturities from one to five years, and long-term loans, with maturities in excess of five years.

Business Installment Loans

Traditional loans to businesses were single-payment loans, but today **business install-ment loans** have become more and more important in the banking industry. The installment loans are used primarily for durable goods that last several years, e.g., a new delivery truck or other machine. The repayment schedule typically matches the life expectancy of the asset and the unpaid balance follows the depreciated value of the item financed.

Bank Line of Credit

Once a business establishes a relationship with a bank, the bank may set a line of credit in conjunction with a business checking account. A **line of credit** is the maximum amount the bank is willing to lend by honoring checks written for amounts exceeding the current account balance. Lines of credit are established after the bank has thoroughly analyzed the customer's needs, credit standing, and frequency of cash needs. Once established, a line of credit is much more convenient for the bank and for the customer; the customer can borrow needed amounts within the line without the formalities of a new credit investigation, analysis, and credit decision. A line of credit can be adjusted by the bank at any time as the perceived risk varies. The line of credit provides a flexible, immediate source of funds for the customer but does not obligate the business to use the entire amount.

When establishing a line of credit, a bank may set two requirements. One is that the customer maintain a **compensating balance** on the deposit at all times—that is, a fraction of the line of credit that the borrower is expected not to withdraw. Generally, compensating balance requirements range from 10 to 20 percent. This rule, though not uniformly applied, is customary in many banks. Some banks institute variations of the principle by requiring borrowers to maintain on deposit a fraction of the total loans made. The other requirement is that the borrower *clean up* loans periodically. This assures the bank that the loan is fulfilling its proper purpose and is not being used for long-term investment purposes. Businesses' temporary and seasonal needs are the basis for a line of credit, and loans used to meet such needs should be self-liquidating. Firms unable to meet this requirement from their own funds must borrow from other banks to clean up their loans and at the same time have their financial affairs scrutinized by other banks.

Secured or Unsecured Loans

Bank loans are also classified according to security—either secured or unsecured. A **secured loan** relies not only on the borrower's promise to pay, but also on the pledge of some specified property. The bank can exercise its lien on the collateral in the event the borrower does not pay. Banks prefer security that can be readily converted into cash. Government bonds, for example, which are easily converted into cash, are the highest quality of collateral. Businesses may, and often do, pledge inventories, stocks, bonds, mortgages, equipment, real estate, accounts receivable, and other property of value.

An **unsecured loan** is based solely on the creditworthiness of the borrower. Sometimes called a *signature loan,* evidence of this type of loan is usually the borrower's signed promissory note. Obviously, the creditworthiness of the borrower must be very high.

In addition to asking for a specific pledge of property as collateral, a bank may insist on other agreements before a loan is made. In smaller, closely held corporations, for example, the president of the firm might be asked to sign a **personal guarantee,** an agreement to pledge personal assets for the repayment of a loan that otherwise would not be available since the corporation is considered a separate entity under the law. A business borrower may also agree to **restrictive covenants,** an agreement listing prohibited acts or required activities that must be adhered to while a loan is outstanding. The borrower, for example, may not be allowed to pay high dividends to stockholders, merge with another business, or sell certain business assets. Other restrictions might involve maintaining certain financial ratios regarding assets and liabilities, or buying certain insurance coverages. If the restrictions are not followed, the loan will typically become due and payable immediately.

Typical Commercial Bank Loans

- Business installment loans
- Secured loans
- Unsecured loans
- Business line of credit
- Single-payment note loans

BANK INTEREST RATES—DISCOUNT RATES

Interest rates on bank loans are determined by a number of factors. An established rate of interest does not apply to all customers. Rather, the rate charged a business customer is determined by the amount and term of the loan, the borrower's credit standing, the tightness or abundance of bank funds, the compensating balance maintained on deposit with the lending bank, the bank's geographic location, and the demand for loans. In general, small businesses pay higher rates than large ones, and rates vary inversely with the size of loan.

A closely monitored interest rate is the **prime rate,** the best, lowest interest rate a commercial bank would offer its best business customer. The prime rates of major U.S. banks are published daily in financial newspapers and fluctuate according to general economic conditions. If the Federal Reserve System raises its own interest rates, these banks usually increase their prime rates. Although few businesses actually borrow at the prime rate, many business loans are tied to the prime rate by variable interest rate agreements. For example, a business loan might carry an interest rate of "prime plus 2 percent." As the prime rate changes, the interest rate on this loan would also change at predetermined adjustment points, e.g., on the first of each month.

Commercial banks employ two methods of collecting interest charges. In the case of short-term loans of 30, 60, or 120 days, banks may deduct the interest charge at the time the loan (advance) is made. Technically, this charge is referred to as the discount, bank discount, or discount rate. The **discount rate** a customer pays is not the same as the rate of interest paid on other loans. For example, if a $10,000 note that is to mature in six months is discounted at 14 percent, the discount would be 0.07 of $10,000, or $700. The business borrower receives $9,300 as the proceeds of the loan, and on maturity of the note a payment of $10,000 is due the bank. The borrower has use of $9,300 and not $10,000, and hence the discount rate is higher than the interest rate. Interest on other loans is usually calculated on the daily balance of the loan and charged to the borrower monthly.

ACTIVITIES OF THE SMALL BUSINESS ADMINISTRATION (SBA)

In 1953 Congress created the **Small Business Administration** (http://www.sba.gov) as a permanent, independent government agency to help small businesses grow and prosper. Small manufacturers, wholesalers, retailers, service concerns, and other businesses can borrow from the agency to construct, expand, or convert facilities; purchase buildings, equipment, or materials; or obtain working capital. One important restriction applies to all SBA loans. By law, the agency cannot make a loan if a business can obtain funds from a bank or some other private source. Businesses, therefore, must first seek private financing before applying to the SBA; that is, they must apply to a local bank or other lending institution for a loan.

To be eligible for SBA loan assistance, the business must be operated for profit and qualify as small under SBA criteria (except for sheltered workshops under the handicapped assistance loan program). Loans cannot be made to businesses involved in the creation or distribution of ideas or opinions such as newspapers, magazines, and academic institutions. Other types of ineligible borrowers include businesses engaged in speculation or investment in (rental) real estate.

For business loans, size standard eligibility is based on the average number of employees for the preceding 12 months or on sales volume averaged over a three-year period. Some industry standards are shown here.

Manufacturing: Maximum number of employees may range from 500 to 1,500, depending on the type of product manufactured.

Wholesaling: Maximum number of employees may not exceed 100. Services: Annual receipts may not exceed $3.5 to $14.5 million, depending on the industry.

Retailing: Annual receipts may not exceed $3.5 to $13.5 million, depending on the industry.

Construction: General construction annual receipts may not exceed $9.5 to $17 million, depending on the industry.

Special trade
construction: Annual receipts may not exceed $7 million.

Agriculture: Annual receipts may not exceed $0.5 to $3.5 million, depending on the industry.

Basic Types of Business Loans

The SBA offers two basic types of business loans:

1. Guaranty loans. **Guaranty loans** are made by private lenders, usually banks, and guaranteed up to 90 percent by the SBA. Most SBA loans are made under this program. The maximum guaranty of loans exceeding $155,000 is 85 percent. The SBA can guarantee up to $750,000 of a private-sector loan. The lender plays the central role in the loan delivery system. The small business submits the loan application to the lender, which makes the initial review and if approved forwards the application and analysis to the local SBA office. If approved by the SBA, the lender closes the loan and disburses the funds.

In addition to general business loan guarantees, the SBA provides a variety of specialized loan-guarantee programs, including:

1. Export revolving lines of credit.
2. International trade loans.
3. Seasonal lines of credit.
4. Small general contractor financing.
5. Lender incentives for small loans of less than $50,000.
6. Pollution control loans.
7. Community economic development loans.

2. SBA direct loans. **SBA direct loans** have an administrative maximum of $150,000 and are available only to applicants unable to secure an SBA-guaranteed loan.

The applicant must have first sought financing from his or her bank and been refused. In cities of over 200,000 population, one other lender must have refused the loan. Direct loan funds are very limited and at times are available only to certain types of borrowers (e.g., borrowers located in high-employment areas, or owned by low-income individuals, handicapped persons, Vietnam-era veterans, or disabled veterans).

Terms of Loans

Working capital loans generally have maturities of five to seven years, with a maximum maturity of 25 years. The longer maturities are used to finance fixed assets such as purchase or major renovation of business premises. Interest rates in the guaranty program are negotiated between the borrower and lender and are subject to SBA maximums. Interest rates for loans generally cannot exceed 2.75 percent over the New York prime rate. Interest rates on direct loans are based on the cost of money to the federal government and are calculated quarterly.

Collateral Needed

The SBA requires that sufficient assets be pledged to adequately secure the loan to the extent required. Personal guaranties are required from all the principal owners and from the chief executive officer of the business. Liens on the personal assets of the principals also may be required when business assets are considered insufficient to secure the loan.

Statistics on Small Business Administration loans to all small businesses from 1980 and 1985 through 1994 are shown in Exhibit 13–1.

ACCOUNTS RECEIVABLE FINANCING

In accounts receivable financing, a financing agency either makes loans to a borrower secured by an assignment of its accounts receivables or purchases the accounts receivables outright. Basically, the firm is able to raise cash immediately after an account receivable is created instead of waiting until the account is paid.

The credit executive needs to have knowledge of accounts receivable financing because such financing may be used by the credit manager's own company or by its suppliers. Equally important, a firm's customers may finance certain phases of their operations this way, and familiarity with this type of financing is essential. Also, the opportunity to convert receivables into cash may help pay a past-due obligation.

The two basic types of accounts receivable financing—ordinary accounts receivable financing and factoring—are subject to much misunderstanding. Ordinary financing of accounts receivable differs from factoring in the following major respects:

1. Commercial banks and commercial finance companies are the principal *sources* of ordinary accounts receivable financing, whereas specialized companies generally known as factors are the source for factoring.

Exhibit 13–1   Small Business Administration Loans to All Small Businesses: 1980 and 1985 to 1994 (For fiscal year ending in year shown. A small business must be independently owned and operated, must not be dominant in its particular industry, and must meet standards set by the Small Business Administration as to its annual receipts or number of employees. Loans include both direct and guaranteed loans to small business establishments. Does not include Disaster Assistance Loans.)

Loans Approved	Unit	1980	1985	1986	1987	1988	1989	1990	1991	1992	1993	1994
Loans, all businesses	1,000	31.7	19.3	16.8	17.1	17.1	17.0	18.8	19.4	25.1	28.0	38.8
Loans, minority-owned businesses	1,000	6.0	2.8	2.0	2.1	2.2	2.4	2.4	2.9	3.6	4.3	6.9
Percent of all business loans	Percent	19	15	12	12	13	14	13	15	14	15	18
Value of total loans[1]	Mil. dol.	3,858	3,217	3,013	3,232	3,434	3,490	4,354	4,625	6,339	7,412	8,426
Value of loans to minority-operated businesses[2]	Mil. dol.	470	324	265	299	343	385	473	601	808	928	1,328

[1] Includes both SBA and bank portions of loans.
[2] SBA direct loans and guaranteed portion of bank loans only.

Source: U.S. Small Business Administration, unpublished data.

2. Businesses finance their accounts receivable for fundamentally different *reasons* than they engage in factoring.

3. The *methods of operation,* procedures, costs, and service charges are basically different in each type of financial arrangement.

4. Finally, there is a marked difference in the *relationship between the parties* involved in accounts receivable financing as contrasted with factoring.

The following definitions point out the differences and similarities of these methods.

1. **Ordinary accounts receivable financing** involves an agreement under which a financing institution (*a*) purchases the open accounts receivable of its customers or advances them loans secured by the pledge of such receivables, generally on a one-time basis (*b*) with recourse to them for any losses and (*c*) without notice to their trade debtors. **Recourse** is an arrangement where the purchaser of the accounts receivable retains the right to return them for a refund if the debtor does not pay.

2. **Factoring** involves a continuing agreement under which a financing institution (*a*) makes credit decisions, collects the accounts, and assumes the credit and collection function for its clients and (*b*) purchases open accounts receivable as they arise (*c*) without recourse to the firm for credit losses and (d) with notice to their trade debtors.

The above definitions imply the reasons a business may enter into one or the other type of financing arrangement. Businesses use ordinary accounts receivable financing for one major reason—to acquire needed capital. Factoring, on the other hand, is entered into for two reasons—first, to acquire operating capital by selling the receivables outright, and second, to shift the entire credit and collection burden to the financing institution.

Ordinary Accounts Receivable Financing

Commercial banks and commercial finance companies are the sources that normally finance accounts receivable. A **commercial finance company** is an organization without a bank charter that makes loans to businesses and provides accounts receivable financing for profit. Commercial banks often follow the procedure of making a loan with the accounts receivable as security. Finance companies may purchase the receivables for some stated amount of cash or accept assigned receivables as security for a loan much as a bank does.

Both types of lenders normally make their advances with recourse to the borrowing firm, but without notice to the borrower's trade debtors. Recourse gives the lending institution protection against slow-paying accounts and losses that occur due to uncollectible accounts. Because of the recourse provision of the transaction, the lender assumes little or no risk; in essence, the assigner guarantees payment of all assigned accounts. The lending institution, whether bank or finance company, examines the quality of the accounts receivable offered. To be acceptable, the major proportion (about 75 to 80 percent) of the assigned receivables must have the high or the second-high rating granted by Dun & Bradstreet or some other credit reporting agency. The contract between the parties under the non-notification plan:

1. Sets forth the lender's advances and charges.

2. Provides that the assigner act as the assignee's agent in collecting accounts.

3. Establishes the method and time by which the assigner transmits collections to the lending firm.

4. Provides for the assigner to guarantee all assigned accounts.

5. Provides that the assignee may inspect the accounting records of the assigner at any time.

These and other provisions of the contract, as well as other technicalities of the transaction, dictate that the borrower give a precise accounting of all funds received that are to be credited to the assigned accounts receivable.

The American Bankers Association recommends that the loans based on accounts receivables should be no more than 80 percent of the face value of the receivables, less trade and other discounts allowed to customers and consideration for merchandise returns. Commercial finance companies may advance 70 to 95 percent of the face value of the receivables. Each of the quoted percentages depends on the quality of the receivables and the lender's standards of acceptability. The difference between the percentage and the net value of the receivables is a margin of safety against deductions, shrinkages, and bad-debt losses.

Rates on this type of lending vary widely and are determined by a group of complex factors. The rate may be set on the basis of the risk involved, the credit standing of the trade debtor's accounts that are assigned, the assigner's terms of sale, the borrower's credit and collection practices, and other factors previously discussed.

Some executives and lenders view accounts receivable financing as undesirable. Their principal objection seems to be that assigning receivables deprives trade creditors of protection against losses. Yet this objection is not as valid as it was before the 1930s. Many creditors now recognize the need for this type of financing as a desired alternative method of acquiring capital, and a large number of banks presently make such loans. Furthermore, the American Bankers Association has recognized that: (1) accounts receivable financing is becoming increasingly important, (2) the security is often the most liquid asset a borrower has to offer, (3) the necessity to borrow arises not from failure but from growth problems, and (4) as a business grows, it faces financial stress from its large volume of receivables, and it is logical to resort to this asset for necessary relief.

Borrowing on the basis of accounts receivable is also an alternative to other financing possibilities. Most businesses face short-term financial problems. Rather than gain relief by increasing its long-term debt, a business can increase its line of credit at the bank. If this is not possible, it can secure an additional loan from the bank by pledging its accounts receivable. Some businesses do not qualify for an additional bank loan or prefer to seek financial aid from a commercial finance company. Whatever the source of the funds, businesses are usually better off with a self-liquidating loan than a long-term debt burden.

Factoring Accounts Receivable

Factoring is the only known arrangement that completely assumes the entire credit and collection function for clients. The financing aspect of factoring is often secondary to the desire and need to make such a shift.

The factor purchases accounts receivable from clients without recourse for credit losses and assumes all credit risks involved. Trade debtors, accordingly, are notified that payments are to be made directly to the factor. Usually the factor decides which orders are shipped and, afterwards, assumes the risk of collecting the funds. As the funds are collected, an account is established that the firm can draw upon as needed. If the account is temporarily empty or insufficient for a current financial need, factors advance cash for receivables before the accounts are paid in the form of a loan. Factors, in addition to their primary activity, make loans to businesses on their inventory, fixed assets, open accounts, and other security. Most factors maintain an advisory service to counsel customers on production, marketing, and financial matters.

Method of Operation

A factor may deal differently with different clients. The specific relationship and the responsibilities of the parties are set forth in the factoring contract.

1. Before clients ship any merchandise to a customer as a result of sales, they must submit the list of customers, amounts of the orders, terms of sale, and any other essential information to the factor for approval.

2. The factor investigates each account and makes the credit decision to accept or reject the order. The order copies with the proper notations "accepted" or "rejected" are returned to the clients. If, at this point, the clients want to ship to rejected accounts, they do so at their own risk.

3. After shipments are made on the approved orders, clients sell the accounts to the factor by signing and transmitting to the factor an assignment schedule supported by a copy of each invoice and shipping order. The assignment schedule provides space for a complete description of the sale and shipment (e.g., customer name, address, terms of sale, due dates, and amounts of invoices). The invoices in turn are stamped before mailing, giving notification to the account that payment must be made directly to the factor. Sufficient copies of each instrument are made so that the factor and the client have complete records.

4. The factor credits the client's account for all accounts receivable purchased and remits the proceeds as mutually agreed on by the factor and the client. If a client doesn't want to withdraw the funds immediately, withdrawal can be made at regular intervals. The method of paying the client is normally geared to the client's working capital needs. The factor pays the client interest on all money that accrues on matured accounts and isn't withdrawn.

5. Clients receive a monthly statement (called an *account current*) showing their financial standing with the factor. This record lists accounts receivable purchased, charges for returns and allowances, the factor's commission and interest charges, and other items that may affect the account.

Factor Terms and Charges

Factoring charges include (1) a commission or service charge and (2) an interest charge. Factors determine the exact amount of commission by taking into consideration the kind of industry the client represents, the client's annual sales volume, the credit standing of the client's customers, and so on. Commission is based on the actual value of the accounts receivable, less cash discounts, merchandise returns, and other normal allowances. The interest charge is computed on the average daily net debit balance.

In comparing factoring costs with the costs of borrowing funds from other sources, a business must consider the factors' other services including complete credit and collection management.

Use of Factoring Operations by Businesses

Contrary to a once common opinion, factoring does not imply a financially weak business. Although a factoring service may be used by a business whose credit isn't acceptable elsewhere, many financially strong companies use factoring to good advantage. Factoring helps firms avoid the costs of maintaining a commercial credit department, including overhead, investigation costs, accounting costs, collection expenses, and the ever-present expense of bad debts. A firm that factors all of its accounts receivables, as many textile companies do, can eliminate this important but often costly business function. Another advantage is that factoring frees management from credit and collection problems so it can concentrate on production and other marketing problems. In a sense factoring provides a form of complete credit insurance and at the same time frees the business from its investment in accounts receivable. Finally, factoring increases the client's net working capital, provided the cash received is put to work to pay current obligations.

The principal objection to factoring accounts receivable is cost. However, only the interest rate should be considered when comparing this method of financing with alternatives. The factoring commission is not entirely a charge for advancing funds but, more accurately, a charge for credit and collection management.

COMMERCIAL FINANCE COMPANIES

Commercial finance companies were mentioned above as a participant in accounts receivable financing. Beyond this activity, commercial finance companies make many other types of loans, including loans on inventory; installment financing of machinery and equipment, and other durable goods; loans on fixed assets and other collateral; and note loans to businesses. Many businesses find that finance companies are more flexible to deal with and more closely meet their needs. Because finance companies provide such a wide variety of financial services, they enjoy a close working relationship with their customers. Because these companies operate on a branch-office basis and are not hampered by the restrictions imposed on banks, they can acquire a more diversified group of risks and hence accept greater risk.

Generally, commercial finance companies are not depository institutions. Because they do not have deposits available to lend to others, these organizations must often raise funds through the sale of corporation notes, bonds, and other forms of commercial paper. The higher costs of raising these funds, coupled with the willingness to accept greater risks, often means their finance charges are higher.

LEASING

Leasing is a method of acquiring assets and equipment for use in a business and, many times, is an alternative to purchasing the asset. A **lease contract** is an agreement that allows the use of equipment or other assets by a lessee in return for rental payments made to the lessor during a specified period of time. Although legal title remains with the lessor, full use is provided the lessee who often commits to lengthy payment periods. The contract specifies many details such as cancellation rights, conditions for renewal, payment configuration, servicing responsibilities, and purchase options at the end of the lease. Often the lessee is responsible for insurance, upkeep, and repairs. If the asset is damaged beyond normal use, additional charges may occur at the end of the lease.

In many instances, the total value of the asset is transferred from the lessor to the lessee when equipment, for example, is leased for most of its lifetime. In these cases, when substantially all the benefits and risks of ownership are transferred by the lease, accountants refer to the agreement as a **capital lease.** The sum of the rental payments often equals the total cost of the asset plus an amount equivalent to interest on a loan to finance the asset. For accounting purposes, the leased equipment may be considered an intangible asset and the agreed to payments a liability.

Operating leases are short-term rentals of equipment that may be canceled at any time. The lessee often rents the equipment for only a fraction of its useful life and is able to deduct the lease payments as an expense. The most significant difference between an operating lease and a capital lease is the commitment to a series of rental payments.

Sometimes a firm will be in a weak cash position and will enter into a **sale-leaseback arrangement.** In this situation, a company sells property to an investor and arranges for a long-term lease. The stream of lease payments represents the amortized value of the asset plus a return on investment for the investor. The liquidity shown on the balance sheet can suddenly improve, but the analyst should recognize that payment obligations increase and profit may decrease. The lessee generally pays all the costs an owner would pay, e.g., insurance, property taxes, etc.

COMMERCIAL PAPER AS A SOURCE OF FUNDS

The growth in the use of **commercial paper**—short-term corporate IOUs—reshaped the commercial lending business and changed the competitive picture in many ways. These ways are still developing today. Businesses' issuance and sale of commercial paper is a relatively simple way for them to enter the marketplace and secure funds for short-term needs. Unlike loans, however, such paper is not renewable. Usually, in times of tight money, cash is still available in the money market—the large pool of funds that financial institutions and individuals lend temporarily. Another reason businesses sell commercial paper is that it may cost less to borrow in the commercial paper market than at a bank even without the cost of keeping cash idle in "compensating balances."

Over a period of time, some commercial banks began playing a role in commercial paper, ranging from privately placing some of the instruments to providing letters of credit to back them up.

The increasing use of commercial paper in recent years has been accompanied by the boom in **securitization** of many kinds of debt. An important part of this change is asset-backed commercial paper, a market estimated at $40 billion by Lehman Brothers.

Asset-backed commercial paper is essentially a combination of traditional forms of bank finance and credit market funding obtained by issuing commercial paper. Credit card receivables, auto and equipment lease receivables, and trade receivables are among the type of assets that have been included in this form of structured finance.

LONG-TERM LOANS

Up to this point, we have discussed businesses' short- and intermediate-term financing needs. Yet long-term borrowing is often one of the first forms of financing a business uses. When a business acquires funds through long-term borrowing arrangements, it is using its **investment credit.**

The Need for Long-Term Financing

Almost all firms need and use **long-term financing.** Firms often use long-term financing at start-up to provide costly production or marketing facilities. Such fixed assets include land, buildings, equipment, and machinery. (Owners may avoid using investment credit if they furnish their own capital—equity capital.)

As they grow and prosper over the years, many businesses need to expand or replace their facilities. They use long-term financing both to expand their fixed assets and to increase current assets. Often a portion of the needed current-asset expansion is financed by long-term methods rather than the previously discussed short-term methods. During periods of rapid expansion, firms may find it more desirable to rely on long-term financing rather than short-term financing to keep a reasonable balance between current assets and current liabilities. In addition, such financing can be used to renew existing indebtedness, to retire some debts, and to acquire the assets of another company under merger arrangements.

Forms and Sources of Long-Term Borrowing

Long-term financing may take one or a combination of the following three forms: (1) long-term loans, (2) real estate mortgage loans, and (3) the issuance of secured or unsecured bonds. In each instance the business uses its investment credit as a power to obtain funds in exchange for its promise to pay an equivalent value at some date in the relatively distant future.

Long-term loans are those with maturities longer than five years. Although not a major lending function of commercial banks, some do deal in this type of loan. Evidence of the transaction is the promissory note, either secured or unsecured. Loans made over long periods are often renewed again and again, thus resulting in a more or less "permanent" obligation on the part of the business borrower. Usually, such loans are repaid at specified intervals mutually agreed on by the lender and borrower. The borrower then gives the lender a series of notes maturing, say, at six-month intervals over the years until the entire loan is repaid. Some borrowers arrange to have the payments gradually increase with each succeeding interval.

Real estate mortgage loans for business concerns may be a single-payment type, also known as the **straight-payment loan,** whereby the borrower makes no payment on the principal until the entire amount is due. Usually, borrowers pay interest on such loans at stated intervals and have prepayment privileges if they want to make partial or full payment on the mortgage before maturity. The direct-reduction mortgage loan, also known as the **amortized loan,** is the other common type of mortgage contract. This instrument specifies monthly, quarterly, semiannual, or annual repayments of principal plus interest.

Corporations that issue bonds to acquire investment capital guarantee to pay a specified sum at some future date, with interest at a fixed rate. Maturity dates usually exceed 10 years (dates of 15, 20, 25, or 30 years are common). When borrowing by this method, the business sells the entire issue to investment bankers, who in turn sell the bonds to the general public or to a single holder, such as a life insurance company.

Some firms sell stock for long-term financing. It is important to understand the differences between stocks and bonds from both sides of the transaction—the firm's position in trying to raise funds, and the investor's involvement in trying to obtain a good return.

STARTING OR EXPANDING AN INDIVIDUAL'S BUSINESS

The need for financing is an important concern for owners of small businesses. Many small businesses are started with the resources of their owners. But the stage can be quickly reached where the owner must look to the credit market for financial help in expanding operations. However, owners may not realize that applying for credit is a more complicated process than obtaining consumer credit and requires a great deal of preparation by the business applicant.

The individual seeking financial help should have a well thought-out and documented business proposal. The proposal should clearly state the purpose of the financial aid, the amount needed and for how long, and a repayment schedule. It should also include the following information:

1. Business description.
2. Personal profile.

3. Proposal.

4. Business plan.

5. Repayment plan.

6. Supporting documentation.

7. Collateral.

8. Financial statements.

9. Personal guarantees.

Alternative Sources of Capital

- Banks.
- Friends, relatives.
- Savings and loan associations.
- Insurance companies.
- Finance companies.
- Mortgage companies.
- Small business investment companies.
- Venture capital firms.
- State government financing sources.
- Pension funds.
- Credit unions.
- Government agencies.
- Private foundations.

Before submitting this proposal to a lender, it is recommended that the advice of another, more experienced individual be sought. One source of counseling is the Service Corps of Retired Executives (SCORE), which is sponsored by the SBA.

Important Terms

amortized loan   279
asset-backed commercial paper   278
business installment loans   267
capital lease   277
commercial bank   266
commercial paper   277
compensating balance   267
discount rate   269

factoring   273
financial capital for business operations   263
guaranty loan   270
investment credit   278
lease contract   277
line of credit   267
long-term financing   278
operating leases   277

Discussion Questions

1. In what ways can bank loans be classified? Distinguish each type.
2. Distinguish between bank interest rates and bank discount rates.
3. What are the principal reasons commercial banks have high credit standards and requirements?
4. Discuss the activities of the Small Business Administration.
5. What are the principal differences between ordinary accounts receivable financing and accounts receivable factoring?
6. Is ordinary accounts receivable financing a desirable or undesirable business practice? Why?
7. Under what circumstances can a business use factoring to good advantage?
8. Explain the use of commercial paper as a source of funds for business concerns.
9. What is investment credit?
10. Which of the alternative sources of capital are best for business concerns?

Suggested Readings—Part IV

Understanding Business Credit

Fagel, Allen J. "Selling on Consignment Another Tool in the Credit Arsenal." *Business Credit,* October 1996, p. 6.

Hadary, Sharon G. and Julie R. Weeks. "Women Business Owners Make Progress in Access to Capital." *Credit World,* November/December 1996, p. 28.

Navarro, Alfred. "Selecting the Right Credit Terms." *Business Credit,* July/August 1996, p. 12.

Whiteside, David E. "Cranking Out Small-Business Loans." *Collections and Credit Risk,* September 1996, p. 37.

Internet Sites

http://www.sba.gov   Small Business Administration

MANAGEMENT AND ANALYSIS OF BUSINESS CREDIT

14

RESPONSIBILITIES OF THE BUSINESS CREDIT MANAGER

Learning Objectives

After studying this chapter, you should be able to:

- Understand the status, place, and functions of the business credit executive.
- Explain the changing status and qualifications of credit management.
- Discuss where the credit department fits into a company's organizational framework.
- Spell out the basic functions of business credit management.
- Explain the classification of the sources of business credit information.
- Point out the factors that should be considered in selecting sources of business credit information.
- Compare internal information and direct investigation.
- Explain the problems leveraged buyouts (LBOs) create for the business credit manager.

The position of the present-day business credit manager continues to grow in importance. The reasons for this are: (1) practically all production and marketing institutions rely on business credit for short-term financing; (2) business credit is a customary means of selling goods and services; (3) the volume of business credit is far larger than other types of credit; and (4) credit executives are assuming the duties of business advisers, one of the most dramatic changes in credit management in recent years.

Some indication of the importance of the credit executive can be gained from estimating the volume of business credit. Ninety to 95 percent of all transactions between business executives are made on the basis of business credit. Because the receivables item is one of the largest and most liquid assets on most manufacturers' and wholesalers' balance sheets, business credit management is concerned with a financial aspect of business as demanding, important, and significant as many other financial tasks. Business credit management must safeguard the receivables asset with sound, intelligent, and effective credit and collection policies.

Business Credit Executive—Status, Place, and Functions

Business credit managers occupy a respected and responsible position in their companies' organizational structures. They manage the acceptance of customers' credit and the collection of their debts. Simple as this appears, effective credit management involves several major tasks, all of which depend on numerous routine operations.

Credit managers have the same aim as their companies—to earn a profit. Their policies also have a significant impact throughout a company. If credit managers' attitudes and policies are too conservative, customers whose credit is less than prime must buy elsewhere. On the other hand, if their attitudes and policies are too lenient, a company may be stuck with low-quality receivables. In the former instance the company's sales and financial gains suffer; in the latter, sales may increase, but the company suffers financial losses on low-quality credit customers. Managing credit sales is the efficient employment of all the devices at one's command to create the most profitable balance between company sales and company revenue.

Responsibilities of the business credit executive include:

1. Analyzing the risk in creating accounts receivable.
2. Conducting credit investigations.
3. Analyzing financial statements.
4. Determining credit terms for customers.
5. Setting credit lines.
6. Handling invoices, posting payments, and maintaining documentation.
7. Analyzing receivables.
8. Collections efforts to collect payments.
9. Customer counseling.
10. Cooperating with other departments within the company.

Changing Status and Qualifications of Credit Management

A major factor contributing to the changing status and qualifications of credit management has been the rapid and tremendous growth of American industry and commerce. When most businesses were small sole proprietorships, credit approval was a simple, personal matter. Fifty to 75 years ago, buyers visited markets once or twice a year. Proprietors had an opportunity to "size up" buyers and either approve or disapprove their credit. As commerce developed, the personal relationship was lost, and business needed some other basis to manage credit.

This task logically fell on someone within the company, usually the "bookkeeper." But as commerce and industry grew, one person couldn't handle both bookkeeping and credit duties.

National Association of Credit Management (http://www.nacm.org)

With the organization of the **National Association of Credit Management (NACM)** in 1896, the significance of professional credit management was realized. Improved sources of credit information developed, better accounting methods became universal, and the techniques of financial statement analysis were refined. Managers recognized the professional character of credit work and its significant relationship to their marketing and financial operations. An increased number of highly qualified people sought credit work as a career and profession. The complexities of modern-day business and the need for specialization fostered the status held by today's credit managers. Credit management is now an established business profession, with prerogatives, responsibilities, standards, and ethics.

Qualifications for success in credit management had to change, too. Bookkeeping knowledge is not sufficient, as it was many years ago. Nor does credit management rely solely on knowledge of accounting principles and financial statement analysis, as some businesspeople and educators still believe. Modern business techniques and the operation of an effective credit department demand that credit management be intimately knowledgeable of credit's relationships to the financial, production, marketing, and other aspects of the business. As a result, credit managers need broader qualifications, with greater emphasis on formal training in both specialized and general areas of credit management.

The NACM has continually recognized the importance of education for its members. In 1918 it added the **National Institute of Credit** to its list of major services provided to members. In 1949 the **Credit Research Foundation, Inc.,** which maintains a close affiliation with the NACM, was established to carry on research and education in credit and financial management.

The National Institute of Credit (NIC), administered by the Credit Research Foundation, is the oldest and broadest-based educational activity of the NACM, benefiting people with different educational and business backgrounds. NIC chapters cooperate with educational institutions through a college affiliation program. Students also may undertake a coordinated program leading to a credit management certificate or degree. Approved courses also prepare people for the credit business associate (CBA), credit business fellow (CBF), and certified credit executive (CCE) designations, which are recognized nationally. The CCE designation is based on a satisfactory review of personal data and successful completion of a comprehensive written examination.

The NACM Graduate School of Credit and Financial Management, conducted by the Credit Research Foundation, offers an executive professional development program for experienced credit executives. Registrants attend a two-week resident session for each of three years. The programs are offered at Dartmouth College and Santa Clara University. Other graduate programs include the advanced credit executive studies (ACES), held at Northwestern University, designed for those who have completed the Graduate School of Credit and Financial Management or its equivalent and other lower division programs for middle management and supervisory-level people; that is, the Mid-Career School, Pine Mountain, Georgia, and the Credit Management Leadership Institute, Baylor University.

Short-term, on-campus residential programs and conferences of one to four days on topics of interest to credit administrators are held nationwide. The Credit Research Foundation conducts basic and applied research in business credit and receivables management and publishes studies on significant trends.

In addition to the above specialized and general educational programs, many colleges and universities offer day and evening programs designed to help equip the credit manager. Schools of business administration usually offer the best programs including specialized training in marketing, management, finance, economics, and accounting. In addition, many firms conduct their own training programs. There is no cut-and-dried formula for a successful training program; each firm must determine the type and extent of training that best suits its needs.

Thus most people, regardless of educational background, can develop the personal, experience, and educational qualifications necessary for the credit management profession.

The Credit Department in the Organization Framework of the Company

Well-run organizations clearly define lines of authority and responsibility to ensure effective performance of the credit function. The credit department must be organized to conduct numerous routine activities, decision-making processes, collection phases of the operation, and supplemental services to customers and the company.

When a business organizes a credit department, the question of its place in the company's organizational framework arises. This question cannot be easily resolved due to variations in company and department size, and the firm's principal business activity. Service companies generally have fewer credit problems and less opportunity to fulfill all the basic credit functions. Manufacturers and wholesalers, especially large ones, need a full-fledged, effective department. Small firms frequently delegate credit and collection functions among the owners, salespeople, or accounting personnel.

In large companies where the credit function plays an integral role in accomplishing major objectives, the credit department may be part of the sales, financial, or accounting areas, or it may be separate and independent.

Credit Department in the Sales Area

It is common to have the credit department as part of the sales area if the company is in a highly competitive industry, if company policies are almost entirely sales oriented, and if the company emphasizes credit service to customers. The principal arguments advanced for and against this type of organizational plan are:

For	*Against*
1. Both sales and credit have the same objective—to maximize sales.	1. The sales philosophy is too liberal with respect to credit risk.
2. Salespeople can help gather credit information.	2. An overly liberal credit policy can as easily create ill will among customers as an overly strict one.
3. Closer cooperation results between sales and credit personnel.	3. The decision-making process is not free from subjective influences.
4. Credit manager has a better opportunity to build goodwill by keeping alert to weak customers and new customers, as reported by sales personnel.	
5. The processing of sales orders is facilitated.	

Credit Department in the Financial Area

Many credit managers are under the supervision of company treasurers. Such companies place great emphasis on utilizing invested capital efficiently. The arguments for and against this type of organizational plan are:

For	*Against*
1. The control of funds invested in accounts receivable is improved.	1. The maximizing of the sales function is likely to suffer under the financial-oriented and not sales-oriented department.
2. A better working relationship between the treasurer and credit manager is fostered.	2. The treasurer is more importantly charged with managing company debt, not customers' credit.
3. The current financing of the company is closely related to the performance of the credit department.	3. Credit and collection policies tend to be conservative and harsh, creating poor customer relations.
4. The total financial plan of the company includes accounts receivables, and the treasurer needs control to forecast the company's financial requirements.	

Credit Department in the Accounting Area

While most credit departments are placed under the sales department or the treasurer's office, there are some advantages to placing them in the accounting area. The main advantage of this type of organizational setup involves recordkeeping. Both accounting and credit personnel need access to the accounts receivable ledger, which is usually maintained by accounting personnel to satisfy both accounting and credit activities. All pertinent data on current and inactive accounts are then centralized, mutually available, and readily accessible. In this arrangement, credit management and accounting management should have positions of coordinate rank. The principal objection to this arrangement is that credit managers may become too concerned with "crunching numbers" and fail to provide adequate customer service and sales emphasis.

The Independent Credit Department

If the credit department does not have some independence, it may be best to change the company's organizational structure. Whether or not this is necessary depends on the management personalities involved. If the credit manager is incapable in certain activities, the credit department should remain under the control of another executive. Conversely, it may be best to establish a separate credit operation if a dominant but shortsighted sales executive, financial officer, or accounting head lacks appreciation of credit's role.

If an independent credit department is organized, it is the responsibility of the senior executives and the credit manager to see that close cooperation between function and operation exists among the various departments in the company. Furthermore, the credit manager should occupy a place in the structure coordinate with that of other executives. Independent credit departments should be able to function more effectively because they are free of the supervision of other department managers. Without the one-sided dominance of another department, the credit department can enhance its cooperation with all other departments.

Credit Department Placement

- In the sales area.
- In the financial area.
- In the accounting area.
- Independent department.

PLANNING THE BUSINESS CREDIT INVESTIGATION

Business credit management confronts the inherent uncertainties and risks caused by the time element in the credit transaction. Because of this, decision making is the core of business credit management, as it is for other types of credit. The decision maker attempts to improve the quality of the credit accepted and to assure a more profitable relationship by minimizing risk on the one hand and increasing sales on the other. Confidence in the decision process is enhanced with a thorough credit investigation to help evaluate the risk a particular customer represents.

The questions of whether an account can and will pay can be answered only after a series of more specific questions about the risk have been answered. Even though no two customers are alike, the same specific questions usually arise and the types of information needed to answer them are usually quite similar. To answer the "can" and "will" question, credit managers must get answers to the following questions:

1. Can we establish this account's identity and legal responsibility so we know the order comes from a bona fide business?
2. What is the history and business background of this account?
3. What is the general character and responsibility of the account's management? Can we anticipate a continuous and healthy business relationship?
4. What is the financial ability and capability of this account?
5. What is the financial strength and outlook of this account?
6. Does the account's past and present payment record inspire confidence? What can we expect in the future?

Forms of Business Organization

An important consideration in business credit decisions is the legal form of organization of a business customer. The business form will often influence outcomes when trying to collect a debt. For example, what is the likelihood that the business will continue at the death or illness of a key owner or employee? How easily can the business raise funds if needed? Finally, are the personal assets of the business owners available to help pay company debts?

Sole Proprietorship

A **sole proprietorship** is a business owned and operated by one person, called the *proprietor.* This form of business is the easiest to establish and the most common. A single, self-employed owner simply begins operating the business with or without a specific trade or business name.

The advantages of this form of business include maximum flexibility in making decisions and responding to customers' needs. The owner has complete freedom to determine products, prices, and overall success. Legal requirements are minimal since the business owner and the business are the same entity. Since the two cannot be separated, both personal assets and business assets are available to pay debts.

Unfortunately, this form of business may represent the greatest risk to a credit grantor. The business owner must do everything from marketing to production and distribution. Although employees are often involved, the burden of management nevertheless rests with the individual owner. If the owner becomes ill or dies, the business ceases to exist and repayment of any debts may have to wait for the distribution of the estate. Also, the ability to raise funds by borrowing is often restricted with this form of business organization.

Sole Proprietorships

Advantages

- Ease of organization.
- Flexibility.
- Simplicity.

Disadvantages

- Unlimited liability of owner.
- Difficulty raising funds.
- Limited management ability.
- Personal assets at risk.
- Business often terminates at death.

Partnership

A **partnership** is an association of two or more persons who combine their skills and capital to carry on a business as co-owners for profit. Although no formal requirements exist to organize a partnership, e.g., the agreement can be oral, it is generally preferable to create a written agreement. Still, the organization of a partnership is relatively easy with the partners generally agreeing to share profits and expenses based on their percentage ownership of the business. The business may benefit from a broader range of expertise since more than one individual is engaged in the management of the firm. Raising capital may also be enhanced since prospective lenders can see the advantages to the business due to its cooperative nature. Also, the partners are liable for all assets and debts of the business with personal assets available to satisfy any claims.

The partnership often terminates, however, with the death or departure of a partner. The estate of the deceased partner, for example, will often require liquidation of assets to allow withdrawal of the value contained in the business. Another important disadvantage for an individual partner is the unlimited liability mentioned above. The personal assets of one partner are usually vulnerable and at risk due to any poor decisions, criminal acts, and failures of the other partners.

Partnerships

Advantages

- Ease of organization.
- Broader range of expertise.
- Greater potential for capital.

Disadvantages

- Unlimited liability of partners.
- Limited life of the partnership.
- Lack of flexibility.

Limited Partnership

All states allow the establishment of this special form of partnership. A **limited partnership** is a partnership with two types of partners: general partners and limited partners. General partners actively carry on the business with full, unlimited personal liability. Limited partners take no active part in the business and can only lose their capital contribution.

Corporations

The Supreme Court has described a **corporation** as "an association of individuals united for some common purpose, and permitted by law to use a common name and to change its members without dissolution of the association." The individuals who wish to begin a corporation must apply to the state that may issue a charter. Once the charter is issued, the corporation operates as a separate entity. As any entity or individual, the corporation can enter into contracts, sue, and be sued. The corporation exists separate from its individual members and, as a result, the personal assets of the individuals are not available to satisfy any claims on the corporation. Furthermore, the corporation has an unlimited life since the corporate shares can be sold, passed on to heirs, or held by anyone.

The most important feature of this form of business is the limited liability enjoyed by the stockholders. This aspect became essential as our economy expanded and businesses needed to raise huge amounts of capital, often from strangers and those in distant locations. If shareholders thought their personal assets were at risk, they would only invest in businesses and managers they knew very well.

Corporations

Advantages

- Operates as a separate entity.
- Enhanced ability to raise capital.
- Limited liability for owners.
- Unlimited life.

Disadvantages

- Difficult to organize.
- May be inflexible.
- Control is shared among owners.

The corporation has some disadvantages. Since many sole proprietorships and partnerships are forced to adopt this form of organization to continue growing, the former owners are forced to share their ownership with others. A board of directors is elected by the stockholders, and if a majority of the voting rights fall into the hands of others, a former owner can lose complete control of the business. Also, as the corporation grows it often becomes less flexible and more bureaucratic.

A very important disadvantage of the corporate form of business organization is **double taxation.** The problem arises because the corporation, as a separate entity, is required to pay federal (and sometimes state) corporate income taxes. If the corporation later distributes part of its after-tax net income to stockholders in the form of dividends, this income is again subject to income taxes for these recipients. Sometimes the corporation elects the **sub-chapter S corporation** form of organization since this special situation avoids double taxation. There are limitations regarding the number of stockholders and types of stock, but the corporation does not pay income taxes. All income is taxable to the individual shareholders at the end of each year.

Limited Liability Companies

A fairly recent form of business organization is the limited liability company or LLC. A **limited liability company** is a partnership that operates like a partnership but affords limited liability to the owners. The owners, generally referred to as "members," must sign an operating agreement or articles of organization which must be filed with the state government. Two members are usually required to operate an LLC. This form of organization has some of the same benefits as a sub-chapter S corporation, e.g., avoidance of double taxation, but it is without the restrictions. Variations exist where this form of business is allowed, and not all states currently have laws for this type of organization.

CLASSIFICATION OF SOURCES OF BUSINESS CREDIT INFORMATION

Credit investigations give credit analysts answers to these questions. There are numerous sources and types of credit information. Credit management may use several sources or vary their use depending on the firm's particular needs. Experienced and resourceful credit managers can select the most suitable combination of sources to supply useful data quickly, economically, and accurately.

The sources of credit information available to business-type creditors can be classified as internal or external as follows:

I. Internal information.
    A. Credit manager's personal knowledge.
    B. In-file information on previously established accounts.
II. External information.
    A. Mercantile agencies.
        1. General.
        2. Special.
        3. Interchange bureaus.
    B. Trade association bureaus.
    C. Interviews.
        1. By sales representatives.
        2. By credit manager and other authorized representatives of the creditor.
    D. Financial statements furnished by the account or new customer directly to the creditor.
    E. Banks.
    F. Attorneys.
    G. Public records.
    H. Correspondence with subject, creditors, or references.
    I. Investors' manuals and services.
    J. Newspapers, magazines, trade journals, and other publications.

Sources of credit information are not only internal or external but are also commercialized or noncommercialized. Commercialized sources are mercantile agencies, trade association bureaus, and investors' manuals and services. A commercialized source is an organization whose main function is supplying credit information for compensation.

On the other hand, internal sources of information are not commercial ventures, so these sources are called *noncommercialized*. The credit manager's personal knowledge and in-file information on previously established accounts are available to most credit analysts. Several external sources of credit information are also noncommercialized (e.g., banks, attorneys, references, interviews, and other creditors). These external sources are often willing to supply information because of reciprocity, custom, courtesy, or informal compensation. Most noncommercialized sources are available to all credit personnel on an equal basis. The amount and usefulness of information from these sources depend on the type of business activity, the creditor's contacts, and the efficiency of the credit department.

Credit managers must be thoroughly familiar with the various sources of credit information and the types of credit information each supplies. They must know how the available types of information will best serve the needs of their firms and what each source can contribute toward sound credit decisions. By having an intimate knowledge of the sources, credit managers can get information at the proper time, of adequate amount and quality, and within the cost limits imposed by their budgets and the characteristics of each account.

Selecting Sources of Credit Information

The particular sources of credit information chosen depend on the characteristics of each source. The most important factors that should be considered are: accuracy of information, content of reports, speed of reporting, cost of the service, trade coverage, geographic coverage, variety and number of reports, and supplemental services that fulfill particular or occasional creditor needs.

Accuracy of Information

Accuracy of information supplied to a creditor is paramount. While most sources report all facts accurately, human frailties cause some errors. Today, automatic processing and duplicating equipment help safeguard against such errors. Foremost to take advantage of these technological improvements were the mercantile agencies. Much information, particularly financial data supplied to the agencies by firms being reported on, is now duplicated mechanically. These more reliable methods of recording facts contrast starkly to the once-prevalent manual operations.

Content of Credit Reports

Credit report content varies depending on the source and the characteristics of the business. Businesses need comprehensive and detailed reports to answer questions on new accounts; they can periodically revise existing accounts with limited information of a specific nature. In appraising the creditworthiness of most accounts, business credit management may need a complete financial picture. If adequate financial information is not available from mercantile agencies, credit managers should request such information from the customer or other sources. This type of information is essential to the appraisal and decision-making functions. Each credit instance dictates the kind and amount of additional information needed to reach a decision. The situation may warrant obtaining information on the aging of accounts payable, the aging of accounts receivable, or even the current status of inventories. Payment record (ledger) information is required for most new accounts because it reveals the likely payment pattern a creditor can expect. There are sources available for all information needs, but cost and time often restrict the choices.

Speed of the Reporting Service

Speed is important to assure credit decisions are made within a reasonable time. Modern communications systems and duplicating devices greatly speed the compilation of credit information. Despite these improvements, some types of information can be gathered only with time and effort. Furthermore, credit departments cannot delay a sale or shipment until they tap all sources of information. Competitive conditions in the market establish the speed required to prevent lost sales. While many credit losses occur when decisions are based on inadequate information, credit managers have to decide when to sacrifice adequacy for speed, or vice versa.

Cost of Credit Information

Credit costs must be evaluated and justified in the same way as other marketing costs. Creditors dealing with a nominal number of accounts may spend a few hundred dollars a year to acquire credit information. But large businesses with thousands of accounts may spend tens of thousands of dollars with a single source. Mercantile agencies usually scale their fees so unit costs decrease as quantity of reports and services increases.

The cost of acquiring and maintaining up-to-date information on each account is nominal with a sizable unit sale. On the other hand, the cost of investigating small orders is frequently disproportionate to their value. To compensate for this relatively high cost, the credit department may conduct a less thorough investigation. Some businesses do not investigate exceptionally small orders. Whether or not a credit investigation is warranted depends on the profit involved, whether the order is from a one-time customer, and whether the overall losses justify the costs.

Another aspect of costs involves risk. Obviously, exposure to more risk dictates more effort, greater costs, and more complete information. Alert credit managers keep costs in line with risk and profit.

Trade and Geographic Coverage

Information sources should cover the same geographic area as the creditor. Businesses that sell in a number of markets and to different types of customers need sources capable of supplying broad information. Not all agencies have national and international coverage, nor do they report on customers in all lines of trade. Credit managers must know these factors to select the most effective source. The variations in these factors become apparent in the next few chapters.

Variety and Number of Reports

Sources differ considerably in the variety and number of reports they supply. Some accounts can be appraised most accurately with particular types of reports supplied by credit department request. Other accounts, particularly those where the degree of risk is high and continuous, require a series of reports supplied at specified intervals. Again, the characteristics of individual accounts must correspond to the services rendered.

Supplemental Services

Supplemental services fulfill particular or occasional credit needs. Credit information sources may maintain credit reference books, make recommendations or decisions, render opinions, and supply foreign credit reports and standardized financial statements. Credit reference books are particularly valuable for preliminary credit checks and in appraising small orders that do not warrant a complete credit investigation. Some sources make recommendations with regard to the acceptability of an account—a valuable service if the credit department is staffed by a part-time credit manager or other circumstances make it desirable to shift the decision-making process. Most creditors' needs are not completely satisfied by the basic credit information services. Supplemental services help refine the decision-making process and overcome peculiar circumstances inherent in trading with a diverse group of customers.

Selecting Sources of Credit Information

- Accuracy of information.
- Content of credit reports.
- Speed of reporting service.
- Cost of credit information.
- Trade and geographical coverage.
- Variety and number of reports.
- Supplemental services.

INTERNAL INFORMATION AND DIRECT INVESTIGATION

In some respects there is no better source of information than the internal information on the debtor business itself, or the information gathered by direct investigation. However, in today's economy, large-scale production, more complex organizational structures, and the increasing distance between customers and suppliers all restrict a creditor's ability to gather sufficient credit information directly. Yet, even though it is seldom possible for a credit manager to interview a customer personally, other company representatives may have a chance to do so.

Typically, a creditor's sales force has direct contact with the account, and it may be mutually beneficial for both the credit and sales departments to cooperate in the gathering of credit information. Many business credit managers require application forms from prospective customers. Traditionally, the direct gathering of credit information has been thwarted (limited) by sales staff involvement and concerns regarding customer harassment. Without detailed information from the prospective customer, the credit manager is more dependent on other sources.

Internal Information

The credit office is a storehouse of credit facts. Each time a credit department accepts a new account, a file on the customer is established. The information contained in these files is known as in-file information. This source of information and the credit manager's own knowledge are the principal sources of **internal information.**

Perhaps the most arbitrary factor affecting the credit risk, and yet a valuable source of information, is the credit manager. The information credit managers acquire through experience and what they already know about their customers sharpen their decisions and methods of operation. Much of what they know they acquire through their attention to in-file information in making decisions and through the help they give their office associates in making routine decisions.

The customer's ledger record is also a valuable source of information. Each time an active or inactive account reorders, credit analysts can review the recorded data, basing a decision on the assumption that past experience will be repeated. They may note the size of the new order and compare it with previous orders. If they see radical differences and the time between orders is lengthy, they may initiate a new investigation.

Direct Investigation

The term **direct investigation** applies when a creditor is directly involved in gathering basic facts from any noncommercialized sources of information. Such an investigation involves either (1) direct contact with the customer to acquire credit information or (2) direct contact with individuals and institutions that may have useful credit information bearing on the account. It does not involve information supplied by any commercialized source.

Customer-Supplied Information

Credit managers often get the most accurate information about a firm's operation and financial condition from its owners or principals. But although customers can supply financial data, trade and bank references, and other pertinent information, limitations affect the use of this source. Direct contact with the customer depends on the customer's degree of cooperation, the distance from the creditor, the time available to conduct the investigation, and the amount of the credit requested. Exhibit 14–1 shows an application form available from NACM used to gather information from a business credit applicant.

Direct contact (by mail, phone, or personal interview) gives the creditor an opportunity to establish goodwill and an enduring business relationship. Creditors can

EXHIBIT 14–1 **Credit Application**

BUSINESS DATA

Name of Company (hereafter "Company")   Date of Application

List D/B/A(s)   DUNS #

| Mailing Address | City | County | State | Zip |

| Street Address | City | County | State | Zip |

Business Phone   Business Fax   E-mail address

Company is a   ❑ Corporation   ❑ LLC   ❑ Partnership   ❑ Sole Proprietorship

If a Corporation or LLC, Date of Incorporation or Formation _____

Federal Tax Identification Number

Owner(s) or Officers:

| Name | Title | Address |

| Name | Title | Address |

| Name | Title | Address |

Accounts Payable Contact Name: _____ Phone: _____

Type of Business: _____ Years in Business: _____

Related Previous Business Ventures: _____

_____

_____

BANK REFERENCES

Name:_____   Name:_____

Address:_____   Address:_____

City/State/Zip:_____   City/State/Zip:_____

Checking Account Number:_____   Checking Account Number:_____

Bank Contact Name:_____   Bank Contact Name:_____

Phone Number:_____   Phone Number:_____

Does a bank, insurance company, or other creditor hold a security interest in your accounts receivable and/or inventory for loans advanced?   ❑ Yes ❑ No If yes, please state names of security interest holders:

_____

The Company hereby authorizes the above banks to release all information requested. It is understood that all information will be kept confidential.

EXHIBIT 14–1 (continued)

BALANCE SHEET

Please supply the following balance sheet information or attach a current copy of your Company's balance sheet.

Balance Sheet at (date): _____

CURRENT ASSETS

Cash .... $ _____ _____

Marketable Securities .... _____ _____

Accounts Receivable
(less allowance for doubtful accounts) .... _____ _____

Inventory .... _____ _____

Prepaid Expenses .... _____ _____

Total Current Assets .... _____ _____

Plant Assets
Land .... _____ _____

Buildings (less accumulated depreciation) .... _____ _____

Equipment (less accumulated depreciation) .... _____ _____

Total Plant Assets .... _____ _____

Total Assets .... $ _____

CURRENT LIABILITIES

Accounts Payable .... _____ _____

Notes Payable .... _____ _____

Salaries Payable .... _____ _____

Total current liabilities .... _____ _____

Long-Term Liabilities
Notes payable .... _____ _____

Total Liabilities .... $ _____

STOCKHOLDERS' EQUITY

Paid in Capital .... _____ _____

Excess of issue price over par .... _____ _____

Total paid-in capital .... _____

Retained Earnings .... _____ _____

Total retained earnings .... $ _____

Total stockholders' equity .... $ _____

Total Liabilities and Stockholders' Equity .... $ _____

300

EXHIBIT 14–1   (concluded)

TRADE REFERENCES

Name	Name
Address	Address
City/State/Zip	City/State/Zip
Account Number	Account Number
Contact	Contact
Phone Number Fax	Phone Number Fax
Average or High Monthly Purchases: $ _____	Average or High Monthly Purchases: $ _____

CREDIT APPLICATION PROVISIONS

ARBITRATION. The terms and conditions of this Application shall, upon extension of credit by the Company, constitute an agreement of sale. The Applicant agrees to be bound to the terms and conditions stated in this Application. The payment for all sales of goods or services will be according to the terms stated on the Company's invoice for the sale of goods or services. The failure to pay on the due date on each invoice shall deem the debt to be delinquent. In the event of a delinquency, the Company may impose a finance charge of the lower of (a) one and one half per cent per month or (b) the highest rate permitted by law on the delinquent balance until paid. In the event of a delinquency, the Company may recoup any discounts to be applied to the Applicant's debt. In the event of a delinquency, all collection expenses and attorneys' fees in connection with the collection of the delinquent debt shall be due and payable by the Applicant.

The Company and the Applicant agree that any claim or dispute between or among them, their agents, employees, successors or assigns, related to this Application, the credit extended thereafter or otherwise (other than the exercise of rights under security interests created by purchases or otherwise), including disputes related to the applicability of this Agreement, regardless against whom made, shall be resolved by binding arbitration by and under either (a) the Code of Procedure of the National Arbitration Forum or (b) the Rules of the American Arbitration Association. Any award may be entered and enforced as a judgment in any court of competent jurisdiction. Claims may be filed at any office of the (a) National Arbitration Forum or (b) American Arbitration Association. This Agreement shall be subject to and interpreted under the Federal Arbitration Act.

The Applicant certifies under the penalty of perjury that the statements contained in this Application are true and correct.

Authorized signature _____   Capacity of signer _____

PERSONAL GUARANTY

The undersigned individual(s) in consideration of the Company's extension of credit to the Applicant hereby agrees to personally guarantee any and all obligations of the Applicant and the Company. This guaranty shall be continuing and unlimited and may be terminated only on thirty days' written notice to the Company. The Company may exercise its rights under this guaranty without first taking any action against the Applicant. The undersigned waives notice of default and non-payment and consents to the extension or modification of credit terms to the Applicant without notice.

Dated: _____

Witness_____   Guarantor_____

Witness_____   Guarantor_____

also use direct contact to clarify credit and collection policies and to answer customers' questions. The first contact with a customer is perhaps the most important. If creditors state their information requirements firmly but courteously during the first contact, customers should remain cooperative in subsequent dealings.

Salespeople are frequently in an excellent position to furnish the credit department with valuable information on their customers. Few salespersons, however, are suited to be good credit reporters because their interests, experiences, and temperaments usually are not conditioned toward this goal. On the other hand, it is in their interest to supply information to the credit department when possible, so the account can be adequately appraised and credit approved quickly.

A salesperson usually has the first contact with a customer; if all goes well, the salesperson may be the only company representative who calls on the account. During these calls, the salesperson can become acquainted with the customer's operation and local reputation. Salespeople should be able to furnish information on business identity and legal responsibility, management ability, habits, local reputation, desirability of location, local conditions, bank and creditor references, and the financial status of the business.

Direct Interchange

Another source of credit information is other creditors who have experience with the customer. It is common practice for creditors to exchange their experience as evidenced by accounting records. Some credit managers believe this source is one of the most valuable at their disposal.

Banks are often asked to provide credit and account information regarding a credit applicant. The bank is obviously concerned that the information is used for credit purposes only and that the facts remain confidential. Exhibit 14–2 shows an NACM *Request for Bank Credit Information.* The second page of this form includes a statement of principles for the exchange of credit information and some guidelines for reporting account information.

Creditors may exchange ledger information by correspondence or personal contact or through **trade group meetings** sponsored by the National Association of Credit Management. Personal contact is the most costly method, because it consumes the valuable time of credit managers or their representatives. This method should be limited to cases involving substantial credit exposure in which other methods are not feasible. On the other hand, correspondence with other interested creditors is low cost and takes little of the credit manager's time. However, respondents do not always reply promptly.

Trade group meetings sponsored by the National Association of Credit Management take place each month throughout the country. Credit executives in the same or allied lines of business, or who sell to the same customers, meet to discuss their joint problems and their experiences with individual accounts.

Although the quantity of information supplied by direct interchange may vary with the approach used and the type of creditors contacted, this source can supply the age of the account, the highest recent credit approved, the manner in which the account has been

Exhibit 14–2   Request For Bank Credit Information

Request For Bank Credit Information

Date: _____

To: _____
_____
_____
_____

RE: _____

Company

Street Address

City/State/Zip

The above referenced account has applied to us for an open credit line of $_____ and has given your bank as a reference. Please fill in the information requested below. We would appreciate any additional information which would prove helpful.

We will be pleased to reciprocate at any time.

Sincerely,

Please return a copy of this completed form to my attention at the following address:

_____
Name   Title

_____
Company

_____
Street Address

_____
Signature

_____
City/State/Zip

_____
Phone Number   Fax Number

_____
Bank Account Number

CHECKING ACCOUNT:

Opened: _____   Average Balance: _____

Returned Items: ☐ Yes ☐ No
Satisfactory: ☐ Yes ☐ No

LOANS:

Opened: _____   High Credit: _____   Balance: _____
Secured by: _____   Unsecured: _____
Payment History: _____
_____

Opened: _____   High Credit: _____   Balance: _____
Secured by: _____   Unsecured: _____
Payment History: _____
_____

COMMENTS: _____
_____
_____

_____   _____   _____
Signature   Title   Date

**To be submitted in duplicate,
Bank to retain one copy.**

This form and the "Statement of Principles" (see reverse side) have been approved by the Robert Morris Association and the National Association of Credit Management.

Additional copies of this form may be purchased from NACM Publications Dept., 8815 Centre Park Dr, #200 Columbia, MD 21045-2158

Form 19

NACM

rma

Exhibit 14-2 (concluded)

STATEMENT OF PRINCIPLES
FOR THE EXCHANGE OF CREDIT INFORMATION

(1) Confidentiality is the cardinal principle in the exchange of credit information. The identity of inquirers and sources should not be disclosed without their permission.

(2) All parties involved in the exchange of credit information must base inquiries and replies on fact.

(3) The purpose of the inquiry and the amount involved should be clearly stated.

(4) If the purpose of an inquiry involves actual or contemplated litigation, the inquirer should clearly disclose this fact.

(5) The inquirer should make every effort to determine the subject's bank(s) of account before placing an inquiry.

(6) Proper identification should be provided in all credit communications.

(7) Replies should be prompt and contain sufficient facts commensurate with the purpose and amount of the inquiry. If specific questions cannot be answered, the reasons should be clearly stated.

RMA GENERAL FIGURE RANGES

To ensure accuracy and consistency when exchanging credit information, the RMA General Figure Ranges should be used. It may be necessary, at times, to clarify these terms so that the inquirer and respondent are "speaking the same language." For example:

Low   1 to 1.9
Moderate   2 to 3.9
Medium   4 to 6.9
High   7 to 9.9

Low 4 figures = $1,000 to $1,999
Moderate 4 figures = $2,000 to $3,999
Medium 4 figures = $4,000 to $6,999
High 4 figures = $7,000 to $9,999

The ranges are adjustable to accommodate all amounts in the following manner:
"Nominal" = Under $100
"3 figures" = From $100 to $999
"4 figures" = From $1,000 to $9,999
"5 figures" = From $10,000 to $99,999
"6 figures" = From $100,000 to $999,999 and so on.

paid, the terms of sale, the current status of the account, and any trade abuses. The advantages of soliciting information from other creditors are:

- Because the information is the result of the other creditors' experiences, the inquirer can reasonably expect any future experience to be similar.
- The information comes from people qualified to recognize the problems confronting a fellow creditor.
- The inquirer tries to solicit data from credit managers who have demonstrated their cooperativeness, reliability, and good judgment.
- The information, under most circumstances, can be obtained quickly.
- The information is up to date and therefore of current value.

The financial conditions of a mutual customer change from time to time. Contacts with others who are selling the same account prevent debtors from becoming seriously past due without other businesses knowing about it.

Banks and business creditors can be mutually helpful in gathering credit information because typical businesses have many credit dealings with banks. Similarly, most companies depend on business credit to meet their inventory, equipment, and miscellaneous requirements. They complement each other in that they both maintain extensive credit files.

Despite the help each could be to the other, both banks and business creditors fall short in cooperation. Some banks refuse to reveal some or all of the data requested, and business creditors are more inclined to inquire of banks than banks are to inquire of them. To improve their relationships with banking institutions, businesses should examine their methods of approach and the content of their requests. One of the best ways to get complete information from a bank is by personal contact. Credit managers should become well acquainted with the members of their bank's credit department. Furthermore, credit managers may be able to influence the placing of their companies' deposits. Once this relationship is cultivated and mutual confidence develops, credit managers should be able to acquire more complete information.

Evaluation of Internal Information and Direct Investigation

Noncommercial sources of credit information can be used by most credit managers. The types of information supplied by these sources can be helpful in determining the creditworthiness of new accounts and in revising the credit lines of existing accounts. The credit analyst needs various types of credit information when deciding whether to accept a customer's credit. Before business creditors can adequately appraise an account, they have to answer questions involving an account's identity and legal responsibility, history and business background, managerial character and responsibility, financial ability and capacity, financial strength and outlook, and payment record.

By tapping the nonbusiness sources, credit managers may be able to acquire the information needed to make a logical and sound credit decision. All information, whether acquired directly or indirectly, originates with the account under investigation. Practically, however, a single source of information seldom supplies all the data needed. Credit managers should check other nonbusiness sources. They can check the subject's record by examining their own files; they can ask other creditors about their experiences; they can develop financial information and verify financial statements by contacting the customer's bank; or they can tap any other "free" source.

Despite all these possibilities, credit managers should not rely entirely on the limited number of nonbusiness sources. Weak accounts can keep their records clean with a limited number of suppliers. They may even be highly regarded by their banks, close business associates, and the creditor's salespeople. In other circles, their financial deterioration is recognized.

More important to all credit managers is the fact that they are too concerned with other financial problems of the business to become expert credit investigators. Therefore, nonbusiness sources are best utilized as a supplemental source of credit information; purchased information comes from a much greater storehouse of credit facts.

Of all the sources of credit information available to the credit analyst, the most extensive are the reports of commercialized organizations, which are discussed in the next chapter. The major purpose of these organizations is to gather and report all types of information that affect the quality of a firm's credit.

Leveraged Buyouts

In recent years, one of the biggest challenges confronting the business credit manager has been understanding and working with leveraged buyouts (LBOs). A **leveraged buyout** is a special type of acquisition where a company is purchased using substantial amount of debt secured by the assets of the company being acquired. The process is often used to *take a company private,* that is, buy up all the stock and no longer offer stock to the general public. Many times the process is initiated by the current company management who are able to acquire the company with a small personal investment. Often, the plan is to return the company to a publicly owned status by selling stock at a later time for a big profit. The current management is helped in its efforts by venture capitalists and other investment companies who contribute significant funds. The bulk of the funds to buy the stock, however, is provided by lenders who use the company's assets as collateral for the loans.

The credit analyst must recognize that considerable debt is involved in this situation. Following the LBO, the company in question is often riskier from a credit perspective than it was before the buyout. Equity is replaced with debt, often creating significantly greater interest payments. The LBO will be successful only if sufficient earnings are forthcoming to pay the huge interest price tag.

The profit margin is often squeezed because of astronomical interest payments due to the increased debt load. In extreme situations, the company is forced to sell portions of its own assets to enable it to make the interest payments on its debt.

A credit manager needs to be able to spot an LBO that may cause trouble. Determining the specific background of all new owners is vital. The credit manager should attempt to discover any silent partners and their complete background. On the positive side, if prior management is involved, they often have significant investments themselves and are committed to making the firm successful in its new format.

Important Terms

business credit managers   286
corporation   292
Credit Research Foundation, Inc.   287
direct investigation   298
double taxation   293
internal information   298
leveraged buyouts (LBOs)   306
limited liability companies   294
limited partnership   292

NACM Graduate School of Credit & Finance
  Management   287
National Association of Credit Management
  (NACM)   286
National Institute of Credit (NIC)   287
partnership   291
sole proprietorship   291
sub-chapter S corporation   293
trade group meetings   302

Discussion Questions

1. Explain why the position of the business credit manager continues to grow in importance.

2. What is the Credit Research Foundation, Inc.? The National Institute of Credit?

3. Comment on the changing status and qualifications of business credit management.

4. What are the arguments for the business credit department to be under the sales area? Under the financial area?

5. Discuss the general questions that should be answered before a credit customer can be appraised objectively.

6. Explain the classification of sources of business credit information. How do these vary from those used in consumer credit transactions?

7. What should be considered in selecting sources of business credit information?

8. Should salespersons be required to gather credit information? Explain your position.

9. What is meant by the term *direct investigation*?

10. Explain why leveraged buyouts have created problems for the business credit manager.

11. Describe the advantages and disadvantages of the various forms of business organization.

15 BUSINESS CREDIT REPORTING AGENCIES

Learning Objectives

After studying this chapter, you should be able to:

- Describe commercialized sources of business credit information.
- Discuss the origin and development of Dun & Bradstreet.
- Explain the present-day activities of Dun & Bradstreet Information Services.
- Explain the principal types of credit reports prepared by D&B.
- Clarify the use of the *Reference Book of American Business.*
- Evaluate the services of Dun & Bradstreet.
- Describe reports and services offered by Experian and Veritas Business Information, Inc.
- Explain the organization and activities of the National Association of Credit Management (NACM).
- Cover the activities of the Business Credit Services of TRW.
- Appraise the credit services of specialized agencies.

Credit management has at its disposal a variety of commercialized sources of credit information, in addition to the noncommercialized sources discussed in the previous chapter. A commercialized source of credit information supplies credit information for compensation. There are three types of commercialized sources of credit information:

1. General mercantile agencies such as Dun & Bradstreet Information Services which report on any business enterprise in response to subscribers' credit inquiries.
2. The Business Credit Reporting Service of the National Association of Credit Management operates for the systematic exchange of ledger information among members.
3. The specialized mercantile agencies report on business enterprises in particular lines of trade on a subscriber's request.

The services of the commercialized sources of credit information are quite varied and somewhat complex, so credit management must be thoroughly familiar with these sources. To arrive at a sound judgment of a credit risk, credit managers must have a wealth of information at their disposal. One of the most important of the commercialized sources is the general mercantile agency.

THE GENERAL MERCANTILE AGENCY—DUN & BRADSTREET

A **general mercantile agency**'s primary function is to supply credit reports on business concerns of all sizes, in all lines of trade, located anywhere in the United States and many foreign countries. **Dun & Bradstreet Information Services** (http://www.dnb.com), the acknowledged leader in this field, provides extensive services as a general credit reporting organization. However, even with its widespread operations and numerous services, Dun & Bradstreet does not have a monopoly in the field of credit reporting. Traditional consumer credit reporting agencies, such as Experian (formerly TRW), Equifax, and Trans Union, are working to provide more business reporting services and continue to challenge D&B's domination in this field. Veritas, a credit reporting agency established in Europe in 1989, began offering commercial credit reports to U.S. companies in 1994. Dun & Bradstreet must also compete with various specialized agencies that often serve the creditor's interests more completely, economically, and effectively.

Despite the competitive atmosphere in credit investigation, Dun & Bradstreet has grown and prospered. It remains the most frequently used source of business credit information. D&B has offices in the principal cities of the United States and leading centers of world trade.

Origin and Development of Dun & Bradstreet

A century ago or even less, the possibility of securing organized and factual data was remote. Credit decisions were often hit-or-miss affairs. Terms were long, the relationship between debtor and creditor was often personal, and some credit transactions were based solely on references furnished by customers. As a result, business experienced large credit losses that had to be offset by greater margins of profit.

During the panic of 1837, Arthur Tappan and Company failed. Lewis Tappan, who was associated with the firm, had gained a wide reputation as an excellent judge of credit risk. His personal interest in credit investigation, his reputation in appraising a credit risk, and the steady growth of the nation's economy suggested the idea of organizing a central credit reporting bureau. In 1841 he organized The Mercantile Agency to collect and disseminate information for the benefit of creditors.

The impetus for developing organized sources of credit information grew out of the uncertainties and losses experienced during the panic of 1837, the rapid changes in the country's economic structure, and the expansion of trading areas. Manufacturers and suppliers needed credit to trade over wider geographic areas. This meant that credit judgment could no longer be based on personal relationships, nor could adequate information be gathered in the immediate vicinity of the creditor. Consequently, a system of organized credit reporting evolved to eliminate some of the major uncertainties of trade.

Soon after Lewis Tappan founded The Mercantile Agency in New York, he developed a branch office system to penetrate major trade centers. Reporters visited each community to interview new and established business executives. R. G. Dun, an employee of The Mercantile Agency in 1851, became the sole proprietor of the company in 1859 and changed the name to R. G. Dun & Co. In 1849 John M. Bradstreet, an attorney in Cincinnati, founded The Bradstreet Company. This company operated in a manner similar to The Mercantile Agency and served the same fields of trade for many years. In 1933 the two firms merged into Dun & Bradstreet, Inc.

In 1973, following more than a decade of expansion and diversification, Dun & Bradstreet Companies, Inc., was formed as the parent corporation Dun & Bradstreet Information Services and a number of subsidiaries, including the Reuben H. Donnelley Corporation and Moody's Investors Service, Inc. In 1979, The Dun & Bradstreet Corporation succeeded the so-called Companies as the parent company.

The Organization, Services, and Activities of Dun & Bradstreet Information Services

To facilitate the tremendous task of collecting, assembling, analyzing, and disseminating business, commercial credit, and business-marketing information, Dun & Bradstreet employs trained analysts in 300 offices worldwide. These people gather credit information from business firms throughout the world for the D&B database which provides online access to more than 217 countries.

By early 1974, Dun & Bradstreet had equipped its U.S. offices with computer installations, and in 1975, the computers were linked to the D&B National Business Information Center in Berkeley Heights, New Jersey. In the early 1980s, a similar center was established in England, and in the late 1980s another center was established in Australia. This network forms one of the largest private computer operations in the world. Through their own terminals, the offices are able to transmit data electronically to the centers and retrieve any of the report information maintained in the D&B information base, which contains information on 40 million companies worldwide.

Principal Activities of Dun & Bradstreet

Dun & Bradstreet's principal activity is supplying business information, and over the years it has developed a number of services for the business community. Its diverse activities include the following:

1. *Report services*—D&B investigates, analyzes, and writes Business Information Reports on commercial and industrial enterprises. All reports have the same basic characteristics, but each is prepared to reflect the complexities of varied financial

structures. International Reports cover the rapidly expanding overseas markets. In recent years, many different report formats have been developed, such as Payment Analysis Reports and Dun's Financial Profiles. An example of a Payment Analysis Report is shown in Exhibit 15–1.

2. *Automated services*—Rapidly developing technology has permitted D&B to develop a wide range of refined services. Automated systems offered by D&B now include Change Notification Service (CNS), Exception Credit Update Service (ECUS), and Key Alert. Under these systems, a subscriber's own account list can be entered into D&B computers for regular monitoring and subsequent notification of significant changes occurring in the D&B information file. The primary difference between the two systems is that CNS and Key Alert output can be printed, while ECUS is intended for computer-to-computer interchange.

Delivery systems (previously the mail) have been expanded to include DunsDial, DunsPrint, and DunsLink. These systems allow subscribers direct access to D&B's computerized business information center.

3. *Reference Book service*—D&B compiles and publishes the *Dun & Bradstreet Reference Book of American Business* six times a year. This book contains businesses' names, telephone number, their SIC (standard industrial classification) number, and when available, a key showing their estimated financial strength and composite credit appraisal rating. The January, March, July, and September revisions also are published in state editions. *The Reference Book* is useful to credit, marketing, and purchasing professionals and salespersons active in the field. International reference books also are available.

4. *Apparel trades service*—This service meets the special needs of business firms in the apparel field. It is rendered through the Credit Clearing House, a D&B unit that gives credit reports and recommendations especially designed to fit the needs of the apparel trades. *The Apparel Trades Book,* containing listings on approximately 200,000 retailers and wholesalers in the apparel industry, is revised four times a year. Many customers use DunsPrint, whereby credit and marketing information is electronically transmitted to terminals in the offices of customers.

5. *Commercial collections*—This service offers accounts receivable control and collection of past-due accounts when necessary.

6. *Publications*—D&B publishes a wide variety of business statistics and operating ratios useful to business management.

7. *Directories*—D&B publishes various directories and other reference books used for credit, sales, publishing, and executive reference, including *Reference Book of Manufacturers, Reference Book of American Business, Reference Book of Corporate Managements,* and *Directory of Principal International Businesses.*

8. *Duns Reference Plus*—This service uses the latest CD-ROM technology to give customers faster access to information with great flexibility. Customers now have instant access to the exact level of D&B information needed to make a wide variety of business decisions.

Duns Reference Plus is a high-speed workstation that combines:

- A compact disk that gives electronic access to reference data on more than 4 million companies and trade styles.

EXHIBIT 15–1   Payment Analysis Report

payment analysis **PAR** report   **Dun & Bradstreet**

a company of
The Dun & Bradstreet Corporation

Prepared for

THIS REPORT MAY NOT BE REPRODUCED IN WHOLE OR IN PART IN ANY MANNER WHATEVER

DUNS: 00-007-7743
GORMAN MANUFACTURING CO., INC.
492 KOLLER STREET
SAN FRANCISCO, CA 94110
(SUBSIDIARY OF GORMAN HOLDING COMPANIES, INC.)

TEL: (415) 555-0000

LESLIE SMITH, PRES

DATE PRINTED
OCT. 26, 199-

COMMERCIAL PRINTING

SIC NOS.
2752

STARTED 1965
SALES $ 13,007,229

PAYDEX 67

★★★ KEY ★★★

PAYDEX	PAYMENT
100	ANTICIPATE
90	DISCOUNT
80	PROMPT
70	SLOW TO 15
50	SLOW TO 30
40	SLOW TO 60
30	SLOW TO 90
20	SLOW TO 120
UN	UNAVAILABLE

PAR GRAF GUIDE

SOLID LINE (——)
IS FIRM'S SCORE,

DOTTED LINE (. . .)
IS MEDIAN INDUSTRY
SCORE

TOP AND BOTTOM
BORDERS OF SHADED
AREA ARE UPPER AND
LOWER INDUSTRY
QUARTILE SCORES

SIC: 2752
OF ESTAB: 1,313

PRIOR QTRS   CURRENT 12 MONTHS

P A Y D E X 96 84 72 60 48 36 24 12 0

	'89 DEC	'90 MAR	'90 JUN	'90 SEP	'90 NOV	'90 DEC	'91 JAN	'91 FEB	'91 MAR	'91 APR	'91 MAY	'91 JUN	'91 JUL	'91 AUG	'91 SEP	'91 OCT
FIRM	79	80	82	82	77	77	75	74	74	74	71	71	63	67	66	67

DETAILED SUMMARY OF FIRM'S PAYMENT HABITS
% OF DOLLAR AMOUNT

	# OF EXP #	DOLLAR AMOUNT $	ANTIC- PROMPT %	SLOW 1-30 %	SLOW 31-60 %	SLOW 61-90 %	SLOW 91+ %
IN FILE							
12 MOS ENDING 10/91	21	784,600	64	19	17	-	-
3 MOS ENDING 10/91	10	118,750	32	39	29	-	-
CREDIT EXTEND. OF $100,000 +	3	550,000	73	9	18	-	-
50-99,999	2	140,000	25	50	25	-	-
15-49,999	3	70,000	68	32	-	-	-
5-14,999	2	15,000	50	50	-	-	-
1- 4,999	6	8,000	66	28	-	6	-
LESS THAN 1,000	5	1,600	69	31	-	-	-
CREDITS OFFERING NET TERMS	4	10,000	90	5	-	5	-
CREDITS OFFERING DISC TRMS	4	127,500	61	39	-	-	-
CASH EXPERIENCES	-		-				
PLACED FOR COLLECTION	-		-				
UNFAVORABLE COMMENTS	-		-				

* INDICATIONS OF SLOWNESS CAN BE THE RESULT OF DISPUTES OVER MERCHANDISE, SKIPPED INVOICES, ETC.

(continued)

EXHIBIT 15–1   (concluded)

payment analysis PAR report   Dun & Bradstreet

Prepared for

a company of
The Dun & Bradstreet Corporation

OCT. 26, 199-
* PAYMENT HABITS BY INDUSTRY *

LINE OF BUSINESS	# EXP	DOLLAR AMOUNT $	HIGHEST CREDIT $	AVERAGE HGH CR $	ANT PPT %	SLO 1-30 %	SLO 31-60 %	SLO 61-90 %	SLO 91+ %
AIR TRANS	1	7,500	7,500	7,500	100	-	-	-	-
BUSN SVCS MISC	1	100	100	100	100	-	-	-	-
ELEC MACHY MF	1	2,500	2,500	2,500	50	50	-	-	-
INDUSL MACHY WH	2	2,000	1,000	1,000	50	50	-	-	-
NON DURBL MISC WH	1	15,000	15,000	15,000	50	50	-	-	-
PAPER PDTS WH	8	747,500	250,000	93,438	64	18	18	-	-
PHOTO EQUIP MF	1	500	500	500	100	-	-	-	-
REPAIR SVCS	2	7,500	7,500	7,500	-	100	-	-	-
SVCS MISC	2	750	500	375	33	67	-	-	-
SYN MATERIAL MF	1	250	250	250	100	-	-	-	-
TRANS SVCS	1	1,000	1,000	1,000	50	-	-	50	-

* PAYMENT SUMMARY *

COMPOSITE PAYDEX CURRENT 12 MONTHS = 72

COMPOSITE PAYDEX PRIOR 12 MONTHS = 81

AVG. HIGH CREDIT = $39,230

HIGHEST CREDIT = $250,000

(Mail Version)

- Advanced communication software that automatically links the customer to the D&B database and lets full reports be retrieved on more than 9 million U.S. firms.
- Report management capabilities that store D&B reports on the customer's hard disk, giving the flexibility to view, store, print, update, or delete at the customer's convenience.
- Yet the most important activity of Dun & Bradstreet is the collecting, assembling, and analyzing of credit information. Many of D&B's other activities are dependent on this one.

Methods of Collecting Credit Information

To accomplish the tremendous task of collecting credit information, Dun & Bradstreet uses personal investigations (both direct and telephone) and mail inquiries. Personal investigations are made by reporters, who are usually assigned a specific territory so they become more intimately acquainted with the sources of credit information and with local business managements. Reporters revise and update reports at stated intervals, so Dun & Bradstreet files contain the latest available information.

Most credit investigations of businesses follow a similar pattern. Reporters first interview the principals of a business, confirm ownership, note details of its operations and methods, obtain a financial statement, and discuss future plans and sales trends. They may also check court and other public records or investigate outside the business (i.e., interview bankers, accountants, and other informed sources) to gather additional facts or verify existing information.

D&B also collects payment data in many forms. It uses the traditional methods of collecting payment data from suppliers by mail and phone. On a daily basis, the National Business Information Center machine generates payment experience request forms and mails them to 700,000 suppliers nationwide. Reporters also ask for payment experiences when they update the Business Information Report.

The primary method of collecting payment data is **Dun-Trade** and, for banking information, **Dun-Bank.** These two methods eliminate all paperwork and phone calls by regularly collecting the same data as the traditional methods (e.g., manner of payment, high credit, amount owing, past dues, terms of sale, and date of last sale) on computer tapes, diskettes, and disks. D&B is also developing a method to accept payment data directly from customers' computers via communication lines. The payment information collected by mail, phone, and computer is added to the business data gathered by reporters and other third-party sources to make up the Business Information Report.

As a further means of ensuring that its reports are accurate and fair, Dun & Bradstreet's policy has always been to make copies available to businesses being reported on. For some years, D&B mailed a copy of pertinent report data to millions of companies covered by D&B reports. More recently, D&B sends a copy of the entire report (either an initial report or a full revision) to the chief executive of the firm being reported on with a request for review and, if appropriate, suggested revisions. The costs of writing a report are assumed by D&B subscribers, never by the subjects themselves.

PRINCIPAL TYPES OF REPORTS

Most D&B reports contain the same basic elements, but some reports use specialized forms to fit the credit and sales requirements of various subscribers. VIP Reports are custom written for each customer to cover its specific needs and may cover short-term credit and management problems and contain highly detailed information along with a specific credit recommendation. International Reports are written on overseas concerns in principal free-world markets.

Senior business analysts handle the more complex and active cases, and, generally, the largest companies are handled by a group of highly trained national business analysts.

Business Information Reports

D&B sends the **Business Information Report** (see Exhibit 15–2) to subscriber inquiries from its National Business Information Center. This is only one type of D&B report, but it is the one most frequently used (about 39,000 a day). A computer-merged Business Information Report is divided into 10 basic sections, 6 of which appear in all cases: summary, payments, finance, banking, history, and operation. Four other elements appear as necessary: special events, changes, update, and public filings.

Most report information is developed through direct contact with principals of the company on which the report is being written, but many details also come from public records, suppliers, and other sources.

EXHIBIT 15–2   The Business Information Report

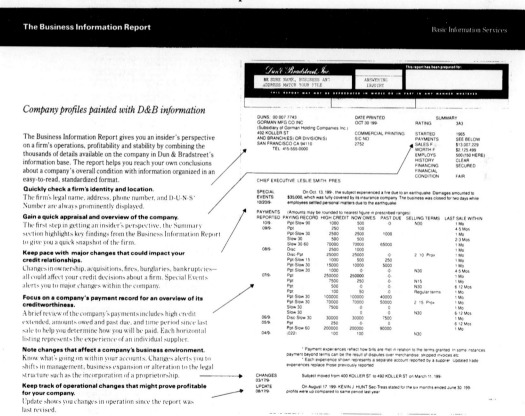

(continued)

EXHIBIT 15–2   (continued)

The Business Information Report   Basic Information Services

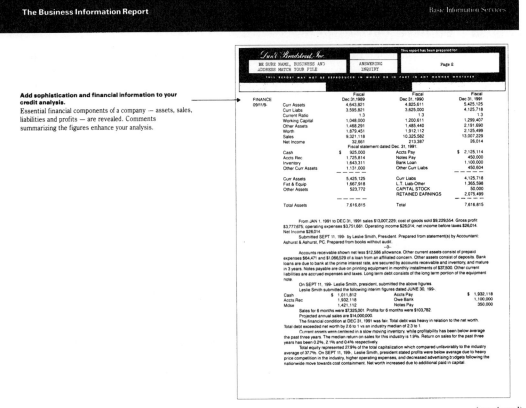

Add sophistication and financial information to your
credit analysis.
Essential financial components of a company — assets, sales,
liabilities and profits — are revealed. Comments
summarizing the figures enhance your analysis.

(continued)

Since a Business Information Report reflects investigations conducted at different times, no single date is applicable to all of the information in the report. The lead date at the top is merely the date on which the report was printed out by computer in response to an inquiry.

Heading and Summary of the Business Information Report

This section provides a concise, at-a-glance picture of a business. Reading across the top, an analyst can quickly obtain the basic identification information about a company: the name and address, telephone number, principal owner or executive, four-digit U.S. standard industrial classification code (designating the company's product line and function), and a written description of the company's line of business.

In the upper left-hand corner is the DUNS number, a unique nine-digit identification code assigned to every company in the D&B computerized files. (Each location of a company has its own separate number.)

Exhibit 15–2   (concluded)

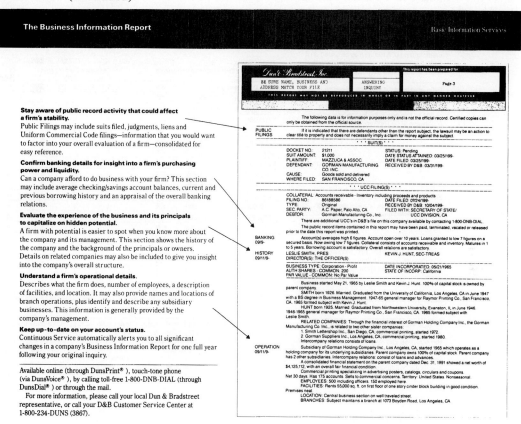

The Business Information Report   Basic Information Services

Stay aware of public record activity that could affect a firm's stability.
Public Filings may include suits filed, judgments, liens and Uniform Commercial Code filings—information that you would want to factor into your overall evaluation of a firm—consolidated for easy reference.

Confirm banking details for insight into a firm's purchasing power and liquidity.
Can a company afford to do business with your firm? This section may include average checking/savings account balances, current and previous borrowing history and an appraisal of the overall banking relations.

Evaluate the experience of the business and its principals to capitalize on hidden potential.
A firm with potential is easier to spot when you know more about the company and its management. This section shows the history of the company and the background of the principals or owners. Details on related companies may also be included to give you insight into the company's overall structure.

Understand a firm's operational details.
Describes what the firm does, number of employees, a description of facilities, and location. It may also provide names and locations of branch operations, plus identify and describe any subsidiary businesses. This information is generally provided by the company's management.

Keep up-to-date on your account's status.
Continuous Service automatically alerts you to all significant changes in a company's Business Information Report for one full year following your original inquiry.

Available online (through DunsPrint®), touch-tone phone (via DunsVoice®), by calling toll-free 1-800-DNB-DIAL (through DunsDial®) or through the mail.
   For more information, please call your local Dun & Bradstreet representative, or call your D&B Customer Service Center at 1-800-234-DUNS (3867).

Above the company name is the Dun & Bradstreet Capital-and-Credit Rating, designating the estimated financial strength and the composite credit appraisal (see the key to ratings in Exhibit 15–3). In addition, for quick review, the Summary at the upper right gives important points derived from more detailed report information. Besides the D&B rating, these points usually include the year started, payments, sales, worth, number of employees, history, financing, condition, and trend.

Started
Ordinarily, this figure is the year the present ownership came into financial control of the business. In older, family-owned businesses and publicly owned companies, however, it may be the year the business originally commenced operations.

Payments
This section always says SEE BELOW because the trade data is updated daily and any abbreviated description may be inconsistent due to recently received data.

EXHIBIT 15–3   D&B Ratings and Symbols

D&B Rating System

The D&B Rating System is a widely used tool that uses a two-part code to represent a firm's estimated financial strength and composite credit appraisal. A Rating may be based on a book financial statement or on an estimated financial statement submitted by the company.

	Estimated Financial Strength		Composite Credit Appraisal			
			High	Good	Fair	Limited

Estimated financial strength, based on an actual book financial statement.

For example, if a company has a Rating of "3A3," this means its financial strength is between $1,000,000 and $9,999,999 and its composite credit appraisal is "fair."

Estimated Financial Strength			Code	High	Good	Fair	Limited
$50,000,000	and over		5A	1	2	3	4
$10,000,000	to	$49,999,999	4A	1	2	3	4
$1,000,000	to	$9,999,999	3A	1	2	3	4
$750,000	to	$999,999	2A	1	2	3	4
$500,000	to	$749,999	1A	1	2	3	4
$300,000	to	$499,999	BA	1	2	3	4
$200,000	to	$299,999	BB	1	2	3	4
$125,000	to	$199,999	CB	1	2	3	4
$75,000	to	$124,999	CC	1	2	3	4
$50,000	to	$74,999	DC	1	2	3	4

Estimated financial strength, based on either an actual book financial statement or an estimated financial statement.

Estimated Financial Strength			Code	High	Good	Fair	Limited
$35,000	to	$49,999	DD	1	2	3	4
$20,000	to	$34,999	EE	1	2	3	4
$10,000	to	$19,999	FF	1	2	3	4
$5,000	to	$9,999	GG	1	2	3	4
	up to $4,999		HH	1	2	3	4

Estimated financial strength, based on an estimated financial statement (when an actual book financial statement is not available to us).

Estimated Financial Strength			Code	High	Good	Fair	Limited
$125,000	and over		1R		2	3	4
$50,000	to	$124,999	2R		2	3	4

Symbols in the Rating column — what do they mean?

-- (Absence of a Rating)

A Business Information Report is available on this business, and other information products may be available as well. However, a D&B Rating has not been assigned. A "--" symbol should not be interpreted as indicating that credit should be denied. It simply means that the information available to Dun & Bradstreet does not permit us to classify the company within our Rating key and that further inquiry should be made before reaching a credit decision.

In many cases, a "--" symbol is used because a current financial statement on the business is not available to us. Some other reasons for using a "--" symbol include:

☐ Unavailability of the source and amount of starting capital -- in the case of a new business
☐ A deficit net worth
☐ Bankruptcy proceedings
☐ A critical financial condition

ER (Employee Range)

Certain lines of business, primarily banks, insurance companies and other service-type businesses, do not lend themselves to classification under the D&B Rating System. Instead, we assign these types of businesses an Employee Range symbol based on the number of people employed. No other significance should be attached to this symbol.

For example, a Rating of "ER7" means there are between 5 and 9 employees in the company.

"ERN" should not be interpreted negatively. It simply means we don't have information indicating how many people are employed at this firm.

Key to Employee Range			
1000	or more employees		ER 1
500	to	999	ER 2
100	to	499	ER 3
50	to	99	ER 4
20	to	49	ER 5
10	to	19	ER 6
5	to	9	ER 7
1	to	4	ER 8
Not available			ER N

INV (Investigation being conducted)

"INV" means that at the time the listings were extracted for this Reference Book, we were conducting an investigation on this business to get the most current details.

Questions? Please call your D&B Customer Service Center at 1-800-234-DUNS (1-800-234-3867).
Our Customer Service Representatives will be happy to help you interpret the D&B Rating System and other symbols.

Sales

This figure is the company's annual sales or revenue. It may be shown as a range of annual sales.

Worth

This figure—sometimes referred to as the estimated financial strength—attempts to show the tangible net worth of a business after all intangible assets have been deducted. Some specific intangible assets are not deducted in computing net worth. When an F precedes the figure, sales or worth is based on figures taken from the books of account. (Such figures have not necessarily been prepared by a public accountant and are an opinion expressed. That can be determined from the Finance section in the body of the report.) When the sales or worth figure is based on signed estimates from the owner or management, the amount is preceded by an E. If there is neither an F nor an E, the figure has been estimated by the management or by others.

Employees

The figure for number of employees includes all those who are paid wages for their services, including full-time and part-time employees, as well as the owner, partners, or officers. In some instances the figure is the latest one available; in others it represents an average number employed over a year's time. If the company's employment is seasonal, a range is usually shown.

History

One of four descriptive words are used in this category: clear, business, management, or incomplete.

Clear indicates that nothing in the background of a business or its management is likely to be of special interest to the report reader, including such items as significant suits, judgments, liens, or business failures.

Business indicates that something in the background of a business or its management is likely to be of interest to the reader. Management indicates that the report contains similar items pertaining to one or more of those who manage or own the business. Incomplete indicates that the identity of one or more of the owners or managers is incomplete or significant background information is unavailable or could not be satisfactorily confirmed.

Financing

The caption "Financing" appears when a business is borrowing and the loan is secured by receivables and/or inventory. If the caption is followed by the word *secured,* either there are such loans outstanding or a financing statement has been filed that makes such loans available to the business. If the caption is followed by *secured-unsecured,* both types of loans are outstanding.

Condition

One of four descriptive words follow this caption: strong, good, fair, or unbalanced. This word describes the financial strength of the business but generally also ties in closely with the composite credit appraisal, as reflected in the second part (the letter) of the D&B rating (i.e., strong = high, good = good, fair = fair, and unbalanced = limited). However, there are exceptions. If business through the trade is slow, the rating could be "good" or "fair" while the firm's condition is "strong." Or the rating may be "blank" ("—-") by reason of a criminal conviction even though the firm's condition is "strong" or "good."

Trend

Trends in earnings, worth, and sales are all important, but the "Trend" caption usually reflects earnings. In some cases large withdrawals of earnings may make the worth trend more significant. If earnings and worth information is unavailable, the trend will reflect sales. In instances of conflicting factors, the D&B analyst must judge which is most significant.

Other Sections of the Business Information Report

Payments

This section shows a company's payment position with its vendors, as reported by suppliers. Each listing in the section will include one or more of the following: the paying record, high credit, amount owing, amount past due (if any), selling terms, and period of time since the last sale. A separate line shows a supplier's comments (e.g., "Account in dispute" or "Special agreement"). The dates to the left of the paying record indicate when that particular information was reported.

Some "slowness" generally appears in every representative trade section, and small percentages are not usually considered significant by credit executives. A fair way to calculate the percentage of prompt payments is to count the number of 1s (prompt or better), 2s (mixed, such as "prompt-slow" or "disc-slow"), and 3s (slow). Each user should establish guidelines for an acceptable amount of slowness. Even in the strongest companies, 20 percent of payments may show some slowness. Where the risk is greater, some analysts prefer a deeper analysis, such as dollar weighting.

From the Payments section, a supplier intending to open a new account receives a good indication of what to expect when dealing with the customer—based on the previous payment experiences of others.

Finance

This section includes essential facts for determining the financial condition and trend of a business. Many reports contain financial information in the form of audited figures prepared by a certified public accountant (with or without qualification in the accountant's opinion), unaudited figures from the books of account (not prepared by an outside accountant), or management's own estimate of assets, liabilities, sales, expenses, and profit. In any event, no audit is conducted by Dun & Bradstreet.

Principals of some concerns decline to furnish detailed figures, and financial figures may therefore be based on bank and supplier comment, investigation of public records, or the D&B business reporter's own estimates of certain estimated tangible balance sheet items.

Financial information is also frequently supplemented with information regarding leases, insurance coverage, and other pertinent details. Comment in the Finance section is devoted to further necessary explanation of the figures and to a description of sales and profit trends. D&B bases its ratings to a large extent on the degree of financial stability and the trend reflected in this section.

Banking

Information on banking relations may include average balances, previous and current loan experience, whether loans are secured or unsecured, the length of time the bank has had the account, and whether the bank considers the account satisfactory. A date to the left indicates when this information was reported to D&B.

Sometimes the report provides the names of some or all of the account's banks, though not necessarily in order of importance.

History

This section contains the names and past business experience of the firm's principals or owners. Such information is usually obtained from the firm's management. Past business experience and outside affiliations of principals are important considerations in evaluating a company's management. D&B uses its own files where feasible to verify and augment the information provided by management. Other background information is usually not verified.

D&B reports any criminal proceedings it learns of for as long as they are pending. If a conviction results, it is reported for 25 years. In general, historical information is not repeated after 25 years, except for such items as corporate charter or trade-style registration dates and principals' educational background and date of birth.

The History section can be used to verify ownership; identify owners, partners, or officers; and reveal the outside interests of the principals.

Operation

This section describes what a company does and the nature of the premises, the neighborhood, and the size of floor space. Also described—wherever applicable—are the lines of merchandise it sells or the kinds of services it supplies, as well as the price range, classification of customers, selling terms, percentage of cash and credit sales, number of accounts, seasonal aspects, and number of employees.

By describing the machinery of production and distribution, the Operation section gives the reader a better understanding of the company's balance sheet and profit and loss figures. The report user is also better able to judge whether capital is adequate or debt is excessive. Sales departments use this section to determine whether the company could be a profitable outlet for their lines of merchandise. Purchasing departments use the information to determine the vendor's capacity to deliver an order or support guarantees.

Special Events

This section highlights significant events that might vitally affect a present credit relationship or pending credit decision, including recent changes of chief executive, legal structure, partners, control, business location, or business name, bankruptcy updates, business discontinuances, criminal proceedings, burglaries or embezzlements, and fires and other disasters.

The Special Events section appears after the Heading and Summary so it can be noticed immediately.

Public Filings

This section identifies public civil filings, such as bankruptcies, suits, judgments, Uniform Commercial Code filings, liens, and record item updates and releases. While it is impossible to provide coverage of all public record information, D&B provides many significant items. The Public Filings section appears between the Finance and Banking sections of the report.

Payment Analysis Reports (PAR)

These reports (see Exhibit 15–1) provide an in-depth but concise report card on a firm's payment habits. Subscribers use **Payment Analysis Reports (PAR)** as a complement to the D&B Business Information Report on new or important accounts or by itself to periodically check smaller or more established customers. The key to PAR is the PAYDEX, a single numerical value that serves as an at-a-glance indicator of a company's current payment posture. The PAYDEX is used to compare the payments of an individual company with other companies in the same line of business and same size range. PAR provides a valuable monthly summary of a firm's payment habits for the previous 12 months and summarizes both the amounts of "credit extended" and the firm's "manner of payment" in an easy-to-read format.

Dun's Financial Profiles

These **financial profiles** provide extensive financial spreadsheets on over 1 million U.S. firms, publicly held and private, large and small, in a format that makes it possible for readers to quickly and easily evaluate financial trends and analyze how these firms compare with their own line-of-business groups (by standard industrial classification number and by asset size range). The profiles also provide a screening service to identify qualified prospects for marketing acquisition or investment purposes using a wide variety of selection criteria provided by the subscriber.

Continuous Service

Continuous service provides automatic notification of recent developments affecting accounts on which the subscriber has ordered a D&B report. It is a "watchdog" service for monitoring key or marginal accounts that a subscriber has registered with D&B. Continuous PAR, another monitoring service, notifies subscribers when any of the accounts that they have registered with D&B undergoes a change in payment score of more than 10 points up or down.

VIP Reports/Special Purpose Reports

Subscribers who need information beyond that found in the Business Information Report or supplied by Continuous Service can use D&B's VIP Reports. Each of these reports furnishes comprehensive and detailed information in answer to specific questions raised by individual subscribers. VIP Reports provide facts on important customers in answer to subscribers' questions.

Subscribers indicate the nature of their question or problem on a special request form. After a comprehensive investigation and analysis, D&B prepares a report to meet the particular need. Because of their comprehensive nature, the detailed and lengthy investigation, and the time necessary to complete them, these reports cost more than the Business Information Reports.

Use of Credit Reports by Subscribers

Subscribers use detailed credit reports for a variety of business purposes. While credit reports usually serve credit purposes, much of the same information is valuable for other business activities. Subscribers normally request reports for the following credit purposes:

1. To appraise the creditworthiness of a new account for which the subscribers have no data on file and for which the D&B *Reference Book* rating is not a sufficient basis for a credit decision.
2. To review active credit files to keep informed of the progress and current condition of accounts. Periodic review of accounts is the basis on which customers' lines of credit and terms of sale are adjusted to their financial standing.
3. To determine the underlying causes of slow and doubtful accounts. Current information often helps subscribers convert such accounts into profitable customers.
4. To provide a sound basis for decision making when customers want to expand their line of credit or when marked changes in paying habits occur.

In addition to the uses cited above, credit reports should be requested whenever the credit manager's confidence in the debtor has been shaken. A number of circumstances can create this condition, such as radical fluctuations in a firm's buying policies and financial dealings, suspected fraud or misrepresentation, legal proceedings, and "acts of God."

Sales departments can use credit reports on new businesses and prospective customers not only to provide a basis for extending credit but also to determine the prospect's sales potential. Salespeople are better equipped to sell when they have advance knowledge of a prospect's operations, scope of activities, and financial capacity. Similarly, such reports help sales departments determine if a firm warrants a higher line of credit or has not reached its full sales potential.

The coordinated use of detailed credit reports as suggested above results in the greatest possible advantages to the subscriber. When credit reports serve more than one purpose, it is easy to justify their costs.

THE DUN & BRADSTREET REFERENCE BOOK OF AMERICAN BUSINESS

The *Dun & Bradstreet Reference Book of American Business* (also referred to as the *Reference Book*) contains the names and credit ratings of almost 3 million business, industrial, and service enterprises located throughout the United States, Puerto Rico, and the U.S. Virgin Islands. Although D&B is well known for this activity, the preparation of credit reports is the backbone of the organization. Information gathered for credit reports contributes to the financial ratings and changes that occur in the *Reference Book.* *Reference Book* ratings are frequently referred to by credit managers. In fact, checking a firm's capital-and-credit rating is frequently the first step in credit risk appraisal. In many instances this rating alone is sufficient to reveal a high degree of creditworthiness.

Contents of the Reference Books

The *Reference Book,* which is prepared in four separate sections, is published every two months and leased to subscribers. It contains a complete listing of most businesses in every city, town, and village in the United States, Puerto Rico, and the U.S. Virgin Islands. Other editions of the *Reference Book* are also available: one covers only the United States, a *State Sales Guide* covers each state, and a number of regional editions include listings of several states. These smaller editions are exact copies of the state or metropolitan information contained in the larger volumes and are published in a convenient 9-by-11-inch briefcase size. Company representatives, especially salespeople, use the state editions to appraise customers conveniently, build prospect lists, and gain helpful information about their territories.

The books contain ratings on manufacturers, wholesalers, retailers, and other businesses on which Dun & Bradstreet has written a Business Information Report. Listings are alphabetical by state, then by town within the state. Following the town name is the population and the county in which the community is located. This information is followed by an alphabetical listing of businesses.

Each business name is preceded by a U.S. standard industrial classification code number, which indicates the nature of the business. For example, 52 51 is the SIC code designating retail hardware, and all hardware stores have this code number preceding the business name. The number immediately after some of the business names indicates the business was started within the last 10 years. The number is the last digit of the year within the 10-year period. To the extreme right, and following this information, is the firm's rating. If the business is new to the current edition of the *Reference Book,* the letter A is posted to the left of the business classification code; the letter C in the same place means a rating change occurred with the current edition. An illustration of a *Reference Book* page is shown in Exhibit 15–4.

Explanation of Ratings

A Dun & Bradstreet rating consists of two elements: (1) a firm's established financial strength and (2) its composite credit appraisal. The estimated financial strength is expressed in the letter portion of the rating. (See Exhibit 15–3 for the Dun & Bradstreet

EXHIBIT 15–4   Page from *Reference Book*

How to interpret Reference Book listings

Reference Book listings give you select summary information on a company, so you can begin to assess the risk of doing business with that firm.

To help you become more familiar with the Reference Book and its coding system, we've organized the listings into the following information categories.

Demographic information

This area gives you information about the city, town or village in which a company is located. Reading left to right, you'll see:

Name of the city, town or village, as designated by the U.S. Postal Service (You'll see a cross-reference if the town is not a primary U.S.P.S. town.)

Telephone area code (For states with one area code, the code appears at the top of the page.)

Population, according to the 1990 U.S. Census (listed for U.S.P.S. towns in which Census figures are available)

County or parish in which the firm is located

Company name, phone number and corporate relationships

In this section you'll see the company's name and telephone number. Use the phone number to obtain more information through an online computer search (Duns-Print® or DunsLink®), by calling an 800 number (DunsDial®) or using a touchtone phone (DunsVoice®).

(If there's an asterisk [*] after the name, this means the business is a corporation and the words "Corporation," "Corp.," "Incorporated," "Inc.," "Limited" or "Ltd." have been omitted.)

Below the company's name, you may see the following indicators:

Sub of ... Uncover hidden business-development opportunities by finding out whether the firm is part of a larger corporate structure. "Sub of" means the firm is a subsidiary, and the parent company guarantees the subsidiary's contract obligations. To locate the listing for the parent company, see the information following "Sub of ... ."

Br of ... Who's ultimately responsible for paying invoices? "Br of" means the firm is a branch. To locate the listing for the company's headquarters, see the town and state following "Br of ... ."

Newbury (904) 1,826 Alachua

2512	Jones AF & Co.	464-5051	DC3
7392	K & B Resources Inc.	464-0204	ER6
A 52x11	Keeton Lumber Corp.	464-0859	– –
2952	Lakeside Roofing Company Inc.		INV
		464-3366	
C 5399	Lane Bros. Inc.	464-4402	DD2 P
7231	Laura's Beauty Place	464-2121	ER5 F
3469	Mark Boring Parts Inc.	464-9163	EE3
5621	Paris Fashions of		
	Crestview, Inc.	464-3004	3A1 P
	Sub of Paris Fashions, Inc.		
	Longview, VA		
54x11	Russell AF	464-2512	1A1 PF
5541	Thomas Bros. Industrial Corp.		2A1
		464-0023	
	Br of Johnstown, PA		
1211	Wells Coal Co.*	464-5550	1A2
	Br of Pittsburgh, PA		
2321	Wilson John Jacob & Co., Inc.		EE3
		464-6222	
5042	Zindler & Dahl	464-5664	FB
5912	Zoby John*	464-1073	8 2R2 P

Newport (See St. Marks)

Change indicators and Standard Industrial Classification codes

Here you'll find the following information:

A Looking for prospects? "A" tells you a business is less than two years old, or that we've added it to the Reference Book.

C Want to monitor changes in the financial condition of your customers or suppliers? "C" means the firm's D&B Rating has changed within the past two months.

2512 Need to identify prospects by
7392 general function (manufacturer,
52x11 wholesaler, retailer or service) and
etc. specific line of business? Four-digit Standard Industrial Classification codes will help. For a list of Standard Industrial Classification codes and a more detailed explanation, please see page 1.4.

Note: When you see an "x" between the second and third digits, this means the company is involved in another line of business within the same general function.

Ratings/Symbols, product availability indicators and year started

Here you'll find the following information:

DC3 This column gives you a quick
ER6 snapshot of the company's estimated
– – financial strength and composite credit
etc. appraisal or a signal that you might need more information before making a decision. Details on interpreting these D&B Ratings and Symbols are on the reverse of this card.

P When are you likely to be paid? For a detailed analysis of a firm's payment habits, check for the "P"—it means a Payment Analysis Report is available on this business.[†] A "P" also signals that a Credit Advisory System and a Credit Scoring Report may be available. See page 3.8 or 3.6 for more information.[*]

F Need an in-depth, analytical look into a firm's finances? Look for the "F"—it means you can get a Duns Financial Profile[†] or that a financial statement on this business is available in the firm's Credit Advisory System report. See page 3.9 or 3.6 to find out more.[*]

[*]Payment and Financial information are often available, even if you don't see a "P" or "F" indicator, in a Business Information Report. See page 3.4 for details.

FB Looking to do business internationally? Check for the "FB"—it means the company is a branch of a foreign firm. See page 3.3 for information on International Services.

8 A single-digit number indicates the year the firm was established or current management took control. For example, "8" means the firm was established in 1988. If there is no number, the firm was established more than 10 years ago. (This feature is not used for branch listings.)

For more background on the firm, you can check the "History" section of the Business Information Report or Credit Advisory System.

If the company you want isn't listed ...

You can still get information—just call us at 1-800-DNB-DIAL (1-800-362-3425). If you still don't find the firm you want, we can conduct an investigation and deliver the information to you in as little as 24 hours.

[†]Indicators reflect report availability at the time of printing.

If you have questions or need additional copies of this tear-out card please call your Customer Service Center at 1-800-234-DUNS (1-800-234-3867).

←   *Tear out along perforated line.*

key to ratings.) These 15 codes (5A to HH) designate the company's range of net worth or financial strength. The composite credit appraisal is a general credit grade of high, good, fair, or limited, expressed by number.

Estimated financial strength is a conservative estimate of the firm's tangible net worth. This is arrived at by analyzing the firm's financial statements or other financial data, after allowances for intangible items such as goodwill or patents.

The composite credit appraisal, an evaluation of the firm's ability and willingness to pay and of its past history in meeting its obligations, is based on the length of time in business, the abilities of management, general financial condition, the trend of the business, payment record data, and the like. If these factors are judged to be strong, D&B may assign the firm a high credit rating; if they are judged to be weak, it may assign a lower rating. The exact credit rating used depends on the strength or weakness of all the above factors in relation to one another.

The assignment of the rating is made by the reporter at the time of report revision. An automated rating assistance algorithm (RATE) suggests a rating to the reporter based on the company's position relative to industry norms and D&B guidelines.

As new data such as late financial information, changes in manner of payment, or courthouse information is added, the RATE algorithm compares the existing rating to the proposed rating. Each case or revision is reviewed by a D&B specialist, and a new rating, based on the latest data, may be applied.

In some instances, D&B isn't able to assign a capital or credit rating, or both. The symbols used to denote these uncommon circumstances are explained in Exhibit 15–3 in the key to ratings.

Use of the D&B Reference Book by Credit Managers

The D&B *Reference Book* contains a large amount of useful information for credit managers. In general, the books are highly regarded throughout the credit profession because they frequently offer a basis for quick approval of orders. Experienced credit managers, however, use them with caution; although a new *Reference Book* is published every two months, the information is not always current. In any event, *Reference Books* are not normally used as a basis to refuse credit but rather may indicate the need for additional information. Any publication as vast in scope and detail as the *Reference Book* cannot be produced without some errors. However, D&B now uses computers and advanced printing technology, and timeliness has been improved.

Serious shortcomings may be due not to the publication task but to the nature of the investigating task. It is impossible to investigate each name immediately before a revised edition. Furthermore, ratings are the result of human judgment based on the information available. No rating system is infallible, and the merits of a rating system cannot compensate for the deficiencies in human judgment. Credit reporters may gather insufficient information or rely too heavily on certain sources. Some businesses will not reveal their financial condition and other facts, so the reporter must rely on the best available sources of indirect information. In these cases, estimates of financial condition are made, errors in judgment occur, and the actual status of the company may not be fully ascertained. However, since 1974 D&B has assigned no full capital-and-credit rating without book figures if tangible net worth exceeds $50,000.

Despite these limitations, subscribers to the *Reference Book* can use it to advantage in the following circumstances:

Credit departments can:

Set up credit lines by ratings.

Check small and sample orders.

Review continuously important changes in customers and prospects.

Purchasing departments can:

Locate sources of supply.

Verify credit standings of suppliers.

Determine responsibility of vendors.

Sales departments can:

Brief salespersons on accounts.

Estimate purchasing power.

Build and revise prospect files.

Spot new prospects (names prefixed by A).

Reclassify prospects (rating changes highlighted by C).

Select prospective distributors.

Guide sales research in selected areas.

OTHER ACTIVITIES

DunsDial

Within seconds, this direct, toll-free telephone service gives regular subscribers access to information on any one of the businesses with data stored in the D&B computerized business information files. Since early 1989 computerized delivery of the reports via fax transmission has been available.

DunsPrint

This access system puts hard-copy Business Information Reports and other information formats in D&B subscribers' hands within minutes. DunsPrint is the ultimate in business information communications—the instant relay of information to personal computers and/or print terminals located on the customer's premises. (A two-page Business Information Report ordinarily takes less than one minute to print.) Formats available are:

Business Information Reports (full display).

Credit Advisory Service (CAS).

Bankers Advisory Service (BAS).

Payment Analysis Reports (PAR).

Dun's Financial Profiles.

Rating & Verification Display.

Summary Display.

Family Tree Service.

Credit Clearing House Recommendation.

EVALUATION OF DUN & BRADSTREET

Dun & Bradstreet follows the previously set criteria in selecting and supplying the information credit analysts need. The important selection factors are: accuracy of information, contents of reports, speed of reporting, cost of service, trade coverage, geographic coverage, variety and number of reports, and supplemental services offered. And credit managers need the following information: identity and legal responsibility, history and business background, character and responsibility of management, financial ability and strength, and payment experience.

While D&B is not free of limitations and errors, it meets the above criteria. The agency's interest is to report facts as accurately and completely as possible. As the most comprehensive source of commercial credit information, D&B reports the facts as it knows them. The procedures of reporting are constantly being improved, and Dun & Bradstreet requests that its subscribers report errors.

D&B's trade and geographic coverage are the most complete in the credit reporting industry. With its large number of reporters, the agency can supply a credit report on any business located anywhere in the country. Dun & Bradstreet does not claim to gather information from sources that would be unavailable to creditors; it acquires its information from the same sources available to all credit managers. Creditors can undertake their own direct investigation, but Dun & Bradstreet's facilities are tailored to this purpose.

Dun & Bradstreet reports give creditors much of the information necessary to make an informed credit decision. If certain types of credit information are not available or the firm has failed to supply financial statements, such shortcomings in the data are clearly apparent to the subscriber. Subscribers can then conduct direct investigations to acquire any necessary missing data. The agency's variety of reports, Continuous Service, *Reference Books,* and collection services fulfill the requirements of most commercial creditors. The broad scope of the agency's services alleviates problems associated with making credit decisions, controlling and collecting accounts receivable, and periodically revising information.

The final responsibility for the credit decision, however, rests with the credit executives. They must decide the amount of information they need, the sources they should use, the reliability of the information, and the weight they should give to the various data they have.

It should be recognized that Dun & Bradstreet has been changing its focus from being simply a "credit reporting" agency to selling customers information at every point in their business decision cycle. D&B sells information to help customers find prospects in the beginning of the cycle as well as services to help them collect on unpaid accounts at the end of the cycle.

OTHER GENERAL MERCANTILE AGENCIES

Other business credit reporting agencies that try to respond to inquiries for any business include Experian and Veritas Business Information, Inc.

Experian (formerly TRW) Business Information Services (http://www.experian.com)

In 1976, TRW pioneered on-line delivery of business credit reports with the formation of TRW Business Information Services. TRW Business Information Services proceeded to build a business credit database of 14 million businesses and offers reports on companies worldwide. In 1996, TRW Business Information Services was acquired by another firm (See Chapter 10) and the name was changed to **Experian Business Information Services.** Experian not only helps businesses determine if their customers can pay, it gives them a predictive indication of when they will pay.

Businesses contribute their accounts receivables to Experian Business Information Services monthly or quarterly, providing a continuously updated database of trade payment information. Experian's business credit report, the Experian Business Profile, uses a business's actual trade payment experiences as the key predictor of future payment behavior. Third-party trade data also provide a more accurate and objective picture of a business's credit behavior.

Experian expresses a business's risk potential in the form of a Days Beyond Terms score (DBT). The DBT score represents the average number of days late a business pays its suppliers past the payment due date on its invoices. Experian augments this information on the Business Profile with the following sections:

Executive summary: identifies the key elements from the body of the report.

Trade payment information: shows trade payment experiences, payment totals, payment trends, and payment history.

Public record information: presents details of bankruptcies; federal, state, and county tax liens; judgments; and attachment liens.

UCC profile: lists UCC filings with the most recent displayed first.

Commercial finance relationships: identifies the name, address, and phone number of the primary bank utilized by the business along with specific account information if available.

Company background information: includes home state of business, year business registered with the state, charter number, current status of business, principal officers, and most recent filing date.

Inquiries: summarizes all inquiries made on the subject during the past nine months.

Standard and Poor's information: contains key financial information on publicly held U.S. companies as well as Summary Business Background Information on both publicly and privately held firms.

Federal government information: reports selected financial and contract data reflecting the company's dealings with federal government agencies.

Experian provides only verified information. It cannot be manipulated by the principal or trade creditors. Financial statements are provided by Standard & Poors on publicly held companies.

Experian Business Information Services offers over 30 business-to-business risk management, credit evaluation, and marketing services including:

- Intelliscore services. Standard and/or custom-built credit risk scoring models that use statistical analyses to determine a company's risk potential in the form of a risk score. Experian offers Industry Intelliscore (Telecom, Leasing, Commercial All Industry), Custom Intelliscore, and Small Business Intelliscore Integrating data for the most predictive risk analysis on small businesses.

- Small Business Advisory Report (SBAR). Proprietor reports that present the personal credit behavior of small business proprietors/partners so that informed business credit decisions can be made.

- International report services. Credit information on companies worldwide with on-line ordering and delivery within 3 to 10 business days. Canadian reports are available on-line.

- Trade payment guides. Summary credit information on up to 3 million businesses in reference books, updated quarterly.

Veritas Business Information, Inc.

Veritas Business Information, Inc. (originally called *European Business Contact, Inc.*) was incorporated in 1989 to provide credit reports on domestic and Canadian companies for European clients. In 1992 the original firm acquired Veritas, S.A., a credit reporting firm in Argentina. During 1992–1995, Veritas opened offices around the world and now produces credit reports on any company in North, South, and Central America.

Each report is freshly investigated featuring current payment and financial trends. Every customer has the ability to ask specific questions which customize the report for their eyes only. Report contents include:

Identification

Executive summary

Veritas rating

Legal information

Related companies

Technical information

History

Financial figures

Industry analysis

Bank reference

Payment history

Trade references

Public record

Conclusion

NATIONAL ASSOCIATION OF CREDIT MANAGEMENT

The **National Association of Credit Management (NACM)** (http://www.nacm.org) is the oldest professional and service association representing business and financial credit personnel in the United States. In 1896, when the association was formally organized, credit managers operated in a vastly different climate. Fraud and misrepresentation were common, and creditors lacked adequate commercial laws to prosecute the guilty and protect their business. For example, it was almost impossible to prosecute debtors who, on the verge of insolvency, sold the assets of their business and pocketed the proceeds. Such actions ignored the interests of creditors and violated the present-day theory that an insolvent business belongs to its creditors. This situation was further aggravated by the rapid growth of interstate commerce and the absence of a uniform federal bankruptcy law to deal with financially distressed businesses. The few state laws at the time were contradictory and complex and generally failed to protect creditors.

Financial statements, though used infrequently in analyzing a risk's creditworthiness, could not be relied on, and no laws protected the creditor. Credit managers did not exchange credit information, and many creditors deliberately attempted to deceive by revealing inadequate or incorrect information.

Any individual attempt to improve the ethical standards of the profession or to raise the quality of the credit structure was recognized as futile. All credit managers, however, working together, could impose ethical standards on the industry, raise the quality of the credit structure, and develop a scientific approach to the mutual problems of credit management. The National Association of Credit Management realized that cooperation was necessary to cope with such problems, which were intensifying through a growing demand for credit. From a humble beginning of less than 600 members, NACM today numbers more than 35,000 members from leading manufacturing, wholesaling, and financial institutions.

Organization

Today, with headquarters in Columbia, Maryland, the association is organized into affiliated local chapters representing most of the nation's major and minor markets. Each local chapter is governed by elected officers, and most chapters employ a full-time administrator of association activities as well as full-time clerical help. Local units are organized into departments for the various services they render, such as legislation, education, business credit reporting, and collection.

The coordinating unit is NACM, which is governed by elected officers and a board of directors. The activities of the national association are directed by a full-time president and a paid staff. Dues grant membership in both the local chapter and the national association.

Activities

In addition to operating credit interchange bureaus, the association fulfills its objectives and meets the individual needs of its membership by engaging in the following activities:

1. *Loss prevention.* The loss prevention department detects and prosecutes perpetrators of commercial frauds.

2. *Education.* The National Institute of Credit offers educational opportunities in the credit, banking, business law, and merchandising fields to members, their associates and assistants, and others who want to train for a career in credit work. Credit institutes and seminars are conducted at major universities throughout the country.

3. *Legislation.* The legislative department has a continuing program for the correction, modification, repeal, or enactment of both federal and state laws that affect credit and finance.

4. *Adjustments.* Adjustment bureaus of NACM are maintained throughout the United States and specialize in the orderly administration of distressed businesses. The bureaus function for the benefit of creditors by acting as assignee, trustee, or receiver and by attending creditors' meetings and making recommendations.

5. *Collections.* NACM operates a nationwide collection service for members.

6. *Publications.* NACM publishes the *Credit Manual of Commercial Laws* annually and *Business Credit,* a monthly magazine.

7. *Research.* The Credit Research Foundation, founded by NACM in 1949, sponsors and encourages credit research concerned with credit conditions and practices of either a general or specific nature. It has prepared and edited the *Credit Management Handbook* and other publications.

8. *Industry and trade group meetings.* NACM sponsors industry and trade group meetings made up of credit and financial management people who meet regularly to discuss credit problems and economic trends. Trade group meetings also give members the opportunity to discuss their experiences with specific accounts.

9. *Foreign credit interchange.* Finance, Credit, and International Business, established in 1919, provides a ready source of payment record data on thousands of foreign buyers located throughout the world. Members of NACM may subscribe to its services on a cost basis.

10. *Government receivables department.* The department serves members interested in the practice of credit and collections for goods and services sold to governments, particularly the federal government. Member benefits include personal assistance in obtaining government payment information, a monthly newsletter, and advance notice of quarterly seminars and account discussions.

Exhibit 15–5 is a list of documents available from NACM's Fax on Request service. The list is updated regularly to incorporate timely and important topics for NACM members.

NATIONAL BUSINESS CREDIT REPORTING SERVICE (NACM)

Originally called *credit interchange bureaus,* the **National Business Credit Reporting Service** was at first operated on a local-market basis. It was soon found that information gathered from one market was insufficient for members' requirements, and a system for interchanging ledger experience among bureaus was developed. In 1919, a central bureau was organized in St. Louis so various bureaus, although independently operated, could exchange their information and reports. Not until 1921 did NACM take over the central bureau, and with 15 participating bureaus it established the National Credit Interchange System.

Exhibit 15–5

Information on Request...By Fax• 1-800-519-3329 • NACM

Fax on request . . . available 24-hours-a-day from your touch-tone phone. Just follow the voice prompts and have the NACM PIN number (6226) and the document number at hand. This index is updated regularly.

General NACM Information/Membership

Special Offers

NACM Mastercard	1111
NACM-MCI Affinity Program	1112
GEICO Preferred Insurance	1113
Overnight Shipping	1114
Business Week Subscription	1115
Member Travel Program	1116

Conventions & Meetings

1995/1996 Meetings Calendar	2221
100th Annual Credit Congress & Exposition	2222
1996 Exhibitor Information	2223
CRF Credit and A/R Open Forum	2224

GRD Seminar:

Defense Finance & Accounting Service	2225
Doing Business w/ the Federal Government	2226
Loss Prevention/Business Credit Fraud Symposium	2227
1996 Legislative & Critical Issues Conference	2228

Education

Professional Designation Program	3331
CBA Exam Study Outline	3332
CBF Exam Study Outline	3333
CCE Exam Study Outline	3334
Self-Study Program	3335

Executive Education Certificate Programs

CMLI Level	3336
Mid-Career School Level	3337
ACES Level	3338

Graduate School of Credit

& Financial Management	3339
NACM-ASU Managing Risk	3340
FCIB-Georgetown University Global Management	3341

Publications

NACM Publications List w/Order Form	4441
Credit Manual Brochure	4442
LienWriter Brochure	4443
Compensation of Credit Executives Brochure	4444

Sample Forms:

Credit Application Form	4445
Credit Approval Form	4446
Proof of Claim Form	4447
Request for Bank Credit Information Form	4448

Communications

Hot Topic: Reengineering

Reengineering the Credit Profession	5551
The Credit Manager's Reengineering Primer	5552

Best Practices: Working Capital

The Study of Working Capital	5553
Understanding Cash Flow Statements	5554
Quarterly Survey of Economic Indicators	5555
Web Site Information	5556

Business Credit Preview

In the upcoming issue . . .	6661
Editorial Calendar/Writers' Guide	6662
Advertising Information	6663
Subscription Information	6664

Government Affairs

Bankruptcy Reform Act of 1994-Summary	7771
Carmack Shipping Amendments of 1995	7772
Procurement Reform Legislation	7773
Pending Bankruptcy Legislation-Summary	7774
Bankruptcy Reform Commission-Update	7775
Equal Credit Opportunity Act	7776
Uniform Commercial Code	7777

Congressional Communications-

Writing to Congress	7778

Government Receivables

Member Benefits	8881

Loss Prevention

Loss Prevention News	9991
Business Credit Loss Prevention Department	9992
Loss Prevention Online	9993
Leasing Industry Loss Prevention	9994
Loss Prevention Special Services	9995

Credit Research Foundation

About the Credit Research Foundation	1001
Membership Application	1002
Benchmarking:The Credit and A/R Function	
(annual survey)	1003
Quarterly Survey of Domestic Trade Receivables	1004
Reengineering the Credit Function	1005
Measuring Your A/R Efficiency	1006
Complete CRF Publications List	1007
Calendar of Events	1008

Finance, Credit & International Business

FCIB Fact Sheet	1101
International Credit Reporting Service	1102
Country Reports	1103
Membership Application	1104

Credit and Financial Development Division

About the CFDD	1201
Conference Calendar	1202
CFDD Chapter Locations and Requirements	1203

National Association of Credit Management
8815 Centre Park Drive • Suite 200
Columbia, Maryland • 21045-2158
voice (410) 740-5560 / fax (410) 740-5574

Organization

Today the National Business Credit Reporting Service is entirely an operation of the National Association of Credit Management. The system comprises a coordinating unit, the Service Corporation of NACM, and 59 local bureaus (plus bureaus in Hawaii and Canada) covering major and minor markets. Each local bureau operating in the system is member owned and member operated under the supervision of the local NACM association. Membership is open to manufacturers, wholesalers, other middlemen, and bankers, regardless of trade line or geographic location. The underlying principles of each bureau are (1) member direction and control and (2) service charges just adequate to cover the costs of operation. The bureaus serve as mediums for assembling and disseminating the credit information supplied and used by member-creditors.

The entire system is administered by NACM.

Method of Operation

The successful and efficient operation of the National Business Credit Reporting Service depends almost entirely on the cooperation of its members. To encourage member cooperation and to perpetuate an efficient system, the mechanics of the operation have been coordinated and standardized.

The system operates on the basis of information accumulated in a national databank; each participating member furnishes aged trial balance information every 30 days.

Knowing how a customer company or a prospective customer company pays its bills is the base of any sound credit decision. NACM credit reports have been providing this information since 1904. In the fast-paced economy of the 1990s, when credit decisions must be made quickly, NACM associations use automation instead of the old mail/telephone system of gathering credit information.

NACM associations today offer their members fast, accurate, current, and objective information within minutes after a request for a credit report has been received. Information in the automated files of NACM is supplied by a broad spectrum of local, regional, and national firms.

National Business Credit Reports answer many key questions about a customer. Does it pyramid its buying? Does it pay one creditor on time but not others? Is it using the creditor's working capital? Are its total purchases within safe limits? What is the trend of its business?

CONTENTS AND INTERPRETATION OF
NACM NATIONAL BUSINESS CREDIT REPORT

An illustrative National Business Credit Report is shown in Exhibit 15–6. Unlike many other types of credit reports, this one offers no recommendations or opinions. Personal views that are not based on actual ledger experience are not included. The report merely presents facts based on creditors' actual ledger experiences arranged in an orderly manner

EXHIBIT 15–6   NACM Business Credit Report

Business credit reports are prepared for NACM members in and through cooperation with NACM affiliates.

Call your local NACM office for credit reporting services.

NACM South Central Region's business credit report was designed by credit experts working directly with experienced technical personnel. This has ensured a standardized format that's objective and easy to read.

The report displays the following categories of information:

Payment History—

1 Ledger experience from individual member and non-member companies, including: member and non-member number identification • business category • year opened • date information reported • last activity • high credit • total owing • account balances displayed in current and past due categories • payment terms • member and non-member remarks.

Trade Line Total—

2 Summary of the individually reported trade experiences both in dollar totals and percentages of the columns pertaining to "Account Balance" and aging of "Account Status."

Trade Current Total—

3 Summary of all individual trade experiences reported within the last 90 days.

Quarterly Payment Trend—

4 Derived from summaries within the previous three calendar quarters, this feature shows the trend of the subject's paying habits.

NACM — South Central Region — National Association of Credit Management

Louisville Division	Lexington Division	Mid-Tennessee Division
436 South Seventh St.	1029 Industry Road	1100 Kermit Drive
P.O. Box 1062	P.O. Box 5154	Suite 208
Louisville, KY 40201-1062	Lexington, KY 40555-5154	Nashville, TN 37217-2121
(502) 583-4471	(606) 254-7733	(615) 366-1906
Fax: (502) 585-5453	Fax: (606) 254-7932	Fax: (615) 366-1906

BUSINESS CREDIT REPORT

REPORT ON: ID# 138145   DATE 11/19/90
QUESTIONABLE REMODELING
BOX 000
ANYWHERE USA   12345
ON FILE SINCE 9/06 PH: 987 654 3210

REPORT FOR MEMBER #   06-09999
NACM South Central Region
P.O. Box 1062
Louisville, KY 40201
To: SANDRA JONES

BUSINESS CATEGORY	YR OPEN	DATE REPTD	LAST ACTIVITY	HIGH REPTD	ACCOUNT BALANCE	CURRENT	DAYS BEYOND TERMS 1-30	31-60	61 & OVER	PAYMENT TERMS	CMNTS
0500004BPL&H		1190	1190	38000	36061	12000	8876	1185	14000	N30DAYS	SLO
0600333ZLSU		1190	890	9800	9800				9800		COL
0600445BLMT	90	1190	890	2245	2245				2245		RTC
0600512PL&H	YR	1190	990	45000	45000	32000	8000	4000	1000	N10PK	PRN
0610354BLMF	YR	1190	1090	10000	12000		2000	10000		24?0N30	30/60
0657689IRST		1190	990	23000	23000	10000	2000	8000	3000		CON
3700397	YS	1190	890	9800	9800				9800		COL
0600949ELSU	83	1090	590	5500	5500				5500		60/90
0601139LMBR	83	1090	790	30000	26900	6500	5000	4200	11200	N10PK	COL
0601237BLMT		1090	790	2000	2000		2000				COD
0604465LMBR		1090	590	10000	2000				2000		CSR
0657678BLMT	11	1090	690	2524	1100			1100			LNS
2200252	85	1090	790	1450	1450		1450				PMT
0600079BLMT		990	590	5000	5000	2500	500	2000			SPT
0600289ELSU	75	990	490	5396	5385	278	88	2236	2793		5MOS
0601361BLMT		990	490	9046	5578	2000	1500	1578	500		CSR
0657679		990	790	4898	4898		4698				30
0601662MFNG		890	490	5818	5818		1000	3018	1000	N30DAYS	RDS
0603999BLMT		890	590	7500	6000	4500	1000	500			60
0604289ELSU		890	390		5477			2595	2882	N10PK	ATT
0657696BLMT	YS	890	690	13000	12576	3255	3971	316	5034		60/90
TRADE LINE TOTAL	21 ACCOUNT				227598	73033 32.1%	42283 18.6%	41528 18.2%	70754 31.1%		
TRADE CURR TOTAL	21 ACCOUNT				227598	73033 32.1%	42283 18.6%	41528 18.2%	70754 31.1%		
QUARTERLY	1/90	23 ACCOUNT			228661	74533 32.6%	40833 17.9%	42541 18.6%	70754 30.9%		
QUARTERLY	4/90	23 ACCOUNT			228661	74533 32.6%	40833 17.9%	42541 18.6%	70754 30.9%		
QUARTERLY	7/90	23 ACCOUNT			230111	74533 32.4%	42283 18.4%	42541 18.5%	70754 30.7%		
QUARTERLY	10/90	23 ACCOUNT			230111	74533 32.4%	42283 18.4%	42541 18.5%	70754 30.7%		

CONFIDENTIAL   The accuracy of this report is not guaranteed. Its contents have been gathered in good faith from members, but no representations can be made as to the accuracy of the information gathered and contained in the report. This bureau disclaims liability for the negligence of any person or entity resulting in an inaccuracy in the report. This report is prepared and distributed for use in the extension only of commercial and business credit.

EXHIBIT 15–6   (concluded)

NACM South Central Region National Association of Credit Management	Louisville Division 436 South Seventh St. P.O. Box 1062 Louisville, KY 40201-1062 (502) 583-4471 Fax: (502) 585-5453	Lexington Division 1029 Industry Road P.O. Box 5154 Lexington, KY 40555-5154 (606) 254-7733 Fax: (606) 254-7932	Mid-Tennessee Division 1100 Kermit Drive Suite 208 Nashville, TN 37217-2121 (615) 366-1906 Fax: (615) 366-1906

BUSINESS CREDIT REPORT

REPORT ON: ID# 138145 DATE 11/19/90	REPORT FOR MEMBER # 06-09999
QUESTIONABLE REMODELING BOX 000 ANYWHERE USA 12345 ON FILE SINCE 9/06 PH: 987 654 3210	NACM South Central Region P.O. Box 1062 Louisville, KY 40201 To: SANDRA JONES

BUSINESS CATEGORY	YR. OPEN	DATE REPTD	LAST ACTIVITY	HIGH REPTD	ACCOUNT BALANCE	CURRENT	DAYS BEYOND TERMS 1-30	31-60	61 & OVER	PAYMENT TERMS	CMNTS
57600BANK	1/82	490	CHKG	MID 5 FIGURES							

GEN INFO AS OF 9/90
PRES: I.M. QUESTIONABLE   YRS IN BUS: 36
NO OF EMP: 42   ESM SALES: $6,000,000
TRADESTYLE: COMMERCIAL/RESIDENTIAL BUILDER/REMODELING

STATE TAX LIEN: 8/06/90 $19,687
MECH LIEN 8/10/90 WOOD LUMBER CO $6,500

```
* ACCOUNTS PLACED FOR COLLECTIONS
  DATE  4/23/90   AMT     312.50   MEMB#86412 N CL.CREDITOR REQ
  DATE  4/23/90   AMT   1,473.89   MEMB#86413 N CL.CREDITOR REQ
  DATE  4/23/90   AMT   1,150.98   MEMB#86414 N CL.CREDITOR REQ
  DATE  4/23/90   AMT   1,212.03   MEMB#86415 N CL.CREDITOR REQ
  DATE  4/23/90   AMT   2,882.07   MEMB#86416 N CL.CREDITOR REQ

  609999B06  11/19/90  INQUIRY    0602240FINA  4/20/90  INQUIRY
  604081BANK  4/20/90  INQUIRY    0609021      3/20/90  INQUIRY
  600894INSU  3/05/90  INQUIRY    0604406BLMT  2/20/90  INQUIRY
  604485      2/20/90  INQUIRY    06090228ERV 12/06/89  INQUIRY

  BU06 NACM SOUTH CENTRAL REGION
```

CONFIDENTIAL   The accuracy of this report is not guaranteed. Its contents have been gathered in good faith from members, but no representation the information gathered and contained in the report. This bureau disclaims liability for the negligence of any person or entity re This report is prepared and distributed for use in the extension only of commercial and business credit.

7 Legal Information—

Mechanic liens and releases, state and federal tax liens and releases, judgments, suits, and bankruptcies.

8 Accounts Placed for Collection—

Accounts placed for collection with NACM automatically default from the collection files to the credit reporting file.

9 Inquiry Record—

A listing of previous inquiries on the subject business showing date and type of company that has inquired. Indicates the level of credit requests with other member companies.

5 Bank Information—

Bank and branch reference information. Banks contribute credit history and loan information on commercial accounts.

10 Business Categories and Comments Code—

A complete directory of business categories and a comments code appear on the reverse side of every page of the report.

6 Historical Information—

(As Available) Date of incorporation, principals, type of business, years in existence, affiliated entities, and trade styles.

NACM
South Central Region
National Association of Credit Management

for rapid appraisal. Because the report contains a large amount of information, it should be appraised carefully and properly. A quick and superficial appraisal may result in faulty interpretation and failure to uncover the true significance of the data.

Comments

This part of the report provides space for information that can clarify the ledger facts recorded in preceding columns. The trend of payments experienced by creditors often appears in this column. In general, data that show no change, improvement, slowness, and the like are valuable in determining the stability of the risk. Any report that shows a large number of unfilled orders in this column should signal further investigation. When comments are particularly unfavorable, such as "collect" or "legal," users should appraise the general character of the report—particularly, the date of the transaction involved so that unfavorable information of long standing is not regarded as current.

NACM recommends that creditors request a National Business Credit Report to investigate a new order, when they receive an unusually large order from a customer, and when they receive a large number of direct inquiries on a customer. Likewise, a report should be requested on all slow-paying accounts and when the creditor is anticipating special collection action against the debtor. Furthermore, the association recommends that creditors keep close watch on important customers and doubtful accounts, by using the automatic revision service. This service gives members a series of new, up-to-date reports at intervals they designate. Such reports permit creditors to keep a close check on the paying habits of their customers and also to determine the share of volume secured from good customers.

APPRAISAL OF THE NACM CREDIT SYSTEM

The NACM credit system is one of the most widely and frequently used sources of credit information. The system's strength accrues from its operation by NACM, which is one of the nation's largest, most respected, and most influential trade associations. Each company represented in the association is either a National Business Credit Report user or a potential member of the system. The varied services of the association and the high esteem with which members regard these services add to the system's strength and overall value.

Perhaps the system's greatest weakness stems from the fact that it is a cooperative venture and hence must depend on its many members reacting in a like manner in supplying ledger information and answering subsequent inquiries. For maximum total effectiveness of the system, each member must be prompt, thorough, and truthful. In addition, each credit department member who answers inquiries and analyzes reports affects the quality of the system. Unless these people are trained to understand the reports and the workings of the system, the system itself cannot operate with maximum effectiveness. In areas where communication is easy and where members of the NACM credit system are actively interested in using and promoting the system, it seems to work well. In some areas, though, these qualities are lacking.

Despite these weaknesses, a cooperative method of gathering ledger information is the most efficient method known in the industry. To overcome the shortage of trained credit department personnel, the association has developed educational programs and publishes a great deal of literature.

Other than what users can imply from a careful analysis, the National Business Credit Report does not reveal information concerning either the subject's business background or the character and responsibility of management. The credit report is most comprehensive when it deals with a customer's immediate past and present payment record. The report does not estimate the subject's financial condition (but users can do so if they analyze the data properly). For these reasons, some credit executives regard the report as supplemental to other types of reports.

Despite the fact that the National Business Credit Report does not fill all the needs of credit management, ledger information is one of the most important types of information used in the industry, followed by the financial statement, the creditor's past experience, and then history and antecedents. While credit management needs several types of credit information, there is considerable variation in the value attached to each and in the frequency with which some kinds of data are needed. The superiority of the National Business Credit Report stems from the frequency with which ledger data can change; antecedents, method of operation, and financial statements change only over extended periods of time. The rapidity with which ledger data change contributed to the development of NACM's credit system. Because ledger information changes frequently, each new credit report should assist the creditor in making proper and current revision of a customer's accounts. Finally, the National Business Credit Report is not intended to replace financial and operating statements but to be used in conjunction with these statements. When credit management does this, it marshals the most valuable data used in making a credit decision.

SPECIALIZED BUSINESS CREDIT REPORTING AGENCIES

The network of business credit reporting comprises an undetermined number of **specialized credit reporting agencies.** Some of these agencies are corporate enterprises, others are operated by trade associations. Specialized agencies differ from general agencies in the following ways: (1) all of them restrict the credit information they gather and the reports they render to a single line of trade or to a limited number of allied trades; (2) some restrict geographic coverage to a particular territorial region; and (3) some restrict their credit information to a special type of activity or concentrate on services valuable to the trade involved. Generally, these reporting services develop at the request of industry members who feel the large reporting agencies are not meeting their specialized needs.

Manufacturers, wholesalers, and other suppliers who merchandise their products to businesses in a particular line or in a few allied fields use specialized agencies' services. Much of the value in using these sources of credit information stems from the specialized nature of their activities.

The following list includes examples of specialized agencies and associations that provide credit reporting services:

- Chicago Mercantile Exchange
- Gift Associates Interchange Network
- Lumbermans Credit Association
- Lyon Mercantile Group (furniture industry)
- Jewelers Board of Trade
- Motor Equipment Manufacturers Association
- National Telecommunications Data Exchange
- Creditor's Information Network

Riemer Credit Groups

The **Riemer network** includes several credit associations that exchange historical and factual information regarding common customers. Information is exchanged by mail, fax, and at industry group meetings. There are more than 70 credit associations with membership numbers ranging from only a few members to 150 members.

Appraisal of Specialized Agencies

Most specialized agencies follow the same method of operation as the general agency, except for distinctive features developed to meet the needs of credit management in particular trades. Although major contributors to the field of credit reporting, some agencies limit their scope of trade coverage. Thus they have somewhat fewer members or subscribers and the information exchanged among creditors is less complete. In general, the services performed by more limited agencies are highly flavored with such sources of trade information as trade bulletins, advisory information pertinent to the trade, and trade-specific rating books.

Specialized agencies are an important source of credit information, and their contributions to better credit judgment are significant. Specialized credit reporting agencies, just like the general agency, meet the needs of credit management by supplying data on a subject's identity and legal responsibility, history and business background, managerial character and responsibility, financial ability and strength, and payment record experience. Their credit services should be measured against these criteria. Specialized agencies are also more flexible in adapting their services to the needs of a particular trade.

Many people believe that credit investigators and correspondents employed by specialized agencies gain a more thorough knowledge of their particular field. By confining activities, they frequently have more intimate contact with and knowledge of their subjects, a factor that may contribute to more complete and more satisfactory credit reporting. By specializing research in particular trade lines, it may be possible to get more detailed information of broader significance to the credit manager.

Specialized agencies have some disadvantages too. The information they gather has little significance for credit managers whose businesses operate in a wide variety of markets. Because there are no specialized credit reporting agencies in such trade lines as tobacco, coal, eating and drinking places, and many others, the general agency is an indispensable source of credit information for the many marketers who sell in a large number and wide variety of markets. A common criticism of credit managers is that the ledger experiences of the specialized sources are often incomplete. Agency reporters, because of their preoccupation with a particular trade, may fail to investigate markets in which subjects do the greater proportion of their purchasing.

Important Terms

Business Information Report (D&B)   315
continuous service   322
D&B Reference Book of American Business   311
Dun and Bradstreet Information Services   309
Dun-Bank   314
Dun-Trade   314
Experian Business Information Services   329
financial profiles   322
General Mercantile Agency   309

key to ratings   326
National Association of Credit Management   331
National Business Credit Reporting Service   332
Payment Analysis Reports (PAR)   322
Riemer network   339
specialized credit reporting agencies   338
Veritas Business Information, Inc.   330

Discussion Questions

1. Why is it necessary for credit managers to have knowledge of a variety of sources of credit information, even though they use only a few?

2. Why is Dun & Bradstreet referred to as a "general agency"?

3. How did economic and business developments in the early 1900s influence credit risk and the need for organized sources of credit information?

4. List the principal activities of Dun & Bradstreet, and explain each one briefly.

5. Of the various activities of Dun & Bradstreet, which one is the "backbone" of the agency's business? Why?

6. Discuss the credit managers' need for and the usefulness of D&B's Key Accounts Reports and its Continuous Service.

7. Under what circumstances would you request the agency's credit reports? Why

wouldn't you request them for each credit decision?

6. What is the basis for the ratings used in D&B's *Reference Book*?

9. What qualifications do you believe a reporter of Dun & Bradstreet should have?

10. What is the Standard Industrial Classification?

11. Who has the ultimate responsibility for the credit decision? Why?

12. Describe the products, services, and reports offered by Experian (formerly TRW) and Veritas Business Information, Inc.

13. Compare and contrast the activities of NACM with those of Dun & Bradstreet.

14. Why is it important to analyze the entire NACM Business Credit Report?

15. What are the advantages and disadvantages of specialized credit reporting?

16 FINANCIAL STATEMENTS— ANALYSIS AND INTERPRETATION

Learning Objectives

After studying this chapter, you should be able to:

- Explain the importance of financial statement analysis in credit decision making.
- Point out the reasons for financial statements.
- Show the sources from which financial statements can be obtained.
- Discuss the various types of accounting opinions appearing on financial statements.
- Explain the importance of cash flow.
- Set forth the steps involved in the preliminary appraisal of financial statements.
- Discuss financial statement legislation.
- Review briefly some of the most important accounting terms.

REASONS FOR FINANCIAL STATEMENTS

Financial statements, prepared according to established formats, show the profitability and financial health of business firms. These statements are used by a variety of individuals. Business owners and stockholders use these statements to decide if they should invest in a particular firm, i.e., buy stock in a corporation. Existing owners use financial statements to monitor the growth and success of the firm. Internal managers use financial statements to evaluate performance and to uncover departments, activities, or products that are performing well—or those that are not meeting established standards. If accounts receivable climb too high, for example, it may be an indication the collections department needs attention. If a business needs a loan from a financial institution or other lender, a financial statement will always be requested. Also, a firm will sometimes request statements from suppliers to ensure financial health and profitability. The purchasing managers may want to make sure the supply of inventory will be steady and available when needed.

Because financial information most often reveals the financial strength and capacity of a business enterprise, credit managers rely heavily on financial statements to guide their decision-making processes. Financial statements also reflect the ability of a firm's management, which handles the decision-making functions of the business. However, statement analysis is not the sole basis of the credit decision; it is only one segment of a larger process known as credit analysis. Supplementary information is often required to correctly interpret what the financial statement reveals.

Requests for financial statements have increased tremendously in recent years, not only between the cash lender and the business borrower but also between the seller and the buyer of goods. One of the reasons for this increased demand is that a growing number of executives at the credit management level have been trained in financial statement analysis. As more firms and banks have called for balance sheets and income statements from their prospective customers, credit applicants have improved their ability to deliver accurate financial statements.

SOURCES OF STATEMENTS

The credit grantor can obtain financial statements either from the applicant, from the applicant's bank or accountant, or from a credit agency.

Directly from Risk

The grantor may ask the credit seeker to supply financial statements. Some firms have adopted a policy of asking for a financial statement before the initial credit acceptance and for interim and annual statements. Such a practice becomes almost automatic for the credit customer. Often a standardized form, similar to the one illustrated in Exhibit 16–1, is furnished to the customer for completion.

Commercial banks and accounting firms are also regarded as "direct" sources of financial statements. Banks sometimes supply financial statements for credit purposes with the prior approval of the business involved. Accounting firms that have certified to the correctness of the customer's accounting procedures, as well as prepared the financial statements, may also supply statements to creditors. Also, corporations whose stock is bought and sold in national stock exchanges generally publish reports containing statements for current and prospective shareholders.

Indirectly from Mercantile Credit Agencies

The reports furnished by Dun & Bradstreet Information Services, Experian (TRW), and other credit reporting agencies often contain financial statements that have been furnished

EXHIBIT 16–1   **Financial Statement Form Approved by the National Association of Credit Management**

(This form approved and published by The National Association of Credit Management)   **FORM 8**

FINANCIAL STATEMENT OF

DATE_____ 19____

FIRM NAME_____

Address_____City_____

At close of business on_____19____State_____

ISSUED TO_____ ←— { NAME OF FIRM
                                                                        Requesting Statement

[PLEASE ANSWER ALL QUESTIONS. WHEN NO FIGURES ARE INSERTED, WRITE WORD "NONE"]

ASSETS	Dollars	Cents	LIABILITIES	Dollars	Cents
Cash in Bank	$		Accounts Payable	$	
Cash on Hand			(For Merchandise)		
			Notes and Acceptances Payable		
Accounts Receivable			(For Merchandise)		
(Amounts Pledged $_____)			For Borrowed Money:		
Notes and Trade Acceptances Receivable			Notes Payable—Unsecured		
(Amounts Pledged $_____)					
Merchandise Inventory			Notes Payable—Secured		
(Not on Consignment or Conditional Sale)					
			Income Taxes Payable or Owing		
(Amounts Pledged $_____)					
Other Current Assets: (Describe)			Other Taxes, including Sales Tax, Owing		
			Rental, Payrolls, Etc., Owing		
			Other Current Liabilities: (Describe)		
TOTAL CURRENT ASSETS			TOTAL CURRENT LIABILITIES		
Land and Buildings (Depreciated Value)			Mortgage on Land and Buildings		
Leasehold Improvements (Amortized Value)			Chattel Mortgage on Merchandise or Equipment		
Machinery, Fixtures and Equipment (Depreciated Value)			Other Liabilities, Unsecured		
Due From Others — Not Customers			Other Liabilities, Secured (Describe)		
Other Assets: (Describe)					
			TOTAL LIABILITIES		
			Capital { Capital Stock $_____ } { Surplus $_____ }		
TOTAL ASSETS	$		TOTAL LIABILITIES AND NET CAPITAL	$	

BUY PRINCIPALLY FROM THE FOLLOWING FIRMS:

NAMES	ADDRESSES	AMOUNT OWING
		$

(continued)

EXHIBIT 16–1   (concluded)

STATEMENT OF PROFIT AND LOSS FOR PERIOD FROM_____TO_____

NET SALES FOR PERIOD	$		DETAILS OF OPERATING EXPENSES:	$	
Cash $			Salaries — Officers (or owner.)		
Credit $					
			Salaries — Employees		
Inventory at start of Period $			Rent, Heat, Light		
			(Include Amortization of Leasehold)		
Purchases for Period $_____			Advertising		
TOTAL $			Delivery		
Less: Inventory at					
Close of Period $_____			Insurance		
COST OF GOODS SOLD			Taxes, Including Sales Taxes		
GROSS PROFIT			Depreciation (Fixtures, Trucks, etc.)		
Less: Operating Expense			Miscellaneous (Other Operating Expenses)		
NET OPERATING PROFIT			TOTAL OPERATING EXPENSE	$	
Other Additions and Deductions (net)			SUPPLEMENTAL INFORMATION (DETAILED)	$	
NET PROFIT BEFORE FEDERAL INCOME TAXES			If Incorporated, Amount of Dividends Paid	$	
Less: Federal Income Taxes			Interest Paid (Expense)		
NET PROFIT AFTER TAXES	$		Cash Discount Earned (Income)	$	

Fire Insurance Carried: On Merchandise $_____On Furniture and Fixtures $_____Other Buildings $_____

Liability Insurance Carried On Premises $_____On Auto and Truck $_____Other Insurance (Type and Am't)_____

Name of Bank_____

Title to Business Premises is in the name of_____

If Premises leased state Annual Rental $_____Lease Expires_____

> The foregoing statement (both sides) has been carefully read by the undersigned (both the printed and written material) and is, to my knowledge, in all respects complete, accurate, and truthful. It discloses to you the true state of (our) (my) financial condition on the date indicated. Since that time there has been no material unfavorable change in (our) (my) financial condition other than indicated below under "Remarks."
> (We) (I) make the foregoing financial statement in writing intending that you should rely upon it for the purpose of our obtaining merchandise from you on credit. You have my (our) permission to disclose this information in confidence to others in order to facilitate the establishment of additional credit lines with them.

Name of Individual or Firm_____

If Partnership, name partners_____

If Corporation, name officers_____

How long established_____Previous business experience_____
_____where_____

Date of signing Statement_____Street_____City_____State_____

Witness_____Signed by_____

Residence Address
of Witness_____Title_____

REMARKS: (Attach separate sheet if necessary)

by the prospective credit customer. In order to show financial trends occurring in the business operation, such reports often contain financial information covering three to five years. These agencies have made a concentrated attempt in recent years to gather financial statements on the business firms they investigate, thus improving their coverage of the financial aspects of credit information for their subscribers.

TYPES OF FINANCIAL STATEMENTS

The **balance sheet** is a statement of the financial condition of a company as of a moment in time. In other words, it is a photograph of the business showing its assets, liabilities, and net worth as of the instant in time the "picture is taken." The **income statement** is a summary of the revenue and expenses of business for a specific period of time, such as a month, quarter, or year. It shows the sales, cost of goods sold, expenses, and net profit or loss during the interval covered. The **statement of cash flows** shows the sources and uses of funds during a specified time period, generally the same period used for the income statement. This statement is typically presented with three sections: cash flows from operating activities, cash flows from investing activities, and cash flows from financing activities. Finally, the **statement of retained earnings** is often provided along with the other statements to provide a link between the income statement and the balance sheet. This statement shows how net income was used, either retained by the business or distributed to the owners in the form of dividends.

Balance Sheet Classifications

Assets are resources, property, and other items of value used in the operation of a business. The assets may be owned outright, or claims of others connected to an asset may exist if it is not owned free and clear. The assets are nevertheless listed, but a liability will also be shown to account for the claim or debt. Assets minus liabilities equals net worth: the equity or value actually owned by the business owners. Some of the most commonly used classifications are as follows.

Current Assets
The **current assets** include cash and other assets that are converted into cash within the operating cycle of the company. The operating cycle is the time it generally takes to move inventory from acquisition to sale. In many cases, the operating cycle will not be longer than a year. Current assets are listed in the order of liquidity, which is the time it takes to convert them into cash. Examples of current assets include cash, marketable securities, accounts receivable, and prepaid items.

Long-Term Assets
Long-term assets are investments and property that generally last beyond one operating cycle. As a result, long-term property, e.g., machinery, is generally depreciated over its lifetime. The value is divided according to established methods and a portion of the total value is listed as an expense on individual income statements. Examples include long-term investments and assets such as land, buildings, machinery, and equipment.

Intangible Assets
Intangible assets are long-lived assets used in the operation of a business that do not have physical properties. Goodwill, for example, is a value assigned to the reputation and name recognition of a firm. Another example is the value assigned to any patents controlled by a business.

Current Liabilities

On the liability side of the balance sheet, **current liabilities** are obligations and debts to be paid within one operating cycle, usually the next year. Examples of current liabilities include accounts payable, notes payable, salaries payable, and taxes payable. These liabilities are generally paid using current assets, such as income from the sale of inventory.

Long-Term Liabilities

Debts not falling due until more than a year from the date of the balance sheet are usually classified as **long-term liabilities.** If the debt is being paid in installments, the payments due within one year are listed as current liabilities. Examples include mortgage notes payable and long-term notes payable.

Owners' equity can be divided into two parts: the amount invested by the owners directly and the retention of net earnings. In a corporation, the owners' equity is frequently called *stockholders' or shareholders' equity.* Another well-known label is simply net worth. This category is a residual claim against the assets of a business after the liabilities are deducted from total assets.

Balance Sheet Classification

Assets

- Current assets
- Long-term assets
- Intangible assets

Classification of Liabilities and Equity

- Current liabilities
- Long-term liabilities
- Owners' equity

Income Statement Classifications

The **income statement** is a flow statement and shows how much revenue is received during a period of time, usually one year. Also listed are the expenses to be subtracted from revenues to arrive at net income.

Net sales may be described as operating revenues. If a company is selling material goods, the **cost of goods sold** is computed and deducted from net sales to give the **gross margin. Operating expenses** may be classified as selling expenses and as general and administrative expenses and are deducted from gross margin to obtain operating revenue. Federal income taxes and interest expenses are also listed, often as separate entries. The excess of revenue over the expenses required to earn the revenue is **net income**, the "bottom line." If the expenses exceed the revenue, the difference is a **net loss.**

Income Statement Classification

Net sales
 less: Cost of goods sold
Gross margin
 less: Selling expenses
  General and administrative expenses
Earnings before interest and taxes
 less: Interest expenses
Earnings before taxes
 less: Taxes
Net income or (net loss)

PRELIMINARY APPRAISAL OF FINANCIAL STATEMENTS

The first step in appraising financial statements should be to test the validity of the stated values. Financial statements present certain facts that, if good accounting practices are followed, the preparer states as accurately as possible. Credit analysts, on the other hand, approach the analysis as outsiders. Because of this, they are likely to be skeptical about some features of the statements and hence will examine them critically. Often they will try to determine whether the business management has presented a statement that overstates the financial condition. Most businesses, for obvious reasons, want their financial statements to appear as favorable as circumstances permit. At times, even with no intention of dishonesty, management attempts to present facts in a more favorable light than the situation justifies. Window dressing, undue optimism, inability to reflect current facts, and actual falsification are some of the ways financial statements may be adjusted to present a more favorable appearance.

Window Dressing or "Putting the Best Foot Forward"

Window dressing is not an attempt to falsify anything but merely to present the business's various aspects in as favorable a light as possible. Knowing that credit analysts look for certain relationships in the statement as a test of goodness, the firm may attempt to manipulate its affairs immediately before statement time to make these relationships highly favorable. For example, knowing that a good cash balance and a very liquid current position are considered desirable by creditors, the firm may, for the month immediately preceding the year-end, work strenuously to collect its accounts receivable and accumulate cash for statement purposes. Thus at the year-end it may have a better-than-normal cash position. It may also defer certain spending to avoid increasing liabilities or draining cash.

Just before the statements are prepared, the firm may deposit in the bank a number of items that may be returned unpaid. These items may include NSF and other bad checks that have been held as collection items; they may even include some checks, drafts, or notes that have been previously presented and refused. Opinions differ as to whether this step is window dressing or actual falsification. It's hard to prove falsification in such cases.

Undue Optimism or "Reluctance to Face Unpleasant Realities"

Like window dressing, **undue optimism** is not usually considered a form of falsification. Instead, it simply reflects the firm's natural hope that certain items on the financial statement will in time return to the value at which they are being carried. For example, certain inventory items or securities may be carried at a much higher figure than their present market value, reflecting the firm's reluctance to face the unpleasant reality that it has done a poor job of buying, selling, or both.

Inability to Reflect Current Facts

The beginner in credit work tends to take the figures shown in financial statements as definite and absolutely accurate. While the depreciated value of certain fixed assets, for example, may be quite accurate from an accounting point of view, their actual value on the present-day market is much more useful and realistic. **Depreciation** is the process of allocating the cost of long-term assets over the life of these assets. A fully depreciated item, for example, may have no value remaining for accounting purposes, yet have a high market value. Some accounts receivable may also be carried at a value higher than reality since the likelihood of collecting these accounts is low. Also, financial statements may overstate the value of intangible assets, e.g., goodwill, but contain no entries for the value of "human capital", e.g., the best engineers in the industry.

PURPOSES OF STATEMENT ANALYSIS

In general, the analysis of financial statements can determine three major factors: a firm's liquidity, solvency, and profitability. The **liquidity** of a business is its ability to meet day-to-day, current obligations. The **solvency** of a business is its financial strength indicated by its level of debts and the investment by owners. **Profitability** indicates the firm's ability to operate efficiently and successfully over a period of time. Whether the analyst approaches the credit case to uncover one, two, or all three financial conditions depends on the nature of the risk and what the analyst must know to arrive at an objective decision. A credit manager might only be interested in liquidity, for example, if the customer is making a one-time purchase with 30-day terms. If a longer relationship is anticipated, however, the analyst is also concerned with solvency and profitability.

METHODS OF STATEMENT ANALYSIS

Simple Evaluation

This method depends heavily on the analyst's experience and judgment. The **simple evaluation method** involves the credit manager inspecting the dollar items shown, and using selected mental or handwritten calculations, arriving at a personal judgment regarding the financial health of the applicant. If the credit manager has statements from prior years, trends and changes can be easily spotted. This relatively unscientific approach is obviously not a technique for beginners.

Percentage Comparison

To facilitate comparison of firms of different sizes, and the results of several years, the **percentage comparison method** expresses each item in the statement as a percentage of the base value. In the balance sheet, the base value is total assets, which is the same number as liabilities plus net worth. In the income statement, the net sales figure usually is taken as 100 percent and the other items are computed as a percentage of this total. This has also been called the *common size method* or *vertical analysis.* If each number is expressed as a percentage of the base, it is easier to compare firms or results from one period to the next.

If customer A maintains operating expenses at 25 percent of sales, and customer B experiences operating expenses at only 10 percent of sales, the credit manager can make some initial observations about efficiency regardless of how large or small the customer firm is. Also, if this percentage for the same company were to change significantly from one year to the next, more behind-the-numbers analysis would be called for. Trend analysis is very useful if the credit manager can take some variable as a percent of sales of a long period of time and observe how it has changed. For example, the analyst may see that cost of goods sold as a percentage of net sales has climbed significantly each year for the last five years. This would provide important insight into the reasons for net income declines.

Ratio Analysis

Ratio analysis involves the use of mathematical calculations to show the relationship between components of financial statements. An individual number by itself provides little information. For example, knowing only the dollar value of net sales is useless unless we also know about expenses. Furthermore, what good is knowing the volume of assets used in the operation of a business unless we know who owns the assets, owners or creditors? Ratio analysis provides an opportunity to calculate relationships and to use these ratios to compare customers to one another or to standard industrial ratios.

Standard industrial ratios are published by several business credit agencies, such as Dun and Bradstreet and Robert Morris Associates. These agencies collect financial statements from many different firms in the same industry and show typical ratios from each group. The standard ratios help the analyst determine what are average, below-average, and above-average results from the calculations for an individual applicant firm. Of course, extenuating circumstances and special situations may explain why a particular firm demonstrates ratios different from other firms in the same industry. Ratios in general provide only one piece of the puzzle, and should never be used as the sole basis for making credit decisions.

There are three levels of understanding in ratio analysis: (1) being able to do the math to come up with a number or ratio; (2) being able to determine if the ratio has improved or deteriorated from one period to the next; and (3) coming up with explanations about why it has improved or gotten worse. For example, if the stock turnover ratio has fallen from one year to the next, is that good or bad? If it has deteriorated, why has the change occurred?

TYPICAL FINANCIAL RATIOS

Credit managers typically have favorite ratios in all three areas: liquidity, solvency, and profitability. Modern computer technology has improved the ability of credit managers to analyze financial statements and calculate many ratios from the same set of data. Trends are also easier to analyze since the annual data of a customer can be retained and, as additional information is gathered, be used to uncover patterns of change. Many financial statement analysis software packages exist and analysts also develop their own computer models using electronic spreadsheets. Since only a few ratios are shown here, those with an interest in ratio analysis will want to study the topic in greater depth. Additional ratios and benchmarks are also discussed in Chapter 20, which deals with measuring the efficiency of a credit department.

Liquidity

The liquidity ratios are designed to test the ability of a firm to "find" the cash when needed to pay ongoing operating costs and short-term obligations. These ratios are important to a credit manager who is offering 30-day terms of sale, for example. A loan officer may also want to ensure that payments on a short-term loan will materialize from short-term operations.

$$\text{Current ratio} = \frac{\text{Current assets}}{\text{Current liabilities}}$$

The **current ratio** is computed by dividing total current assets by total current liabilities, and it shows the number of times current assets exceed current liabilities. An excess of current assets over current liabilities may show sufficient cash on hand to meet the business obligations without difficulty. The standard most commonly accepted is that current assets should be twice current liabilities—a two-to-one ratio. This ratio alone, however, can be misleading since the composition of the current assets is more important than the amount by which they exceed the current liabilities. A firm with an unusually high level of obsolete inventory, for example, would have a high current ratio since inventory is a part of current assets. This ratio is still the most widely known liquidity ratio, however, and should be calculated and understood by credit managers.

$$\text{Acid-test ratio} = \frac{\text{Current assets} - \text{Inventory}}{\text{Current liabilities}}$$

The **acid-test ratio**, also known as the quick ratio, is computed by dividing total current assets less inventory by total current liabilities. Converting inventory into cash is the primary reason most firms exist and any firm is always trying to speed this process with higher sales. Since inventory is the slowest of the current assets; when it is deducted from the total, the remaining current assets are more readily converted into cash without shrinkage. The standard minimum for this ratio is one to one, although variations occur between various lines and during different economic conditions.

$$\text{Stock turnover} = \frac{\text{Net sales}}{\text{Inventory}}$$

The **stock turnover** may be computed in at least two ways, if the information is available:

$$\text{Stock turnover (for retailers only)} = \frac{\text{Net sales at retail}}{\text{Average inventory at retail}}$$

$$\text{Stock turnover} = \frac{\text{Cost of goods sold}}{\text{Average inventory at cost}}$$

This ratio indicates how often the inventory is theoretically turned over, that is, purchased and sold. The ratio is related to sales levels, of course, since higher sales with the same inventory will produce a higher stock turnover from one period to the next. The ratio also provides some insight into inventory management, since a firm that keeps too much inventory on hand will have lower turnovers than firms with more appropriate inventory levels. If the inventory is too old, or obsolete, the turnover ratio will also be lower. The ratio shows overall efficiency and indicates how quickly a firm can raise cash from the conversion of inventory. Generally, a high turnover is desirable, although too high a ratio may indicate that the firm does not maintain enough inventory and customer service suffers.

$$\text{Receivables turnover} = \frac{\text{Net credit sales}}{\text{Average receivables}}$$

The **receivables turnover**, computed by dividing net credit sales by average accounts receivable, shows the number of times during the fiscal period that the receivables are turned. This indicates the efficiency with which the receivables are being collected. If a firm has difficulty collecting funds owed by its customers, it will have difficulty paying its own bills. A declining ratio may also result from poorer-quality customers, that is, selling goods to more firms with weak sales or poor liquidity.

The turnover ratio can be used to calculate the average number of days it takes the firm to collect its sales on account. The analyst can divide the number of days in one year, approximately 360, by the receivables turnover. Thus, if the turnover is 6 times a year, it collects in 60 days; if 12 times a year, it collects in 30 days; and if 10 times a year, in 36 days.

$$\text{Sales to net working capital} = \frac{\text{Net sales}}{\text{Current assets} - \text{Current liabilities}}$$

The **net working capital ratio** is computed by dividing net sales figure by net working capital (current assets less current liabilities). A larger number is generally desirable since it would indicate that a firm is generating lots of sales from a given volume of working capital. It shows how efficiently the firm is utilizing net working capital to produce the desired results—sales.

Solvency

In interpreting the solvency ratios, the analyst is answering such questions as: "Is the net worth adequate?" and "Is the borrowing proper?"

$$\text{Debt to net worth} = \frac{\text{Current debt} + \text{Long-term liabilities}}{\text{Net worth}}$$

The ratio of **debt to net worth** is computed by dividing total debt by net worth. It shows the proportion of investments by outside creditors in relation to capital investment by the owners. In other words, how does the investment of creditors, lenders, and others providing goods and services compare with the investment of the owners of the firm. Obviously, if most of the assets are provided by others through credit extensions, there is little investment by the owners themselves. It may be easier for owners to "walk away" from the business or manage it less productively with this little at risk.

Aside from the proportional investment question, this ratio is simply a measure of debt. Given two firms with relatively equal net worth values, a higher debt-to-net worth ratio for one represents more claims on the assets of the business. Common sense will lead anyone to the conclusion that too much debt is bad and this situation can threaten the repayment of any loans or credit extended. However, analysts should not be tempted to believe that this ratio should be as low as possible. Few businesses are successful without using credit and debt to obtain assets for productive use. If a business can use someone else's assets through a credit arrangement, and then use these assets to generate more revenue than the cost of the credit, a profit will be made.

$$\text{Times interest earned} = \frac{\text{Net income or earnings}}{\text{Interest expense}}$$

Times interest earned is computed by dividing net income by interest expense. This ratio tests the premise mentioned above, that borrowing and using someone else's assets is fine as long as earnings exceed the expense of using those assets. It is also a measure of debt since a firm with a lower ratio may demonstrate too much borrowing.

Profitability

The profitability ratios illustrate the ability of the firm to generate sales and the ability to retain a significant portion of each dollar of sales as income. A firm that produces a high level of sales while controlling costs will obviously be more profitable.

$$\text{Sales to total assets} = \frac{\text{Net sales}}{\text{Total assets}}$$

This ratio, **sales to total assets**, is computed by dividing net sales by total assets. It shows the number of dollars in sales generated by the total assets invested in the business. More efficient use of the assets results in more dollars of sales; less efficient use results in a falling ratio.

$$\text{Net profit margin} = \frac{\text{Net income}}{\text{Net sales}}$$

The **net profit margin** shows the percentage of each dollar of sales retained as income. A high profit margin may indicate several situations. The products and services of the firm may be desired by many buyers who are willing to pay a large price for these items. A high profit margin may also indicate a market situation where there is modest competition. Finally, a firm may be controlling costs and, as a result, keeping a higher percentage of each sales dollar.

$$\text{Return on assets} = \frac{\text{Net income}}{\text{Average total assets}}$$

Return on assets is computed by dividing net income by average total assets during a specific time period. It is a measure of profitability since a well-managed firm will generate more income from a given level of assets than a poorly managed firm. As is the case with nearly all profitability ratios, a higher number is generally a better number.

$$\text{Return on investment} = \frac{\text{Net income}}{\text{Average owner's equity}}$$

Return on investment, also called *return on equity,* is computed by dividing net income by average owner's equity or average net worth. This ratio shows the financial return provided to those who have personally invested in this firm. A low return on investment would be an indication that the owners are not receiving a significant gain from their involvement. As in any investment, an insufficient return may result in investors moving the investment elsewhere.

IMPORTANCE OF CASH FLOW

A basic part of every business operation is cash flow. Since the most important and the most frequently used source of funds for loan repayment comes from the business's normal operations, it is vital that primary consideration be given to cash flow in any credit appraisal. For purposes of financial analysis, **cash flow** is considered to be the net income for a period, after adding back items deducted as expenses that currently do not involve the use of cash funds. Depreciation, for example, is not an actual cash flow item. It is an accounting entry designed to allocate the total cost of a fixed asset to different accounting periods, rather than a representation of how the asset is actually paid for. Likewise, items that are not a current source of funds may be deducted from the net income figure.

Cash flow is one of the most difficult and complicated areas to forecast because many intermixed forces can affect the outcome of business operations. A firm's ability to meet its short-term obligations is important to both the credit analyst and the firm's management, so cash flow forecasting benefits both parties.

A **cash flow forecast** is a planned procedure for estimating cash receipts and disbursements over a specified time period, usually one year. Since cash is usually budgeted on a monthly basis, management has time to arrange for necessary financing; in turn, the credit analyst can be alerted to situations that may create difficulties in repaying obligations. Although the cash forecast is based primarily on historical data, it also must consider many other factors, including projected expenditures for new plant and equipment, expansion in future sales volume, and the effect of economic conditions on collections and selling terms.

The credit analyst's goal is to predict loan repayment, which is directly correlated with future cash flows. The installment loan officer must know the loan-seeking firm's plans and market estimates before earnings and cash flows can be accurately predicted. In making such predictions, he or she evaluates historical information, forming opinions as to the competency and consistency of the firm's management and evaluating the degree of asset protection. As a general rule, a small business term loan is paid out of earnings rather than out of a liquidation of inventory and receivables, as in business credit transactions. Therefore, anticipated earnings, along with the other elements of cash flow, should exceed repayment requirements by a reasonable amount.

Exhibit 16–2 illustrates a statement of cash flows. This statement, used with the information contained in other financial statements, will give the analyst valuable insight into the sources and uses of cash.

Statement Analysis Should Answer These Questions

- Does the company earn adequate profits?
- Can the company pay its bills promptly?
- Does the company have sufficient liquidity?
- Is the company a safe investment?

Actual Falsification

As a matter of routine procedure, credit analysts should begin their examination by determining whether the statement presents any false conditions. The first thing to do when handling a new statement is to make sure the statement is correctly totaled, to see that it is dated and signed, and, if possible, to see that the evidence of mailing is preserved. The statement with round figures that are clearly estimated rather than book figures should be viewed with suspicion. The business should have noted this condition to forestall any claims of falsification. While credit analysts see few **false financial statements**, they need to test every statement for correctness and honesty in the

Exhibit 16–2   Illustrative Example of the Statement of Cash Flows
(direct method)

ENTERPRISE, INC.
Statement of Cash Flows
For the Year Ended July 31, 19—

Cash flows from operating activities:		
Cash received from customers	$ 14,635	
Cash paid to suppliers and employees	(13,220)	
Income taxes paid	(360)	
Interest received	25	
Net cash provided by operating activities		$1,080
Cash flows from investing activities:		
Proceeds from sale of building	205	
Purchase of equipment	(120)	
Net cash provided in investing activities		85
Cash flows from financing activities:		
Proceeds from issuance of stock	45	
Dividends paid	(23)	
Net cash provided by financing activities		22
Net increase in cash and cash equivalents		1,187
Cash and cash equivalents at beginning of year		13
Cash and cash equivalents at end of year		$1,200
Reconciliation of net income to net cash provided by operating activities:		
Net income		$ 900
Adjustments to reconcile net income to net cash provided by operating activities:		
Depreciation of fixed assets	$ 125	
Amortization of deferred organization expenses	3	
Provision for losses on trade accounts receivable	15	
Payment of deferred organization expenses	(16)	
Changes in assets and liabilities:		
Increase in trade accounts receivable	(46)	
Decrease in inventories	49	
Increase in accrued liabilities and other payables	32	
Increase in interest and taxes payable	18	
Total adjustments		180
Net cash provided by operating activities		$1,080

Disclosure of accounting policy:

Cash in excess of daily requirements is invested in U.S. government obligations whose maturities are three months or less. Such marketable investments are deemed to be cash equivalents for purposes of the statement of cash flows.

Source: Dennis F. Wasniewski, "Statement of Cash Flows," *Business Credit*, September 1988, p. 27. Permission granted by the National Association of Credit Management, *Business Credit*.

presentation of facts. Nothing can be gained by analyzing a statement that has been falsified or doctored to present a more favorable position. Examples of falsification are as follows:

Cash

Cash on hand is sometimes exaggerated because the cash drawer may include certain items that are not cash. Examples include IOUs from owners and advances to salespeople that are incorporated in petty cash accounts. Of course, fictitious bank accounts can also be invented.

Accounts Receivable

This is another item that may be adjusted to show a more favorable situation than the true circumstances warrant. Firms can include in accounts receivable items that are not likely to be collected, or that are definitely going to become bad-debt losses. The firm may further falsify this item by arbitrarily including certain amounts that are not actually trade receivables, such as amounts due from the business officers and employees that will never be repaid. Finally, some firms attempt more deliberate falsification by writing up fictitious accounts receivable. They may set up receivables with existing firms for imaginary transactions or with imaginary firms. This increases the accounts receivable asset falsely and also increases sales figures.

Inventory

Merchandise is a very difficult item to evaluate properly. There are numerous opportunities for honest differences of opinion as to the actual value of the merchandise inventory, and it is difficult to arrive at an inventory valuation that is agreed to by all the people concerned. In addition to unduly optimistic valuations, which may deceive the credit analyst, firms can falsify their statements more deliberately by including in the merchandise inventory certain goods whose invoices are not included in the liability item of accounts payable. This has the double effect of increasing the assets and decreasing the liabilities, thus making the statement even more favorable than would be the case if just one of these items changed.

Fixed Assets

Fixed assets may be even more difficult to value than the inventory. Fixed assets, e.g., machinery and equipment, may be very unique to a particular industry. This makes the valuation task more difficult and can produce more opportunity for fraud since the financial statement analyst may not have a basis for knowing the true value of fixed assets listed on the statements.

Accounts Payable

The liability, accounts payable, may be reduced by omitting an invoice as a liability while entering the merchandise received as an asset. The accounts payable item may be checked by contacting trade creditors as part of a more complete credit investigation. If the total of the amount owed as reported by creditors is significantly more than reported on the financial statements, a problem may exist. Also, a business that reports a highly liquid position, but is slow in paying routine accounts payable, may be falsifying information.

Actual Falsification May Involve

- Cash
- Accounts receivable
- Inventory
- Fixed assets
- Accounts payable
- Other payables

Types of Accounting Opinions on Financial Statements

A common method used to enhance the accuracy of financial statements used for analysis is to request that the statements be audited. Independent auditors are often engaged to prepare and verify the accuracy of financial statements. The auditors typically prepare a certificate that outlines the scope of the audit, the degree to which the statements follow standard accounting procedures, and their opinions regarding accuracy. It is obviously important for credit managers to look for and read the auditors' opinions.

Depending on their findings, accountants may express: (1) an **unqualified opinion**, (2) **an unqualified opinion with qualification as to scope**, or (3) a **qualified opinion.** Accountants express only one kind of opinion on any particular set of financial statements. If they cannot give an opinion under the circumstances, they may present an **adverse opinion** or a **disclaimer of opinion.**

Unqualified Opinion

Accountants express unqualified opinions when satisfied that the financial statements present a firm's financial position and results of operations fairly and in conformity with generally accepted accounting principles and practices consistently applied. Accountants should not express unqualified opinions unless they are satisfied in all material respects and have adequate grounds for their opinion.

Unqualified Opinion with Qualification as to Scope

At times the section of an accountant's report dealing with the scope of the examination states that the accountant has not, for example, confirmed the accounts receivable and has not actually observed inventories. If the receivables and inventories are substantial, the accountant should make a qualification as to the scope of these items. A qualification as to the scope of the examination does not mean the opinion is qualified.

Qualified Opinion

Accountants express qualified opinions when they believe the statements are a generally fair presentation but they are not completely satisfied on some point or they feel that some part of the financial position or operations is not fairly presented. In general, accountants express qualified opinions when they are not permitted or are otherwise unable to conduct an examination complete enough to warrant an unqualified opinion or when they discover departures from accepted accounting principles that the firm is not willing to correct.

Adverse Opinion

In an adverse opinion, the auditor states that as a whole the financial statements are not presented fairly in conformity with generally accepted accounting principles. The auditor should have definite evidence of lack of fair presentation, and the exceptions should be so material that a qualified opinion cannot be issued.

Disclaimer of Opinion

Sometimes an auditor is unable to form an opinion as to the fairness of the financial statements and thus disclaims an opinion. For example, an unusual uncertainty may be very material, and the auditor may wish to issue a disclaimer. A disclaimer also should be given if an auditor is not independent.

FINANCIAL STATEMENT LEGISLATION

Because the financial statement may be a vital factor in a firm's decision to sell its goods on credit, safeguards must be provided to prevent the furnishing of false and misleading information to creditors. For this reason, most of the states and the federal government have enacted legislation that holds certain abuses of financial statements to be a misdemeanor subject to civil and criminal prosecution. Exhibit 16–3 compares state and federal requirements for prosecuting credit seekers who have submitted false financial statements. Although there is no express federal legislation for prosecuting makers of false financial statements, Section 215 of the U.S. Criminal Code is the basis for controlling those who use the mails to transmit false statements to obtain credit.

The requirements for prosecution under various state laws are similar to those under the federal enactment pertaining to offenses against the Postal Service. Under each set of laws, the prosecution must prove that the financial statement was submitted in writing and was signed, that the maker of the statement knew that the statement was false, that the statement was made for credit purposes with the intent that it be relied on in any credit decision, and that the false part of the statement misrepresented the facts to such a degree

EXHIBIT 16–3 **Prosecution of Makers of False Statements**
(state and federal laws)

Requirements	State Laws	Federal Law
In writing and signed	Must be proved	Must be proved
Made knowingly	Must be proved	Must be proved
For credit purposes	Must be proved	Must be proved
To be relied on	Must be proved	Must be proved
Materially false	Must be proved	Must be proved
Fraudulent	Need not be proved	Must be proved
Use of mails	Need not be proved	Must be proved
Place of prosecution	County where statement is made	Where statement is made or received

that the decision would have been otherwise if the true facts had been known. For federal purposes, the use of the mails must be proven. Finally, the burden of proving intent to defraud is significant since it must often be shown that the individual intended to "cheat" someone out of property or value.

ILLUSTRATIVE USE OF RATIO ANALYSIS

Exhibit 16–4 provides an illustration of statement analysis. The credit manager may interpret these figures as follows.

Both total assets and total liabilities have decreased. The inventory has decreased $15,000, from 36 to 31 percent of total assets. This decline in inventory has, however, been nearly counteracted by the increase in receivables, so that current assets make up almost as large a part of total assets as before. The current assets-to-current liability ratio shows that current assets are still considerably in excess of current liabilities, indicating the firm is not in a dangerous condition in this respect.

The acid-test ratio indicates that, even with inventory omitted, the current assets are equal to the current liabilities. For this ratio, the minimum for satisfactory conditions is often stated as one to one. The debt-to-net worth ratio has improved. Despite the decline in net worth, there is a still greater decline in liabilities. Credit managers believe that owners should have, as a general rule, a larger stake in the business than creditors.

The sales-to-inventory ratio indicates the efficiency with which the management turns its investment in merchandise into sales. This firm has shown a decline in efficiency in this respect, and many firms of this type have a sales-to-inventory ratio of at least seven or eight to one.

The sales-to-receivables ratio is alarming. It has deteriorated sharply and shows that the management is not efficient in collecting. This ratio not only has decreased greatly but also has reached the point where it is evident that the firm has accepted credit unwisely. (Assume there has been no change in the type of credit offered.)

EXHIBIT 16–4   **The Fashion Shop**
(retailer of ladies' ready-to-wear)

	19—	Percent	19—	Percent
Cash	$ 10,483	6	$ 4,550	3
Receivables	14,977	9	22,657	15
Inventory	60,642	36	45,318	31
Total current assets	86,102	51	72,525	49
Fixed assets	82,349	49	74,026	51
Total assets	$168,541	100	$146,551	100
Current liabilities	$ 26,872	15	$ 23,880	16
Fixed liabilities	38,000	23	30,000	21
Net worth	104,669	62	92,671	63
Total liabilities and net worth	$168,541	100	$146,551	100
Sales	$225,000		$151,688	
Net profit	7,532		5,221	

Ratio Analysis	19—	19—
Current assets to current liabilities	3.33	3.04
Current assets less inventory to current liabilities (acid test)	0.98	1.14
Debt to net worth	0.61	0.58
Sales to inventory	3.71	3.35
Sales to receivables	15.02	6.69
Sales to net worth	2.15	1.64
Percent net profit to sales	3.35	3.44
Percent net profit to total assets	4.47	3.56
Percent net profit to net worth	7.20	5.63

The deterioration of both these ratios can be partially explained by the decrease in sales. However, the firm did not adjust to this decline by reducing either its inventory or its receivables to bring them in line with the lessened sales volume. This has kept it from turning these assets into cash and reducing current liabilities accordingly. It has meant the sacrifice of cash and the loss of opportunities to take cash discounts.

The ratio of sales to net worth shows how efficiently owners' capital is being used. Too low a ratio here means that owners' capital is not being used efficiently; too high a ratio shows insufficient capital for the volume of business being attempted. In this case the ratio is too low and is getting worse. The large investment in fixed assets that are not fully productive partially explains the low ratio here.

The three profit percentages are important in this situation. The net profit-to-sales ratio appears better than it really is because adequate reserves against losses on bad debts have not been set up. The ratios of net profit to total assets and to net worth, although not large, are satisfactory.

Credit managers reviewing this situation will find some indication of satisfactory conditions and some of very unsatisfactory conditions. They have only the two statements. If they had one or two more, they could determine the trend. They must decide whether the trend of sales is a result of national and local economic conditions and whether an improvement can be expected in the near future. Or is this drastic drop a reflection of poor management? There are ample assets to protect creditors, and there appears to be no immediate danger of failure. They might expect payments to be somewhat slow but would feel safe in accepting a moderate amount of credit if they are able to resolve the declining sales figure. Any decision made involves a compromise.

The firm's future prospects depend on what steps management takes to correct the unsatisfactory conditions. The firm must stage a vigorous selling drive to clean out its surplus stock and at the same time must wage an effective campaign to collect debts from delinquent customers. The firm may then use the funds realized from these sources to pay off its own current liabilities, bringing them down to manageable proportions and making the firm liquid enough to take advantage of cash discounts. It also would bring about a proportion of assets to liabilities such that when business conditions improved, the firm could increase its inventory and receivables to keep pace with increased sales. These increases could be managed on credit when accompanied by increased sales, but the wisdom of incurring additional current debt is subject to considerable speculation.

Important Terms

acid-test ratio   351
adverse opinion   357
assets   345
balance sheet   345
cash flow forecast   354
cost of goods sold   346
current assets   345
current liabilities   346
current ratio   350
debt to net worth   352
depreciation   348
disclaimer of opinion   357
false financial statements   354
gross margin   346
income statement   345
intangible assets   345
liquidity   348
long-term assets   345
long-term liabilities   346
net income   346
net loss   346
net profit margin   353
net sales   346

net working capital ratio   352
operating expenses   346
owners' equity   346
percentage comparison method   349
profitability   348
qualified opinion   357
ratio analysis   349
receivables turnover   351
return on assets   353
return on investment   353
sales to total assets   353
simple evaluation method   349
solvency   348
standard industrial ratios   349
statement of cash flows   345
statement of retained earnings   345
stock turnover   351
times interest earned   352
undue optimism   348
unqualified opinion   357
unqualified with qualification as to scope   357
window dressing   347

Discussion Questions

1. Distinguish clearly between a balance sheet and an income statement.

2. From what sources are financial statements usually available? What are the advantages of using one source over another?

3. Assume a prospective customer refuses to furnish a balance sheet and an income statement. How would you acquire the needed information? Would refusal of this request influence your credit decision? Discuss.

4. Should the loyalty and effectiveness of a firm's personnel be included in its assets? Why or why not?

5. Why has there been an increasing demand for financial statement analysis and interpretation in recent years?

6. How do you account for the different types of accounting opinions on financial statements?

7. Do all credit problems require the same degree of financial analysis to arrive at a sound credit decision? Why or why not?

8. What is meant by the following expressions:
   a. The liquidity position of a firm.
   b. The solvency condition of a firm.
   c. The profitability of a firm.

9. Distinguish clearly between window dressing, undue optimism, and actual falsification.

10. What are the most common techniques used to exaggerate or falsify the following: cash, accounts receivable, fixed assets, and accounts payable?

11. In what respects do the state laws and the federal law differ in regard to making and issuing false financial statements?

12. Discuss three commonly accepted methods of financial statement analysis. Explain the most important features of each method.

13. What are the most important liquidity ratios? Explain what each ratio reveals.

14. What are some ratios generally accepted as capable of showing the solvency condition of a firm? Explain what each ratio reveals.

15. List the profitability ratios that are considered in this chapter, and explain what each of these ratios reveals.

16. How are standard industrial ratios used in financial statement analysis?

17. Study Exhibit 16–4. Assume you have received an initial order amounting to $1,750 from the Fashion Shop. The order is to be made up of women's coats and dresses.
   a. On the basis of the analysis accompanying Exhibit 16–4, would you accept or reject this order? Why or why not?
   b. Would you want additional information on this case? What type of information would be particularly helpful?
   c. If you have rejected the order, would you accept it on COD terms? Explain your decision.

18. The Happy Shoe Store. Situation: Assume you are the credit manager for the Royal Shoe Company. Your firm manufactures a complete line of shoes—men's, women's, and children's—and distributes them directly to retail outlets. Your merchandising method is to establish the line with one of the better retail stores and to get the major portion of the trade from the selected outlet rather than to sell to all possible outlets. Thus the number of accounts handled is small, but each account is rather substantial.

   The Happy Shoe Store has been an outlet for approximately 50 years; it became a major outlet during the years 1940 to 1945. During these years, you favored it by allotting it something more than its share of your production, and it expanded substantially. During the past few years, its purchases have been close to $30,000 a year, and the account with you has tended to increase. From a running balance of approximately $3,000, the balance has mounted until it is currently $10,348. The payments that had been discounted have deteriorated, so that now the account would be classified as slow, even unsatisfactory.

You receive a current financial statement direct from the Happy Shoe Store (see Exhibit 16–5), which prompts you to review the account completely and to order a current credit report.

Required:

a. Make a complete analysis of the financial data.

b. Make a careful analysis of the credit information on hand.

c. Recommend appropriate action, and state the reasons for your recommendations.

d. What payment experience could the Royal Shoe Company expect?

e. What collection experience is the Happy Shoe Store having with its accounts receivable?

f. What additional information, if any, would you like to have to make a more complete analysis?

g. Should your firm reconsider its approach which concentrates receivables with only a few customer firms?

Financial information: Copies of standardized financial statements for the last four years are given.

Credit information: Pertinent information from the credit reports arranged under appropriate headings is presented below.

History and method of operation: The Happy Shoe Store was organized in 1933. During the first five years of operation, the store barely broke even, but it made more rapid progress following 1939. In 1941, the owners obtained new quarters, the store was expanded, and substantial progress was made. The rate of progress slowed in later

years, but the store is considered the leading store in its line.

Operated as a family shoe store, the Happy Shoe Store carries a complete line of men's, women's and children's shoes. Its principal line is Royal, which is featured in its advertising and display. The store's fixtures are modern and attractive; its windows are attractive; and its stock is orderly and well arranged. It is regarded as a promotional store, and it frequently emphasizes special promotions that are advertised heavily. At the end of 1996, the Happy Shoe Store started promoting its own revolving credit plan. Within the past two years, it decided also to accept the Visa credit card.

Walter Green, the owner, is 55 years old, married, and experienced in the line. He employs an assistant manager and two salespeople on a full-time basis, with additional personnel employed on a part-time basis for the weekend and special sales.

The Happy Shoe Store is located in the downtown section of Middleville, a city of 20,000 people. Middleville is an expanding industrial center and also a trading center for the surrounding area. Within the last 18 months, an outlying shopping center has been established. A competing shoe store is located in the shopping center.

Ledger clearance: By direct inquiry of sources, the following information is obtained:

HC	Owes Now	Payments
$2,234	$2,234	$600 now due, balance past due
294	264	Now on COD basis
900	400	Pays when due, formerly discounted
634	—	Discounts
7,600	736	30 to 60 days slow
1,000	—	Pays when due

EXHIBIT 16-5   **Happy Shoe Store**

	12/31/94	12/31/95	12/31/96	12/31/97
Assets				
Current assets:				
Cash	$ 10,526	$ 8,236	$ 8,684	$ 7,744
Receivables	2,344	2,190	3,172	13,430
Inventory	48,420	47,526	49,946	51,634
Other current assets	4,200	4,338	5,190	5,248
Total current assets	65,490	62,290	66,992	78,056
Furniture and fixtures	14,244	13,948	13,462	12,852
Total assets	$ 79,734	$ 76,238	$ 80,454	$ 90,908
Liabilities and Net Worth				
Accounts payable	$ 14,116	$ 13,966	$ 18,438	$ 25,284
Notes payable (less than one year)	7,724	4,230	3,948	4,086
Accrued taxes and expenses	2,206	1,962	2,234	2,436
Total current liabilities	$ 24,046	$ 20,158	$ 24,620	$ 31,806
Net worth	55,688	56,080	55,834	59,102
Total liabilities and net worth	$ 79,734	$ 76,238	$ 80,454	$ 90,908
Sales	$148,534	$140,236	$131,634	$141,232
Cost of goods sold	93,504	90,688	85,162	93,226
Gross margin	55,030	49,548	46,472	48,006
Total expenses	44,756	42,526	40,238	41,426
Net profit	$ 10,274	$ 7,022	$ 6,234	$ 6,580

17

BUSINESS CREDIT— ANALYSIS, DECISION MAKING, AND CREDIT LINES

Learning Objectives

After studying this chapter, you should be able to:

- Discuss the basic purposes and challenges for a business credit department.
- Describe decision alternatives available to a credit manager.
- Explain decision-making goals.
- Describe significant sections in a written credit policy.
- Point out the importance of credit lines.
- Explain how to set credit lines.
- Discuss business credit decision guidelines.
- Describe possible forms of security in business credit.
- Describe common examples of business credit fraud.
- Explain how automatic initial orders systems might be used.
- Illustrate the importance of automation in the business credit department.

The basic purpose of the credit department is to make credit decisions. The challenge is to analyze the risk that each credit applicant or each new purchase order presents. The credit manager must balance the risk of loss with the risk of lost sales. The lost sales may extend beyond the purchase offer at hand. A customer who is denied credit terms, or other credit extensions, will possibly begin buying goods and services from competitors. The firm loses not only the sale currently presented, but all future sales if an applicant is turned down or not treated well.

DECISION ALTERNATIVES

The outcomes of the decision-making process are not as clear cut as the uninformed person may believe. Many possible decisions lie on a continuum extending between "Yes" and "No."

Yes ... Order or Applicant Approved

In this instance, the decision is affirmative. Perhaps the order is from a long-term good customer whose total indebtedness is low. A new applicant may have provided complete documentation, the reports from Dun and Bradstreet and other reporting agencies are excellent, trade references are good, and the requested order amount is reasonable. In these cases it is easy for a credit manager to approve the order. The emphasis turns to delivering good customer service and shipping the goods as soon as possible.

No ... Order or Applicant Rejected

There are many reasons an applicant or order might be turned down. The internal files of the credit department may reveal collections problems in the past and the credit manager believes future business promises greater losses than profits. For new applicants, the credit investigation may reveal excessive indebtedness, derogatory information from reporting agencies, or poor trade references. The financial statements, if any, show high debts, low net worth, or poor liquidity. It is obvious that the customer represents potential loss and the terms of sale are not offered. In many cases, however, the credit manager will carefully turn down the client and will recommend that the applicant try again. The current sale may be salvaged on a cash basis, and a future customer may materialize, if the turndown is properly conducted.

Maybe ...

Many decisions will fall within this category. Some facts would indicate approval; others show a need for caution. Alternatives to approving the order or applicant as presented do exist, however. A new applicant may be approved, but for a smaller initial order. Perhaps additional security will be sought, such as a personal guarantee from the major stockholders of the corporation. An existing client may be required to pay the account down to a certain point before more orders are approved. Also, the terms of sale offered may be more restrictive than normal, requiring earlier payment. Sometimes a "maybe" is implied when a new applicant is turned down, but invited to apply again within a certain period of time.

How Much? ... Setting a Credit Line

Most business credit departments establish credit lines for their customers. A **credit line** is the maximum indebtedness that would be allowed a credit customer without additional investigation of creditworthiness. The credit line typically operates like a red flag, an indication that total debt has climbed to a point where the credit manager should reevaluate the credit relationship with a particular customer. A related maximum, a **credit limit,** is a level of indebtedness that will not be extended under any circumstances. Credit lines permit the credit manager to delegate the credit decision below the line to others; in some cases, to computers that approve all orders below the credit line established for a particular customer.

DECISION-MAKING GOALS

Valid Decisions

Certainly the most important goal is to arrive at good decisions. The majority of approved orders and customers *must* pay their accounts in full on or before the date due, or the firm will suffer losses. An analysis of collection results will often reveal if recent credit decisions are getting better or worse than in the past. If bad-debt expense, delinquency, or collections expense increases, it may be caused by poor decision making. Unfortunately, there are few good methods for determining if applicants who are turned away would have been good customers. However, the credit manager can monitor the percentage of new applicants or orders denied to determine changing trends in department approvals.

Speed and Efficiency

The decision-making process must be smooth and efficient. Taking too much time to arrive at a decision is frustrating for many participants in the exchange process: sales representatives, potential buyers, and other employees within the firm selling goods and services. Efficiency is enhanced by clearly defining decision inputs and the process needed to approve or reject an order. A written credit policy should exist to inform everyone what standards and procedures exist. Sales representatives, for example, should know what data is required from new customers and they may be asked to collect this information when possible. The process should also require reasonable investigation efforts which provide important data, but which do not slow down the process unnecessarily. When possible, delegation of decision-making responsibilities will also make the process more efficient, e.g., using credit lines.

Consistency

Customers, sales representatives, and other firm managers desire consistency in decision making. The set of standards used to deny or approve requests for credit terms should be the same from one period to the next. By understanding what is expected, each participant can modify credit requests and purchase orders to match the requirements of the credit department.

Reasonable Decisions

Decisions should be reasonable and, to some extent, understood by the applicant and others involved in the process. If a young college student with a short-term job is turned down for a bank loan to buy an expensive automobile, most observers would understand why this might occur. The firm trying to buy inventory with a promise to pay should understand what the requirements for credit terms are and why they do not meet these requirements. Also, the selling firm's own sales representatives may depend on approved orders before they receive sales commissions and should also understand why an applicant is denied a credit sale.

Adherence to Credit Laws

Many laws affect credit decisions and credit terms. Consumer protection laws require credit decisions that are nondiscriminatory, valid, and communicated to applicants. Other laws, e.g., Robinson-Patman Act, recognize that credit terms are a part of the price of goods and require similar terms for customers in the same category. Otherwise, illegal price discrimination may occur.

Decision-Making Goals

- Valid decisions.
- Speed and efficiency.
- Consistency.
- Reasonable decisions.
- Adherence to credit laws.

DEVELOPING A WRITTEN CREDIT POLICY

Many of the goals for credit decision making can be met with a **written credit policy.** The credit policy will provide important guidelines to employees and others who are involved in credit extensions. Although the level of detail in a written credit policy will vary from one firm to another, the policy will help everyone understand why, how, and when credit decisions are made. If general credit policies are written, a separate *credit manual* may be used to provide more detailed procedures, rules, and guidelines for employees. The following sections are often incorporated into a written credit policy or credit manual.

Credit Department Mission

The credit department is interested in extending credit terms to worthy customers in an effort to increase sales. What constitutes creditworthiness, however? How much risk will the firm tolerate in its effort to increase sales? The credit department mission statement provides an opportunity to explain the firm's **house standard,** a description of the acceptable level of risk for the firm. Some firms rely on a strict collections system to provide acceptable cash flow and will be more lenient in making credit decisions. Other firms extend credit to only the best firms and, as a result, can get by with less strict collection activities. This section also provides an opportunity to state nondiscrimination policies and other provisions that are required by law.

Credit Department Goals

The goals may be written in general terms or they may be very specific. A general goal would simply state that the credit department attempts to control receivables. A more specific goals section might use collections data such as number of days sales are outstanding, accounts receivable turnover statistics, bad-debt percentages, and other carefully outlined numbers. These specific goals provide benchmarks for others to follow, but they also reduce flexibility.

Credit Department Organization and Authority

This section might outline reporting channels and the placement of authority within the firm. If credit lines are used, for example, many persons within the department may be authorized to approve orders as long as they fall within the maximum credit allowed. Procedures may also be included for resolving disputes among customers, sales representatives, and finance department personnel.

Required Documentation and Investigations

Some firms will require specific credit documents such as financial statements, credit applications, or credit agency ratings. Other requirements might involve a minimum number of trade references or banking relationships. Specific verifications may also be outlined so participants can understand what steps, and input, are involved in the decision-making process.

Credit Lines

If the firm uses credit lines, some indication of how they are established and used might be beneficial. If the firm does not inform customers of their credit line, this section may not be included in the written credit policy. What happens if a customer sends in an order that exceeds the current credit line? Is there a procedure for requesting a higher credit line? When are credit lines reviewed and why are they typically changed?

Terms of Sale

This section will include information about typical or desired terms of sale. Some firms have many different terms of sale and, obviously, will not incorporate a long list. A firm may outline, however, the point at which a delinquent firm might be denied terms of sale and, instead, be placed on a COD or cash-in-advance status.

Security Requirements

A section may be included to outline typical security requirements. Types of security desired and the procedures for obtaining and filing security interests can be described.

Collections Policy

The credit department may want to indicate what collections devices and systems are employed. Who is responsible for collecting past-due accounts? When are orders withheld? At what point is an account turned over to a collection agency or is legal action initiated?

CREDIT LINES

As described earlier, a firm generally uses a credit line as a warning signal or as a red flag on the amount of credit to be approved. It does not mean that orders exceeding this limit are automatically refused, but that the limit acts as a guide to force further analysis of the account and a decision on whether to accept or reject the larger order.

Developing a Written Credit Policy

- Credit department mission.
- Credit department goals.
- Required documentation and investigations.
- Credit lines.
- Terms of sale.
- Security requirements.
- Collections policy.

Advantages

The use of credit lines increases the efficiency of the credit department. The credit manager should not have to give the final approval for every order. If handled properly, credit lines save the credit manager's time for really important decisions, permit delegation of authority but still allow the credit manager to retain control of the accounts, and place routine tasks in the hands of subordinate personnel. In addition, credit lines force overall consideration of the entire account, not merely consideration on a transaction-by-transaction basis. This should in turn lead to better decision making. Likewise, credit lines protect the buyer; they act as a check on reckless buyers who for the moment may be unduly optimistic and want to buy excessive amounts.

Limitations

Firms that establish lines of credit for their customer and then do not keep them up to date defeat the basic purpose of credit lines. Such revisions are time consuming and costly, but periodic review is necessary to establish the customer's current ability to pay. Failure to keep credit lines updated may result in lost sales to good customers who limit their orders to the credit-line amount.

Another limitation of credit lines is that approval of orders within the credit line is generally performed by clerical personnel and not by the credit manager. Thus the credit manager may lose contact with an account and not develop its full business potential.

Methods of Setting Credit Lines

Some firms do not use credit lines and allow customers as much credit as they wish, as long as they pay as agreed. Such an arrangement stresses the "increasing sales volume" function of the credit department and does not create any real problems for the credit manager—unless the customer cannot or will not pay as agreed. As long as payment is prompt and automatic, this situation is a highly desirable one. On the other hand, some observers recognize that this approach is dangerous unless customers are carefully monitored.

The credit department is never in a better position to establish a credit line for a customer than when the credit investigation is first completed. Generally, at this time the credit department examines the credit data more carefully, analyzes the account more completely, and gives more thought as to whether to accept future orders than at any other time in the life of the account. The question then arises—just how do credit managers set credit lines? Credit managers generally report that they follow certain techniques, but they are not sure these are the best methods possible.

Five methods are commonly used:

1. Allow the customer as much as the other creditors are allowing.
2. Allow a small dollar volume of purchases and raise the amount gradually as the customer proves to be a good risk.
3. Allow purchases based on a time interval.
4. Base on reporting agency ratings.
5. Use a formula approach based on facts or numbers drawn from financial statements or other source documents.

As Much as Other Creditors Are Allowing

This method is based on the premise that a firm can discover the amount of credit its competitors are allowing the customer in question. While exact figures may be hard to obtain, a firm can often acquire approximations through direct interchange of such information and from reporting agencies. A high credit amount is often quoted which indicates the highest indebtedness ever extended or available to a customer. Of course, this amount allowed by others may exceed what the seller believes the limit should be.

If a firm adopts this method, it should ask, "How did the competitors decide what the credit line should be?" In certain cases, extenuating circumstances (such as a desire not to offend a long-time customer) may cause others to allow excessive amounts of indebtedness. Many firms rely on their own analysis and interpretation of the credit information to set the credit line, using their competitors' experiences only as a guide in particular cases.

Start Low and Raise with Experience

A very common and practical procedure is to start with a small dollar amount and raise it gradually as the customer proves to be a good risk. The credit department may start a customer with a low limit or with enough to take care of the first purchase. As experience with the account accumulates and the customer proves able to pay larger amounts, the credit department raises the limit to take care of larger purchases. If the customer proves incapable of paying, the credit department holds the limit to restrain the customer's purchases, or it even lowers it.

Base Purchases on a Time Interval

Some credit departments attempt to limit an account's total debt to the typical purchases during a specific time period. For example, a firm that generally buys $10,000 of goods each month will be assigned a credit line of $30,000, or three months worth of purchases. Obviously, the actual time frame will vary in different situations and industries. The advantage, however, is the ease and uniformity of this credit line method. This approach also emphasizes sales since customers who buy increasingly larger amounts will receive expanded credit lines.

Base on Reporting Agency Ratings

Dun and Bradstreet and other reporting agencies provide ratings to indicate financial strength and overall creditworthiness. Specific credit lines can be assigned based on the two-part rating provided by Dun and Bradstreet which includes a capital rating and a composite credit appraisal. For example, a firm with a CC2 rating may be assigned a $10,000 credit line and an EE2 customer may be given a credit line of $15,000. Delinquency scores and other statistics computed by reporting agencies are growing in popularity and may become more useful in setting credit lines in the future.

Formula Approach

This method may be based on certain financial data, such as net worth, current assets, net working capital, and inventory. As the use of computers increased, many credit managers have developed systems and models to assist them with credit decisions and credit lines. Financial ratios, economic conditions, agency ratings, profit margins, and other data can be built into computer models which help make decisions. One advantage of this approach is the lack of bias and its usefulness when the firm is subjected to antidiscrimination laws. Disadvantages include a lack of flexibility and the mistaken impression that scientific approaches are automatically appropriate.

The formula approach is similar to credit scoring systems used in consumer credit decisions. Points or scores can be assigned to specific qualities or characteristics presented by a credit applicant. For example, a firm with more years of operation or a higher current ratio might receive more points in a credit scoring system. If the total score is sufficient, the application for an open credit account is approved. Credit scores can also be used to determine credit lines. Again, there are obvious advantages when bias is removed from the decision process, but the long-term success of this approach requires use of valid characteristics and appropriate weights in the formulas.

To Inform or Not to Inform Customers

There are different schools of thought as to whether customers should be advised of their credit limit as soon as it is established. Some executives claim that notification permits the seller to discuss the entire credit picture with the customer and to offer suggestions on improving the credit standing, if necessary. Likewise, customers know the amount of credit they can rely on from the seller.

On the other hand, some observers point out that notification may cause customers to restrict their buying to the dollar amount of the credit line; that is, customers may interpret the word *line* to mean an inflexible limit. Because such an interpretation may hurt goodwill and sales volume, some executives view the credit line only as an instrument of internal control.

Order Limits

Some credit managers use an order limit as an additional notification and monitoring tool. An **order limit** is a maximum single order amount that can be approved without notification of the credit manager or higher authority. A particular customer, for example, may have a $50,000 credit line and a $10,000 order limit. Thus, a $12,000 order will be brought to the attention of the credit manager even though the total indebtedness will remain below $50,000. The order limit provides an additional opportunity to monitor customer purchases and activity.

BASIC DECISION GUIDELINES

The most important C's of credit decision making described in Chapter 9 are *character, capacity, capital, and collateral.* These terms are typically used to describe and categorize the concerns of credit decision makers in both consumer credit and business credit.

Character in the credit management world is used to indicate an applicant's willingness to pay debts as agreed. The best measure is an analysis of how a particular firm or individual has paid others in the past. Of course, the past may be a poor predictor of future activities, but the payment record is the best indication available. Sometimes, an effort is made to incorporate the personal payment records of the principals of a business, especially when the business is not incorporated.

Capacity is the ability to pay debts and make payments as agreed. Many of the ratios used in analyzing financial statements are designed to uncover liquidity and profitability. These characteristics, of course, are closely aligned with the ability to pay financial obligations as they come due. Other considerations such as industry trends, general economic conditions, and age of the business enter into this analysis.

Capital is the financial strength of a firm shown by the level of reserve assets available for payment of its debts. If a firm experiences an economic downturn, or another unexpected financial catastrophe, these reserve assets may be important for its long-term survival. Again, analyzing the financial statements, especially the capital or net worth accounts, is important.

Collateral is the assignment of ownership rights in property in the event a customer does not pay. If the client loses both the willingness and the ability to pay, this may provide the only means for collecting the amounts due. If the ownership rights are carefully documented and recorded according to law, the creditor may be able to recover inventory or other property to pay the amounts due. In business credit, the Uniform

Commercial Code (UCC) is especially important, since this law outlines the creditor's rights and the processes required to establish them.

Other forms of security involve personal guarantees, letters of credit, subordination agreements, or mechanic's liens. A **guarantee** is a written promise by persons or firms to pay an obligation if the debtor does not pay. A personal guarantee, for example, is an agreement by one or more officers of a corporation to pay a debt from personal assets if the firm defaults. An **irrevocable letter of credit** is an agreement by a bank to pay debts on behalf of an individual or firm. A **subordination agreement** provides enhanced status for a creditor by establishing a prior claim to the customer's assets in the event of nonpayment or liquidation.

A **mechanic's lien** is a claim created by state statute for the purpose of securing priority of payment for work or materials furnished in constructing a building or other structure, and as such, the lien generally attaches to the land as well as the improvements on it. For example, if a building materials supplier furnishes goods in the construction of an office building, the supplier is often granted a lien on the property to support payment. The lien would have to be paid and satisfied before the property could be sold or transferred. Each state has its own statute, but this rather unique form of security can be worthwhile.

Creditor's Rights Under the UCC

The **Uniform Commercial Code** (UCC) regulates sales and leases of goods, commercial paper, secured transactions, letters of credit, bills of lading, certain aspects of banking and fund transfers, and warehouse receipts. Article 9 of the UCC, entitled Secured Transactions, deals with the creation of security interests in personal property, that is, all property that is not real property. The most common forms of property used as security include inventory, equipment, and accounts receivable. A creditor seeking security to ensure payment of a debt will obtain a security agreement from the debtor. This agreement may be specific, giving the supplier a security interest in the inventory being sold and the proceeds resulting from its sale. It may also designate specific inventory, accounts receivable, or equipment; or it may be general and cover all these items.

The security agreement must be **perfected** before the rights of the creditor are superior to the rights of third parties, such as other creditors or trustees in bankruptcy. The process of perfecting a security agreement involves preparing a financing statement and filing it with the appropriate state or county office, or both. Filing requirements vary from one state to another, so the credit manager must check filing deadlines, fees, and other statutes to ensure that security interests are properly established.

PROTECTING YOURSELF FROM BUSINESS FRAUD

Business credit operations are sometimes vulnerable to fraudulent activities since business is often conducted by mail, fax machine, or between distant locations. Fraudulent debtors and con artists use deceitful practices and devices to steal property or money from unsuspecting businesses. Especially in competitive industries, the desire to approve a big order may result in significant losses for a credit department.

Some common scams include bust outs, hit and run, advance fee scams, and fraudulent loans. A bust out involves a business obtaining large quantities of merchandise without paying for it. A fictitious business may begin operating and ordering relatively small amounts from a few suppliers. The early bills are paid in full and these payment records are used to extend credit lines and add additional suppliers. Eventually, however, large orders are received and the business disappears leaving many creditors with unpaid accounts.

A hit-and-run operation will order merchandise COD and pay with bogus certified or cashier's checks. The business moves quickly and will be gone by the time creditors find out the payments were no good.

Advance fee scams involve payments for services that are never delivered.

Fraudulent loans are obtained using nonexistent inventory, fake trade references, and false financial statements.

The best protection is to develop consistent, disciplined credit investigation procedures. These scams generally rely on finding credit managers who will act too quickly without doing thorough credit checks and risk assessment. In every case, it is important to verify the identity and financial health of customers.[1]

Business Credit Frauds and Scams

- Bust out
- Hit and run
- Advance fee scam
- Fraudulent loans

Automatic and Nonautomatic Initial Orders

Credit managers need to make a distinction between **initial orders** and **follow-up orders.** It is essential, whenever possible, that the first order from a new customer be processed as quickly and expeditiously as possible, without lengthy and extensive investigation. A new order is the first contact between buyer and seller; initial impressions often mean the difference between a long-range series of follow-up orders and a one-time, one-order customer. Some firms consider old customers who have not bought during the preceding year as "new" customers.

---

[1]See "How to Protect Yourself from Business Fraud," at the Dun and Bradstreet web site—http://www.dbisna.com

Automatic Initial Orders

To expedite the processing of initial orders, credit departments may give blanket approval to all first orders below a specified amount. This amount is influenced by the type of product involved, the nature of the company's operation, its overall credit policy, general market conditions, competitive credit terms, and prior experience in collecting small credit accounts approved in this manner. However, a follow-up procedure is vital for successful future operation.

Some firms appraise initial orders on the basis of ratings given by credit agencies such as Dun & Bradstreet and the various specialized agencies. They assign maximum amounts to each Dun & Bradstreet credit rating. For example, if the initial order of a customer with a certain credit rating falls below the maximum, approval is automatic. Of course, each company that uses such a technique establishes its own first-order limits to meet its own needs and conform to its own policies.

Nonautomatic Initial Orders

If the company has no established procedures such as blanket and agency-rating approvals, it must decide how to handle initial orders. It may base this decision on answers to the following questions:

1. Is the profit margin on the order large enough to cover the cost of investigation?
2. Should the account be cultivated because of the potential future sales volume?
3. What public relations benefits might the company gain because of the sale?

If the company decides to investigate, a further decision must be made as to how extensive the investigation should be. Where present and expected sales potential justifies an intensive and direct investigation, the credit department should seek all available information regarding historical and forecast data, reputation and ability of principles, marketability and competitive forces related to products, and so on.

HANDLING ORDERS FROM ESTABLISHED CUSTOMERS

When an old, established account orders merchandise, credit department procedures are greatly simplified. The credit department refers to in-file information to determine whether the account is in good standing or not. Most business credit departments periodically accumulate credit information and revise credit limits on established accounts. Hence in-file data is usually reasonably current, leading to a rapid credit decision. If the order is acceptable and within the assigned credit limit when added to any existing balances, it is approved and sent to the shipping department, where the order is filled and shipped to the customer.

However, if the account is not in good standing because previous balances remain unpaid or if filling the order would greatly exceed the account's credit limit, the order is sent to the credit manager for decision. With all in-file data available, the credit manager may revise the credit limit upward, seek additional credit information from external sources or, rather than assume greater risk from the customer, notify the customer of the negative decision. If the account is seriously overdue, the company may withhold shipment pending receipt of payment from the customer to defray the previous balance. In this event, the customer should be notified as to the reason for the shipping delay.

Speed—Essential to Handling Orders

In the operation of a business credit department, speed in processing and acting on orders is imperative. Much of this speed is accomplished by routinizing the credit-decision task through the maintenance of the department's in-file information. Current in-file information on customers and credit limits safely permits automatic approval of a large volume of orders. New accounts on which no in-file data exist and revived old accounts must be processed quickly and the credit investigation started without delay.

Speed is necessitated by the strong competitive environment in which many companies operate. Speed is one of the most important considerations when customers have the alternative of purchasing elsewhere. Delays, withheld shipments, and unreasonable requests for credit information destroy the desirable customer relationships developed by the salespeople. Retaining present customers and gaining new ones depend as much on speed as they do on price, quality, service, personalities, and the like.

EDI or electronic data interchange is another electronic or computer development being used by more business credit departments. EDI is defined as the business-to-business exchange of business documents, such as purchase orders, shipping notices, or invoices using electronic transmissions.

Surveys of companies using EDI show the main benefits of using EDI, including the following:

- Cost efficiency.
- Faster response time.
- Potential increase in customer base.
- Convenience.

Companies mention some disadvantages of EDI:

- Initial setup cost.
- Lack of standardized formats.
- Incompatibility between company computers and software.
- Lack of total management commitment.

Automation in business credit departments is constantly changing, and it is impossible to predict what the future will hold. But a few things seem inevitable. These include that technology will continue to improve the operation and speed of computers due to new microprocessor chips, new forms of mass data storage, and faster networks based on fiber optics or wireless communications.

The continued automation and integration of virtually all business technologies will continue, and with this merging of technologies a problem for the credit department is evolving; that is, the problem of having too much data versus too little. The ability to sort the pertinent data out of a sea of information will become increasingly important.

REVIEW OF DECISIONS

Business conditions change. The credit standing of customers changes. The outlook of sellers changes. In fact, in credit operations change is a certainty, and successful credit managers recognize that decisions and credit lines must be regularly reviewed to bring them up-to-date. Otherwise, a company will not be able to increase sales volume, cut bad-debt losses, reduce the costs of credit administration, and efficiently manage the investment of receivables.

Unfortunately, despite all the safeguards of analyzing credit information from a number of sources, making careful and complete credit decisions, setting realistic lines of credit, and constantly reviewing all of these steps—not all credit accepted is repaid on time, and in some instances it is never repaid.

Important Terms

capacity   373

capital   373

character   373

collateral   373

credit limit   366

credit line   366

electronic data interchange (EDI)   377

follow-up orders   375

guarantee   374

house standard   368

initial orders   375

irrevocable letter of credit   374

mechanic's lien   374

order limit   373

perfected   374

subordination agreement   374

Uniform Commercial Code (UCC)   374

written credit policy   368

Discussion Questions

1. What purpose does the business credit department serve for a typical business? Why are its efforts important to the survival and profitability of a firm?

2. What decision alternatives are available for a business credit manager?

3. What goals are important in making business credit decisions?

4. List and describe possible sections for a written credit policy. Why is a written credit policy helpful?

5. Explain the usefulness of credit lines. What are typical methods for establishing credit lines?

6. What basic considerations enter into a business decision regarding the C's of credit decision making?

7. What types of security can be used in business credit? What does "perfecting" a security interest involve?

8. What are some examples of business credit fraud? How can a credit manager protect his or her firm?

9. What are the advantages and disadvantages of automatic initial order programs?

10. Describe some examples of automation in business credit departments.

Suggested Readings—Part V

Management and Analysis of Business Credit

Adler, Jane. "D&B: Meet the Competition." *Collections & Credit Risk,* April 1996, p. 30.

Dennis, Michael. "How To Get Financial Statements From Your Customers." *Business Credit,* July/August 1995, p. 5.

Dennis, Michael. "The Limitations of Financial Statement Analysis." *Business Credit,* February 1995, p. 32.

"Financial EDI: Improving the Business Cycle." *Business Credit,* April 1996, p. 21.

Gomez, Lucas. "Time for Change." *Business Credit,* November/December 1995, p. 4. (Business Credit Investigation)

Hanson, Randall. "What Credit Managers Should Know About Secured Transactions Under the UCC." *Business Credit,* January 1995, p. 10.

Hill, Ned C. and Michael J. Swenson. "The Impact of EDI on Credit and Sales." *Business Credit,* January 1995, p. 24.

Jeschke, Katherine R. "Full Faith and Credit." *Business Credit,* July/August 1996, p. 15. (Fraud)

Kristy, James E. "Conquering Financial Ratios: The Good, the Bad, and the Who Cares." *Business Credit,* February 1994, p. 14.

Miller, Barry. "Cause-and-Effect Ratio Analysis Adds Decision-Making Value to Credit Scoring Models." *Business Credit,* February 1994, p. 27.

Millis, Robert. "How To Handle Waivers of Lien." *Business Credit,* January 1995, p. 14.

Naff, Kevin. "Teams Approach to Credit Management Gaining in Popularity." *Business Credit,* April 1995, p. 35.

Scherr, Frederick C. "Credit Department Structure and Policy-Making: Rethinking the Basics for a Competitive World." *Business Credit,* February 1996, p. 20.

Selby, Glenda K. "Credit Versus Sales? A Customer Service Approach." *Business Credit,* March 1996, p. 29.

Thorpe, Paula. "Financial Analysis for Today's Credit Profession." *Business Credit,* February 1996, p. 18.

Whiteside, David E. "Commercial Credit Data Gets Crowded." *Collections and Credit Risk,* December 1996, p. 39.

Zanolini, Ken. "Spotting the Bad Credit Risk—Ask Before, During, and After the Sale." *Business Credit,* June 1995, p. 15.

Zuckerman, Marc A. "Automating Financial Statement Analysis." *Business Credit,* May 1995, p. 29.

Internet Sites

http://www.dbisna.com   Dunn and Bradstreet Information Services

Many companies provide their financial statements and other information on-line. Here are some:

http://www.chryslercars.com	Chrysler
http://www.cocacola.com	Coca Cola
http://www.dupont.com	DuPont
http://www.gm.com	General Motors
http://www.jnj.com	Johnson & Johnson
http://www.landsend.com	Lands' End

INTERNATIONAL TRADE CREDIT

18

INTERNATIONAL TRADE CREDIT

Learning Objectives

After studying this chapter, you should be able to:

- Explain the importance of credit in international trade.
- Discuss the credit problems of export trade.
- Describe protection offered by Eximbank (the Export-Import Bank of the United States).
- Explain different terms of sale in export operations.
- Discuss sources of foreign credit information.
- Describe the use of a letter of credit (L/C) in foreign credit operations.
- Comment on the credit card boom outside America's shores.

The United States is one of the world's leading exporters and importers of merchandise. However, the U.S. balance of payments has shown deficits for more than a decade, and this has caused the U.S. government to reevaluate its foreign policy and to institute certain necessary adjustments to help reduce these deficits. As one adjustment, the government has enlarged its existing federal export expansion program to encourage exports by manufacturers not currently exporting and to expand sales among manufacturers currently exporting.

Japan, the Pacific Basin, and several Western European countries have dramatically increased their exports since World War II. We are increasingly involved in a true *world economy* as products from overseas are commonplace. Many foreign suppliers and manufacturers are locating facilities in the United States or buying former U.S. firms. Trying to buy only goods "made in America" is becoming very difficult to do. If U.S. citizens buy more foreign goods than are sold by U.S. firms to purchasers overseas, the balance of payments account shows a deficit, that is, there is a net loss of spending.

Selling products overseas requires specialized export marketing skills. And of course these export marketing skills include skill in the use of credit. A company's credit policy, or lack of one, is vital to the success or failure of its international marketing program. The fact that a customer trading on credit is located in a foreign country does not alter the basic principles and procedures of sound credit management. Foreign customers must still be investigated, the risk carefully analyzed, logical credit limits imposed, and collections made. There are, however, some basic differences in practice and some problems not encountered in domestic credits and collections.

CREDIT PROBLEMS OF EXPORT TRADE

The principal problem area for most credit managers stems from their need to judge the credit risk accurately. A foreign credit customer usually represents greater risk and is more difficult to evaluate. The increased degree of risk and difficulty in evaluation does not mean credit losses are higher on foreign customers than domestic customers. Risk and evaluation problems intensify, though, because of the following factors, which must be considered when judging the foreign credit risk: government, economic stability, currency and exchange, business practices, distance, the status of export credit insurance, and collections.

Foreign Government Policies

Any nation's economy and business climate are directly influenced by the attitudes and policies of its government. A government's political orientation, whether right or left, also affects its economic policy and the degree to which it regulates both internal commerce and external trade. Different economic systems exist throughout the world, some involve limited private ownership and significant government controls. Governments often implement various regulations, quotas, taxes, and restrictions regarding foreign trade. The resulting situations are very complex and can often change quickly.

In deciding whether to sell to customers in a particular country, business executives have to consider the type of government involved. Although it is desirable to avoid politics in international business, American firms have found they cannot ignore local government because it influences so many phases of business activity. For example, the right to conduct business activities and the extent of foreign investment permitted are determined by government policy.

Economic Stability

Likewise, export credit executives must be alert to and understand the general economic situation in any foreign country in which they have customers. Although most Americans understand recessions, inflation, and interest rate changes, our economy is relatively stable. Some foreign economies, however, are very unstable. Business cycle fluctuations, sometimes brought on by government changes, can be severe and long-lived. The general standard of living in a foreign country can also be dramatically different from our own.

Currency and Exchange

One of the inherent risks of export trade stems from the instability of some currencies. At a given point in time, a foreign currency can be exchanged for a certain number of U.S. dollars. Unfortunately, the exchange rate will vary constantly and the number of dollars received in the exchange will change.

This risk must be assumed by one of the parties to the transaction. If the exporter bills the foreign customer in the native currency (pounds, pesos, francs, rupees, and so on), the exporter runs the risk that when the importer pays the bill, the exchange into dollars may yield a smaller amount than anticipated. If the foreign currency should drop in value, the seller will receive less as the foreign currency is converted into dollars. If, on the other hand, the exporter bills the foreign customer in dollars (this is more common), the risk of devaluation is placed on the importer.

Not only does risk surround the relative value of currencies, but each foreign country also rigidly enforces exchange regulations. In general, foreign money can be obtained only from designated exchange authorities usually controlled by the central banking system. Exchange regulations fluctuate with the country's political and economic conditions. In the past, importers in some countries have been prevented from remitting dollars to the United States; or, due to an unfavorable exchange situation, the foreign buyer may delay settlement of the account until more favorable exchange rates prevail.

A credit manager whose firm sells to foreign customers must be a student of international financial developments. The sufficiency of dollar reserves, the likelihood of foreign currency devaluation, and monetary restrictions all must be considered in evaluating the foreign credit risk.

Business Practices

Management techniques and the tools of efficient business management are not as advanced in most foreign countries as they are in the United States. This deficiency takes on particular significance in the area of accounting and preparation of financial statements. Foreign merchants, except for those in the largest trade centers, may not have trained accountants available. Furthermore, some foreign merchants still hold to the archaic view that their "names" and integrity are sufficient evidence on which to base credit appraisal. Foreign buyers are often highly irritated by what they think are unnecessary requests for credit information from U.S. sellers. Often these foreign firms have been in business many years and have done business with U.S. firms on an open account basis for fairly long periods. Unthoughtful actions in requesting certain information have proved distasteful to some foreign companies. Many are also reluctant to supply financial statements even though they have them, because they fear revealing business secrets. While these arguments have diminished in recent years as more firms adopt advanced business practices, gathering adequate financial information on foreign buyers still remains a problem.

The lack of, or the poor quality of, financial data is further complicated by language difficulties. Despite great emphasis on the foreign language requirement for those concerned with foreign trade, neither party is usually well versed in technical terms, business definitions, and trade names. Hence, there is a greater possibility of misunder-standings, disputes, and rejection of the shipment.

Business practices also are influenced by the diversity of commercial laws of foreign countries. Commonly, such things as import restrictions and licenses, laws of contract and title, bankruptcy, commercial arbitration, and patents are highly technical and complex. Because of the wide variety of such foreign regulations, most creditors should consult an attorney who is familiar with international law before getting involved for the first time with importers of products from a particular country.

Distance

The distance between the exporter and the importer compounds the problem of risk evaluation. If financial information on domestic customers is inadequate, the credit manager or a representative often can visit the prospective customer's place of business and make a judgment on nonfinancial factors. The opportunity for personal contact with foreign customers is limited, particularly where small accounts are involved. Conse-quently, the credit decision must be based almost entirely on data supplied by credit investigation agencies and other sources. In addition, good credit information cannot always be obtained on customers in other countries, even by well-known credit reporting agencies. Sufficient staff personnel are not always available in the foreign offices of these agencies, and access to important information is not always forthcoming.

Furthermore, the distance factor influences the terms of sale. Usually, there is a relatively long lapse of time between the purchase or shipment of goods and their receipt by the importer. Because of this, foreign terms of sale are often longer than domestic terms of sale, and hence accounts receivable remain unpaid for extended periods. Credit managers report that in recent years, as competition for foreign customers has increased, the demands of these customers for longer credit terms have also increased. Because the credit manager is not close to the foreign customer, it is extremely difficult to know whether the customer is actually playing one creditor against another or is taking advantage of a plausible situation. Whatever the circumstances, firms need greater financial capacity to carry foreign accounts than domestic accounts. The long lapse of time and longer terms granted to compete with other sellers aggravate exchange risks and risks created by the possibility of new import regulations.

Government-Sponsored Programs to Encourage Exports

Most of the major exporting nations have adopted either **export credit insurance** plans or guarantees that protect creditors against defaulting foreign customers. The **Export-Import Bank** of the United States (http://www.exim.gov) is the government agency responsible for assisting businesses involved in export sales. The agency assists with financing of U.S. goods through a variety of loan, guarantee, and insurance programs.

Working Capital Guarantee
This guarantee program assists small businesses in obtaining working capital to fund their export activities. Generally, the program guarantees 90 percent of the principal and

interest on loans extended by commercial lenders to eligible U.S. exporters. The loan proceeds can be used for pre-export activities such as purchase of inventory, raw materials, or the manufacture of a product for export.

Export Credit Insurance

An exporter can reduce risks by purchasing Ex-Im Bank export credit insurance through insurance brokers or directly from Ex-Im Bank. The insurance protects the exporter against the failure of foreign buyers to pay their credit obligations. Ex-Im Bank often assumes 95 percent of the commercial risk and 100 percent of the political risk involved in extending credit overseas. The insurance encourages exporters to offer competitive terms of sale and supports penetration into higher-risk foreign markets.

Direct Loans and Guarantees

Ex-Im Bank also provides direct loans and guarantees of commercial financing to foreign buyers of U.S. goods and services. Both programs cover up to 85 percent of the U.S. export value, with repayment terms of one year or more.

Seminars and Briefing Programs

Ex-Im Bank offers seminars, group briefings, and individual discussions at Ex-Im Banks and at locations around the United States.

Collections

Another problem area of concern to the export credit manager is collections. As with domestic customers, the collection of foreign accounts is an inherent risk in the adoption of a credit policy. The cost of collecting overdue export accounts, the variance in commercial laws from one foreign country to another, and the factors already discussed compound the problem. Because of the greater collection problem, standards of acceptability are generally higher for foreign accounts than for domestic accounts. Despite the higher standards, creditors should expect to experience some difficulty with collections and some bad-debt losses.

The variety of reasons or conditions that cause export customers to become delinquent and the collection procedures and devices necessary to effect settlement are similar to those for domestic customers. Due to the conditions that influence the collection of foreign accounts, it is particularly important that the credit manager establish internal controls to detect overdue accounts at an early date. Prompt follow-up of the account by mail, telephone, or cable will usually elicit the reason for the delay. Once the specific reason is known, the credit manager can plan collection action more intelligently and can expect the actions taken to be more effective.

The credit manager confronts a particularly knotty problem when collection devices fail to bring results and the export account is eventually classified as "placed for collection" or "legal action." At this stage in the life of the account, the credit manager must decide whether it is worthwhile to proceed further. Litigation abroad is both costly and time consuming, and the effort outweighs the potential results. Obviously, only sizable accounts and large unpaid balances should be considered for legal action. If legal action is necessary, creditors should consult with their banks, their own legal counsel, or an export agency for advice on competent legal counsel in the foreign country. In some countries only nationals are permitted to practice law. American exporters' experiences with foreign lawyers have not all been positive; exporters frequently feel that their rights are not wholeheartedly enforced.

If a foreign account is to be placed for collection (as distinguished from collection by legal action), a number of well-known agencies may provide valuable help. Dun & Bradstreet and the FCIB of the National Association of Credit Management are two such agencies. Each of these services uses "moral suasion" letters that emphasize the importance of maintaining a good credit standing.

Business arbitration also is used to try to bring about speedy and inexpensive settlement of overdue accounts. A worldwide system of arbitration, organized by the American Arbitration Association and cooperating trade associations and chambers of commerce, has been in operation for many years.

Factors in Judging Foreign Credit Risk

- Foreign government policies
- Economic stability
- Currency and exchange
- Business practices
- Distance
- Government-sponsored programs
- Collections

EXPORT TERMS OF SALE

In recent years, competition for foreign customers has become particularly intense in a number of international markets. When this condition exists, importers do considerable bargaining for lenient credit terms. So prevalent is such bargaining today that credit managers believe the particular credit terms granted may be a deciding factor in making a sale. The export credit manager must, however, be careful to avoid those firms that take advantage of a competitive situation but still have a marginal or deteriorating financial condition. Even though the present-day competitive scene magnifies the exporter's credit problems, the future outlook is somewhat brighter. As competition improves, some international markets will have overcome their perplexing political and economic situations, and hence the risk of exchange and monetary restrictions is likely to decrease substantially.

Terms of sale used in export trade, to some extent at least, denote the quality of the risk, just as terms of sale in domestic trade classify accounts by risk or unique circumstances. **Export terms of sale** may be classified in order of decreasing risk as follows:

1. Open account.
2. Consignment.
3. Drafts drawn by the seller on the buyer.
4. Authority to purchase.
5. Export letter of credit.
6. Cash payment before delivery.

Open Account

The **open account** with terms to compensate for the distance factor and other normal delays is used in a minority of export credit transactions. Again the exporter must have the utmost confidence in the customer, and the exchange provisions must be favorable to the use of these terms. In some countries, applications for exchange to settle dollar draft obligations receive priority over applications to settle open account obligations.

Consignment

Consignment sales are not widely used in export trade and are never used when exchange and monetary restrictions are not favorable to converting foreign currency into dollars. Laws on passing title to goods are not the same in all foreign countries, and such laws alone may preclude the use of this device. If, however, exporters are shipping to customers of long standing in whom they have the utmost confidence or to foreign subsidiaries and sales agents, consignment terms may be desirable. Customers of these types must be located in established foreign markets where the trade and banking facilities are capable of coping with the technicalities of consigned shipments.

Drafts

Time and sight drafts are widely used credit instruments in export credit sales. A **draft** is an order for the payment of money from one person to another. A **sight draft** requires immediate payment when presented while a **time draft** is payable at a future specified date. Drafts may be either dollar or foreign currency drafts, depending on the arrangements previously made between the exporter and the buyer.

Usually, the drafts (whether time or sight) are documentary drafts as contrasted with clean drafts. The **documentary draft** is accompanied by all the title documents and papers essential to the shipment, such as bills of lading, insurance certificates, and shipping documents. The **clean draft** is free of these attachments. In this case the importer may have already received the shipment, and the exporter forwards the clean draft through banking channels to collect the amount due.

In using a draft to collect the accepted credit, the exporter should consult the *Credit Manual of Commercial Laws,* published annually by the National Association of Credit Management. This volume contains much helpful information on terms of sale, trade definitions, and the various documentary requirements. Furthermore, the instructions to the bank regarding collection of the draft, remittance of the funds by the foreign bank, the handling of collection charges and taxes, and other charges must be clearly set forth to avoid misunderstandings, delays, and more complicated collection procedures.

Authority to Purchase

Export sales may involve payment by documentary draft with **authority to purchase,** which is an authorization to a bank to purchase, on behalf of a foreign bank, the documentary draft drawn by the seller on the buyer. Such authority provides a place where the exporter may negotiate a draft with documents attached and thus obtain funds immediately.

Export Letter of Credit

The exporter who wants greater certainty of payment, other than cash before delivery, should request the importer to arrange for an export letter of credit.

The Uniform Commercial Code (UCC) defines a **letter of credit (L/C)** as "an engagement by a bank . . . made at the request of a customer . . . that the issuer will honor drafts or other demands for payment upon compliance with the conditions specified in the credit."

On a sale that calls for payment by means of a letter of credit, foreign importers arrange with their banks that a credit for the amount be established in favor of the exporter. Payment generally is made against documents evidencing shipment of the goods. Thus, under an export letter of credit, the importer's bank undertakes to pay the exporter.

A letter of credit issued by a foreign bank and accepted by an American bank is known as an **irrevocable export letter of credit.** An irrevocable letter of credit also may be issued by an American bank, or may be issued by a foreign bank but unconfirmed by an American bank. Drafts drawn under this type of letter of credit are paid by the foreign bank, not by the American bank. A **revocable export letter of credit** may be issued. Because this instrument may be revoked or amended at any time, the exporter has only day-to-day assurance that the issuing bank will accept sight and time drafts drawn against it. Exporters much prefer the two former instruments, which are widely used.

The preference of export creditors for the irrevocable export letter of credit stems from their ability to convert accepted drafts into cash almost immediately. All the exporter must do is draw a draft, support it with the necessary shipping documents, and present it to the accepting bank. After verifying the exporter's claim, the bank accepts the draft. Once the bank accepts the draft on the irrevocable letter of credit, the exporter can in turn discount it on the open market and receive full payment for the shipment less the discount charge. For all practical purposes, then, the irrevocable letter of credit parallels a cash sale. If, however, the exporter wants to save the discount charge, the draft can be held until maturity.

The possible problems in using letters of credit are shown in Exhibit 18–1.

Exhibit 18–1 Problems in Using Letters of Credits

Look for These L/C Red Flags:

DRAFTS

Amount in numbers and words do not agree with invoice amount.

Drawn to purchaser instead of issuing bank.

Letter of credit number and date of issuance are not shown or are incorrectly shown.

Drawer's name does not agree with invoice name.

Draft is drawn to beneficiary and beneficiary's name is missing on reverse side.

Drafts are not presented, even though it is required by letter of credit terms.

Tenor of draft differs from letter of credit.

Credit amount exceeded.

Amount disproportionate to quantity invoiced.

INVOICES

Invoice name and address do not agree with letter of credit.

Quantity does not agree with other supporting documents.

Unit price and extensions of unit price are incorrect.

Terms of sale omitted or incorrect (FOB, C&F, CIF, etc.).

Certification, which may be required by letter of credit terms, is missing.

Signatures, if required, are missing.

Marks and numbers differ from other documents.

Merchandise description is different from letter of credit.

Invoice shows excess shipment, short shipment, or partial shipment, which may be prohibited by terms of the letter of credit.

Insufficient copies are presented.

Adjustments on previous shipments or charges are contained, which are not allowed under the letter of credit terms (cable, air mail, storage, financing, or messenger fees).

BILLS OF LADING

Full set not presented, if required by letter of credit terms.

Unclean bills of lading (contains a notation as to a defect or qualification in packing or condition of merchandise).

Charter party bills of lading presented.

Does not show that the merchandise is actually "Shipped On-Board."

Shipments between ports differ from letter of credit terms.

Does not indicate whether freight is prepaid or not.

Shows that merchandise is shipped "On-Deck."

Indicates a later date than that allowed by letter of credit terms.

Not signed by carrier/agent/owner.

Merchandise description inconsistent with other documents.

INSURANCE DOCUMENTS

Coverage other than that required by letter of credit terms.

Claims payable in currency other than that of letter of credit.

Insurance policy/certificate not signed or properly endorsed.

Coverage effective after shipping date.

Amount of coverage insufficient.

Merchandise description inconsistent with other documents.

Incomplete sets presented.

Corrections not authenticated.

Not in negotiable form, unless letter of credit terms permit.

Not countersigned.

Transshipments not covered when bills of lading show it will take place.

Insurance certificate presented when policy is required.

OTHER DOCUMENTS

Certificates of origin should comply with importing country requirements.

Weight/packing/measurement list, analysis certificates, and inspection certificates, if required, must be fully detailed and conform strictly to the letter of credit terms.

Documents should be notarized, where required, as per letter of credit terms.

Note: Also see Erice R. Anderson, "Coming to Terms with Importers," *Business Credit*, March 1993, p. 15; and Sidney S. Goldstein and Bruce S. Nathan, "How Strict Is Strict Compliance?" *Business Credit*, May/June 1990, p. 39.

Source: Herman J. Ortmann, "The Pitfalls of Letters of Credit," *Business Credit*, November-December 1990, p. 24. Permission granted by the National Association of Credit Management, *Business Credit*.

Cash before Delivery Terms

The circumstances under which an exporter may demand CBD terms are much the same as those in domestic sales. When importers cannot qualify to meet the demand for a letter of credit or when their credit standing is clearly unsatisfactory, it is desirable to ask for

cash before delivery (CBD). Not all circumstances that call for this arrangement are the importer's responsibility. Exporters may request these terms when the foreign country's exchange conditions are such that long delays are likely if more lenient terms are used. A few products have customarily been sold on CBD terms to domestic customers, and the same terms apply to foreign customers.

Export Terms of Sale

- Open account.
- Consignment.
- Drafts.
- Authority to purchase.
- Export letter of credit.
- Cash payment before delivery.

SOURCES OF FOREIGN CREDIT INFORMATION

The evaluation of the foreign credit customer is much the same as that for a domestic customer. The exception to this, of course, is the close evaluation of factors peculiar to export trade. Likewise, the sources of credit information and the content and format of credit reports are much the same as those frequently consulted in domestic credit analysis. However, as mentioned earlier, reasonably good credit information cannot always be obtained on customers in foreign countries. Foreign credit reporting offices are not always adequately staffed, nor do they always have access to all necessary information.

The sources of information on the foreign buyer can be classified as domestic and foreign. The domestic sources can be subdivided into business credit reporting agencies, the exporter's bank, the U.S. Department of Commerce, and foreign trade publications. The foreign sources include the buyer, the buyer's bank, and the exporter's foreign sales representatives.

Commercial Credit Reporting Agencies

As exports and the world's trading areas have expanded in recent years, improved credit reporting services have also expanded. Dun & Bradstreet and the FCIB of the National Association of Credit Management are two well-known sources of foreign credit information. Both agencies write credit reports on manufacturers, wholesalers, sales agents, and other business enterprises located in most of the free nations of the world. Dun & Bradstreet also supplies reports on companies located in the East bloc. Competition continues to expand with the increased involvement of Equifax Information Services and Experian (formerly TRW).

Dun and Bradstreet

Dun & Bradstreet maintains offices in a large number of foreign countries, supplemented by an international network of credit correspondents. These Dun & Bradstreet facilities serve as a viable source of credit information for both domestic and foreign manufacturers, distributors, and bankers. Reports prepared on customers in foreign countries are of the same general type as those prepared for domestic use, except that more emphasis may be placed on background and reputation and less on financial standing. Most of the information shown in the credit reports and international publications is gathered through detailed investigations performed by credit reporters operating out of the Dun & Bradstreet foreign offices.

Dun & Bradstreet has a worldwide communication network that allows access to databases in Europe, North America, and the Pacific. Customers may gain access to these databases through their standard print terminals or personal computers. The European database offers summarized information in a choice of six languages.

Dun & Bradstreet publishes more than a dozen major international reference books and directories, including the *Exporters' Encyclopedia*. This reference book can be a valuable aid for the credit executive, as it details the facts and rules needed to function effectively in over 180 countries. Highlights include: documentation requirements, import licensing and exchange regulations, and key contacts.

Other services of Dun & Bradstreet include: (1) worldwide business collection service through its network of offices and agents, (2) marketing research, (3) specialized investigations, (4) export support, (5) advertising, and (6) direct marketing.

FCIB-NACM

The FCIB is the international arm of the National Association of Credit Management, serving those association members who are interested or engaged in international trade activities.

Since 1919 the National Association of Credit Management has operated the member-owned **FCIB-NACM Corporation** in order to help exporters with the many credit problems inherent in international selling. Like its domestic counterpart, FCIB functions as a clearinghouse for payment experiences—in this case, exporters' payment experiences with overseas customers. This information, rather than being historical and financial in character, is the actual ledger and credit experience of American export creditors. The body of the foreign report is essentially the same as the Business Credit Report. However, in the foreign report, each member who reports on a particular account also rates the customer as high, good, satisfactory, unsatisfactory, or undesirable by using the respective code letters Q, R, S, T, and U.

Other services of the FCIB include:

1. Worldwide collection service.
2. Free reciprocal copy of all foreign credit interchange reports to which the member contributes experience.
3. Biweekly bulletins.
4. Minutes of monthly roundtable conferences on foreign credit, collection, and exchange problems, with participation by either mail or attendance.
5. Consultation and market research service.

Equifax International Operations

Equifax is organized into three main international divisions: Equifax Canada, Equifax Europe, and Equifax South America. A variety of services are provided by these divisions, including: consumer credit information, accounts receivable services, check guarantee services, marketing information, credit scoring, and collections.

Experian (formerly TRW)

In November 1996, the former TRW Information Services operation was acquired and merged with the CCN Group of Nottingham, United Kingdom. This new global information provider—which is first or second in every market it serves—provides many credit-related services. Experian holds minority interest in the Central Communication Bureau, Japan's third-largest consumer credit firm. The CCN Group has operations in the United Kingdom, the Netherlands, Italy, France, Germany, Spain, Belgium, Canada, South Africa, Australia, Hong Kong, and the United States.

Commercial Banks

Often the bank through which the exporter conducts international business has credit information on foreign customers. This is in direct contrast to the role of banks as a source of credit information for domestic customers. Banks accumulate a great deal of foreign information because they are often directly involved in export credit sales. Drafts and letters of credit are frequently used in export credit transactions, and hence banks have a great interest in the same types of credit information as do export credit managers.

The information contained in banks' extensive files may be available to clients who request it for credit purposes. In requesting such information, the creditor should completely reveal the details of the export credit transaction. Complete information on the transaction helps the bank make the most accurate and usable reply possible. Banks also write or cable for information not in their files. This is possible because their foreign offices and correspondent banks have firsthand experience with importers in the payment of their foreign trade obligations.

Bank information on foreign customers is highly regarded by export credit managers. The information that may be obtained from a bank includes the importer firm's history and antecedents; the importer firm's financial strength and capacity, when available; and the bank's record of the payment performance experienced by its overseas branches and correspondents. In general, this source of information has the advantages of completeness, high quality, and speed.

Other Sources

A number of other sources supply valuable information. Foreign trade publications, exporters' associations, and the importer's bank may provide supplemental information of value. An export credit manager closely associated with foreign trade groups has little difficulty picking up essential information on particular markets and on the exchange problems encountered by other members. Not to be overlooked are the exporter's salespeople, foreign representatives, and, of course, the customer.

The U.S. Department of Commerce supplies valuable facts about foreign firms; its World Trade Data Reports are also valuable to exporters. U.S. foreign service offices are in a position to secure information that may be valuable to an American exporter in making credit decisions.

The so-called Edge Law banks should be mentioned briefly. The Edge Law, passed in December 1919 as part of the Federal Reserve Act, provides for the federal incorporation of businesses to engage solely in international or foreign banking or in other types of foreign financial operations. These banks are an excellent source of valuable credit information.

CREDIT CARD BOOM OUTSIDE THE UNITED STATES

The bank credit card is now one of America's most successful exports. As countries throughout the world grow and prosper economically, more demand for credit services is developing. Foreign citizens are embracing the concept of credit cards and the use of these cards is expanding rapidly. The hot spots today are Japan, Taiwan, South Korea, and many countries in Europe. Even Latin America is showing some promise as some countries start to get inflation under control. European charge volume continues to grow rapidly, especially in the United Kingdom and Germany.

Important Terms

authority to purchase   390
cash before delivery (CBD)   392
clean draft   389
consignment sales   389
documentary draft   389
draft   389
export credit insurance   386
Export-Import Bank   386

export terms of sale   389
FCIB-NACM Corporation   393
irrevocable export letter of credit   390
letter of credit (L/C)   390
open account   389
revocable letter of export credit   390
time and sight drafts   389
tools of efficient business management   385

Discussion Questions

1. How do you account for the fact that the balance of payments of the United States has shown deficits for more than a decade?

2. How do you explain the increased interest in export marketing among U.S. manufacturers?

3. What conditions magnify the problem of credit risk evaluation on foreign creditors? Explain each of the conditions you have listed.

4. Would you expect credit operations to be more or less advanced overseas than in the United States?

5. What is the basic purpose of export credit insurance?

6. What are some services provided by Ex-Im Bank?

7. Under what conditions would you use consignment terms? Open account terms?

8. What is the difference between a time draft and a sight draft?

9. Discuss the statement, "For all practical purposes, an irrevocable letter of export credit results in a cash sale."

10. Why would American industries prefer to sell on CBD terms?

11. How do you account for the differences and similarities between domestic and foreign sources of credit information?

12. Why are commercial banks a source of information on foreign customers?

13. What is the FCIB? Explain what it attempts to accomplish.

Suggested Readings—Part VI

International Trade Credit

Bocchino, Ralph. "Improving Your Collections of Foreign Receivables." *Business Credit,* November/December 1996, p. 47.

Burd, Laura. "Export Credit Insurance: The Risk Management Tool With an Edge." *Business Credit,* July/August 1995, p. 23.

"Distant Neighbors: Prospects for a First World Credit Economy in Mexico." *Credit World,* July/August 1996, p. 24.

Feely, Mary. "The Obstacle Course in Overseas Markets." *Collections & Credit,* April 1996, p. 49.

Flock, Michael. "Doing Business Abroad: Open Account or Letter of Credit?" *Business Credit,* March 1995, p. 23.

"Managing Risks by Selling Internationally on Open Account." *Business Credit,* January 1996, p. 13.

McIntosh, Paul F. "Export Credit Management—Is It Different?" *Business Credit,* November/December 1996, p. 7.

Moses, Max G. and Murray S. Lubitz. "Selling and Collecting Internationally: A Survey for Credit Grantors—Part 1: From Australia to Ireland." *Business Credit,* November/December 1996, p. 25.

Richards, Leslie A. and Stephen F. Borde. "International Trade Financing: An Exposition and Update." *Business Credit,* November/December 1996, p. 19.

Roth, Louis A. "Export and Domestic Trade Insurance." *Business Credit,* March 1995, p. 4.

Stroh, Leslie. "Safe Harbors for Overseas Shipments: A Guide to Protecting Your Exports." *Business Credit,* November/December 1994, p. 21.

Wagoner, Jeffrey L. "Extending International Credit and Collecting Foreign Debts." *Business Credit,* November/December 1996, p. 29.

Williamson, Irene K. "Entering New Markets: The Practical Pilgrim." *Credit World,* November/December 1995, p. 11. (International Trade)

Internet Sites

http://www.exim.gov   Export-Import Bank of the U.S.

PART

VII

COLLECTIONS MANAGEMENT AND CONTROL

19 COLLECTION POLICIES AND PRACTICES

Learning Objectives

After studying this chapter, you should be able to:

- Describe the goals of a good collections system.
- Explain common reasons for nonpayment of debts.
- Discuss the factors affecting a collection policy.
- Explain the important ingredients in a collections system.
- Describe four stages found in a general collection system.
- Discuss the various types of actions and collection devices that might be used during each collection stage.
- Describe the use of automated collections systems.

Collections are an inherent part of any credit business. Some customers will take longer than expected to pay their financial obligations. Some will not pay at all. Obviously, the profitability of the credit operation will suffer in either situation.

GOALS OF A GOOD COLLECTION SYSTEM

Any collection system must get the money. Yet this objective becomes difficult to attain when the company also has to retain customer goodwill, rehabilitate the debtor, encourage prompt payment, and operate economically. Each organization must sort through these goals to determine priorities. If promptness is the firm's major objective, it may use strenuous collection activity immediately after a payment is missed. However, the methods it uses may be very costly in dollars and goodwill. On the other hand, if a firm's major objective is to retain goodwill, its appeals and techniques will be very gentle, even delicate, and collections will be slow. The firm must try to understand the relationship between profits and collection efforts to determine the best methods to use.

Aid the Working Capital Position of the Firm

Every firm needs cash to operate. If collections fall behind, the firm may be required to borrow funds to pay its own bills. The collections department must generally work closely with the financial officers of a larger firm to predict cash receipts and the amount of cash that will become available in the months ahead. The payments must be collected promptly, and in full, if the creditor wants to avoid cash flow problems.

Reduce Operating Expenses and Bad Debt

Although getting the money is important, the collections system should not generate excessive costs for the firm. These costs include telephone expense, mail costs, legal fees, collection agency expenses, and the wages of those involved in the collection activity. Typically, the longer a bill goes without payment, the less likely the creditor is to receive the funds. As time goes by without consistent follow up of delinquent debtors, the collection effort also becomes more expensive since more elaborate methods are typically required.

An especially costly type of expense is bad debt. **Bad debt** is an operating expense that occurs when an account is determined to be uncollectible and the entire amount owed is charged as an expense against the firm's sales. The purpose of bad-debt expense is to stop the ongoing collection expenses after the account becomes uncollectible. The event that prompts the decision to charge off an account varies but may involve the closing of a debtor's business, the disappearance of the debtor, or the belief the client will never be able to pay. The creditor may not give up completely, however, and may occasionally investigate the debtor's situation to see if conditions (and possible avenues of collection) have improved. Some reasons for bad debt, e.g., the barring of collections activities by the statute of limitations or bankruptcy, may prevent any follow up of any kind.

Retain Customer Goodwill

Collections can be an emotion-charged activity. Few customers want to admit that they have been unable to meet their responsibilities regarding payment. In fact, if the initial collection call is made because of a creditor error, or because an unusual event has occurred such as the loss of the original invoice, the client may have not knowingly defaulted. Even if misfortune has prevented the client from paying as agreed, many customers will again be desirable customers after a temporary problem has passed. A collection system should not be too aggressive too early. The collection devices and activities should be matched to the known seriousness of the delinquency. Retaining customer goodwill is important to prompt repeat sales from quality customers and to the overall reputation of a firm in the community.

Rehabilitate the Customer

Some customers are indeed delinquent and have fallen behind in their payments. A part of the collection process may involve working with some customers to help them identify the causes for their nonpayment and to help them improve their credit behavior. They may suffer from procrastination, overindebtedness, or a noncaring attitude toward their obligations. If they are overextended, they may benefit from help identifying total indebtedness, analyzing sources of income, and working out a realistic plan for repayment. Assisting customers who will benefit from rehabilitation efforts may help cement lifelong relationships with a particular credit grantor.

Aid the Sales Effort

A good collections department will often improve sales. Credit customers will generally buy goods from firms where they are up-to-date with their payments and where their status is good. Borrowers will return for more loans from lenders that have helped them make regular payments as agreed. Also, previous collection problems that were not handled well may cause embarrassment which prevents future sales. In this case, the customer will buy from competing firms.

Promote Good Communications with Customers

Sometimes the actual cause for collection difficulties is the failure of communications. The contacts and communications that occur between the creditor and the debtor must be timely and effective. Sometimes invoices are not sent promptly and the creditors themselves fail to communicate properly. Legitimate misunderstandings can also occur that will prevent a customer from paying a bill when due. Communication involves following up promptly after payments are missed or arrangements are broken. For example, if a payment should have arrived by Monday, a follow-up communication should occur on Tuesday to inquire about why payment was not received. The debtors must also be reminded occasionally of the seriousness of their delinquency. Collection efforts revolve around effective communication skills and the ability to understand human behavior. Good collectors are persistent, understanding, and above all else, good communicators.

Goals of a Good Collections System

- Aid the working capital position of the firm.
- Reduce operating expenses and bad debt.
- Retain customer goodwill.
- Rehabilitate the customer.
- Aid the sales effort.
- Promote good communications with customers.

REASONS FOR NONPAYMENT

The reasons a customer does not pay are many. They obviously vary in the level of seriousness and the likelihood that collections will proceed without difficulty. The collector, of course, needs to determine as quickly as possible why payment has not been made. The collection devices employed, and the assertiveness of the overall collection effort, will vary depending on the reason payment was not made.

Debtor Misunderstood Terms

If the debtor misunderstood the terms of the credit, the individual may not have known that payment was due. Perhaps the invoice or bill was lost, never arrived, or was unclear. Occasionally in business credit situations, sales representatives, in an effort to close a sale, will tell the customers to take additional time as needed. This can be used as an excuse, of course, since customers might pretend they didn't realize they were late with payment. In the interest of maintaining goodwill, the collector must generally believe that the customer misunderstood the terms. If this excuse is used too often, however, the collector will be justified in no longer believing the customer did not know payment was due.

Disputed Amount

Sometimes customers feel they were overcharged or that the goods received were inferior. In other cases, they believe that the bill is incorrect. In these cases, the collector needs to carefully gather the facts and perhaps investigate the situation further. Once the dispute is solved, payment will generally be forthcoming.

Careless or Inefficient Customer

Collecting from this customer should not be a major problem. Pressed with a variety of other problems and cares, this customer has just overlooked making payment. The debtor may use an inefficient system to keep track of when bills are due or may just be careless or even forgetful. In most cases a simple reminder that the amount is due and immediately payable brings in payment with no loss of customer goodwill.

Small Amount Involved and Customer Ignores

A small number of accounts payable personnel and customers feel that if the indebtedness is small, they may ignore it for the time being, wait until the account becomes larger, and then write just one check to cover the entire amount. In such cases the debtor firm is making no attempt to escape payment; it is simply pursuing a delaying action that results in "future" payment to the creditor. In addition to the nuisance and trouble involved in having to start the collection procedure, there is always the problem that what is small to one firm may not be small to another.

Slow by Habit and by Nature

Some customers are notoriously slow in making payment. Payment is attained only after various types of collection devices are used and various degrees of persuasion applied. The firm that sells to this type of customer, and knows beforehand that the customer is of this type, should carefully analyze the gross margin on any sale and compare it with the expenses involved in making the sale. Such expenses tend to be high because of the cost of the collection process. Even at the risk of losing a customer, the executive assigned the collection task should adopt a strict policy toward the firm that is slow by habit and nature. Such customers have a poor concept of responsibility and generally are undesirable and unprofitable accounts.

Poor Financial Management

Customers falling into this category account for perhaps the largest number of difficulties for the collection manager. Often these customers are honest and optimistic, but they overbuy. Because of poor financial management, they find they can't meet the terms to which they agreed. The creditor must decide whether there is any hope that such a customer will learn to conduct buying activities profitably before determining whether to follow a strict or a lenient collection policy. Can the debtor be salvaged and made into a good customer? If the answer is no, the relationship should be terminated quickly.

Temporarily Out of Funds but Good

This type of customer is usually delinquent because of conditions beyond his or her control, such as illness, loss of income, poor business conditions or other developments. The debtor is not actually attempting to avoid payment, and the delinquency should not be viewed as a reflection on the debtor's integrity, but this should not delay the collection action. An amicable adjustment or extension of the credit period should be made as quickly as possible, and the creditor should insist that the terms of the new agreement be carried out to the limit of the debtor's ability.

Could Pay but Must Be Forced

This type of customer is somewhat similar to the customer who is slow by habit and by nature. However, in dealing with this group, more persuasion and even threats must be used to obtain payment. Most of the time, unless they are pursued vigorously, payment is unduly delayed or never occurs. Credit standing means very little to this customer who has become accustomed to severe collection methods. For this reason, in its dealings with these chronic delinquents the collection department should force the issue immediately and strongly, at the very moment when the account becomes past due. Less severe actions have little value, and the creditor will get no return for the expense involved.

Terms Chiseler

This customer is primarily a business credit phenomenon. At least two types of chiselers might be included in this classification. One is the type who regularly deducts cash discounts even when making payments after expiration of the cash discount period. Firms vary as to their policies in such a situation. Is it best to return the check and request full payment or to accept the check and bill the customer for the balance owing. Whichever procedure is followed, the action taken should be accompanied by a clear, concise statement that credit terms are being violated. How strong and threatening the statement should be largely depends on how profitable the customer is to the firm and on how much the customer's future business is desired.

Another type of chiseler is the customer who makes only a partial payment, sends a postdated check with deductions for cash discounts, or dates a check back so that the date is within the discount period. The chronic offender who operates this way should be told "the facts of credit" much more emphatically than the first-time offender who simply may have been careless.

A Skip

A **skip** is a debtor who deliberately moves or changes location in an attempt to avoid payment. Collectors often uncover this fact when mail is returned as undeliverable, or they find disconnected telephone numbers. The first calls in skip tracing will be to verify if a skip truly exists, or to see if the debtor simply forgot to keep the creditor informed of the new address. The original application for credit should be pulled and a new round of verifications and credit checks completed. In this way, the true situation can generally be quickly uncovered. If a skip has occurred, references should be called and every effort made to locate the debtor.

A Fraud

The creditor should show this dishonest debtor no consideration, nor should it make any effort to retain this debtor's goodwill or possible future business. Just as soon as the creditor is convinced that the debtor is dishonest and is engaged in fraudulent actions, the account should be turned over to an attorney, or possibly to a collection agency, with instructions to take legal action against the debtor. Time is of the essence in dealing with such offenders, and there is little reason to go through all the steps normally followed in a collection process.

Reasons for Nonpayment

- Debtor misunderstood terms.
- Disputed amount.
- Careless or inefficient customer.
- Small amount involved and customer ignores.
- Slow by habit and by nature.
- Poor financial management.
- Temporarily out of funds but good customer.
- Could pay but must be forced.
- Terms chiseler.
- A skip.
- A fraud.

FACTORS AFFECTING A COLLECTION POLICY

Collectors need collection policies and guidelines to help them decide whom to pursue. A collection policy will outline the collection devices that will be used and will indicate how long a collector will normally wait between the stages of collection. The collector, of course, will always match the collection tools and time frames to the individual case. In deciding which type of collection policy to adopt, a firm must recognize that many factors influence policy. Capital, competition, type of goods, and class of customers are among the most important and influential factors, although they by no means constitute a complete list.

Capital

One of the most important factors affecting collection policy is the amount of capital the firm owns or has available. Regardless of how liberal a collection policy creditors may wish to follow, if they are operating with a limited capital structure, they are usually forced to adopt a "strict" collection policy in order to meet the demands of their own creditors. Most business firms are not blessed with an overabundance of working capital; they depend on the turnover of their goods to provide needed funds. But a mere turnover of goods is not enough, if these goods are sold on credit. One step is added to the process—completion of the credit transaction by receipt of cash payment. How quickly this step must be completed depends on how badly the firm needs capital. Thus capital availability and need play a vital role in determining what type of collection policy a firm must adopt, despite the fact that a different policy might be more desirable in view of some of the other factors involved.

Competition

Another influence in a collection policy is, "What is the competition doing?" Community size plays a role; there is generally more room for different policies among large-city competitors than among small-town competitors. Regardless of community size, however, customers become aware of widely varying credit and collection policies, and a firm must know what its direct and indirect competitors are offering these mutual customers.

Type of Goods

The type of goods handled by the firm also influences the determination of collection policy. The greater the perishability of the good, the greater is the need for prompt payment of the account and thus the stricter is the collection policy. On the other hand, if the goods involved are durable goods and repossession (although undesired) is possible, the need for a strict collection policy is lessened. This is not to say, however, that a strict collection policy is never followed by a firm handling hard goods, but it does point up that such a policy is dictated by some factor other than the type of goods involved.

Class of Customers

Collection work would be easier and the results better if there were some magic way to classify each account as to the reason for nonpayment and identify the collection method that would be most effective. Sorting devices to perform such miracles unfortunately are not yet available. Until such devices become economically and mechanically feasible, the responsibility for any classification rests with credit personnel.

Some customers pay regularly and automatically. Those in this desirable classification solve one part of the classification problem and remove themselves as possible collection cases.

Thus, in deciding on what collection policies and practices to adopt, many firms attempt to decide whether their customers will pay promptly and need only slight reminders, if any. In these cases, if pressure is ever needed, it will be applied gradually and slowly. Included in this classification are debtors who, although they may be having difficulty in making payment, respond fully to any inquiry by explaining the reason for nonpayment and indicating when full payment may be expected.

With customers at the other extreme, if the company realizes it made a mistake in accepting their credit in the first place, little is gained by using gradual and weak devices. Experience shows that such individuals respect only strong efforts. An immediate threat of legal action may be the only way to get results.

Between prompt payers and known deadbeats is the group of debtors with whom judgment and experience play a vital role in determining how strict to be, how severe a collection method to use, and when to apply pressure. With these debtors the problem of classification is most acute.

IMPORTANT INGREDIENTS IN A COLLECTIONS SYSTEM

Coordination of Credit and Collection Policies

The firm must decide on the combination of credit policy and collection policy it believes is appropriate. The following combinations are possible.

1. Liberal credit—strict collection.
2. Strict credit—liberal collection.
3. Liberal credit—liberal collection.
4. Strict credit—strict collection.

The first two combinations are probably the most common. An exclusive men's clothing store might have very high credit standards, for example, and thus be able to ease off on collections. Others might be very liberal in their decisions to extend credit to customers, but should also be prepared to handle collection more aggressively. The third combination, unfortunately, often occurs among small business operations that fail to handle credit management functions well.

Flexibility

A good collections system should match the collection device and the level of assertiveness with the reason for nonpayment. Early in the collections process, the collector needs to determine why the payment was not made. An overly aggressive approach may jeopardize customer relationships, yet an overly meek approach will often result in further payment delays.

Flexibility is also required in determining the length of time the collection process will run for an individual customer. In some cases, additional time to pay will be freely allowed. In others, severe collection devices and techniques will be started very quickly.

Prompt Response to Missed Payments

The collections system must be prompt in identifying and responding to missed payments. Many firms now employ computer systems that monitor payments as they are posted. In the early collection stages, when routine form letters or notices are being mailed, the computer actually prepares and sends these pieces. Some customer accounts, however, should be coded so that this step is actually skipped since the routine letters are not likely to be successful with certain customers.

Persistence

A key ingredient to successful collections is persistence. If a payment is missed and an arrangement is made, a telephone call or other response should be quickly completed. If the new arrangement is broken, another communication must quickly occur. The most successful collectors are those that persist and don't give up easily in their efforts. The collection system also needs a way to efficiently place accounts into a **suspense file**, a file for further action from which the accounts that are out for review can be pulled when the arrangements are broken.

Cost Effective

An important concern is the level of expenses generated by the collections activity. If expenses are too high, the income from finance charges (if they exist) will be quickly eaten up by these costs. Using third parties, e.g., collection agencies and attorneys, is especially expensive and should be avoided except in the most serious cases. An awareness of these costs is the first step and may often lead to more diligent in-house collection efforts before the delinquent accounts are passed on.

Legal Considerations

Various laws, both state and federal, have an impact on the collections process. Many times laws define harassment and outline various prohibited activities that can be carried on during the collection of an account. Restrictions on repossession, garnishment, and contract provisions also have an impact on collections. It is extremely important that collectors be knowledgeable about these laws.

Important Ingredients in a Collections System

- Coordination of credit and collection policies.
- Flexibility.
- Prompt response to missed payments.
- Persistence.
- Cost effective.
- Legal considerations.

A GENERAL COLLECTION SYSTEM

A well-designed collection system can be compared to a series of screens that sift delinquent customers into various categories. Earlier screens are low in cost and handle the customer gently to preserve goodwill. Later screens are less routine, cost more to apply, and may be somewhat sharper in action. They may not preserve goodwill with such certainty. The screens tend to classify reluctant debtors into much smaller and more exact assortments.

A general collection system progresses through four stages based on the collection effort involved:

1. The impersonal routine stage.
2. The impersonal appeals stage.
3. The personalized appeals stage.
4. The drastic or legal action stage.

The collection devices appropriate to each stage and the classes of debtors expected to respond at that stage are indicated in Exhibit 19–1.

Self-classification on the part of debtors is accomplished at each stage. The devices suggested for each stage are too numerous to incorporate into one operating system. When developing a system to use in a particular situation, credit managers select the devices most appropriate to their collection task and determine the frequency of use and the time that should elapse between uses. They tailor the devices used to their own situation, considering the needs of their firm and the character of their customers. They should also conform to the customs of their lines of business and territory and should deviate from custom only on the basis of well-informed judgment.

This general system conforms to the principles of effective collection. It assures that lower-cost and routine methods are used for the majority of accounts and that customers

---

EXHIBIT 19–1   A General Collection System

Stage of System	Collection Devices Available for Use	Debtors Involved
Impersonal routine	Statement—1st, 2nd, 3rd, etc. Statement inserts and stickers Notes on statements Form letters of reminder type (Note: These refer only to devices used after expiration of credit period.)	Those awaiting notice Honestly overlooked Temporarily financially embarrassed Careless or procrastinating
Impersonal appeals	Form letters appealing to: "Anything wrong" tone "Tell us your story" tone Pride in credit responsibilities Sense of fair play Seeking reply from debtor: Telephone Special letters: Registered Special delivery Trick reply	Honestly overlooked Careless or procrastinating Temporarily embarrassed Overbought Accident or misfortune Disputed account
Personalized appeals	Personal collector: Telephone Personal interview Personal letters to: Debtor Employer Credit bureau	Overbought Eventual insolvents Accident or misfortune Frauds—no intent to pay Disputed account
Drastic or legal action	Extension agreement Composition arrangement Collection agency Garnishment or wage assignment Repossession Attorney Suit Other actions	Same as debtors shown in the *personalized appeals* stage (all should have assets)

---

with more desire and means to pay meet their obligation during the early stages of the system. After the bulk of the accounts has been reduced by various low-cost methods that also preserve goodwill, the higher-cost methods are applied selectively to the remaining small number of accounts. These stronger and more emphatic methods have lower percentage returns because the potential of the group to which they are applied is lower. At this point, creditors aren't as concerned about retaining goodwill because the self-classification process has already eliminated accounts whose goodwill is important. Thus, through the four stages, the collection department gradually increases pressure up to the point that the debtor should (but, unfortunately, does not always) feel that there is no more desirable alternative than paying and that there is no escape from this conclusion.

The general system will give a sound, effective, and logical organization to the collection efforts. Skill in selecting the devices, the quality of the devices individually prepared, and appropriate timing should assure that the system is properly adapted to the firm's situation and the nature of its customers.

The Impersonal Routine Stage

In this stage the self-classification of debtors begins. Many debtors pay within the established credit period and thus are never considered in any of the four collection stages. The impersonal routine stage begins when the established credit period expires.

Some common collection devices used in this stage are impersonal statements (or bills) sent to customers, statement inserts and stickers, stamped or written notes on the statements, and various form letters of the reminder type (see Exhibits 19–2 and 19–3). Debtors who respond to the collection devices of this stage are generally those who are simply awaiting some notice that the account is overdue, those who have honestly overlooked making payment, careless or procrastinating debtors, and those who are temporarily financially embarrassed.

Mail is one of the most important means of contacting debtors. Whether using statements, inserts, or form letters, creditors should remember that their collection device is attempting to sell the debtor on the idea that the account must be paid at once. Frequent change in the wording of notes on statements and form letters is advisable. In fact, some firms keep a record of the pulling power of each form letter they use. Some firms also experiment with colored paper or colored printing to see whether it increases the effectiveness of the collection device.

In this impersonal routine stage, the firm uses a gentle nudging without giving the idea that it is seriously concerned over nonpayment. Just how soon this gentle nudging starts after expiration of the credit period varies depending on company policy as well as the type of credit account involved. Thus with weekly or semimonthly payments, a three-day grace period is common. Since installment accounts generally are paid from current income, a missed payment usually means the debtor must wait until the next pay period for future payments. Such considerations are often overlooked in planning a collection system.

The Impersonal Appeals Stage

If the mild notices in the first stage fail to produce payment or to gain some response from the debtor, a more forceful means is used to bring the indebtedness to a speedy conclusion. That is the purpose of this second stage. In this stage, collection efforts are still "impersonal" but change from a routine procedure to a nonroutine one or an appeals basis. The form letters used are no longer the routine impersonal type; they take the "anything wrong?" or "tell us your story" tone or appeal to the customers' pride in meeting their credit responsibilities or to their sense of fair play.

The use of the telephone as a collection device has increased tremendously over the past several years. In addition to its direct appeal, the telephone has a cost advantage over the use of the mails. Many firms, recognizing the value of the telephone as a collection

EXHIBIT 19–2   **Examples of Impersonal Routine Stage (stickers for statements)**

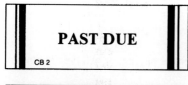

PAST DUE

CB 2

PLEASE

CB 1

WON'T YOU PLEASE
TELL US IF THERE IS ANY REASON WHY
PAYMENT HAS BEEN WITHHELD?

Thank You

CB 3

SOURCE: Courtesy of International Credit Association

EXHIBIT 19–3   **Example of Impersonal Routine Stage (form letter)**

We've searched HIGH . . .

. . . and LOW for
Your payment.

We haven't found it yet.

Will you please send it?

device, consider (when deciding to accept credit) whether an individual has a telephone listing.

After writing to a person who does not respond but who gives every indication of residing at the address used, the creditor has several alternatives that may be more effective but involve increased costs. Unusual letters such as special delivery or registered mail are used to secure some indication of whether the debtor received the inquiry. The use of certified mail, restricted delivery to addressee only, returned postage receipt showing the name of the person who signed for it, and return receipt showing address where delivered are other alternatives.

Debtors involved in this stage generally include those who: have honestly overlooked the amount in arrears, are in a temporarily embarrassing financial position, are careless in making payments or are procrastinators, have suffered a misfortune since incurring the debt, have overbought, believe the amount owed is incorrect, or have questions involving some phase of the transaction and thus dispute the amount.

The Personalized Appeals Stage

This third stage incorporates both the personal aspect and the appeals approach. All efforts are directed toward the debtor on a highly personalized basis—efforts that are the last ones before the creditor takes some type of drastic or legal action (see Exhibit 19–4). Debtors who force the creditor to this stage include those who: overbought, will eventually become insolvent (and may even resort to bankruptcy), met with some accident or misfortune, are habitual frauds with no intent of paying, or believe the amount owed is incorrect and dispute the bill.

The collection devices commonly used in this stage include personal letters (usually a series, spaced at different intervals) pointing out the drawn-out procedure the creditor has been forced to go through up to this stage. In this stage the creditor may notify the local credit bureau of the impairment of the debtor's credit standing. Personal collectors and personal contacts by phone are also commonly used at this stage.

The costs of the actions in this stage are greater than those involved in the first two stages. Personally dictated letters are one of the main weapons employed. Although personally dictated letters are initially expensive, they permit more varied and persuasive appeals than do stock form letters. Debtor reaction is generally more favorable, and the result is greater pulling power.

Drastic or Legal Action Stage

In the previous three stages, creditors consider customer goodwill before taking any action, but in this last stage the gloves are off and the honeymoon is over. Debtors involved at this stage are of much the same type as the debtors of the third stage, but the creditor now should consider what assets the debtor owns before undertaking a legal action, such as law suit. Many firms don't use the techniques discussed in this section, however, because of the possible ill feelings they can create.

Extension Agreement

An **extension agreement** is the allowance of more time to repay a debt. Under this agreement, honest and sincere people who are temporarily unable to meet their obligations may be given a longer time to pay their debts. Creditors should allow this only when they are convinced that both parties will benefit from such an arrangement.

Composition Arrangement

A **composition arrangement** is a settlement in which a group of creditors agree to accept a reduced amount as payment of their indebtedness in full. Often this type of arrangement is acceptable to the creditors only when the debtor is on the brink of bankruptcy. It also generally requires the cooperation of all creditors since no one will be willing to accept less than full payment unless everyone else does. This scaling down is done only if the debtor is honest and sincere and free from any taint of fraud. Such an arrangement enables the debtor to recover a debt-free position, while creditors receive x cents on the dollar of their indebtedness without any more drastic action.

EXHIBIT 19–4   Example of Personalized Appeals Stage

Date

Mr. John C. Slow
000 Main Street
Your City, Your State

Dear Mr. Slow:

You expect fairness from us, don't you?

Our entire collection procedure has been based on courtesy and consideration. We have been willing to cooperate with you in every way.

All, alas, to no avail.

Now, our last message to you . . . sent in all fairness.

Your account will be placed with a professional collection agency unless you pay it in full, or make satisfactory arrangements, within the next five days.

Be fair to yourself . . . your immediate action will prevent serious trouble.

Cordially yours,

(Signature)
Name typed
Title

SOURCE: Courtesy of International Credit Association

Box 19–1   Credit Management Tips . . .

Steps in Making an Effective Collection Call

1. Identify the debtor and check the address.
   Use the debtor's full name and take precautions to ensure that you are talking to the person truly responsible for payment.

2. Provide your name and the name of your employer.
   It is important that you not misrepresent yourself or the purpose of your call.

3. Ask for payment in full, of amounts due.
   In a business-like fashion ask for full payment since this is the only amount acceptable.

4. Strategic pause
   Wait for the debtor to explain when you can expect this payment or, if not forthcoming, why not.

5. Identify the true reason for nonpayment.
   If you suspect you are not getting the full story, courteously question the debtor further. Try to determine the debtor's attitude toward payment.

6. Make a realistic arrangement for payment.
   The arrangement must be realistic for both the debtor and your firm. Help the debtor uncover ways to pay the past-due amount.

7. Motivate the debtor to pay.
   Outline the benefits for payment in full and explain the importance of maintaining a good credit rating.

8. Review the arrangement and mark the rcords.
   Explain to the debtor that you will expect the payment on the arranged date and that you have written the information down.

9. Thank the debtor for their cooperation.
   Explain that they should contact you immediately in the future if payments will be delayed.

A related action is to waive or forgive interest charges when a debtor is burdened with excessive debt. This may occur when a debtor is working with a debt counseling service that is collecting funds and paying bills on behalf of the distressed debtor. The creditor agrees to accept lesser payments as part of a repayment plan and, in some cases, will apply the full amount received to the outstanding principal as long as the debtor continues to work with an approved debt counseling agency. Also, some nonprofit debt counseling agencies are funded by the lenders in a community who agree to post higher payments to an account than are actually received. For example, the debt counseling agency might retain 15 percent from a $100 payment allotted to a particular creditor. Even though the creditor receives only $85, the full $100 payment is credited to the account. The participating creditors normally require that only debtors referred by the creditors involved are eligible for this treatment.

Collection Agency

Another drastic action that a creditor can take is referring an account to a collection agency. Although there are thousands of collection agencies in the country, one of the better known groups is the Collection Service Division of Associated Credit Bureaus, Inc. Members are located in all parts of the United States and Canada and form what might be termed a *network collection service.* Each local collection service office may (and does) call on any one of the other offices for help in locating the debtor of a local creditor. The account is usually forwarded to any of the other offices involved, and personal collection effort is expended on the local level to collect the account. These local collection service offices generally have their own established collection systems, which may closely resemble the four stages just outlined.

The costs of collecting through such an agency vary considerably, although the average runs between one-third and one-half of the amount collected. The 50 percent figure is used primarily with accounts $25 or under, accounts 12 months past due, accounts that require skip tracing or litigation, and when necessary to receive payments of $5 or less.

Once an account is turned over to a collection agency, the creditor should insist that all dealings be made through the agency, that the agency furnish periodic progress reports, and that arrangements be made as to how and when collections should be remitted.

The American Collectors Association, Inc. (ACA) is a trade association representing collection agencies located in the United States, Canada, and more than 100 countries overseas. To become a member of ACA, a collection service makes an application to an affiliated state or multistate association. Once accepted at that level, it becomes an ACA member. All association members are bonded as required by their state or through ACA. ACA provides educational programs not only for collectors but for creditors and consumers as well. Since more than two-thirds of the states license or regulate collection services in some way, one of ACA's functions is to keep members informed of changing state (and federal) regulations.

Garnishment or Wage Assignment

These two actions are combined to illustrate techniques available for collecting amounts due by securing part of the debtor's income. The two actions vary considerably, however, in how they are carried out.

The right of garnishment exists in some form or other in practically every state, although it is called by varying names. **Garnishment** is a legal proceeding whereby property or money due a creditor, but in the hands of a third party, is applied to the payment of the debt. The most common outcome is a court order that requires an employer to deduct money from each paycheck and send it to the creditor. It requires a court order, in which a creditor may acquire a right to hold a third party (in whose possession goods, money, or credits of the debtor are found) liable for the debt of the defendant.

Title III of the Consumer Credit Protection Act places some restrictions on garnishment. The law limits weekly garnishments to either (1) 25 percent of after-tax pay or, (2) after-tax pay minus 30 times the federal minimum wage, whichever is less. Federal law applies only to activities related to interstate commerce, but this classification includes nearly every business that operates. The law also prohibits employers from firing an employee because his wages are subject to garnishment for one indebtedness. Every time the minimum wage rate is increased as set forth in the Fair Labor Standards Act, the amount immune from garnishment also increases.

A **wage assignment** is an agreement signed by a debtor, usually at the time the credit transaction is made, that provides in case of nonpayment, the creditor may seek a certain portion of the debtor's wages without a court order. Such an arrangement is pertinent only to the employer named in the wage assignment. In an effort to protect the wage earner, most states have placed restrictions on the use of wage assignments. Sometimes wage assignments are allowed, but the customer has the right to revoke the wage assignment at any time, a feature that will generally make the wage assignment useless. Wage assignments have sometimes been declared invalid because the employee does not receive due process, the legal protection afforded an individual by the judicial system and the ability to be heard in a court of law.

There are other restrictions on the use of garnishments and wage assignments. In some states, state employees cannot be bound by garnishment proceedings and wage assignments. Federal government employees and members of the armed forces are not generally subject to these collection devices. However, effective April 22, 1978, the U.S. Postal Service was required to honor valid court-ordered wage garnishments. This decision was based on the fact that five federal appellate courts had held that the U.S. Postal Service was not entitled to the defense of sovereign immunity in wage garnishments.

Repossession

Repossession is the legal process to take possession of goods for failure to pay amounts as agreed. A debtor may have pledged an automobile as security on a loan, for example. Repossession is the process a creditor would use to claim legal rights to possession of the automobile.

Although generally the creditor's last desire is to retake merchandise that is not paid for, this may be the only action left. The **right of replevin** specifies that if the creditor can show a title or a possessory right superior to that of the debtor, then the merchandise can be retaken in case of nonfulfillment of the terms of the contract. If a major appliance was purchased using a conditional sales contract, for example, missed payments will generally show that the title to the merchandise still belongs to the creditor since regular payments were a condition of the sale. However, the varying state laws set forth widely different provisions as to the circumstances under which replevin is applicable.

Repossession can take place only when the creditor has a secured interest in the merchandise and when a writ of replevin has been obtained after suit has been filed and judgment rendered.

Attorneys

Another technique is to turn the account over to an attorney who will act like a collection agency in attempting to secure payment. Two different approaches are found under this arrangement: (1) use of the company's own attorney, who usually contacts the debtor as a private lawyer and not as an employee of the company; and (2) use of a separate and independent attorney who attempts to collect the indebtedness on a fee or commission basis.

Suit

Collection by suit is generally considered when all other collection methods fail and when the debtor has sufficient assets against which to execute a judgment. Suit action, which is generally looked on with disfavor by the creditors of consumer debt because of possible bad publicity, accomplishes two things: (1) it establishes the legal fact that the debt exists and that it is of such an amount; and (2) it provides the creditor with a legal remedy and aid in collecting the debt. However, just obtaining a judgment does not guarantee payment. Creditors should make sure the debtor has sufficient assets against which the judgment can be entered before instituting suit.

The effectiveness of collection by suit is reduced by two modifications. First, a debt cannot be held forever. Every state has statutes of limitations that spell out in detail the length of time during which a debt may be collected and the provisions for renewing the limitation period. Second, various state laws stipulate what property and what percentage of earnings are not subject to seizure by suit. These exemptions are allowed because of the traditional belief it is an injustice to society and to the debtor to strip the debtor of all personal assets and income.

Other Actions

Small amounts can be collected in various small claims courts or, as they are known in some states, justice of the peace (JP) courts. Again, state laws governing the actions of these courts vary. No attempt has been made to list all possible drastic or legal means.

AUTOMATED COLLECTIONS SYSTEMS

The use of computers and automated systems is increasing at a very rapid rate. Modern technology has had an impact on every phase of credit management. In the area of collections, computers and automation are also taking on more responsibilities and improving overall results. Modern computer systems organize collection efforts and provide management with a vast array of useful information.

Organize Collection Efforts

In computerized collection systems, paper and pencils have been largely eliminated. The collector sits down at the computer terminal each day, types in a password and identification code, and begins working on a computer-organized list of clients. The highest priority call will appear on the screen along with data regarding the customer and the payment record. When a telephone call is made, the collector inputs the details of the arrangement, and moves on to the next customer that appears on the computer screen. Since all payments are posted on the computer system, a broken arrangement will be noticed by the computer and this customer's record will once again appear on a collector's screen for a follow-up call.

Handle Routine Communications

In many automated systems the first late notices and form letters are sent automatically after a predetermined number of days have passed beyond the payment due date. If the computer-initiated notices do not result in a payment, the customer's file will then show up in a collector's work day. Customers can be coded differently so a certain type and number of notices can be sent automatically. For example, customers who are known to ignore form letters can be drawn into the personalized appeal stage more quickly so that a telephone call will occur sooner to discuss arrangements for a payment.

Analyze Delinquency

The computer systems will constantly analyze the level of outstanding accounts and the nature of the delinquency involved. **Age analysis** is the classification of accounts according to the length of time since the last payment. Classifications of delinquent accounts typically include 30-day, 60-day, 90-day, and 90-day plus account classifications. A 30-day account, for example, is a delinquent account where a payment has not been received for at least 30 days. The account becomes a 60-day account when the payment lapse exceeds 60 days from the date of last payments. Most organizations monitor this delinquency to help them predict cash flows and analyze the success of their collections efforts.

Monitor Customer Payment Patterns

Sophisticated computer systems monitor the payment patterns of individual customers to identify their normal credit behavior. Customers who consistently pay on time will find their credit lines expanded. Good-paying customers will perhaps receive more informal notices and more gentle collection responses if a payment is missed. If the computer detects a significant slowdown in payment patterns, it often begins to reduce credit lines to lessen the exposure of the firm to potential losses. Some systems actually include programs to predict bankruptcies and other payment problems.

Evaluate Collection Personnel

Since the computer systems include all data related to payments and collection efforts, it can also be used to assess the ability of the collection department and individual collectors. The computer system, in some cases, actually totals the number of telephone calls placed by an individual collector, the number of arrangements made, and the success or failure of the communications. Employees who are successful collectors welcome the opportunity to be recognized.

Conduct Collection Calls

Although still not widely used, some systems are experimenting with computerized collection calls. Since modern computer systems include devices that can dial telephone numbers and afterwards relay verbal messages, some systems allow the computer to actually make the call and record the results. Some means must be used to determine, of course, that the correct person has answered the phone before the collection message is delivered. In the some systems, a human collector will come on the line to verify the identity of the person called, but will immediately allow the computer to deliver the appropriate message. Obviously, there are some concerns regarding the protection of individual privacy. In some of the early experiments, however, these systems are able to complete hundreds of calls in a single hour.

Automated Collections Support

- Organize collection efforts.
- Handle routine correspondence.
- Analyze delinquency.
- Monitor customer payment patterns.
- Evaluate collection personnel.
- Conduct collection calls.

Important Terms

age analysis   418
bad debt   400
composition arrangement   412
extension agreement   412
garnishment   415

right of replevin   416
repossession   416
skip   404
suspense file   407
wage assignment   416

Discussion Questions

1. Explain why collections are an inherent part of any credit business.
2. What is bad debt? What are some of the events that determine when an account is charged to bad-debt expense?
3. How can an effective collections department contribute to increased sales in a retail department store?
4. List and describe common reasons for nonpayment of debts. As you describe each reason, explain what you would do in each case to bring forth a payment.
5. What is skip tracing? Make a list of all possible contacts that could be used to locate a skip.

6. Describe four important factors that influence the collection policy outlined by a particular firm.
7. List and explain important ingredients in a collection system.
8. Describe the four stages in a general collections system. Explain how each varies in terms of tone, devices used, and goals regarding customer relations.
9. Describe six collection devices or techniques that are examples of drastic actions.
10. Explain six ways computers and automated collection systems are used in collection activities.

CASE PROBLEM

Collecting a Past-Due Payment

Bill and Betty Stevens have fallen behind in their auto loan payments. Today is January 10 and they have not made a payment since November 25. Other information regarding the loan follows:

Original balance	=	$11,000
Terms of loan	=	36 months at $349.80
Number of payments made	=	15
Current balance	=	$6,773
Date last paid	=	November 25
Previous times past due	=	2

You place a telephone collection to the Stevens' residence and speak to Betty. Choose a partner to role-play the collection calls and conversations that follow. Each situation represents a different "excuse" and will probably require different responses on your part. Follow the steps in making an effective telephone collection call.

1. Christmas Expenses

    Betty explains that they spent more for Christmas gifts than they should have. She tells you that they have just filed their income taxes and will catch up on or before April 15.

2. Problems at the Office Products Store

    Some unexpected expenses occurred at the office products store operated by Bill. He had to invest some more funds from their personal savings accounts. He doesn't know when things will pick up so they will be able to pay.

3. Check Is in the Mail.

    There must be a mistake according to Betty. They already sent the payment.

4. Unexpected Medical Bills.

    Bill hurt his back moving boxes at the store. They will pay as soon as they can.

5. Marital Problems.

    Bill and Betty may be getting a divorce. Bill moved out and took the car with him. Betty doesn't know where he has gone and she cannot afford to pay the payments.

CHAPTER

20

CONTROLLING ACCOUNTS AND MEASURING EFFICIENCY

Learning Objectives

After studying this chapter, you should be able to:

- Discuss the areas of consumer credit and business credit insurance.
- Describe options for restructuring an original agreement.
- Explain the features of an extension agreement.
- Explain what composition settlements attempt to accomplish.
- Explain an assignment for the benefit of creditors.
- Outline the process and problems connected with consumer and business bankruptcy.
- Describe debt counseling services.
- Explain the benefits and calculation of various tests of credit department operations.

In the previous chapter, coverage was placed on collection policies and practices. Emphasis was given to developing collection policy, factors affecting such a policy, and stages in an effective collection system. In this chapter, on the other hand, the role of credit insurance is explored, special situations arising in collections are treated, and tests and measurements in credit management are covered.

CONSUMER CREDIT INSURANCE

It is important to recognize a collection device used in certain consumer credit transactions: consumer credit insurance. **Consumer credit insurance** is designed to make payments on a debtor's behalf in the event of death, sickness, disability, or lost income.

422

During recent years, the use of life and disability insurance in connection with consumer credit transactions has risen rapidly. Many different types of credit-granting institutions now offer debtors this special kind of insurance, called *consumer credit insurance*. The insurance names the creditor as the first beneficiary. If the insured dies, the insurance company pays the debt in full. If the insured becomes disabled, the insurance company pays his or her periodic installments. Consumer credit insurance is divided, then, into two major categories: credit life insurance and credit accident and health insurance. Some lenders also now offer unemployment coverage in the event the borrower faces an involuntary unemployment situation.

Credit grantors can make the insurance available to their customers by offering individual policies, for which the debtor usually pays the premium, or by offering certificates of insurance under a group policy. The cost of group coverage may be paid by the creditor, or it may be shifted to the debtor through an identifiable charge. Unfortunately, some customers believe credit insurance is automatically included with their loan, while others have the misconception that it is required to obtain a loan. Misunderstandings about product features of the credit insurance are an even greater problem.

Nature of the Insurance

Credit insurance is written for the duration of a consumer loan or installment sale contract in an amount equal to the indebtedness. It is issued to debtors without benefit of a medical examination, with no restrictions for physical impairment or occupational hazards, and with a uniform charge regardless of the insured person's age.

Individual credit life insurance policies may be written either on a decreasing-term or a level-term basis. **Decreasing-term coverage** provides a benefit that decreases as the installment debt reduces, so that the protection is always equal (or approximately equal) to the debt. With **level-term coverage**, the amount of insurance in force remains the same for the duration of the debt. Decreasing-term coverage is the more popular of the two.

There are two basic kinds of **credit accident and health insurance** policies: those with an elimination period and those with a retroactive period. Under either plan, the insurance company assumes installment payments only after a stated period of disability—usually 14 days. If the policy has an elimination period, the disabled debtor is not reimbursed by the insurance company for any payments made during the waiting period. If coverage is retroactive, the insurance company reimburses the debtor for payments made during the waiting period.

Consumer credit insurance benefits both debtors and creditors. Debtors benefit because the insurance gives them protection and peace of mind, permits them to make greater use of their credit, enables them to get cosigners when needed, and is available without exclusions. Creditors benefit because the insurance serves as an added security device and relieves them of troublesome collection duties. In addition, goodwill accrues to the creditor when benefits are paid as the result of death or disability and because large numbers of consumer-debtors want such coverage.

The growth of consumer credit insurance in recent decades has been the result of several factors:

1. The public's desire for security.
2. The benefits provided by the insurance.
3. The increased use of consumer credit.
4. The passage of favorable state laws.
5. The great variety of creditors offering protection.
6. The competitive selling efforts of the insurance companies.
7. The favorable publicity it has received.
8. The "fee income" revenue to the creditor institution from the sale of the credit insurance to the debtor.

However, states regulate consumer credit insurance because: (1) the consumer is in an inferior bargaining position and is generally not versed in matters relating to insurance; (2) the insurance companies, as a selling device to creditors, tend to grant higher commissions than necessary; and (3) unscrupulous creditors, in the absence of effective laws, might use the insurance as a means of extracting extra charges from their customers.

The following rules help prevent abuses:

1. Charges for individual and group insurance and the compensation received by creditors must be limited.
2. Coverage must never exceed the amount of the debt or the term of indebtedness.
3. Debtors must be free to acquire the insurance from sources other than the creditor.
4. Creditors must give insured persons a statement or copy of the policy that describes the coverage.
5. Insurance must be canceled and unearned charges refunded when debts are prepaid or refinanced.
6. Claims must be paid by the insurance company rather than by the credit grantor.
7. Insurance companies writing the policies must be authorized to do business in the state.
8. Creditors selling individual or group coverage must be licensed or authorized by the state insurance department.
9. All policies must be reviewed and approved by the insurance department.

Business Credit Insurance

Business credit insurance is an arrangement between an insurance company and a business under which the insured firm is guaranteed payment against abnormal credit losses arising from the failure of business debtors to pay their obligations. In addition, the insured firm often receives other services and benefits from the insurance company.

Purpose of Business Credit Insurance

In Chapter 1 credit was defined as a medium of exchange of limited acceptance. Credit is of limited acceptance because of two elements: time and risk. Thus in every credit transaction there is an element of risk, and the credit manager must decide whether to bear this risk alone or to share it with someone else. The firm that factors its accounts receivable has decided to let another institution bear the task of credit acceptance and credit collection without recourse. For this service, the firm pays a fee to the factor. Credit insurance is another method of sharing this risk with others—this time with an insurance institution rather than with a financial institution. For a charge, the risk accompanying the credit transaction is shared with a specialist, just as fire, theft, storm, and public liability dangers are passed on to other types of insurance companies. Credit insurance insures against unusual loss—it does not protect the insured against normal (or primary) loss.

Life insurance certainly does not eliminate the need for doctors and attention to good health practices, and business credit insurance does not eliminate the need for credit departments and managers. But this type of insurance, which is still unused by a large segment of the business world, is a valuable management tool.

Basic Features of Business Credit Insurance

Business credit insurance is used primarily to protect manufacturers, jobbers, wholesalers, and certain types of service organizations.

Since business credit insurance is offered in a wide variety of policy forms, endorsements, and stipulations, a business credit insurance policy can be tailored to meet the needs of the policyholder. In the past, insurers wrote individual account policies, along with general coverage policies. The individual account policies covered only single accounts selected by the insured company. In recent years, very few individual account policies have been written because of the possible adverse selection of risk against the insurance company. Practically all policies now being written are of the general coverage type.

Policies may be written with or without a provision for the insurance company to handle all phases of the collection of past-due accounts. When the policy is written on an optional collection basis, the insured firm may turn over any past-due account for collection; no fees are charged on accounts collected within 10 days. The policy lists an agreed-on schedule of fees for collections beyond 10 days. Policies also may be written with no collection provision.

In a business credit insurance policy there may be two deductibles: coinsurance and primary loss. The purpose of the insurance is to cover *abnormal losses* and these deductibles allow the absorption of normal losses by the business credit department.

The insurance company and the insured agree on a **primary loss** figure as a percentage of the insured's covered sales, with a definite minimum spelled out in the policy. This deductible represents the "normal" loss for the credit department and is not reimbursed by the insurance company. The primary loss percentage varies with the risk covered, the size of the sales volume, and the insured's actual loss experience in the past.

Coinsurance is an arrangement by which an insured firm bears a specified percentage of its total losses on all insured accounts. The business credit department (the insured) participates in every loss covered by the insurance company. The coinsurance usually amounts to approximately 10 to 20 percent, although on many policies it can be waived. For example, the insurance company would only reimburse $800 for a $1,000 loss with a 20 percent coinsurance clause. The percentage paid by the insured may be higher for customers who are not rated in the first or second credit appraisal category of recognized mercantile agencies or who carry no credit appraisal at all.

Advantages of Business Credit Insurance

When a firm suffers an abnormal bad-debt loss, credit insurance has more to offer than just financial coverage.

Improved Ability to Predict Profit

Advocates of business credit insurance point out that users can have a clear idea in advance of what costs they will incur during the coming year in the form of excessive or abnormal credit losses. By combining normal losses with the premium cost paid for credit insurance, the credit manager can estimate the maximum cost fairly accurately. If a firm's expense control system is working properly and other expense items are subject to accurate prediction, the firm can then make a fairly good approximation of anticipated profits. This use of credit insurance depends on the type of policy written because some policies do not cover all possible losses on all classes of risks.

Increased Sales

Credit insurance also works on the sales side of the credit manager's operations. Some credit managers believe that purchasing credit insurance makes them more careful about accepting credit. Care is necessary in order to stay within the provisions of the credit insurance policy. Other credit managers argue that the opposite effect results. By shifting extraordinary losses to the insurance company, the insured can afford to take greater risks in credit acceptance and thus can increase sales volume. Since the insurance company covers and the insured firm retains any increased profits, credit insurance may work for freer credit acceptance on the part of some companies.

Improvement in Collection

The longer an account remains unpaid, the more difficult it is to collect. The insurance company usually stipulates that to be proved as claims, delinquent accounts must be turned over to the company within 12 months of the shipping date or within 3 months of the due date, whichever is longer. The insurance company usually takes vigorous collection action, thus increasing the chances of early collection and greater return to the creditor company. The psychological impact of collection by a third party—when the third party is an insurance company—cannot be overlooked.

Improvement in Borrowing Capacity

Most firms have to borrow funds periodically to carry on their operations. Some of these loans are unsecured; some involve assignment of accounts receivable as collateral.

Disadvantages of Business Credit Insurance

Some credit executives believe the weaknesses connected with business credit insurance overshadow any benefits. Some even go so far as to say there is no legitimate place or need for credit insurance in an efficient and well-run credit department. Despite its widespread use, not all firms need business credit insurance. Some types of firms may find credit insurance unnecessary or of little or no advantage.

Some of the most important disadvantages generally listed are cost, a false sense of security, restrictions in placing accounts for collection, limiting features of the policy provisions, and need for credit insurance as opposed to other types of insurance.

Cost

Premium payments on business credit insurance are an expense item for a business. Although credit insurance is designed to cover an abnormal or unusual credit loss, some firms find that amounts recovered from such accounts are frequently less than the premium cost over a number of years. Of course, a company cannot overlook the fact that it enjoyed protection from excess loss during the period and in one sense was fortunate that its bad debts stayed within a normal range. Similarly, individuals who buy health and accident insurance and are fortunate enough to stay well for five years may reason that they would have been ahead at the end of the five-year period if they had not taken out the insurance. Their reasoning would be very different, however, if they had required a month's hospital stay during the first year the policy was in effect. Even if no claim is made against the business credit insurance (or the health and accident insurance), remember that protection has been obtained for the premium paid.

False Sense of Security

Another important objection raised against business credit insurance is that it may cause some credit managers to rely more on insurance protection than on their own judgment. Credit insurance thus may give credit managers a false sense of security. Because excessive bad-debt losses are covered, credit managers may have less incentive to lower bad-debt losses and may exercise a freer hand in credit acceptance to receive a return from the credit insurance policies.

Collection Restrictions

Under most business credit insurance policies, accounts that have gone unpaid are turned over to the insurance company within the stipulated period of 12 months from the shipment date. Previously, this period was only six months, which sometimes precluded a credit department from exploring all friendly means of collecting the entire amount or an acceptable and fair reduced amount (composition settlement as discussed later). Lengthening this period from 6 to 12 months recognized the fact that circumstances often prevent a firm from paying within the specified credit period and that a carefully worked out arrangement between seller and buyer may result in complete recovery of the indebtedness and the maintenance of goodwill.

Limiting Policy Features

Business credit insurance does not cover all losses. Creditors must bear normal (or primary) bad-debt losses, and some criticism is leveled at the method by which this primary loss is computed.

Another debatable feature of credit insurance policies is that the insurable risk of any one customer may depend primarily on the ratings given by Dun & Bradstreet and by special mercantile agencies. To base credit decisions primarily on agency ratings fails to give due weight to all the other credit information normally available to the credit analyst. While the required limitation is justifiable from the insurance company's view, such a restriction seems to infringe on the credit manager's responsibility to weigh all the factors involved and analyze pertinent sources of information before arriving at a decision.

Credit versus Other Types of Insurance

Simply to say that a firm needs to protect its accounts receivable by insurance because insurance protects its inventory, building, and equipment against fire or "acts of God" fails to recognize the difference in the two needs. The company that has all of its inventory and equipment in one building faces the threat that a fire, flood, tornado, or windstorm could wipe out these assets in a short time. To protect against this calamity, companies carry insurance. There are companies, of course, whose plants are so widely scattered and whose danger of financial ruin because of fires and acts of God is so remote that they provide their own form of insurance through some system of reserves.

The chances that a firm's accounts receivable will be wiped out in a single disaster are very remote. Even though receivables are concentrated industrywide or geographically, it is hard to imagine a firm losing the major portion of its accounts in any one year. Nevertheless, protection against excessive loss in large accounts has proved a desirable activity for many firms.

The insurance company should never be considered as a replacement for the firm's credit department and manager. Business credit insurance is not intended to make credit executives careless in credit acceptance. Its primary purpose is to protect against the unexpected and unpreventable accidental losses that sometimes occur despite the precautions and safeguards taken by the insuring concern.

SPECIAL SITUATIONS IN COLLECTIONS

Most collection activity is relatively routine. Invoices, telephone calls, collection letters, and perhaps legal action are used to collect funds owed. Sometimes these activities and devices fail to produce payments, however, and the customer remains seriously past due. The customer usually has severe financial problems and may be contemplating bankruptcy. These situations can arise in either business or consumer credit environments. Whenever these more serious situations occur, the credit manager must be equipped to deal with these nonroutine solutions.

Business Credit Insurance

Advantages
- Improved ability to predict profit.
- Increased sales.
- Improvements in collections.
- Improvement in borrowing capacity.

Disadvantages

- Costs.
- False sense of security.
- Collection restrictions.
- Limiting policy features.
- Credit versus other types of insurance.

Restructuring the Original Agreement

This solution involves setting aside the original credit terms or contract and entering into a new agreement. In business credit, the normal terms of sale generally do not involve interest charges, so a business credit debtor may be asked to also sign a **promissory note**, an agreement to pay a sum in the future. The note will often incorporate interest charges for the time period exceeding the net credit period. In consumer credit, it is not uncommon to **rewrite a loan** which involves negotiating a new loan with the proceeds used to pay an existing loan. Even though no new dollars are typically advanced, the debtor can be brought up-to-date and given a fresh start. The new loan may also carry lower payments if the loan repayment period is extended. The creditor must believe that the new loan will be honored or the existing loan should not be rewritten. An alternative is to provide the debtor with a **payment deferral**, the agreement by the creditor to allow a payment to be skipped and added to the end of the contract. Some state statutes allow a deferral charge which often equals the interest on the unpaid balance for the remaining time period until the loan is paid in full.

If a loan agreement incorporates an **acceleration clause**, the original contract with fixed payments and an established repayment period may set aside. The acceleration clause usually requires full and immediate payment of the outstanding loan balance because the debtor has fallen behind by a specified number of payments. Since the debtor is generally not able to pay the loan, interest is charged on a daily basis at the rate stated in the original contract. This clause provides the creditor with additional interest payments that would not have occurred in the original precomputed payment schedule.

Extension Agreement

An **extension agreement**, which may be either a single-creditor or a group-creditor action, is essentially a moratorium under which the debtor proposes to pay creditors in full at some future date. This agreement is binding only on those creditors who sign it, and no creditor is compelled to do so. For this reason, if larger creditors want to grant an extension to a debtor but some smaller creditors do not agree, the smaller creditors sometimes are paid in full by the other creditors to prevent them from filing involuntary bankruptcy proceedings. Credit managers have learned to be careful in estimating the extent of the debtor's difficulties, however, before granting an extension.

Composition Settlement

This **composition settlement**, either with or without an extension of time, is a contractual arrangement under which the creditors that sign the agreement offer to accept less than the full amount of their indebtedness and in turn agree to discharge the debtor from any future obligation to make a full settlement. A group of creditors, for example, may agree to accept 75 percent of the amounts owed them as payment in full. Generally, all creditors must be involved, otherwise some will be paid in full and others will not.

Again, care should be taken to grant such settlements only to debtors who could probably operate profitably in the future if relieved of their present excessive debt burden. Also, evidence of fraud should cause any composition settlement to be set aside and the offender prosecuted to the limit.

Assignment

When an extension is not warranted and a composition settlement cannot be agreed on, "friendly" liquidation of the business and settlement of the indebtedness may come about through assignment proceedings.

Assignment for the benefit of creditors is generally considered a voluntary, out-of-court action taken by debtors who usually are insolvent (liabilities exceed assets). The debtors transfer in trust some or all of their assets to a third party, an assignee, so that these assets or proceeds from their sale can be applied to pay their debts. Such an assignment may be made under either common law or state law—every state has some form of law that spells out the provisions for an assignment.

At first glance, it may appear that assignment prevents all the ills of bankruptcy (described in the subsequent section). Advocates of this method point out that it is fast, relatively inexpensive, free from court restraints, and private, and that it provides more money for distribution to the creditors. Critics of the plan point out that:

- Assignment constitutes an act of bankruptcy.
- Debtors cannot be examined under oath.
- Recovery of preferential payments is not provided for.
- Debtors are not freed of their remaining indebtedness without the creditors' consent.
- There is a lack of uniformity in state laws concerning the procedure.
- There is little or no direct supervision over the assignee in estate administration.

Bankruptcy

Bankruptcy is a legal process in federal court whereby a debtor is declared insolvent and certain assets are liquidated by a court appointed trustee with the proceeds equitably distributed to creditors. The process has two basic purposes: to provide the insolvent debtor a fresh start and to ensure that creditors receive a fair division of available assets.

Who May File Bankruptcy?

Any person who lives in the United States, owns property, or operates a business can file for protection under the federal bankruptcy laws. It is referred to as *protection* since all legal action to collect debts must cease under an **automatic stay** provision once the individual or business has filed for bankruptcy. Banks, insurance companies, railroads, savings and loan associations, and government units cannot file for bankruptcy, although provisions do exist to help them reorganize their operations.

Types of Bankruptcy

The various types of bankruptcy are often identified by the chapter number found in the Federal Bankruptcy Code. **Chapter 7** is sometimes referred to as *straight bankruptcy* and involves the liquidation of all nonexempt assets with most remaining debts discharged. **Chapter 9** applies to municipalities; **Chapter 11** is most often used to reorganize corporations. **Chapter 12** is designed to assist family farmers in reorganizing the farm and its financial structure. **Chapter 13** is often called the **wage earner's plan** since it involves a court-approved plan to pay debts from future income. Exhibit 20–1 shows bankruptcy petitions filed in recent years.

Filing for Bankruptcy

Anyone, except the types of businesses mentioned above, may file a **voluntary petition** for bankruptcy. A husband and wife can file an individual or a joint petition. Most individuals and businesses can by forced into **involuntary bankruptcy** if a required number of creditors with sufficient debts file a petition. If a failing business continues to lose money every day, it may be in the best interest of the creditors to force a bankruptcy to save the assets that currently exist. In an involuntary bankruptcy, the first step for the court is to determine if the debtor is indeed insolvent.

The Bankruptcy Process

The bankruptcy procedures provide for an orderly process to locate assets, pay bills, and discharge debts. The following steps occur in a Chapter 7 liquidation:

1. Filing a petition. The voluntary or involuntary petition is filed in federal court. In an involuntary filing, the petitioning creditors must show that the debtor is guilty of failing to pay debts when due, or the debtor appointed a receiver or made a general assignment for the benefit of creditors within 120 days. The debtor may also be granted a trial to contest insolvency and, if the debtor wins, it can collect damages from the creditors.

2. The judge issues an order for relief that halts collection proceedings and appoints a trustee. The trustee is responsible for representing the creditors by preserving assets and

EXHIBIT 20–1   Bankruptcy Petitions Filed and Pending, by Type and Chapter: 1986 to 1994

(For years ending June 30. Covers only bankruptcy case filed under the Bankruptcy Reform Act of 1978. Bankruptcy: legal recognition that a company or individual is insolvent and must restructure or liquidate. Petitions "filed" means that commencement of a proceeding through the presentation of a petition to the clerk of the court; "pending" is a proceeding in which the administration has not been completed.)

Item	1986	1987	1988	1989	1990	1991	1992	1993	1994
Total, filed	477,856	561,278	594,567	642,993	725,484	880,399	972,490	918,734	845,257
Business[1]	76,281	88,278	68,501	62,534	64,688	69,193	72,650	66,428	56,748
Nonbusiness[2]	401,575	473,000	526,066	580,459	660,796	811,206	899,840	852,306	788,509
Voluntary	476,214	559,658	593,158	641,528	723,886	878,626	971,047	917,350	844,087
Involuntary	1,642	1,620	1,409	1,465	1,598	1,773	1,443	1,384	1,170
Chapter 7[3]	332,679	397,551	423,796	457,240	505,337	612,330	679,662	638,916	578,903
Chapter 9[4]	7	10	3	7	7	20	15	9	17
Chapter 11[5]	24,443	22,566	18,891	17,465	19,591	22,495	24,029	20,579	17,098
Chapter 12[6]	(X)	4,824	3,099	1,717	1,351	1,358	1,634	1,434	976
Chapter 13[7]	120,726	136,300	148,771	166,539	199,186	244,192	267,121	257,777	248,246
Section 304[8]	1	27	7	25	12	4	29	19	17
Total, pending ..	728,577	808,504	814,195	869,340	961,919	1,123,433	1,237,357	1,183,009	1,134,036

NOTE: X Not applicable.
[1]Business bankruptcies include those filed under Chapters 7, 9, 11, or 12.
[2]Bankruptcies include those filed under Chapters 7, 11, or 13.
[3]Chapter 7, liquidation of nonexempt assets of businesses or individuals.
[4]Chapter 9, adjustment of debts of a municipality.
[5]Chapter 11, individual or business reorganization.
[6]Chapter 12, adjustment of debts of a family farmer with regular annual income, effective November 26, 1986.
[7]Chapter 13, adjustment of debts of an individual with regular income.
[8]11 USC., Section 304, cases ancillary to foreign proceedings.
SOURCE: Administrative Office of the U.S. courts, *Annual Report of the Director.*

overseeing the liquidation. The creditors have an opportunity to select a permanent trustee later in the process if desired.

3. First meeting of creditors. A First Meeting of Creditors is scheduled and is attended by the trustee, the debtor, and the creditors. The debtor provides schedules that list income and all debts. Creditors also have a chance to examine the debtor and ask questions about assets and liabilities. Creditors also have an opportunity to file claims or to ask that their debts not be included in the process due to fraud.

4. Trustee collects assets. The trustee collects nonexempt assets, resolves secured creditor decisions, and recovers assets from fraudulent conveyances and preferences. A **preference** is simply the payment of a debt, usually within 90 days preceding a bankruptcy filing, that helps an individual creditor at the expense of the entire group. A **fraudulent conveyance** involves transferring assets to others in an effort to hide the assets or to withhold them from creditors by selling them at less than fair value.

A secured creditor must make a selection to either retain his or her security interest or to participate in the bankruptcy process. If the secured creditor elects to retain the security, the property is removed from the available property list. Generally, the debtor will retain the security and the creditor retains the security interest.

5. Debtor selects exemptions. Exemptions identify assets that will not be liquidated by the trustee. These assets remain with the debtor and are the basis for the "fresh start." The exemptions are controlled by state law, although in some states the debtor can choose between a state list of exempt assets or the federal exemptions. In most states the following assets are exempt: limited cash, residence or homestead, clothing, tools of a trade, insurance, and some equity in an automobile.

6. Distribution of nonexempt assets. The trustee must adhere to the following list of priorities in the distribution:

    a. Expenses of the bankruptcy.

    b. Debts arising from the ordinary course of business after the filing.

    c. Wages earned by employees during the 90 days preceding the filing.

    d. Fringe benefits for employees earned during the 180 days preceding the filing.

    e. Claims of grain farmers and fishermen against storage facilities.

    f. Claims by consumers for goods and services paid for but not received.

    g. Claims against the debtor for alimony payments, maintenance payments, or child support.

    h. Debts owed to the government, e.g., taxes owed for the three previous years.

    i. Remaining funds, if any, are available to the general unsecured creditors.

7. Discharge of debts. Debts are wiped out by the judge with a recommendation of the trustee. The discharge cancels the debts and further payment is not required. Certain debts continue to be fully enforceable even though the debtor has received a discharge. Some of the debts not affected by a discharge include:

    a. Taxes due any government unit.

    b. Loans where the proceeds were used for federal taxes.

    c. Debts acquired by fraud, e.g., obtained by lying about financial condition.

    d. Claims not included in bankruptcy schedules,

    e. Debts related to embezzlement or theft.

    f. Alimony.

g. Child support.

h. Fines imposed by a governmental unit.

i. Student loans, unless the loan is at least five years in arrears.

j. Purchases and cash advances from creditors that represent "loading up" prior to a bankruptcy.

The steps in a Chapter 11 or a Chapter 13 bankruptcy proceeding are obviously different since the goal is to reorganize the financial state of affairs. In a Chapter 13 bankruptcy, a plan is devised for an individual to pay creditors reduced amounts based on available income and a carefully constructed budget. Eligibility limits for a Chapter 13 debtor were increased by the Bankruptcy Reform Act of 1994 to allow unsecured debts up to $250,000 and secured debt up to $750,000. Chapter 13 bankruptcies carry less stigma of failure and are obviously preferred by creditors. Exhibit 20–2 shows how companies reorganize under Chapter 11. Again, the goal is to allow a business to survive and emerge from the process as a viable operation.

Responsibilities of Credit Managers

When becoming a party to an involuntary petition or when receiving notice of the filing of either a voluntary or an involuntary petition, credit managers should immediately take steps to protect their firms' interests. These necessary steps are as follows:

1. Stop all further credit. Mark all records to indicate that credit lines are suspended.

2. Recover as much as can be recovered. Hold up or stop payment on all checks and other remittances going to the bankrupt. Issue stoppage orders on goods in transit. Stop work on all goods in process or on order. File suit to recover goods already in the debtor's possession whenever there is a legal ground for doing so. Seize and hold all the debtor's property in your possession or that can be placed in your possession lawfully.

3. Start foreclosure proceedings on all secured claims, or take possession of all collateral or other property against which you have a lien claim; attempt possession wherever possible.

4. File proof of claim.

5. Attend creditors' meeting; cooperate in the election of a capable trustee; and see, so far as is in your power, that the estate comes under the influence of a reputable lawyer.

6. Whenever there is the slightest suspicion of fraud, assist other creditors by contributing to an investigation fund to expose further evidence of fraud. Postpone the examination of the bankrupt until the investigation is completed.

7. Assist in the examination of the bankrupt, and help other creditors to set aside voidable preferences or conveyances where they are present in the case.

8. Resist the final discharge whenever there are any grounds for opposing it; and if such grounds are present, assist in the criminal prosecution of the bankrupt.

The most important responsibility of credit managers arises out of the fact that they often have the power to decide whether to place a debtor in bankruptcy or to attempt other means

EXHIBIT 20–2   How Companies Reorganize under Chapter 11*

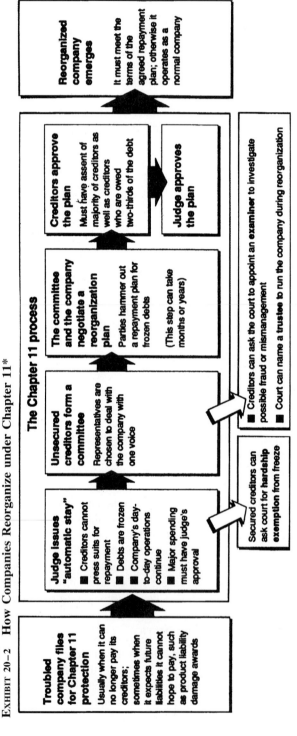

The Chapter 11 process

Troubled company files for Chapter 11 protection

Usually when it can no longer pay its creditors; sometimes when it expects future liabilities it cannot hope to pay, such as product liability damage awards

Judge issues "automatic stay"

■ Creditors cannot press suits for repayment
■ Debts are frozen
■ Company's day-to-day operations continue
■ Major spending must have judge's approval

Unsecured creditors form a committee

Representatives are chosen to deal with the company with one voice

The committee and the company negotiate a reorganization plan

Parties hammer out a repayment plan for frozen debts

(This step can take months or years)

Creditors approve the plan

Must have assent of majority of creditors as well as creditors who are owed two-thirds of the debt

Judge approves the plan

Reorganized company emerges

It must meet the terms of the agreed repayment plan; otherwise it operates as a normal company

Secured creditors can ask court for hardship exemption from freeze

■ Creditors can ask the court to appoint an examiner to investigate possible fraud or mismanagement
■ Court can name a trustee to run the company during reorganization

Note: *Chapter 11 refers to the chapter in the Federal Bankruptcy Act that provides for court-supervised reorganization of debtor companies.

Source: *St. Petersburg Times*, January 16, 1990, p. 2A. Adapted with permission from AP/Times art.

of working out a bad situation. Hastening to place every difficult collection into bankruptcy means overburdening the bankruptcy courts with unnecessary cases. Liquidation by bankruptcy may be more costly and less advantageous than liquidation by other means. The creditor, then, should consider carefully whether all other possible means of collecting the debt have been canvassed before consenting to be a party to a bankruptcy petition.

Another consideration is the debtor's attitude. If the debtor is giving preference to favored creditors or is dissipating the estate by conveyances, transferences, or concealment of property with the intent to hinder, delay, or defraud creditors, the estate must be put into bankruptcy to protect all creditors and to secure a fair and equitable distribution of the assets. If, however, the debtor is trying to be fair and is doing everything possible to protect the creditor's interests, intelligent creditors help the debtor avoid the stigma of bankruptcy and find some better way to work out the debtor's difficulties.

Adjustment Bureaus

Recognizing the need to speed up the collection process, especially in cases of insolvent and embarrassed debtors, many industries have organized some form of **adjustment bureau** or agency to help their members, particularly those in the larger market centers, deal with their overdue accounts. The National Association of Credit Management has been an outstanding leader in the development and widespread use of such bureaus, through the establishment of local adjustment bureaus within its own organization.

Adjustment bureaus have a long history. The earliest known instance of merchants organizing to help solve the problems of distressed debtors occurred in 1868 in San Francisco. Since that time, other such organizations have evolved. There is a real need for adjustment bureau intervention in many cases. Adjustment bureau administration usually is less expensive than administration by the bankruptcy court; such administration gives creditors a more immediate sense of participation; and adjustment bureaus are often able to work out long-term solutions not readily achieved through the courts.

The National Collection Service was established in 1971 by the National Association of Credit Management and has as its primary goal the development of new collection business from national and regional companies. These companies' claims are forwarded to an approved National Collection Service Bureau nearest the debtor for action.

This section should also mention the **bulk sales laws**. While not strictly a collection device, state laws generally provide that prior to the sale of a business "in bulk," the seller must give the buyer a sworn list of creditors (names, addresses, and amounts owing), an inventory of the business must be taken, and the creditors must be notified that such a sale is scheduled to take place. These laws are designed to prevent debtors from selling out at so many cents on the dollar and leaving the creditors in a precarious position in trying to collect the full amount due them—a definite problem before the passage of such laws.

Consumer Credit Counseling Service

The consumer can get credit counseling from a number of sources: nonprofit counseling centers, for-profit counseling centers, credit unions, lawyers, and many more. However, the consumer should choose his or her adviser carefully.

Nonprofit credit counseling centers are helpful to people having trouble paying their debts because the centers contact the creditors and try to arrange a repayment plan. The

Consumer Credit Counseling Service (CCCS) has more than 350 nonprofit offices in 47 states. CCCS counselors help the consumer set up a realistic budget and, on the basis of that budget, try to arrange a repayment plan. Counselors also aid consumers in developing a spending plan to cover living expenses, debt payments, and other financial obligations. The meeting between counselor and client is an opportunity for the consumer to discuss any financial-related concerns and to plan for future expenses.

If the consumer's debt is beyond a monthly budget, CCCS may suggest a debt management plan, in which creditors are asked to accept smaller payments over a longer period. CCCS disburses funds monthly until all accounts are paid in full. Some creditors stop finance charges for clients on the CCCS debt management plan. Clients agree to incur no further credit obligations while in the program.

The National Foundation for Consumer Credit is engaged primarily in efforts to inform and educate people who use consumer credit. This program of education is conducted not only for young people who will become the consumers of tomorrow but also for adult consumers who have allowed themselves to become overburdened with debt and who need immediate professional advice. The National Foundation for Consumer Credit has been dealing with the problem of consumer credit for more than 25 years through the sponsorship of locally organized and managed Consumer Credit Counseling Service offices nationwide.

MEASURING EFFICIENCY IN THE CREDIT DEPARTMENT

Too often in the rush of getting the day's work done, credit managers lose themselves in the numerous details of their work and never stop to ask exactly what their objectives are or whether they still are on the right road to accomplishing them. Without clearly defined objectives and the means of measuring progress, credit executives may waste much precious time, effort, and money exploring side roads and bypaths that do not lead to the end desired. Although they spend considerable time evaluating the success of their customers, credit managers may fail to evaluate their own performance.

Credit executives should be prepared to answer the following questions:

1. What are the responsibilities and appropriate policies for my firm's credit department in view of current and anticipated conditions?
2. What measures can I use to determine whether these policies are reached?

Responsibilities of the Credit Department

In setting the proper objectives of the credit department, credit executives have an implied responsibility to three interests:

1. To the firms that employ them.
2. To the debtors whose credit they accept.
3. To the business and social community whose well-being may be—and undoubtedly will be—affected by their actions.

The responsibility to their own firms is the most direct and readily apparent. The main objective of business management is to make profits; the intermediate objective of the credit function is to achieve maximum sales and minimum losses. This is its contribution to the profit objective. At times the credit department emphasizes the sales portion of the task; at other times, the loss-avoidance portion. Most frequently, however, it keeps both objectives in mind. To accept this ideal, however, the phrase "minimum losses" must be interpreted in the widest possible sense. By a policy of careful and persistent collections, a firm can attain low bad-debt losses, but maximum profits may not result because of high collection costs and expenses and the high costs of carrying receivables. The final result may even be considerably less profit, and in times of stress such a policy may seriously handicap the firm's operations because capital is frozen in slow-moving receivables. Nor can the time element be ignored. Over what period shall the minimum of losses and the maximum of sales be calculated? Taking substandard business may mean some customers will cause losses, but some may become tomorrow's volume buyers. Perhaps a better statement of the ideal might be to seek minimum costs and maximum gains in both the present and the future.

Credit managers also serve the interests of the debtor. Credit managers have a responsibility to the debtor just as definite and exacting as their responsibility to their own firms. As enlightened sales departments have discovered that satisfaction is one of the most vital stages in a sale, so have credit departments recognized the need for customer satisfaction in every credit transaction.

The third interest involved is the interest of society at large. The economic community in general is not a party to the transaction arranged between debtor and creditor. It occupies the role of the innocent bystander. As such, society at large is frequently injured by the actions of the immediate participants, unless the debtor exercises care in seeking additional credit and the creditor exercises care in making sure acceptance of the additional amount benefits all concerned.

Tests of Credit Department Operations[1]

Credit management's responsibility to the firm, the debtor, and society having been recognized and the objectives of credit department operations having been clearly stated, the next step should be to measure the attainment of these objectives—to test the manner in which the credit department is meeting its responsibility. The object of tests and measurements is to evaluate individual, departmental, and company performance. There is little agreement regarding which measures to use, but most firms attempt to monitor performance in some way.

Appropriate tests and measures are very helpful. They can be used to identify areas of expertise among department employees and areas where additional training is needed. Employees who are doing a good job will be recognized and measures can be used as a basis for performance appraisals and salary increases. Measures of performance can also improve policies and procedures, reduce customer complaints, and improve cash flow.

---

[1]See *Measures of Performance,* a comprehensive treatment of credit department tests and measurements published by the Credit Research Foundation and NACM.

Some of the measuring devices used for this purpose are fairly well known to most credit personnel; some of them may be familiar only to credit management personnel who have studied this phase of credit work. Many credit departments operate without any checks on their operations other than the bad-debt loss index. The tools or indexes are designed to provide credit management with some means for testing the efficiency of its credit operations. These tools help credit managers determine whether their departments are bringing about maximum sales and minimum losses. Some of the tools are described in the sections below.

The Credit Research Foundation has initiated an extensive effort to standardize many of these calculations and to provide survey information to participants. CRF publishes an *Annual Benchmarking Report* which provides comparisons by SIC code and by industry. The published data assists credit departments in checking their performance compared to others.

Bad-Debt Loss

A credit department's efficiency is often judged by rule of thumb. Successful operation is assumed to be evidenced by the manager's ability to reduce bad-debt losses or to keep them at a minimum. Even today, some credit managers boast that their businesses have lost practically nothing during the year or that losses amounted to an insignificant fraction of credit sales or total sales. Such rule-of-thumb judgments are misleading although, unfortunately, they often appeal to certain segments of top management. An exceedingly small loss record alone is not indisputable evidence of efficient credit administration. In fact, it may be an inferior basis on which to judge performance efficiency because credit managers can easily accomplish such a feat by practicing conservatism and accepting only the best risks. Such a policy often diverts business to competitors and results in lost profits.

The bad-debt loss index was one of the first tests to be developed and still is one of the tests most generally used by credit managers. The relationship is generally shown by dividing bad debts incurred during a period by total credit sales during the same period, as follows:

$$\text{Bad debt loss index} = \frac{\text{Bad debt written off}}{\text{Total credit sales}}$$

However, there is little uniformity in calculating this proportion. Some firms calculate the percentage of bad debts to total sales; others calculate the percentage of bad debts to credit sales. Also, there is no uniform practice as to the time when an account is classified as bad. Some firms leave it to an official's discretion to decide when to call an account bad; others so classify accounts after the passage of some definite time without payment; still others, after the occurrence of some definite act, such as the return of an unsatisfied judgment or a similar event. A big margin of error also exists because some accounts may be written off as bad debts shortly after they become overdue, while others may be carried for many months before they are eventually written off. Consequently, a substantial portion of the bad debts recorded for a given year may have resulted from credit decisions or collection procedures in the preceding year. Yet they are compared with credit sales in the current year, and conclusions drawn from the ratio are applied to the current year's credit and collections policies. Furthermore, because of this lag in bad-debts recording, a substantial change in sales volume may introduce a misleading variation in the bad-debt ratio. Thus, when sales for credit are increasing while cash sales are remaining fairly stationary, the base on which the index is computed will increase and cause a more favorable showing than is justified.

Percentages of bad-debt losses naturally vary with different lines of business, competitive conditions, the month or season of the year, and general business conditions. Proper interpretation of bad-debt losses requires comparison between the current year's business, business for previous periods, and bad-debt losses by other firms operating under similar conditions. Data for comparison with other firms is increasingly available from various credit and trade associations and the federal government. However, credit managers should be cautious when using the bad-debt ratios of other sellers to determine a "sound" ratio for their own companies. The bad-debt ratio of any other business for a single year is of little value as a guide because of the lag factor just discussed. Furthermore, if the other company operates on a higher or lower profit margin, its "sound" bad-debt ratio should be smaller or larger. If the difference in profit margins is known, an adjustment should be made for it. Trend analysis of a company's bad-debt ratios over a few years does not, by itself, indicate whether its credit or collection policies are becoming more strict or more lax. General business fluctuation and particular regional and trade developments influence the bad-debt ratio more profoundly than changes in a firm's credit and collection policy.

Too great a reliance on the test of bad-debt losses is dangerous since it tends to overemphasize caution in accepting credit. The company's policy should be to hold the proportion within normal limits. And these normal limits should be determined, for each firm, on the basis of the profit margin it works on.

Days Sales Outstanding (DSO)

This is the most common measure of performance for credit and collection departments. It is basically the level of accounts receivable measured by the number of days worth of sales outstanding. The base calculation is as follows:

$$\frac{\text{Outstanding accounts receivable}}{\text{Average daily sales}} = \text{Days sales outstanding}$$

To complete this calculation for a calendar quarter, a credit manager would divide average accounts receivable for the three months by average daily sales for the quarter. Mathematically, the formula eventually becomes:

$$\text{DSO} = \frac{\text{Last three months ending total receivable balance}}{\text{Credit sales for the quarter}} \times 30$$

$$\text{DSO} = \frac{\$15,000 + \$16,000 + \$17,000}{\$45,000} \times 30 = 32 \text{ days}$$

The calculation would suggest that this firm has 32 days worth of sales invested in its accounts receivable. If the DSO number grows, the general feeling is that the credit department is not doing as well and not collecting accounts effectively.

Those who have carefully studied DSO results, however, point out that the calculation incorporates significant sales bias. In other words, DSO calculations may be dramatically different as sales vary over a period of time. Opponents of DSO say that it fails to allow for seasonal sales changes or for periods of poor sales. As the DSO number varies, it will be largely unrelated to the efficiency of the credit department. Recently, much has been written about DSO in popular periodicals and alternative calculations have been discussed. Among the newer calculations are: Best Possible DSO, Sales-Weighted DSO, Average Days Delinquent, and True DSO.

Past-Due Index

This test of credit management measures the proportion on all past-due accounts, in amount or in number. It is computed by dividing the total past due by the total outstanding as follows:

$$\text{Past-due index} = \frac{\text{Total accounts receivable past due}}{\text{Total accounts receivable}}$$

When this past-due index is computed for several successive periods, it serves as a barometer indicating whether the general trend of poor pay is up or down. If this percentage increases faster than it should at any given time, credit management can take steps to curb the trend or bring it back to its normal position (which can be ascertained from records maintained over a period of years).

Collections Effectiveness Index (CEI)

This percentage calculation expresses the effectiveness of collections efforts over a period of time. Better collections efficiency is indicated as the resulting number moves closer to 100 percent. CEI was developed by Dr. Venkat Srinivasan of SR Research in cooperation with the Credit Research Foundation as another measure of performance. It is generally agreed that sales bias is removed in the following:

$$\text{CEI} = \frac{\text{Beg Tot Recv} + (\text{qrtly credit sales}/3) - \text{End Tot Recv}}{\text{Beg Tot Recv} + (\text{qrtly credit sales}/3) - \text{End Current Recv}} \times 100$$

Beg = Beginning

Tot = Total

Recv = Receivables

qrtly = Quarterly

End = Ending

This calculation compares the amount collected (numerator) with the total amount collectable (denominator). The collection effectiveness index has an advantage over the bad-debt loss calculation because it can often be figured earlier and can help forecast difficulties in collection far enough in advance for the company to take corrective measures. Collection percentages, when decreasing, generally show an accumulation of poor accounts or a slackening of collection efforts. These measures of credit activity should enable credit management to detect the effects of unsound policies. For example, a falling collection percentage may indicate unduly lenient terms, solicitation of unsound classes of customers, and a yielding to competitive temptations to outdo others in credit. In addition, unduly stringent collection activity, overly conservative credit acceptance, and undue hesitation in taking risks can be detected earlier by studying the trend of collection percentages.

Credit Department Cost Calculations

Several calculations are possible to monitor the costs of operating a credit department. Although offering credit purchase options may not be a choice for top management, an attempt to follow credit department cost is worthwhile.

$$\text{Cost per credit sales dollar} = \frac{\text{Total operating costs for dept.}}{\text{Credit sales}}$$

$$\text{Cost per credit employee} = \frac{\text{Total operating costs for dept.}}{\text{Number of employees}}$$

$$\text{Cost per transaction} = \frac{\text{Total operating costs for dept.}}{\text{Number of transactions}}$$

Comparisons between different firms, even in the same industry, can be difficult due to different organizational structures and cost allocation systems. Costs should include wages, fees and dues for credit information, legal expenses for collections, equipment, and collection agency fees. When comparing this index over time, costs should be added and assigned in the same fashion from one period to the next.

Acceptance Index

The number of acceptances indicates the firm's attitude toward applications, the quality of the applicants, and the credit policy currently being followed. The acceptance index shows the percentage of applications for credit that are accepted.

This is computed as follows:

$$\text{Acceptance index} = \frac{\text{Applications accepted}}{\text{Applications submitted}}$$

The acceptance index varies considerably, depending on the firm's line of business, the leniency or strictness of its credit-granting policies, and the stage of the business cycle.

Number of New Accounts Opened

The credit department's activity is reflected by the number of new accounts it opens during the period in question. This figure indicates the extent to which the business emphasizes credit service and whether or not it is alert to opportunities for attracting new trade. The number of new accounts opened may also measure the effectiveness of credit publicity. This figure, together with the acceptance percentage, measures the leniency or strictness of the business's credit policy.

Age Analysis of Accounts Receivable

Age analysis is classifying accounts according to the period of time they are past due. Typical categories include: current or not due, 30-days past due, 60-days past due, 90-days past due, and more than 90-days past due. This activity stems from the fact that there is a direct and important relationship between the length of time that an account has been outstanding, the rate of collection, and the probable net loss from bad debts. Age analysis helps credit workers identify the most important collection tasks and assists in predicting cash flow.

Aging of accounts can be supplemented with a detailed itemized list of overdue accounts, showing both the name and present status of such accounts. A list of this kind is valuable in authorizing additional requests for credit.

Interpreting Results

These figures and calculations should be compared with those for previous months and with those for the same month of as many preceding years as possible. Such an accumulation of figures over a period of years helps the credit manager to recognize seasonal trends that should be considered in any analysis. Likewise, comparisons with similar firms give some indication of the subject firm's relative standing.

These indexes reflect only averages; certain accounts may be falling behind in payments at the same time that overall collection tests disclose a favorable picture. Credit management personnel should recognize this situation and allow for it in any analysis based on averages.

Improvement in a firm's collection percentage may reflect improved economic conditions even before an increase in credit and cash sales. This situation arises because consumers tend to repay previously incurred debts before assuming new ones. Conversely, a decline in economic conditions is more likely to be reflected earlier in declining credit sales than in declining collection percentages. This results from the debtors' reluctance to make additional credit purchases until they are sure they can pay for them. Proper analysis of these pending changes should enable credit management to carry out its obligation to the firm, the firm's customers, and society.

Presenting the Measured Results

Justifying credit operations as an important division of the business is easier and more certain when the credit department can show the facts of its own operations. Computers have obviously improved the ability of everyone to collect, retain, and manipulate data related to accounts receivable and performance. Computer-generated charts and reports may be used to present various measures of the department's success—or failure—to top management. For example, by using bar charts showing the aging of receivables and line charts illustrating the seasonal influence on collection ratios, the credit manager can give "the boss" much of the story at a glance and be better prepared to present information justifying the credit department's operation and budget.

Important Terms

Discussion Questions

1. How do you account for the fact that collections are an inherent part of any credit business?

2. What is the purpose of consumer credit insurance? How does it help both the debtor and the creditor?

3. Explain the two main categories of consumer credit insurance.

4. Explain why states should regulate this type of insurance.

5. Explain why a firm might use business credit insurance.

6. Are collections stimulated by business credit insurance coverage?

7. What are some options for restructuring an original agreement as part of a collection effort?

8. When would you recommend that an extension agreement be used? A composition settlement?

9. What is the primary purpose of bankruptcy?

10. What are the important steps in a Chapter 7 bankruptcy?

11. Explain the purposes of consumer credit counseling services.

12. It is said that the credit executive has an implied responsibility to three interests. What are these interests?

13. How can various tests and measurements of a credit department operation be used?

14. How would you define a bad-debt loss?

15. Discuss why accounts receivable should be aged.

Suggested Readings—Part VII

Collections Management and Control

Blakeley, Scott E. "Chapter 9 Bankruptcy and Unsecured Creditors." *Business Credit,* March 1995, p. 8.

Briggs, Janet M. "Highlights of the Bankruptcy Reform Act of 1994." *Credit World,* March/April 1995, p. 14.

Callahan, W. Terrence. "Improving Performance through Benchmarking." *Business Credit,* January 1996, p. 42.

Chek, Larry. "When Filing an Involuntary Bankruptcy Petition Makes Sense." *Business Credit,* October 1995, p. 41.

Daly, James J. "It's Getting Harder to Hide." *Collections & Credit Risk,* March 1996, p. 57. (Skiptracing)

Dockery, Darrell. "Deductions: 'Cashflow Killer.' " *Business Credit,* March 1995, p. 44.

Fishman, Robert M. and Brian L. Shaw. "The Involuntary Bankruptcy Proceeding." *Business Credit,* October 1996, p. 16.

Flock, Michael. "Automation in the Collections Industry." *Credit World,* November/December 1996, p. 19.

Henderson, Michael J. "How to Elude Bankruptcy Preference Claims." *Business Credit,* March 1995, p. 12.

Hutnyan, Joseph D. "Congress Changes Bankruptcy Rules." *Credit Union Magazine,* December 1994, p. 38.

Laughlin, Alex. "Top Ten Things to Do When a Bankruptcy Is Filed." *Business Credit,* April 1996, p. 7.

Leibowitz, David P. "Organization of Creditors' Committees in Chapter 11." *Business Credit,* October 1996, p. 27.

Middleton, Martha. "Is DSO DOA?" *Collections and Credit Risk,* December 1996, p. 21.

Mines, Ron. "Listening + Training + Negotiating = Successful Collections." *Credit World,* January/February 1996, p. 16.

Snyder, Jesse. "Credit Coverage: Nutty or Nifty?" *Collections and Credit Risk,* December 1996, p. 45.

Weinberg, Joel B. "Non-Bankruptcy Alternatives for the Financially Distressed Business." *Business Credit,* October 1995, p. 19.

Whiteside, David E. "Collections Goes Online," *Collections and Credit Risk,* January 1996, p. 35.

Internet Sites

http://www.abiworld.org   American Bankruptcy Institute

CASE PROBLEM

Measuring Collections Efficiency at Office Supply, Inc.

Bill has gathered the following information from the quarterly financial records of Office Supply, Inc. Use the information to calculate the tests and measurements indicated.

Beginning total receivables for the quarter	$12,500
Ending total receivables for the quarter	13,500
Ending current receivables for the quarter	8,000
Quarterly credit sales	50,000
Ending total receivables by month	
Month 1	17,000
Month 2	18,000
Month 3	13,500
Bad-debt loss this quarter	$ 1,000
Twenty five new credit applications were received.	
Twenty accounts were opened.	

Calculate the following:

Days sales outstanding

Collections effectiveness index

Past-due index

Bad-debt index

Acceptance index

GLOSSARY

AOG (Arrival of Goods)   Terms of sale where the time period for cash discounts and payment periods begins when the goods arrive at their destination.

Acceleration Clause   A credit installment contract clause which provides that in the event a specified number of payments is past due, all remaining payments are due and payable at once, or on the demand of the contract holder.

Acceptance Index   A ratio that shows the percentage of applications for credit that are accepted.

Account Receivable   An accounting entry which records the funds due on accounts from customers arising from sales or services provided.

Acid-Test Ratio   Also called the *quick ratio,* a ratio that divides the most liquid current assets, not including inventory, by current liabilities.

Add-On Method   The amount of finance charge is computed before the loan is made and is added to the loan amount.

Adjustable Rate Mortgage   A real estate loan that provides for periodic adjustments in the interest rate during the repayment period.

Adjusted Balance Method   The finance charge on the previous month's ending balance less any payments or credits.

Adjustment Bureau   Agencies that assist in the collection of debts.

Adjustment Period   This describes how often the interest rate on the mortgage will be adjusted.

Adverse Opinion   The auditor states that as a whole, the financial statements are not presented fairly in conformity with generally accepted accounting principles.

Affinity Cards   General-purpose credit cards issued to members of a group that share a common bond, such as members of the same organization.

Age Analysis   The classification of accounts according to the length of time since the last payment.

Aging of Accounts   A detailed analysis of accounts, such as: not due, 30-days past due, 60- days past due, and over one-year past due.

Amortization   The systematic and continuous payment of the principal balance on an obligation through installments until the debt has been paid in full.

Amortization Table   A listing of payments for an installment loan which shows the interest paid, the principal due, and the remaining balance after each payment.

Amortized Loan   A direct-reduction mortgage loan.

Annual Percentage Rate   A standardized calculation that incorporates interest and other fees to show the total cost of the loan averaged over the entire loan term.

Anticipation Rate   Added inducement to get the buyer to pay early by allowing him or her to deduct interest for the number of days he or she is paying ahead of the due date.

Asset Resources, property, and other items of value used in the operation of a family or business.

Assignment for the Benefit of Creditors A voluntary, out-of-court action taken by debtors who are usually insolvent and who transfer in trust some or all of their assets to a third party so these assets, or the proceeds from their sale, can be used to pay debts.

Assumption Clause A prospective buyer of a home may be able to keep the mortgage currently in force for the seller.

Authority to Purchase An authorization to a bank to purchase, on behalf of a foreign bank, the documentary draft drawn by the seller on the buyer.

Authorization The control of the quantity of credit used by the customers.

Automated Teller Machine (ATM) Equipment that enables consumers to perform various banking transactions such as deposits, cash withdrawals, inquiries as to account balances, and account transfers using remote terminals without the aid of a human teller.

Automatic Stay A provision of the bankruptcy process that halts all legal action to collect debts once a petition has been filed.

Average Daily Balance Method The finance charge varies according to the point in the billing cycle when the customer makes a payment.

Bad Check A check (order to pay) for which payment is refused by the financial institution, usually due to insufficient funds in the account the check is written on.

Bad-Debt Expense An expense category in a firm's financial records for recording uncollectible debts.

Bad-Debt Loss Index A ratio that is computed by dividing the amount of bad debts written off by total credit sales during a period of time.

Balance Sheet A statement of the financial condition of a company as of a moment of time.

Balloon Mortgage A type of loan that can be computed on a fixed rate for any number of years payback with a balloon payment for the remainder of the loan placed at any given year.

Balloon Payment Clause In a mortgage, requires that a fixed-rate, long-term loan be paid off at the end of a specified time period.

Banker's Acceptance Drafts or bills of exchange drawn against the buyer's bank.

Bank Holding Company A company that holds a controlling interest in one or more commercial banks.

Bankruptcy In addition to the condition of insolvency, there must also be some legal and public recognition of the condition, coupled with some specific act or acts on the part of the debtor or creditor or both.

Base Interest Rate The interest rate that the various caps are figured on, generally the sum of the index and the margin rate at the time the loan is applied for.

Bond A written contract that contains a promise to pay a sum of money at a fixed future time.

Bulk Sales Laws State laws that are designed to prevent debtors from selling their assets and inventory at bargain prices prior to going out of business; protects general creditors.

Business Credit The credit relationships involved in purchasing goods for resale, or obtaining funds to operate, using credit as the medium of exchange.

Business Credit Insurance Used primarily to protect manufacturers, jobbers, wholesalers, and certain types of service organizations by paying the insurance holder for abnormal credit losses.

Business Credit Manager An occupation involved in the promotion, analysis, and collection of business credit.

Business Cycle The up and down variations in the levels of total spending and productive activity that occur within our economic system.

Business Information Report (BIR) A credit report issued by Dun & Bradstreet which incorporates several sections regarding the payment history, financial strength, and operations of a business.

Business Report A report prepared by a consumer credit reporting agency regarding a small business and its owners, often a partnership or sole proprietorship.

Capacity The ability of a credit applicant to pay a specific dollar obligation when it is due.

Capital The financial strength of a credit applicant, primarily determined by the level of reserve assets.

Capital Lease   A situation where substantially all of the benefits and risks of ownership are transferred by a lease.

Cash Advance   A loan obtained with a general-purpose credit card that provides the borrower with cash up to the existing cash-advance limit and at terms specified at the time the card is issued.

Cash Credit   An arrangement where a borrower obtains funds from a lender in exchange for an agreement to repay the funds later, generally with interest charges.

Cash Discounts   This may be allowed for early payment of an account.

Cash Discount Period   Period of time the cash discount is allowed.

Cash Flow Estimate   A calculation to estimate discretionary income; income minus estimated expenses.

Cash Flow Forecast   A planned procedure for estimating cash receipts and disbursements over a specified period of approximately 10 days from the date of invoice.

Cashier's Check   A draft issued by a bank drawn on its own funds and signed by an official or officer of the bank.

Cash Terms   Do not indicate the immediate payment of cash but the acceptance of credit for a period approximately 10 days from the date of invoice.

CBD (Cash before Delivery)   Prepayment terms that require payment before the goods will be shipped to the buyer.

Certified Check   An ordinary check that has been accepted by an official of the drawee bank; the check is generally stamped and the funds set aside for payment.

Character   An intangible sum of personal attributes related to integrity and the moral strength of a person.

Charge Card   A card, plate, or any other single device that may be used from time to time to obtain credit that is not subject to a finance charge.

CIA (Cash in Advance)   Prepayment terms that require payment before the goods will be shipped to the buyer.

Class Action Suit   Occurs when a plaintiff initiates a lawsuit on their own behalf and on behalf of any others who may have the same claim against the defendant.

Clean Draft   A draft used in international trade without title documents, often used when the importer has already received the goods and the draft is being sent through banking channels to obtain payment.

COD (Cash on Delivery)   A term of sale where the buyer must pay the agent delivering the goods.

Coinsurance   A provision of an insurance policy where the insured bears a specific percentage of all losses.

Collateral   The assignment of ownership rights of property in the event a credit customer does not pay.

Collateral Note   A promissory note secured by personal property.

Collection Activities   Any effort to get credit customers to pay their bills, or payments, in a timely manner.

Collection Effectiveness Index   A percentage calculation that measures the effectiveness of collection efforts over a period of time.

Collection Policy   A guideline to help credit workers decide which collection devices to employ and how to proceed when attempting to collect amounts owed to the firm.

Commercialized Reporting Agencies   Agencies that collect, retain, and sell information about the credit histories of consumers and businesses.

Commercial Finance Company   A principal source of accounts receivable financing.

Commercial Paper   Short-term, unsecured debt instruments (IOUs) issued by major corporations in need of funds.

Common Sense   This is simply good judgment.

Community Property State   A state that has laws that provide equal ownership of all property by spouses obtained during a marriage regardless of how the property is titled.

Compensating Balance   A fraction of the line of credit the borrower is expected not to withdraw.

Composition Arrangement   A contractual agreement under which the creditors that sign the agreement offer to accept less than the full amount of the indebtedness.

Conditional Sales Agreement   A contract that outlines the terms and payments required to purchase an item on credit and which also provides that actual ownership of the item does not pass to the buyer until all payments have been made.

Conditions   A credit analysis category that looks at how the applicant fits into the economic system and how economic events will affect the ability and willingness to pay.

Consignment Terms   Transferring goods for sale to another person or business without a transfer of ownership; seller does not hold title to the goods but sells them on behalf of the owner.

Consumer Credit   The use of credit as a medium of exchange for the purchase of finished goods and services by the ultimate user.

Consumer Credit Insurance   Written for the duration of a consumer loan or installment sales agreement, a policy that pays on death or disability of the debtor.

Consumer Credit Reporting Agencies   Credit reporting agencies that prepare credit reports regarding the credit histories and creditworthiness of consumers as opposed to businesses.

Consumer Finance Companies   Corporations that make loans to consumers under state-enacted regulations.

Continuous Service   Automatic notification of recent developments affecting accounts.

Control   A management task that involves verifying or checking progress of an activity followed by efforts to correct deviations.

Control Functions   Used to monitor an account to ensure that total indebtedness is appropriate for an individual customer.

Cost Analysis   Helps make sounder policy decisions regarding credit activities by uncovering the true costs of different activities, e.g., credit costs per credit employee, costs per credit sales dollar.

Cost of Goods Sold   The cost of the manufactured product or inventory sold by a business.

Credit   A medium of exchange with limited acceptance.

Credit Accident and Health Insurance   Insurance that pays installment loan payments on behalf of a disabled debtor.

Credit Bureau   A firm that collects, retains, and sells information related to the credit histories of consumers.

Credit Bureau Inquiries   Listings that show what creditors or parties have requested a particular credit file.

Credit Bureau Report   Contains payment histories along with other information gathered from public records, collection agencies, and others.

Credit Card   A card that is subject to a finance charge.

Credit Card Bank   A special bank with limited functions that can only offer credit card lending.

Credit Character   The willingness of credit customers to pay their payments as agreed.

Credit Counseling Centers   Helpful to people having trouble paying their debts; place where budgets are constructed and repayment plans are worked out.

Credit Decision   A judgment made by the credit manager to accept or reject an application for a credit purchase.

Credit Investigation   A series of steps undertaken to verify information on the credit application and determine how the customer has handled past financial obligations.

Credit Limit   The maximum dollar amount that can be charged to a credit account for the account to remain in good standing.

Credit Line   A preauthorized spending limit that is assigned to a credit customer which automatically allows additional purchases up to a certain amount.

Credit Manager   An individual within a business organization responsible for evaluating customer applications for credit who holds the power to commit business resources in a credit transaction.

Credit Management Process   A series of steps that involves promoting credit purchase options, analyzing the risk of credit applications, and collecting the payments after the debt is created.

Credit Period   The length of time allowed the buyer before payment is considered past due.

Credit Policy   A written policy statement used by a credit department to define the types of credit offered and to state the basic characteristics of an acceptable risk.

Credit Scoring System   A statistically based form, or computer program, that assigns points to different facts reported on the application and on the credit bureau report.

Credit Terms   Same as terms of sale; understanding between buyer and seller regarding payment for goods and services.

Credit Union   An association of people who decide to save their money together and make loans to each other at relatively low interest rates.

Creditor The party that is owed value or payment in a credit transaction.

Creditworthiness The ability of a business or consumer to obtain goods, services, or money by using its promise to deliver payments in the future.

Cross-Selling Looking for opportunities to sell other services offered by the firm.

Current Assets Include cash and other assets that in the normal course of events are converted into cash during one operating cycle.

Current Liabilities Obligations to be paid within the next year or within the next operating cycle.

Current Ratio A ratio computed by dividing current assets by current liabilities.

Cycle Billing The names in the credit files are divided systematically and statements are rendered to a different group of customers each working day of the month.

CWO (Cash with Order) Prepayment terms that require payment before the goods will be shipped to the buyer.

Daily Simple Interest Method This is different from the add-on method in that it is figured on a daily interest rate—usually 1/365th of the annual finance charge—that is added to the daily outstanding balance of the cash loan.

Days Sales Outstanding The number of days worth of sales currently owed a business, computed by dividing total accounts receivable by average daily sales.

Dealer Reserve An account maintained at a bank as part of an agreement between a retailer who wishes to sell installment contracts and the financing organization that will be purchasing contracts.

Debenture A note generally issued by a business that is unsecured and, as such, is backed only by the earning power of the business.

Debit Card A plastic card used to electronically access funds stored elsewhere for payment for goods and services.

Debtor The party that owes value or payment in a credit transaction.

Debt Ratio Total monthly debt payments divided by monthly income.

Debt-to-Net Worth Ratio A ratio computed by dividing total debt by owners' equity or net worth.

Decreasing Term Coverage Life insurance coverage where the death benefit decreases over time, often equal to the declining balance on an installment loan.

Default Insurance Provides a mortgage payoff on behalf of the borrower if he or she does not pay.

Demographic Information Data related to the identity and location of the family.

Depreciation The process of allocating the cost of a long-term asset over the life of the asset.

Direct Inquiry The process of contacting employers, credit grantors, and other individuals who can verify facts and provide information about an applicant's willingness and ability to pay.

Disclaimer of Opinion An auditor's opinion where the auditor declines to provide an opinion regarding the preparation and accuracy of financial statements, often due to incomplete information.

Discount Loan A loan arrangement where the interest for the entire loan period is deducted at the time the loan proceeds are distributed.

Discount Rate The interest charged by the Federal Reserve System for loans made to commercial banks that belong to the system.

Descriptive Billing A machine-produced monthly statement showing various financial figures pertaining to a customer.

Disclaimer of Opinion When an auditor is unable to form an opinion as to the fairness of the financial statements and thus disclaims an opinion.

Documentary Draft Drafts accompanied by the title documents and papers essential to the shipment, such as bills of lading, insurance certificates, and shipping documents.

Down Payment A cash payment made by the buyer to cover a portion of the full purchase price.

Draft An order to pay a certain sum on demand, or at a definite time, to another person.

Durable Goods Manufactured products with a relatively long life and long-term utility.

EDI (Electronic Data Interchange) Business-to-business exchange of documents using electronic transmission.

Electronic Funds Transfer System Utilize telephone lines and electronic messages to transfer funds.

Employment Information   Data related to the name of an individual's employer, position held, income, and length of service.

Export Credit Insurance   Protection to the creditor against defaulting foreign customers.

Export-Import Bank (Exim Bank)   A government agency responsible for assisting businesses involved in export sales by providing a variety of loans, loan guarantees, and insurance services.

Export Terms of Sale   The understanding between buyer and seller regarding payment for goods and services in export trade.

Extension Agreement   A moratorium under which the debtor proposes to pay creditors in full at some later date.

Extortionate Credit Transactions   Transactions with exorbitant or excessive charges.

Extra Dating   A term of sale that provides extra time for buyers to pay in an effort to encourage them to order early.

Fact   Information that has been objectively verified as real information.

Factor   A financial institution, or other agency, that purchases the accounts receivable of a business from clients and assumes all credit risks involved.

Factoring   A service that involves accounts receivable financing where the financing institution purchases accounts receivable as they arise and assumes all credit risk.

Fair Credit Reporting Act   Effective 1971, regulates the credit reporting agencies, provides access to information by consumers, and includes methods and formats, so that today treatment of consumers is uniform.

Falsification of Financial Statements   Placing untrue conditions on a statement in order to deceive credit analysts.

FDIC (Federal Deposit Insurance Corporation)   Provides protection of deposits in commercial banks.

FIRREA (Financial Institutions Reform, Recovery, and Enforcement Act of 1989)   Changed the savings and loan industry and its federal regulation.

Finance Charge   An additional amount that must be paid over and above the value received by the debtor in the credit exchange process.

Financial Capital   The money needed to start, maintain, and operate a business.

Financial Statement Analysis   The calculation of various financial ratios, and other computations, using numbers drawn from financial statements.

First Mortgage   Provides the lender with the first claim on the value of the real estate in the event the borrower defaults on the loan and cannot pay.

Fiscal Policy   Controlled by Congress, it implements laws to change taxes and the levels of government spending.

Fixed-Rate Mortgage   A loan secured by real estate that carries a predetermined, fixed rate of interest for the term of the repayment period.

Foreclosure   A legal procedure in which the lender exercises their security interest in the property and forces the sale of the property to try to pay off the mortgage if the borrower does not pay.

Formal Application   A comprehensive form that is used to gather information about the applicant's credit qualities followed by a personal interview with a credit analyst to go over the facts outlined.

Fraudulent Conveyance   Transferring assets to others in an effort to hide the assets or to withhold them from creditors by selling them at less than fair value.

Full Recourse   Dealers sell or sign over to the bank installment sale paper that they have originated, with their unconditional guarantee and with full responsibility for the paper should the purchaser become delinquent.

Garnishment   A legal proceeding whereby property or money due a creditor, but in the hands of a third party, is applied to the payment of the debt.

General Mercantile Agency   A business credit reporting agency whose primary function is to supply credit reports on business concerns of all sizes and types.

General-Purpose Credit Cards   Revolving credit card accounts used to purchase a wide variety of goods and services from merchants that have agreed to accept these cards in lieu of cash.

Grading the Credit   The examination of evidence and the recording of the quality judgment drawn from specific evidence bearing on specific factors in an orderly manner.

Gross Margin   Net sales less cost of goods sold.

Halo Effect   A problem in making credit decisions arising from the inability to consider all facts if one fact becomes overwhelming, i.e., a high income.

Home Equity Line of Credit   An open-end credit plan with a loan reserve based on the equity owned by the borrower in real estate.

Home Equity Loan   An installment loan secured by the equity, or net worth, in real estate after subtracting outstanding first mortgage balance from the market value.

House Standard   Guide by which credit managers may judge the pertinent qualities of credit risks seeking to purchase from their firms.

Identification   The technique of making sure the person purchasing is the party who has an account and not an imposter.

Income Statement   Covers a period of time and reflects the sales, costs of goods sold, expenses, and net profit or loss during the interval covered.

Independent Sales Organizations (ISOs)   Provide banks with outside assistance in finding and signing up additional cardholders and retail and service concerns in order to expand their bank credit card programs.

Index   An arbitrary index that is outside the control of the lender and is used to determine the changes in the interest rates when each adjustment occurs with an adjustable rate mortgage.

Indirect Lender   A financial institution, e.g., bank or consumer finance company, that purchases installment credit contracts as they are created by the seller of the goods.

Industrial Banks   Banking companies organized under the industrial loan laws that exist in some states primarily for the purpose of making consumer installment loans.

In-File Credit Report   The most common report; involves the credit bureau providing all the information as it currently exists in the bureau files.

Inflation   A general rise in the prices of goods and services.

Informal Application   A relatively short credit form that is completed by the customer and delivered to the credit grantor for processing.

Initial Interest Rate   The beginning interest rate for the loan which may be used as a marketing device to attract borrowers.

Initial Screening   The efforts by credit personnel to make quick, cost-effective checks to see if a credit applicant meets the basic criteria for opening a credit account.

Installment Loans   Loan arrangements where a series of fixed, regular payments are made by a borrower to repay the funds over a period of time in the future.

Installment Terms   Found in the installment credit agreement; outline the amount, frequency, and timing of the regular payments.

Intangible Asset   Assets used in the operation of a business that do not have physical properties, e.g., goodwill, patents.

Inventory Financing   A form of credit extended by a lender to a retail dealer to enable the dealer to carry an adequate supply of goods for display and sale.

Investigation Policy   A written guideline to help credit investigators gather sufficient information to arrive at a sound decision.

Investigative Consumer Reports   Credit reports that contain information about a consumer's character, general reputation, personal characteristics, or mode of living obtained through personal interviews as well as traditional sources.

Judgmental Decision Making   The ability to make decisions based on experience, personal knowledge, and intuition.

Ledger Information   The recorded monetary transactions of a business and, in this context, shows how an individual credit customer has handled his or her credit account.

Letter of Credit (L/C)   A written engagement by a bank that it will honor drafts or other demands for payment; commonly used in international trade.

Level Term Coverage   Life insurance coverage where the death benefit remains the same while the insurance is in force.

Leveraged Buyouts   When a company is bought out using borrowed money to finance the purchase.

Lifetime Interest Rate Cap   A clause in an adjustable rate mortgage that will limit the total increase during the lifetime of the mortgage and will define a maximum interest rate.

Limited Acceptance   It is because of two elements, risk and time, found in every credit transaction that credit has limited acceptance.

Liquidity   This is concerned with a firm's ability to meet day-to-day current obligations.

Liquidity Ratios   Seven ratios that generally are considered significant in analyzing a firm's ability to meet its debts.

Line of Credit   By prior arrangement, the maximum amount a financial institution will lend a customer by honoring checks written for amounts exceeding the current account balance.

Lockboxes   A central payment point; a service offered by a financial institution that receives mail payments for a customer for processing and posting to an account.

Long-Term Asset   Investments and property that is expected to last beyond one business operating cycle and is depreciated to spread the value over its years of life.

Long-Term Liability   Debts not falling due until more than one year from the date of the balance sheet.

Managerial Efficiency   As revealed by financial statement analysis, this determines a firm's ability to operate profitably and successfully over a long period.

Margin Rate   The interest rate at each adjustment point will equal the index plus the margin rate.

Marketing   The process and functions that facilitate the movement of goods and services from the producer to the ultimate consumer.

Mechanics Lien   A claim created by state statute for the purpose of securing priority for payment for work or materials furnished in constructing a building.

Medium of Exchange   Something of value acceptable to the seller in exchange for the good or service delivered.

Merchandise Credit   Used to obtain goods, raw materials, and inventory for resale.

Microfiche   A sheet of microfilm that contains many pages of data in reduced, miniature form that is read with special magnifying machines.

Monetary Policy   Controlled by the Federal Reserve System and involves several different policy tools designed to expand, or contract, the money supply to control interest rates.

Money Market Mutual Fund   Invests funds in short-term, unsecured money market investments such as corporate bonds, treasury securities, and commercial paper (notes).

Mortgage   A debt secured by real estate.

Mortgage Bankers   Companies or individuals who originate mortgage loans, sell them to other investors, service the monthly payments, and may act as agents to dispense funds for taxes and insurance.

Monthly Payment Cap   A limit on the annual increase in monthly payments.

Mutual Fund   An investment company that pools the funds of a group of investors and buys securities of a particular type.

Negative Amortization   A situation with a mortgage or other loan where the outstanding balance grows since the payments are not sufficient to pay the interest due.

Negotiable Instruments   Promissory notes, checks, and drafts used in business transactions to borrow funds, pay for purchases, or transfer value to another.

Net Profit   Also called *net income,* the amount by which revenue exceeds expenses for a period of time.

Net Profit Margin   A ratio computed by dividing net income by net sales; shows the percentage of each dollar of sales retained as income.

Net Credit Period   In terms of sale, the length of time allowed the buyer before payment is considered past due.

Networking   Sharing resources with several computers that are linked together with cables.

Net Working Capital Ratio   Net sales divided by net working capital (current assets minus current liabilities).

Nominal Annual Rate   The nominal rate must be converted to a nominal annual rate if the period involved is less than or more than one year.

Nominal Rate   Simply the dollar amount of interest charge divided by the dollar amount of credit desired by the customer.

Nonbank Banks   An innovative species allowed to offer checking accounts or make commercial loans but cannot do both.

Nonrecourse   Under this plan, dealers are not contingently responsible for the customer's credit failure.

Numerical Decision Making   A number-based decision-making approach that assigns weighted values to different qualities or observations to calculate a total score to help make a decision.

Open Account Transaction A credit sale documented by accounting entries in the business records of both buyer and seller.

Open-Market Operations The buying and selling of government securities by the Federal Reserve System.

Operating Lease Short-term rentals of equipment that may be canceled at any time.

Opinion A belief or conclusion that is not substantiated by proof or positive knowledge.

Optima Credit Card A credit card plan launched by American Express in March 1987.

Order Limit The maximum single order that can be approved without notification of the credit manager or higher authority.

Ordinary Accounts Receivable Financing An agreement under which a financing institution purchases the open accounts receivable of its customers, with recourse and without notice to trade debtors.

Ordinary Terms Including two component parts—the net credit period and the cash discounts.

Organizing A management function that involves grouping activities and assigning these activities to individual employees.

Overdraft Plan Provides a borrower with a preapproved loan reserve, generally incorporated into a checking account, that is used at the convenience of the borrower when funds are needed.

Owners' Equity A residual claim against the assets of a business after the liabilities are deducted from total assets; also called *stockholders' equity, shareholders' equity, capital account,* or *net worth.*

Past-Due Index A ratio computed by dividing total accounts receivable past due by total accounts receivable.

Pawnbroker A lender licensed to loan money at a specified interest rate with personal property left with the pawnbroker as security.

Payment Terms Same as terms of sale; understanding between buyer and seller regarding payment for goods and services.

Percentage Comparison Method Also called the *100 percent* or *common size method* where balance sheet entries are expressed as a percent of the balance sheet total and income statement items are expressed as a percent of net sales.

Perfect a Security Interest The process of documenting a security interest by preparing and filing a statement with the appropriate government agency.

Personal Guarantee An agreement to pledge personal assets for the repayment of a loan if the debtor does not pay.

Personnel Report A report prepared by a consumer credit reporting agency for a prospective employer which includes information on an individual being considered for hire.

P.M.I. (Private Mortgage Insurance) Guarantees conventional home mortgage loans, that is, nongovernment loans.

Point Equals 1 percent of the face value of the mortgage and is an additional charge required to obtain a mortgage loan.

Preference A payment of a debt, usually within 90 days preceding a bankruptcy filing, that helps an individual creditor at the expense of the entire group.

Prepayment Clause Requires the mortgage holder to pay specified fees or penalties if the mortgage is paid off early.

Prepayment Terms These reduce or eliminate the element or risk that is inherent in credit transactions.

Prestige Card Both Visa and Mastercard have consolidated a wide array of bank products into a single prestige product.

Previous Balance Method The finance charge is based on the previous month's balance without deducting payments or credits made during the month if the account is not paid in full.

Primary Loss The portion of total losses that are considered normal losses which must be suffered before an insurance company would begin covering loss.

Prime Rate The best interest rate a commercial bank will offer its best business customer.

Private Credit Credit used by individuals and businesses carrying on exchanges in the private sector of our economy.

Private Mortgage Insurance Guarantees the repayment of conventional home mortgage loans in exchange for a premium paid by the mortgage holder.

Procedures Step-by-step instructions which are designed to bring about a consistent course of action when performing a task.

Promissory Note A written promise to pay money at a specified time.

Promotion   Advertising or other efforts undertaken to encourage product sales or increased use of services.

Public Credit   Borrowing by a level of government to finance the goods, services, and welfare programs it offers to its citizens.

Public Record Information   The data maintained by governments, the court systems, and other public agencies that make this information available to anyone who is interested.

Qualification as to Scope   Accountants express this generally when they have not confirmed the accounts receivable and have not actually observed the taking of inventories.

Qualified Opinion   Accountants express this when they believe the statement is a generally fair presentation but they are not completely satisfied on some point.

Ratio Analysis   Certain fundamental relationships of items in a financial statement are emphasized by stating them in the form of ratios.

Real Estate Credit   Credit that involves funds being extended to the borrower with a loan that uses real property as security or collateral for the loan.

Real Estate Investment Trust   An investment comprised of shares which, once issued, are traded on stock exchanges. The proceeds from the original offering are used to invest in mortgages or real estate properties.

Real Estate Mortgage Note   A promissory note secured by real property.

Rebate for Prepayment   The return of a portion of the total precomputed interest included in an installment credit agreement if it is paid early.

Receivables Turnover   Net credit sales divided by average accounts receivable.

Recourse   One arrangement of ordinary accounts receivable financing where the purchaser of the accounts retains the right to return them for a refund if the debtor does not pay.

Redlining   Setting aside certain areas in a community as undesirable credit risk zones.

Repossession   The legal process to take possession of goods for failure to pay amounts as agreed.

Repurchase   In case of consumer default on the terms of the contract, dealers are responsible for buying back the property for the unpaid balance after it has been retaken from the installment buyer.

Residential Mortgage Credit Report   A comprehensive updated consumer credit bureau report prepared as part of a residential mortgage transaction; often paid for by the borrower as a closing cost.

Reserve Requirements   Funds that depository institutions (banks, credit unions, saving and loan associations, etc.) must keep on hand or on deposit with the Federal Reserve System.

Retail Credit   A category of credit used by consumers to purchase final goods and services directly from sellers using revolving credit, installments contracts, or service credit.

Retail Installment Credit   A credit plan or program that allows purchasers to pay for goods in the future by making a series of fixed, regular payments.

Retail 30-Day Charge Account   Provides a retail customer with the opportunity to charge a series of purchases to an account operated by a retailer who will send one bill or statement at the end of a predetermined time period (usually once a month).

Restrictive Covenants   An agreement listing prohibited acts or required activities that must be adhered to while a loan is outstanding.

Return on Assets   A ratio computed by dividing net income by average total assets during a specific time period.

Return on Investment   A ratio computed by dividing net income by average owners' equity during a specific time period.

Revocable Letter of Credit   An agreement by a bank to pay debts on behalf of an individual or firm that can be rescinded or canceled.

Revolving Credit   A credit agreement that allows consumers to purchase a variety of items using credit up to a predetermined maximum amount.

Right of Replevin   If the creditor can show a title or a possessory right superior to that of the debtor, then the merchandise can be retaken in case of nonfulfillment of the terms of the contract.

Right of Rescission   Provides signers of a contract with the opportunity to cancel, annul, or void a contractual obligation within a stated period of time.

Robinson-Patman Act   A federal law that prohibits price discrimination, including the terms of sale, which restricts competition or promotes monopolies.

ROG (Receipt of Goods) Terms of sale where the time period for cash discounts and payment periods begins when the goods arrive at their destination.

RTC (Resolution Trust Corporation) Established to dispose of thrift institutions that failed and were taken over by regulators after January 1, 1989.

Rule of 78s A method used to calculate the amount of the rebate of precomputed finance charges when an installment credit agreement is paid early.

Rules Statements that outline prohibited activities and define acceptable behavior.

Sales Finance Company A specialized type of institution that engages primarily in buying consumer installment contracts from retail dealers and in providing wholesale financing for these dealers and that charges rates competitive with those of commercial banks and other lenders for equivalent services.

Sale Leaseback Arrangement A situation where a seller transfers property to another and arranges for continued use of the asset by a lease.

Sales to Total Assets A ratio computed by dividing net sales by total assets.

Savings and Loan Associations Depository thrift institutions originally organized to accept savings deposits and provide mortgage financing.

Savings Banks Receive their charters from the state governments, and the regulations governing their operations have a wide range of variations.

Season Dating A special situation where an invoice is dated for the season of sale, not according to the date order or shipped, often designed to induce the buyer to order early.

Secondary Mortgage Market Mortgage contracts are purchased by various federal agencies and later sold to investors.

Second-Layer Lenders They conduct secondary market activities in the buying and selling of loans and provide credit to primary lenders in the form of borrowed money.

Secured Credit Cards Usually general-purpose credit cards issued to borrowers without good credit histories often secured by savings account balances.

Self-Liquidating Credit Obtaining goods and services for resale, providing the means to repay when the goods are later resold.

Service Credit Service providers agree to wait for payment from their customers.

Settlement Costs Costs associated with the transfer of ownership to the real estate property and the settling of accounts with the buyer, seller, and real estate agent, financial institution, and others who deliver services required by the transfer of title.

Share Draft A unique type of financial instrument, payable by a credit union out of a member's share draft account.

Sight Draft An order to pay that is payable on sight or on presentation to the payee or holder of the draft.

Sight Draft-Bill of Lading Terms Terms of sale that involve the payment of a draft on sight before ownership documents are provided to the buyer of the goods.

Simple Evaluation A form of financial statement analysis where the credit manager merely inspects the dollar items shown.

Simple Interest Method Charges interest on a daily basis using a daily interest rate, usually 1/365th of the annual finance charge, which is deducted first from each payment.

Single-Payment Loans Generally short-term loans where funds are advanced for a year or less with an arrangement that the funds will be repaid in one payment at the end of the period.

Single-Payment Terms In reality a special form of dating, in which customers are allowed to accumulate their obligations over a short time.

Skip A debtor who deliberately moves or changes location in an attempt to avoid payment.

Smart Card A debit card that stores value which can be accessed for purchases electronically.

Solvency Indicated by a concern's dependence on finance support from creditors as contrasted to the financial investment by its owners.

Solvency Ratios Seven ratios that are generally accepted as capable of showing a firm's solvency condition.

Specialized Credit Reporting Agency A business credit reporting agency that provides reports on businesses in selected industries, size categories, or geographic locations.

Special-Datings Terms Adjusting terms to conditions peculiar to a trade or its customers.

Standard Industrial Ratio Financial benchmarks calculated from survey results and reported by certain credit reporting agencies designed to show average financial ratios.

Statement of Cash Flows   An accounting statement that shows the sources and uses of funds during a specified time period.

Statement of Retained Earnings   An accounting statement that shows how net income was used, either retained by the business or distributed to the owners in the form of dividends.

Stock Turnover   A ratio computed by dividing sales by average inventory, computed using cost or retail prices.

Store Card   A retailer owned and operated credit card program designed to facilitate sales in its own retail outlets.

Student Loans   Loans made to help pay tuition and the other costs related to education.

Subordination Agreement   Provides enhanced status for a creditor by establishing a prior claim to the customer's assets in the event of nonpayment.

Suspense File   A file for further action from which the accounts out for review can be pulled when the arrangements are broken.

Terms Chiseler   One who regularly deducts cash discounts, even though payment is made after expiration of the cash discount period; one who makes only a partial payment.

Terms of Sale   An understanding between the buyer and the seller regarding the conditions for the payment for the goods and services.

Time Draft   An order to pay providing payment after a certain time period.

Times Interest Earned   A ratio computed by dividing net income or earnings by interest expense.

Total Finance Charge   A total of interest, fees, and charges payable by the loan customer and required as a condition of the credit.

Trade Acceptance   A type of draft prepared by the seller of goods which is signed, or accepted, by the buyer.

Trade Discount   Pricing device that bears no relationship to the time of payment.

Trade Group Meeting   Sponsored by NACM to discuss joint problems.

Travel and Entertainment Card   A charge card that allows the cardholder to charge goods and services at member establishments, and then receives one itemized monthly statement of the charges which is paid in full each month.

Underwriting Securities   The practice of an investment banker purchasing the newly issued securities of a corporation with the expectation that the securities will be sold later at a profit.

Undue Optimism   A reflection of a firm's natural hope that certain items on a financial statement will in time return to the value at which they are now being carried.

Uniform Commercial Code (UCC)   A law adopted by nearly every state that regulates sales and leases of goods, commercial paper, secured transactions, letters of credit, bills of lading, and certain aspects of banking and fund transfers.

Unqualified Opinion   Expressed by accountants when satisfied that a financial statement presents fairly the financial position and the results of the operation.

Usury   A premium paid by a consumer for the loan of money.

Voluntary Bankruptcy Petition   A petition for bankruptcy filed by the debtor asking for protection under federal bankruptcy laws.

Wage Assignment   An agreement signed by a debtor, usually at the time the credit transaction is made, that provides in case of nonpayment; the creditor may seek a certain portion of the debtor's wages without a court order.

Wage Earner's Plan   A type of bankruptcy provided in Chapter 13 of the Federal Bankruptcy Code that involves a court-approved plan to pay debts from future income.

Wage Garnishment   A legal proceeding whereby money or property due to a debtor (wages) but in possession of another (employer) is applied to the payment of a debt.

Window Dressing   Presenting the various aspects of a business in as favorable a light as possible.

INDEX

459